T0260717

# HIGH PERFORMANCE
# SWITCHES AND ROUTERS

BICENTENNIAL
1807
**WILEY**
2007
BICENTENNIAL

## THE WILEY BICENTENNIAL–KNOWLEDGE FOR GENERATIONS

*E*ach generation has its unique needs and aspirations. When Charles Wiley first opened his small printing shop in lower Manhattan in 1807, it was a generation of boundless potential searching for an identity. And we were there, helping to define a new American literary tradition. Over half a century later, in the midst of the Second Industrial Revolution, it was a generation focused on building the future. Once again, we were there, supplying the critical scientific, technical, and engineering knowledge that helped frame the world. Throughout the 20th Century, and into the new millennium, nations began to reach out beyond their own borders and a new international community was born. Wiley was there, expanding its operations around the world to enable a global exchange of ideas, opinions, and know-how.

For 200 years, Wiley has been an integral part of each generation's journey, enabling the flow of information and understanding necessary to meet their needs and fulfill their aspirations. Today, bold new technologies are changing the way we live and learn. Wiley will be there, providing you the must-have knowledge you need to imagine new worlds, new possibilities, and new opportunities.

Generations come and go, but you can always count on Wiley to provide you the knowledge you need, when and where you need it!

**WILLIAM J. PESCE**
PRESIDENT AND CHIEF EXECUTIVE OFFICER

**PETER BOOTH WILEY**
CHAIRMAN OF THE BOARD

# HIGH PERFORMANCE SWITCHES AND ROUTERS

H. JONATHAN CHAO and BIN LIU

**WILEY-INTERSCIENCE**
A JOHN WILEY & SONS, INC., PUBLICATION

Copyright © 2007 by John Wiley & Sons, Inc., All rights reserved.

Published by John Wiley & Sons, Inc., Hoboken, New Jersey
Published simultaneously in Canada

No part of this publication may be reproduced, stored in a retrieval system, or transmitted in any form or by any means, electronic, mechanical, photocopying, recording, scanning, or otherwise, except as permitted under Section 107 or 108 of the 1976 United States Copyright Act, without either the prior written permission of the Publisher, or authorization through payment of the appropriate per-copy fee to the Copyright Clearance Center, Inc., 222 Rosewood Drive, Danvers, MA 01923, (978) 750-8400, fax (978) 750-4470, or on the web at www.copyright.com. Requests to the Publisher for permission should be addressed to the Permissions Department, John Wiley & Sons, Inc., 111 River Street, Hoboken, NJ 07030, (201) 748-6011, fax (201) 748-6008, or online at http://www.wiley.com/go/permission.

Limit of Liability/Disclaimer of Warranty: While the publisher and author have used their best efforts in preparing this book, they make no representations or warranties with respect to the accuracy or completeness of the contents of this book and specifically disclaim any implied warranties of merchantability or fitness for a particular purpose. No warranty may be created or extended by sales representatives or written sales materials. The advice and strategies contained herein may not be suitable for your situation. You should consult with a professional where appropriate. Neither the publisher nor author shall be liable for any loss of profit or any other commercial damages, including but not limited to special, incidental, consequential, or other damages.

For general information on our other products and services or for technical support, please contact our Customer Care Department within the United States at (800) 762-2974, outside the United States at (317) 572-3993 or fax (317) 572-4002.

Wiley also publishes its books in a variety of electronic formats. Some content that appears in print may not be available in electronic formats. For more information about Wiley products, visit our web site at www.wiley.com.

*Library of Congress Cataloging-in-Publication Data.*

Chao, H. Jonathan, 1955-
  High performance switches and routers / by H. Jonathan Chao, Bin Liu.
     p.  cm.
  ISBN-13: 978-0-470-05367-6
  ISBN-10: 0-470-05367-4
1. Asynchronous transfer mode. 2. Routers (Computer networks)
3. Computer network protocols. 4. Packet switching (Data transmission)
I. Liu, Bin. II. Title.
  TK5105.35.C454 2007
  621.382′16- -dc22                          2006026971

# CONTENTS

# PREFACE

As increasing voice, audio, video, TV, and gaming traffic is carried over IP, Internet traffic continues to grow rapidly. Many network-related applications are emerging for portable devices. As smart cellular phone technology advances, the price decreases, and the infrastructure to support wireless applications (voice, data, video) is being deployed ubiquitously to meet unprecedented demands from users. All of these fast-growing services translate into the high volume of Internet traffic, stringent quality of service (QoS) requirements, large number of hosts/devices to be supported, large forwarding tables to support, high speed packet processing, and large storage capability. When designing/operating next generation switches and routers, these factors create new specifications and new challenges for equipment vendors and network providers.

Jonathan has co-authored two books: *Broadband Packet Switching Technologies—A Practical Guide to ATM Switches and IP Routers* and *Quality of Service Control in High-Speed Networks*, published by John Wiley in 2001. Because the technologies in both electronics and optics have significantly advanced and because the design specifications for routers have become more demanding and challenging, it is time to write another book. This book includes new architectures, algorithms, and implementations developed since 2001. Thus, it is more updated and more complete than the two previous books.

In addition to the need for high-speed and high-capacity transmission/switching equipment, the control function of the equipment and network has also become more sophisticated in order to support new features and requirements of the Internet, including fast re-routing due to link failure (one or more failures), network security, network measurement for dynamic routing, and easy management. This book focuses on the subsystems and devices on the data plane. There is a brief introduction to IP network management to familiarize readers with how the network is managed, as many routers are interconnected together.

The book starts with an introduction to today's and tomorrow's networks, the router architectures and their building blocks, examples of commercial high-end routers, and the challenging issues of designing high-performance high-speed routers. The book first covers the main functions in the line cards of a core router, including route lookup, packet classification, and traffic management for QoS control described in Chapters 2, 3, and

4, respectively. It then follows with 11 chapters in packet switching designs, covering various architectures, algorithms, and technologies (including electrical and optical packet switching). The last chapter of the book presents the state-of-the-art commercial chipsets used to build the routers. This is one of the important features in this book—showing readers the architecture and functions of practical chipsets to reinforce the theories and conceptual designs covered in previous chapters.

A distinction of this book is that we provide as many figures as possible to explain the concepts. Readers are encouraged to first scan through the figures and try to understand them before reading the text. If fully understood, readers can skip to the text to save time. However, the text is written in such a way as to talk the readers through the figures.

Jonathan and Bin each have about 20 years of experience researching high-performance switches and routers, implementing them in various systems with VLSI (very-large-scale integration) and FPGA (field-programmable gate array) chips, transferring technology to the industry, and teaching such subjects in the college and to the industry companies. They have accumulated their practical experience in writing this book. The book includes theoretical concepts and algorithms, design architectures, and actual implementations. It will benefit the readers in different aspects of building a high-performance switch/router. The draft of the book has been used as a text for the past two years when teaching senior undergraduate and first-year graduate students at the author's universities. If any errors are found, please send an email to chao@poly.edu. The authors will then make the corresponding corrections in future editions.

## Audience

This book is an appropriate text for senior and graduate students in Electrical Engineering, Computer Engineering, and Computer Science. They can embrace the technology of the Internet so as to better position themselves when they graduate and look for jobs in the high-speed networking field. This book can also be used as a reference for people working in the Internet-related area. Engineers from network equipment vendors and service providers can also benefit from the book by understanding the key concepts of packet switching systems and the key techniques of building high-speed and high-performance routers.

# ACKNOWLEDGMENTS

This book would not have been published without the help of many people. We would like to thank them for their efforts in improving the quality of the book.

Several chapters of the book are based on research work that was done at Polytechnic University and Tsinghua University. We would like to thank several individuals who contributed material to some sections. They are Professor Ming Yu (Florida State University) on Section 1.5, Professor Derek C. W. Pao (City University of Hong Kong) on Section 2.4.2, and Professor Aleksandra Smiljanic (Belgrade University) on a scheduling scheme she proposed in Chapter 7. We would like to express our gratitude to Dr. Yihan Li (Auburn University) for her contribution to part of Chapter 7, and the students in Bin's research group in Tsinghua University for their contribution to some chapters. They are Chenchen Hu, Kai Zheng, Zhen Liu, Lei Shi, Xuefei Chen, Xin Zhang, Yang Xu, Wenjie Li, and Wei Li. The manuscript has been managed from the beginning to the end by Mr Jian Li (Polytechnic University), who has put in tremendous effort to carefully edit the manuscript and serve as a coordinator with the publisher.

The manuscript draft was reviewed by the following people and we would like to thank them for their valuable feedback: Professor Cristina López Bravo (University of Vigo, Spain), Dr Hiroaki Harai (Institute of Information and Communications Technology, Japan), Dr Simin He (Chinese Academy of Sciences), Professor Hao Che (University of Texas at Arlington), Professor Xiaohong Jiang (Tohoku University, Japan), Dr Yihan Li (Auburn University), Professor Dr Soung Yue Liew (Universiti Tunku Abdul Rahman, Malaysia), Dr Jan van Lunteren (IBM, Zurich), Professor Jinsoo Park (Essex County College, New Jersey), Professor Roberto Rojas-cessa (New Jersey Institute of Technology), Professor Aleksandra Smiljanic (Belgrade University, Serbia and Montenegro), Professor Dapeng Wu (University of Florida), and Professor Naoaki Yamanaka (Keio University, Japan).

Jonathan would like to thank his wife, Ammie, and his children, Jessica, Roger, and Joshua, for their love, support, encouragement, patience, and perseverance. He also thanks his parents for their encouragement.

Bin would like to thank his wife, Yingjun Ma, and his daughter, Jenny for their understanding and support. He also thanks his father-in-law for looking after Jenny to spare his time to prepare the book.

# CHAPTER 1

# INTRODUCTION

The Internet, with its robust and reliable Internet Protocol (IP), is widely considered the most reachable platform for the current and next generation information infrastructure. The virtually unlimited bandwidth of optical fiber has tremendously increased the data transmission speed over the past decade. Availability of unlimited bandwidth has stimulated high-demand multimedia services such as distance learning, music and video download, and videoconferencing. Current broadband access technologies, such as digital subscriber lines (DSLs) and cable television (CATV), are providing affordable broadband connection solutions to the Internet from home. Furthermore, with Gigabit Ethernet access over dark fiber to the enterprise on its way, access speeds are expected to largely increase. It is clear that the deployment of these broadband access technologies will result in a high demand for large Internet bandwidth. To keep pace with the Internet traffic growth, researchers are continually exploring faster transmission and switching technologies. The advent of optical transmission technologies, such as dense wave division multiplexing (DWDM), optical add-drop multiplexers, and ultra-long-haul lasers have had a large influence on lowering the costs of digital transmission. For instance, 300 channels of 11.6 Gbps can be wavelength-division multiplexed on a single fiber and transmitted over 7000 km [1]. In addition, a 1296 × 1296 optical cross-connect (OXC) switching system using micro-electro-mechanical systems (MEMS) with a total switching capacity of 2.07 petabits/s has been demonstrated [2]. In the rest of this chapter, we explore state-of-the-art network infrastructure, future design trends, and their impact on next generation routers. We also describe router architectures and the challenges involved in designing high-performance large-scale routers.

*High Performance Switches and Routers*, by H. Jonathan Chao and Bin Liu
Copyright © 2007 John Wiley & Sons, Inc.

## 1.1 ARCHITECTURE OF THE INTERNET: PRESENT AND FUTURE

### 1.1.1 The Present

Today's Internet is an amalgamation of thousands of commercial and service provider networks. It is not feasible for a single service provider to connect two distant nodes on the Internet. Therefore, service providers often rely on each other to connect the dots. Depending on the size of network they operate, Internet Service Providers (ISPs) can be broken down into three major categories. Tier-1 ISPs are about a dozen major telecommunication companies, such as UUNet, Sprint, Qwest, XO Network, and AT&T, whose high-speed global networks form the Internet backbone. Tier-1 ISPs do not buy network capacity from other providers; instead, they sell or lease access to their backbone resource to smaller Tier-2 ISPs, such as America Online and Broadwing. Tier-3 ISPs are typically regional service providers such as Verizon and RCN through whom most enterprises connect to the Internet. Figure 1.1 illustrates the architecture of a typical Tier-1 ISP network.

Each Tier-1 ISP operates multiple IP/MPLS (multi-protocol label switching), and sometimes ATM (asynchronous transfer mode), backbones with speeds varying anywhere from T3 to OC-192 (optical carrier level 192, ~10 Gbps). These backbones are interconnected through peering agreements between ISPs to form the Internet backbone. The backbone is designed to transfer large volumes of traffic as quickly as possible between networks. Enterprise networks are often linked to the rest of the Internet via a variety of links, anywhere from a T1 to multiple OC-3 lines, using a variety of Layer 2 protocols, such as Gigabit Ethernet, frame relay, and so on. These enterprise networks are then overhauled into service provider networks through edge routers. An edge router can aggregate links from multiple enterprises. Edge routers are interconnected in a pool, usually at a Point of Presence (POP)

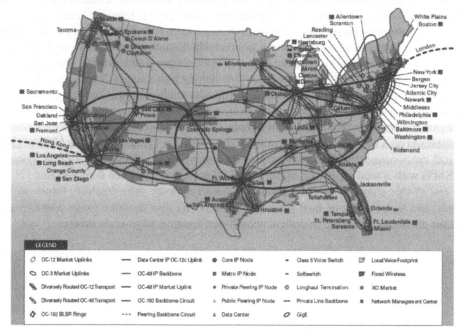

**Figure 1.1**    Network map of a Tier-1 ISP, XO Network.

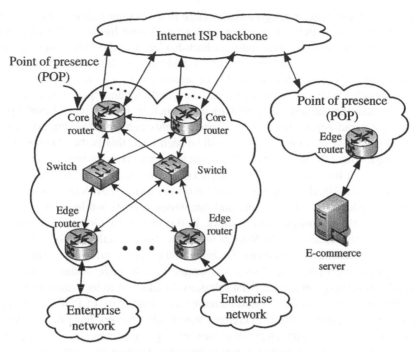

**Figure 1.2**    Point of presence (POP).

of a service provider, as shown in Figure 1.2. Each POP may link to other POPs of the same ISP through optical transmission/switching equipment, may link to POPs of other ISPs to form a peering, or link to one or more backbone routers. Typically, a POP may have a few backbone routers in a densely connected mesh. In most POPs, each edge router connects to at least two backbone routers for redundancy. These backbone routers may also connect to backbone routers at other POPs according to ISP peering agreements. Peering occurs when ISPs exchange traffic bound for each other's network over a direct link without any fees. Therefore, peering works best when peers exchange roughly the same amount of traffic. Since smaller ISPs do not have high quantities of traffic, they often have to buy *transit* from a Tier-1 provider to connect to the Internet. A recent study of the topologies of 10 service providers across the world shows that POPs share this generic structure [3].

Unlike POPs, the design of backbone varies from service provider to service provider. For example, Figure 1.3 illustrates backbone design paradigms of three major service providers

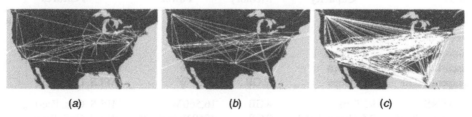

|  |  |  |
|:---:|:---:|:---:|
| (a) | (b) | (c) |

**Figure 1.3**    Three distinct backbone design paradigms of Tier-1 ISPs. (*a*) AT&T; (*b*) Sprint; (*c*) Level 3 national network infrastructure [3].

in the US. AT&T's backbone design includes large POPs at major cities, which in turn fan out into smaller per-city POPs. In contrast, Sprint's backbone has only 20 well connected POPs in major cities and suburban links are back-hauled into the POPs via smaller ISPs. Most major service providers still have the AT&T backbone model and are in various stages of moving to Sprint's design. Sprint's backbone design provides a good solution to service providers grappling with a need to reduce capital expenditure and operational costs associated with maintaining and upgrading network infrastructure. Interestingly, Level 3 presents another design paradigm in which the backbone is highly connected via circuit technology such as, MPLS, ATM or frame relays. As will be seen later, this is the next generation of network design where the line between backbone and network edge begins to blur.

Now, let us see how network design impacts on the next generation routers. Router design is often guided by the economic requirements of service providers. Service providers would like to reduce the infrastructure and maintenance costs while, at the same time, increasing available bandwidth and reliability. To this end, network backbone has a set of well-defined, narrow requirements. Routers in the backbone should simply move traffic as fast as possible. Network edge, however, has broad and evolving requirements due simply to the diversity of services and Layer 2 protocols supported at the edge. Today most POPs have multiple edge routers optimized for point solutions. In addition to increasing infrastructure and maintenance costs, this design also increases the complexity of POPs resulting in an unreliable network infrastructure. Therefore, newer edge routers have been designed to support diversity and are easily adaptable to the evolving requirements of service providers. This design trend is shown in Table 1.1, which lists some properties of enterprise, edge, and core routers currently on the market. As we will see in the following sections, future network designs call for the removal of edge routers altogether and their replacement with fewer core routers to increase reliability, throughput, and to reduce costs. This means next generation routers would have to amalgamate the diverse service requirements of edge routers and the strict performance requirements of core routers, seamlessly into one body. Therefore, the real question is not whether we should build highly-flexible, scalable, high-performance routers, but how?

### 1.1.2 The Future

As prices of optical transport and optical switching sharply decrease, some network designers believe that the future network will consist of many mid-size IP routers or MPLS

**TABLE 1.1   Popular Enterprise, Edge, and Core Routers in the Market**

| Model | Capacity[a] | Memory | Power | Features |
|---|---|---|---|---|
| Cisco 7200 | – | 256 MB | 370 W | QoS, MPLS, Aggregation |
| Cisco 7600 | 720 Gbps | 1 GB | – | QoS, MPLS, Shaping |
| Cisco 10000 | 51.2 Gbps | – | 1200 W | QoS, MPLS |
| Cisco 12000 | 1.28 Tbps | 4 GB | 4706 W | MPLS, Peering |
| Juniper M-320 | 320 Gbps | 2 GB | 3150 W | MPLS, QoS, VPN |
| Cisco CRS | 92 Tbps | 4 GB | 16,560 W | MPLS, Qos, Peering |
| Juniper TX/T-640 | 2.5 Tbps/640 Gbps | 2 GB | 4550 W/6500 W | MPLS, QoS, Peering |

[a]Note that the listed capacity is the combination of ingress and egress capacities.

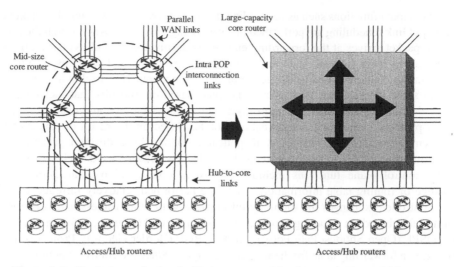

**Figure 1.4**   Replacing a cluster of mid-size routers with a large-capacity scalable router.

switches at the network edge that are connected to optical crossconnects (OXCs), which are then interconnected by DWDM transmission equipment. The problem for this approach is that connections to the OXC are usually high bit rates, for example, 10 Gbps for now and 40 Gbps in the near future. When the edge routers want to communicate with all other routers, they either need to have direct connections to those routers or connect through multiple logical hops (i.e., routed by other routers). The former case results in low link utilization while the latter results in higher latency. Therefore, some network designers believe it is better to build very large IP routers or MPLS switches at POPs. They aggregate traffic from edge routers onto high-speed links that are then directly connected to other large routers at different POPs through DWDM transmission equipment. This approach achieves higher link utilization and fewer hops (thus lower latency). As a result, the need for an OXC is mainly for provisioning and restoring purposes but not for dynamic switching to achieve higher link utilization.

Current router technologies available in the market cannot provide large switching capacities to satisfy current and future bandwidth demands. As a result, a number of mid-size core routers are interconnected with numerous links and use many expensive line cards that are used to carry intra-cluster traffic rather than revenue-generating users' or wide-area-network (WAN) traffic. Figure 1.4 shows how a router cluster is replaced by a large-capacity scalable router, saving the cost of numerous line cards and links, and real estate. It provides a cost-effective solution that can satisfy Internet traffic growth without having to replace routers every two to three years. Furthermore, there are fewer individual routers that need to be configured and managed, resulting in a more efficient and reliable system.

## 1.2   ROUTER ARCHITECTURES

IP routers' functions can be classified into two categories: datapath functions and control plane functions [4].

The datapath functions such as forwarding decision, forwarding through the backplane, and output link scheduling are performed on every datagram that passes through the router. When a packet arrives at the forwarding engine, its destination IP address is first masked by the subnet mask (logical AND operation) and the resulting address is used to lookup the forwarding table. A so-called longest prefix matching method is used to find the output port. In some applications, packets are classified based on 104 bits that include the IP source/destination addresses, transport layer port numbers (source and destination), and type of protocol, which is generally called 5-tuple. Based on the result of classification, packets may be either discarded (firewall application) or handled at different priority levels. Then, time-to-live (TTL) value is decremented and a new header checksum is recalculated.

The control plane functions include the system configuration, management, and exchange of routing table information. These are performed relatively infrequently. The route controller exchanges the topology information with other routers and constructs a routing table based on a routing protocol, for example, RIP (Routing Information Protocol), OSPF (Open Shortest Path Forwarding), or BGP (Border Gateway Protocol). It can also create a forwarding table for the forwarding engine. Since the control functions are not performed on each arriving individual packet, they do not have a strict speed constraint and are implemented in software in general.

Router architectures generally fall into two categories: centralized (Fig. 1.5a) and distributed (Fig. 1.5b).

Figure 1.5a shows a number of network interfaces, forwarding engines, a route controller (RC), and a management controller (MC) interconnected by a switch fabric. Input interfaces send packet headers to the forwarding engines through the switch fabric. The forwarding engines, in turn, determine which output interface the packet should be sent to. This information is sent back to the corresponding input interface, which forwards the packet to the right output interface. The only task of a forwarding engine is to process packet headers and is shared by all the interfaces. All other tasks such as participating in routing protocols, reserving resource, handling packets that need extra attention, and other administrative and maintenance tasks, are handled by the RC and the MC. The BBN multi-gigabit router [5] is an example of this design.

The difference between Figure 1.5a and 1.5b is that the functions of the forwarding engines are integrated into the interface cards themselves. Most high-performance routers use this architecture. The RC maintains a routing table and updates it based on routing protocols used. The routing table is used to generate a forwarding table that is then downloaded

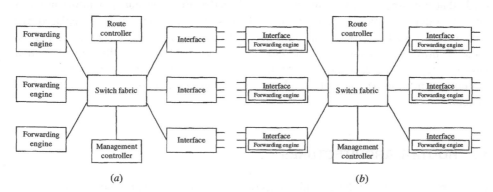

(a)                                                      (b)

**Figure 1.5** (a) Centralized versus (b) distributed models for a router.

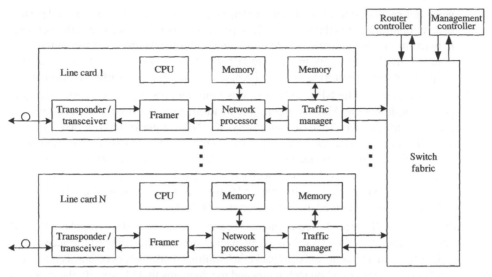

**Figure 1.6**   Typical router architecture.

from the RC to the forwarding engines in the interface cards. It is not necessary to download a new forwarding table for every route update. Route updates can be frequent, but routing protocols need time, in the order of minutes, to converge. The RC needs a dynamic routing table designed for fast updates and fast generation of forwarding tables. Forwarding tables, on the other hand, can be optimized for lookup speed and need not be dynamic.

Figure 1.6 shows a typical router architecture, where multiple line cards, an RC, and an MC are interconnected through a switch fabric. The communication between the RC/MC and the line cards can be either through the switch fabric or through a separate interconnection network, such as a Ethernet switch. The line cards are the entry and exit points of data to and from a router. They provide the interface from physical and higher layers to the switch fabric. The tasks provided by line cards are becoming more complex as new applications develop and protocols evolve. Each line card supports at least one full-duplex fiber connection on the network side, and at least one ingress and one egress connection to the switch fabric backplane. Generally speaking, for high-bandwidth applications, such as OC-48 and above, the network connections support channelization for aggregation of lower-speed lines into a large pipe, and the switch fabric connections provide flow-control mechanisms for several thousand input and output queues to regulate the ingress and egress traffic to and from the switch fabric.

A line card usually includes components such as a transponder, framer, network processor (NP), traffic manager (TM), and central processing unit (CPU).

*Transponder/Transceiver.*  This component performs optical-to-electrical and electrical-to-optical signal conversions, and serial-to-parallel and parallel-to-serial conversions [6, 7].

*Framer.*  A framer performs synchronization, frame overhead processing, and cell or packet delineation. On the transmit side, a SONET (synchronous optical network)/SDH (synchronous digital hierarchy) framer generates section, line, and path overhead. It performs framing pattern insertion (A1, A2) and scrambling. It generates section, line, and path bit interleaved parity (B1/B2/B3) for far-end performance monitoring. On the receive side, it processes section, line, and path overhead. It performs frame delineation, descrambling, alarm detection, pointer interpretation, bit interleaved parity monitoring (B1/B2/B3), and error count accumulation for performance monitoring [8]. An alternative for the framer is Ethernet framer.

*Network Processor.* The NP mainly performs table lookup, packet classification, and packet modification. Various algorithms to implement the first two functions are presented in Chapters 2 and 3, respectively. The NP can perform those two functions at the line rate using external memory, such as static random access memory (SRAM) or dynamic random access memory (DRAM), but it may also require external content addressable memory (CAM) or specialized co-processors to perform deep packet classification at higher levels. In Chapter 16, we present some commercially available NP and ternary content addressable memory (TCAM) chips.

*Traffic Manager.* To meet the requirements of each connection and service class, the TM performs various control functions to cell/packet streams, including traffic access control, buffer management, and cell/packet scheduling. Traffic access control consists of a collection of specification techniques and mechanisms that (1) specify the expected traffic characteristics and service requirements (e.g., peak rate, required delay bound, loss tolerance) of a data stream; (2) shape (i.e., delay) data streams (e.g., reducing their rates and/or burstiness); and (3) police data streams and take corrective actions (e.g., discard, delay, or mark packets) when traffic deviates from its specification. The usage parameter control (UPC) in ATM and differentiated service (DiffServ) in IP performs similar access control functions at the network edge. Buffer management performs cell/packet discarding, according to loss requirements and priority levels, when the buffer exceeds a certain threshold. Proposed schemes include early packet discard (EPD) [9], random early packet discard (REPD) [10], weighted REPD [11], and partial packet discard (PPD) [12]. Packet scheduling ensures that packets are transmitted to meet each connection's allocated bandwidth/delay requirements. Proposed schemes include deficit round-robin, weighted fair queuing (WFQ) and its variants, such as shaped virtual clock [13] and worst-case fairness WFQ (WF$^2$Q+) [14]. The last two algorithms achieve the worst-case fairness properties. Details are discussed in Chapter 4. Many quality of service (QoS) control techniques, algorithms, and implementation architectures can be found in Ref. [15]. The TM may also manage many queues to resolve contention among the inputs of a switch fabric, for example, hundreds or thousands of virtual output queues (VOQs). Some of the representative TM chips on the market are introduced in Chapter 16, whose purpose it is to match the theories in Chapter 4 with practice.

*Central Processing Unit.* The CPU performs control plane functions including connection set-up/tear-down, table updates, register/buffer management, and exception handling. The CPU is usually not in-line with the fast-path on which maximum-bandwidth network traffic moves between the interfaces and the switch fabric.

The architecture in Figure 1.6 can be realized in a multi-rack (also known as multi-chassis or multi-shelf) system as shown in Figure 1.7. In this example, a half rack, equipped with a switch fabric, a duplicated RC, a duplicated MC, a duplicated system clock (CLK), and a duplicated fabric shelf controller (FSC), is connected to all other line card (LC) shelves, each of which has a duplicated line card shelf controller (LSC). Both the FSC and the

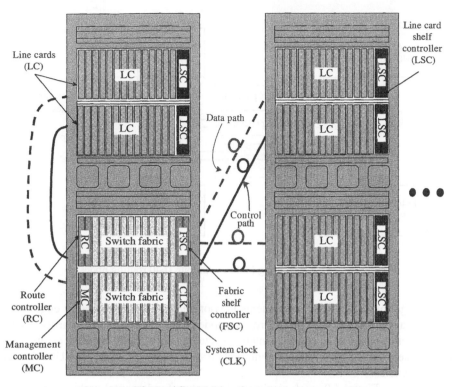

**Figure 1.7**  Multi-rack router system.

LSC provide local operation and maintenance for the switch fabric and line card shelves, respectively. They also provide the communication channels between the switch/line cards with the RC and the MC. The duplicated cards are for reliability concerns. The figure also shows how the system can grow by adding more LC shelves. Interconnections between the racks are sets of cables or fibers, carrying information for the data and the control planes. The cabling usually is a combination of unshielded twisted path (UTP) Category 5 Ethernet cables for control path, and fiber-optic arrays for data path.

## 1.3  COMMERCIAL CORE ROUTER EXAMPLES

We now briefly discuss the two most popular core routers on the market: Juniper Network's T640 TX-Matrix [16] and Cisco System's Carrier Routing System (CRS-1) [17].

### 1.3.1  T640 TX-Matrix

A T640 TX-Matrix is composed of up to four routing nodes and a TX Routing Matrix interconnecting the nodes. A TX Routing Matrix connects up to four T640 routing nodes via a three-stage Clos network switch fabric to form a unified router with the capacity of 2.56 Terabits. The blueprint of a TX Routing Matrix is shown in Figure 1.8. The unified router is controlled by the Routing Engine of the matrix which is responsible for running routing protocols and for maintaining overall system state. Routing engines in each routing

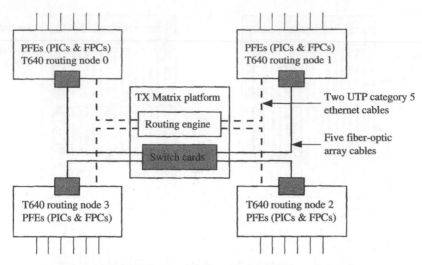

**Figure 1.8** TX Routing Matrix with four T640 routing nodes.

node manage their individual components in coordination with the routing engine of the matrix. Data and control plane of each routing node is interconnected via an array of optical and Ethernet cables. Data planes are interconnected using VCSEL (vertical cavity surface emitting laser) optical lines whereas control planes are interconnected using UTP Category 5 Ethernet cables.

As shown in Figure 1.9, each routing node has two fundamental architectural components, namely the control plane and the data plane. The T640 routing node's control plane is implemented by the JUNOS software that runs on the node's routing engine. JUNOS is a micro-kernel-based modular software that assures reliability, fault isolation, and high availability. It implements the routing protocols, generates routing tables and forwarding tables, and supports the user interface to the router. Data plane, on the other hand, is responsible for processing packets in hardware before forwarding them across the switch fabric from the ingress interface to the appropriate egress interface. The T640 routing node's data plane is implemented in custom ASICs in a distributed architecture.

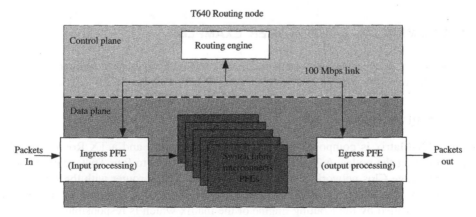

**Figure 1.9** T640 routing node architecture.

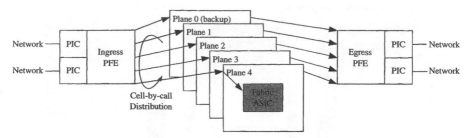

**Figure 1.10**   T640 switch fabric planes.

The T640 routing node has three major elements: Packet forwarding engines (PFEs), the switch fabric, and one or two routing engines. The PFE performs Layer 2 and Layer 3 packet processing and forwarding table lookups. A PFE is made of many ASIC components. For example, there are Media-Specific ASICs to handle Layer 2 functions that are associated with the specific physical interface cards (PICs), such as SONET, ATM, or Ethernet. L2/L3 Packet Processing, and ASICs strip off Layer 2 headers and segment packets into cells for internal processing, and reassemble cells into Layer 3 packets prior to transmission on the egress interface. In addition, there are ASICs for managing queuing functions (Queuing and Memory Interface ASIC), for forwarding cells across the switch fabric (Switch Interface ASICs), and for forwarding lookups (T-Series Internet Processor ASIC).

The switch fabric in a standalone T640 routing node provides data plane connectivity among all of the PFEs in the chassis. In a TX-Routing Matrix, switch fabric provides data plane connectivity among all of the PFEs in the matrix. The T640 routing node uses a Clos network and the TX-Routing Matrix uses a multistage Clos network. This switch fabric provides nonblocking connectivity, fair bandwidth allocation, and distributed control. In order to achieve high-availability each node has up to five switch fabric planes (see Fig. 1.10). At a given time, four of them are used in a round-robin fashion to distribute packets from the ingress interface to the egress interface. The fifth one is used as a hot-backup in case of failures. Access to switch fabric bandwidth is controlled by the following three-step request-grant mechanism. The request for each cell of a packet is transmitted in a round-robin order from the source PFE to the destination PFE. Destination PFE transmits a grant to the source using the same switch plane from which the corresponding request was received. Source PFE then transmits the cell to the destination PFE on the same switch plane.

### 1.3.2   Carrier Routing System (CRS-1)

Cisco System's Carrier Routing System is shown in Figure 1.11. CRS-1 also follows the multi-chassis design with line card shelves and fabric shelves. The design allows the system to combine as many as 72 line card shelves interconnected using eight fabric shelves to operate as a single router or as multiple logical routers. It can be configured to deliver anywhere between 1.2 to 92 terabits per second capacity and the router as a whole can accommodate 1152 40-Gbps interfaces. Router Engine is implemented using at least two route processors in a line card shelf. Each route processor is a Dual PowerPC CPU complex configured for symmetric multiprocessing with 4 GB of DRAM for system processes and routing tables and 2 GB of Flash memory for storing software images and system configuration. In addition, the system is equipped to include non-volatile random access

**Figure 1.11** Cisco CRS-1 carrier routing system.

memory (NVRAM) for configurations and logs and a 40 GB on-board hard drive for data collection. Data plane forwarding functions are implemented through Cisco's Silicon Packet Processor (SPP), an array of 188 programmable reduced instruction set computer (RISC) processors.

Cisco CRS-1 uses a three-stage, dynamically self-routed Benes topology based switching fabric. A high-level diagram of the switch fabric is shown in Figure 1.12. The first-stage (S1) of the switch is connected to ingress line cards. Stage-2 (S2) fabric cards receive cells from Stage-1 fabric cards and deliver them to Stage-3 fabric cards that are associated with the appropriate egress line cards. Stage-2 fabric cards support speedup and multicast replication. The system has eight such switch fabrics operating in parallel through which cells are transferred evenly. This fabric configuration provides highly scalable, available, and survivable interconnections between the ingress and egress slots. The whole system is driven by a Cisco Internet Operating System (IOS) XR. The Cisco IOS XR is built on a micro-kernel-based memory-protected architecture, to be modular. This modularity provides for better scalability, reliability, and fault isolation. Furthermore, the system implements check pointing and stateful hot-standby to ensure that critical processes can be restarted with minimal effect on system operations or routing topology.

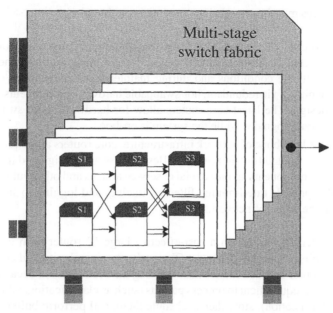

**Figure 1.12**    High-level diagram of Cisco CRS-1 multi-stage switch fabric.

## 1.4  DESIGN OF CORE ROUTERS

Core routers are designed to move traffic as quickly as possible. With the introduction of diverse services at the edges and rapidly increasing bandwidth requirements, core routers now have to be designed to be more flexible and scalable than in the past. To this end, design goals of core routers generally fall into the following categories:

*Packet Forwarding Performance.* Core routers need to provide packet forwarding performance in the range of hundreds of millions of packets per second. This is required to support existing services at the edges, to grow these services in future, and to facilitate the delivery of new revenue-generating services.

*Scalability.* As the traffic rate at the edges grows rapidly, service providers are forced to upgrade their equipment every three to five years. Latest core routers are designed to scale well such that subsequent upgrades are cheaper to the providers. To this end, the latest routers are designed as a routing matrix to add future bandwidth while keeping the current infrastructure in place. In addition, uniform software images and user interfaces across upgrades ensure the users do not need to be retrained to operate the new router.

*Bandwidth Density.* Another issue with core routers is the amount of real estate and power required to operate them. Latest core routers increase bandwidth density by providing higher bandwidths in small form-factors. For example, core routers that provide $32 \times$ OC-192 or $128 \times$ OC-48 interfaces in a half-rack space are currently available on the market. Such routers consume less power and require less real estate.

*Service Delivery Features.* In order to provide end-to-end service guarantees, core routers are also required to provide various services such as aggregate DiffServ classes, packet filtering, policing, rate-limiting, and traffic monitoring at high speeds.

These services must be provided by core routers without impacting packet forwarding performance.

*Availability.* As core routers form a critical part of the network, any failure of a core router can impact networks dramatically. Therefore, core routers require higher availability during high-traffic conditions and during maintenance. Availability on most core routers is achieved via redundant, hot-swappable hardware components, and modular software design. The latest core routers allow for hardware to be swapped out and permit software upgrades while the system is on-line.

*Security.* As the backbone of network infrastructure, core routers are required to provide some security related functions as well. Besides a secure design and implementation of their own components against denial of service attacks and other vulnerabilities, the routers also provide rate-limiting, filtering, tracing, and logging to support security services at the edges of networks.

It is very challenging to design a cost-effective large IP router with a capacity of a few hundred terabits/s to a few petabit/s. Obviously, the complexity and cost of building a large-capacity router is much higher than building an OXC. This is because, for packet switching, there is a requirement to process packets (such as classification, table lookup, and packet header modification), store them, schedule them, and perform buffer management. As the line rate increases, the processing and scheduling time associated with each packet is proportionally reduced. Also, as the router capacity increases, the time interval for resolving output contention becomes more constrained. Memory and interconnection technologies are the most demanding when designing a large-capacity packet switch. The former very often becomes a bottleneck for a large-capacity packet switch while the latter significantly affects a system's power consumption and cost. As a result, designing a cost-effective, large capacity switch architecture still remains a challenge. Several design issues are discussed below.

*Memory Speed.* As optical and electronic devices operate at 10 Gbps (OC-192) at present, the technology and the demand for optical channels operating at 40 Gbps (OC-768) is a emerging. The port speed to a switch fabric is usually twice that of the line speed. This is to overcome some performance degradation that otherwise arises due to output port contention and the overhead used to carry routing, flow control, and QoS information in the packet/cell header. As a result, the aggregated I/O bandwidth of the memory at the switch port can be 120 Gbps. Considering 40-byte packets, the cycle time of the buffer memory at each port is required to be less than 2.66 ns. This is still very challenging with current memory technology, especially when the required memory size is very large and cannot be integrated into the ASIC (application specific integrated circuit), such as for the traffic manager or other switch interface chips. In addition, the pin count for the buffer memory can be several hundreds, limiting the number of external memories that can be attached to the ASIC.

*Packet Arbitration.* An arbitrator is used to resolve output port contention among the input ports. Considering a 40-Gbps switch port with 40-byte packets and a speedup of two, the arbitrator has only about 4 ns to resolve the contention. As the number of input ports increases, the time to resolve the contention reduces. It can be implemented in a centralized way, where the interconnection between the arbitrator and all input line (or port) cards can be prohibitively complex and expensive. On the other hand, it can be implemented in a distributed way, where the line cards and switch cards are involved in the arbitration. The distributed implementation may degrade throughput and delay performance due to lack of the availability of the state information of all inputs and outputs. As a result, a higher speedup is required in the switch fabric to improve performance.

*QoS Control.* Similar to the above packet arbitration problem, as the line (port) speed increases, the execution of policing/shaping at the input ports and packet scheduling and buffer management (discarding packet policies) at the output port (to meet the QoS requirement of each flow or each class) can be very difficult and challenging. The buffer size at each line card is usually required to hold up to 100 ms worth of packets. For a 40-Gbps line, the buffer can be as large as 500 Mbytes, which can store hundreds of thousands of packets. Choosing a packet to depart or to discard within 4 to 8 ns is not trivial. In addition, the number of states that need to be maintained to do per-flow control can be prohibitively expensive. An alternative is to do class-based scheduling and buffer management, which is more sensible at the core network, because the number of flows and the link speed is too high. Several shaping and scheduling schemes require time stamping arriving packets and scheduling their departure based on the time stamp values. Choosing a packet with the smallest time stamp in 4 to 8 ns can cause a bottleneck.

*Optical Interconnection.* A large-capacity router usually needs multiple racks to house all the line cards, port cards (optional), switch fabric cards, and controller cards, such as route controller, management controller, and clock distribution cards. Each rack may accommodate 0.5 to 1 terabit/s capacity depending on the density of the line and switch fabric cards and may need to communicate with another rack (e.g., the switch fabric rack) with a bandwidth of 0.5 to 1.0 terabit/s in each direction. With current VCSEL technology, an optical transceiver can transmit up to 300 meters with 12 SERDES (serializer/deserializer) channels, each running at 2.5 or 3.125 Gbps [18]. They have been widely used for backplane interconnections. However, the size and power consumption of these optical devices could limit the number of interconnections on each circuit board, resulting in more circuit boards, and thus higher implementation costs. Furthermore, a large number of optical fibers are required to interconnect multiple racks. This increases installation costs and makes fiber reconfiguration and maintenance difficult. The layout of fiber needs to be carefully designed to reduce potential interruption caused by human error. Installing new fibers to scale the router's capacity can be mistake-prone and disrupting to the existing services.

*Power Consumption.* As SERDES technology allows more than a hundred bi-directional channels, each operating at 2.5 or 3.125 Gbps, on a CMOS (complementary metal-oxide-semiconductor) chip [19, 20], its power dissipation can be as high as 20 W. With VCSEL technology, each bi-directional connection can consume 250 mW. If we assume that 1 terabit/s bandwidth is required for interconnection to other racks, it would need 400 optical bi-directional channels (each 2.5 Gbps), resulting in a total of 1000 W per rack for optical interconnections. Each rack may dissipate up to several thousands watts due to the heat dissipation limitation, which in turn limits the number of components that can be put on each card and limits the number of cards on each rack. The large power dissipation also increases the cost of air-conditioning the room. The power consumption cannot be overlooked from the global viewpoint of the Internet [21].

*Flexibility.* As we move the core routers closer to the edge of networks, we now have to support diverse protocols and services available at the edge. Therefore, router design must be modular and should evolve with future requirements. This means we cannot rely too heavily on fast ASIC operations; instead a balance needs to be struck between performance and flexibility by ways of programmable ASICs.

## 1.5 IP NETWORK MANAGEMENT

Once many switches and routers are interconnected on the Internet, how are they managed by the network operators? In this section, we briefly introduce the functionalities, architecture, and major components of the management systems for IP networks.

### 1.5.1 Network Management System Functionalities

In terms of the network management model defined by the International Standard Organization (ISO), a network management system (NMS) has five management functionalities [22–24]: performance management (PM), fault management (FM), configuration management (CM), accounting management (AM), and security management (SM).

*PM.* The task of PM is to monitor, measure, report, and control the performance of the network, which can be done by monitoring, measuring, reporting, and controlling the performance of individual network elements (NEs) at regular intervals; or by analyzing logged performance data on each NE. The common performance metrics are network throughput, link utilization, and packet counts input and output from an NE.

*FM.* The goal of FM is to collect, detect, and respond to fault conditions in the network, which are reported as trap events or alarm messages. These messages may be generated by a managed object or its agent built into a network device, such as Simple Network Management Protocol (SNMP) traps [25] or Common Management Information Protocol (CMIP) event notifications [26, 27], or by a network management system (NMS), using synthetic traps or probing events generated by, for instance, Hewlett-Packard's OpenView (HPOV) stations. Fault management systems handle network failures, including hardware failures, such as link down and software failures, and protocol errors, by generating, collecting, processing, identifying, and reporting trap and alarm messages.

*CM.* The task of CM includes configuring the switch and I/O modules in a router, the data and management ports in a module, and the protocols for a specific device. CM deals with the configuration of the NEs in a network to form a network and to carry customers' data traffic.

*AM.* The task of AM is to control and allocate user access to network resources, and to log usage information for accounting purposes. Based on the price model, logged information, such as call detailed records (CDR), is used to provide billing to customers. The price model can be usage-based or flat rate.

*SM.* SM deals with protection of network resources and customers' data traffic, including authorization and authentication of network resources and customers, data integrity, and confidentiality. Basic access control to network resources by using login and password, generation of alarms for security violation and authorization failure, definition and enforcement of security policy, and other application layer security measures such as firewalls, all fall under the tasks of security management.

### 1.5.2 NMS Architecture

Within a network with heterogeneous NEs, the network management tools can be divided into three levels: element management system (EMS), from network equipment vendors that specialize in the management of the vendor's equipment; NMS, aimed at managing networks with heterogeneous equipment; and operational support systems (OSS), operating support and managing systems developed for network operator's specific operations, administration, and maintenance (OAM) needs. A high-level view of the architecture of a typical NMS is shown in Figure 1.13. In this architecture, the management data are collected and processed in three levels.

*EMS Level.* Each NE has its own EMS, such as EMS1, EMS2, and EMS3, shown in Figure 1.13. These EMS collect management data from each NE, process the data, and forward the results to the NMS that manages the overall network. In this way, the EMS and NMS form a distributed system architecture.

*NMS Level.* Functionally, an NMS is the same as an EMS, except an NMS has to deal with many heterogeneous NEs. The NMS station gathers results from the EMS

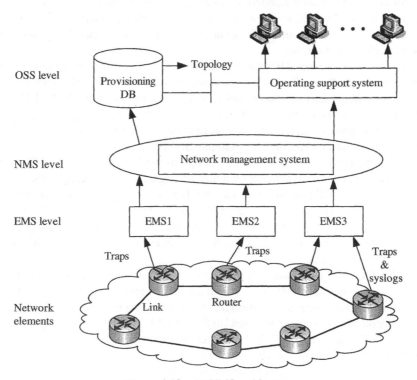

**Figure 1.13**   An NMS architecture.

stations, displays information, and takes control actions. For example, an NMS aggregates the events from all the related NEs in handling a specific fault condition to identify the root cause and to reduce the number of events that are sent to the OSS for further processing. Note that the NMS is independent of specific NEs.

*OSS Level.* By combing the network topology information, the OSS further collects and processes the data for specific operational needs. Therefore, the OSS can have subsystems for PM, FM, AM, and SM.

A key feature of this architecture is that each of the three levels performs all of the network management functions by generating, collecting, processing, and logging the events to solve the scalability issues in large-scale networks.

There are many NMS tools that are commercially available [28, 29]. For example, Cisco's IOS for the management of LANs (local area networks) and WANs (wide area networks) built on Cisco switches and routers; and Nortel's Optivity NMS for the management of Nortel's ATM switches and routers. To manage networks with heterogeneous NEs, the available tools are HPOV, Node Manager, Aprisma's SPECTRUM, and Sun's Solstice NMS. These tools support SNMP and can be accessed through a graphical user interface (GUI) and command line interface (CLI). Some of them also provide automated assistance for CM and FM tasks.

### 1.5.3    Element Management System

As a generic solution for configuring network devices, monitoring status, and checking devices for errors, the Internet-standard framework for network management is used for the management tasks of an NE, as for an IP network. Therefore, functionally, an EMS and NMS have the same architectures. The same five functions for network management are also used for element functions.

The architecture of a general EMS is shown in Figure 1.14. On the device side, the device must be manageable, that is, it must have a management agent such as the SNMP agent (or server), corresponding data structures, and a storage area for the data. On the EMS station side, the station must have a management client such as the SNMP manager (or client). In between the management station and the managed device, we also need a protocol for the communications of the two parties, for example, SNMP.

The core function to manage a device is implemented by using an SNMP manager. Whenever there is a command issued by a user through the user interface, the command is received by the SNMP manager after parsing. If it is a configure command, the SNMP manager issues an SNMP request to the SNMP agent inside the device. From the device, the SNMP agent then goes to the management information bases (MIBs) to change the value of a specified MIB object. This is shown as 'Config' in Figure 1.14. Config can be done by a simple command such as 'set'.

Similarly, if the command issued by the user is to get the current status of the device, the SNMP manager issues an SNMP request to the SNMP agent inside the device. From the device, the SNMP agent then goes to the MIBs to get the value of a specified MIB object by a 'get' command, which is shown as 'View' in Figure 1.14. Then, the SNMP agent forwards the obtained MIB values to the SNMP manager as response back. The response is finally sent to the user for display on the GUI or CLI console.

In some cases, the device may send out messages to its SNMP agent autonomously. One example is the trap or alarm, where the initiator of the event is not the user interface but

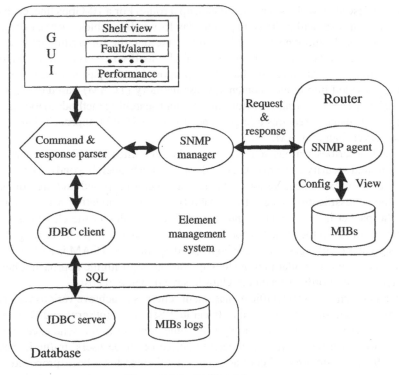

**Figure 1.14**   EMS archtiecture.

the device. Here, the most important communications are regulated by the SNMP protocol, including the operations and protocol data unit (PDU) format.

Note that all the configuration data and performance statistics are usually saved in a separate database. For example, for disaster recovery purposes, the changes in the configuration of a device will also be saved in the database. The database saves both MIB information and log messages. The communications between the database and the management client are implemented by using a database client inside the management client and database server inside the database. As shown in Figure 1.14, a popular choice is a JDBC (Java Database Connectivity) client and a JDBC server in the two sides. The commands and responses between the EMS and the device are parsed and converted into structured query language (SQL) commands to access the database and get the view back.

## 1.6  OUTLINE OF THE BOOK

Chapter 1 describes present day and future Internet architecture, the structure of Points of Presence, where core and edge routers are interconnected with Layer-2 switches. It shows a router architecture, where a large number of line cards are interconnected by a switch fabric. It also includes a router controller that updates the forwarding tables and handles network management. Two commercial, state-of-the-art routers are briefly described. It also outlines the challenges of building a high-speed, high-performance router.

Chapter 2 describes various schemes to look up a route. For a 10-Gbps line, each lookup is required to complete within 40 ns. In present day forwarding tables, there can be as many as 500,000 routes. As more hosts are added to the Internet, the forwarding table will grow one order of magnitude in the near future, especially as IPv6 emerges. Many high-speed lookup algorithms and architectures have been proposed in the past several years and can be generally divided into ternary content address memory (TCAM)-based or algorithmic-based. The latter uses novel data structure and efficient searching methods to look up a route in a memory. It usually requires a larger space than the TCAM approach, but consumes much less power than a TCAM.

Chapter 3 describes various schemes for packet classification. To meet various QoS requirements and security concerns, other fields of a packet header, beyond the IP destination address, are often examined. Various schemes have been proposed and are compared in terms of their classification speed, the capability of accommodating a large number of fields in the packet headers, and the number of filtering rules in the classification table. Because more fields in the packet header need to be examined, in prefix or range formats, it imposes greater challenges to achieve high-speed operations. TCAM is a key component in packet classification, similar to route lookup. Various algorithmic approaches have been investigated by using ordinary memory chips to save power and cost.

Chapter 4 describes several traffic management schemes to achieve various QoS requirements. This chapter starts by explaining Integrated Services (IntServ) and Differentiated Service (DiffServ). Users need to comply with some contract to not send excessive traffic to the network. As a result, there is a need to police or shape users' traffic if they don't comply with the predetermined contract. Several schemes have been proposed to meet various QoS requirements. They are divided into two parts, packet scheduling to meet various delay/bandwidth requirements and buffer management to provide different loss preferences.

Chapter 5 describes the basics of packet switching by showing some fundamental switching concepts and switching fabric structures. Almost all packet switching fabrics can route packets autonomously without an external configuration controller, as circuit switches do. One of the important challenges in building large-scale, high-performance switches is to resolve packet contention, where multiple packets are heading to the same output and only one of them can be transmitted at a time. Buffers are used to temporarily store those packets that lost the contention. However, the placement of the buffers, coupled with contention resolution schemes, determines much of the switch's scalability, operation speed, and performance.

Chapter 6 describes the shared-memory switch, which is the best performance/cost switch architecture. Memory is shared by all inputs and outputs, and thus has the best buffer utilization. In addition, delay performance is also the best because of no head-of-line blocking. On the other hand, the memory needs to operate at the speed of the aggregated bandwidth of all input and output ports. As the line rate or the port number increases, the switch size is limited due to the memory speed constraint. Several architectures have been proposed to tackle the scalability issue by using multiple shared-memory switch modules in parallel. The difference between various proposed ideas lies in the ways of dispatching packets from the input ports to the switch modules.

Chapter 7 describes various packet scheduling schemes for input-buffered switches. The complexity of resolving packet contention can cause the system to bottleneck as the switch size and the line speed increase. The objective is to find a feasible scheduling scheme (e.g., in a time complexity of $O(\log N)$ where $N$ is the switch size), close to 100 percent throughput, and low average delay. Several promising schemes have been proposed to achieve 100 percent throughput without speeding up the internal fabric operation speed. However, their time complexity is very high and prohibits them from being implemented for real applications. One practical way to maintain high-throughput and low delay is to increase the internal switch fabric's operation speed, for example, twice the line rate, to compensate for the deficiency of contention resolution schemes. However, it requires output buffers and, thus, increases the implementation cost. Most packets are delivered to the output buffers and wait there. Thus, some kind of backpressure mechanism is needed to throttle the packets from jamming at the output buffers and from being discarded when buffers overflow.

Chapter 8 describes banyan-based switches. They have a regular structure to interconnect many switch modules that can be $2 \times 2$ or larger. The multistage interconnection network was investigated intensively in early 1970s for interconnecting processors to make a powerful computer. The banyan-based switches received a lot of attention in early 1980s when people started fast packet switching research. One of the reasons is that the switch size can be scaled to very large by adding more stages. However, the interconnection wire can be very long due to the shuffle type of interconnections and they can occupy a large space, inducing considerable propagation delay between the devices, and difficulty in synchronizing the switch modules on the same stage. As a result, one can rarely find a commercial switch/router that is built with the banyan structure.

Chapter 9 describes Knockout switches. It has been proven that output-buffered or shared-memory switches demonstrate the best performance, where packets from all inputs need to be stored in an output buffer if they all are destined for the same output. The memory speed constraint limits the switch size. However, what is the probability that all incoming packets are destined to the same output? If the probability is very low, why do we need to have the output buffer receive all of them at the same time? A group of researchers at Bell Labs in the late 1980s tried to resolve this problem by limiting the number of packets that can arrive at an output port at the same time, thus relaxing the speed requirement of the memory at the output ports. Excessive cells are discarded (or knocked out) by the switch fabric. Various switch architectures using the knockout principle are presented in this chapter.

Chapter 10 describes the Abacus switch that was prototyped at Polytechnic University by the first author of the book. It takes advantage of the knockout principle by feeding back those packets that are knocked out in the first round to retry. As a result, the packets will not be discarded by the switch fabric. The Abacus switch resolves contention by taking advantage of the cross-bar structure of the switch. It can also support the multicasting function due to the nature of the cross-bar structure and the arbitration scheme used in each switch element. The switch fabric has been implemented on ASICs.

Chapter 11 describes crosspoint buffered switches. There are several variants depending where the buffers are placed – only at the crosspoints, both at the inputs and the crosspoints, or at the inputs, the crosspoints, and the outputs. The crosspoint buffer increases performance from input-buffered switches, where performance degradation is due to the head-of-line blocking. In the crosspoint switches, packets are temporarily stored in the crosspoint buffer, allowing multiple packets to be sent out from the same input, which is not possible for the input-buffered switch. However, the trade-off is to implement the memory within the switch fabric. With today's very large scale integration (VLSI) technology, the on-chip memory can be a few tens of megabits, which is sufficient to store a few tens of packets at each crosspoint. Another advantage of this switch architecture is that it allows packet scheduling from inputs to the crosspoint buffers and packet scheduling from the crosspoint buffers to the outputs to be independent, thereby creating the possibility of exploring different scheduling schemes individually to maximize the overall performance.

Chapter 12 describes Clos-network switches. This structure was proposed by Charles Clos for making a scalable telephone circuit switch. It has been used in packet switch fabrics because of its regular interconnections and scalability. Multiple switch modules are interconnected in a Clos-type structure. Each switch module's size is usually determined by the input/output pin count of a chip or the connectors of a printed circuit board. Each switch module can be a crossbar switch with or without buffers. If without buffers, a global contention resolution scheme is required. If with buffers, the contention can be done within the switch modules in a distributed manner. As the switch grows larger and larger, it is more practical to resolve the contention in a distributed manner. However, because of multiple possible paths between each input and each output pair, the challenge becomes choosing a switch module in the center stage. If not carefully chosen, the load is not balanced among the switch modules in the center stage, causing some center modules to be more congested than others. In addition, due to various delays of the multiple paths between an input/output pair, maintaining the order of the packets in the same flow becomes very challenging.

Chapter 13 describes a practical multi-plane, multi-stage buffered switch, called True-Way. It has the features of scalability, high-speed operations, high-performance, and multicasting. It resolves the issues of: (1) How to efficiently allocate and share the limited on-chip memories; (2) How to intelligently schedule packets on multiple paths while maximizing memory utilization and system performance; (3) How to minimize link congestion and prevent buffer overflow (i.e., stage-to-stage flow control); and (4) How to maintain packet order if the packets are delivered over multiple paths (i.e., port-to-port flow control). A small-scale TrueWay switch has been prototyped using field programmable gate array (FPGA) and SERDES chips with signals running at 3.125 Gbps at the backplane.

Chapter 14 describes load-balanced switches. The idea of this type of switch is very interesting. Packets from each input are temporarily and evenly distributed to all other output ports. They are then forwarded to their final destinations. By doing this, the switch fabrics can operate in a cyclic-shifting configuration at each time slot and still achieve 100 percent throughput. One challenging issue of this kind of switch is to maintain packet order. The difference of several proposed schemes lies in the way of resolving the packet out-of-order issue. Since the packets traverse from the input to a temporary output and then from that port to the final output port, one either needs to use two separate switch fabrics or have one switch fabric running at twice the speed of the input. People will argue that the 100 percent throughput is achieved because of the speedup factor of 2. However, the biggest incentive for this kind of switch is that there is no need for an arbitrator to resolve packet contention.

Chapter 15 describes optical packet switches. Depending on whether the contended packets are stored in the optical or in the electrical domain, these switch architectures are classified into opto-electronic packet switches and all-optical packet switches. In either case, contention resolution among the arriving packets is handled electronically. It is very challenging to store contending packets in an optical buffer, which is usually implemented by an optical delay line. The storage size and the time that a packet can be stored are quite limited when using optical delay lines. Another challenging issue is to align the optical packets before storing them on the optical delay lines. It requires tremendous effort to align them when traversing different distances from different sources. Until there is a major breakthrough in optical buffering technology, it will remain very difficult to implement all-optical packet switches.

Chapter 16 describes high-speed router chip sets. This is the most unique section of the book. Up to this point, emphasis has been on learning the background information necessary to implement a high-performance router, including IP address lookup, packet classification, traffic management, and various techniques to build large-scale, high-speed switch fabrics. This section describes practical commercial chips that are used to implement all the above. Thus, it paves a way for tightly combining theory with practice. These chips include: (1) Network processors for flexible packet processing; (2) Co-processors for route lookup and packet classification; (3) Traffic managers; and (4) Switch fabrics.

## REFERENCES

[1] G. Vareille, F. Pitel, and J. F. Marcerou, '3-Tbit/s (300 × 11.6 Gbit/s) transmission over 7380 km using C + L band with 25 GHz channel spacing and NRZ format,' in *Proc. Optical Fiber Communication Conference and Exhibit*, Anaheim, California, vol. 4, pp. PD22-1-3 (Mar. 2001).

[2] R. Ryf *et al.*, '1296-port MEMS transparent optical crossconnect with 2.07 petabit/s switch capacity,' in *Proc. Optical Fiber Communication Conference and Exhibit*, Anaheim, California, vol. 4, pp. PD28-P1 (Mar. 2001).

[3] N. Spring, R. Mahajan, and D. Wetherall, 'Measuring ISP topologies with rocketfuel,' in *Proc. ACM SIGCOMM*, Pittsburgh, Pennsylvania, pp. 133–145 (Aug. 2002).

[4] N. Mckeown, 'A fast switched backplane for a gigabit switched router,' *Business Communications Review*, vol. 27, no. 12 (Dec. 1997).

[5] C. Partridge *et al.*, 'A fifty gigabit per second IP router,' *IEEE/ACM Transactions on Networking*, vol. 6, no. 3. pp. 237–248 (June 1998).

[6] *VIT10: 10G transponder and VSC8173/75: physical layer multiplexer/demultiplexer*, Vitesse. [Online]. Available at: http://www.vitesse.com

[7] *CA16: 2.5 Gbit/s DWDM with 16-channel 155 Mb/s multiplexer and demultiplexer and TB64: Uncoded 10 Gbit/s transponder with 16-channel 622 Mbit/s Multiplexer and Demultiplexer*, Agere. [Online]. Available at: http://www.agere.com

[8] M. C. Chow, *Understanding SONET/SDH: Standards and Applications*, Andan Publisher, 1995.

[9] A. Romanow and R. Oskouy, 'A performance enhancement for packetized ABR and VBR + data,' *ATM Forum 94-0295*, Mar. 1994. [Online]. Available at: http://www.mfaforum.org

[10] S. Floyd and V. Jacobson, 'Random early detection gateways for congestion avoidance,' *IEEE/ACM Transactions on Networking*, vol. 2, no. 4, pp. 397–413 (Aug. 1993).

[11] *Quality of Service (QoS) Networking*, Cisco System, June 1999, white paper.

[12] G. Armitage and K. Adams, 'Package reassembly during cell loss,' *IEEE Network*, vol. 7, no. 5, pp. 26–34 (Sept. 1993).

[13] D. Stiliadis and A. Varma, 'A general methodology for design efficient traffic scheduling and shaping algortihms,' in *Proc. IEEE INFOCOM'97*, Kobe, Japan, pp. 326–335 (Apr. 1997).

[14] J. C. R. Bennett and H. Zhang, 'Hierarchical packet fair queuing algorithms,' *IEEE/ACM Transactions on Networking*, vol. 5, no. 5, pp. 675–689 (Oct. 1997).

[15] H. J. Chao and X. Guo, *Quality of Service Control in High-Speed Networks*, John Wiley & Sons, Inc., Sept. 2001.

[16] 'Juniper networks t-series core platforms,' Juniper Inc. [Online]. Available at: http://www.juniper.net/products/tseries/

[17] R. Sudan and W. Mukai, *Introduction to the Cisco CRS-1 Carrier Routing System*, Cisco Systems, Inc, Jan. 1994.

[18] *Plugable fiber optic link* (12 × 2.5 *Gbps*), Paracer. [Online]. Available at: http://www. paracer.com

[19] *M21150 and M21155 144 × 144 3.2 Gbps Crosspoint Switch*, Mindspeed. [Online]. Available at: http://www.mindspeed.com

[20] *VC3003 140 × 140 Multi-Rate Crosspoint Switch with Clock, Data Recovery at Each Serial Input*, Velio. [Online]. Available at: http://www.velio.com

[21] M. Gupta and S. Singh, 'Greening of the Internet,' in *Proc. ACM SIGCOMM03*, Karlsruhe, Germany, pp. 19–26 (Aug. 2003).

[22] 'ISO 9596, information processing systems, open system interconnection, management information protocol specification, common management information protocol.' ISO, Nov. 1990.

[23] 'ISO 7498, information processing systems, open system interconnection, basic reference model part 4, OSI management framework.' ISO, Oct. 1986.

[24] 'ISO/IEC DIS 10165-1, ISO/IEC DIS 10165-2, ISO/IEC DIS 10165-4, information processing systems, open system interconnection, structure of management information.' ISO, July 1990.

[25] J. Case, R. Mundy, D. Partain, and B. Stewart, *Introduction to Version 3 of the Internet-standard Network Management Framework*, RFC 2570 (Informational), Apr. 1999, obsoleted by RFC 3410. [Online]. Available at: http://www.ietf.org/rfc/rfc2570.txt

[26] U. Black, *Network Management Standards: SNMP, CMIP, TMN, MIBs, and Object Libraries*, 2nd ed., McGraw-Hill, 1994.

[27] W. Stallings, *SNMP, SNMPv2, SNMPv3, and RMON 1 and 2*, Addison-Wesley, Massachusetts 1999.

[28] *SNMPv1, SNMPv2, and SNMPv3*, SNMP Research International. [Online]. Available at: http://www.snmp.com

[29] *MIB compiler, MIB browser, and SNMP APIs*, AdventNet, Inc. [Online]. Available at: http://www.adventnet.com/products/javaagent/snmp-agent-mibcompiler.html

# CHAPTER 2

# IP ADDRESS LOOKUP

## 2.1 OVERVIEW

The primary role of routers is to forward packets toward their final destinations. To this purpose, a router must decide for each incoming packet where to send it next, that is, finding the address of the next-hop router as well as the egress port through which the packet should be sent. This forwarding information is stored in a forwarding table that the router computes based on the information gathered by routing protocols. To consult the forwarding table, the router uses the packet's destination address as a key – this operation is called *address lookup* [1]. Once the forwarding information is retrieved, the router can transfer the packet from the incoming link to the appropriate outgoing link.

***Classful Addressing Scheme.*** IPv4 IP addresses are 32 bits in length and are divided into 4 octets. Each octet has 8 bits that are separated by dots. For example, the address 10000010 01010110 00010000 01000010 corresponds in dotted-decimal notation to 130.86.16.66. The bits in an IP address are ordered as shown in Figure 2.1, where the 1st bit is the most significant bit (MSB) that lies in the leftmost position. The 32nd bit is the least significant bit (LSB) and it lies in the rightmost position.

The IP address consists of two parts. The first part contains the IP addresses for networks and the second part contains the IP addresses for hosts. The network part corresponds to the first bits of the IP address, called the *address prefix*. We will write prefixes as bit strings of up to 32 bits in IPv4 followed by an asterisk(*). For example, the prefix 10000010 01010110* represents all the $2^{16}$ addresses that begin with the bit pattern 10000010 01010110. Alternatively, prefixes can be indicated using the dotted-decimal notation, so the same prefix can be written as 130.86/16, where the number after the slash indicates the length of the prefix.

*High Performance Switches and Routers*, by H. Jonathan Chao and Bin Liu
Copyright © 2007 John Wiley & Sons, Inc.

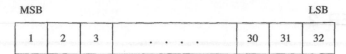

**Figure 2.1**   IP address bit positions.

Since routing occurs at the network level to locate the destination network, routers only forward packets based on network level IP addresses. Thus, all hosts attached to the network can be stored in the router's forwarding table by a single network IP address, known as *address aggregation*. A group of addresses are represented by prefixes. An example of a router's forwarding table is shown in Table 2.1. Each entry in the forwarding table contains a prefix, next-hop IP address, and output interface number. The forwarding information is located by searching for the prefix of the destination address.

The Internet addressing architecture was first designed using an allocation scheme known as *classful addressing*. Classful addressing defines three different sized networks of classes: A, B, or C (Fig. 2.2). The classes are based on the amount of IP addresses contained in the network partition. With the IPv4 address space of 32 bits, Class A has a network size of 8 bits and a host size of 24 bits. Class B has a network size of 16 bits and a host size of 16 bits. Class C has a network size of 24 bits and a host size of 8 bits. Class D is for multicasting applications.

The classful addressing scheme created very few class A networks. Their address space contains 50 percent of the total IPv4 address space ($2^{31}$ addresses out of a total of $2^{32}$). Class B address space contains 16,384 ($2^{14}$) networks with up to 65,534 hosts per network. Class C address space contains 2,097,152 ($2^{21}$) networks with up to 256 hosts per network.

***Classless Inter-Domain Routing (CIDR) Addressing Scheme.*** The evolution and growth of the Internet in recent years has proven that the classful address scheme is inflexible and wasteful. For most organizations, class C is too small while class B is too large. The three choices resulted in address space being exhausted very rapidly, even though only a small fraction of the addresses allocated were actually in use. The lack of a network class of a size that is appropriate for mid-sized organizations results in the exhaustion of the class B network address space. In order to use the address space efficiently, bundles of class C addresses were given out instead of class B addresses. This causes a massive growth of forwarding table entries.

CIDR [2] was introduced to remedy the inefficiencies of classful addressing. The Internet Engineering Task Force (IETF) began implementing CIDR in the early 1990s [2, 3]. With CIDR, IP address space is better conserved through arbitrary aggregation of network

**TABLE 2.1   Router's Forwarding Table Structure [1]**

| Destination Address Prefix | Next Hop IP Address | Output Interface |
| --- | --- | --- |
| 24.40.32/20 | 192.41.177.148 | 2 |
| 130.86/16 | 192.41.177.181 | 6 |
| 208.12.16/20 | 192.41.177.241 | 4 |
| 208.12.21/24 | 192.41.177.196 | 1 |
| 167.24.103/24 | 192.41.177.3 | 4 |

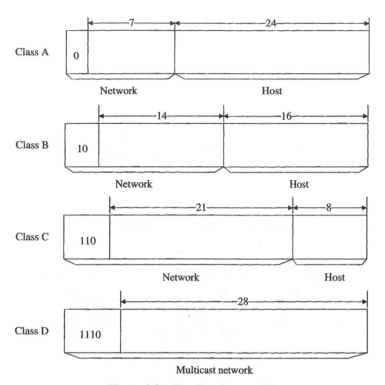

**Figure 2.2** Classful addresses [1].

addresses rather than being limited to 8, 16, or 24 bits in length for the network part. This type of granularity provides an organization with more precise matches for IP address space requirements. The growth of forwarding table entries is also slowed by allowing address aggregation to occur at several levels within the heirarchy of the Internet's topology. Backbone routers can now maintain the forwarding information at the level of the arbitrary aggregates of networks, instead of at the network level only.

For example, consider the networks represented by the network numbers from 208.12.16/24 through 208.12.31/24 (see Fig. 2.3) and in a router all these network addresses are reachable through the same service provider. The leftmost 20 bits of all the addresses in this range are the same (11010000 00001100 0001). Thus, these 16 networks can be aggregated into one 'supernetwork' represented by the 20-bit prefix, which in decimal notation gives 208.12.16/20. Indicating the prefix length is necessary in decimal notation, because the same value may be associated with prefixes of different lengths; for instance, 208.12.16/20 (11010000 00001100 0001*) is different from 208.12.16/22 (11010000 00001100 000100*).

Address aggregation does not reduce entries in the router's forwarding table for all cases. Consider the scenario where a customer owns the network 208.12.21/24 and changes its service provider, but does not want to renumber its network. Now, all the networks from 208.12.16/24 through 208.12.31/24 can be reached through the same service provider, except for the network 208.12.21/24 (see Fig. 2.4). We cannot perform aggregation as before, and instead of only one entry, 16 entries need to be stored in the forwarding table. One solution is aggregating in spite of the exception networks and additionally storing

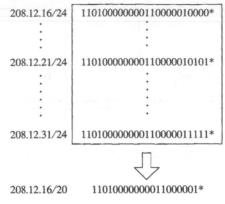

**Figure 2.3**   Prefix aggregation [1].

**Figure 2.4**   Prefix ranges [1].

entries for the exception networks. In this example, this will result in only two entries in the forwarding table: 208.12.16/20 and 208.12.21/24 (see Fig. 2.5 and Table 2.1). However, now some addresses will match both entries because of the prefixes overlap. In order to always make the correct forwarding decision, routers need to do more than search for a prefix that matches. Since exceptions in the aggregations may exist, a router must find the most specific match, which is the longest matching prefix. In summary, the address lookup problem in routers requires searching the forwarding table for the longest prefix that matches the destination address of a packet.

Obviously, the longest prefix match is harder than the exact match used for class-based addressing because the destination address of an arriving packet does not carry with it the information to determine the length of the longest matching prefix. Hence, we need to search among the space of all prefix lengths, as well as the space of all prefixes of a given length. Many algorithms have been proposed in recent years regarding the longest prefix match. This chapter provides a survey of these techniques. But before that, we introduce some performance metrics [4] for the comparison of these lookup algorithms.

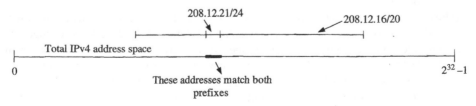

**Figure 2.5**   Exception prefix [1].

*Lookup Speed.* The explosive growth of link bandwidth requires faster IP lookups. For example, links running at 10 Gbps can carry 31.25 million packets per second (mpps) (assuming minimum sized 40-byte IP packets).

*Storage Requirement.* Small storage means fast memory access speed and low power consumption, which are important for cache-based software algorithms and SRAM (static RAM)-based hardware algorithms.

*Update Time.* Currently, the Internet has a peak of a few hundred BGP (Border Gateway Protocol) updates per second. Thus, a certain algorithm should be able to perform 1k updates per second to avoid routing instabilities. These updates should interfere little with normal lookup operations.

*Scalability.* It is expected that the size of forwarding tables will increase at a speed of 25k entries per year. Hence, there will be around 250 k entries for the next five years. The ability of an algorithm to handle large forwarding tables is required.

*Flexibility in Implementation.* Most current lookup algorithms can be implemented in either software or hardware. Some of them have the flexibility of being implemented in different ways, such as ASIC, a network processor, or a generic processor.

## 2.2  TRIE-BASED ALGORITHMS

### 2.2.1  Binary Trie

A trie structure is a multi-way tree where each node contains zero or more pointers to point its child nodes, allowing the organization of prefixes on a digital basis by using the bits of prefixes to direct the branching. In the binary trie (or 1-bit trie) structure [5], each node contains two pointers, the 0-pointer and the 1-pointer.

***Data Structure.*** A node $X$ at the level $h$ of the trie represents the set of all addresses that begin with the sequence of $h$ bits consisting of the string of bits labeling the path from the root to that node. Depending on the value of the $(h + 1)$th bit, 0 or 1, each pointer of the node $X$ points to the corresponding subtree (if it exists), which represents the set of all route prefixes that have the same $(h + 1)$ bits as their first bits. An example data structure of each node (i.e., the entry in a memory) is shown in Figure 2.6, including the next hop address (if it is a prefix node), a left pointer pointing to the left node location (with an address bit 0) and a right pointer pointing to the right node location (with an address bit 1).

A prefix database is defined as a collection of all prefixes in a forwarding table. A prefix database example is shown in Figure 2.6 [6], where the prefixes are arranged in an ascending order of their lengths for easy illustration.

To add a route prefix, say 10111*, simply follow the pointer to where 10111 would be in the trie. If no pointer exists for that prefix, it should be added. If the node for the prefix already exists, it needs to be marked with a label as being in the forwarding table (for example, $P_i$). The nodes in gray are prefix nodes. When deleting a route prefix that has no children, the node and the pointer pointing to it are deleted and the parent node is examined. If the parent node has another child or it is a gray node, it is left alone. Otherwise, that node is also deleted and its parent node is examined. The deletion process is repeated up to the trie until a node that has another child or a gray node is found.

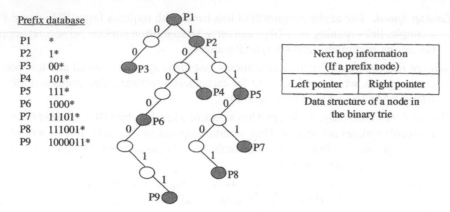

**Figure 2.6** Data structure of a 1-bit binary trie.

***Route Lookup.*** Each IP lookup starts at the root node of the trie. Based on the value of each bit of the destination address of the packet, the lookup algorithm determines whether the left or the right node is to be visited. The next hop of the longer matching prefix found along the path is maintained while the trie is traversed. An example is shown in Figure 2.6. Suppose that a destination address 11101000 is given. The IP lookup starts at the root, traverses the path indicated by the destination address, and remembers the last time a gray node was visited. The first bit of 11101000 is 1, so we go to the right and get to the node 1*, which is a gray node, the longest prefix match so far. The 2nd–5th bits of the key are 1, 1, 0, and 1, respectively. So, we turn right, right, left, and right in sequence, and come to a leaf node P7. It is a prefix node and its associated next hop information is returned.

***Performance.*** The drawback of using the binary trie structure for IP route lookup is that the number of memory accesses in the worst case is 32 for IPv4. To add a prefix to the trie, in the worst case it needs to add 32 nodes. In this case, the storing complexity is $32N \cdot S$, where $N$ denotes the number of prefixes in the forwarding table and $S$ denotes the memory space required for each node. In summary, the lookup complexity is $O(W)$, so is the update complexity, where $W$ is the maximum length of the prefix. The storage complexity is $O(NW)$.

***Variants of Binary Tries.*** The 1-bit binary trie in Figure 2.6 can be expanded to a complete trie, where every bottom leaf node is a prefix. There will be 128 leaf nodes. The data structure will be a memory with 128 entries. Each stores a prefix and can be directly accessed by a memory lookup using the seven bits of the destination address. One drawback is that the memory size becomes too big to be practical when the address has 32 bits, requiring a memory with $2^{32}$ entries.

One way to avoid the use of the longest prefix match rule and still find the most specific forwarding information is to transform a given set of prefixes into a set of disjoint prefixes. Disjoint prefixes do not overlap, and thus no address prefix is itself a prefix of another. A trie representing a set of disjoint prefixes will have prefixes at the leaves but not at internal nodes. To obtain a disjoint-prefix binary trie, we simply add leaves to nodes that have only one child. These new leaves are new prefixes that inherit the forwarding information of the closest ancestor marked as a prefix. Finally, internal nodes marked as prefixes are unmarked.

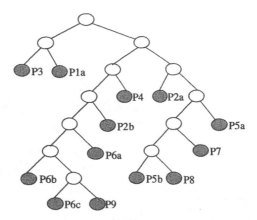

**Figure 2.7**   Disjoint-prefix binary trie.

For example, Figure 2.7 shows the disjoint-prefix binary trie that corresponds to the trie in Figure 2.6. Prefixes P2a and P2b have inherited the forwarding information of the original prefix P2, similar to other nodes such as P1a, P5b, P6a, P6b, and P6c. Since prefixes at internal nodes are expanded or pushed down to the leaves of the trie, this technique is called 'leaf pushing' by Srinivasan and Varghese [7].

### 2.2.2   Path-Compressed Trie

Path compression technique was first adopted in the Patricia trees [8]. A path-compressed trie is based on the observation that each internal node of the trie that does not contain a route prefix and has only one child node can be removed in order to shorten the path from the root node.

**Data Structure.**   By removing some internal nodes, the technique requires a mechanism to record which nodes are missing. A simple mechanism is to store in each node:

- A number, the skip value, that indicates how many bits have been skipped on the path.
- A variable-length bit-string, segment, that indicates the missing bit-string from the last skip operation.

The path-compressed version of the binary trie in Figure 2.6 is shown in Figure 2.8. The node structure has two more fields – skip value and segment. Note that some gray nodes have a skip value $= 1$ or $> 1$. For instance, for node P9, its skip value $= 2$ and the segment is '11'. As compared to P9 in Figure 2.6, the P9 node in Figure 2.8 moved up the level by 2 and missed the examination of two bits '11'. Therefore, when we traverse the trie in Figure 2.8 and reach P9, the immediate two bits of the key need to be checked with the 2-bit segment.

**Route Lookup.**   Suppose that a destination address 11101000 (i.e., the key) is given. The route lookup starts at the root and traverses the path based on the destination address bits. It also records the last gray node that was visited. The first bit of 11101000 is 1, so we go to the right and get to the prefix node P2. As the second bit of the key is 1, we go right again,

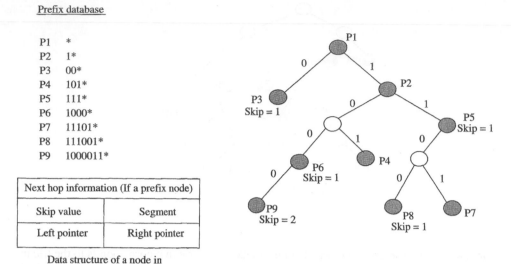

Prefix database

| | |
|---|---|
| P1 | * |
| P2 | 1* |
| P3 | 00* |
| P4 | 101* |
| P5 | 111* |
| P6 | 1000* |
| P7 | 11101* |
| P8 | 111001* |
| P9 | 1000011* |

| Next hop information (If a prefix node) | |
|---|---|
| Skip value | Segment |
| Left pointer | Right pointer |

Data structure of a node in
the path-compressed trie

**Figure 2.8**    Path-compressed trie example.

and reach node P5. This node has a skip value of 1, meaning that a node is skipped on the path. We then use the 3rd bits of the key to compare with the segment field '1' (to verify we have arrived at the correct node in the path). If a match is found, it indicates that we have arrived at P5 correctly. As the 4th bit of the key is 0, we turn left; no skip value is found so we move on. With the 5th bit a 1, we again turn right and get to node P7. Here, we reach a leaf and no skip value is found. So, the lookup stops here, and the next hop information corresponding to P7 is returned.

**Performance.** Path compression reduces the height of a sparse binary trie. When the tree is full and there is no compression possible, a path-compressed trie looks the same as a regular binary trie. Thus, its lookup and update complexity (the worst case) is the same as a binary trie, $O(W)$. Considering a path-compressed trie as a full binary trie with $N$ leaves, there can be $N - 1$ internal nodes between the root and each leaf node (including the root node), as shown in Figure 2.9. Since the path can be significantly compressed to reduce the internal nodes, the space complexity becomes $O(N)$, independent of $W$.

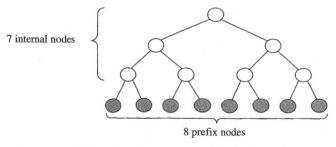

7 internal nodes

8 prefix nodes

**Figure 2.9**    Example of path-compressed trie with $N$ leaves.

### 2.2.3 Multi-Bit Trie

The lookup performance can be improved by using a multi-bit trie structure [7]. The multi-bit trie structure examines several bits at a time, called the lookup stride, while the standard binary trie only examines one bit at a time.

***Data Structure.*** A multi-bit trie example is shown in Figure 2.10. Its prefix database is the same as the one in Figure 2.6. Suppose we examine the destination address three bits at a time, that is, the lookup stride is 3. Then a problem arises for the prefixes like P2 = 1* that do not fit evenly in multiples of three bits. One solution is to expand a prefix like 1* into all possible 3 bit extensions (100, 101, 110, and 111). However, prefixes like P4 = 101 and P5 = 111 are selected because they have longer length matches than those of expanded prefixes of P2. In other words, prefixes whose lengths do not fit into the stride length are expanded into a number of prefixes that fit into the stride length. However, expanded prefixes that collide with an existing longer length prefix are discarded.

Figure 2.10 shows an expanded trie with a fixed stride length of 3 (i.e., each trie node examines three bits). Notice that each trie node has a record of eight entries and each has two fields: one for the next hop information of a prefix and one for a pointer that points to the next child node. Consider, for example, entry 100 in the root node. It contains a prefix (P2 = 100) and a pointer to the trie node containing P6. The P6 pointer also points to another trie containing P9.

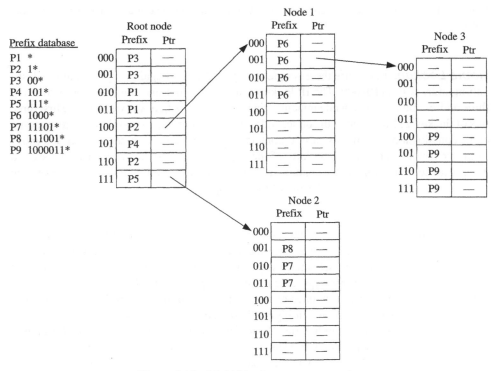

**Figure 2.10** Multi-bit trie structure example.

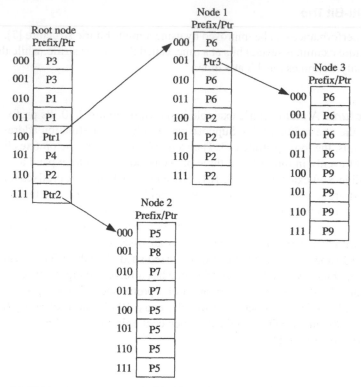

**Figure 2.11**   Multi-bit trie structure example with each entry a prefix or a pointer to save memory space.

*Route Lookup.* Let us use the example in Figure 2.10 and again suppose that the destination address is 11101000. The IP lookup starts at the root and traverses the path using three address bits at a time while remembering the last prefix that was visited. The first three bits of the key 111 are used as the offset address in the root node to find if the corresponding entry contains a prefix (in this case, it contains P5). We then follow the pointer and move to the next node. Then the 4–6th bits of the key 010 are used as an offset in the second node. The corresponding entry contains P7's next hop information and a pointer pointing to a NULL address, indicating the end of the lookup.

*Performance.* The advantage of the $k$-bit trie structure is that it improves the lookup by $k$ times. The disadvantage is that a large memory space is required. One way to reduce the memory space is to use a scheme called 'leaf pushing' described in Section 2.2.1. Leaf pushing can cut the memory requirements of the expanded trie in half by making each node's entry contain either a pointer or next hop information but not both (as shown in Figure 2.11 versus the one shown in Figure 2.10). The trick is to push down the next hop information to the leaf nodes of the trie. The leaf nodes only have the next hop information, since they do not have a pointer. For instance, P6's next hop information at the entry 001 of the top middle node is pushed down to the vacant locations of its child node (i.e., the right most node).

The lookup is performed in strides of $k$ bits. The lookup complexity is the number of bits in the prefix divided by $k$ bits, $O(W/k)$. For example, if $W$ is 32 and $k$ is 4, then 8 lookups in the worst case are required to access that node. An update requires a search through $W/k$ lookup iterations plus access to each child node ($2^k$). The update complexity is $O(W/k + 2^k)$. In the worst case, each prefix would need an entire path of length ($W/k$) and each node would have $2^k$ entries. The space complexity would then be $O((2^k * N * W)/k)$.

### 2.2.4 Level Compression Trie

The path-compressed trie in Section 2.2.2 is an effective way to compress a trie when nodes are sparsely populated. Nilsson and Karlsson [9] have proposed a technique called level compression trie (LC-trie), to compress the trie where nodes are densely populated. The LC-trie actually combines the path-compression and multi-bit trie concepts to optimize a binary trie structure.

**Data Structure.** The fixed-stride multi-bit trie (in Section 2.2.3) can improve lookup performance, but it may incur redundant storage. However, from an angle of local scopes, if we only perform multi-bit lookup wherever the sub-trie structures are full sub-trees, then no redundant storage is needed in those nodes. The construction of the LC-trie is, in fact, a process of transforming a path-compressed trie to a multi-bit path-compressed trie. The process is to find the full sub-trees of a path-compressed trie, and transform them into multi-bit lookup nodes. Therefore, information stored in each node of the LC-trie includes those that are needed for both the path-compressed trie and the multi-bit trie lookup.

The LC-trie algorithm starts with a disjoint-prefix binary trie as described in Section 2.2.1, where only leaf nodes contain prefixes. Figure 2.12 shows three different tries: (*a*) 1-bit binary trie with prefixes at leaf nodes; (*b*) path-compressed trie; and (*c*) LC-trie. The LC-trie needs only three levels instead of the six required in the path-compressed trie. Furthermore, Figure 2.12 shows a straight-forward transformation from path-compressed trie to LC-trie, as shown in the dashed boxes in Figures 2.12*b* and *c*, where the first three levels of the path-compressed trie that form a full sub-trie are converted to a single-level 3-bit sub-trie in the LC-trie.

**Route Lookup.** Let us again use the 8-bit destination address 11100000 as an example to explain the lookup process. The lookup starts at the root node of the LC-trie in Figure 2.12*c*. In this node, the multi-bit and path-compression trie lookup information shows 'stride = 3' and 'skip = 0'. 'Stride = 3' indicates that there would be $2^3 = 8$ branches in this node and that we should use (the next) 3 bits of the address to find the corresponding branch. 'Skip = 0' indicates that no path compression is involved here. The first three bits of the address 111 are inspected, and we should take the $(7 + 1) = 8$th branch of this node. Then, at the branched node, we have 'stride = 1' and 'skip = 3'. 'Stride = 1' indicates that there are only $2^1 = 2$ branches in this node. 'Skip = 3' indicates that the following path of the trie is path-compressed, and we should compare with the stored segment, and if it matches then skip the next three bits of the IP address. We skip the next three bits 000 and examine the fourth bit, 0. The bit 0 indicates that we should take the left branch of this node, and then we come to node 13. On finding that node 13 is a leaf node, the lookup stops here, and the next hop information corresponding to node 13 is returned.

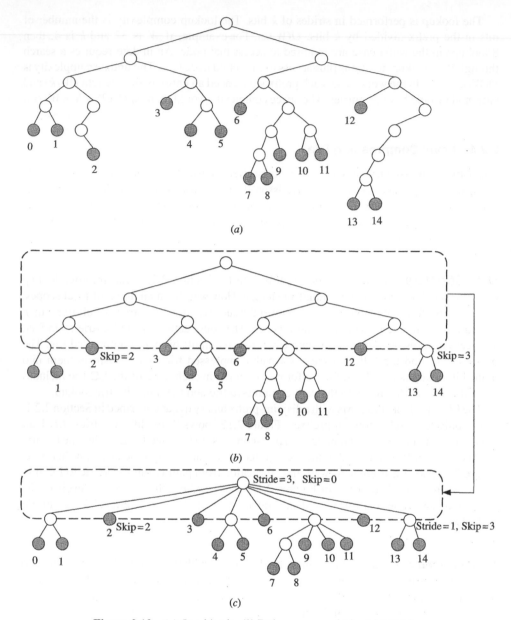

**Figure 2.12** (*a*) One-bit trie; (*b*) Path-compressed trie; (*c*) LC-trie.

***Performance.*** Instead of only transforming strictly full sub-tries in the path-compressed trie, we could transform nearly full sub-tries as well. An optimization proposed by Nilsson and Karlsson [9] suggests this improvement under the control of a fill factor $x$, where $0 < x < 1$. The transformation could be performed on this sub-trie when a $k$-level sub-trie has more than $2^k \cdot x$ leaf nodes available.

Less than 1-Mbyte memory is required and 2 Mpackets/s (assuming average packet size of 250 bytes) search speed is achieved when running on a SUN Sparc Ultra II workstation [9]. This is for an LC-trie built with a fill factor of 0.5 and using 16 bits for branching at the root and a forwarding table with around 38,000 entries. However, using a node array to store the LC-trie makes incremental updates very difficult.

An LC-trie searches in strides of $k$ bits, and thus the lookup complexity of a $k$-stride LC-trie is $O(W/k)$. To update a particular node, we would have to go through $W/k$ lookups and then access each child of the node ($2^k$). Thus, the update complexity is $O(W/k + 2^k)$. The memory consumption increases exponentially as the stride size ($k$) increases. In the worst case, each prefix would need an entire path of length ($W/k$) and each node has $2^k$ entries. The space complexity would then be $O((2^k * N * W)/k)$.

### 2.2.5 Lulea Algorithm

Degermark et al. [10] have proposed a data structure that can represent large forwarding tables in a very compact form. This solution is small enough to fit entirely in the Level 1/Level 2 cache. This provides an advantage in that this fast IP route-lookup algorithm can be implemented in software running on general-purpose microprocessors at high speeds.

The key idea of the Lulea scheme is to replace all consecutive elements in a trie node that have the same value with a single value, and use a bitmap to indicate which elements have been omitted. This can significantly reduce the number of elements in a trie node and save memory.

Basically, the Lulea trie is a multi-bit trie that uses bitmap compression. We begin with the corresponding multi-bit 'leaf-pushing' trie structure given in Section 2.2.3. For instance, consider the root node in Figure 2.11. Before bitmap compression, the root node has the sequence of values (P3, P3, P1, P1, ptr1, P4, P2, ptr2), where ptr1 is a pointer to the trie node containing P6 and ptr2 is a pointer to the trie node containing P7. If we replace each string of consecutive values by the first value in the sequence, we get P3, −, P1, −, ptr1, P4, P2, ptr2. Notice the two redundant values have been removed. We can now get rid of the original trie node and replace it with a bitmap 10101111 where the '0's indicate the removed position and a compressed list (P3, P1, ptr1, P4, P2, ptr2). The result of doing bitmap compression for all four trie nodes is shown in Figure 2.13.

***Data Structure.*** The multi-bit trie in the Lulea algorithm is a disjoint-prefix trie as described in Section 2.2.1. As shown in Figure 2.14, level one of the data structure covers the trie down to depth 16, level two covers depths 17 to 24, and level three depths 25 to 32. A level-two chunk describes parts of the trie that are deeper than 16. Similarly, chunks at level three describe parts of the trie that are deeper than 24. The result of searching a level of the data structure is either an index into the next-hop information or an index into an array of chunks for the next level.

The first level is essentially a complete trie with 1–64k children nodes, which covers the trie down to depth 16. Imagine a cut through the trie at depth 16. Figure 2.15 shows an example of partial cut. The cut is stored in a bit-vector, with one bit per possible node at depth 16. Thus, $2^{16}$ bits = 64 kbits = 8 kbytes are required for this. The upper 16 bits of the address are used as an index into the bit-vector to find the bit corresponding to the initial part of an IP address.

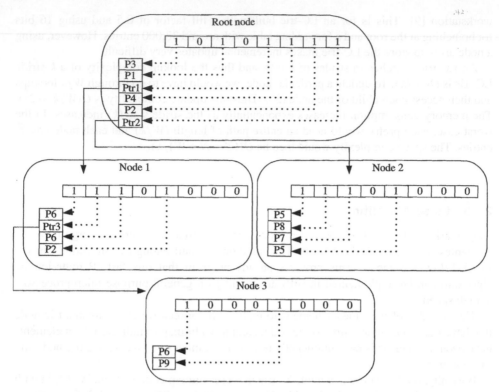

**Figure 2.13** Example of a Lulea trie.

As shown in Figure 2.15, a bit in the bit-vector can be set to:

- One representing that a prefix tree continues below the cut. They are called a root head (bits 6, 12, and 13 in Fig. 2.15).
- One representing a prefix at depth 16 or less. For the latter case, only the lowest bit in the interval covered by that prefix is set. They are called a genuine head (bits 0, 4, 7, 8, 14, and 15 in Fig. 2.15).
- Zero, which means that this value is a member of a range covered by a prefix at a depth less than 16 (bits 1, 2, 3, 5, 9, 10, and 11 in Fig. 2.15).

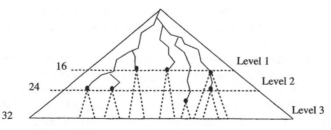

**Figure 2.14** Three levels of the data structure [10].

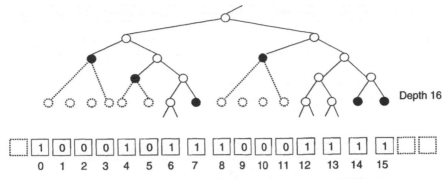

**Figure 2.15**   Part of cut with corresponding bit-vector [10].

A pointer to the next-hop information is stored for genuine heads. Members behind the genuine head use the same index. A pointer to the level two chunk that represents the corresponding sub-trie is stored in the root heads.

The head information is encoded in 16-bit pointers stored in an array. Two bits of the pointer encode what kind of pointer it is. The 14 remaining bits are either indices into the next-hop information or into an array containing level two chunks. Note that there are as many pointers associated with a bit-mask as its number of set bits.

***Finding Pointer Groups.***   The bit-vector is divided into bit-masks of length 16 and there are $2^{12} = 4096$ of those. Figure 2.16 is an illustration of how the data structure for finding pointers corresponds to the bit-masks. The data structure consists of an array of code words of all bit-masks and an array of base indices of one per four code words. The code words consist of a 6-bit offset $(0, 3, 10, 11, \ldots)$ and a 10-bit value $(r1, r2, \ldots)$.

The first bit-mask in Figure 2.16 has three set bits. The second code word thus has an offset of three because three pointers must be skipped over to find the first pointer associated with that bit-mask. The second bit-mask has seven set bits and consequently the offset in the third code word is $3 + 7 = 10$.

After four code words, the offset value might be too large to represent with six bits. Therefore, a base index is used together with the offset to find a group of pointers. There can be at most 64k pointers in a level of the data structure, so the base indices need to be at most 16 bits $(2^{16} = 64k)$. In Figure 2.16, the second base index is 13 because there are 13 set bits in the first four bit-masks. This explains how a group of pointers is located. The first 12 bits of the IP address are an index to the proper code words. The first 10 bits are an index to the array of base indices.

How to find the correct pointer in the group of pointers will now be explained. This is what the 10-bit value is for $(r1, r2, \ldots$ in Fig. 2.16). The value is an index into a table that maps bit-numbers in the IP address to pointer offsets. Since bit-masks are generated from a complete trie, not all combinations of the 16 bits are possible. As shown by Degermark et al. [10], the number of possible bit-masks with length 16 is only 678. They are all stored in a table, called `maptable`, as shown in Figure 2.17. An index into a table with an entry for each bit-mask only needs 10 bits. The content of each entry of the `maptable` is a bit-mask of 4-bit offsets. The offset specifies how many pointers to skip over to find the wanted one, so it is equal to the number of set bits smaller than the bit index. For instance, if the 2nd 4-bit mask in Figure 2.16 is chosen and the low 4 of high 16 bits of IP address is

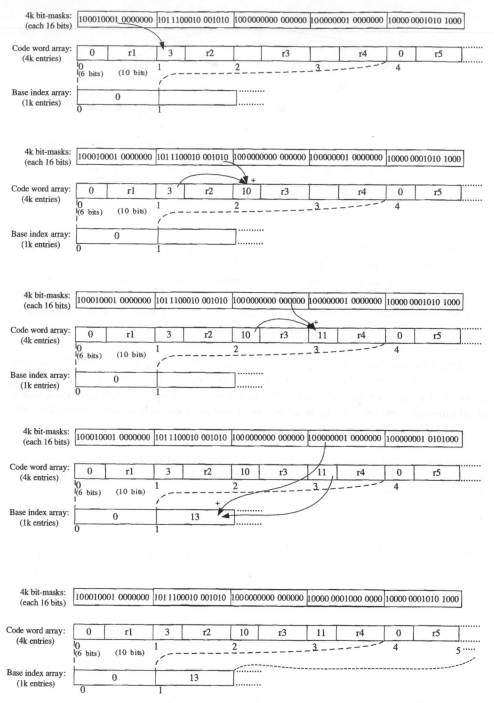

**Figure 2.16**   Bit-masks versus code words and base indices.

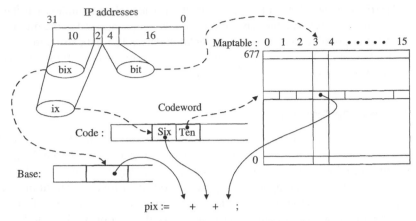

**Figure 2.17**    Finding the pointer index [10].

'1010', the 4-bit offset in the `Maptable` will be 5, counting five '1' from the left to the bit location of '1010'.

***Route Lookup.*** The following steps are required to search the first level of the data structure. The array of code words is called `code` and the array of base addresses is called `base`. Figure 2.17 illustrates the procedure. The variables are defined as below:

`ix` := high 12 bits of IP address
`bit` := low 4 of high 16 bits of IP address
`code word` := code[ix]
`ten` := ten bits from codeword
`six` := six bits from codeword
`bix` := high 10 bits of IP address
`pix` := base[bix] + six + maptable[ten][bit]
`pointer` := level1_pointers[pix]

The index of the code word (`ix`), the index of the base index (`bix`), and the bit number (`bit`) are first extracted from the IP address. Then the `code word` is retrieved and its two parts are extracted into `ten` and `six`. The pointer index (`pix`) is then obtained by adding the base index, the 6-bit offset `six`, and the pointer offset obtained by retrieving column `bit` from row `ten` of `maptable`. After the `pointer` is retrieved from the pointer array, it will be examined to determine if the next-hop information has been found or if the search should continue on to the next level.

***Performance.*** The Lulea algrorithm provides a very compact data structure and fast lookups. The data structure has 150–160 kbytes for the largest forwarding tables with 40,000 routing entries, which is small enough to fit in the cache of a conventional general-purpose processor. A 200 MHz Pentium Pro or a 333 MHz Alpha 21164 with the table in the cache can perform a few million IP lookups per second without special hardware and no traffic locality is assumed. Lulea does not support incremental updates because of the algorithm's tight coupling property. In many cases, the whole table should be reconstructed. Thus, routing protocols that require frequent updates make this algorithm unsuitable.

The Lulea trie uses the $k$-bit stride multi-bit method. The lookup complexity is the same as a multi-bit trie, $O(W/k)$. The bitmap compression technique applied to the multi-bit trie makes it almost impossible to perform incremental updates. The data structure may need to be completely rebuilt. The memory consumption is the same as the $k$-bit stride multi-bit trie. Thus, the space complexity is $O((2^k * N * W)/k)$.

### 2.2.6 Tree Bitmap Algorithm

Eatherton et al. [11] have proposed a data structure of lookup scheme based on multi-bit expanded tries without any leaf pushing and bitmap compression, called Tree Bitmap. The lookup scheme simultaneously meets three criteria: scalability in terms of lookup speed and table size, the capability of high-speed updates, and feasibility in size to fit in a Level 3 forwarding engine or packet processor with low overhead. Tree Bitmap has flexibility to adapt to the next generations of memory technology. To the best of our knowledge, Cisco CRS-1 uses this lookup scheme.

***Data Structure.*** In the Tree Bitmap algorithm, a trie node, as shown in Figure 2.18, is fixed in size, containing a head pointer to the block of child nodes, an extending paths bitmap, an internal next hop information bitmap, and a pointer to the external result array of next hop information associated with prefixes stored in the node. Since update time is bounded by the size of a trie node, Tree Bitmap uses trie nodes of no more than eight strides. By taking advantage of modern burst-based memory technologies, Tree Bitmap keeps the trie nodes as small as possible to be within the optimal memory burst size. Thus, all information about the node being examined can be fetched into the processor in one memory reference and processed to find the longest prefix match.

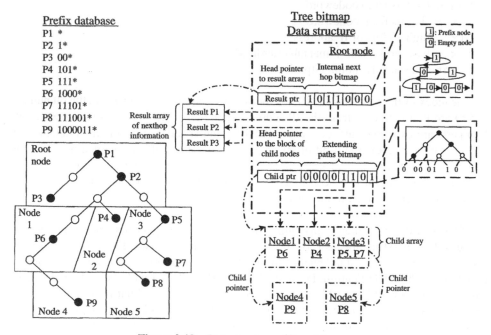

**Figure 2.18** Data structure of Tree Bitmap.

A multi-bit node could be seen as a unibit node of multiple levels. It has to have two functions: it has to point to all its child nodes and it has to point to next hop information for prefix nodes within its internal structure. Tree Bitmap uses two bitmaps to implement these two functions individually. Tree Bitmap uses different multi-bit node grouping schemes from the multi-bit trie described in Section 2.2.3. As shown in Figure 2.18, all length 3 prefixes are pushed and stored along with the length 0 prefixes in the next node down. For example, P5 is pushed down to Node 3 in Level 2; P4 is pushed down to Node 2, which is created to store P4. However, in the multi-bit trie of Figure 2.10, P4 and P5 are stored in the root node.

All child nodes of a given trie node are stored contiguously. In Figure 2.18, all child nodes of the root node, Node 1, Node 2, and Node 3, are contiguous in memory. Thus, only one head child pointer is needed in the root node to point to all its children with the help of the extending paths bitmap, which contains a bit for all possible $2^r$ child nodes ($r$: stride size) and is used to calculate the offset from the head pointer. In Figure 2.18, of the eight possible leaves, only the fifth, the sixth, and the eighth leaf nodes have pointers to children. Thus, the extending paths bitmap is 00001101 by setting the corresponding bit positions from the left to be '1'.

The next hop information associated with the internal prefixes of each trie node is stored in a separate array associated with the trie node. Only the head pointer to the array is necessarily kept in the trie node, together with an internal next-hop information bitmap, which is used to record every prefix stored within the node and to calculate the offset from the head pointer. In a $r$-bit trie, the first bit of the bitmap is associated with prefix of length 0. The two following bits are associated with prefixes of length 1, the four following bits are associated with prefixes of length 2, ... and $2^{r-1}$ following bits are associated with prefixes of length $r - 1$ for a total of $2^r - 1$ bits. In Figure 2.18, the internal bitmap of the root node is obtained by traversing through the 3-level unibit trie nodes from top to bottom and from left to right, and replacing the prefix nodes with 1s and non-prefix nodes with 0s.

***Route Lookup.*** Figure 2.19 illustrates how to search for the longest prefix match of '11101100' in the Tree Bitmap data structure. According to the stride of the root node, three in the example, the first three bits of '11101100', '111', are used as an index to look up the extending path bitmap, resulting in a '1' (Step 1). This means there is a valid child pointer. The number of 1s is counted to the left in the bitmap to compute the offset, $I = 3$ (Step 2). Since the head pointer to the block of child nodes, $H$, is known as well as the size of each child node, $S$, the pointer to the child node can be easily calculated as $H + (I \times S)$, which points to Child Node 3 (Step 3).

Then, the internal next hop information bitmap is checked to see if there is a prefix match (Step 4). It uses a completely different calculation from Lulea. As mentioned earlier, in a $r$-bit trie, Tree Bitmap pushes length $r$ prefixes down to be stored as length 0 in the next level. Thus, the right most bit of '111' is removed at first, resulting in '11*'. From the previous example about how to construct an internal bitmap, it is easy to conceive that '11*' corresponds to the seventh bit of the internal bitmap, where '0' is found. No prefix is found (Step 5). One more right most bit of '11*' is removed, resulting in '1*'. The corresponding third bit of the internal bitmap is checked. '1' is found, meaning there is a prefix found (Step 6). The number of '1's before the matched prefix at Step 6 is 1. It indicates the offset of the prefix match in the result array. The pointer to the matched prefix is calculated by using the head pointer to the result array and the offset, resulting in P2, which is stored as

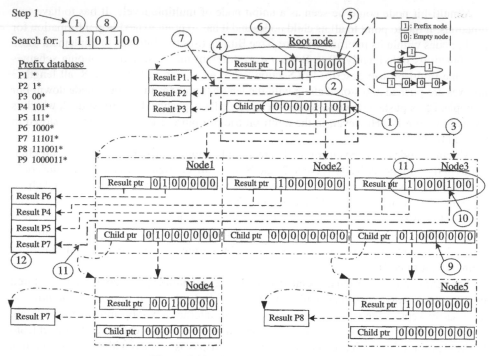

**Figure 2.19**    Example of route lookup.

prefix match (Step 7). The information of Child Node 3 is loaded from memory and another iteration begins.

The next 3-bit chunk from '11101100', '011', is extracted (Step 8). No extending path with index '011' is found in Node 3 (Step 9). The right most bit of '011' is removed, resulting in '01*'. The fifth bit of the internal bitmap is found to be '1', indicating a prefix found (Step 10). The number of 1s to the left of the matched prefix is 1. The prefix match is P7 (Step 11). The prefix match found in the lowest level is the longest one. When there are no more child nodes, the search stops. The next hop information of P7 is retrieved from the result array (Step 12).

**Performance.** Similar to the Lulea algorithm, described in Section 2.2.5, Tree Bitmap uses multi-bit tries and bitmaps to compress wasted storage in trie nodes and achieve fast lookup speeds. However, Tree Bitmap uses a completely different encoding scheme that relies on two bitmaps per node to avoid leaf pushing, which makes update inherently slow as in the Lulea algorithm. Tree Bitmap allows not only fast searches comparable to the Lulea algorithm, but also fast update.

Tree Bitmap takes advantage of memory technology and processing power. It performs complex processing in one memory access per trie node, as opposed to three memory references required by the Lulea algorithm. It trades off algorithm complexity for less memory access. Tree Bitmap is tunable over a wide range of architectures.

### 2.2.7 Tree-Based Pipelined Search

Most tree-based solutions for network searches can be regarded as some form of tree traversal, where the search starts at the root node, traverses various levels of the tree, and typically ends at a leaf node. The tree-based solution has optimal memory utilization but needs multiple times memory access per packets according to the depth of searching tree. Tree-based pipelined searching methods are then introduced to avoid the bottleneck in memory access. It allows different levels of the tree to be partitioned onto private memories associated with the processing elements. Tree-based searches are pipelined across a number of stages to achieve high throughput, but this results in unevenly distributed memory. To address this imbalance, conventional approaches use either complex dynamic memory allocation schemes (dramatically increasing the hardware complexity) or over-provision each of the pipeline stages (resulting in memory waste). The use of large, poorly utilized memory modules results in high system cost and high memory latencies, which can have a dramatic effect on the speed of each stage of the pipelined computation, and thus on the throughput of the entire architecture.

***Balance Memory Distribution in a Pipelined Search Architecture.*** A novel architecture for a network search processor, which provides both high execution throughput and balanced memory distribution by dividing the searching tree into subtrees and allocating each subtree separately has recently been described [12]. This method allows searches to begin at any pipeline stage to balance the separated memory rather than the prior pipelined network search algorithms, which require all searches to start from the first pipeline stage (the root node of searching tree), going next to the second, and so on.

Figure 2.20 shows a tree-based search structure. To keep the explanation simple, let us assume that the tree has four subtrees, called $S_1, \ldots, S_4$. The separation of the subtree can be determined by using a hash function based on information in the packet header. For IP lookups the hash function is made up of a set of variable length IP prefixes. For packet classification, the hash function may use some of the most significant bits in two or three different fields of the packet header. Furthermore, the search structure is implemented on a four-stage pipeline, called $P_1, \ldots, P_4$, corresponding to the depth of each subtree with four levels. Each level in the subtree can handle multiple bits lookup, for example, by 'Tree Bitmap' scheme [11] in Section 2.2.6. The first level of the subtree $S_1$, called $S_1^1$, is stored

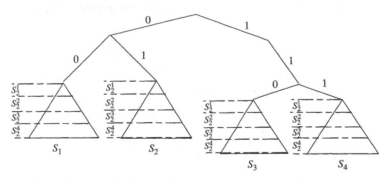

**Figure 2.20** Example of a basic tree-based search structure. The tree is split into four subtrees $S_1, \ldots, S_4$. Each subtree has up to four levels. We call $S_i^j$ the level $j$ into the subtree $S_i$ [12].

and processed by the pipeline stage $P_1$. The second level $S_1^2$ is stored and processed by the pipeline stage $P_2$, and so on. The second subtree is processed starting with pipeline stage $P_2$, $S_2^1$ on $P_2$, $S_2^2$ on $P_3$, $S_2^3$ on $P_4$ and $S_2^4$ on $P_1$, respectively. Similarly, the third subtree $S_3$ starts on stage $P_3$, while the fourth subtree $S_4$ starts on pipeline stage $P_4$. This allocation scheme tries to balance the load on each of the pipeline stages. By doing so, the pipeline allocates nearly equal amounts of memory to each stage.

In practice, the number of subtrees should be more than or equal to the number of pipeline stages (processing elements), thus implying multiple subtrees may have the same start node. The number of the maximum depth of each subtree should be less than or equal to the number of pipeline stages. However, this tree-based pipelined search architecture with balanced memory distribution by allowing search tasks to start execution from any pipeline stage impacts the throughput of the system. This is because of potential conflicts in memory access between the new tasks and the ones that are in execution.

***Avoid Memory Access Conflicts in the Pipelined Search Architecture.*** A random ring pipeline architecture with two data paths is described and shown in Figure 2.21 to eliminate the possible conflicts. All tasks are inserted at the first pipeline stage and traverse the pipeline twice, irrespective of their starting stage (for execution) in the pipeline. Each pipeline stage accommodates two data paths (virtual data paths – they can share the same physical wires). The first data path (represented by the top lines) is active during the odd clock cycles and it is used for a first traversal of the pipeline. The second data path is traversed during even cycles and allows the task to continue its execution on the pipeline stages that are left. Once a task finishes executing, its results are propagated to the output through the final stage. Each pipeline stage works at a frequency $f = 2 \times F$ where $F$ is the maximum throughput of the input.

For example, consider the four-stage pipeline in Figure 2.21. A task that must start executing in pipeline stage 3 is inserted in pipeline stage 1. It traverses the pipeline only in the odd cycles until it reaches stage 3 where it starts executing. Its results are forwarded to pipeline stage 4 also during an odd cycle. However, the results of the execution on stage 4 are moved forward to pipeline stage 1 for execution during the next even cycle. The task finishes its execution on pipeline stage 2. The final results are moved to the output via pipeline stages 3 and 4 during even cycles.

This solution guarantees the following features: (1) an output rate equal to the input rate; (2) all the tasks exit in order; and (3) all the tasks have a constant latency through the pipeline equal to $M \times (1/F)$ where $M$ is the total number of pipeline stages.

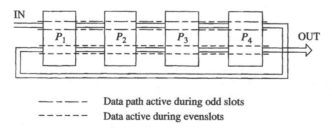

    ————— Data path active during odd slots
    —————— Data active during evenslots

**Figure 2.21** Random ring pipeline architecture with two data paths: first path is active during the odd clock cycles, used during the first traversal of the pipeline; second path is active during the even clock cycles to allow a second traversal of the pipeline [12].

### 2.2.8 Binary Search on Prefix Lengths

The idea of this algorithm is that the longest prefix matching operation can be decomposed into a series of exact matching operations, each performed on the prefixes with the same length. This decomposition can be viewed as a linear search of the space of $1, 2, \ldots, W$ prefix lengths. An algorithm that performs binary searches on this space was proposed by Waldvogel et al. [13].

***Data Structure.*** The prefixes of a forwarding table are stored by length respectively, say sub-table $H_1, H_2, \ldots, H_w$. More specifically, a sub-table (say $H_i$) stores all the prefixes with a length of $i$. To reduce the exact matching time during route lookup, this algorithm uses hashing for the exact matching operation among prefixes of the same length (in the same sub-table). In other words, each sub-table uses a different hash function to hash all its prefixes. Each prefix will be associated with a hash value. If there are more than one prefix hashed to the same value, it is called 'hash collision'. They are linked together for one by one exact matching during route lookup.

***Route Lookup.*** Given a destination address, a linear search on the space of prefix lengths requires probing each of the $W$ hash tables, $H_1, H_2, \ldots, H_w$. It requires $W$ hash operations and $W$ hashed memory accesses. To shoot the probing process, the algorithm first probes $H_{w/2}$. If a node is found in this hash table, there is no need to probe tables $H_1, H_2, \ldots, H_{w/2-1}$. This is due to the requirement of longest prefix match. If no node is found, hash table $H_{w/2+1}, \ldots, H_w$ need not be probed. The remaining hash tables are probed again in a binary search manner.

Figure 2.22 illustrates how the algorithm works. The table on top of Figure 2.22 gives the five example prefixes in the forwarding table. There are three different lengths, 8, 16, and 24, of these prefixes, so three hash tables $H_8$, $H_{16}$, and $H_{24}$ are constructed in Figure 2.22. In addition to five prefixes in the three sub-tables, there is an entry ⟨90.2⟩ in $H_{16}$. It is called a marker because it is not a prefix in the forwarding table but an internal node to help determine the direction of the next branch, either going to the lower part or the higher part. Given an IP address ⟨90.1.20.3⟩, we start the lookup from $H_{16}$ (since $W = 32$ for IPv4 and $W/2 = 16$) and find a match at the entry ⟨90.1⟩. Then, we process to $H_{24}$ and another match is found at the entry ⟨90.1.20⟩. The lookup terminates here because no more hash tables are available to be searched. The prefix ⟨90.1.20⟩ is returned as the result. Figure 2.23 illustrates an example of the binary search on prefix lengths.

***Performance.*** The algorithm requires $O(\log_2 W)$ hashed memory accesses for one lookup operation, taking no account of the hash collision. So does the update complexity. This data structure has storage complexity of $O(NW)$ since there could be up to $W$ markers for a prefix-each internal node in the trie on the path from the root node to the prefix. However, not all the markers need to be kept. Only the $\log_2 W$ markers that would be probed by the binary search algorithm need be stored in the corresponding hash tables. For instance, an IPv4 prefix of length 22 needs markers only for prefix lengths 16 and 20. This decreases the storage complexity to $O(N \log_2 W)$.

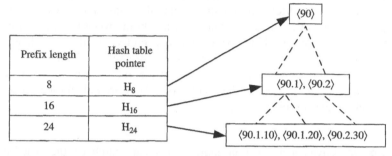

| Example prefixes |
|:---:|
| 90/8 |
| 90.1/16 |
| 90.1.10/24 |
| 90.1.20/24 |
| 90.2.30/24 |

| Prefix length | Hash table pointer |
|:---:|:---:|
| 8 | $H_8$ |
| 16 | $H_{16}$ |
| 24 | $H_{24}$ |

⟨90⟩

⟨90.1⟩, ⟨90.2⟩

⟨90.1.10⟩, ⟨90.1.20⟩, ⟨90.2.30⟩

**Figure 2.22**   Binary search example on prefix lengths.

### 2.2.9   Binary Search on Prefix Range

Lampson et al. [14] showed how to apply a binary search to perform longest prefix matching lookup. This algorithmic approach to IP lookups views a prefix database as a set of intermingled ranges, where each prefix is expanded to two endpoints in a number line.

***Data Structure.***   The left column of Figure 2.24*a* shows a sample prefix database with an assumption of 6-bit addresses. To apply a prefix-range-based binary search on this set, two endpoints are generated for each prefix by padding 0s and 1s, respectively, as shown in the right column of Figure 2.24*a*. These endpoints are mapped to a number line as shown in 2.24*b*. A table containing six endpoints based on these expanded prefixes is shown in Figure 2.24*c*. Each of the endpoints (excluding the last one) actually denotes the left boundary of a specific prefix range (total of five prefix ranges in the example). Another two fields (the '=' and the '>' fields) are created for each endpoint. This indicates the corresponding longest matching prefix when the destination address falls within the prefix range ('>') following the boundary or just falls on the (left) boundary ('=') of the prefix range, as shown in the right column of Figure 2.24*c*. These are all pre-computed.

***Route Lookup.***   The lookup process of a given destination address is actually the process of a linear search for the nearest left boundary to the destination address in the forwarding table (since we only keep the '=' and '>' fields, but not '<', we only find the left but not right boundary). Let us use the prefix database in Figure 2.24 as an example and assume the destination address to be 101011. Then lookup the address in the forwarding table is actually to find which of the six entries is the nearest left boundary to 101011. For instance, we can see that the key falls into the range of P2 by mapping the given key to the number line. Binary search is a very efficient way to search a linear space. The first time, the key (destination address) 101011 is compared with the $\lceil 6/2 \rceil$ = third entry 101111. Then a '<'

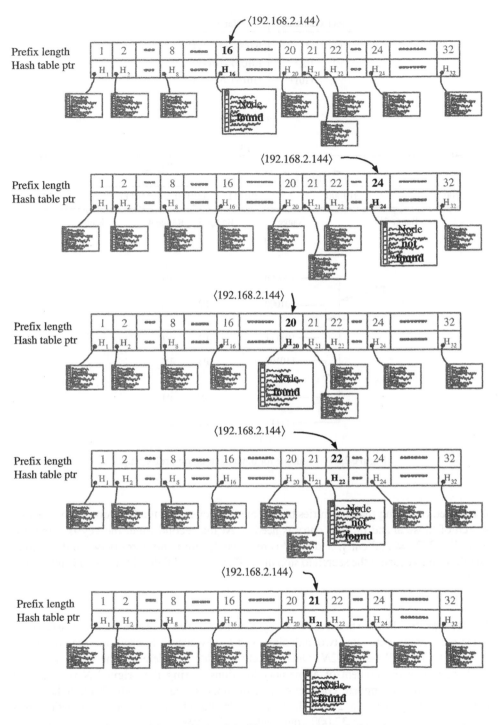

**Figure 2.23**    Example of the binary search on prefix lengths.

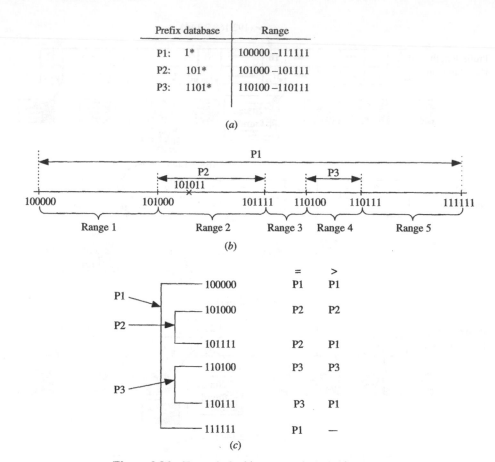

**Figure 2.24** Example for binary search on prefix range.

is returned (meaning that the entries behind the third one need not be probed), so a second search of those ahead of third entry is needed. At the second time, the key is compared with the $\lceil 3/2 \rceil = 2$nd entry, and a '>' is returned. There is no entry between the second and third ones causing the search to stop there. P2 in the '>' field of the second entry is the result.

***Performance.*** There should be $2N$ segment points for a prefix database size of $N$ when each prefix generates two endpoints. If a $k$-way search is used, the search time in the worst case will be $\log_k 2N$. Once a prefix is added or deleted, the range sequence is changed and the content of $N$ memory locations storing the original $N$ ranges need to be updated. The update complexity and memory space are both $O(N)$. It has been reported that by using a 200-MHz Pentium Pro-based machine and a practical forwarding table with over 32,000 route entries, the worst-case time of 490 ns and an average time of 100 ns for IP route lookups were obtained [14]. Only a 0.7-Mbyte memory was used. A drawback of this algorithm is that it does not support incremental updates.

## 2.3  HARDWARE-BASED SCHEMES

### 2.3.1  DIR-24-8-BASIC Scheme

Gupta et al. [15] proposed a route lookup mechanism that can achieve one route lookup every memory access when implemented in a pipeline fashion in hardware. It is called the DIR-24-8-BASIC scheme. This corresponds to approximately 100 Mlookups/sec with the 10-ns SDRAM technology.

***Data Structure.***  The DIR-24-8-BASIC has two level searches as shown in Figure 2.25. The first-level search uses the first 24 bits and the second-level search (if necessary) uses the combination of index and the remaining 8 bits. The scheme makes use of the two tables shown in Figure 2.26, both stored in SDRAM. The first table (called TBL24) stores all possible route pre-fixes that are up to, and including, 24 bits long. This table has $2^{24}$ entries, addressed from 0.0.0 to 255.255.255. Each entry in TBL24 has the format shown in Figure 2.27. The second table (TBL*long*) stores all route prefixes in the forwarding table that are longer than 24 bits.

Assume for example that we wish to store a prefix $X$ in an otherwise empty forwarding table. If $X$ is less than or equal to 24 bits long, it needs only be stored in TBL24: the first bit of the entry is set to zero to indicate that the remaining 15 bits designate the next hop information. If, on the other hand, the prefix $X$ is longer than 24 bits, we then use the entry

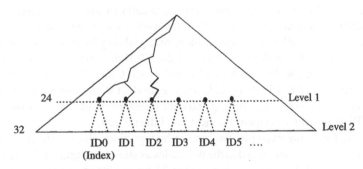

**Figure 2.25**  Two levels of the data structure.

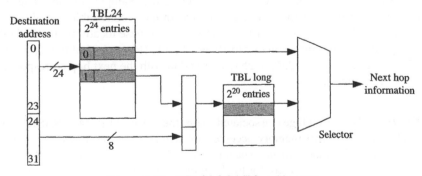

**Figure 2.26**  DIR-24-8 BASIC architecture.

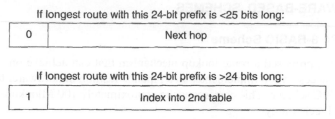

**Figure 2.27**    TBL24 entry format.

in TBL24 addressed by the first 24 bits of $X$. We set the first bit of the entry to one to indicate that the remaining 15 bits contain a pointer to a set of entries in TBL*long*.

In effect, route prefixes shorter than 24 bits are expanded. For example, the route prefix 128.23/16 will have entries associated with it in TBL24, ranging from the memory address 128.23.0 through 128.23.255. All 256 entries will have exactly the same contents (the next hop corresponding to the routing prefix 128.23/16). With the cost of a large memory, we can find the next hop information within one memory access.

TBL*long* contains all route prefixes that are longer than 24 bits. Each 24-bit prefix that has at least one route longer than 24 bits is allocated $2^8 = 256$ entries in TBL*long*. Each entry in TBL*long* corresponds to one of the 256 possible longer prefixes that share the single 24-bit prefix in TBL24. It needs to be only 1 byte wide if we assume that there are fewer than 255 next-hop routers, this assumption could be relaxed if the memory was wider than 1 byte because we simply store the next-hop in each entry of the second table.

When a destination address is presented to the route lookup mechanism, the following steps are taken: (1) We perform a single memory read yielding 2 bytes using the first 24 bits of the address as an index to the first table TBL24; (2) If the first bit equals zero, then the remaining 15 bits describe the next hop information; (3) Otherwise (if the first bit is one), we multiply the remaining 15 bits by 256, add the product to the last 8 bits of the original destination address (achieved by shifting and concatenation), and use this value as a direct index into TBL*long*, which contains the next hop information.

Consider the following example, we can see how prefixes, 10.54/16 (A), 10.54.34/24 (B), 10.54.34.192/26 (C), are stored in the two tables as shown in Figure 2.28. The first route includes entries in TBL24 that correspond to the 24-bit prefixes from 10.54.0 to 10.54.255 (except for 10.54.34). The second and third routes require that the second table be used. This is because both of them have the same first 24 bits and one of them is more than 24 bits long. In TBL24, we insert a one followed by an index (in the example, the index equals 123) into the entry corresponding to the 10.54.34 prefix. In the second table, we allocate 256 entries starting with memory location $123 \times 256$. Most of these locations are filled in with the next hop information corresponding to 10.54.34 route (B), and 64 of them [those from $(123 \times 256) + 192$ to $(123 \times 256) + 255$] are filled in with the next hop corresponding to the 10.54.34.192 route (C).

**Performance.** The advantages associated with the basic DIR-24-8-BASIC scheme include: (1) Generally, two memory accesses are required. These accesses are in separate memories that allow the scheme to be pipelined; (2) This infrastructure will support an unlimited number of routes, except for the limit on the number of distinct 24-bit prefixed routes with length greater than 24 bits; (3) The total cost of memory in this scheme is the

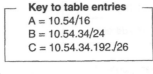

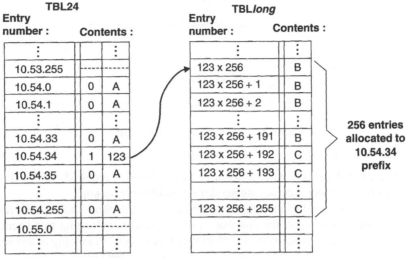

**Figure 2.28**  Example of two tables containing three routes.

cost of 33 Mb of SDRAM. No exotic memory architectures are required; and (4) The design is well-suited for hardware implementation.

The disadvantages are: (1) Memory is used inefficiently and (2) Insertion and deletion of routes from this table may require many memory accesses.

### 2.3.2  DIR-Based Scheme with Bitmap Compression (BC-16-16)

Huang [16] proposed a route lookup scheme combining the concepts of Lulea algorithms' bitmap compression (Section 2.2.5) and DIR-24-8's direct lookup. The most straightforward way to implement a lookup scheme is to have a forwarding table in which an entry is designated for each 32-bit IP address, as depicted in Figure 2.29. This design needs only one memory access for each IP route lookup, but the size of the forwarding table, next-hop array (NHA), is huge ($2^{32}$ bytes $= 4$ GB).

An indirect lookup can be employed to reduce the memory size (see Fig. 2.30). Each IP address is split into two parts: (a) segment (the higher 16 bits) and (b) offset (the lower 16 bits). The segmentation table has 64K entries ($2^{16}$) and each entry (32 bits) records either the next hop information (port number, if value $\leq 255$) or a pointer (if value $>255$) pointing to the associated NHA. Each NHA consists of 64K entries ($2^{16}$) and each entry (8 bits) records the next hop (port number) of the destination IP address. For a destination IP address $a.b.x.y$, the $a.b$ is used as the index of the segmentation table and the $x.y$ is employed as the index of the associated NHA, if necessary. For a segment $a.b$, if the length of the longest prefix belonging to this segment is less than or equal to 16, then the corresponding entries of the segmentation table store the output port directly, and the associated NHA is not necessary. On the other hand, if the length of the longest prefix belonging to this

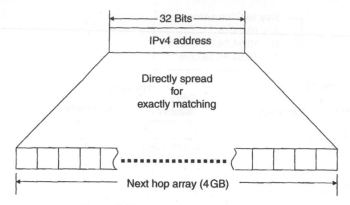

**Figure 2.29**   Direct lookup mechanism.

segment is greater than 16, then an associated 64 KB NHA is required. In this design, a maximum of two memory accesses are needed for an IP route lookup.

Although the indirect-lookup scheme furnishes a fast lookup (up to two memory accesses), it does not consider the distribution of the prefixes belonging to a segment. A 64 KB NHA is required as long as the length of the longest prefix belonging to this segment is greater than 16. The size of the associated NHA can be reduced further by considering the distribution of the prefixes within a segment. The IP address is still partitioned into segment (16 bits) and offset ($\leq 16$ bits).

***Data Structure.*** Figure 2.31 shows Huang's lookup mechanism. Four tables are used, the $2^{16}$-entry Segment Table (Seg Table), the Code Word Array (CWA), the Compressed Next Hop Array (CNHA), and the Next Hop Array (NHA).

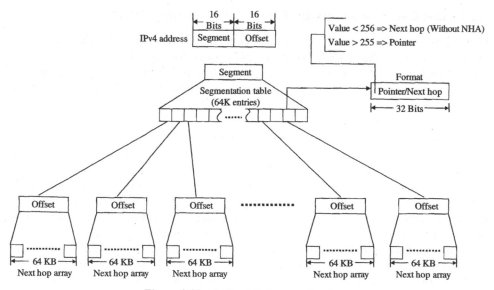

**Figure 2.30**   Indirect-lookup mechanism.

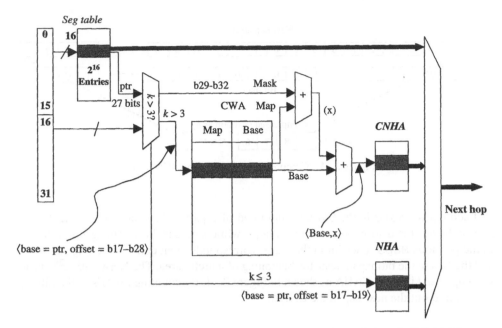

**Figure 2.31**    Multi-bit trie algorithm with bitmap compression technique in BC-16-16.

Similar to the DIR-24-8, the segment table in BC-16-16 is with the size of 64 KB entries, and each one (32 bits) is divided into three fields: $F$ (Flag, 1 bit), pointer/next hop (27 bits) and offset length (4 bits) (as shown in Fig. 2.32). The first field indicates if the second field contains a pointer to the next level table structure or a next hop index; the second field records either the next hop (port number, if value $\leq 255$) of the routing, or a pointer (if value $>255$) pointing to the associated NHA or a second level table structure (CWA-CNHA). The offset length field shows the size of NHA table, in terms of the power of 2. If the size is not greater than eight (i.e., field value $k \leq 3$), the pointer will point to an entrance of a common NHA (a table containing a series of next hop index). If the size is greater than eight (i.e., field value $>3$), the pointer will point to a CWA. We can decode the CNHA and find out the next hop by searching the CWA. The frameworks of the CWA and the CNHA are shown in Figures 2.33 and 2.34, respectively.

| $F$ (1 bit) | Pointer/Next hop (27 bits) | Offset length $k$ (4 bits) |
|---|---|---|

**Figure 2.32**    Segment table entry format.

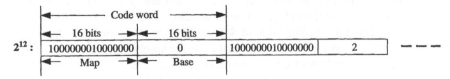

**Figure 2.33**    Code word array (CWA).

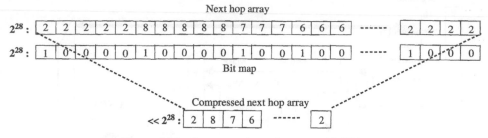

**Figure 2.34** Compressed next hop array (CNHA).

Each Code Word in the CWA is composed of 2 parts: Map and Base. The (Bit) Map indicates the distribution of the next hops, while Base is the summing-up of the '1's in the previous Maps. Each bit in the Maps corresponds to an entry in the original NHA, and the '1's in the bitmap indicate the beginning of a prefix area. The NHA with $2^{28}$ entries is compressed into the CNHA as shown in Figure 2.34. By counting the '1's in the bitmap, we can find out the next hop in the CNHA.

***Route Lookup.*** The first 16 bits (segment) of the incoming IP address are used to lookup the Seg Table. If the most significant bit ($F$ field) is a '0', indicating the following field contains a next hop index (output port number), then the lookup process stops and the next hop index is returned. Otherwise, if the $F$ field is a '1', then we inspect the offset length field. If the offset length $\leq 3$, we use the pointer field as the base address, and the $(16 + 1)$th to $(16 + $ offset length)th bits of the IP address as the offset address to lookup the NHA table, and return the associated result. If offset length $>3$, we should then lookup the CWA table with the following steps: (1) Use the pointer field as the base address, and the 17th to 28th bits as the offset address to find the corresponding Code Word in the CWA table, and get the corresponding Map and Base; (2) Define the 29th to 32nd bits of the IP address to be $p$, and calculate the number of '1's in the most significant $p$ bits in the Map field of the Code Word, say $x$; (3) Use Base as the base address and $x$ as the offset address to lookup the CNHA table, and return the associated result (next hop index).

***Performance.*** The basic idea of this lookup scheme is derived from the Lulea algorithm in Section 2.2.5, which uses bitmap code to represent part of the trie and significantly reduce the memory requirement. The main difference between BC-16-16 and the Lulea algorithm is that the former is hardware-based and the latter is software-based. The first-level lookup of the BC-16-16 uses direct 16-bit address lookup while the Lulea scheme uses bitmap code to look up a pointer to the next level data structure.

BC-16-16 needs only a tiny amount of SRAM and can be easily implemented in hardware. Based on the data obtained from [17], a large forwarding table with 40,000 routing entries can be compacted to a forwarding table of 450–470 kbytes. Most of the address lookups can be done by one memory access. In the worst case, the number of memory accesses for a lookup is three. When implemented in a pipeline in hardware, the proposed mechanism can achieve one route lookup every memory access. This mechanism furnishes approximately 100 M route lookups per second with current 10 ns SRAM.

However, this algorithm does not support incremental updates. When the CWA table needs to be updated, the whole second level table, including the associated CWA and CNHA should be reconstructed.

### 2.3.3 Ternary CAM for Route Lookup

*Basic TCAM Scheme.* CAM is a specialized matching memory that performs parallel comparison. The CAM outputs the location (or address) where a match is found. Conventional CAM can only perform exact matching, when presenting a parallel word to the input, and cannot be applied to CIDR 1P route lookup. A ternary CAM (TCAM) stores each entry with a (val, mask) pair, where val and mask are both $W$-bit numbers. For example, if $W = 6$, a prefix 110* is stored as the pair (110000, 111000). Each TCAM element matches a given input key by checking if those bits of val for which the mask bit is 1 match those in the key.

The logical structure of a TCAM device is shown in Figure 2.35. Whenever a matching operation is triggered, the 32-bit destination IP address will be compared with all the TCAM entries bit by bit, respectively and simultaneously. Since there may be multiple matches found at the same time, priority resolution should be used to select a match with the highest priority as the output. Many commercial TCAM products are order-based, such that the priority is determined by the memory location. The lower the location, the higher is the priority. Namely the $i$th TCAM has higher priority than the $j$th TCAM, if $i < j$. The priority arbitration unit selects the highest priority matched output from the TCAMs. For instance, an IP address 192.168.0.177 fed to the TCAM in Figure 2.35 results in four matches at the locations of 1, 1003, 1007, and 65535. The location of 1 is selected.

The forwarding table is stored in the TCAM in decreasing order of prefix lengths, so that the longest prefix is selected by the priority encoder. As shown in Figure 2.35, the group of 32-bit prefixes are at the bottom of the TCAM. Note that there are some empty spaces

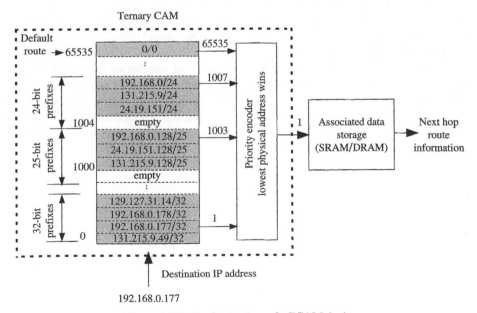

**Figure 2.35** Logic structure of a TCAM device.

in some groups reserved for adding prefixes in the future. The default route is located at the very top of the TCAM chip. Its mask value is 0, which guarantees that it will match with any input IP address. Only when there is no match from all the locations below it, will it be selected by the priority arbitrator. The output from the TCAM is then used to access RAM, in which the next hop information is stored in the same location as the prefix in the TCAM.

**Performance.** TCAM returns the result of the longest matching prefix lookup within only one memory access, which is independent of the width of the search key. And the implementation of TCAM-based lookup schemes are commonly used because they are much simpler than that of the trie-based algorithms. The commercially available TCAM chips [18, 19] can integrate 18 M-bit (configurable to $256\,k \times 36$-bit entries) into a single chip working at 133 MHz, which means it can perform up to 133 million lookups per second. However, the TCAM approach has the disadvantage of high cost-to-density ratio and high-power consumption (10–15 Watts/chip) [20].

### 2.3.4  Two Algorithms for Reducing TCAM Entries

TCAM-based IP route lookup is fast and easy to implement, but it also has high system cost and power consumption. Liu et al. [21] proposed two simple schemes to circumvent the above drawbacks. The TCAM size can be reduced by minimizing the amount of redundancy that exists among the prefixes in the forwarding table. Reducing the TCAM size will save on cost and power consumption.

**Prefix Pruning.** Figure 2.36 shows a situation where a part of the prefix trie is given. Assume that P1 and P2 have the same forwarding information. Then, P2 is actually a redundant prefix because deleting P2 will not affect the lookup result in any way. The direct ancestor of P2 (i.e., P1) on the prefix trie contains the same forwarding information (to port 2) with P2. For a longest matching prefix lookup that should terminate at P2 originally, it will terminate at P1 if P2 is pruned.

Many real-life IP forwarding tables have a substantial number of redundant prefixes. Pruning the redundant prefixes before storing them into TCAM will significantly reduce the TCAM requirement. For instance, an original prefix table in Figure 2.37 with seven prefixes can be reduced to a table with only four prefixes. It is reported that ~20–30 percent of the prefixes are redundant. This equates to ~20–30 percent TCAM space that can be saved by using the prefix pruning technique [21].

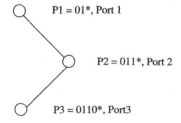

**Figure 2.36**   Pruning example.

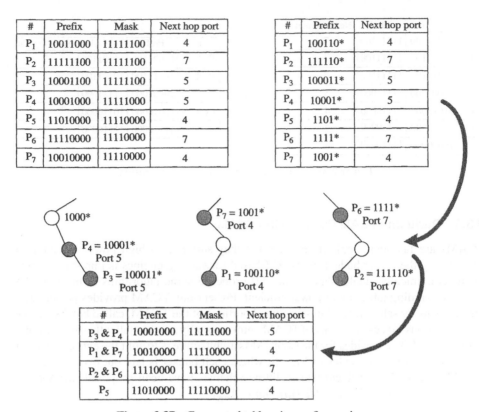

| # | Prefix | Mask | Next hop port |
|---|---|---|---|
| $P_1$ | 10011000 | 11111100 | 4 |
| $P_2$ | 11111100 | 11111100 | 7 |
| $P_3$ | 10001100 | 11111100 | 5 |
| $P_4$ | 10001000 | 11111000 | 5 |
| $P_5$ | 11010000 | 11110000 | 4 |
| $P_6$ | 11110000 | 11110000 | 7 |
| $P_7$ | 10010000 | 11110000 | 4 |

| # | Prefix | Next hop port |
|---|---|---|
| $P_1$ | 100110* | 4 |
| $P_2$ | 111110* | 7 |
| $P_3$ | 100011* | 5 |
| $P_4$ | 10001* | 5 |
| $P_5$ | 1101* | 4 |
| $P_6$ | 1111* | 7 |
| $P_7$ | 1001* | 4 |

1000*

$P_4 = 10001*$
Port 5

$P_3 = 100011*$
Port 5

$P_7 = 1001*$
Port 4

$P_1 = 100110*$
Port 4

$P_6 = 1111*$
Port 7

$P_2 = 111110*$
Port 7

| # | Prefix | Mask | Next hop port |
|---|---|---|---|
| $P_3$ & $P_4$ | 10001000 | 11111000 | 5 |
| $P_1$ & $P_7$ | 10010000 | 11110000 | 4 |
| $P_2$ & $P_6$ | 11110000 | 11110000 | 7 |
| $P_5$ | 11010000 | 11110000 | 4 |

**Figure 2.37**   Compacted table using prefix pruning.

***Mask Extension.*** TCAM is used for ternary matching, and not just prefix matching. The main difference between these two kinds of matching is that prefix matching needs the mask to be all '1's in the most significant bit and all '0' in the rest less significant bit. Ternary matching uses free types of mask. The main idea of mask extension is to extend the prefix-match-kind of masks to the ternary-match-kind of masks in the TCAM-based route lookup scheme. In this case, some TCAM entries in the prefix-match-kind can be represented by only one ternary-match-kind entry. For instance, the seven entries in an original prefix table can be fully represented by the five entries in the mask extended table (Fig. 2.38), when ternary-match-kind of masks are used. It is reported that nearly 20–30 percent of the original TCAM entries can be further saved if the mask extension technique is adopted [21].

***Performance.*** Real-life forwarding tables can be represented by much fewer TCAM (ternary match) entries, typically 50–60 percent of the original size by using the above two techniques. Prefix pruning would cause no change in prefix update complexity. Mask extension increases update complexity. Many prefixes are associated with others after mask extension, which results in the obstacles of performing incremental updates.

| # | Prefix | Mask | Next hop port |
|---|--------|------|---------------|
| $P_1$ | 10011100 | 11111100 | 7 |
| $P_2$ | 10001100 | 11111100 | 7 |
| $P_3$ | 11011100 | 11111100 | 7 |
| $P_4$ | 10001000 | 11111000 | 5 |
| $P_5$ | 11010000 | 11110000 | 4 |
| $P_6$ | 11110000 | 11110000 | 7 |
| $P_7$ | 10010000 | 11110000 | 4 |

| # | Prefix | Mask | Next hop port |
|---|--------|------|---------------|
| $P_1$ & $P_2$ | 10001100 | 11101100 | 7 |
| $P_1$ & $P_3$ | 10011100 | 10111100 | 7 |
| $P_4$ | 10001000 | 11111000 | 5 |
| $P_5$ & $P_7$ | 10010000 | 10110000 | 4 |
| $P_6$ | 11110000 | 11110000 | 7 |

**Figure 2.38**   Compacted table using mask extension.

### 2.3.5   Reducing TCAM Power – CoolCAMs

TCAMs are fast and simple to manage, but they suffer from high power consumption. Minimizing the power budget for TCAM-based forwarding engines is important to make them economically viable. Zane et al. [22] proposed some algorithms to make TCAM-based forwarding tables more power efficient. Present-day TCAM provides power-saving mechanisms by selectively addressing small portions of the TCAM, called blocks. A block is a contiguous, fixed-size chunk of TCAM entries, usually much smaller than the size of the entire TCAM. The key idea for the CoolCAMs architecture is to split the entire forwarding table into multiple sub-tables or *buckets*, where each bucket is laid out over one or more TCAM blocks. Two different table-splitting schemes have been proposed: *Bit-Selection Architecture* and *Trie-Based Table Partitioning* [22].

***Bit-Selection Architecture.*** Figure 2.39 shows a fixed set of bits (labeled as *suitable ID*) of the input IP address used to hash to one of the buckets (the shaded area in the *data TCAM*). Then, the IP address is compared to all the entries within the selected buckets and the index of the matched entry is used to address the associated SRAM to get the next hop information. The bit-selection logic in front of the TCAM is a set of muxes that can be programmed to extract the hashing bits from the destination address and use them to index to the appropriate TCAM bucket. For example, in Figure 2.39, each of the three 32 : 1 muxes uses a 5-bit value ($c0$, $c1$, and $c2$) to pick one bit from the incoming 32-bit address. The set of hashing bits can be changed over time by reprogramming the selectors of the muxes.

Because only a very small percentage of the prefixes in the core forwarding tables (less than 2 percent [22]) are either very short ($<16$ bits) or very long ($>24$ bits), they are grouped into the minimum possible number of TCAM blocks and will be searched for every lookup. The remaining 98 percent of the prefixes that are 16 to 24 bits long, called *split set*, are partitioned into buckets.

Assume that the total number of buckets $K = 2^k$ is a power of 2. Then the bit selection logic extracts a set of $k$ hashing bits from the destination address and selects a bucket to be searched. As in the example of Figure 2.39, the total number of buckets is $K = 8$ and the number of hashing bits is $k = 3$. The hashing bits should be chosen from the first 16 bits, which is the minimum length of a prefix in the split set. On the other hand, if $k'$ of the hashing bits are in bit positions larger than the length of a prefix, this prefix needs to be replicated in $2^{k'}$ buckets. For example, if we choose $k' = 2$ bits from bit positions 19 and

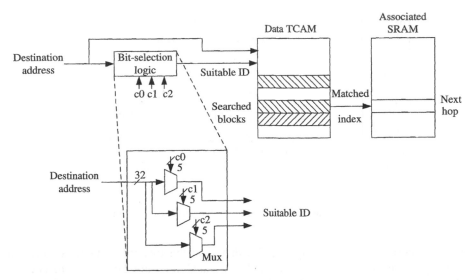

**Figure 2.39** Forwarding engine architecture for using bit selection to reduce power consumption. The three hashing bits are selected from the 32-bit destination address by setting the appropriate 5-bit values of $c0$, $c1$, and $c2$.

20 as hashing bits, then for a 18-bit prefix, it should be extended to $2^{k'}$ (or 4) 20-bit prefixes and stored in the four corresponding buckets.

***Trie-Based Table Partitioning.*** This approach uses a prefix trie (i.e., the 1-bit trie as shown in Fig. 2.6) to get the ID of the proper TCAM bucket. Figure 2.40 illustrates the prefix trie contained in a small-sized TCAM called the *index TCAM*. Each input is first fully searched in the index TCAM and then addressed into an *index SRAM* which contains the ID of the TCAM bucket.

Trie-based table partitioning works in two steps. In the first step, a binary routing trie is constructed from a given forwarding table. In the second step, subtrees or collections of subtrees of the 1-bit trie are successively carved out and mapped into individual TCAM buckets. The second step is called the *partitioning step*. There are two different partitioning schemes and are described below. Figure 2.41 shows a 1-bit trie that will be used as an example in both schemes. Here, the number of forwarding table prefixes in the subtree rooted at a node $v$ is defined as the *count* of $v$. For any node $u$, the prefix of the lowest

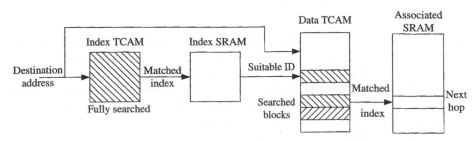

**Figure 2.40** Forwarding engine architecture for the trie-based power reduction schemes.

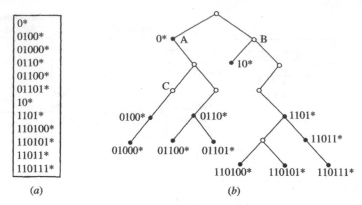

**Figure 2.41** (*a*) Example of forwarding table; (*b*) corresponding 1-bit trie.

common ancestor of *u* (including *u* itself) that is in the forwarding table is called the *covering prefix* of *u*. For example, both nodes A and C in Figure 2.41*b* have the covering prefix A. If there are no nodes in the path of a certain node to the root whose prefix is in the forwarding table, the covering prefix of this node is nil, such as B.

*Subtree Splitting.* Let *N* denote the number of prefixes in a forwarding table and *b* the maximum number of prefixes in a TCAM bucket. This algorithm produces a set of $K \in [\lceil N/b \rceil, \lceil 2N/b \rceil]$ TCAM buckets, each with a size in the range $[\lceil b/2 \rceil, b]$ (except possibly the last bucket, whose size is in the range $[1, b)$), and an index TCAM of size *K*. During the partitioning step, the entire trie is traversed in post-order looking for a *carving node*, which is a node *v* whose count is at least $\lceil b/2 \rceil$ and whose parent exists and has a count greater than *b*. Every time a carving node *v* is encountered (not necessary a prefix), the entire subtree rooted at *v* is carved out and the prefixes in the subtree are placed into a separate TCAM bucket. Next, the prefix of *v* is placed in the index TCAM and the covering prefix of *v* is added to the TCAM bucket. This ensures a correct result is returned when an input address that matches an entry in the index TCAM has no matching prefix in the corresponding subtree. Finally, the counts of all the ancestors of *v* are decreased by the count of *v*. When there are no more carving nodes left in the trie, the remaining prefixes (if any) are put in a new TCAM bucket with an index entry of an asterisk (∗) in the index TCAM.

Figure 2.42 shows how subtrees are carved out of the 1-bit trie from Figure 2.41. The number at each node *u* denotes the current value of *count(u)*. The arrows show the path along with *count(u)* is updated in each iteration, while the circle denotes the subtree that is carved. Table 2.2 shows the final results.

*Post-order Splitting.* This algorithm partitions the forwarding table into buckets that each contain exactly *b* prefixes (except possibly the last bucket). The algorithm traverses the 1-bit trie in post-order and successively carves out subtree collections that form a bucket. If a node *v* is encountered such that the count of *v* is *b*, a new TCAM bucket is created, the prefix of *v* is put in the index TCAM and the covering prefix of *v* is put in the TCAM bucket. If *count(v)* is *x* such that $x < b$ and the count of *v*'s parent is $>b$, then a recursive carving procedure is performed. Denote the node next to *v* in post-order traversal as *u*. Then the subtree rooted at *u* is traversed in post-order, and the algorithm attempts to carve out a

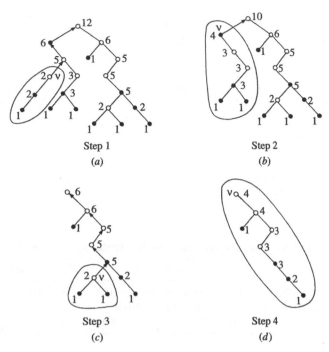

**Figure 2.42** Four iterations of the subtree-split algorithm (with parameter $b$ set to 4) applied to the 1-bit trie from Figure 2.41.

**TABLE 2.2  Four Resulting Buckets from the Subtree-Split Algorithm**

| Index | Bucket Prefixes | Bucket Size | Covering Prefix |
|---|---|---|---|
| 010* | 0100*, 01000* | 2 | 0* |
| 0* | 0*, 0110*, 01100*, 01101* | 4 | 0* |
| 11010* | 110100*, 110101* | 2 | 1101* |
| * | 10*, 1101*, 11011*, 110111* | 4 | — |

subtree of size $b - x$ from it. In addition, the $x$ entries are put into the current TCAM bucket (a new one is created if necessary), and the prefix of $v$ is added to the index TCAM and made to point to the current TCAM bucket. Finally, when no more subtrees can be carved out in this fashion, any remaining prefixes less than $b$ in number are put in a new TCAM bucket. An asterisk ($*$) entry in the index TCAM points to the last bucket. Figure 2.43 shows a sample execution of the algorithm with $b = 4$ and Table 2.3 lists the final result.

***Performance.*** The complexity for the post-order traversal is $O(N)$. Updating the counts of nodes all the way to root when a subtree is carved out gives a complexity of $O(NW/b)$. This is where $W$ is the maximum prefix length and $O(N/b)$ is the number of subtrees carved out. The total work for laying out the forwarding table in the TCAM buckets is $O(N)$. This makes the total complexity for subtree-split $O(N + NW/b)$. It can be proved that the total

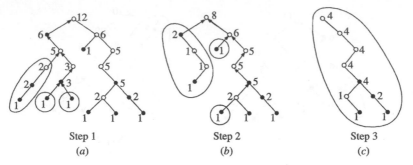

**Figure 2.43**    Three iterations of the post-order split algorithm (with parameter $b$ set to 4) applied to the 1-bit trie from Figure 2.41.

**TABLE 2.3    Three Resulting Buckets from the Post-Order Split Algorithm**

| $i$ | $Index_i$ | Bucket Prefixes | Size | Covering Prefix |
|---|---|---|---|---|
| 1 | 010*, 01100*, 01101* | 0100*, 01000*, 01100*, 01101* | 4 | 0*, 01100*, 01101* |
| 2 | 0*, 10*, 110100* | 0*, 0110*, 10*, 110100* | 4 | 0*, 10*, 110100* |
| 3 | 1* | 110101*, 1101*, 11011*, 110111* | 4 | — |

running time for post-order split is also $O(N + NW/b)$. The drawback of subtree-split is that the smallest and largest bucket sizes vary by as much as a factor of 2.

This method requires the entire index TCAM to be searched every time. The algorithm has to ensure that the index TCAM is small enough as compared to the data TCAM and does not contribute significantly to the power budget. The size of index TCAM for subtree-split is exactly the number of buckets in data TCAM. Post-order split adds at most $W + 1$ entries to the index TCAM and $W$ covering prefixes to the bucket in the data TCAM because the maximum number of times for carve-exact procedure is $W + 1$, which equals the number of prefixes added to the index TCAM for any given TCAM bucket.

Experimental results with real-life prefix database show that all three methods can dramatically reduce power consumption in practice. Even with only eight buckets, the bit-selection algorithm results in reduction factors of about 7.55; and subtree-split and post-order split of 6.09 and 7.95, respectively.

### 2.3.6  TCAM-Based Distributed Parallel Lookup

Zheng et al. [23] proposed an ultra-high throughput and power efficient TCAM-based lookup scheme. The throughput of TCAM-based lookup is determined by the TCAM access speed. The memory access rate increases ~7 percent per year. This is far behind the optical transmission increase rate that roughly doubles every year [24]. By using the chip-level-parallelism technique, we can improve the lookup throughput and so meeting the needs of the next generation routers. However, if one just duplicates a forwarding table into multiple copies and stores each copy into a TCAM device, the cost and power consumption will be prohibitively high.

By analyzing several real-life forwarding tables, it has been observed that the prefixes in a forwarding table can be approximately evenly partitioned into groups, called ID groups.

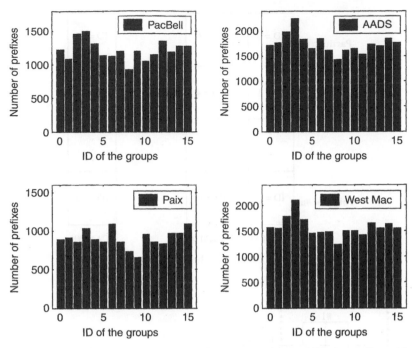

**Figure 2.44**  Prefixes distribution among ID groups in four real-life forwarding tables.

The partition is based on a few certain bits of the prefixes. Figure 2.44 illustrates 16 ID groups created by using the 10–13th bits of the prefixes in the forwarding table of the routers at four popular sites. Note that using more significant bits of the IP address may not obtain uniform classification, while using less significant bits may need to expand many short prefixes to long ones. Using the 10–13th bits of the IP addresses as their ID bits seems to be a good choice.

***Data Structure.***  Suppose that there are $K$ (e.g., $K = 4$) TCAM chips and each TCAM chip has $n$ (e.g., $n = 5$) partitions. Each ID group is approximately equal to $N/16$ prefixes, where $N$ denotes the total number of prefixes in the forwarding table. These ID groups are then distributed to $K$ TCAM chips (each ID group is stored in a TCAM). The goal is to have incoming packets that belong to different ID groups access the TCAM chips as evenly as possible. More TCAM chips working in parallel results in a higher lookup throughput.

In order to further balance the lookups among the TCAM chips, some of the ID groups with large traffic load ratio may be stored in multiple TCAM chips. For example, ID group 0, 4 and 11 are stored twice in the example in Figure 2.45. Therefore, the lookups for these three ID groups may be shared between the TCAM chips that have copies of them.

***Route Lookup.***  An implementation architecture for the distributed parallel lookup scheme is shown in Figure 2.46. For a given IP address to be searched, firstly, 4 bits (10–13th bits) are extracted to determine which TCAM chips contain the ID group that matches the IP address. This is implemented by the Indexing Logic. The output will be multiple TCAM candidates because of the redundant storage. A Priority Selector will pick

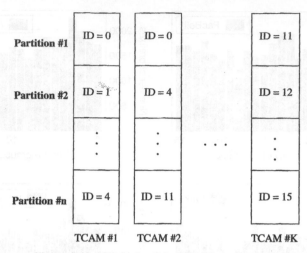

**Figure 2.45**    Example of the TCAM organization.

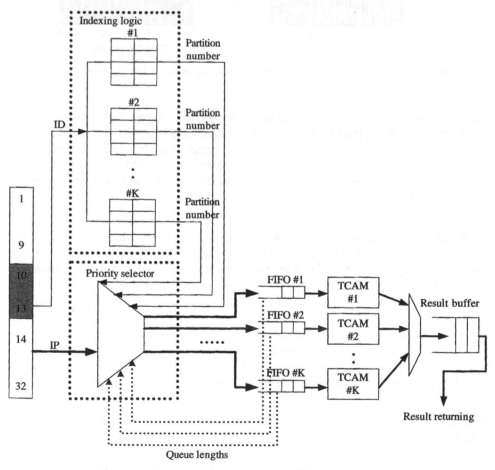

**Figure 2.46**    Implementation of the parallel lookup scheme.

a TCAM chip that is the least busy among the candidates (e.g., by comparing the first-in first-out (FIFO) queue lengths of the TCAM chips).

During the TCAM access cycle, each of the K TCAM chips fetch an assigned IP address from the FIFO queue, and performs a longest prefix match lookup independently. At the output ports of the TCAM chips, an Ordering Logic reads out the lookup results and returns them in their original sequence according to the time stamps attached to them.

*Performance.* The lookup throughput can be significantly improved with chip level parallelism. The proposed scheme can achieve a peak lookup throughput of 533 million packets per second (mpps) using four 133 MHz TCAM chips and having 25 percent more TCAM entries than the original forwarding table [24]. This performance can readily support a line rate of 160 Gbps. The disadvantage is that route update can be quite complicated.

## 2.4 IPV6 LOOKUP

### 2.4.1 Characteristics of IPv6 Lookup

Internet Protocol Version 6 (IPv6) is one of the key supporting technologies of the next generation network. According to the Internet Architecture Board (IAB), a unicast IPv6 address consists of two parts: a 64-bit network/sub-network ID followed by a 64-bit host ID. To enable a smooth transition from IPv4 to IPv6, the *IPv4-mapped address* and *IPv4-compatible address* formats were introduced. The former is defined by attaching the 32-bit IPv4 address to a special 96-bit pattern of all zeros. The IPv4-mapped address starts with 80 bits of zeros and 16 bits of ones, followed by the 32-bit IPv4 address.

The IAB and IESG [25] recommend that, in general, an address block with a 48-bit prefix be allocated to a subscriber. Very large subscribers could receive a 47-bit prefix or slightly shorter prefix, or multiple 48-bit prefixes. A 64-bit prefix may be allocated when it is known that one, and only one, subnet is needed; and a 128-bit prefix is allocated when it is absolutely known that one, and only one, device is connecting to the network. It is also recommended that mobile devices be allocated 64-bit prefixes.

From related recommendations in request for comments (RFC) and Réseaux IP Européens (RIPE) documents, the following important characteristics can be obtained: (1) It is obvious but important to note that there is no prefix with lengths between 64 bits and 128 bits (excluding 64 bits and 128 bits); (2) The majority of the prefixes should be the '/48s' and '/64s' the secondary majority. Other prefixes would be distinctly fewer than the '/48s' and '/64s'; (3) Specifically, the number of '/128s' should be tiny, which would be similar to the ratio of the '/32s' in the case of IPv4. Figure 2.47 shows the prefix length distribution of an IPv6 routing table reported in [26]. In this routing table, there are a total of 567 prefixes where only one prefix is longer than 64 bits.

### 2.4.2 A Folded Method for Saving TCAM Storage

Because of the high lookup rate and simplicity of table management, TCAM is currently the most popular solution for address lookup and packet classification. Commercial TCAM

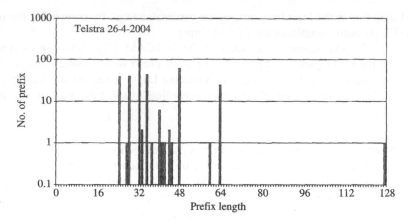

**Figure 2.47**    Prefix length distribution of an IPv6 routing table.

devices available today support configurable word-lengths of 36-, 72-, 144-, 288-, and 576-bits, and there are 72 input/output (I/O) pins for inputting the search key [27]. Double data rate I/O is supported, so there will be no extra overhead in handling search keys that are up to 144 bits in length. In a straightforward implementation of a route lookup engine using TCAM, a word-length of 144-bits will be selected. However, as mentioned in Section 2.4.1, the majority of IPv6 prefixes are no longer than 64 bits. Hence, over 50 percent of a TCAM word will store the 'don't care' value. Pao [28] has recently presented a simple but effective approach to improve the space efficiency by over 40 percent.

In his approach [28], the TCAM is configured with 72-bit words. The route prefixes are divided into two groups, $G_S$ and $G_L$. $G_S$ contains all the prefixes with no more than 72 bits, and $G_L$ contains all the prefixes with more than 72 bits. The TCAM blocks are divided into two partitions, $P_S$ and $P_L$. Prefixes in $G_S$ are stored in $P_S$. Prefixes in $G_L$ are grouped by the value of the first 72 bits. Routes $a$ and $b$ are put in the same subgroup if $a$ and $b$ share a common 72-bit prefix $M$. Assume the number of subgroups of long prefixes is less than 64k. Each subgroup is assigned a distinct 16-bit tag $T$. The common prefix $M$ of a subgroup is inserted into the partition $P_S$ of the TCAM to serve as a *marker*. An entry in the routing table is a six-tuple $\langle$ *prefix, p, m, v, next-hop, T* $\rangle$, where the flags $p$ and $m$ indicate whether the entry is a prefix, a marker, or both. If the next-hop value is valid, then $v = 1$; otherwise, $v = 0$. For a marker, the next-hop field records the next hop of the longest prefix in $G_S$ that matches $M$, if any. Let $a$ be a prefix with $l$ bits where $l > 72$. The bits are numbered from 1 to $l$ starting from the left. We define the suffix of $a$ as the substring consisting of bits 73 to $l$. The first 72 bits of $a$ will be stored in partition $P_S$, and the suffix (concatenated to the tag $T$) is stored in partition $P_L$. The entries in the two partitions are ordered by their lengths. An example of the two-level routing table organization is shown in Figure 2.48, where a full-length address has 12 bits and a tag has 4 bits. A wildcard entry is inserted into $P_S$ to represent the default route, and a wildcard entry with $v = 0$ is inserted into $P_L$ to serve as a sentinel to simplify the handling of the boundary condition.

Address lookup is a two-step process. First, the most significant 72 bits of the destination address $A$ is extracted and the partition $P_S$ is searched. If the best matching entry found is not a marker, then the packet is forwarded to the next-hop value returned by the address lookup engine. If the best matching entry is a marker, then the 56-bit suffix of $A$ is extracted and concatenated with the 16-bit tag of the marker to form a key to search the partition

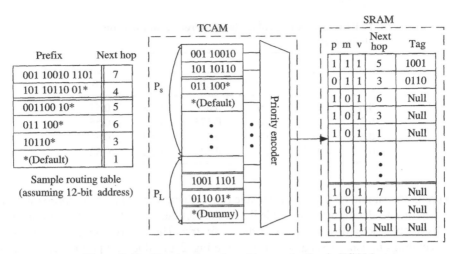

**Figure 2.48**   Two-level routing table organization in TCAM.

$P_L$. If the search result is invalid, that is, $v = 0$, then the packet will be forwarded to the next-hop value found in step 1; otherwise, the packet will be forwarded using the next-hop found in step 2.

If there are more than 64k subgroups of long prefixes, one can further divide $P_L$ into two or more partitions. In addition to the tag value, a partition ID is associated with the marker. When a partition is searched, the other partitions are disabled. Hence, each partition can support 64k subgroups of long prefixes, that is, a tag value only has local context within a partition.

***Performance.***  Let the total number of prefixes be $N$ and the fraction of prefixes with no more than 72 bits be $S$. Hence, the number of prefixes in group $G_S$ is $SN$ and the number of prefixes in $G_L$ is $(1 - S)N$. In the basic scheme, a 144-bit word is used to store a prefix regardless of the actual length of the prefix. The total TCAM space used is $144N$ bits. For the folded approach, let the average size of a subgroup of long prefixes in $G_L$ be $\beta$. The number of markers required is equal to $(1 - S)N/\beta$. The total TCAM space required is $72(SN + (1 - S)N/\beta) + 72(1 - S)N = 72N(1 + (1 - S)/\beta)$ bits. Let $R_s$ be the ratio of the space used by the folded scheme over the space used by the basic scheme. We have $R_s = (1 + (1 - S)/\beta)/2$. Table 2.4 lists the values of $R_s$ for various combinations of $S$ and $\beta$. One can expect a space saving of more than 40 percent using the two-level routing table organization.

### 2.4.3  IPv6 Lookup via Variable-Stride Path and Bitmap Compression

By considering the discrepancies among different parts of the prefix trie, and taking advantage of the wide-word memory architecture, Zheng et al. [29] proposed a scalable IPv6 route lookup scheme by combining the techniques of path compression and Lulea bitmap compression. In addition, variable-stride was introduced to enhance the efficiency of compression.

The viability and effectiveness of the combination of path and bitmap compression are based on the facts that the prefix density of IPv6 is much smaller than that of IPv4. Hence, the

**TABLE 2.4   Values of $R_S$ for Different Combinations
of $S$ and $\beta$**

| | $\beta$ | | | | |
|---|---|---|---|---|---|
| $S$ | 1.0 | 1.5 | 2.0 | 2.5 | 3.0 |
| 0.6 | 0.7 | 0.63 | 0.6 | 0.58 | 0.57 |
| 0.7 | 0.65 | 0.6 | 0.575 | 0.56 | 0.55 |
| 0.8 | 0.6 | 0.57 | 0.55 | 0.54 | 0.53 |
| 0.9 | 0.55 | 0.53 | 0.525 | 0.52 | 0.52 |

IPv6 prefix trie should be more compressible (for both bitmap and path compression). The efficiency of introducing variable-stride lies in the fact that the bitmap compression ratios vary distinctly among different parts of the prefix trie. Thus, a fixed compression stride, such as cuttings in depth 16 and 24 in Lulea (see Fig. 2.14), does not provide efficiency in route table lookup, storage, and update costs due to the uneven distribution of prefixes.

***Data Structure.***  A prefix trie is partitioned into sub-tries with variable heights, as shown in Figure 2.49. A subtrie is defined to be a full binary trie that is carved out from a prefix trie. It can be specified by a 2-tuple (*root*, *SubTrieHeight*), where *root* is the root node of a subtrie, and *SubTrieHeight* specifies the height/stride of this subtrie. The nodes on the bottom of the subtrie are called edge nodes and each subtrie should have $2^{SubTrieHeight}$ edge nodes.

Each trie node carries next hop IP address (NIP) or trie structure information. We use a data structure called pointer array (PA) to hold the route information carried by the edge node of a subtrie, with each pointer representing the memory location of either the NIP or the next level subtrie structure, as shown in Figure 2.50.

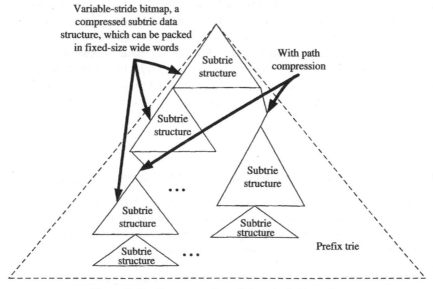

**Figure 2.49**   Demonstration of the subtrie hierarchy.

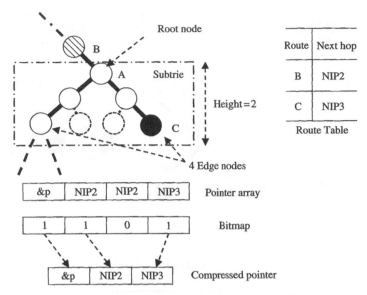

**Figure 2.50**  PA and corresponding compressed PA.

As depicted in Figure 2.50, Node A is the root of a two-layer subtrie, which consequently contains four edge nodes and they are associated with a PA of four pointers, each of which contains the memory location of either the NIP or the next subtrie structure. Node B carries the route information with NIP2, which descends to the root of the subtrie. Hence, two successive pointers (for the second- and third-edge nodes) within in the PA contain the same value (NIP2). In order to reduce the storage requirement, we can only keep such

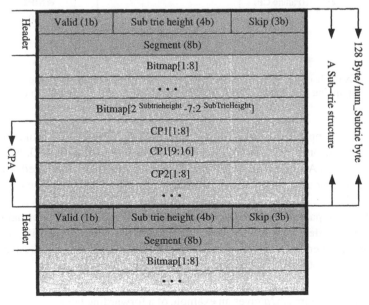

**Figure 2.51**  Data structure of a word frame.

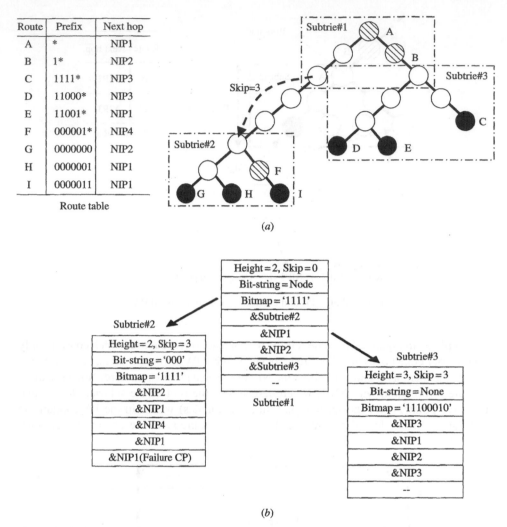

| Route | Prefix | Next hop |
|-------|--------|----------|
| A | * | NIP1 |
| B | 1* | NIP2 |
| C | 1111* | NIP3 |
| D | 11000* | NIP3 |
| E | 11001* | NIP1 |
| F | 000001* | NIP4 |
| G | 0000000 | NIP2 |
| H | 0000001 | NIP1 |
| I | 0000011 | NIP1 |

Route table

(a)

(b)

**Figure 2.52** Example of variable-strike trie with path and bitmap compression trie. (a) Forwarding table and corresponding binary trie; (b) Corresponding data structure of example in (a).

information in a compressed pointer array (CPA) through introducing a bitmap to indicate which value can be omitted. As illustrated in the lower part of Figure 2.50, NIP2 appears only once in the CPA, but twice in the PA. Bitmap stores the compressed information. Such an idea/technique is called bitmap compression, which has been discussed in detail in Section 2.2.2.

The subtries are packed in fixed-size wide words with compressed information, if any. One wide word, called word frame, may contain one big subtrie when its compressing potential is high; otherwise, several subtries are enclosed in one wide word. An example of the word frame data structure is depicted in Figure 2.51.

**Route Lookup.** Figure 2.52a gives an example of a forwarding table and the corresponding binary trie. Through path-compression, some internal nodes are omitted. The heights

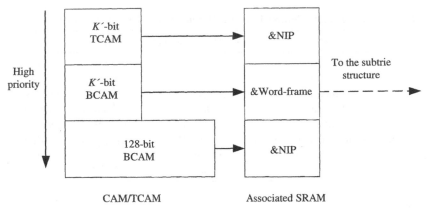

**Figure 2.53**  CAM organization for lookup.

of the three subtries are 2, 2 and 3, respectively. Figure 2.52*b* illustrates the corresponding data structure of the example. Note that the 'skip' value of subtrie #2 is 3 (>0), so the corresponding word frame contains a failure CP.

The lookup process starts with the destination IP address as the search key and a compressed pointer to the root of the prefix trie (as subtrie #1 in Fig. 2.52*b*). The lookup proceeds by using the key and the pointer to find the successive word frames and get the corresponding pointers iteratively. When the NIP containing the next IP address is encountered, the lookup process terminates.

A delicate CAM lookup mechanism is also introduced based on the following two observations: (1) the number of prefixes with the shortest length (say $k_{min}$) or with the length that is slightly longer than $k_{min}$ (say $k'$) are tiny; (2) the number of 128-bit prefixes is also very small. Therefore, (1) a $k'$-bit wide TCAM is used to store the prefixes no longer than $k'$-bit; (2) a $k'$-bit wide BCAM (binary CAM) is used for the prefixes between $k'$-bit and 64-bit; and (3) a 128-bit wide BCAM is used to store the 128-bit prefixes. The architecture is shown in Figure 2.53.

An incoming search key will be first sent to the mixed-CAM for a match. The matching result with the highest priority is returned, along with the pointer to a word frame containing either the associated next-hop IP address (for prefixes less than $k'$ bits or exactly 128 bits) or the subtrie structure whose root node exactly matches the first $k'$th bits of the key.

***Performance.***  The experimental results show that for an IPv6 forwarding table containing over 130k prefixes, generated by an IPv6 generator [29], the scheme can perform 22 million lookups per second even in the worst case with only 440 kbytes of SRAM and no more than 3 kbytes of TCAM. This means that it can support 10 Gbps route lookup for back-to-back 60-byte packets using on-chip memories.

## 2.5  COMPARISON

Table 2.5 summarizes several IP route lookup schemes with the asymptotic complexity for worst case lookup, storage, and update [1]. They are categorized into five classes, Class I–V, based on data structure and lookup mechanism. Class I includes the basic 1-bit trie and

**TABLE 2.5   Complexity Comparison of Different Route Lookup Schemes**

| Case | Scheme | Worst-case Lookup | Storage | Update |
|------|--------|-------------------|---------|--------|
| I | 1-bit trie | $O(W)$ | $O(NW)$ | $O(W)$ |
|   | PC-trie | $O(W)$ | $O(N)$ | $O(W)$ |
| II | k-bit trie | $O(W/k)$ | $O(2^k NW/k)$ | $O(W/k + 2^k)$ |
|   | LC-trie | $O(W/k)$ | $O(2^k NW/k)$ | $O(W/k + 2^k)$ |
|   | Lulea | $O(W/k)$ | $O(2^k NW/k)$ | $O(W/k + 2^k)$ |
| III | Binary search on prefix lengths | $O(\log_2 W)$ | $O(N \log_2 W)$ | $O(\log_2 W)$ |
| IV | k-way range search | $O(\log_k N)$ | $O(N)$ | $O(N)$ |
| V | TCAM | $O(1)$ | $O(N)$ | — |

the path-compressed trie structures. The latter improves the average lookup performance and storage complexity. But its worst-case lookup performance is still $O(W)$, because there may be some paths from the root to the leaves that are $W$ bits long. The path-compressed trie has the property of keeping the total number of nodes, both leaf nodes and internal nodes, below $2N$, resulting in the storage complexity of $O(N)$.

The schemes in Class II are based on the multi-bit trie, which is a very powerful and generalized structure. Besides the four schemes listed in Table 2.5, the DIR-24-8-BASIC and BC-16-16 also belong to this class. The worst case lookup is in $O(W/k)$ because a chunk of $k$ bits of the destination address is inspected at a time, as opposed to one bit at a time in Class I. The Lulea algorithm has the same order of storage complexity as the others, but with a smaller constant factor, making it attractive in implementation.

The schemes in Classes I and II perform the lookup by linearly traversing the trie levels from top to bottom. The algorithm in Class III deploys a binary search over trie levels and performs hash operations at each level. Although the algorithm in Class III seems to have a small lookup complexity, it is based on the assumption of perfect hashing (no hash collision and thus one hash operation at each level). In reality, the time complexities of searches and updates over the hash tables are non-deterministic and can be quite large.

The algorithm in Class IV solves the IP lookup problem by treating each prefix as a range of the address space. The ranges split the entire address space into multiple intervals, each of which is associated with a unique prefix. Then a two-way (binary) or $k$-way search is deployed to determine which interval the prefix belongs to. Its lookup performance is $O(\log_k N)$ in the worst case.

TCAM is specialized hardware that completes the lookup in a constant time by simultaneously comparing the IP address with all prefixes in the table. We left '−' in the update complexity column due to its dependence on the data management schemes used for the TCAM.

Making a choice among these IP lookup schemes depends on the speed and storage requirements. For instance, in a low-end or a medium router, packet processing and forwarding are usually handled by general purpose processors. The trie-based schemes, such as LC-trie, Lulea algorithm, and binary search on trie levels are good candidates in these conditions. Typically, low-end or medium routers perform packet processing and forwarding with generic processors allowing for the algorithms to be easily implemented in software. However, for a core/backbone router, where the link speed is high and the forwarding table is large, the lookup time becomes more stringent. Assuming 40-byte packets are back-to-back at a 10 Gbps (OC-192) link, the lookup time is only 32 ns. In this case, the hardware-based algorithms, such as DIR-24-8-BASIC, BC-16-16, and TCAM, become more feasible.

## REFERENCES

[1] M. Sanchez, E. W. Biersack, and W. Dabbous, "Survey and taxonomy of IP address lookup algorithms," *IEEE Network*, vol. 15, no. 2, pp. 8–23 (Mar. 2001).

[2] V. Fuller, T. Li, J. Yu, and K. Varadhan, "Classless inter-domain routing (CIDR): an address assignment and aggregation strategy," RFC 1519 (Proposed Standard), Sept. 1993. [Online]. Available at: http://www.ietf.org/rfc/rfc1519.txt

[3] Y. Rekhter and T. Li, "An architecture for IP address allocation with CIDR," RFC 1518 (Proposed Standard), Sept. 1993. [Online]. Available at: http://www.ietf.org/rfc/rfc1518.txt

[4] P. Gupta, "Routing lookups and packet classifications: theory and practice," in *Proc. HOT Interconnects* 8, Stanford, California (Aug. 2000).

[5] D. Knuth, *Fundamental Algorithms Vol. 3: Sorting and Searching*. Addison-Wesley, Massachusetts, 1973.

[6] W. Eatherton, "Hardware-based internet protocol prefix lookups," M. S. Thesis, Washington University, St. Louis, Missouri (May 1999).

[7] V. Srinivasan and G. Varghese, "Faster IP lookups using controlled prefix expansion," in *Proc. ACM SIGMATICS*, Madison, Wisconsin, pp. 1–10 (June 1998).

[8] D. R. Morrison, "PATRICIA - Practical algorithm to retrieve information coded in alfanumeric," *IEEE/ACM Transactions on Networking*, vol. 17, no. 1, pp. 1093–1102 (Oct. 1968).

[9] S. Nilsson and G. Karlsson, "IP-Address lookup using LC-tries," *IEEE Journal on Selected Areas in Communications*, vol. 17, pp. 1083–1092 (June 1999).

[10] M. Degermark, A. Brodnik, S. Carlsson, and S. Pink, "Small forwarding tables for fast routing lookups," in *Proc. ACM SIGCOMM*, Cannes, France, pp. 3–14 (Sept. 1997).

[11] W. Eatherton, G. Varghese, and Z. Dittia, "Tree Bitmap: hardware/software IP lookups with incremental updates," *ACM SIGCOMM Computer Communications Review*, vol. 34, no. 2, pp. 97–122 (Apr. 2004).

[12] F. Baboescu, D. M. Tullsen, G. Rosu, and S. Singh, "A tree based router search engine architecture with single port memories," *ACM SIGARCH Computer Architecture News*, vol. 33, pp. 123–133 (May 2005).

[13] M. Waldvogel, G. Varghese, J. Turner, and B. Plattner, "Scalable high-speed IP routing lookups," in *Proc. ACM SIGCOMM*, Cannes, France, pp. 25–36 (Sept. 1997).

[14] B. Lampson, V. Srinivasan, and G. Varghese, "IP lookups using multiway and multicolumn search," in *Proc. IEEE INFOCOM'98* San Francisco, California, vol. 3, pp. 1248–1256 (Apr. 1998).

[15] P. Gupta, S. Lin, and N. McKeown, "Routing lookups in hardware at memory access speeds," in *Proc. IEEE INFOCOM'98*, San Francisco, California, vol. 3, pp. 1240–1247 (Apr. 1998).

[16] N. Huang, S. Zhao, J. Pan, and C. Su, "A fast IP routing lookup scheme for gigabit switching routers," in *Proc. IEEE INFOCOM'99*, New York, pp. 1429–1436 (Mar. 1999).

[17] *IDT75P52100 Network Search Engine*, IDT, June 2003. [Online]. Available at: http://www.idt.com

[18] *CYNSE10512 Network Search Engine*, CYPRESS, Nov. 2002. [Online]. Available at: http://www.cypress.com

[19] *Ultra9M – Datasheet from SiberCore Technologies*. [Online]. Available at: http://www.sibercore.com

[20] P. Gupta, "Algorithmic search solutions: features and benefits," in *Proc. NPC-West 2003*, San Jose, California (Oct. 2003).

[21] H. Liu, "Routing table compaction in ternary CAM," *IEEE Micro*, vol. 22, no. 1, pp. 58–64 (Jan. 2002).

[22] F. Zane, G. Narlikar, and A. Basu, "Cool CAMs: power-efficient TCAMs for forwarding engines," in *Proc. IEEE INFOCOM'03*, San Francisco, California, pp. 42–52 (Apr. 2003).

[23] K. Zheng, C. C. Hu, H. B. Lu, and B. Liu, "An ultra high throughput and power efficient TCAM-based IP lookup engine," in *Proc. IEEE INFOCOM'04*, Hong Kong, vol. 3, pp. 1984–1994 (Mar. 2004).

[24] J. L. Hennessy and D. A. Patterson, *Computer Architecture: A Quantitative Approach*, 2nd ed., Morgan-Kaufmann, San Francisco, California, 1995.

[25] X. Zhang, B. Liu, W. Li, Y. Xi, D. Bermingham, and X. Wang, "IPv6-oriented 4 OC-768 packet classification with deriving-merging partition and field-variable encoding algorithm," in *Proc. IEEE INFOCOM'06*, Barcelona, Spain (Apr. 2006).

[26] "Route-view v6 database." [Online]. Available at: http://archive.routeviews.org/routeviews6/bgpdata/

[27] Netlogic Microsystems. [Online]. Available at: http://www.netlogicmicro.com

[28] D. Pao, "TCAM organization for IPv6 address lookup," in *Proc. IEEE Int. Conf. on Advanced Communications Technology*, Phoenix Park, South Korea, vol. 1, pp. 26–31 (Feb. 2005).

[29] K. Zheng, Z. Liu, and B. Liu, "A scalable IPv6 route lookup scheme via dynamic variable-stride bitmap compression and path compression," Computer Communication, vol. 29, no. 16, pp. 3037–3050 (Oct. 2006).

# CHAPTER 3

# PACKET CLASSIFICATION

## 3.1 INTRODUCTION

Traditionally, Internet routers only provide best effort service by processing each incoming packet in the same manner. With the emergence of new applications, Internet Service Providers (ISPs) would like routers to provide different QoS levels to different applications. To meet these QoS requirements, routers need to implement new mechanisms, such as admission control, resource reservation, per-flow queuing, and fair scheduling. However, a prerequisite to deploying these mechanisms is that the router is able to distinguish and classify the incoming traffic into different flows. We call such routers flow-aware routers. A flow-aware router is distinguished from a traditional router in that it is capable of keeping track of flows passing by and applying different classes of service to each flow.

Flows are specified by *rules* and each rule consists of operations comparing packet fields with certain values. We call a set of rules a *classifier*, which is formed based on the criteria to be applied to classify packets with respect to a given network application. Given a classifier defining packet attributes or content, packet classification is the process of identifying the rule or rules within this set to which a packet conforms or matches [1]. To illustrate the kinds of services that could be provided by a flow-aware router with packet classification capability, we use an example classifier shown in Table 3.1. Assume this classifier is stored in the router $R$ in the example network shown in Figure 3.1.

*High Performance Switches and Routers*, by H. Jonathan Chao and Bin Liu
Copyright © 2007 John Wiley & Sons, Inc.

**TABLE 3.1  Classifier Example**

| | Network-Layer | | Transport-Layer | | Application-Layer | |
|---|---|---|---|---|---|---|
| Rule | Destination | Source | Protocol | Destination | Protocol | Action |
| $R_1$ | 128.238/16 | * | TCP | = telnet | * | Deny |
| $R_2$ | 176.110/16 | 196.27.43/24 | UDP | * | RTP | Send to port III |
| $R_3$ | 196.27.43/24 | 134.65/16 | TCP | * | * | Drop traffic if rate > 10 Mbps |
| $R_4$ | * | * | * | * | * | Permit |

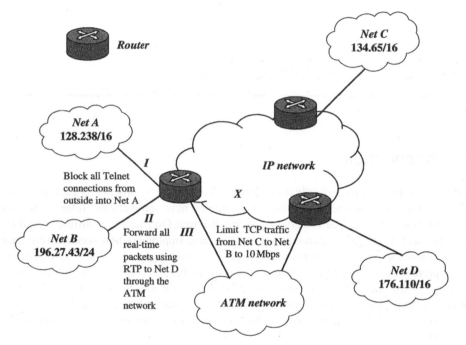

**Figure 3.1**  Network example with classifier.

With only four rules in the example classifier, the router $X$ provides the following services:

*Packet Filtering.*  Rule $R_1$ blocks all telnet connections from outside into Net A, which may be a private research network.

*Policy Routing.*  Rule $R_2$ enables the router to forward all real-time traffic using real-time transport protocol (RTP) in the application layer from Net B to Net D through the ATM network at the bottom of Figure 3.1.

*Traffic Policing.*  Rule $R_3$ limits the total transmission control protocol (TCP) traffic rate from Net C to Net B up to 10 Mbps.

A formal description of the rule, classifier, and packet classification is given in the work of Lakshman and Stiliadis [2]. We will use these symbols and terminologies throughout this chapter.

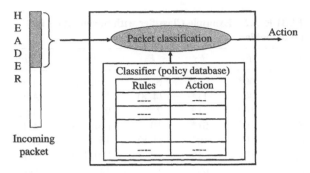

Matching the packet header to the rules in the classifier

**Figure 3.2**   Packet classification [11].

1. A classifier $C$ consists of $N$ rules, $R_j$, $1 \le j \le N$, where $R_j$ is composed of three entities:
    (a) A regular expression $R_j[i]$, $1 \le i \le d$, on each of the $d$ header fields of a packet.
    (b) A number, $Pri(R_j)$, indicating the priority of the rule in the classifier.
    (c) An action, referred to as $Action(R_j)$.
2. An incoming packet $P$ with the header considered as a $d$-tuple $(P_1, P_2, \ldots, P_d)$ is said to match $R_j$, if and only if, $P_i$ matches $R_j[i]$, where $1 \le i \le d$.
3. Given an incoming packet $P$ and thus the $d$-tuple, the $d$-dimensional packet classification problem is to find the rule $R_m$ with the highest priority among all the rules $R_j$ matching the $d$-tuple. As shown in Figure 3.2, a packet header, consisting of IP source address (32 bits), destination address (32 bits), source port number (16 bits), destination port number (16 bits), and protocol type (8 bits)[1], is used to match the rule(s) in the classifier. The one with the highest priority is chosen and its corresponding action is applied to the packet.

In the example classifier shown in Table 3.1, each rule has five regular expressions on five packet-header fields from network layer to application layer. Each expression could be a simple *prefix/length* or *operator/number* specification. The prefix/length specification has the same definition as in IP lookups, while the operator/number could be more general, such as equal 23, range 256–1023, and greater than 1023. Furthermore, a wildcard is allowed to be inserted to match any value. Note that $R_4$ in Table 3.1 matches with any incoming packet due to its 'all-wildcards' specification, which means the priorities of rules take effect when a packet matches both $R_4$ and the other rules.

Suppose there is a rule set $C = R_j (1 \le j \le N)$ and each rule $R_j$ has $d$ fields. The fields are labeled as $F_i (1 \le i \le d)$ and $R_j$ is denoted as $\langle R_{j1}, R_{j2}, \ldots, R_{jd} \rangle$. Table 3.2 shows an example classifier with seven rules in four fields. The first two fields, $F_1$ and $F_2$, are specified in prefixes and the last two fields, $F_3$ and $F_4$, are specified in ranges. The last column shows the action associated with the rules. $F_1$ and $F_2$ can be handled more efficiently by using tries or TCAM as in Chapter 2. On the other hand, $F_3$ and $F_4$ can be handled more efficiently

---

[1] Herein, the classification is for IPv4 scenario only.

**TABLE 3.2    Example Classifier with Seven Rules in Four Fields**

| Rule | $F_1$ | $F_2$ | $F_3$ | $F_4$ | Action |
|------|-------|-------|-------|-------|--------|
| $R_1$ | 00* | 110* | 6 | (10, 12) | $Act_0$ |
| $R_2$ | 00* | 11* | (4, 8) | 15 | $Act_1$ |
| $R_3$ | 10* | 1* | 7 | 9 | $Act_2$ |
| $R_4$ | 0* | 01* | 10 | (10, 12) | $Act_1$ |
| $R_5$ | 0* | 10* | (4, 8) | 15 | $Act_0$ |
| $R_6$ | 0* | 1* | 10 | (10, 12) | $Act_3$ |
| $R_7$ | * | 00* | 7 | 15 | $Act_1$ |

by projecting the numbers into different ranges and then performing range lookup, to be described in later sections of this chapter. The seven rules are listed in the order of descending priorities, that is, $R_1$ has the highest priority. This rule set will be used to illustrate some of the algorithms described later.

Several performance metrics [3] are used to compare and analyze packet classification algorithms:

*Search Speed.* High-speed links require fast classification. For example, assuming a minimum-sized 40-byte IP packet, links running at 10 Gbps can carry 31.25 million packets per second (mpps). The classification time is limited to 32 ns.

*Storage Requirement.* Small storage means fast memory access speed and low power consumption, which are important for cache-based software algorithms and SRAM-based hardware algorithms.

*Scalability in Classifier Size.* The size of the classifier depends on the applications. For a metro/edge router performing microflow recognition, the number of flows is between 128k and 1 million. Obviously, this number increases as the link speed increases.

*Scalability in the Number of Header Fields.* As more complex services are provided, more header fields need to be included.

*Update Time.* When the classifier changes, such as an entry deletion or insertion, the data structure needs to be updated. Some applications such as flow-recognition require the updating time to be short. Otherwise, the performance of classification is degraded.

*Flexibility in Specification.* The ability of an algorithm to handle a wide range of rule specifications, such as prefix/length, operator/number, and wildcards, enables it to be applied to various circumstances.

Linear search is the simplest algorithm for packet classification. The rule set can be organized into an array or a linked list in order of increasing costs. Given an incoming packet header, the rules are examined one by one until a match is found. For a $N$-rule classifier, both the storage and query time complexity are $O(N)$, making this scheme infeasible for large rule sets.

Many efficient packet classification schemes have been proposed and are described in the following sections.

## 3.2  TRIE-BASED CLASSIFICATIONS

### 3.2.1  Hierarchical Tries

Hierarchical trie is a simple extension of a one-dimension trie to a multiple-dimension trie, with each dimension representing a field. It is also called multi-level tries, backtracking-search tries, or trie-of-tries [3].

***Rule Storing Organization.*** A two-dimensional hierarchical trie representing the first two fields of rule set $C$ in Table 3.2 is shown in Figure 3.3. Here, we only consider $F_1$ and $F_2$ because they are prefixes and can be easily processed by using tries. The ellipse nodes belong to the $F_1$-trie and round nodes belong to $F_2$-tries. The bold curved arrow denotes the next-trie pointer. Note that there are four $F_2$-tries because we have four distinct prefixes in the $F_1$ field of $C$. Each gray node is labeled with a rule $R_j$, which means that if this node is reached during a search, $R_j$ is matched. In general, the hierarchical trie can be constructed as follows: a binary radix trie, called $F_1$-trie is first built for the set of prefixes $\{R_{j1}\}$ that belong to $F_1$ of all the rules. Secondly, for each prefix $p$ in the $F_1$-trie, a $(d-1)$-dimensional hierarchical trie $T_p$ is recursively constructed for those rules that exactly specify $p$ in $F_1$, that is, the set of rules $\{R_j | R_{j1} = p\}$. Trie $T_p$ is connected to $p$ by a next-trie pointer stored in node $p$.

***Classification Scheme.*** Classification for an incoming packet with the header $(v_1, v_2, \ldots, v_d)$ should be carried out in the following procedure: The query algorithm traverses the $F_1$-trie based on $v_1$; if a next-trie pointer is encountered, the algorithm goes on with the pointer and queries the $(d-1)$-dimensional hierarchical trie recursively.

For the above rule set $C$, given an incoming packet $(001, 110)$, the search process starts from the $F_1$-trie to find the best matching prefix of '001'. After node 'D' in the $F_1$-trie is reached, the next-trie pointer is used to guide the search into the $F_2$-trie to find all matching prefixes of '110'. Apparently, both node $R_1$ and node $R_2$ are reached; however, only $R_1$ is recorded due to its higher priority. Now the search process backtracks to node 'B', which is the lowest ancestor of node 'D' in the $F_1$-trie. Again, we use the next-trie pointer here to

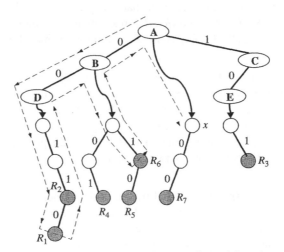

**Figure 3.3**  Hierarchical trie data structure for $F_1$ and $F_2$ of the rule set in Table 3.2.

search the $F_2$-trie. This procedure is repeated until no ancestor node of node 'D' is available to be searched. In this example, the search process ends up at node $x$ and the entire traversing path is depicted by the dashed line in Figure 3.3. During this traversal, three matches are found, $R_1$, $R_2$, and $R_6$. $R_1$ is returned as the highest priority rule matched. The backtracking process is necessary since '001' of the incoming packet may match several prefixes in the first field and we have no knowledge in advance which $F_2$-trie contains prefix(es) that match '110'. Furthermore, all matches must be found to ensure that the highest priority one is returned.

***Performance Comments.*** Hierarchical trie is one of most storage-economic algorithms. For a $N$-rule set, each of which is with $d$ sub-fields and the maximum field length of each field is $W$, then the storage complexity is $O(dW)$. The data structure is straightforward and easy to maintain at the expenses of a longer searching time. Traversing the trie brings backtracking in an attempt to find all the matching rules since the priority level cannot be effectively reflected by this data structure. The search time complexity is $O(W^d)$. $F_d$-trie has a depth of $W$ and thus takes $O(W)$ to search. $F_{d-1}$-trie also has a depth of $W$, where each node has a $F_d$-trie. The worst-case search time for the $F_{d-1}$-trie is thus $O(W^2)$. With induction, the time complexity becomes $O(W^d)$. Incremental updates can be implemented in $O(d^2W)$ because each field of the updated rule is stored in exactly one location at $F$ maximum depth $O(dW)$.

### 3.2.2   Set-Pruning Trie

The set-pruning trie is a modified version of the hierarchical trie. Backtracking is avoided during the query process in a set-pruning trie.

***Rule Storing Organization.*** In a set-pruning trie, each trie node (with a valid prefix) duplicates all rules in the rule sets of its ancestors into its own rule set and then constructs the next dimension trie based on the new rule set.

An example of the 2-dimensional set-pruning trie denoting $F_1$ and $F_2$ fields of the rule set $C$ (Table 3.2) is shown in Figure 3.4. Note that in Figure 3.3 the rule sets of $F_1$-trie node A, B, and D are $\{R_7\}$, $\{R_4, R_5, R_6\}$, and $\{R_1, R_2\}$, respectively. While in Figure 3.4, they are $\{R_7\}$, $\{R_4, R_5, R_6, R_7\}$, and $\{R_1, R_2, R_4, R_5, R_6, R_7\}$, where rules have been duplicated.

***Classification Scheme.*** The search process for a $d$-tuple consists of $d$ consecutive longest prefix matching on each dimension of the set-pruning trie. Given a 2-tuple $(001, 110)$, the query path is depicted by the dashed line in Figure 3.4. $R_1$ is returned as the highest priority rule matched. Multiple rules may be encountered along the path and the one with the highest priority is recorded. The $R_2$ node on the path is supposed to include rules $R_2$ and $R_6$, but only $R_2$ is kept due to its higher priority.

***Performance Comments.*** Hierarchical trie needs backtracking because the rule sets associated with the $F_1$-trie nodes are disjointed with each other. The set-pruning trie eliminates this need and decreases the query time complexity to only $O(dW)$ at the cost of increased storage complexity, $O(N^d dW)$, since a rule may need to be duplicated up to $N^d$ times. The update complexity is also $O(N^d)$.

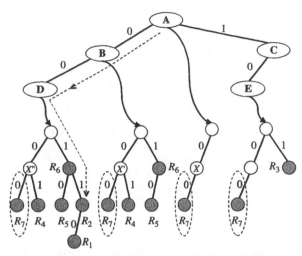

**Figure 3.4**   Set-pruning trie data structure for the rule set in Table 3.2.

### 3.2.3  Grid of Tries

Srinivansan et al. [4] proposed the grid-of-tries data structure for 2D (2-dimensional) classi-fication, which reduces the storage complexity to $O(NdW)$, as in the hierarchical trie, while still keeping the query time complexity at $O(dW)$ by pre-computing and storing the so-called switching pointers in some $F_2$-trie nodes. It is mentioned above that the $F_1$-trie node of the set-pruning trie duplicates rules belonging to its ancestors. This procedure could also be interpreted that the $F_1$-trie node merges the $F_2$-tries of its ancestors into its own $F_2$-trie. For instance, $R_7$ in $F_2$-trie of node A in Figure 3.4 is duplicated three times. Assuming that the $F_2$-trie belonging to node B is denoted as $F_2$-B-trie, the only difference between the two $F_2$-B-tries in Figures 3.3 and 3.4 is that node $R_7$ is duplicated in the set-pruning trie. Now instead of node duplication, a switching pointer labeled with '0' is incorporated at node $x'$ and points to node $R_7$ in the $F_2$-A-trie as shown in Figure 3.5. The switching pointers are depicted by the dashed curved arrows. In fact, the switching pointer labeled '0' at node $x'$ replaces the 0-pointer in the set-pruning trie.

   If the hierarchical trie and set-pruning trie have been built for a classifier $C$, the grid-of-tries structure of $C$ could be constructed by adding switching pointers to the $F_2$-tries of the hierarchical trie with comparison to that of the set-pruning trie. A switching pointer, $p_s$, labeled with 0/1 is inserted at node $y$ whenever its counterpart in the set-pruning trie contains a 0/1-pointer to another node $z$ while $y$ does not. Node $z$ may have several counterparts in the hierarchical trie, but $p_s$ points to the one contained in the $F_2$-trie that is 'closest' to the $F_2$-trie containing node $y$. For instance, node $x$ and node $x'$ in Figures 3.4 and 3.5 are both counterparts of node $x''$ in Figure 3.4. However, the switching pointer at node $y$ points to node $x'$ since node B is closer to node D than node A. If the switching pointers are viewed the same as 0/1-pointers, the query procedure is identical as in the set-pruning trie.

   The grid-of-tries structure performs well on both query time and storage complexity, but incremental updates are complex since several pointers may point to a single node. If the node is to be removed, a new node needs to be created and the pointers need to be updated to point to the new node.

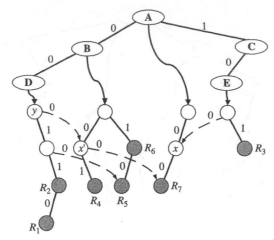

**Figure 3.5**   Example of the grid-of-tries structure for the rule set in Table 3.2.

### 3.2.4   Extending Two-Dimensional Schemes

Baboescu et al. [5] introduced a novel classification method EGT-PC for core routers. The key idea was to make use of the characteristics of rule databases they discovered in core routers to reduce the complexity of multi-dimensional search to that of a 2D search. By observing statistics from classifiers in Tier 1 ISP's core routers, they found that every packet matches at most a few distinct source–destination prefix pairs (SIP, DIP) presented in the rule set. In other words, if we project the rule set to just the source and destination fields, no packet matches more than a small number of rules in the new set of projected rules. Note that this is emphatically not true for single fields because of wildcards: a single packet can match hundreds of rules when considering any one field in isolation. Based on this character, they present the idea of a simple 2D classification method, as shown in Figure 3.6.

The idea is first to use any efficient 2D matching scheme to find all the distinct source–destination prefix pairs $(S_1, D_1), \ldots, (S_t, D_t)$ that match a header. For each distinct pair $(S_i, D_i)$ there is a linear array or list with all rules that contain $(S_i, D_i)$ in the source and

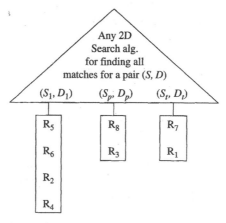

**Figure 3.6**   Extended 2D search policy [5].

destination fields. As shown in Figure 3.6 $(S_1, D_1)$ contain rules, $R_5$, $R_6$, $R_2$, and $R_4$. Note that a rule can only be associated with a source–destination prefix pair. On the other hand, one may wish to replicate rules to reduce the number of source–destination prefix pairs considered during the search to reduce the searching time. When searching for a rule for a given key, multiple source–destination prefix pairs can match with the key. For instance (*, 000) and (1*, 0*) match with a prefix key (111, 000). As a result, the rules in each matched $(S, D)$ pair will be further searched against with the rest part of the key. For example, if $(S_1, D_1)$ is matched, all its rules, $R_5$, $R_6$, $R_2$, and $R_4$, are searched against with, for instance, the port numbers of the key.

### 3.2.5 Field-Level Trie Classification (FLTC)

A field-level trie classification (FLTC) uses a field-level trie (FLT) structure that is organized in a hierarchical structure field by field [6]. The classification data structure has been optimized so that TCAM and multiway search are deployed for prefix and range fields, respectively. The query (search) process is also carried out field by field. With proper implementation, each query only requires a few memory accesses on average, and thus very high-speed classification can be achieved. The storage requirement of the FLTC is reasonable due to the node-sharing property of the FLT. Although node sharing makes the updating processes (insertion and deletion) less straightforward, the complexity of the update operation remains low because each operation only affects a small part of the data structure. The FLTC can easily support large classifiers, for example, with 100,000 to 1 million rules, without compromising query performance.

The FLT structure targets classifiers with multiple fields, each one of which is specified in either prefix format or range format. Figure 3.7 shows the FLT constructed from the classifier in Table 3.2. The FLT is defined to have the following properties:

1. It is organized in a hierarchical structure field by field. The depth of an FLT equals the number of fields, $d$. In Figure 3.7, there are four levels of nodes, organized from $F_1$ to $F_4$.[2]

2. Each node in the FLT contains a rule set, which is also a subset of its parent node's rule set. The root node of the FLT is defined to contain all the rules in the classifier.

3. Node $a$ in the $i$th level[3] generates its child nodes in the $(i + 1)$th level based on the $F_i$ values of all the rules contained in node $a$. Depending on $F_i$'s specification, there are two different procedures for child-node generation:

   - If $F_i$ is specified in prefix format, the number of child nodes of $a$ equals the number of different prefixes contained in the $F_i$ field of $a$'s rule set. Each child node is associated with a different prefix. Assuming that child node $b$ is associated with prefix $p$, the $F_i$ value of rule $r$ contained in $b$'s rule set is either the same as or a prefix of $p$. For instance, the root node in Figure 3.7 contains all seven rules and there are four different prefixes, *, 0*, 00*, and 10*, in field $F_1$, so four child nodes are generated. Node $x$ associated with prefix 0* contains four rules, $R_4$–$R_7$. The $F_1$ value of $R_4$–$R_6$ is 0*, which is the associated prefix; the $F_1$ value of $R_7$ is *, which is a prefix of 0*.

---

[2]Note that the gray nodes in the bottom do not form a separate level. They are shown only to indicate which rule is matched when the query (classification) process terminates at the fourth level.

[3]The root node is defined to be in the first level.

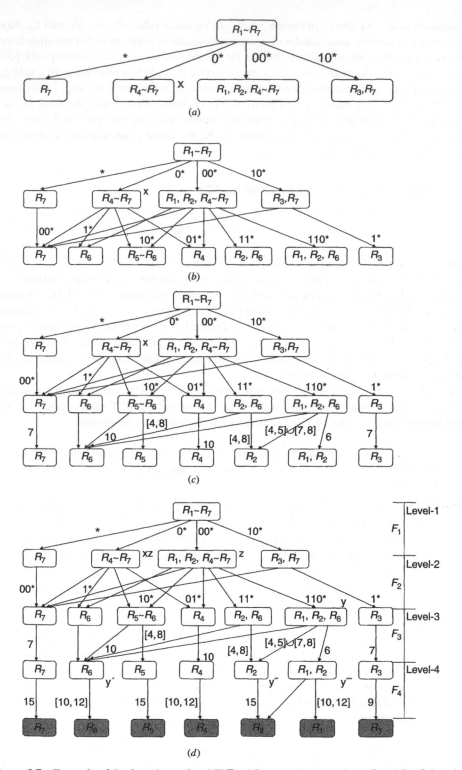

**Figure 3.7** Example of the four-dimensional FLT. (*a*) Level 1; (*b*) Level 2; (*c*) Level 3; (*d*) Level 4.

- If $F_i$ is specified in range format, we first project all the ranges (taken from the $F_i$ fields of $a$'s rule set) onto a number line and obtain a set of intervals. For each interval $I$, a child node $b$ is generated. A rule $r$ is contained in $b$'s rule set if, and only if, the range specified by the $F_i$ field of $r$ covers $I$. For instance, node $y$ generates three child nodes, node $y'$ with interval $[10, 10]$, which is a single point, node $y'''$ with interval $[6, 6]$, and node $y''$ with intervals $[4, 5]$ and $[7, 8]$ (in fact, there are two pointers both pointing to $y''$), as indicated in Figure 3.7.

4. The rule set of a node $a$ in the $i$th level is unique among the rule sets of all the nodes in the $i$th level. If two nodes in the $(i - 1)$th level, $b$ and $c$, have a child node $a$ in common, then only one node, which is $a$, is generated and they share it. Figure 3.7 shows that node sharing happens when a node is pointed to by multiple pointers.

***Fields in Prefix Form.*** Since each field is normally specified in either the prefix or range forms and each specification has its own favored data structure and searching algorithms, we group the fields with the same specifications together. In most cases, a classifier has two groups of fields; the first group in prefix form and the second group in range form. In Table 3.2, $F_1$ and $F_2$ are in the first group and $F_3$ and $F_4$ are in the second. The FLT is organized so that fields of the first group appear in the upper levels and fields of the second one appear in the lower levels.

For the first group where only prefix fields exist, TCAM can be used for storing the prefixes and searching among them. Since TCAM can accommodate multiple fields simultaneously, the query of the first group of fields can be accomplished in a single TCAM access. Figure 3.8 shows the compressed FLT derived from the classifier in Table 3.2 and the trie structure in Figure 3.7. Now there is only one level existing for fields $F_1$ and $F_2$. The root node has seven child nodes initially lying in the third level in Figure 3.7. Each second-level node has an $F_1/F_2$ prefix pair associated with it. Each such prefix pair is the contents

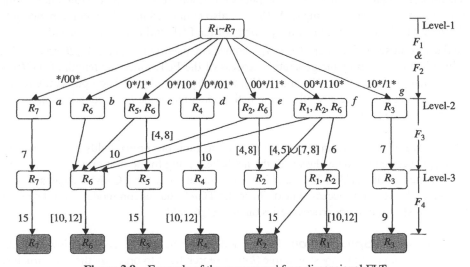

**Figure 3.8**  Example of the compressed four-dimensional FLT.

**TABLE 3.3   TCAM Contents for the Compressed FLT**

| Entry # | Prefix Pair | Node Name | Sum of Lengths from Prefix Pair |
|---------|-------------|-----------|----------------------------------|
| 1 | */00* | *a* | 2 |
| 2 | 0*/1* | *b* | 2 |
| 3 | 0*/10* | *c* | 3 |
| 4 | 0*/01* | *d* | 3 |
| 5 | 10*/1* | *g* | 3 |
| 6 | 00*/11* | *e* | 4 |
| 7 | 00*/110** | *f* | 5 |

of an entry in the TCAM. The prefix pair is derived from the trie structure in Figure 3.7. For each node *a* in the third level in Figure 3.7, corresponding to the node in the second level in Figure 3.8, we find a path from the root node to *a* with the smallest sum of the prefix lengths. The prefixes along this path form the prefix pair associated with *a* in Figure 3.8. All prefix pairs are arranged in decreasing order of prefix length (the sum of the lengths of the two prefixes) in the TCAM. For prefix pairs with the same length, their relative order can be arbitrary. The contents of the TCAM for the compressed FLT in Figure 3.8 is shown in Table 3.3.

By arranging the prefix pairs in ascending order in the TCAM (meaning that the longest matching prefix pair will be found), we can guarantee the search result from the TCAM to be correct, for example, the appropriate node in the second level is determined to continue the entire query process. A brief proof follows.

When searching the TCAM with a key $A/B$, if two entries with prefix pairs $A_1/B_1$ and $A_2/B_2$ are matched, there will be two scenarios. Without loss of generality, we assume $A_1 \prec A_2$, meaning that $A_1$ is a prefix of $A_2$.

- In the first scenario, where $B_1 \prec B_2$, the length of $A_2/B_2$ is larger than that of $A_1/B_1$. Therefore, the entry with $A_2/B_2$ is output as the result. It is a correct result since all the rules in node *a* (corresponding to $A_1/B_1$) are also contained in node *b* (corresponding to $A_2/B_2$), which is guaranteed by the property of the FLT, and node *b* is selected.

- In the second scenario, where $B_2 \prec B_1$, another entry with prefix pair $A_2/B_1$ must exist, which is guaranteed by the generation process of the FLT. Since the length of $A_2/B_1$ is larger than that of both $A_1/B_1$ and $A_2/B_2$, the entry with $A_2/B_1$ is output as the result. It is a correct result because all rules in both node *a* and node *b* are contained in node *c* (corresponding to $A_2/B_1$).

The above conclusion can be easily extended to multiple prefix fields more than two. Given a packet header to be classified, the fields belonging to the first group are extracted and presented to the TCAM for searching. The output from the TCAM indicates a node in the second level to be accessed next. Since the TCAM has accommodated all the prefix fields, the rest of the query process relies on the range fields.

***Fields in Range Specification.*** For the nodes existing in the second or lower levels, we propose using a multiway search tree (*k*-way search tree) to organize the data structure

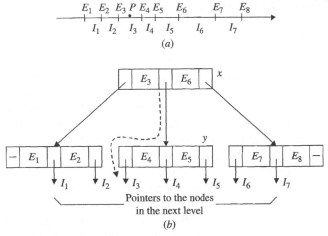

**Figure 3.9**   Example of the node structure organized in three-way search tree. (*a*) Derived intervals by range protection; (*b*) Node structure for a three-way search tree.

at each node. For example, there is a node *a* in the *i*th level ($i > 1$) of the compressed FLT. After projecting the $F_i$ fields of the rules in *a*'s rule set onto a number line, seven intervals, $I_1$ to $I_7$, are obtained with eight end points, $E_1$ to $E_8$, as shown in Figure 3.9*a*. If we use a three-way search tree to organize these intervals, the result is shown in Figure 3.9*b*. It is a two-layer tree with four blocks (to avoid confusion with the terms 'level' and 'node' in the FLT, we use the terms 'layer' and 'block' in the *k*-way search tree). Each block contains up to *k* pointers and $k - 1$ end points. The pointer in an internal block points to another block in the *k*-way search tree, while the pointer in a leaf block points to a $(i + 1)$th level node in the compressed FLT. We use an example to illustrate the searching process in the *k*-way search tree. Assuming point *P* exists in the interval $I_3$, the searching process starts from the root block *x*. By comparing *P* with the two end points, $E_3$ and $E_6$, stored in *x*, we know the order among them is $E_3 < P < E_6$. So the second pointer is followed to block *y* in the second layer. Similarly, by comparing *P* with the two end points, $E_4$ and $E_5$, we know that the first pointer associated with interval $I_3$ should be followed to a node in the next level of the compressed FLT.

The multiway search is an efficient algorithm for range lookup problems. The number of layers of a *k*-way search tree can be determined by $\log_k M$ where $M$ is the number of intervals. From the implementation point of view, each block in the *k*-way search tree is a basic unit stored in memory, which requires one memory access for one read/write operation. Thus, during a search process, the number of memory accesses equals the number of layers of the *k*-way search tree, which is $\log_k M$. The number *k* here is limited by the block size, which is determined by the memory bandwidth.

The query process of an FLT starts from the TCAM for all the prefix fields. After reaching the range field, the query process proceeds one level (or one field) at a time and at each level a *k*-way search is performed to find the next-level node to be accessed. The query process terminates when a leaf node is reached and a matched rule (if it exists) is returned as the result.

## 3.3 GEOMETRIC ALGORITHMS

### 3.3.1 Background

As mentioned before, each field of a classifier can be specified in either a prefix/length pair or an operator/number form. From a geometric point of view, both specifications could be interpreted by a range (or interval) on a number line. Thus, a rule with two fields represents a rectangle in the 2D Euclidean space and a rule with $d$ fields represents a $d$-dimensional hyper-rectangle. The classifier is a set of such hyper-rectangles with priorities associated. Given a packet header ($d$-tuple), it represents a point $P$ in the $d$-dimensional space. The packet classification problem is equivalent to finding the highest priority hyper-rectangle that encloses $P$. Figure 3.10 gives the geometric representation of $F_1$ and $F_2$ of the classifier in Table 3.2 with rectangles overlapped according to their priorities. Given the point $P(0010, 1100)$, it is straightforward to figure out the highest priority matching rule $R_1$.

There are several standard problems in the field of computational geometry that resemble packet classification [7]. One is the point location problem that is defined as finding the enclosing region of a point, given a set of non-overlapping regions. Theoretical bounds for point location in $N$ (hyper-)rectangular regions and $d > 3$ dimensions are $O(\log N)$ time with $O(N^d)$ space, or $O((\log N)^{d-1})$ time with $O(N)$ space. Packet classification is at least as hard as point location since (hyper-)rectangles are allowed to overlap. This conclusion implies that the packet classification is extremely complex in the worst case.

Packet classification algorithms of this category always involve the range interpretation on certain fields of the classifier. If the prefixes or ranges in one field of a classifier are projected on the number line $[0, 2^W - 1]$, a set of disjoint elementary ranges (or intervals) is obtained and the concatenation of these elementary ranges forms the whole number line. For instance, there are four ranges on $F_1$ dimension and five ranges on $F_2$ dimension, as shown in Figure 3.10. Given a number $Z$ on the number line, the range lookup problem is defined as locating the elementary range (or interval) containing $Z$. One way to locate the number on a range is to use the $k$-way search described in previous section. For simplicity, we use range (or interval) instead of elementary range (or interval) unless explicitly specified. It is clear that a prefix represents a range on the number line. On the other hand, an arbitrary

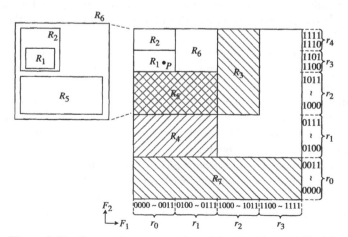

**Figure 3.10**  Geometric representation of the classifier in Table 3.2.

range may need up to $2W - 2$ prefixes for representation [3]. This is a useful conclusion for analyzing the increased storage complexity of some classification algorithms that only support prefix specification well. The process of transforming an arbitrary range into one or several prefixes is called range splitting.

### 3.3.2  Cross-Producting Scheme

Srinivansan et al. [4] proposed a cross-producting scheme that is suitable for an arbitrary number of fields and either type of field specification. The cross-producting scheme works by performing $d$ range lookup operations, one on each field, and composing these results to index a pre-computed table that returns the highest priority rule matched.

Refer to $F_1$ and $F_2$ of classifier $C$ of Table 3.2. For the first step, the rule specifications in the $F_1$ and $F_2$ fields are projected on two number lines vertical to each other and two sets of ranges $\{r_1[0], \ldots, r_1[3]\}$ and $\{r_2[0], \ldots, r_2[4]\}$, are obtained as shown in Figure 3.11. Each pair of ranges $(r_1[i], r_2[j])$, corresponds to a small rectangle with a pre-computed best matching rule written inside ('—' means no matching rule exists). The entire pre-computed table is shown in Figure 3.11 if we organize the table in a 2D matrix format. Thus, given a 2-tuple $(p_1, p_2)$, two range lookups are performed on each range set and the two matching ranges returned are composed to index the pre-computed table. For instance, if $p_1 = 0010$ and $p_2 = 1100$, the two returned ranges $(r_1[0], r_2[3])$, tell us that $R_1$ is the best matching rule. Regarding the generic $d$-dimensional classifier, $d$ sets of ranges are obtained by projecting the rule specification on each dimension and each item in the $d$-dimensional cross-product table could be pre-computed in the same way as the above example.

The cross-producting scheme has a good query time complexity of $O(d \cdot t_{RL})$, where $t_{RL}$ is the time complexity of finding a range in one dimension. However, it suffers from a memory explosion problem; in the worst case, the cross-product table can have $O(N^d)$ entries. Thus, an on-demand cross-producting scheme together with rule caching are proposed [4] for classifiers bigger than 50 rules in five dimensions. Incremental updates require reconstruction of the cross-product table, so it cannot support dynamic classifiers well.

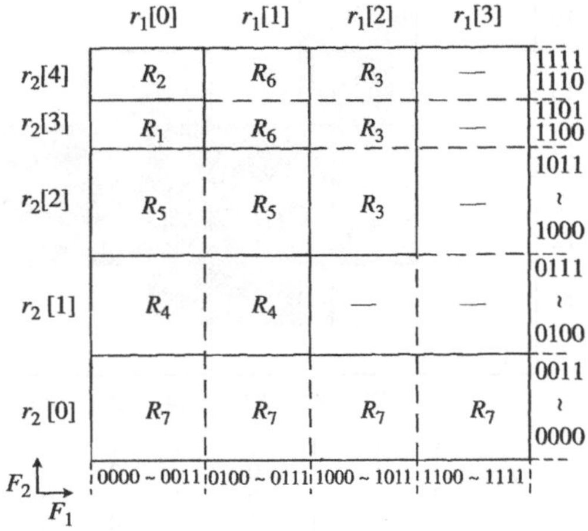

**Figure 3.11**  Geometric representation of the cross-producting algorithm.

### 3.3.3  Bitmap-Intersection

The bitmap-intersection scheme proposed by Lakshman et al. [8] applies to multi-dimensional packet classification with either type of specification in each field. This scheme is based on the observation that the set of rules, $S$, that matches a packet is the intersection of $d$ sets, $S_i$, where $S_i$ is the set of rules that matches the packet in the $i$th dimension alone.

Figure 3.12 contains an example to illustrate how the bitmap-intersection scheme works. Four rules of a 2D classifier are depicted as four rectangles in Figure 3.12 and projected on the two number lines. Two sets of intervals $\{X_1, \ldots, X_6\}$ and $\{Y_1, \ldots, Y_6\}$ are derived in each dimension by the rule projections. Each interval is associated with a precomputed 4-bit bitmap with each bit representing a rule. A '1' in the bitmap of $X_k/Y_k$ denotes that the rule contains (matches) $X_k/Y_k$ in the $X/Y$ dimension. Given a packet $P(p_1, p_2)$, two range lookups (e.g., using a multiway search tree in Fig. 3.9) are performed in each interval set and two intervals, $X_i$ and $Y_j$, which contain $p_1$ and $p_2$, are determined. Then the resulting bitmap, obtained by the intersection (a simple bitwise AND operation) of the bitmaps of $X_i$ and $Y_j$, shows all matching rules for $P$. If the rules are ordered in decreasing order of priority, the first '1' in the bitmap denotes the highest priority rule. It is straightforward to expand the scheme to apply to a multi-dimensional classification.

Since each bitmap is $N$ bits wide, and there are $O(N)$ ranges in each of the $d$ dimensions, the storage space consumed is $O(dN^2)$. Query time is $O(d \cdot t_{RL} + dN/w)$, where $t_{RL}$ is the time to perform one range lookup and $w$ is the memory width. Time complexity can be reduced by a factor of $d$ by looking up each dimension independently in parallel. Incremental updates are not well-supported.

It is reported that the scheme can support up to 512 rules with a 33-MHz FPGA and five 1-Mbyte SRAMs, classifying 1 mpps [8]. The scheme works well for a small number of rules in multiple dimensions, but suffers from a quadratic increase in storage and linear increase in classification time with the size of the classifier.

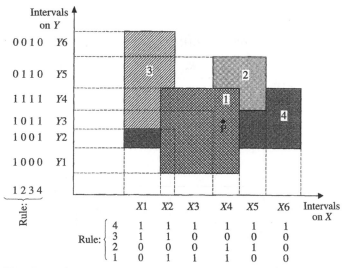

**Figure 3.12**   Geometric interpretation of the bitmap-insertion scheme for a 2D classifier.

### 3.3.4  Parallel Packet Classification (P²C)

Lunteren et al. [9] proposed a fast multi-field classification scheme based on the independent searching and primitive range encoding. The idea is that the ranges in each dimension are first encoded into some code vectors. Then for a specific classification operation, P²C performs irrespective parallel searching in each dimension (sub-range) to get the corresponding code vectors. And then the vectors found in all dimensions are combined together to carry out a ternary match in TCAM to finally gain the multi-field classification outcome. Ranges are defined as the intervals divided by the boundaries of all rules; as shown in Figure 3.13, for example, $X_0$–$X_8$ on axis $X$ and $Y_0$–$Y_6$ on axis $Y$ are all ranges. And it is straightforward that each range has a unique matching condition.

The ranges on each dimension divide the hyper-plane into several 'grids' (as depicted in Fig. 3.13); each of the grids can be represented by a $d$-tuple of the ranges; and the rule with the highest priority that covers one of the grids is defined as 'the rule corresponding to this grid'. For example, as the case shown in Figure 3.13, the grid determined by the 2-tuple $(X_2, Y_2)$ corresponds to $R_4$, and the grid determined by $(X_5, Y_4)$ corresponds to $R_1$, with assumption that $R_1$ is of higher priority.

According to this principle, if the correspondent relationships of the tuple of the ranges and the rules are pre-computed, the classification operation is then carried out to be: (1) to find the corresponding ranges of the given key on each dimension in parallel; (2) to combine the ranges into a key to find the corresponding rule.

In P²C, the ranges are all encoded into code vectors; in the first step, the ranges are found in the form of code vectors and then the code vectors are combined together and put in a TCAM to gain the final multi-dimension classification outcome.

*Encoding the Ranges.* As shown in Figure 3.14, the layers (dashed lines) are defined according to the priority of the rules and the relation of overlap between them. The higher the priority of a rule is, the higher the layer its corresponding range belongs to, on their dimension; non-overlapping rules can be within the same layer.

'Layer' is the minimum unit in the assignment of bits of code. Binary digits above the lines are code vectors assigned to the range on this layer, representing the matching

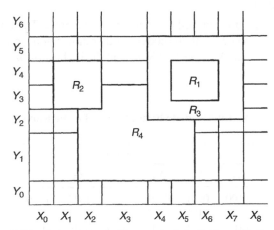

**Figure 3.13**   Rules and primitive ranges in both $X$ and $Y$ dimensions.

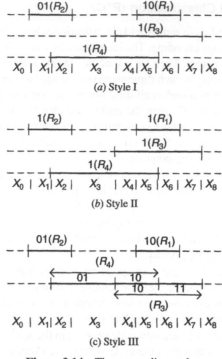

**Figure 3.14** Three encoding styles.

conditions of the corresponding ranges, such as '01' and '10' in Figure 3.14$a$. Three range coding styles, as shown in Figure 3.14, have been proposed to fit for different environments, in order to get the optimal encoding result (with the fewest bits assigned).

The corresponding results produced by the three encoding styles are given by Table 3.4, according to the encoding styles in Figure 3.14. Then, according to the relationship of the rules and the range (as shown in Fig. 3.13), the matching conditions of the rule in dimension $X$ is given by Table 3.5. The ternary form matching conditions for dimension $Y$ can be obtained similarly.

When a packet arrives, it is mapped to a range independently. The range corresponds to a code, which is then combined with the codes of other dimensions' ranges. The combined range code is then used to lookup the TCAM to find the highest priority rule.

**TABLE 3.4 Intermediate Result Vectors for the Range Hierarchies**

|  | Ranges | | | | | | |
|---|---|---|---|---|---|---|---|
|  | $X_1$ | $X_2$ | $X_3$ | $X_4$ | $X_5$ | $X_6$ | $X_7$ |
| Style I | 0100 | 0101 | 0001 | 0011 | 1011 | 1010 | 0010 |
| Style II | 100 | 101 | 001 | 011 | 111 | 110 | 010 |
| Style III | 0100 | 0101 | 0001 | 0010 | 1010 | 1011 | 0011 |

TABLE 3.5    **Ternary-Match Conditions for the Range Hierarchies**

|  | $R_4$ | $R_3$ | $R_2$ | $R_1$ |
|---|---|---|---|---|
| Style I | xxx1 | xx1x | 01xx | 10xx |
| Style II | xx1 | x1x | 10x | 11x |
| Style III | xx01,xx10 | xx10,xx11 | 01xx | 10xx |

***Performance Comments.*** Adopting independent field search makes parallel search in each dimension viable. The time complexity of this algorithm lies on the most time-consuming one of those independent field searches. Every packet classification needs about five memory accesses (four for the longest field search, and one for TCAM access) [9]. The reported memory requirement is relatively good because the coding method is used. The algorithm has been designed such that any rule insertion or removal will not impact the codes for existing rules. Furthermore, compared to most other packet classification schemes, $P^2C$ stores the data related to a single rule at very few locations, typically one location in each field search structure and at one location in the TCAM (e.g., a total of 6 locations for 5-tuple classification). As a result, updates require only incremental modification of very few locations in the data structure, enabling fast efficient updates with a rate $> 10,000$ rules/second. Those updates can be performed without interrupting the classification operation.

### 3.3.5  Area-Based Quadtree

Buddhikot et al. [10] proposed the area-based quadtree (AQT) structure for 2D classification with prefix specification in both fields as shown in Figure 3.15a. Compared with a binary tree, the node of quadtree may have up to four children and four pointers labeled with 00, 01, 10, and 11 as shown in Figure 3.15b. Each node in the AQT represents a 2D space that is evenly decomposed into four quadrants corresponding to its four children. For example, the root node of Figure 3.15b denotes the entire square in Figure 3.15a and thus the four children represent the four quadrants, SW (southwest), NW (northwest), SE (southeast), and NE (northeast), respectively. If the 2D space represented by the root node is expressed as a prefix pair (*, *), the four quadrants are therefore (0*, 0*), (0*, 1*), (1*, 0*), and (1*, 1*) with each prefix denoting a range in one dimension.

For a certain classifier $C$, the AQT is constructed as follows. A rule set $S(u)$ containing all rules of $C$ is associated with the root node $u$. $u$ is expanded with four children (decomposing space (*, *)) each associated with a rule set $S(v_m)$, where $1 \leq m \leq 4$. $S(v_m)$ contains the rules that are fully contained in the quadrant represented by $v_m$. However, there are some rules in $S(u)$ that are not fully contained in any of the four quadrants. Such rules are stored in another so-called crossing filter set (CFS) associated with node $u$. Each rule in the CFS is said to be a crossing node $u$ because it completely spans at least one dimension of the 2D space represented by $u$. For instance, rule $R_7$ denoted by a bold rectangle in Figure 3.15a is said to cross space (*, *) since the rectangle completely spans $x$-dimension of space (*, *). Thus, $R_7$ is stored in the CFS of the root node in Figure 3.15c. Each child node $v_m$ of $u$ is expanded in the same way until $S(v_m)$ is empty. This procedure is carried out recursively and the construction terminates until the rule set $S$ of each leaf node is empty. Note that only the CFS is indeed stored at each node after the construction. Therefore, the storage

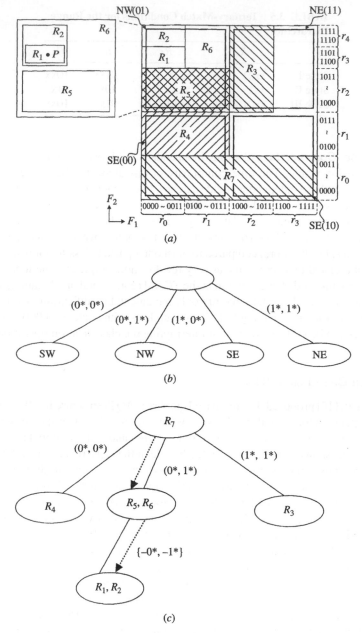

**Figure 3.15** Example of the area-based quadtree structure. (a) Cross-producting scheme; (b) Area-based quadtree with the four quadrants; and (c) Expressed as $(F_1, F_2)$ pairs from each rule in Table 3.2.

complexity of AQT tree is $O(NW)$ since each rule is only stored once at a certain node $v$, where the rule crosses the 2D space of $v$.

Given the 2-tuple, $P(p_1, p_2)$, query of the AQT involves traversing the quadtree from root node to a leaf node. The branching decision at each node is made by two bits, each taken from $p_1$ and $p_2$. $P$ is compared with the rules in the CFS of each node encountered along the traversing path to find matches. The best matching rule is returned after traversing to the leaf node. The CFS at each node could be split into two sets, $x$-CFS and $y$-CFS. The former contains rules completely spanning in $x$ dimension, while the latter spans in $y$ dimension. Because of this spanning, only the $y(x)$ dimension (field) of each rule in $x(y)$-CFS needs to be stored. For instance, $R_7$ completely spans the space (*, *) in $x$ dimension so it belongs to the $x$-CFS of the root node. In fact, only '00*', which is the $y$ field of $R_7$ is kept and used for the range lookup at the root node. Now finding matches of $P$ in the CFS of a node is transformed into two range lookups in $x$-CFS and $y$-CFS. Figure 3.15$c$ shows the AQT for the classifier in Table 3.2 with the geometric interpretation shown in Figure 3.15$a$. The dashed line in Figure 3.15$c$ indicates the traversing path when a 2-tuple (001, 110) (point $P$ in Fig. 3.15$a$) is searched in the AQT.

An efficient update algorithm for the AQT is proposed in [10]. It has $O(NW)$ space complexity, $O(\alpha W)$ search time, and $O(\alpha^\alpha \cdot \sqrt{N})$ update time, where $\alpha$ is a tunable integer parameter.

### 3.3.6 Hierarchical Intelligent Cuttings

Hierarchical intelligent cuttings (HiCuts), proposed by Gupta and McKeown [11], partitions the multidimensional search space guided by heuristics that exploit the structure of the classifier.

***Rule Storing Organization.*** The HiCuts algorithm builds a decision tree data structure by carefully preprocessing the classifier. Each internal node $v$ of the decision tree built on a $d$-dimensional classifier is associated with:

1. A box $B(v)$, which is a $d$-tuple of intervals or ranges: $([l_1 : r_1], [l_2 : r_2], \ldots, [l_d : r_d])$.
2. A cut $C(v)$, defined by a dimension $i$, and $np(C)$, the number of times $B(v)$ is cut (partitioned) in dimension $i$ (i.e., the number of cuts in the interval $[l_i : r_i]$). The cut thus evenly divides $B(v)$ into smaller boxes, which is associated with the children of $v$.
3. A set of rules $S(v)$. The tree's root has all the rules associated with it. If $u$ is a child of $v$, then $S(u)$ is defined as the subset of $S(v)$ that collides with $B(u)$. That is, every rule in $S(v)$ that spans, cuts, or is contained in $B(u)$ is also a member of $S(u)$. $S(u)$ is called the colliding rule set of $u$.

As an example, consider the case of two $W$-bit-wide dimensions. The root node, $v$, represents a box of size $2^W \times 2^W$. We make the cuttings using axis-parallel hyperplanes, which are just lines in two dimensions. Cut $C(v)$ is described by the number of equal intervals we cut in a particular dimension of box $B(v)$. If we decide to cut the root node along the first dimension into $D$ intervals, the root node will have $D$ children, each with an associated box of size $(2^W/D) \times 2^W$.

We perform cutting on each level and recursively on the children of the nodes at that level until the number of rules in the box associated with each node falls below a threshold called *binth*. In other words, the number of rules in each leaf node is limited to at most binth to speed up the linear search in the node. A node with fewer than binth rules is not partitioned further and becomes a leaf of the tree.

**TABLE 3.6    Rule Set Example with Two Dimensions in Ranges**

| Rule | X Range | Y Range |
|------|---------|---------|
| $R_1$ | 0–31 | 0–255 |
| $R_2$ | 0–255 | 128–131 |
| $R_3$ | 64–71 | 128–255 |
| $R_4$ | 67–67 | 0–127 |
| $R_5$ | 64–71 | 0–15 |
| $R_6$ | 128–191 | 4–131 |
| $R_7$ | 192–192 | 0–255 |

To illustrate this process, Table 3.6 shows an example classifier. Figure 3.16 illustrates this classifier geometrically and Figure 3.17 shows a possible decision tree. Each ellipse denotes an internal node $v$ with a triplet $(B(v), \dim(C(v)), np(C(v)))$ and each square is a leaf node containing rules. The root node $u$ denotes the entire space with the box $B(u) = 256 \times 256$. $B(u)$ is evenly cut into four small boxes in dimension $X$ shown in Figure 3.17. In this example, binth $= 2$. Therefore, the set with $R_2, R_3, R_4$, and $R_5$ is further cut in $Y$ dimension.

***Classification Scheme.*** Each time a packet arrives, the classification algorithm traverses the decision tree to find a leaf node, which stores a small number of rules. A linear search of these rules yields the desired matching.

***Performance Comments.*** The characteristics of the decision tree (its depth, degree of each node, and the local branching decision to be made at each node) can be tuned to trade off query time against storage requirements. They are chosen while preprocessing the classifier based on its characteristics. Four heuristics have been proposed when performing the cuts on node $v$ [11].

For 40 real-life 4D classifiers and some of them with up to 1700 rules, HiCuts requires less than 1 Mbyte of storage, has a worst-case query time of 20 memory accesses, and supports fast updates.

### 3.3.7 HyperCuts

Singh et al. [12] have proposed a classification algorithm based on a decision tree, called HyperCuts, the idea of which is somewhat similar with that of the HiCuts algorithm (Section 3.3.6) in that they both allow the leaf nodes to store more than one rule and that linear search is performed at the leaf nodes. HyperCuts makes two improvements over HiCuts:

1. At each node of the decision tree, the rule is cut in multi-dimension at one time and stored in a multi-dimensional array. In other words, it uses HyperCut to cut rules, while HiCuts only considers one-dimensional cutting.
2. If all the children of a node in the tree contain the same subset of rules, the subset is lifted up to be stored in the node to reduce storage space. For instance, R2 in Figure 3.17 can be moved up to the root node and eliminated from the four children nodes.

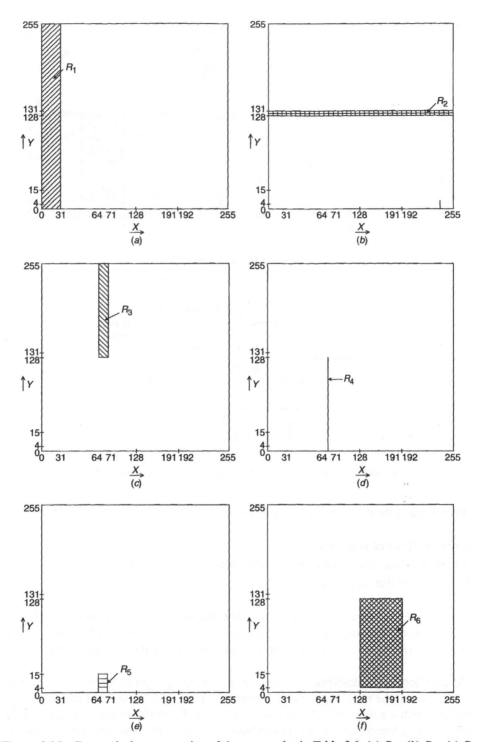

**Figure 3.16**   Geometrical representation of the seven rules in Table 3.6. (*a*) $R_1$; (*b*) $R_2$; (*c*) $R_3$; (*d*) $R_4$; (*e*) $R_5$; (*f*) $R_6$; (*g*) $R_7$; (*h*) All seven rules.

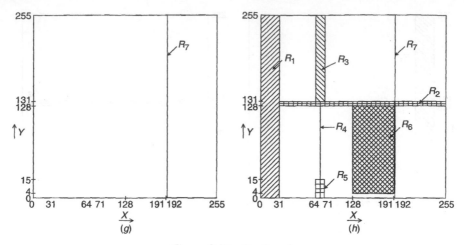

**Figure 3.16** Continued.

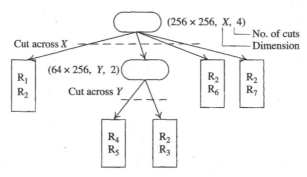

**Figure 3.17** Possible decision tree for classifier in Table 3.6 (*binth* = 2).

Each node in the decision tree has associated with:

- A region $R(v)$ that is covered.
- A number of cuts (NC) and a corresponding array of NC pointers.
- A list of rules that may match.

Figure 3.18 shows HyperCuts in action for classifier in Table 3.7. The tree consists of a single root node that covers the region [0–15, 0–15, 0–3, 0–3, 0–1], which is split into sub-regions with 16 cuts. Note that each dimension is evenly cut into multiple regions.

***Rule Storing Organization.*** The decision-tree-building algorithm starts with a set of $N$ rules, each of the rules containing $d$ dimensions. Each node identifies a region and has associated with it a set of rules $S$ that match the region. If the size of the set of rules at the current node is larger than the acceptable bucket size (i.e., binth in HiCuts), the node is split in a number (NC) of child nodes, where each child node identifies a sub-region of the region associated with the current node. Identifying the number of child nodes as well as the sub-region associated with each of the child nodes is a two-step process, which tries to

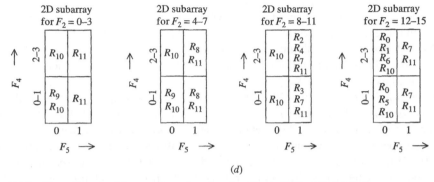

| $F_2$ | Rules associated with $F_2$ |
|-------|------------------------------|
| 0–3 | $R_9$, $R_{10}$, $R_{11}$ |
| 4–7 | $R_8$, $R_9$, $R_{10}$, $R_{11}$ |
| 8–11 | $R_2$, $R_3$, $R_4$, $R_7$, |
| 12–15 | $R_0$, $R_1$, $R_5$, $R_6$, $R_7$, $R_{10}$, $R_{11}$ |

(a)

| $F_4$ | Rules associated with $F_4$ |
|-------|------------------------------|
| 0–1 | $R_0$, $R_3$, $R_5$, $R_7$, $R_8$, $R_9$, $R_{10}$, $R_{11}$ |
| 2–3 | $R_0$, $R_1$, $R_2$, $R_4$, $R_6$, $R_7$, $R_8$, $R_{10}$, $R_{11}$ |

(b)

| $F_5$ | Rules associated with $F_5$ |
|-------|------------------------------|
| 0 | $R_0$, $R_1$, $R_5$, $R_6$, $R_9$, $R_{10}$ |
| 1 | $R_2$, $R_3$, $R_4$, $R_7$, $R_8$, $R_{11}$ |

(c)

(d)

**Figure 3.18** HyperCuts decision tree based on the classifier in Table 3.7. (a) Rules corresponding to fixed values in $F_2$; (b) Rules corresponding to fixed values in $F_4$; (c) Rules corresponding to fixed values in $F_5$; (d) A search through the HyperCuts decision tree (evenly cut in each dimension).

locally optimize the split(s) such that the distribution of the rules among the child nodes is optimal. The detailed cutting process can be found in the work of Singh et al. [12].

***Classification Scheme.*** The search algorithm for a packet with an $i$-dimensional header starts with an initialization phase of setting the current node for searching as the root node

**TABLE 3.7 Range-based Representation of a Classifier with 12 Rules on Five Fields ($F_1$–$F_5$)**

| Rule | $F_1$ | $F_2$ | $F_3$ | $F_4$ | $F_5$ | Action |
|------|-------|-------|-------|-------|-------|--------|
| $R_0$ | 0–1 | 14–15 | 2 | 0–3 | 0 | $act_0$ |
| $R_1$ | 0–1 | 14–15 | 1 | 2 | 0 | $act_0$ |
| $R_2$ | 0–1 | 8–11 | 0–3 | 2 | 1 | $act_1$ |
| $R_3$ | 0–1 | 8–11 | 0–3 | 1 | 1 | $act_2$ |
| $R_4$ | 0–1 | 8–11 | 2 | 3 | 1 | $act_1$ |
| $R_5$ | 0–7 | 14–15 | 2 | 1 | 0 | $act_0$ |
| $R_6$ | 0–7 | 14–15 | 2 | 2 | 0 | $act_0$ |
| $R_7$ | 0–7 | 8–15 | 0–3 | 0–3 | 1 | $act_2$ |
| $R_8$ | 0–15 | 4–7 | 0–3 | 0–3 | 1 | $act_2$ |
| $R_9$ | 0–15 | 0–7 | 0–3 | 1 | 0 | $act_0$ |
| $R_{10}$ | 0–15 | 0–15 | 0–3 | 0–3 | 0 | $act_3$ |
| $R_{11}$ | 0–15 | 0–15 | 0–3 | 0–3 | 1 | $act_4$ |

of the decision tree structure and setting the regions that cover the packet header to the maximum value of the regions for each of the dimensions. Then the decision tree is traversed until either a leaf node or a NULL node is found, with the hyper-regions that cover the values in the packet header being updated at each node traversed. Once a leaf node is found, the list of rules associated with this node is fully searched and the first matching rule is returned. If there is no match, a NULL is returned.

This is further explained by going through an example. Figure 3.19 shows that a packet arrives at a node A that covers the regions 200–239 in the $X$ dimension and 80–159 in the $Y$ dimension. The packet header has the value 215 in the $X$ dimension and 111 in the $Y$ dimension. During the search, the packet header is escorted by a set of registers carrying information regarding the hyper-region to which the packet header belongs at the current stage. In this example, the current hyper-region is $\{[200–239], [80–159], \ldots\}$.

Node A has 16 cuts, with four cuts for each of the dimensions $X$ and $Y$. To identify the child node, which must be followed for this packet header, the index in each dimension is determined as follow: first, $X_{index} = \lfloor 215 - 200/10 \rfloor = 1$. This is because each cut in the $X$ dimension is of size $(239 - 200 + 1)/4 = 10$. Similarly, $Y_{index} = \lfloor 111 - 80/20 \rfloor = 1$. This is because each cut in the $Y$ dimension is of size $(159 - 80 + 1)/4 = 20$. As a result the child node B is picked and the set of registers is updated with the new values describing the hyper-region covering the packet header at this stage. This hyper-region is now: $\{[210–219], [100–119], \ldots\}$. The search ends when a leaf node is reached in which case the packet header is checked against the fields in the list of rules associated with the node.

***Performance Comments.*** By contrast, HyperCuts allows the cutting of both source and destination IP fields in a single node, which not only disperses the rules among the child nodes in a single step but also reduces the effect of rule replication. Furthermore, HyperCuts pushing up common sets of rules reduces the damage due to replication. It is reported in [12] that for real-life firewall databases, this optimization resulted in a memory

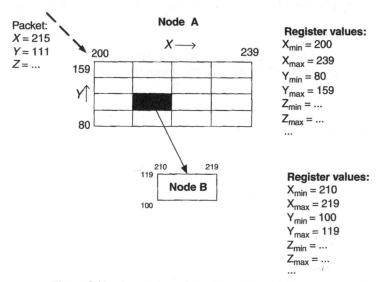

**Figure 3.19**    Search through the HyperCuts decision tree.

reduction of 10 percent. Overall, for firewall databases, HyperCuts uses an amount of memory similar to EGT-PC (Section 3.2.4) while its search time is up to five times better than HiCuts optimized for speed. For synthetic core-router style databases of 20,000 rules size, HyperCuts requires only 11 memory accesses for search in the worst case; for edge-router style databases, HyperCuts requires 35 memory accesses for a database of 25,000 rules. In the case of firewall-like databases, the presence of $\sim$10 percent wildcards in either of the source and destination IP field contributes to a steep memory increase. This is possibly because of a large number of rules replicated in leaf nodes.

## 3.4  HEURISTIC ALGORITHMS

### 3.4.1  Recursive Flow Classification

Gupta and McKeown [3, 7] have proposed a heuristic scheme called Recursive Flow Classification (RFC) and have applied it to packet classification on multiple fields. Classifying a packet involves mapping the $H$-bit packet header to a $T$-bit action identifier (where $T = \log N$, $T \ll H$) for a $N$-rule classifier. A simple, but impractical, method is to precompute the action for each of the $2^H$ different packet headers and store the results in a $2^H \times 2^T$ array. Therefore, only one memory access is needed to yield the corresponding action. But this would require too much memory. The main aim of RFC is to perform the same mapping, but over several stages (phases), as shown in Figure 3.20. The mapping is performed recursively; at each stage, the algorithm performs a reduction, mapping one set of values to a smaller set. In each phase, a set of memories returns a value shorter, that is, expressed in fewer bits, than the index of the memory access. Figure 3.21 illustrates the structure and packet flow of the RFC scheme.

***Rule Storing Organization.*** The construction of the preprocessed tables is explained with a sample rule set $C$ [7] shown in Table 3.8. Note that the address information has been sanitized, which makes it different from what we used in reality.

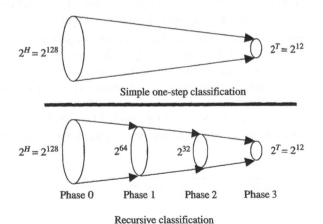

**Figure 3.20**  Basic idea of the recursive flow classification (RFC).

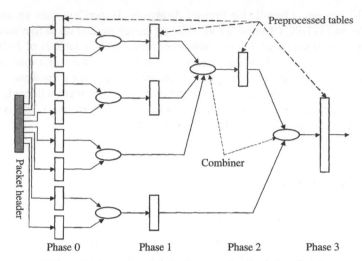

**Figure 3.21**   Packet flow in the recursive flow classification.

**TABLE 3.8   Rule Set Example**

| Destination IP (addr/mask) | Source IP (addr/mask) | Port Number | Protocol |
|---|---|---|---|
| 152.163.190.69/255.255.255.255 | 152.163.80.11/0.0.0.0 | * | * |
| 152.168.3.0/255.255.255.0 | 152.163.200.157/0.0.0.0 | eq www | UDP |
| 152.168.3.0/255.255.255.0 | 152.163.200.157/0.0.0.0 | range 20–21 | UDP |
| 152.168.3.0/255.255.255.0 | 152.163.200.157/0.0.0.0 | eq www | TCP |
| 152.163.198.4/255.255.255.255 | 152.163.160.0/255.255.252.0 | gt 1023 | TCP |
| 152.163.198.4/255.255.255.255 | 152.163.36.0/0.0.0.255 | gt 1023 | TCP |

1. The first step of constructing the preprocessed table is to split the $d$ fields of the packet header into multiple chunks that are used to index multiple memories in parallel. For example, the number of chunks equals eight in Figure 3.21. One possible way of chopping the packet header for rule set $C$ is shown in Figure 3.22.

2. Each of the parallel lookups will map the chunk to an *eqID* according to the rules. Consider a chunk of size $b$ bits. Its mapping table is of $2^b$ entries and each entry contains an *eqID* for that chunk value. The *eqID* is determined by those component(s) of the rules in the classifier corresponding to this chunk. The term 'Chunk Equivalence Set' (CES) is used to denote a set of chunk values that have the same *eqID*. To further understand the meaning of 'CES', consider chunk 3 for the classifier in Table 3.8. If there are two packets with protocol values lying in the same set and have otherwise

| | Source IP | Destination IP | Port | Protocol |
|---|---|---|---|---|
| Width (bits) | 32 | 32 | 16 | 8 |
| Chunks # | 0 | 1 | 2 | 3 |

**Figure 3.22**   Chopping of packet header into chunks for rule set $C$ in the first phase of RFC.

identical headers, the rules of the classifier do not distinguish between them. Then the 'CES' for chunk 3 will be:

(a) {TCP}

(b) {UDP}

(c) {all remaining numbers in the range 0–255}

Each CES can be constructed in the following manner. For a $b$-bit chunk, project the rules in the classifier on to the number line $[0, 2^b - 1]$. Each component projects to a set of (not necessarily contiguous) intervals on the number line. The end points of all the intervals projected by these components form a set of non-overlapping intervals. Two points in the same interval always belong to the same equivalence set. Two intervals are also in the same equivalence set if exactly the same rules project onto them. An example of chunk 2 of the classifier in Table 3.8 with the end-points of the intervals $(I_0 \ldots I_4)$ and the constructed equivalence sets $(E_0 \ldots E_3)$ are shown in Figure 3.23. The four CESs can be decoded using two bits. For example, we can assign '00' to $E_1$, '01' to $E_0$, '10' to $E_2$ and '11' to $E_3$. Then the RFC table for this chunk is filled with the corresponding $eqIDs$, such as $table(20) = $ '01', $table(23) = $ '11', etc.

3. A chunk in the following steps is formed by a combination of two (or more) chunks obtained from memory lookups in previous steps, with a corresponding CES. If, for example, the resulting chunk is of width $b$ bits, we again create equivalence sets such that two $b$-bit numbers that are not distinguished by the rules of the classifier belonging to the same CES. Thus, (20, UDP) and (21, UDP) will be in the same CES in the classifier of Table 3.8 in the second step. To determine the new equivalence sets for this phase, we compute all possible intersections of the equivalence sets from the previous steps being combined. Each distinct intersection is an equivalence set for the newly created chunk. For example, if we combine chunk 2 (port number) and 3 (protocol), then five CESs can be obtained:

(a) $\{(\{80\}, \{UDP\})\}$

(b) $\{(\{20 - 21\}, \{UDP\})\}$

(c) $\{(\{80\}, \{TCP\})\}$

(d) $\{(\{gt1023\}, \{TCP\})\}$

(e) {all the remaining crossproducts}.

These can be expressed in a three-bit $eqID$, as shown in Figure 3.24$e$. From this example, we can see that the number of bits has been reduced from four to three during step one (two bits for chunk 2 and 3, respectively) and step two. For the combination of the two steps, this number has dropped from 24 to 3.

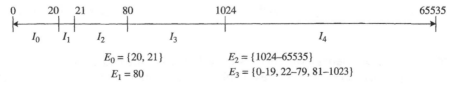

**Figure 3.23**    Example of computing the four equivalence classes $E_0 \ldots E_3$ for chunk 2 (corresponding to the 16-bit transport-layer destination port number) in the rule set of Table 3.8.

| Destination IP (addr/mask) | Chunk Number | eqID (only 2 bits required) |
|---|---|---|
| 152.163.190.69/255.255.255.255 | 0 | 00 |
| 152.168.3.0/255.255.255.0 | 1 | 01 |
| 152.163.198.4/255.255.255.255 | 2 | 10 |

(a)

| Source IP (addr/mask) | Chunk Number | eqID (only 2 bits required) |
|---|---|---|
| 152.163.80.11/0.0.0.0 | 0 | 00 |
| 152.163.200.157/0.0.0.0 | 1 | 01 |
| 152.163.160.0/255.255.252.0 | 2 | 10 |
| 152.163.36.0/0.0.0.255 | 3 | 11 |

(b)

| Port Number | Chunk Number | eqID (only 2 bits required) |
|---|---|---|
| Range 20-21 | 0 | 00 |
| eq www | 1 | 01 |
| gt 1023 | 2 | 10 |
| 0-19,22-79,81-1023 | 3 | 11 |

(c)

| Protocol | Chunk Number | eqID (only 2 bits required) |
|---|---|---|
| tcp | 0 | 00 |
| udp | 1 | 01 |
| all remaining protocols | 2 | 10 |

(d)

| Port Number and Protocol | Chunk Number | eqID (only 3 bits required) |
|---|---|---|
| eq www & udp | 0 | 000 |
| Range 20-21 & udp | 1 | 001 |
| eq www & tcp | 2 | 010 |
| gt 1023 & tcp | 3 | 011 |
| all remaining crossproducts | 4 | 100 |

(e)

**Figure 3.24** Rule storing organization for RFC for the rule set in Table 3.8. (a) Destination IP field made into chunks and epIDs. (b) Source IP field made into chunks and eqIDs. (c) Port number field made into chunks and eqIDs. (d) Protocol field made into chunks and eqIDs. (e) Port number and protocol fields combined and made into chunks and eqIDs.

**Classification Scheme.** The classification of a packet is first split into several chunks to be used as an index; then the required *eqIDs* are combined into chunks of the second phase; this procedure goes on until the final phase is reached when all the remaining *eqIDs* have been combined into only one chunk. The corresponding table will hold the actions for that packet.

**Performance Comments.** The contents of each memory are chosen so that the result of the lookup is narrower than the index. Different combinations of the chunks can yield different storage requirements. It is reported [7] that with real-life 4D classifiers of up to 1700 rules, RFC appears practical for 10 Gbps line rates in hardware and 2.5 Gbps rates in software. However, the storage space and preprocessing time grow rapidly for classifiers larger than 6000 rules. An optimization described in Ref. [7] reduces the storage requirement of a 15,000 four-field classifier to below 4 Mbytes.

### 3.4.2 Tuple Space Search

Srinivansan et al. [13] have proposed a tuple space search scheme for multi-dimensional packet classification with prefix specification. The basic tuple space search algorithm decomposes a classification query into several exact match queries in hash tables. This algorithm is motivated by the observation that while classifiers contain many different prefixes, the number of distinct prefix lengths tends to be small. Thus, the number of distinct combinations of prefix lengths is also small. Then a tuple for each combination of field length can be defined and by concatenating the known set of bits for each field in order, a hash key can be created to map the rules of that tuple into a hash table. Suppose a classifier $C$ with $N$ rules that results in $M$ distinct tuples. Since $M$ tends to be much smaller than $N$ in practice, even a linear search through the tuple set is likely to greatly outperform the linear search through the classifier.

***Rule Storing Organization.*** Each rule $R$ in a classifier can be mapped into a $d$-tuple whose $i$th component specifies the length of the prefix in the $i$th field of $R$. A tuple space is defined as the set of all such tuples of a classifier. For each tuple in the tuple space, a hash table is created storing all rules mapped in the tuple. As an example, Table 3.9 shows the tuples and associated hash tables for the classifier in Table 3.2. For instance, (1, 2) means the length of the first prefix is one and the length of the second prefix is two.

Rules always specify IP addresses using prefixes, so the number of bits specified is clear. For port numbers that are often specified using ranges, the length of a port range is defined to be its nesting level. For instance, the full port number range [0, 65,535] has nesting level and length 0. The ranges [0, 1023] and [1024, 65,535] are considered to be nesting level 1, and so on. If we had additional ranges [30,000, 34,000] and [31,000, 32,000], then the former will have nesting level 2 and the latter 3 (this algorithm assumes that port number ranges specified in a database are non-overlapping).

While the nesting level of a range helps define the tuple it will be placed in, a key to identify the rule within the tuple is also needed. Thus a RangeID is used, which is a unique ID given to each range in any particular nesting level. So the full range always has the ID 0. The two ranges at depth 1, namely, $\leq 1023$ and $>1024$, receive the IDs 0 and 1, respectively. Suppose we had ranges $200 \ldots 333$, $32,000 \ldots 34,230$, and $60,000 \ldots 65,500$ at level 2, then they would be given IDs 0, 1 and 2, respectively.

**TABLE 3.9    Example of the Tuple Space Search Scheme**

| Tuple | Hash Table Entries |
|---|---|
| (0, 2) | $\{R_7\}$ |
| (1, 1) | $\{R_6\}$ |
| (1, 2) | $\{R_4, R_5\}$ |
| (2, 1) | $\{R_2, R_3\}$ |
| (2, 2) | $\{R_1\}$ |

Notice that a given port in a packet header can be mapped to a different ID at each nesting level. For example, with the above ranges, a port number 33,000 will map on to three RangeID values, one for each nesting depth: ID 0 for nesting depth 0, ID 1 for nesting depth 1, and ID 1 for nesting depth 2. Thus, a port number field in the packet header must be translated to its corresponding RangeID values before the tuple search is performed. In summary, the nesting level is used to determine the tuple, and the RangeID for each nesting level is used to form the hash key, the input to the hash function.

***Classification Scheme.*** All rules that map to a particular tuple have the same mask: some number of bits in the IP source and destination fields, either a wild card in the protocol field or a specific protocol ID, and port number fields that contain either a wild card or a RangeID. Thus, we can concatenate the required number of bits from each field to construct a hash key for that rule. All rules mapped to a tuple $U$ are stored in a hash table Hashtable($U$). For instance, rules $R_4$ and $R_5$ are stored in the same hash table, say Hashtable2. A probe in a tuple $U$ involves concatenating the required number of bits from the packet as specified by $U$ (after converting port numbers to RangeID), and then doing a hash in Hashtable($U$). The key will be hashed in each table to find the matched rule. For instance, the key is hashed and matched with $R_4$ in Hashtable2. Thus, given a packet $P$, we can linearly probe all the tuples in the tuple set, and determine the highest priority filter matching $P$.

***Performance Comments.*** The query time complexity of the basic tuple space search scheme is $O(M)$, where $M$ is the number of tuples in the tuple space. Perfect hashing is assumed here, which is chosen to avoid hash collisions.

$M$ is still large for many real cases. Thus, a simple but efficient optimization called tuple pruning is proposed in [13] to improve the query speed and update performance. When a packet header presents to be classified, longest prefix matching is first performed in each dimension. The best matching prefix $P_i$ in each dimension $i$ returns a tuple list $tl_i$ that is precomputed and associated with the prefix. Each tuple in the tuple list from $P_i$ contains at least one rule whose $i$th field equals $P_i$ or is a prefix of $P_i$. Another tuple list, the intersection list, is derived from the intersection of all $tl_i$. For a given query, only the tuples contained in the intersection list need to be searched. It will benefit if the reduction in the tuple space afforded by pruning offsets the extra individual prefix (or range) matches on each field. Reference [13] reports that by having the tuple pruning only in two fields, for example, the source and destination IP address, the number of tuples that needs to be searched is greatly reduced.

The storage complexity for tuple space search is $O(NdW)$ since each rule is stored in exactly one hash table. Incremental updates are supported and require just one hash memory access to the hash table associated with the tuple of the modified rule. However, the use of hashing may have hash collision and cause the search/update nondeterministic.

## 3.5 TCAM-BASED ALGORITHMS

### 3.5.1 Range Matching in TCAM-Based Packet Classification

Ternary content addressable memory (TCAM)-based algorithms are gaining increasing popularity for fast packet classification. In general, a TCAM coprocessor works as a look-aside processor for packet classification on behalf of a network processing unit (NPU) or

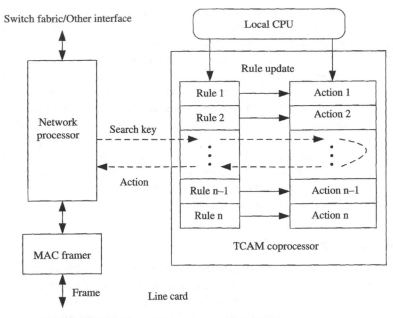

**Figure 3.25** Network processor and its TCAM coprocessor.

network processor. When a packet is to be classified, an NPU generates a search key based on the information extracted from the packet header and passes it to the TCAM coprocessor for classification. A TCAM coprocessor finds a matched rule in $O(1)$ clock cycles and, therefore, offers the highest possible lookup/matching performance. Figure 3.25 is a logic diagram showing how an NPU works with its TCAM coprocessor. When a packet arrives, the NPU generates a search key based on the packet header information and passes it to the TCAM coprocessor to be classified, via a NPU/TCAM coprocessor interface. A local CPU is in charge of rule table update through a separate CPU-TCAM coprocessor interface.

However, despite its fast lookup performance, one of the most critical resource management issues in the use of TCAM for packet classification/filtering is how to effectively support filtering rules with ranges, known as range matching. The difficulty lies in the fact that multiple TCAM entries have to be allocated to represent a rule with ranges. A range is said to be exactly implemented in a TCAM if it is expressed in a TCAM without being encoded. For example, six rule entries are needed to express a range {>1023} in a TCAM, if the range is exactly implemented, as shown in Figure 3.26.

Today's real-world policy/firewall filtering (PF) tables were reported [7, 14–16] to involve significant amounts of rules with ranges. In particular, the statistical analysis of real-world rule databases in [17] shows that TCAM storage efficiency can be as low as

**Figure 3.26** Range >1023 is expressed in terms of 6 sub-ranges in a TCAM.

16 percent due to the existence of a significant number of rules with port ranges. Apparently, the reduced TCAM memory efficiency due to range matching makes TCAM power consumption, footprint, and cost an even more serious concern.

A widely adopted solution to deal with range matching is to perform range preprocessing/encoding by mapping ranges to a short sequence of encoded bits, known as bit-mapping. The idea is to view a $d$-tuple rule as a region in a $d$-dimensional rule space and encode any distinct overlapped regions among all the rules so that each rule can be translated into a sequence of encoded bits, known as rule encoding. Accordingly, a search key, which is based on the information extracted from the packet header, is preprocessed to generate an encoded search key, called search key encoding. Then, the encoded search key is matched against all the encoded rules to find the best matched rule. Unlike rule encoding, which can be pre-processed in software, search key encoding is performed on a per packet basis and must be done in hardware at wire-speed.

### 3.5.2 Range Mapping in TCAMs

As stated above, when the range specification is used for the field without range encoding, range splitting must be performed to convert the ranges into prefix formats to fit the bit boundary. This increases the number of entries and could make TCAMs infeasible for some classifiers that use the range specification. Liu [18] has suggested an efficient encoding scheme of range classifier into TCAM. The basic algorithm expands TCAM horizontally (using more bits per entry), and for a width limited application, an algorithm that allows both horizontal and vertical expansion is proposed.

*Rule Storing Organization.* For each range field, an $n$ bits vector $B = b_1, b_2, \ldots, b_n$ is used to represent it, where $n$ is the number of distinct ranges specified for this field. The $B$ vector for a range $E_i$ has 1 at bit position $i$, that is, $b_i = 1$ and all other bits are set to don't care. This is based on the observation that even though the number of rules in a classifier could be large, the number of distinct ranges specified for any range field is very limited and exact match specification also happens frequently for a range field. The bit vector representation for Table 3.10 is shown in Table 3.11 ($n = 5$ in this case). For example, the range of greater than 1023 in R1 is represented by 'xxxx1'.

*Classification Scheme.* A lookup key $v \in [0, 2k]$ is translated into an $n$ bit vector $V = v_1, v_2, \ldots, v_n$. Bit $v_i$ is set to 1 if the key $v$ falls into the corresponding range $E_i$, otherwise it will be set to 0. Lookup key translation could be implemented as a direct memory lookup since most of the range fields are less than 16-bit wide. A complete lookup key translation

TABLE 3.10   Simple Example Classifier for TCAM
Implementation

| $R_i$ | Dest IP Addr (IP/mask) | Dest Port Range | Action |
|---|---|---|---|
| 1 | 10.0.0.0/255.0.0.0 | >1023 | $Act_0$ |
| 2 | 192.168.0.0/255.255.0.0 | 50–2000 | $Act_1$ |
| 3 | 192.169.0.0/255.255.0.0 | 80(http) | $Act_2$ |
| 4 | 172.16.0.0/255.255.0.0 | 23(telnet) | $Act_3$ |
| 5 | 172.16.0.0/255.255.0.0 | 21(ftp) | $Act_4$ |

**TABLE 3.11    Rules Stored in TCAM**

| $R_i$ | TCAM Rules | |
|---|---|---|
| 1 | 10.x.x.x | xxxx1 |
| 2 | 192.168.x.x | xxx1x |
| 3 | 192.169.x.x | xx1xx |
| 4 | 172.16.x.x | x1xxx |
| 5 | 172.16.x.x | 1xxxx |

table for the example classifier for each possible lookup key value is shown in Figure 3.27. For example, the right most bit vector is set to 1 for all the locations above 1023. Furthermore, the second bit from the right between the locations 50 and 20 (including them) is also set to 1. Next paragraph, some optimization can be further made for exact match. It is possible to reduce the number of bits used to $\log_2(m+1)$, where $m$ is the number of exact matches.

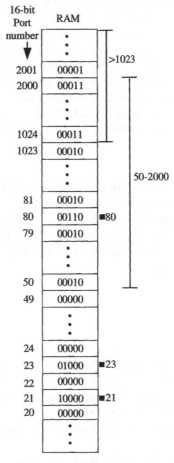

**Figure 3.27**    Lookup key translation table for the example classifier.

**TABLE 3.12   Rules Stored in TCAM with Exact Match Optimization**

| $R_i$ | TCAM Rules | |
|---|---|---|
| 1 | 10.x.x.x | xxxx1 |
| 2 | 192.168.x.x | xxx1x |
| 3 | 192.169.x.x | x01xx |
| 4 | 172.16.x.x | x10xx |
| 5 | 172.16.x.x | x11xx |

The bit representation will contain two parts $\langle B_e, B \rangle$, $B_e$ for exact matches, and $B$ for all others. $B_e = b_1, b_2, \ldots, b_t$ is a $t$ bit vector, where $t \geq \log_2(m + 1)$.

For a normal range, $\langle B_e = 0, B \rangle$ and its $B$ portion is the same as before. For an exact match, $\langle B_e = i, B = 0 \rangle$, if it is the $i$th exact match. In the previous example, if we use bit 2 and 3 as $B_e$ (where bit 1 is the left-most significant bit), the example classifier stored in TCAM is shown in Table 3.12 and now only two bits are needed to represent the three distinct exact matches. The lookup key translation table needs to be changed accordingly. The lookup key also contains two parts $\langle V_e; V \rangle$, $V_e$ corresponding to all exact matches and $V$ to the rest. $V_e = \langle v_1, v_2, \ldots, v_t \rangle$ is a $t$ bit vector (e.g., $b_2$ and $b_3$ of the right column of Table 3.12), and $V_e = i$ if the lookup key $v$ equals to the $i$th exact match, otherwise $V_e = 0$. Assume that the classifier is stored in TCAM as shown in Table 3.12. A new packet arrives with destination IP address 192.169.10.1 and port number 80. First, the port number is indexed into the lookup key translation table (Figure 3.27). The resulting $V = 10$ because 80 falls in range 50–2000 but not range $> 1023$. The resulting $V_e = 01$ because 01 is the value assigned to exactly match the value of 80. Together with destination IP address, the final result is rule 3.

**Performance Comments.** This scheme requires less TCAM storage space. Thus it can accommodate a much larger number of rules in a single TCAM table and reduce system cost and power consumption. Meanwhile, it also keeps the advantage of deterministic execution time of TCAM devices. However, adding/deleting rules causes the change of bit vectors and may require re-computation of the entire translation table, which is a time consuming process.

## REFERENCES

[1] S. Lyer, R. R. Kompella, and A. Shelat, "ClassiPI: an architecture for fast and flexible packet classification," *IEEE Network*, vol. 15, no. 2, pp. 33–41 (Mar. 2001).

[2] P. Gupta, "Routing lookups and packet classifications: theory and practice," in *Proc. HOT Interconnects*, Stanford, California (Aug. 2000).

[3] P. Gupta and N. Mckeown, "Algorithms for packet classification," *IEEE Network*, vol. 15, no. 2, pp. 24–32 (Mar. 2001).

[4] V. Srinivasan, G. Varghese, S. Suri, and M. Waldvagel, "Fast and scalable layer four switching," in *Proc. ACM SIGCOMM*, Vancouver, Canada, pp. 191–202 (Aug. 1998).

[5] F. Baboescu, S. Singh, and G. Varghese, "Packet classification for core routers: Is there an alternative to CAMs?" in *Proc. IEEE INFOCOM'03*, San Francisco, California, vol. 1, pp. 53–63 (2003).

[6] G. Zhang and H. J. Chao, "Fast packet classification using field-level trie," in *Proc. IEEE GLOBECOM'03*, San Francisco, California, vol. 6, pp. 3201–3205 (Dec. 2003).

[7] P. Gupta and N. Mckeown, "Packet classification on multiple fields," in *Proc. ACM SIGCOMM'99*, Harvard University, vol. 29, no. 4, pp. 147–160 (Aug. 1999).

[8] T. V. Lakshman and D. Stiliadis, "High-speed policy-based packet forwarding using efficient multi-dimensional range matching," in *Proc. ACM SIGCOMM*, Vancouver, Canada, pp. 203–214 (Sep. 1998).

[9] J. van Lunteren and T. Engbersen, "Fast and scalable packet classification," *IEEE Journal on Selected Areas in Communications*, vol. 21, pp. 560–571 (May 2003).

[10] M. M. Buddhikot, S. Suri, and M. Waldvogel, "Space decomposition techniques for fast layer-4 switching," in *Conf. Protocols for High Speed Networks*, Holmdel, New Jersey, vol. 66, no. 6, pp. 277–283 (Aug. 1999).

[11] P. Gupta and N. McKeown, "Classification using hierarchical intelligent cuttings," in *Proc. HOT Interconnects VII*, Stanford, California (Aug. 1999).

[12] S. Singh, F. Baboescu, G. Varghese, and J. Wang, "Packet classification using multidimensional cutting," in *Proc. ACM SIGCOMM*, Karlsruhe, Germany, pp. 213–224 (Aug. 2003).

[13] V. Srinivasan, S. Suri, and G. Varghese, "Packet classification using tuple space search," in *Proc. ACM SIGCOMM*, Cambridge, Massachusetts, pp. 135–146 (Aug. 1999).

[14] F. Baboesu and G. Varghese, "Scalable packet classification," in *Proc. ACM SIGCOMM*, San Diego, California, pp. 199–210 (Aug. 2001).

[15] M. E. Kounavis, A. Kumar, H. Vin, R. Yavatkar, and A. T. Campbell, "Directions in packet classification for network processors," in *Proc. Second Workshop on Network Processors (NP2)*, Anahein, California (Feb. 2003).

[16] E. Spitznagel, D. Taylor, and J. Turner, "Packet classification using extended TCAMs," in *Proc. International Conference of Network Protocol (ICNP)*, Atlanta, Georgia, pp. 120–131 (Nov. 2003).

[17] H. Che, Z. Wang, K. Zheng, and B. Liu, "Dynamic range encoding scheme for TCAM coprocessors," Technical report. [Online]. Available at: http://crystal.uta.edu/hche/dres.pdf.

[18] H. Liu, "Efficient Mapping of range classifier into Ternary-CAM," in *Proc. 10th Hot Interconnects*, Stanford, California, pp. 95–100 (Aug. 2002).

# CHAPTER 4

# TRAFFIC MANAGEMENT

## 4.1 QUALITY OF SERVICE

The main task of internetworking is to deliver data from one peer to the other providing a certain minimal level of quality or the quality of service (QoS). QoS can normally be expressed by parameters such as achieved bandwidth, packet delay, and packet loss rates [1]. Achieving QoS guarantee becomes very difficult with the increasing number of users connected to a network, the increasing bandwidth required for applications, the increasing types of QoS requirements, and the increasing usage of multicast. The task becomes even more difficult in a connectionless IP network (the Internet). Congestion control provided by the flow control at the transport layer and to some extent by dynamic routing protocols [such as open shortest path forwarding (OSPF)] is inadequate to provide QoS. Different types of applications have different requirements of how their data should be sent. Some applications require error-free and loss-free transmission without any delay requirements. Some others require timely delivery but can sustain some data loss. Network resources will need to be managed appropriately to deal with these types of traffic.

Traditionally, the Internet has offered a single QoS, best-effort delivery, with available bandwidth and delay characteristics dependent on instantaneous load. Control over the QoS seen by applications is exercised by adequate provisioning of the network infrastructure. In contrast, a network with dynamically controllable QoS allows individual application session to request network packet delivery characteristics according to its perceived needs, and may provide different qualities of service to different applications [1].

The network has been evolving to provide QoS guarantees to the users. For instance, asynchronous transfer mode (ATM) can reserve the bandwidth and buffer size for each virtual connection. Similarly, Internet Integrated Service (IntServ) can also provide QoS for each flow in the IP network, while Internet Differentiated Service (DiffServ) provides

*High Performance Switches and Routers*, by H. Jonathan Chao and Bin Liu
Copyright © 2007 John Wiley & Sons, Inc.

different treatment for packets to different classes, instead of on flow basis, so that it has better scalability than IntServ.

To maximize network resource utilization while satisfying the individual user's QoS requirements, traffic management should be provided with prioritized access to resources at network nodes. In this chapter, three fundamental traffic management techniques, traffic policing/shaping, packet scheduling and buffer management, are presented in detail.

Traffic policing/shaping is normally performed at the network edge to monitor traffic flows and take appropriate actions when they are not compliant to traffic contract. They are either discarded, marked, and delayed. The control can become challenging when the number of flows is large or the line speed is high. Especially, when traffic shaping is performed by delaying arriving packets in a buffer, choosing a packet that is compliant from hundreds or thousands of packets in the buffer is very difficult.

Packet scheduling specifies the queue service discipline at a node, which determines the transmission order of the queued packets. Since packets of many users may leave for the same output interface, packet scheduling also enforces a set of rules in sharing the link bandwidth. One major concern is how to ensure that the link bandwidth is fairly shared among the connections and to protect the individual user's share from being corrupted by malicious users.

Beside packet scheduling algorithms, buffer management is also very critical to the performance of the network. Buffer management mechanisms are needed in the high speed communication devices such as multiplexers, packet switches, and routers to set up the buffer sharing policy and decide which packet should be discarded when the buffer overflows or is getting filled.

### 4.1.1   QoS Parameters

QoS parameters represent the QoS to customers. It should be easy for customers to understand the degree of assuring the service. QoS parameters can be different according to the type of services and layers. Generic QoS parameters required in network service include throughput, packet delay, bandwidth, residual error rate, and so on. The definitions of these parameters are as follows [2, 3].

*Throughput.* Throughput is a connection-mode QoS parameter that has end-to-end significance. It is defined as the total number of bits successfully transferred by a primitive sequence divided by the input/output time, in seconds, for that sequence. Successful transfer of a packet is defined to occur when the packet is delivered to the intended user without error, in proper sequence, and before connection termination by the receiving user.

*Packet Delay.* Packet delay is the time taken for a packet to travel from a service access point (SAP) to a distant target. It usually includes the transport time and queuing delay. The packet delay distribution occurring in a router can be like the one as shown in Figure 4.1. The maximum packet delay for a flow is the $(1 - a)$ quantile of packet delay.

*Bandwidth.* Bandwidth means used capacity or available capacity. Service providers usually assure the maximum bandwidth to customers and it is stated clearly in the Service Level Agreement (SLA, see Section 4.3 for detail).

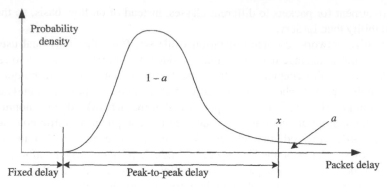

**Figure 4.1**   Packet delay in a router.

**Residual Error Rate.**   Residual error rate (RER) is the ratio of total incorrect, lost and duplicated packets to the total packets transferred between users during a period of time.

**Delay Variation.**   Delay variation may cause the increasing of TCP retransmit timer and unnecessary packet loss. So delay variation parameter is very important, which can be measured by the dispersion of maximum delay and minimum delay during a short measurement interval.

**Loss Rate.**   Loss rate is the ratio of lost packets to the total packets in transit from source to destination during a specific time interval, expressed in percentages.

**Spurious IP Packet Rate.**   Spurious IP packet rate is defined as the rate of the fraction of the spurious IP packets during a specific time interval (number of spurious IP packets per second).

**Availability.**   Availability is the percentage of the feasibility of service in every particular service request, which means connectivity and functionality in the network management layer. Connectivity is the physical connectivity of network elements and functionality means whether the associated network devices work well or not. Traffic service time can be divided into available time and unavailable time. If packet lose rate is under a defined threshold, it is recognized to be available, otherwise unavailable.

### 4.1.2   Traffic Parameters

The following traffic parameters are commonly used to categorize a flow [4].

**Peak Rate.**   The peak rate is the highest rate at which a source can generate traffic. The peak rate is limited by the transmission link rate. The peak rate can be calculated from the packet size and the spacing between consecutive packets.

**Average Rate.**   The average rate is the rate averaged over a time interval. The average rate can be calculated in several ways, and the results can be quite different. It is important to know the exact method and the time interval used in the calculation. Typically the average rate is calculated with a moving time window so that the averaging time interval can start from any point in time.

**Burst Size.** The burst size is defined as the maximum amount of data that can be injected into the network at the peak rate. The burst size reflects the burstiness of the traffic source. To avoid packet losses, the first hop router may have to allocate a buffer for the source larger than its burst size.

## 4.2  INTEGRATED SERVICES

Integrated Services (IntServ) is an end-to-end, flow-based mechanism for providing QoS. Routers need to keep track of every flow. IntServ reserves resources along the path of transmission, via resource Reservation Protocol (RSVP). In other words, IntServ sets up a virtual circuit. During the reservation process, a request goes through admission control, which will either grant or deny the request. This is done based on the resources available on that router, and it is necessary to preserve the QoS requirements for other flows currently active in the router.

### 4.2.1  Integrated Service Classes

In addition to best-effort delivery, IntServ has two additional service classes, and they are:

**Guaranteed Service.** This service class is used for intolerant playback applications without any distortion like H.323 video conferencing. This class offers perfectly reliable upper bound on delay.

**Controlled-Load Service.** Also known as predictive service, this service class is more relaxed on the delay bound. It is fairly reliable, but not perfectly reliable in providing the delay bound. It works well when network is lightly loaded. However, if the network is overloaded, some packet loss or delay can be experienced. This is the middle ground between guaranteed and best effort. It is used for tolerant applications like MPEG-II video. This service class is more efficient in utilizing the network resources because it allows other flows to share its resources when it is not in use. For example, an application can ask for 5 Mbps, but the bit rate can vary between 2 and 5 Mbps. Instead of wasting the extra 3 Mbps, this service class allows other flows to use the extra 3 Mbps.

### 4.2.2  IntServ Architecture

To understand the IntServ model, a reference implementation framework has been specified in RFC 1633. Figure 4.2 shows the key components in the reference model. The model can be logically divided into two planes: the control plane and the data plane. The control plane sets up resource reservation; the data plane forwards data packets based on the reservation state.
    Key elements in the reference model are briefly explained below.

**RSVP.** Connections are established using a reservation setup agent known as RSVP, which makes end-to-end reservations over a connectionless network. RSVP is responsible for changing the traffic control database (used to store classifier and scheduling policies) to

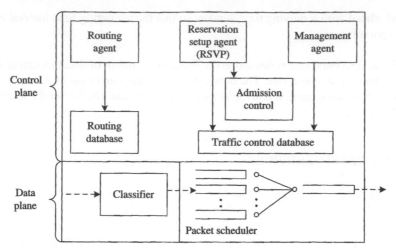

**Figure 4.2**    IntServ reference model for routers.

accommodate the required QoS. The management agent is used to set up the policies for the classifier and scheduler. More details on RSVP are described in Section 4.2.3.

***Classifier.***  Packets need to be mapped into some class for the process of traffic control. Packets from the same class will get the same treatment from the scheduler. A class can be based on network headers, transport headers, application headers, or any combination of them. For instance, an IP flow is normally identified by the five-tuple in the packet header: source IP address, destination IP address, protocol ID, source port, and destination port, as we discussed in Chapter 3.

***Admission Control.***  Admission control is responsible for permitting or denying flows into the router. Admission control is used to decide whether a new flow can be granted the requested QoS without effecting current guarantees. If the router decides that it does not have the required resources to meet the requested QoS, the flow gets a denied admission. Admission control has two basic functions. The first function is to determine if a new reservation can be set up based on the admission control policies. The second one is to monitor and measure available resources. Parameter based approach and measurement based approach are two basic methods to admission control. In the parameter based approach, a set of parameters is used to precisely characterize traffic flows; the admission control agent then calculates the required resources based on these parameters. Instead of relying on a prior traffic characterization, the measurement based approach measures the actual traffic load and uses that for admission control.

***Packet Scheduler.***  The packet scheduler reorders packet transmission so that certain flows can be served based on their service class and levels. For example, packets that require guaranteed service will be served first before those that require controlled-load service or best-effort service. The packet scheduler is responsible for enforcing resource allocation, which directly affects the delay. The key task of a packet scheduler is to select a packet to transit when the outgoing link is ready. We present several packet scheduling schemes in Section 4.5.

### 4.2.3 Resource ReSerVation Protocol (RSVP)

A quick summary about RSVP is given below:

- RSVP is a signaling protocol for establishing a guaranteed QoS path between a sender and (a) receiver(s).
- RSVP establishes end-to-end reservations over a connectionless network.
- RSVP is robust when links fail: Traffic is re-routed and new reservations are established.
- RSVP is receiver-initiated and so is designed with multicast in mind.
- RSVP is simplex (reserves for unidirectional data flow) and receiver-oriented.
- Operates in 'soft state', responds to changes in routing, multicast membership.
- Provides transparent operation through routers that do not support RSVP.
- RSVP is independent of the IP protocol versions – RSVP applies equally well to IPv4 and IPv6.

***RSVP operations.*** Figure 4.3 illustrates how RSVP sets up resource reservation between senders (sources) and receivers (destinations). There are two types of messages in RSVP: PATH messages and RESV messages. PATH messages are sent from traffic sources, while RESV messages are sent between RSVP-aware routers hop by hop after receiving the PATH messages. A PATH messages is addressed to the flow's ultimate destination but it actively interacts with all of the RSVP-aware routers as it travels downstream along the path to its destination, setting up control blocks as it goes. After receiving the PATH message, all of the routers in the path will have the information they need to recognize the flow when it appears at one of their ports. The PATH message also carries the traffic characteristics of the flow which is called 'Tspec', so the routers will know how much the flow is asking for to prevent over-reservation and perhaps unnecessary admission control failures. In addition, the PATH messages can contain a package of OPWA (One Pass With Advertising) advertising information, known as an 'Adspec'. The Adspec received in the PATH message is passed to the local traffic control, which returns an updated Adspec; the

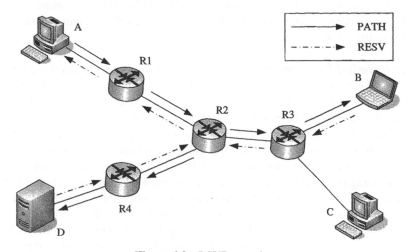

**Figure 4.3** RSVP operations.

updated version is then forwarded in the PATH message sent downstream. When the PATH message finally reaches its destination, the destination can then, if it wants, ask to make a QoS reservation for the flow.

The reservation is made by the RESV message, which follows the path of the PATH message backward, upstream to the data source. However, it is well known that IP networks are asymmetrically routed. That is, the transmission path from user A to user B is often totally different from the one which is from user B to user A. When the PATH message travels from the flow source to the destination, it takes care to place a special PHOP (previous hop) address in each control block that it sets up. Therefore, the RESV message will be able to follow the path message's path backward by looking at the PHOP address stored in all the control blocks. Then it will continue upstream, marking changes in all the routers' control blocks as needed to install the designated QoS reservation, until it finally arrives at the flow source. At that time, the flow source will know if it was able to make the reservation successfully to the flow's destination.

The process of RSVP can be concluded as follows. First, traffic sources send PATH messages towards receivers which contain the information of the sender (bandwidth, delay and jitter it needs) and the path characteristics to the receivers. Second, the routers forward the PATH messages. The forwarding process is determined by the unicast and multicast routing protocols. Third, routers determine if reservation can be fulfilled and forward/merge RESV messages upstream toward the source along the exact reverse path of the PATH message. Fourth, after receiving the RESV messages, the sender can start to transmit packets along the reserved path. When transmission is finished, routers tear down the resource reservation.

**Unicast and Multicast.** For unicast reservation, two applications agree on a specific QoS required to support its service and expect the network to support this QoS. If the network is experiencing congestion, or is on the verge of experiencing it, it may not provide the requested QoS. In that case, the communicating applications will be notified and may choose not to start a session, and instead wait for the network traffic to decrease. They may also choose to start the session, but at a lower QoS.

Multicast transmission is the driving point of RSVP implementation. A multicast transmission can generate an enormous amount of network traffic due to its nature: it could be either a high volume data application (such a video broadcast), or having many scattered subscribers to the same service.

**Receiver-Initiated Reservation.** The approach to resource reservation used in Frame Relay and ATM consists of the source of the data flow requesting a specific set of resources, which works well for unicast traffic. However, this approach does not work well in a multicast environment. And the main reason is that different destinations in a multicast group may have different resource requirements, which is quite common in the current Internet. If a source transmission flow can be divided into component subflows, then some destination members may want to require only one subflow. For example, some receivers may not have enough processing power to handle a high definition video multicast, and choose to receive only low-definition video. In a word, the QoS requirements of different receivers may differ, depending on their hardware capabilities, processing powers, and link speeds.

This is the big plus of RSVP: The receivers specify the QoS of the transmission. Routers can then aggregate multicast resource reservations to take advantage of shared paths along the distribution tree.

***Soft State.*** RSVP makes use of the concept of a soft state. A connection-oriented scheme takes a hard-state approach, in which the nature of the connection along a fixed route is defined by the state information in each of the switching nodes. The soft state approach is characterized by the fact that the each switching node along the path has cached information that is refreshed after a specified time limit. If the state is not refreshed after this time limit, the router considers the state invalid and discards it. It will then propagate its new status to the next hop. The soft state approach is used because membership of a large multicast group and the resulting multicast tree topology are likely to change with time. The RSVP design assumes that state for RSVP and traffic control is to be built and destroyed incrementally in routers and hosts. Of course, the state can also be deleted by a teardown message.

## 4.3 DIFFERENTIATED SERVICES

IntServ and RSVP provide a structure for very detailed control of the QoS of the individual flow as it passes through a network of IP routers. Unfortunately, the scalability of IntServ solution, which is mainly caused by its complex per-flow classification and scheduling, is still in doubt. IntServ requires routers to store and process each individual flow that goes through it, and it becomes overwhelming in the Internet. The Differentiated Services (DS or DiffServ) architecture was then developed in response to the need for relatively simple, coarse methods of providing different levels of service for Internet traffic. The advantage of DS is that many traffic streams can be aggregated into one of a small number of behavior aggregates, forwarded using the same PHBs (per hop behavior) at the router, thereby simplifying the processing and associated storage. PHB is a description of the externally observable forwarding behavior of a DS node applied to a particular DS behavior aggregate. In addition, there is no signaling, other than what is carried out in the DSCP (DS Codepoint) of each packet. No other related processing is required in the core of the DS network, since QoS is invoked on a packet-by-packet basis. Before explaining the details, a quick summary of DS is given below:

- Demands from customers for service differentiation.
- Emerging of new multimedia applications for which the best-effort service in today's Internet cannot support.
- Define the meaning of the DS field, that is, Type of Service (TOS) field in IPv4 or Traffic Class field in IPv6, in the IP packet header for each class of services.
- Mark the DS field of packets based on their service classes and process them differently.
- Offering services for traffic on a per-class basis rather than on a per-flow basis at the internal nodes.
- Forcing as much complexity out of internal nodes of a network to boundary nodes, which process lower volumes of traffic and smaller number of flows.
- Pushing per-flow processing and state management to the boundary nodes.

The DiffServ is different from IntServ in many aspects, and the key difference is that DiffServ distinguishes a small number of forwarding classes rather than individual flows. IntServ uses a signaling protocol (RSVP, discussed in Section 4.2.3) to reserve resources for individual flows, while DiffServ allocates resources on a per-class basis which is based on the ToS octet in IPv4 header or the Traffic Class octet in IPv6 header. Each router along the path examines this octet and makes a QoS decision based on the policies set up on that router. As a result, all the information that the router needs to handle the packet is contained in the packet header; so routers do not need to learn and store information about individual flows. There is no need for soft-state refresh messages. There is no worry about the packets that temporarily don't get their proper QoS handling after they have been rerouted. There is no scalability problem associated with need for the router to handle per-flow packet.

Each router is independent from one another. Therefore to provide consistency in QoS, routers should be configured with similar policies.

### 4.3.1   Service Level Agreement

A Service Level Agreement (SLA) is a service contract between a customer and a service provider that specifies the forwarding service a customer should receive. A customer may be a user organization (source domain) or another DS domain (upstream domain). Here, a DS domain is a contiguous set of nodes which operates with a common set of service provisioning policies and PHB definitions.

A SLA can be dynamic or static. Static SLAs are negotiated on a regular basis, for example, monthly or yearly. Dynamic SLAs use a signaling protocol to negotiate the service on demand.

The SLA typically contains:

- The type and nature of service to be provided, which includes the description of the service to be provided, such as facilities management, network services, and help desk support.
- The expected performance level of the service, which includes two major aspects: reliability and responsiveness. Reliability includes availability requirements – when is the service available, and what are the bounds on service outages that may be expected. Responsiveness includes how soon the service is performed in the normal course of operations.
- The process for reporting problems with the service, which forms a big part of a typical SLA. It includes information about the person to be contacted for problem resolution, the format in which complaints have to be filed, and the steps to be undertaken to resolve the problem quickly, and so on.
- The time frame for response and problem resolution, which specifies a time limit by which someone would start investigating a problem that was reported, and so on.
- The process for monitoring and reporting the service level, which outlines how performance levels are monitored and reported – that is, who will do the monitoring, what types of statistics will be collected, how often they will be collected, and how past or current statistics may be accessed.
- The credits, charges, or other consequences for the service provider when not meeting its obligation (i.e., failing to provide the agreed-upon service level).
- Escape clauses and constraints, including the consequences if the customer does not meet his or her obligation, which qualifies access to the service level. Escape clauses are conditions under which the service level does not apply, or under which it is considered unreasonable to meet the requisite SLAs. For example, when the service provider's equipment has been damaged in flood, fire, or war. They often also impose some constraints on the behavior by the customer. A network operator may void the SLA if the customer is attempting to breach the security of the network.

### 4.3.2 Traffic Conditioning Agreement

An SLA also defines Traffic Conditioning Agreement (TCA) which defines the rules used to realize the service – what the client must do to achieve desired service and what the service provider will do to enforce the limits. More specifically, a TCA is an agreement specifying classifier rules and any corresponding traffic profiles and metering, marking, discarding and/or shaping rules which are to apply to the traffic streams selected by the classifier. A TCA encompasses all of the traffic conditioning rules explicitly specified within a SLA along with all of the rules implicit from the relevant service requirements and/or from a DS domain's service provisioning policy.

A traffic profile specifies the temporal properties of a traffic stream selected by a classifier. It provides rules for determining whether a particular packet is in-profile or out-of-profile. For example, a profile based on a token bucket may look like:

$$codepoint = X, \text{ use token-bucket } r, b$$

The above profile indicates that all packets marked with DS codepoint X should be measured against a token bucket meter with rate $r$ and burst size $b$. In this example out-of-profile packets are those packets in the traffic streams which arrive when insufficient tokens are available in the bucket (details are covered in Section 4.4.3). The concept of in- and out-of-profile can be extended to more than two levels, for example, multiple levels of conformance with a profile may be defined and enforced.

As packets enter the domain, they will be classified into a traffic aggregate based on the specified filter at the domain ingress interface of the border router. The filter must be associated with a traffic profile that specifies committed information rate (CIR) and a description on how it is to be measured. For example, the measurement may be based on a committed burst size (CBS) or an averaging time interval (T1).

The traffic profile may also include other traffic parameters. These parameters may place additional constraints on packets to which the assurance applies or may further differentiate traffic that exceeds the CIR. Such parameters could include: peak information rate (PIR), peak burst size (PBS), excess burst size (EBS), or even a second averaging time interval (T2).

### 4.3.3 Differentiated Services Network Architecture

DS divides a network into several domains as shown in Figure 4.4. A DS domain [5] is a continuous set of nodes which operates with a common set of resource provisioning policies and PHB definitions. It has a well defined boundary and there are two types of nodes associated with a DS domain: boundary nodes and interior nodes. Boundary nodes connect the DS cloud to other domains. Interior nodes are connected to other interior nodes or boundary nodes, but they must be within the same DS domain. The boundary nodes are assigned the duty of classifying ingress traffic so that incoming packets are marked appropriately to choose one of the PHB groups supported inside the domain. They also enforce the TCA between their own DS domain and the other domains it connects to. The TCA defines the rules used to realize the service, such as metering, marking, and discarding.

Interior nodes map the DS codepoints of each packet into the set of PHBs and perform appropriate forwarding behavior. Any non-DS compliant node inside a DS domain results in unpredictable performance and a loss of end-to-end QoS. A DS domain is generally made up of an organization's intranet or an ISP, that is, networks controlled by a single entity.

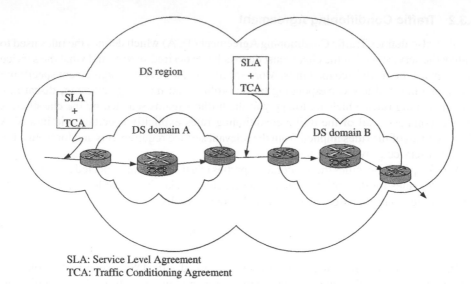

SLA: Service Level Agreement
TCA: Traffic Conditioning Agreement

**Figure 4.4** Differentiated services (DS) network architecture.

DiffServ is extended across domains by SLA between them. An SLA specifies rules such as traffic remarking, actions to be taken for out-of-profile traffic, and so on. The TCAs between domains are decided from this SLA.

Depending on direction of traffic flow, DS boundary nodes can be both ingress nodes and egress nodes. Traffic enters the DS cloud through an ingress node and exits through an egress node. An ingress node is responsible for enforcing the TCA between the DS domain and the domain of the sender node. An egress node shapes the outgoing traffic to make it compliant with the TCA between its own DS domain and the domain of the receiver node.

Flows are classified by predetermined rules so that they can fit into a limited set of class flows. The boundary routers use the eight-bit ToS field of the IP header, called the DS field, to mark the packet for preferential treatment by the interior routers. Only the boundary routers need to maintain per-flow states and perform the shaping and the policing. This is usually advantageous since the links between the customer and service provider are usually slow, so additional computational delay is not that much of a problem for routers interfacing to these links. Therefore, it is affordable to do the computationally intensive traffic shaping and policing strategies at the boundary routers. But once inside the core of the service providers, packets need to be routed (or forwarded) very quickly and so it must incur minimum computational delay at any router/switch. Since the number of flows at the boundary router is much smaller than that in the core network, it is also advantageous to do flow control at the boundary routers.

### 4.3.4 Network Boundary Traffic Classification and Conditioning

Traffic conditioners perform various QoS functions and are located at network boundaries. The boundary routers classify or mark traffic by setting the DSCP field and monitor incoming network traffic for profile compliance. The DSCP field indicates what treatment the packet should receive in a DS domain. The QoS functions can be those of packet classifier, DSCP marker, or traffic metering function, with either the shaper or dropper action.

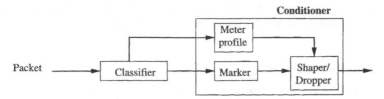

**Figure 4.5**   Packet classifier and traffic conditioning.

Figure 4.5 presents the logical structure of traffic classification and conditioning functions. The classification of packets can be done in one of two ways, depending on the connectivity of the boundary router. Some boundary routers are connected to customer networks, and some others are connected to other ISPs.

A boundary router that is connected to a customer network uses six fields in an incoming IP packet to determine the PHB that the packet should receive in the core network. These six fields are IP source address, IP destination address, protocol ID, DS field in the incoming packet header, source port, and destination port in the transport header respectively. A rule that maps a packet to a PHB does not need to specify all six fields. We refer to these rules as classificaton rules. When a classification rule does not specify any specific value for a field, that specific field is not used for the purpose of classification.

Boundary routers could use just one field in the incoming IP packet to determine the PHB for their network. This field could be the DS field contained in the incoming packet. A boundary router would simply change the DS field to some other value that corresponds to a specific PHB at the core routers. This type of classification would be the one expected at the exchange points of other ISPs. The neighboring ISP domain may have been using a different set of PHBs or may use different DS field values to represent the same PHB.

A boundary router may limit the total number of packets that can be sent into each class. If it is found that a packet cannot be mapped into any of the PHBs because a limit would be exceeded, it may either be mapped into a different PHB or discarded.

The meters check conformance of traffic streams to certain parameters and pass the results to the marker and shaper/dropper. Traffic meters measure the temporal properties of the stream of packets selected by a classifier against a traffic profile specified in a TCA. A meter passes state information to other conditioning functions to trigger a particular action for each packet which is either in- or out-of-profile.

The marker is responsible for writing/rewriting DSCP values. It can mark packets based on classifier match or based on results from the meters. Packet markers set the DS field of a packet to a particular codepoint, adding the marked packet to a particular DS behavior aggregate. The marker may be configured to mark all packets which are steered to it to a single codepoint, or may be configured to mark a packet to one of a set of codepoints used to select a PHB in a PHB group, according to the state of a meter. When the marker changes the codepoint in a packet, it is said to have 're-marked' the packet.

The shaper/dropper is responsible for shaping the traffic to be compliant with the profile and may also drop packets when congested. Shapers delay some or all of the packets in a traffic stream in order to bring the stream into compliance with a traffic profile. A shaper usually has a finite-size buffer, and packets may be discarded if there is no sufficient buffer space to hold the delayed packets. Droppers discard some or all of the packets in a traffic stream in order to bring the stream into compliance with a traffic profile. This process is known as 'policing' the stream. Note that a dropper can be implemented as a special case of a shaper by setting the shaper buffer size to zero (or a few) packets.

### 4.3.5 Per Hop Behavior (PHB)

According to RFC 2475 [5], PHB is the means by which a node allocates resources to aggregate streams. A given example is that a PHB defines a percentage of the capacity of a link. The interior routers in the DS model only need to forward packets according to the specified PHB.

If only one behavior aggregate occupies a link, the observable forwarding behavior will generally only depend on the congestion of the link. Distinct behavioral patterns are only observed when multiple behavioral aggregates compete for buffer and bandwidth resources on a node as shown in Figure 4.6. There are two flows: 'Source 1 → Destination 1' and 'Source 2 → Destination 1.' They have different classifications and will be treated differently by the interior router, for example, using different scheduling and/or discarding preference. A network node allocates resources to the behavior aggregates with the help of the PHBs. PHBs can be defined either in terms of their resources (e.g., buffer and bandwidth), in terms of their priority relative to other PHBs, or in terms of their relative traffic properties (e.g., delay and loss). Multiple PHBs are lumped together to form a PHB group [5] to ensure consistency. PHBs are implemented at nodes through some buffer management or packet scheduling mechanisms. A particular PHB group can be implemented in a variety of ways because PHBs are defined in terms of behavior characteristics and are not implementation dependent.

The standard for DiffServ describes PHBs as the building blocks for services. The focus is on enforcing an SLA between the user and the service provider. Customers can mark the DS octet of their packets to indicate the desired service, or have them marked by the boundary router based on multifield classification (MF), such as IP destination and source addresses, transport port numbers, protocol ID, and so on. Inside the core, packets are forwarded according to their behavior aggregates. These rules are derived from the SLA. When a packet goes from one domain to another, the DS octet may be rewritten by the new network boundary routers. A PHB for a packet is selected at a node on the basis of its DS codepoint. The four most popularly used PHBs are default behavior, class selector, Assured

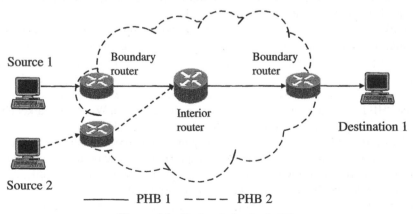

**Figure 4.6** Per hop behavior in DS.

Forwarding (AF), and Expedited Forwarding (EF), described in Section 4.3.6. The mapping from DS codepoint to PHB may be 1 to 1 or $N$ to 1. All codepoints must have some PHBs associated with them. Otherwise, codepoints are mapped to a default PHB. Examples of the parameters of the forwarding behavior that each traffic class should receive are bandwidth partition and the drop priority. Examples of implementations of these are WFQ (weighted fair queuing) for bandwidth partition and RED (random early detection) for drop priority.

### 4.3.6  Differentiated Services Field

The DS values are known as the Differentiated Service Code Point (DSCP). Figure 4.7 illustrates the ToS and DSCP octet formats. In IPv4, only the first three bits were used for QoS purposes. In DiffServ, six bits are used. The same octet is now referred to as the DS field. The DS field is broken up into three-bit class selector and three-bit drop precedence. A more complete mapping between the ToS octet and DS octet is presented in Figure 4.8.

***Default Behavior.*** The default or best-effort PHB corresponds to the default best-effort packet forwarding in the traditional IP network. Packets belonging to this PHB could be forwarded in any manner without any restrictions. The recommended codepoint by IETF for best effort PHB is $0 \times 000000$.

***Class Selector.*** The left most three bits of the DS field/IP ToS define eight classes. They are the DS5 to DS3 bits in Figure 4.7. A packet with a higher numeric value in the Class Selector field is defined to have a better (or equal) relative priority in the network for forwarding than a packet with a lower numeric value. A router does not need to implement eight different priority levels in the network to support the class selector PHBs. It can claim compliance with the standards by supporting only two priority levels, with the eight numeric values mapping to one of the two classes.

***Assured Forwarding (AF).*** The AF PHB is used to provide Assured Services to the customers, so that the customers will get reliable services even in times of network congestion. Classes 1 to 4 are known as the AF service levels. Because making a decision based on only the class selector is very coarse, the AF PHB was created to provide more granularities in buffer management. This class makes use of the drop precedence bits (DS2 to DS0 in Figure 4.7).

When backlogged packets from an AF forwarding class exceed a specified threshold, packets with the highest drop priority are dropped first and then the packets with the lower drop priority. Drop priorities in AF are specific to the forwarding class; comparing two drop priorities in two different AF classes may not always be meaningful. For example, when a DS node starts to drop the packets with the highest drop priority in one forwarding class,

| ToS Octet: | P2 | P1 | P0 | T3 | T2 | T1 | T0 | Zero |
|---|---|---|---|---|---|---|---|---|
| DS Octet: | DS5 | DS4 | DS3 | DS2 | DS1 | DS0 | ECN1 | ECN0 |
|  | (Class Selector) | | | (Drop Precedence) | | | | |

**Figure 4.7**   IPv4 ToS octet and the DS octet.

| IP Precedence (3 bits) | | | DSCP (6 bits) | | | | |
|---|---|---|---|---|---|---|---|
| Name | Value | Bits | Per-Hop Behavior | Class Selector | Drop Precedence | Codepoint Name | DSCP Bits (decimal) |
| Routine | 0 | 000 | Default | | | Default | 000 000(0) |
| Priority | 1 | 001 | AF | 1 | 1: Low | AF11 | 001 010(10) |
| | | | | | 2: Medium | AF12 | 001 100(12) |
| | | | | | 3: High | AF13 | 001 110(14) |
| Immediate | 2 | 010 | AF | 2 | 1: Low | AF21 | 010 010(18) |
| | | | | | 2: Medium | AF22 | 010 100(20) |
| | | | | | 3: High | AF23 | 010 110(22) |
| Flash | 3 | 011 | AF | 3 | 1: Low | AF31 | 011 010(26) |
| | | | | | 2: Medium | AF32 | 011 100(28) |
| | | | | | 3: High | AF33 | 011 110(30) |
| Flash Override | 4 | 100 | AF | 4 | 1: Low | AF41 | 100 010(34) |
| | | | | | 2: Medium | AF42 | 100 100(36) |
| | | | | | 3: High | AF43 | 100 110(38) |
| Critical | 5 | 101 | EF | 5 | | EF | 101 110(46) |
| Internetwork Control | 6 | 110 | — | | | | (48–55) |
| Network Control | 7 | 111 | — | | | | (56–63) |

**Figure 4.8** IPv4 ToS to DSCP mapping.

the packets in other forwarding classes may not experience any packet dropping at all. Each forwarding class has its bandwidth allocation. Dropping takes place only in the forwarding class in which traffic exceeds its own resources.

In general, a DS node may reorder packets of different AF classes but should not reorder packets with different drop priorities but in the same class. The boundary nodes should avoid splitting traffic from the same application flow into different classes since it will lead to packet reordering with a microflow in the network.

***Expedited Forwarding (EF).*** Class 5 is known as EF. The EF PHB is used to provide premium service to the customer. It is a low-delay, low-jitter service providing nearly constant bit rate to the customer. The SLA specifies a peak bit rate which customer applications will receive and it is the customers' responsibility not to exceed the rate.

Expedited forwarding PHB is implemented in a variety of ways. For example, if a priority queuing is used, then there must be a upper bound (configured by the network administrator) on the rate of EF traffic that should be allowed. EF traffic exceeding the bound is dropped.

### 4.3.7 PHB Implementation with Packet Schedulers

This section describes some typical packet schedulers and how they can be used to support the PHBs. Here we only show two implementation examples. Other possible implementations regarding packet scheduling such as WFQ and its variants can be found in Section 4.5. Implementation regarding buffer management such as RED can be found in Section 4.6.

**Static Priority Queues.** Consider a static priority queue scheduler with two levels of priorities. Such a scheduler serves packets in the higher-priority queue if they are available and only serves the lower-priority queue if the higher-priority queue is empty.

This scheduler can support the class selector PHBs by mapping packets with the DS fields of 1000000, 101000, 110000, and 111000 into the higher-priority queue and those with the DS fields of 000000, 001000, 010000, and 011000 into the lower-priority queue. Other mappings are also possible. The DS standards require that packets with the DS fields of 110000 and 111000 should map to the higher-priority queue, and packets with the DS field of 000000 should map to the lower-priority queue. Packets with other DS fields may be mapped to either of the two queues. A network administrator should ensure that the mapping is consistent across all the routers within a single administrative domain.

**Weighted Round Robin (WRR).** A round-robin scheduler with weights assigned to each of multiple queues would be the closest match to implementation of the EF and AF PHBs. The round-robin queues could be assigned weights based on the allocated bandwidth so that they would be able to serve each of the queues proportional to their bandwidth. Class selector PHBs could be supported: packets with the DS field of 110000 and 111000 are mapped to a queue with a larger weight than the queue to which packets with the DS field of 000000 (best effort) are mapped.

If a router were to implement only the EF and the default PHBs, it would need to implement only two queues, which are served round-robin with specific weights assigned to them. If the router were to implement EF, AF, and the default, it would need three queues overall, each with a different assigned weight.

## 4.4 TRAFFIC POLICING AND SHAPING

Traffic policing and shaping functions are performed in both ATM and IP network. ATM has usage parameter control (UPC) and similar mechanisms are required at the edge of autonomous networks for IntServ and DiffServ. Policing functions monitor traffic flows and take corrective actions when the observed characteristics deviate from a specific traffic contract. The mark action or drop action taken by policing functions are determined by an SLA between the user and the network providers. On the other hand, shaping is to control burst data or traffic rate to send data streams to ensure conformance to a traffic contract. If a flow does not conform to the traffic contract, shaping function can be used to delay nonconforming traffic until they conform to the profile. Therefore, a shaper usually has a finite-size buffer, and packets may be discarded if the buffer space is not enough to hold the delayed packets.

Policers and shapers usually identify traffic descriptor violations in an identical manner. They usually differ, however, in the way they respond to violations [6].

- A policer typically drops packets. For example, a committed access rate (CAR) rate-limiting policer will either drop the packet or rewrite its IP precedence code, resetting the packet header's type of service bits.

• A shaper typically delays excess traffic using a buffer, or queueing mechanism, to hold packets and shape the flow when the data rate of the source is higher than expected. For example, general traffic shaping (GTS) uses a weighted fair queue to delay packets in order to shape the flow, and frame relay traffic shaping (FRTS) uses either a priority queue (PQ), a custom queue (CQ), or a first-in-first-out (FIFO) queue for the same, depending on how one configures it.

### 4.4.1 Location of Policing and Shaping Functions

Figure 4.9 shows the generic placement of policing and shaping functions in the network. Usually, first node of the network performs policing and the end user performs the shaping, as shown by the solid box in the figure. One network may police the traffic received from another and shape the traffic before sending to downstream network, but it is optional. Properly shaped traffic never fails a policing check when both functions employ the same traffic contract. The downstream network node should perform policing accounting for accumulated impairments, unless the previous network performs the shaping function.

As illustrated in Figure 4.10, a router or switch is a collection of ports interconnected by a switch fabric. Both input side and output side perform traffic management functions. Beginning on the input side, a policing function determines whether the incoming flow is in conformance to the traffic contract or not. Next, buffer management block determines whether the incoming packets should be accepted or not, and how to discard packets. Also a packet scheduling block is placed next in line to determine which packet to serve next. Buffer management and packet scheduling functions are performed also at the output side. Then a shaping function appears before sending traffic to downstream network. Policing and shaping are discussed in this section. Packet scheduling and buffer management will be explained in Sections 4.5 and 4.6, respectively.

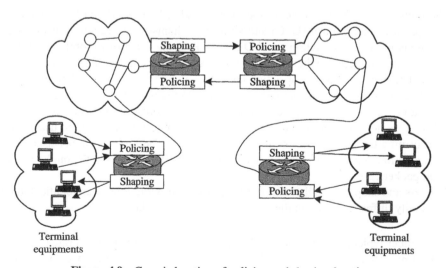

**Figure 4.9** Generic location of policing and shaping function.

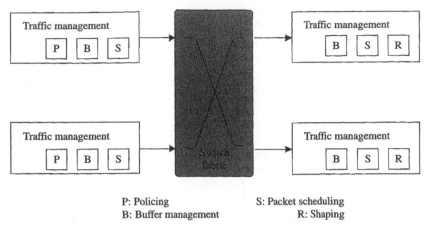

P: Policing                              S: Packet scheduling
B: Buffer management                     R: Shaping

**Figure 4.10**    Generic block diagram of traffic management in router/switch.

### 4.4.2    ATM's Leaky Bucket

The leaky bucket algorithm is a general algorithm that can be effectively used to police and shape real time traffic. ATM networks use a continuous state version of the leaky bucket algorithm called the generic cell rate algorithm (GCRA) to police traffic at the entrance to the ATM network.

The leaky bucket algorithm is the key to define the meaning of conformance. The leaky bucket analogy refers to a bucket with a hole in the bottom that causes it to 'leak' at a certain rate corresponding to a traffic cell rate parameter (e.g., PCR: peak cell rate). The 'depth' of the bucket corresponds to a tolerance parameter (e.g., CDVT: cell delay variation tolerance). Each cell arrival creates a 'cup' of fluid flow 'poured' into one or more buckets for use in conformance checking. The cell loss priority (CLP) bit in the ATM cell header determines which bucket(s) the cell arrival fluid pours into.

In the algorithm, a cell counter represents the bucket. This counter is incremented by one for each incoming cell. The 'leak rate' in the algorithm is the decrement rate which reduces the counter value by one at certain intervals. This rate is given by the cell rate under consideration (e.g., 1/PCR) and is governed by the minimum distance between two consecutive cells. The bucket volume is analogous to the cell counter range, which is represented by the permissible time tolerance for the incoming cells. This value is determined through the traffic contract or is set by the network provider and is called CDVT. If the counter exceeds a certain value, the cells are assumed not to conform to the contract. To counteract this, nonconforming cells can now either be marked (CLP-1) or dropped. The algorithm is called 'dual leaky bucket' if several parameters (e.g., PCR and SCR) are monitored at once, or 'single leaky bucket' if only one parameter is monitored.

The GCRA algorithm is characterized by an increment $I$ and a limit $L$. The increment denotes the average interarrival time between cells. The limit places a bound on the burstiness of the traffic. Figure 4.11 shows the flowchart of GCRA and the equivalent continuous state leaky bucket algorithms.

In GCRA, TAT denotes the theoretical arrival time of the next cell, that is, the time when the next cell is expected to arrive. If the cell arrives after TAT, then the cell is conforming, and TAT is set to the sum of the cell's arrival time and the increment $I$. If the cell arrives

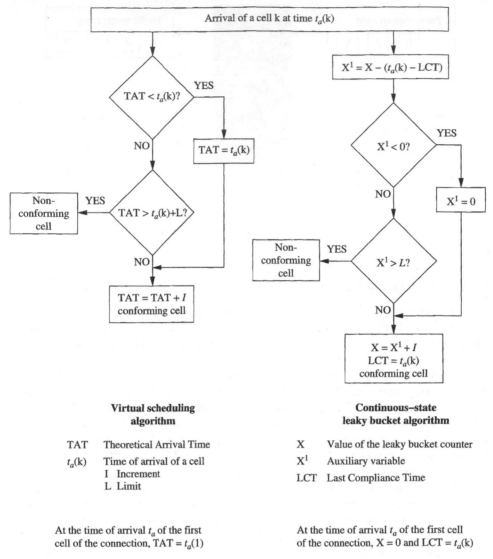

At the time of arrival $t_a$ of the first cell of the connection, TAT = $t_a(1)$

At the time of arrival $t_a$ of the first cell of the connection, X = 0 and LCT = $t_a(k)$

**Figure 4.11** Leaky bucket algorithm for generic cell rate algorithm (GCRA).

before TAT, that is, the actual arrival time $t_a$ of the cell is less than TAT, then the cell can arrive within a limited period before TAT. This period is denoted by limit $L$. If TAT > $t_a + L$ then the cell is marked non-conforming and the TAT is left unchanged. Otherwise, the cell is marked conforming and TAT is incremented by the increment $I$.

In the continuous state leaky bucket algorithm, a counter leaks from a bucket at each time unit. The bucket initially holds 0 counters. The total capacity of the bucket is $L$. The arrival of a cell adds $I$ counters to the leaky bucket. When a cell arrives, if the bucket has leaked enough so that the addition of $I$ counters will not cause the bucket to overflow, then the cell is conforming, else the cell is nonconforming.

### 4.4.3  IP's Token Bucket

In the Internet, a token bucket is used instead of a leaky bucket to control the average transmission rate and burst duration. A token bucket of a traffic regulator has three components:

- Mean rate $r$. It is measured in bytes of IP datagrams per unit time on average permitted by the token bucket. Values of this parameter may range from 1 byte per second to 40 tera-bytes per second [7].
- Bucket depth $b$. It specifies in bits per burst that can be sent within a given unit of time without creating scheduling concerns. Values of this parameter may range from 1 byte to 250 gigabytes [7].
- Time interval, also called the measurement interval. It specifies the time quantum in seconds per burst.

In the token bucket metaphor, tokens are put into the bucket at a certain rate. The bucket itself has a specified capacity. If the bucket fills to capacity, newly arriving tokens are discarded. Each token is the permission for the source to send a certain number of bits into the network. To transmit a packet, the regulator must remove from the bucket a number of tokens equal in representation to the packet size.

If not enough tokens are in the bucket to send a packet, the packet either waits until the bucket has enough tokens or the packet is discarded. If the bucket is already full of tokens, incoming tokens overflow and are not available to future packets. Thus, at any time, the largest burst a source can send into the network is roughly proportional to the size of the bucket.

Figure 4.12 shows the operation of the token bucket algorithm. Algorithm adds the tokens to the bucket at a rate of $r$ bytes per second. An incoming packet conforms to the token bucket traffic specification, if the level of tokens in the bucket $X$ equals or exceeds the length of incoming packet. Specifically, the arbiter checks the incoming packet length $L$ and the current bucket level $X$. If $L \leq X$, then the packet conforms to the token bucket

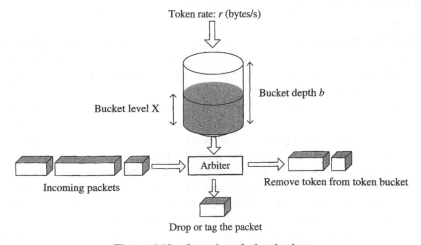

**Figure 4.12**    Operation of token bucket.

traffic specification and $L$ bytes from token bucket are removed. Otherwise, the packet is nonconforming and no tokens is removed. The relationship between token bucket parameters $(r, b)$ and the amount of data sent over time interval $T$, $D(T)$, as follows:

$$D(T) \le rT + b \tag{4.1}$$

This equation limits the maximum amount of data that can arrive over an interval $T$ via a linear function. Therefore, the actual average rate over an interval $T$ can be described as $A(T) = D(T)/T = r + b/T$. Note that, as $T \to \infty$, the actual rate $A(T)$ approaches the desired rate $r$.

### 4.4.4  Traffic Policing

The policing mechanism in ATM network is called UPC/NPC (usage parameter control/network parameter control), which enforces traffic contract between users and network or between networks. Without policing, unfair situations where vicious user greedily take up resources can occur. In Internet, policing function is performed similar to the one in ATM.

A leaky bucket or a token bucket is utilized for policing, thus it can pass temporary bursts that exceed the rate limit as long as tokens are available. Once a packet has been classified as conforming or exceeding a particular rate limit, the router performs one of the following actions to the packet:

*Transmit.*  The packet is transmitted.

*Drop.*  The packet is discarded.

*Set precedence and transmit.*  The ToS bits in the packet header are rewritten. The packet is then transmitted. One can use this action to either color (set precedence) or recolor (modify existing packet precedence) the packet.

*Continue.*  The packet is evaluated using the next rate policy in a chain of rate limits. If there is no another rate policy, the packet is transmitted.

***Multiple Rate Policies.***  A single committed access rate (CAR) policy includes information about the rate limit, conform actions, and exceed actions. Each interface can have multiple CAR policies corresponding to different types of traffic. For example, low priority traffic may be limited to a lower rate than high priority traffic. When there are multiple rate policies, the router examines each policy in the order entered until the packet matches. If no match is found, the default action is to transmit. Rate policies can be independent: each rate policy deals with a different type of traffic. Alternatively, rate policies can be cascading: a packet may be compared to multiple different rate policies in succession. Cascading of rate policies allows a series of rate limits to be applied to packets to specify more granular policies. For example, one could limit total traffic on an access link to a specified subrate bandwidth and then limit World Wide Web traffic on the same link to a given proportion of the subrate limit. One could configure CAR to match packets against an ordered sequence of policies until an applicable rate limit is encountered, for instance, rate limiting several MAC addresses with different bandwidth allocations at an exchange point.

### 4.4.5  Traffic Shaping

Traffic shaping allows one to control the traffic going out of an interface in order to match its flow to the speed of the remote, target interface and to ensure that the traffic conforms to policies contracted for it. Thus, traffic adhering to a particular profile can be shaped to meet downstream requirements, thereby eliminating bottlenecks in topologies with data-rate mismatches.

The primary reasons one would use traffic shaping are to control access to available bandwidth, to ensure that traffic conforms to the policies established for it, and to regulate the flow of traffic in order to avoid congestion that can occur when the transmitted traffic exceeds the access speed of its remote, target interface. Here are some examples:

- Control access to bandwidth when, for example, policy dictates that the rate of a given interface should not, on the average, exceed a certain rate even though the access rate exceeds the speed.

- Configure traffic shaping on an interface if one has a network with differing access rates. Suppose that one end of the link in a frame relay network runs at 256 kbps and the other end of the link runs at 128 kbps. Sending packets at 256 kbps could cause failure of the applications using the link. A similar, more complicated case would be a link-layer network giving indications of congestion that has different access rates on different attached data terminal equipment (DTE); the network may be able to deliver more transit speed to a given DTE at one time than another (this scenario warrants that the token bucket be derived, and then its rate maintained).

- Configure traffic shaping if one offers a subrate service. In this case, traffic shaping enables one to use the router to partition T1 or T3 links into smaller channels.

For traffic shaping, a token bucket permits burstiness but bounds it. It guarantees that the burstiness is bounded so that the flow will never send faster than the token bucket's capacity plus the time interval multiplied by the established rate at which tokens are placed in the bucket. It also guarantees that the long-term transmission rate will not exceed the established rate.

The full RSVP traffic specification starts with the token bucket specification and adds three additional parameters: a minimum-policed unit $m$, a maximum packet size $M$, and a peak rate $p$. The packet size parameters, $m$ and $M$, include the application data and all protocol headers at or above the IP level (e.g., IP, TCP, UDP, etc.). They exclude the link-level header size.

The minimum-policed unit requires that the device removes at least $m$ token bytes for each conforming packet. The parameter $m$ also allows the device to compute the peak packet-processing rate as $b/m$. It also bounds the link-level efficiency by $H/(H + m)$ for a link-level header of $H$ bytes. The maximum packet size $M$ determines the largest permissible size of a conforming packet. In other words, any arriving packet with a length greater than $M$ bytes is nonconforming. The measure for the peak traffic rate $p$ is also bytes of IP datagrams per second, with the same range and encoding as the token bucket parameter $r$. When the peak rate equals the link rate, a node may immediately forward packets that conform to the token bucket parameters. For peak rate values less than the link rate, a leaky bucket shaper following the token bucket conformance checking ensures that the transmitted data $D(t)$ over any interval of time $T$ satisfies the following inequality: $D(T) \leq Min[pT + M, rT + b]$.

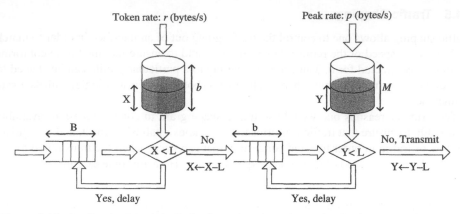

**Figure 4.13** Traffic shaping via buffering in conjunction with a token bucket and peak regulate.

Figure 4.13 shows the block diagram model for a token bucket with parameters $r$ and $b$ operating in conjunction with a peak rate shaper with parameters $p$ and $M$. The shaping buffer must be of size $b$ bytes to admit a burst of packets conforming to the token bucket. The peak rate shaper only operates on packets conforming to the token bucket parameters. The combination of buffers and regulators delays packets until transmission is in conformance with both the token bucket and peak rate parameters. The logic that compares the number of tokens in the bucket with the length of the first packet in the buffer achieves this objective.

## 4.5 PACKET SCHEDULING

Packet networks allow users to share resources such as buffer and link bandwidth. However, the problem of contention for the shared resources arises inevitably. Given a number of users (flows or connections) multiplexed at the same link, a packet scheduling discipline is needed to determine which packets to serve (or transmit) next. In other words, sophisticated scheduling algorithms are required to prioritize users' traffic to meet various QoS requirements while fully utilizing network resources. For example, real-time traffic is delay-sensitive, while data traffic is loss-sensitive. This section presents several packet scheduling schemes. They are typically evaluated along several dimensions, such as tightness of delay bounds, achievable network utilization, fairness and protection, protocol overhead, computational cost, and robustness. Figure 4.14 illustrates a packet scheduler, which, for instance, can be located at the output of a switch/router. The packet scheduler, based on a scheduling algorithm, determines the departure sequences of the packets stored in the memory. Several packet scheduling schemes are discussed below.

### 4.5.1 Max-Min Scheduling

One of the goals for packet scheduling is to fairly allocate the available bandwidth among sessions (see Fig. 4.15 for example). The link bandwidth between user A and router R1 is 10 Mb/s, between user B and router R1 is 100 Mb/s, and between R1 and destination C is 1.1 Mb/s. Here comes the question: what is the 'fair' allocation, 0.55 Mb/s and 0.55 Mb/s or 0.1 Mb/s and 1 Mb/s for A and B, individually?

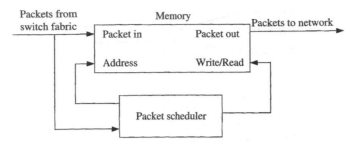

**Figure 4.14**   Packet scheduler.

The classical principle to this problem is the max-min fairness criteria as discussed, for instance, by Bertsekas and Gallager [8]. One possible way to define fairness for a rate allocation scheme is to require that each user should obtain the same transmission rate. For example, when $R$ users access a single link with capacity $C$, a fair allocation would give each user a transmission rate equal to $C/R$. Applying this notion to a network consisting of several links could lead to an inefficient use of link resources [5, 10]. Instead, one could first allocate the same transmission rate to all users, and then share the remaining network bandwidth to fully utilize the network. Or more formally, a max-min fair allocation can be defined as follows.

Considering $N$ flows share a link of rate $C$. Flow $f_i(1 \leq i \leq N)$ wishes to send at rate $W(f_i)$, and is allocated rate $R(f_i)$. We call a rate allocation $\{R(f_1), \ldots, R(f_N)\}$ is feasible, when $\sum_{i=1}^{N} R(f_i) \leq C$. We call a feasible allocation $\{R(f_1), \ldots, R(f_N)\}$ is max-min fair, when it is impossible to increase the rate of a flow $p$ without losing feasibility or reducing the rate of another flow $q$ with a rate $R(f_p) \leq R(f_q)$. Roughly, this definition states that a max-min fair allocation gives the most poorly treated user (i.e., the user who receives the lowest rate) the largest possible share, while not wasting any network resources.

A common way to allocate flows can be described as follows. It is illustrated by an example shown in Figure 4.16, where four flows share a link from router R1.

Step 1. Pick the flow $f_j$ from set $\{R(f_n)\}$ $(1 \leq j \leq N)$, with the smallest requested rate.
Step 2. If $W(f_j) \leq C/N$, then set $R(f_j) = W(f_j)$.
Step 3. If $W(f_j) > C/N$, then set $R(f_j) = C/N$.
Step 4. Set $N = N - 1$, $C = C - R(f_j)$, remove flow $f_j$ from set $\{R(f_n)\}$.
Step 5. If $N > 0$ goto Step 1.

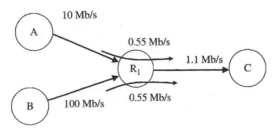

**Figure 4.15**   What is the 'fair' allocation: (0.55 Mb/s, 0.55 Mb/s), or (0.1 Mb/s, 1 Mb/s)? [9].

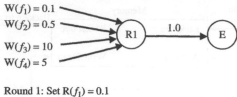

Round 1: Set $R(f_1) = 0.1$
Round 2: Set $R(f_2) = 0.9/3 = 0.3$
Round 3: Set $R(f_3) = 0.6/2 = 0.3$
Round 4: Set $R(f_4) = 0.3/1 = 0.3$

**Figure 4.16** Max-min fairness example [9].

### 4.5.2 Round-Robin Service

In a round-robin (RR) scheduler, newly arriving packets are stored in different queues based on their flow IDs or service classes. The server polls each queue in a cyclic order and serves a packet from any nonempty queue encountered. A misbehaving user may overflow its own queue but will not affect others'. The RR scheduler attempts to treat all users equally and provide each of them an equal share of the link capacity (in other words, providing isolation among the users). It performs reasonably well when all users have equal weights and all packets have the same size (like cells in ATM networks).

When the number of queues is large (e.g., a few thousands or a few hundreds of thousands) and the link rate is high, it is impractical to poll every queue in a round-robin manner to determine which queue has a cell to send. One practical way to implement the RR scheduler is to use a so-called departure queue (DQ) to store the indices of the queues that are non-empty, as shown in Figure 4.17. Here, we consider fixed-length service unit (cell). The packet scheduler at the output of the switch has $M$ flow queues (FQ) and one DQ. There can be up to $N$ cells from the switch fabric arriving at the scheduler in each cell time slot (assuming the switch size of $N$ inputs and $N$ outputs). They are stored in a cell memory (not shown in the figure) and their addresses in the memory (e.g., $A_i$, $A_j$, and $A_k$) are stored in the corresponding FQs. For every nonempty FQ, its FQ index (1 to $M$) will be stored in the DQ (only one copy from each FQ).

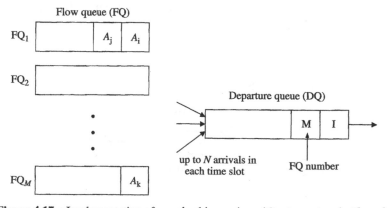

**Figure 4.17** Implementation of round-robin service without a system bottleneck.

In each time slot, the DQ chooses the head-of-line (HOL) index and transmits its HOL cell. If the FQ is nonempty after sending the HOL cell, its index is written back to the tail of the DQ. If the FQ becomes empty, do nothing. When a cell arriving at an empty FQ, its FQ index is immediately inserted to the tail of the DQ.

With this approach, in each time slot there may be up to $N$ cells written to the memory, $N$ memory addresses written to the FQs, one access to the DQ to get the HOL FQ index, and one memory access to transmit the cell. It is independent of the number of FQs ($M$), which is usually much larger than the switch size (e.g., a few tens in general). Thus, it is very scalable. One thing worthy to notice is that the output cell sequence may not be completely identical with the one from the RR service. But, they both achieve the same fairness in the long run.

### 4.5.3 Weighted Round-Robin Service

Consider a weighted round robin (WRR) system in which every connection $i$ has an integer weight $w_i$ associated with it. When the server polls connection $i$, it will serve up to $w_i$ cells before moving to the next connection in the round. This scheme is flexible since one can assign the weights corresponding to the amount of service required. The scheme attempts to give connection $i$ a rate of

$$g_i = \frac{w_i}{\sum_j w_j} \qquad (4.2)$$

For instance, a RR cell system in which there are two users, A and B with their weights $w_A = 3$ and $w_B = 7$ cells, respectively. The scheme attempts to give 30 percent $[= w_A/(w_A + w_B)]$ share of the link capacity to the user A and 70 percent $[= w_B/(w_A + w_B)]$ share to the user B. One possible outgoing cell sequence in a round is *AAABBBBBBB*. A better implementation of WRR operates according to a frame structure and gives *ABBABBABBBA*. That is, user A does not need to wait for seven cell time slots before having its cell sent.

The WRR service can be implemented by using a register storing weight ($w_i$) and a counter ($C_i$) for each FQ ($FQ_i$) as shown in Figure 4.18. The counter keeps track the

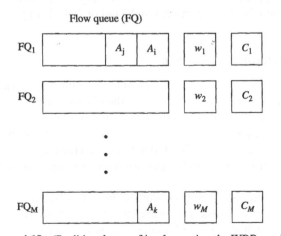

**Figure 4.18** Traditional way of implementing the WRR service.

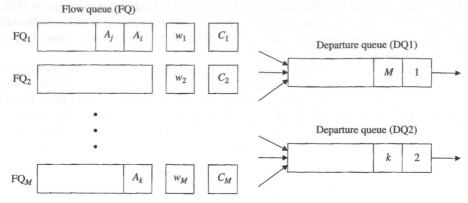

**Figure 4.19** Implementation of WRR service without a system bottleneck.

number of cells that can be sent in a frame, whose size is the sum of all weights. Let us assume the frame size is $F (= \sum w_i)$. A FQ is said to be eligible if it has cells to send and its counter value is not zero. At the beginning of a frame, each counter ($C_i$) is loaded with its weight ($w_i$). Each eligible FQ is served in RR manner. Upon a cell being served from a FQ, its $C_i$ value is reduced by one. After $F$ cells have been served, a new frame starts. However, if prior to $F$ cells being served, no eligible VOQ can be found, a new frame starts. This scheme has a bottleneck from searching an eligible FQ when there are many of them.

To implement the WRR without a system bottleneck, we use two DQs as shown in Figure 4.19. One is active, responsible for transmitting cells, and the other is standby, denoted as $DQ_a$ and $DQ_s$, respectively. The way of storing arriving cells to the memory and their addresses to the FQs is similar to the RR case. $DQ_a$ chooses its HOL FQ to transmit its cell until it becomes empty. When that happens, the role of $DQ_a$ and $DQ_s$ swap. In the system initialization, each counter ($C_i$) is loaded with its weight ($w_i$). When a cell arrives at a FQ (say $FQ_i$), if it is a HOL cell and $C_i$ is nonzero, it joins $DQ_a$ (i.e., its index is inserted to the tail of $DQ_a$). If it is not a HOL cell, it simply joins the tail of its FQ. If it is a HOL cell but its $C_i$ is zero, it joins $DQ_s$. Upon a cell being served from a FQ (say $FQ_i$), its $C_i$ value is reduced by one. $FQ_i$ is then checked. If it is nonempty and $C_i \neq 0$, insert $i$ to the tail of $DQ_a$. If it is non-empty but $C_i = 0$, insert $i$ to the tail of $DQ_s$. If $FQ_i$ is empty, do nothing.

### 4.5.4 Deficit Round-Robin Service

Deficit round robin (DRR) [11] modifies the WRR to allow it to handle variable-sized packets in a fair manner. The basic idea is to use the RR service discipline with a quantum of service assigned to each queue. The only difference from traditional RR is that if a queue was not able to send a packet in the previous round because its packet size was too large, the remainder from the quantum is added to the quantum for the next round. Thus, deficits are recorded. Queues that were shortchanged in a round are compensated in the next round. The detailed algorithm is as follows.

Assume that each flow $i$ is allocated $Q_i$ worth of bits in each round; there is an associated state variable $DC_i$ (Deficit Counter) recording the deficits. Since the algorithm works in rounds, we can measure time in terms of rounds. A round is one RR iteration over the queues that are backlogged. To avoid examining empty queues, an auxiliary list *ActiveList* is kept and consists of a list of indices of queues that contain at least one packet. Packets coming in on different flows are stored in different queues. Let the number of bytes of HOL packet for queue $i$ in round $k$ be $bytes_i(k)$. Whenever a packet arrives at a previously empty queue $i$, $i$ is added to the end of *ActiveList*. Whenever index $i$ is at the head of *ActiveList*, say, in the round $k$, the algorithm computes $DC_i \leftarrow DC_i + Q_i$, sends out queue *is* HOL packet subject to the restriction that $bytes_i(k) \leq DC_i$ (and updates $DC_i \leftarrow DC_i - bytes_i(k)$ if the condition is true). If, at the end of this service opportunity, queue $i$ still has packets to send, the index $i$ is moved to the end of *ActiveList*; otherwise, $DC_i$ is reset to zero and index $i$ is removed from *ActiveList*. The DRR, however, is fair only over time scales longer than a round time. At a shorter time scale, some users may get more service (in terms of bits sent) than others.

An example showing how the DRR works is illustrated in Figure 4.20. At the beginning the counter variables $DC_i$ are initialized to zero. The round robin pointer points to the top of the active list. When the first queue is served the quantum value of 500 is added to the $DC_i$ value. The remainder after servicing the queue is left in the $DC_i$ variable. After sending out a packet of size 200, the queue had 300 bytes of its quantum left. It cannot be served in the current round, since the next packet in the queue is 750 bytes. Therefore, the amount 300 will carry over to the next round when it can send packets of size totaling $300 + 500 = 800$ (deficit from previous round + $Q_i$). The pointer now moves to FQ #2, where its DC is added with 500 bytes, allowing one HOL packet to be sent out.

### 4.5.5  Generalized Processor Sharing (GPS)

Generalized Processor Sharing (GPS) [12, 13] is an ideal scheduling policy in that it provides an exact max-min fair share allocation. The GPS is fair in the sense that it allocates the whole outgoing capacity to all backlogged sessions proportional to their minimum rate (bandwidth) requirements. Basically, the algorithm is based on an idealized fluid-flow model. That is, we assume that a GPS scheduler is able to serve all backlogged sessions instantaneously and the capacity of the outgoing link can be infinitesimally split and allocated to these sessions. However, in real systems only one session can be serviced at each time and packets cannot be split into smaller units. An important class of so-called packet fair queueing (PFQ) algorithms can then be defined in which the schedulers try to schedule the backlogged packets by approximating the GPS scheduler, such as weighted fair queueing (WFQ), virtual clock, and self-clock fair queueing (SCFQ), which are discussed in the following sections. We first introduce the ideal GPS algorithm.

Before getting into the detailed discussion of the GPS, let us use a couple of examples to briefly explain the concept. In Figure 4.21, four flows with equal weights share the link bandwidth. Their rate are 0.1, 0.3, 0.3, and 0.3, respectively. With GPS scheduling, the order of service for the four flows is: $f_1, f_2, f_3, f_4, f_2, f_3, f_4, f_2, f_3, f_4, f_1, \ldots$, where one bit is served at each time. In practice, the link shall serve packet by packet. Figure 4.22 illustrates how packet-mode GPS works, which is called WFQ.

Assume there are four queues labeled A, B, C, and D, sharing the link bandwidth of 4 bps with equal weight. Figure 4.22a shows the initial stage of the scheduling. There are one packet of four bits in queue A (A1), one packet of three bits in queue B (B1), two packets of one bit in queue C (C1 and C2), and two packets of one bit and two bits in queue D (D1 and D2). In round one, the first bit of each queue departs and two packets, A2 (two bits) and C3 (three bits), arrive (Fig. 4.22b). As C1 and D1 has only one bit, they depart in round one. Figures 4.22c and 4.22d show that the GPS scheduler goes on transmitting each

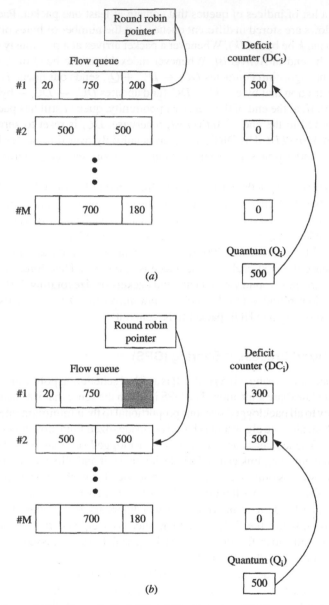

**Figure 4.20**    Example for DRR (*a*) The first step; (*b*) The second step.

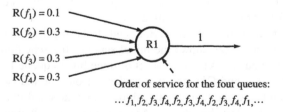

**Figure 4.21**    Weighted bit-by-bit fair queuing (GPS).

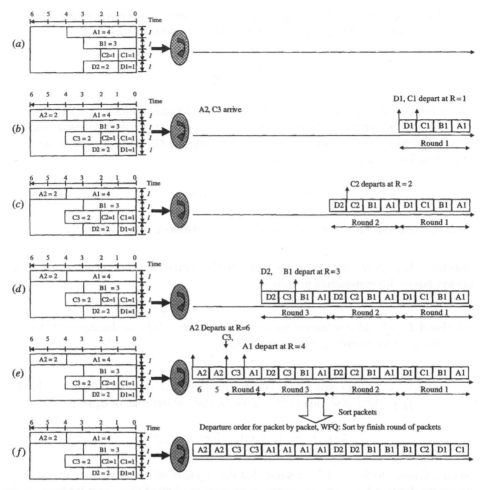

**Figure 4.22** Illustrated example for packet-mode GPS with four queues, sharing 4 bits/sec bandwidth, and equal weights [9].

queue with one bit in each of the second and third rounds. C2 departs in round two, while B1 and D2 depart in round three. After three rounds scheduling, queues B and D become empty, and queues A and C are scheduled during round four as shown in Figure 4.22*e*. At the end of fourth round, only queue A is nonempty. So, A2 is scheduled during round 5 and round 6. Figure 4.22*f* shows the actual departure order for all queued packets, sorted by their finishing rounds.

Assume that a set of $N$ sessions (connections), labeled $1, 2, \ldots, N$, share the common outgoing link of a GPS server. For $i \in \{1, 2, \ldots, N\}$, let $r_i$ denote the minimum allocated rate for session $i$. The associated admission policy should guarantee that

$$\sum_{i=1}^{N} r_i \leq r \tag{4.3}$$

where $r$ is the capacity of the outgoing link.

Let $B(t)$ denote the set of backlogged sessions at time $t$. According to the GPS, the backlogged session $i$ will be allocated a service rate $g_i(t)$ at time $t$ such that,

$$g_i(t) = \frac{r_i}{\sum_{j \in B(t)} r_j} \times r \qquad (4.4)$$

We will use an example to illustrate the service rate allocation principle of GPS servers. Let $A_i(\tau, t)$ be the arrivals of session $i$ during the interval $(\tau, t]$, $W_i(\tau, t)$ the amount of service received by session $i$ during the same interval, and $Q_i(t)$ the amount of session $i$ traffic queued in the server at time $t$, that is,

$$Q_i(t) = A_i(\tau, t) - W_i(\tau, t)$$

Note that, whenever the system becomes idle, all parameters can be reset to zero.

**Definition 4.1.** A *system busy period* is a maximal interval of time during which the server is always busy with transmitting packets.

**Definition 4.2.** A *backlogged period for session $i$* is any period of time during which packets of session $i$ are continuously queued in the system.

**Definition 4.3.** A *session $i$ busy period* is a maximal interval of time $(\tau_1, \tau_2]$ such that for any $t \in (\tau_1, \tau_2]$, packets of session $i$ arrive with the rate greater than or equal to $r_i$, that is,

$$A_i(\tau_1, t) \geq r_i(t - \tau_1), \quad \text{for } t \in (\tau_1, \tau_2]$$

With reference to Figure 4.23, assume that the capacity of the server $r = 1$, and three connections, labeled 1, 2, and 3, share the same outgoing link of the server, where $r_1 = \frac{1}{6}$, $r_2 = \frac{1}{3}$, and $r_3 = \frac{1}{2}$.

Suppose that each packet has a fixed length that needs exactly one unit time to transmit. At time $t = 0$, session 1 starts a session busy period in which packets from session 1 arrive at the server with a rate one packet per unit time. At $t = 1$, packets from session 2 also start to arrive at the server with the same arrival rate. Session 3 starts a session busy period at $t = 3$ with the same packet arrival rate. The arrival curves of these three sessions are given in Fig. 4.24$a$.

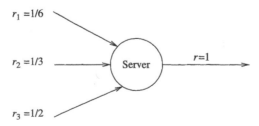

**Figure 4.23**    GPS server with three incoming sessions.

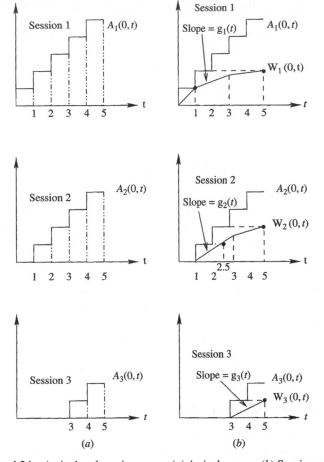

**Figure 4.24**  Arrival and service curves (*a*) Arrival curves; (*b*) Service curves.

The GPS server will allocate a service rate to each session as follows:

$$g_1(t) = \begin{cases} 1 : & 0 < t \le 1 \\ \frac{1}{3} : & 1 < t \le 3 \\ \frac{1}{6} : & t > 3 \end{cases}$$

$$g_2(t) = \begin{cases} 0 : & 0 < t \le 1 \\ \frac{2}{3} : & 1 < t \le 3 \\ \frac{1}{3} : & t > 3 \end{cases}$$

$$g_3(t) = \begin{cases} 0 : & 0 < t \le 3 \\ \frac{1}{2} : & t > 3 \end{cases}$$

The service curves are shown in Figure 4.24*b*. Note that $g_i(t)$ is also the slope of the service curve of session $i$ at time $t$. Furthermore, at any time during the system busy period,

$\sum_{i=1}^{N} g_i(t) = r$ because of the work-conserving property.[1] The departure times of the first packet of sessions 1, 2, and 3 are 1, 2.5, and 5, respectively.

The *fairness index* of backlogged session $i$ can be defined as $W_i(\tau_1, \tau_2)/r_i$. That is, during any time interval $(\tau_1, \tau_2)$, for any two backlogged sessions $i$ and $j$, the scheduler is said to be *perfectly fair* if and only if it always satisfies that

$$\frac{W_i(\tau_1, \tau_2)}{r_i} = \frac{W_j(\tau_1, \tau_2)}{r_j}$$

The GPS server is perfectly fair.

The GPS is an ideal PFQ service policy based on a fluid-flow model. However, because the fluid GPS is not practical, a class of PFQ algorithms has been proposed to emulate the fluid GPS to achieve the desired performance. The objective is to design an efficient and scalable architecture that can support hundreds of thousands of sessions in a cost-effective manner. All of them are based on maintaining a global function, referred to as either *system virtual time* or *system potential*, which tracks the progress of the GPS. This global function is used to compute a *virtual finish time* (or *time stamp*) for each packet or the head-of-line (HOL) packet of each session in the system. The time stamp of a packet is the sum of its *virtual start time* and the time needed to transmit this packet at its reserved bandwidth. Packets are served in an increasing order of their time stamps.

The implementation cost of a PFQ algorithm is determined by two components: (1) Computing the system virtual time function; and (2) Maintaining the relative ordering of the packets via their time stamps in a priority queue mechanism. Several PFQ algorithms are introduced in the following sections.

### 4.5.6 Weighted Fair Queuing (WFQ)

Although the GPS service principle is perfectly fair, the idealized fluid-flow model is not practical to implement. However, we can simulate the GPS server and then schedule the backlogged packets in accordance with the packet behavior of the simulated GPS server. A WFQ (also called Packetized GPS) system is defined with respect to its corresponding GPS system. Let $d_p^{GPS}$ be the time at which packet $p$ will depart (finish service) under GPS. A good approximation of GPS would be a scheme that serves packets in an increasing order of $d_p^{GPS}$. However, this is not always possible without causing the discipline to be nonwork-conserving. This is because when the packet system is ready to choose the next packet to transmit, the next packet to depart under GPS may not have arrived at the packet system yet. Waiting for it requires the knowledge of the future and also causes the system to be nonwork-conserving. In WFQ, the server simply assigns the departure time of a packet in the simulated GPS server as the time stamp of that packet, and then the server transmits packets in an increasing order of these time stamps. When the server is ready to transmit the next packet at time $\tau$, it picks the first packet that would complete service in the corresponding GPS system as if no additional packets were to arrive after time $\tau$.

Weighted fair queuing [12] uses the concept of *virtual time* to track the progress of GPS that will lead to a practical implementation of packet-by-packet GPS. Denote as an *event* each arrival and departure of sessions from the GPS server, and let $t_j$ be the time at which

---

[1] A server is work-conserving if it is never idle whenever there are packets to be transmitted. Otherwise, it is nonwork-conserving.

the $j$th event occurs (simultaneous events are ordered arbitrarily). Let the time of the first arrival of a busy period be denoted as $t_1 = 0$. Now observe that, for each $j = 2, 3, \ldots$, the set of sessions that are busy in the interval $(t_{j-1}, t_j)$ is fixed. We denote this set as $B_j$. Virtual time $V(t)$ is defined to be zero for all times when the server is idle. Consider any busy period, and let the time that it begins be time zero. Then, $V(t)$ evolves as follows:

$$V(0) = 0,$$

$$V(t_{j-1} + \tau) = V(t_{j-1}) + \frac{r\tau}{\sum_{i \in B_j} r_i}, \qquad \text{for } \tau \le t_j - t_{j-1}, \, j = 2, 3, \ldots \quad (4.5)$$

The rate of change of $V$, namely $dV(t_j + \tau)/d\tau$, is $r/\sum_{i \in B_j} r_i$, and each backlogged session $i$ receives service at rate $r_i[dV(t_j + \tau)]/[d\tau]$, that is, $g_i(t_j + \tau)$ according to Eq. (4.4). Thus, $V$ can be interpreted as increasing at the marginal rate at which backlogged sessions receive service.

Now suppose that the $k$th packet from session $i$ arrives at time $a_{i,k}$ and has length $L_{i,k}$. Then, denote the virtual times at which this packet begins and completes service as $S_{i,k}$ (also called *virtual start time* [12] or *start potential* [14]) and $F_{i,k}$ (*virtual finish time* [12] or *finish potential* [14]), respectively. Defining $F_{i,0} = 0$ for all $i$, we have

$$S_{i,k} = \max\{F_{i,k-1}, V(a_{i,k})\},$$

$$F_{i,k} = S_{i,k} + \frac{L_{i,k}}{r_i}. \qquad (4.6)$$

The role of $V(a_{i,k})$ is to reset the value of $S_{i,k}$ when queue $i$ becomes active (i.e., receives one packet after being empty for a while) to account for the service it missed [14, 15]. Therefore, the start time of each backlogged queue can stay close to each other (they are the same in a GPS server).

For the above example, let the $k$th packet from backlogged session $i$ be labeled by $(i, d_{i,k}^{GPS})$, where $d_{i,k}^{GPS}$ is the departure time of this packet in the simulated GPS server. Figure 4.25 shows the service curves and the departure order of packets in the WFQ server for the previous example. As shown in the right-hand side of Figure 4.25, packets depart according to the departure time in the GPS system. For those packets that have the same departure time, they are served arbitrarily.

On the other hand, let each packet be labeled by $(i, F_{i,k})$. Figure 4.26 shows the virtual time $V(t)$ according to [Eq. (4.5)]. Figure 4.27 shows the virtual finish time curves and the departure order of packets for the previous example. $F_i(t)$ denotes a stair-wise function of time $t$ with $F_i(a_{i,k}) = F_{i,k}$, $a_{i,k}$ is the arrival time of the $k$th packet of session $i$ and is calculated according to Eq. (4.6). Note that the departure order is the same with that in Figure 4.25.

In [12], Parekh establishes the following relationships between the GPS system and its corresponding packet WFQ system:

$$d_{i,k}^{WFQ} - d_{i,k}^{GPS} \le \frac{L_{\max}}{r}, \quad \forall i, k \qquad (4.7)$$

$$W_i^{GPS}(0, \tau) - W_i^{WFQ}(0, \tau) \le L_{\max}, \quad \forall i, \tau \qquad (4.8)$$

where $d_{i,k}^{WFQ}$ and $d_{i,k}^{GPS}$ are the times at which the $k$th packet on session $i$ departs under WFQ and GPS, respectively, $W_i^{WFQ}(0, \tau)$ and $W_i^{GPS}(0, \tau)$ are the total amounts of service

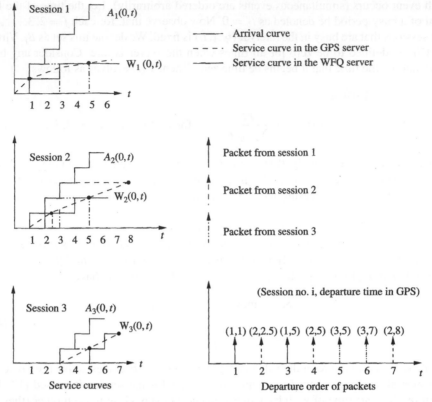

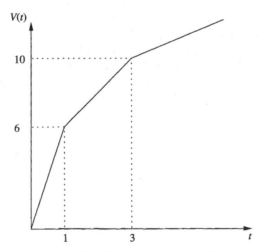

**Figure 4.25** Service curves and the departure order of packets in the WFQ server. Packets depart according to the depart times as if the packets are served by a GPS server.

**Figure 4.26** Virtual time function $V(t)$.

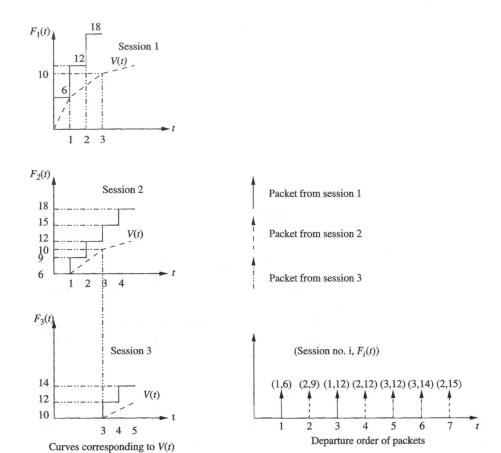

**Figure 4.27** Virtual finish time stamps, $F(t)$, and the departure order of packets. $F(t)$ is calculated with the knowledge of virtual time, $V(t)$. Packets depart according to their $F(t)$ values.

received by session $i$ (the number of session $i$ bits transmitted) by time $\tau$ under WFQ and GPS, respectively, and $L_{max}$ is the maximum packet length among all the sessions.

Another parameter called *latency* [14] can be defined and used to compare the performances of the WFQ and the GPS servers.

**Definition 4.4.** The *latency* of a server $\mathcal{S}$, $\Theta_i^{\mathcal{S}}$, is the minimum non-negative number that satisfies

$$W_{i,j}^{\mathcal{S}}(\tau, t) \geq \max\{0, r_i(t - \tau - \Theta_i^{\mathcal{S}})\}. \tag{4.9}$$

for any time $t$ after time $\tau$ when the $j$th busy period started and until the packets that arrived during this period are served, where $W_{i,j}^{\mathcal{S}}$ is the service received by session $i$ corresponding $j$th busy period.

With reference to Figure 4.28, the inequality (4.9) defines an envelope to bound the minimum service offered to session $i$ during a busy period. It is easy to show that the

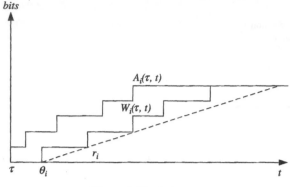

**Figure 4.28** Latency.

latency $\Theta_i^S$ represents the worst-case delay seen by the first packet of a busy period of session $i$.

In the GPS server, the newly backlogged session can get served immediately with a rate equal to or greater than its required transmission rate. As a result, the latency is zero.

In the WFQ server, however, the worst-case delay of the first packet of a backlogged period for session $i$ is $d_{i,1}^{\text{WFQ}} - a_{i,1}$, where $a_{i,1}$ is the arrival time of that packet. From inequality (4.7), we have,

$$d_{i,1}^{\text{WFQ}} - a_{i,1} \le d_{i,1}^{\text{GPS}} + \frac{L_{\max}}{r} - a_{i,1} \le \frac{L_i}{r_i} + \frac{L_{\max}}{r}$$

where $L_i$ is the maximum packet size of session $i$. Thus, we can conclude that the latency of session $i$ in the WFQ server is bounded by $(L_i/r_i) + (L_{\max}/r)$.

The WFQ algorithm has a time complexity of $O(N)$ because of the overhead in keeping track of sets $B_j$, which is essential in the updating of virtual time, where $N$ is the maximum number of backlogged sessions in the server. Other functions of time have been proposed to approach the virtual time function such that the computation complexity of the scheduling algorithm can be further reduced. As shown in the following sections, all PFQ algorithms use a similar priority queue mechanism that schedules packet transmission in an increasing order of their time stamps, but differ in choices of system virtual time function and packet selection policies [14, 15].

### 4.5.7 Virtual Clock

The virtual clock (VC) scheduler uses a real time function to approach the virtual time function. That is, the scheduler assigns

$$V^{\text{VC}}(t) = t, \quad \text{for } t \ge 0. \tag{4.10}$$

The $k$th packet from session $i$ will be assigned a time-stamp $F_{i,k}$ from Eq. (4.6) and Eq. (4.10), that is,

$$F_{i,k} = \max\{F_{i,k-1}, a_{i,k}\} + \frac{L_{i,k}}{r_i}, \tag{4.11}$$

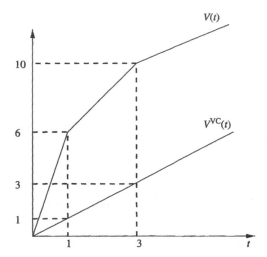

**Figure 4.29** VC scheduler uses real time to approach the virtual time.

where $a_{i,k}$ is the arrival time of the $k$th packet of session $i$. Figure 4.29 shows the curves $V(t)$ and $V^{VC}(t)$, and Figure 4.30 shows the service curves and the departure order of packets for the previous example.

Since the real time is always less than or equal to the virtual time, the VC scheduler can always provide the newly backlogged session with a latency smaller than or equal to that provided by the WFQ server [16].

However, the VC service discipline is defined with reference to the static time system and the calculation of the time stamp is independent of the behaviors of other sessions. As a result, if a connection has sent more packets than specified, it may be punished by the VC, regardless if such misbehavior affects the performance of other connections. For example, suppose there are two sessions 1 and 2 as shown in Figure 4.31.

All packets from both sessions are the same size. The link capacity is normalized as one packet per time slot. Let $r_1 = r_2 = 0.5$ packet/slot, so the time stamp for a session will be advanced by two slots each time its HOL packet is sent based on Eq. (4.11). Initially, at time 0 (in unit of slot), $F_{1,0} = F_{2,0} = 0$. Session 1 source continuously generates packets from time 0, while session 2 source starts to continuously send packet from time 900, as illustrated in Figure 4.31. Up to time 900, 900 packets from source 1 have been transmitted by the VC scheduler, and based on Eq. (4.11), $F_{1,901} = 1802$ at time 900, while $F_{2,1} = 902$. Therefore, the 901th packet arriving from session 1 at time 900 (with its stamp 1802) cannot get any service until the 449th packet from session 2 (arriving at time 1349 and stamped with 1800) finished its service. In other words, session 1 packets that arrived in the interval [900, 1349) are being punished since the session used the server exclusively in the interval [0, 900). But note that this exclusive use of the server was not at the expense of any session 2 packets.

Figure 4.30 also shows that session 1 is punished by the Virtual Clock scheduler when compared with the departure order in the Figure 4.27. In this case, old backlogged sessions must wait for the server to serve the newly backlogged session until its HOL packet has a time stamp larger than or equal to the time stamps of those old backlogged sessions. As a result, there is no fairness bound for the VC scheduling algorithm because there is no bound for $|W_i(\tau_1, \tau_2)/r_i - W_j(\tau_1, \tau_2)/r_j|$ when both sessions $i$ and $j$ are backlogged.

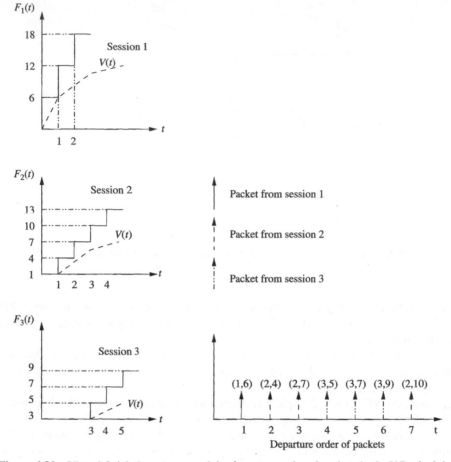

**Figure 4.30** Virtual finish time stamps and the departure order of packets in the VC scheduler.

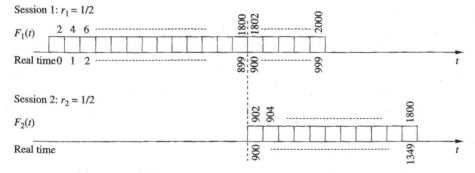

**Figure 4.31** Example showing unfairness of the VC.

### 4.5.8  Self-Clocked Fair Queuing

The self-clocked fair queuing (SCFQ) [17] scheduler updates its virtual time function only when a packet departs, and the assigned value is equal to the time stamp of that packet. That is, the scheduler assigns

$$V^{\text{SCFQ}}(t) = F_{j,l}, \text{ if the } l\text{th packet of session } j \text{ departs at time } t \geq 0. \tag{4.12}$$

Similarly, the $k$th packet from session $i$ will be assigned a time stamp $F_{i,k}$ from Eq. (4.6) and Eq. (4.12), that is,

$$F_{i,k} = \max\{F_{i,k-1}, V^{\text{SCFQ}}(a_{i,k})\} + \frac{L_{i,k}}{r_i}. \tag{4.13}$$

Figure 4.32 shows the curves corresponding to $V(t)$ and $V^{\text{SCFQ}}(t)$, respectively, while Figure 4.33 shows the time stamps and the departure order of packets for the previous example.

Figure 4.34 demonstrates that how the SCFQ is able to provide fairness guarantee for the same situation given in Figure 4.31 where the VC fails to do so. With reference to Figure 4.34, we can see that under the SCFQ, packets from both sessions are served in a round robin fashion according to their time stamps after session 2 becomes active at time 900.

Compared with the VC scheduler, the SCFQ can approach WFQ more accurately. However, the problem is that $V^{\text{SCFQ}}(t)$ can be larger than $V(t)$ as shown in Figure 4.32, and thus the latency can be very large. Consider a worst case situation where $(N-1)$ sessions have backlogged and their $F$ values are the same. Assume where one packet is completely transmitted at $\tau$, the virtual time is updated to the departed packet's virtual finish time $F$, say $V^{\text{SCFQ}}(\tau)$. Also assume session $i$ becomes backlogged at time $\tau$, $(N-2)$ HOL packets from other backlogged sessions have the same time stamp value as $V^{\text{SCFQ}}(\tau)$. Since the first packet of the newly backlogged session has a time stamp with a minimum

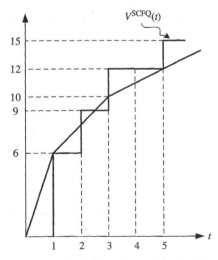

**Figure 4.32**  The SCFQ scheduler uses the time stamp of the last departed packet to approach the virtual time.

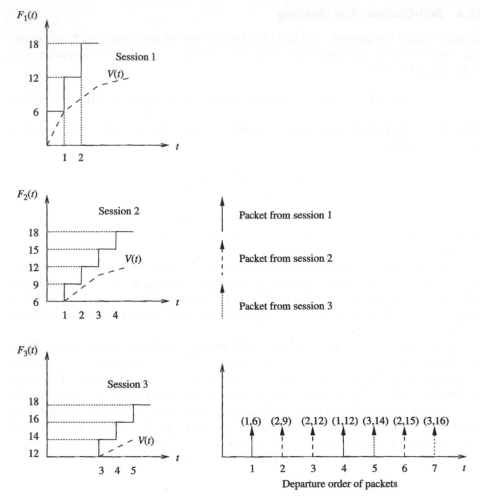

**Figure 4.33** Virtual finish time stamps and the departure order of packets in the SCFQ scheduler.

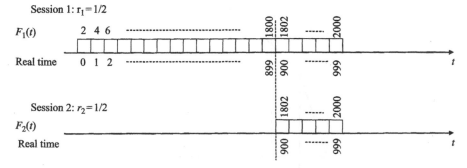

**Figure 4.34** Example showing fairness of the SCFQ.

value $V^{\text{SCFQ}}(\tau) + (L_{i,1}/r_i)$, it may experience the worst-case delay time (i.e., latency) $(L_{i,1}/r_i) + (N-1)(L_{\max}/r)$ [14, 18]. The first $(N-2)(L_{\max}/r)$ is for those $N-2$ HOL packets being transmitted, and the last $(L_{i,1}/r_i) + (L_{\max}/r)$ is the same latency as in WFQ. As a result, the latency of SCFQ scheduler is $(L_{i,1}/r_i) + (N-1)(L_{\max}/r)$.

### 4.5.9 Worst-Case Fair Weighted Fair Queuing (WF²Q)

The results given by Eq. (4.7) and Eq. (4.8) can be easily interpreted to be that WFQ and GPS provide almost identical service except the difference of one packet. What Parekh has proven is that WFQ cannot fall behind GPS with respect to service given to a session by one maximum size packet. However, packets can leave much earlier in a WFQ system than in a GPS system, which means that WFQ can be far ahead of GPS in terms of the number of bits served for a session.

Consider the example illustrated in Figure 4.35$a$ where there are 11 sessions sharing the same link [19]. The horizontal axis shows the time line and the vertical axis shows the sample path of each session. For simplicity, assume all packets have the same size of 1 and the link speed is 1. Also, let the guaranteed rate for session 1 be 0.5, and the guaranteed rate for each of the other 10 sessions be 0.05.

In the example, session 1 sends 11 back-to-back packets starting at time 0 while each of the other 10 sessions sends only one packet at time 0. If the server is GPS, it will take two time units to service a session 1 packet and 20 time units to service a packet from another session. This is illustrated in Figure 4.35$b$. If the server is WFQ, at time 0, all 11 sessions have packets backlogged. Since packet $p_{1,1}$ (i.e., the first session 1 packet) finishes at time 2 while all other $p_{i,1}$ ($i = 2, \ldots, 11$) packets finish at time 20 in the GPS system, WFQ will service $p_{1,1}$ first. In fact, the first 10 packets on session 1 all have finishing times smaller than packets belonging to any other session, which means that 10 packets on session 1 will be served back-to-back before packets on other sessions can be transmitted. This is shown in Figure 4.35$c$. After the burst the next packet on session 1, $p_{1,11}$, will have a larger finishing time in the GPS system than the 10 packets at the head of other sessions' queues. Therefore, it will not be serviced until all the other 10 packets are transmitted, at which time, another 10 packets from session 1 will be served back-to-back. This cycle of bursting 10 packets and going silent for 10 packet times can continue indefinitely. With more sessions, the length of the period between bursting and silence can be larger.

Such oscillation is undesirable for flow and congestion control in data communication networks. To quantify the discrepancy between the services provided by a packet discipline and the fluid GPS discipline, we consider the notion of worst-case packet fair as defined below [19].

**Definition 4.5.** A service discipline $s$ is called *worst-case fair for session i* if for any time $\tau$, the delay of a packet arriving at $\tau$ is bounded above by $[Q_i^s(\tau)/r_i] + C_i^s$, that is,

$$d_{i,k}^s < a_{i,k} + \frac{Q_i^s(a_{i,k})}{r_i} + C_i^s, \tag{4.14}$$

where $r_i$ is the minimum bandwidth guaranteed to session $i$, $Q_i^s(a_{i,k})$ is the queue size of session $i$ at time $a_{i,k}$ when the $k$th packet of session $i$ arrives, and $C_i^s$ is a constant independent of the queues of the other sessions multiplexed at the server.

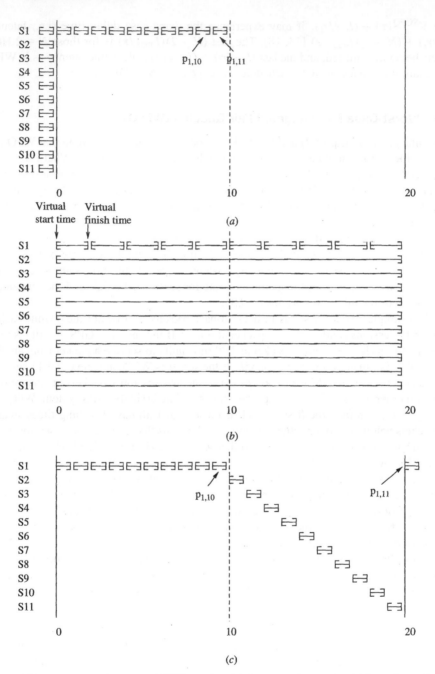

**Figure 4.35** Example of GPS and WFQ service (*a*) Packet arrivals; (*b*) GPS service order and (*c*) WFQ service order (©1996 IEEE).

**Definition 4.6.** A service discipline is called *worst-case fair* if it is worst-case fair for all sessions.

**Definition 4.7.** $C_i^s$ is called the *worst-case fair index* (WFI) for session $i$ at server $s$.

Since $C_i^s$ is measured in absolute time, it is not suitable for comparing $C_i^s$s of sessions with different $r_i$s. To perform such a comparison, the normalized WFI for session $i$ at server $s$ can be defined as

$$c_i^s = \frac{r_i C_i^s}{r}. \tag{4.15}$$

For a server that is worst-case fair, we define its normalized WFI to be

$$c^s = \max_i \{c_i^s\}. \tag{4.16}$$

Notice that GPS is worst-case fair with $c^{\text{GPS}} = 0$. Thus, we can use $c^s$ as the metric to quantify the service discrepancy between a packet discipline $s$ and GPS. It has been shown in [19] that $c^{\text{WFQ}}$ may increase linearly as a function of number of sessions $N$.

To minimize the difference between a packet system and the fluid GPS system, another class of scheduling algorithms called shaper-schedulers [19–23] has been proposed to achieve minimum WFI and have better worst-case fairness properties. With these algorithms, when the server is picking the next packet to transmit, it chooses, among all the *eligible* packets, the one with the smallest time stamp. A packet is eligible if its virtual start time is *no greater than* the current system virtual time. This is called the *eligibility test* or *smallest eligible virtual finish time first* (SEFF) policy [19, 20].

Worst-case fair weighted fair queuing or WF$^2$Q [19] is one such example. Recall that in a WFQ system, when the server chooses the next packet for transmission at time $\tau$, it selects, among all the packets that are backlogged at $\tau$, the first packet that would complete service in the corresponding GPS system. In a WF$^2$Q system, when the next packet is chosen for service at time $\tau$, rather than selecting it from among all the packets at the server as in WFQ, the server only considers the set of packets that have started (and possibly finished) receiving service in the corresponding GPS system at time $\tau$, and selects the packet among them that would complete service first in the corresponding GPS system.

Now consider again the example discussed in Figure 4.35 but in light of WF$^2$Q policy. At time 0, all packets at the head of each session's queue, $p_{i,1}$, $i = 1, \ldots, 11$, have started service in the GPS system [Figure 4.35a]. Among them, $p_{1,1}$ has the smallest finish time in GPS, so it will be served first in WF$^2$Q. At time 1, there are still 11 packets at the head of the queues: $p_{1,2}$ and $p_{i,1}$, $i = 2, \ldots, 11$. Although $p_{1,2}$ has the smallest finish time, it will not start service in the GPS system until time 2; therefore, it won't be *eligible* for transmission at time 1. The other 10 packets have all started service at time 0 at the GPS system; thus, they are eligible. Since they all finish at the same time in the GPS system [Figure 4.35(b)], the tie-breaking rule of giving highest priority to the session with the smallest number yields $p_{2,1}$ as the next packet for service. In contrast, if a WFQ server is used, rather than selecting the next packet from among the 10 packets that have started service in the GPS system, it would pick the packet among all 11 packets, which results in packet $p_{1,2}$. At time 3, $p_{1,2}$ becomes eligible and has the smallest finish time among all backlogged packets, thus it starts service next. The rest of the sample path for the WF$^2$Q system is shown in Figure 4.36 [19].

Therefore, even in the case when session 1 is sending back-to-back packets, its output from the WF$^2$Q system is rather smooth as opposed to the bursty output under a WFQ system. The following theorem summarizes some of the most important properties of WF$^2$Q [19].

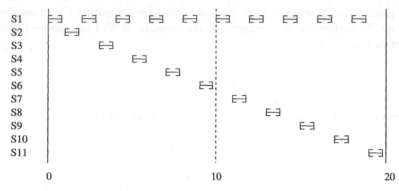

**Figure 4.36**   An example of WF$^2$Q service order (©1996 IEEE).

**Theorem 4.1.** Given a WF$^2$Q system and a corresponding GPS system, the following properties hold for any $i, k, \tau$:

$$d_{i,k}^{\text{WF}^2\text{Q}} - d_{i,k}^{\text{GPS}} \le \frac{L_{\max}}{r}; \tag{4.17}$$

$$W_i^{\text{GPS}}(0, \tau) - W_i^{\text{WF}^2\text{Q}}(0, \tau) \le L_{\max}; \tag{4.18}$$

$$W_i^{\text{WF}^2\text{Q}}(0, \tau) - W_i^{\text{GPS}}(0, \tau) \le \left(1 - \frac{r_i}{r}\right) L_i. \tag{4.19}$$

### 4.5.10   WF$^2$Q+

While WF$^2$Q provides the tightest delay bound and smallest WFI among all PFQ algorithms, it has the same worst-case time complexity of $O(N)$ as WFQ because they both need to compute the virtual time or the system virtual time $V(t)$ by tracing the fluid GPS system.

WF$^2$Q+ [22] and starting-potential fair queuing (SPFQ) [14] have been shown to have worst-case fairness properties similar to WF$^2$Q but is simpler to implement by introducing the following system virtual time function.

$$V(t + \tau) = \max \left\{ V(t) + \tau, \min_{i \in \hat{B}(t)} \{S_i(t)\} \right\}, \tag{4.20}$$

where $\hat{B}(t)$ is the set of sessions that are backlogged in the system at time $t$, and $S_i(t)$ is the virtual start time of the HOL packet of backlogged session $i$. Let $W(t, t + \tau)$ be the total amount of service provided by the server or the bits that have been transmitted during a time interval $(t, t + \tau]$. In the special case of a fixed rate server, $\tau = W(t, t + \tau)/r$, where $r$ is the link capacity. The time complexity is reduced to $O(\log N)$, attributed to the operations of searching for the minimum start time value among all $N$ sessions.

To approximate the GPS, a PFQ algorithm, such as WF$^2$Q+ and SPFQ, maintains a system virtual time function $V(t)$, a virtual start time $S_i(t)$, and a virtual finish time (or time stamp) $F_i(t)$ for each queue $i$. $S_i(t)$ and $F_i(t)$ are updated on the arrival of the HOL packet for each queue. A packet departure occurs when its last bit is sent out, while an HOL packet arrival occurs in either of two cases: (1) a previously empty queue has an incoming packet that immediately becomes the HOL; or (2) the packet next to the previous HOL packet in a non-empty queue immediately becomes the HOL after its predecessor departs. Obviously, a packet departure and a packet arrival in case II could happen at the same time. Therefore,

$$S_i(t) = \begin{cases} \max\{V(t), F_i(t^-)\} & \text{for packet arrival in case I} \\ F_i(t^-) & \text{for packet arrival in case II} \end{cases} \tag{4.21}$$

$$F_i(t) = S_i(t) + \frac{L_i^{\text{HOL}}}{r_i}, \tag{4.22}$$

where $F_i(t^-)$ is the finish time of queue $i$ before the update, and $L_i^{\text{HOL}}$ is the length of the HOL packet for queue $i$. The way of determining $V(t)$ is the major distinction among proposed PFQ algorithms [14, 15].

### 4.5.11 Comparison

WFQ or packet GPS (PGPS) is probably the first PFQ algorithm [12], in which the state of the GPS is precisely tracked. Although, in terms of the number of bits served for a session, the WFQ has proven that it will not fall behind the GPS by one maximum size packet; it can be far ahead of the GPS. In other words, it is not *worst-case fair*, as indicated with a large worst-case fair index (WFI) [19]. Motivated by this, an eligibility test was introduced in the WF$^2$Q [19] (also SPFQ [14]). In this test, when the next packet is chosen for service, it is selected from those 'eligible' packets whose start times are not greater than the system virtual time. It has been proven that the WF$^2$Q can provide almost identical service to that of the GPS, differing by no more than one maximum size packet. However, a serious limitation to the WF$^2$Q (and WFQ) is its computational complexity arising from the simulation of the GPS. A maximum of $N$ events may be triggered in the simulation during the transmission of a packet. Thus, the time for completing a scheduling decision is $O(N)$.

Table 4.1 summarizes the latency, fairness measures, and time complexity of several scheduling algorithms [14]. Note that the $O(\log N)$ complexity of most of the sorted-priority algorithms arises from the complexity of priority queue operations, as explained in detail in the following section.

**TABLE 4.1    Latency, Fairness, and Time Complexity of Several Scheduling Algorithms**

| Scheduler | Reference | Latency | WFI | Complexity |
|---|---|---|---|---|
| GPS | [12] | $0^a$ | 0 | — |
| WFQ | [12] | $(L_i/r_i) + (L_{\max}/r)$ | $O(N)$ | $O(N)$ |
| SCFQ | [17] | $(L_i/r_i) + (L_{\max}/r)(N-1)$ | — | $O(\log N)$ |
| VC | [16] | $(L_i/r_i) + (L_{\max}/r)$ | $\infty$ | $O(\log N)$ |
| DRR | [11] | $(3F - 2\phi_i)/r$ | $O(N)$ | $O(1)$ |
| WF$^2$Q | [19] | $(L_i/r_i) + (L_{\max}/r)$ | $O(L_i/r_i)$ | $O(N)$ |
| WF$^2$Q+ | [22] | $(L_i/r_i) + (L_{\max}/r)$ | $O(L_i/r_i)$ | $O(\log N)$ |

(©1997 IEEE)

$^a$In DRR, $F$ is the frame size and $\phi_i$ is the weighting factor of session $i$ in bandwidth allocation.

### 4.5.12 Priorities Sorting Using a Sequencer

This section describes an architecture to implement the packet schedulers. It uses a sorting device, called sequencer, to arrange the departure order of the cells/packets based on the time stamp values, as shown in Figure 4.37 [24]. The example used to illustrate the architecture has $P$ priority levels, $N$ inputs, and one output, but it can be generally applied to more outputs. The write/read controllers generate proper control signals for all other functional blocks. As shown in Figure 4.37, the cells are time-division multiplexed first and then written into the cell pool with idle addresses stored in a FIFO. A pair of a cell's priority field and its corresponding address, denoted as *PA*, is stored in the sequencer in such a way that higher priority pairs (e.g., smaller time stamp values) are always at the right of lower priority ones so they will be accessed sooner by the read controller. Once the pair has been accessed, the address is used to read out the corresponding cell in the cell pool.

The concept of implementing the Sequencer is very simple, as illustrated in Figure 4.38. Assume that the value of $P_n$ is less than that of $P_{n+1}$ and has a higher priority. When a new cell with priority $P_n$ arrives, all pairs on the right of $A_k$, including the $A_k$ itself, remain at their positions while others are shifted to the left. The vacant position is replaced with a pair of the new cell's priority field ($P_n$) and address ($A_n$).

When the cell pool is full (i.e., the idle-address FIFO is empty), the priority field at the left-most position of the sequencer (e.g., $P_z$) is compared to that of the newly arrived cell ($P_n$). If $P_n$ is smaller than $P_z$, the pair of $P_z$ and $A_z$ is pushed away from the sequencer as the new pair $P_nA_n$ is inserted in the sequencer. Meanwhile, the cell with address $A_z$ in the pool is overwritten with the new cell. However, if $P_n \geq P_z$, the new cell is discarded instead.

Both the traffic shaper's architecture and the queue manager's architecture require a sequencer to sort the cells' departure times (DTs) or departure sequences (DSs) in descending order [25]. In [25], Chao and Uzun implemented the sequencer with a VLSI chip, which is essentially a 256-word sorting-memory chip. Figure 4.39 shows the building block of the

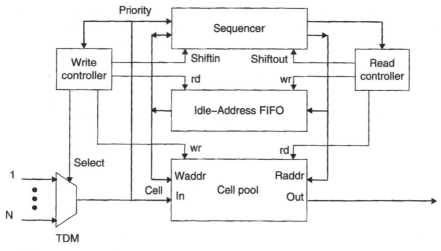

**Figure 4.37** Sorting cell's departure with a sequencer. The sequencer determines the departure sequence for the cells that are stored in the cell pool (©1992 IEEE).

Sequencer

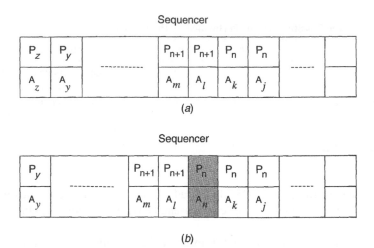

(a)

Sequencer

(b)

**Figure 4.38**  Operations of the sequencer. As a pair of new priority and address is inserted, all pairs with lower priority are pushed to the left.

chip, where the circuit in the dashed box is a module and is repeated 256 times in the chip. Each module has a 24-bit register, which stores the 14-bit DT/DS values and the 10-bit address. A single chip can accommodate a cell pool capacity of up to 256 cells and DT/DS values (or the number of priority levels in some applications) up to $2^{14} - 1$. This provides

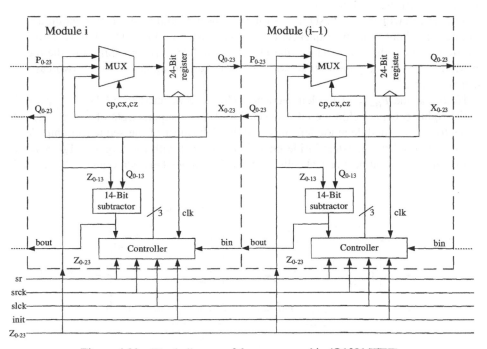

**Figure 4.39**  Block diagram of the sequencer chip (©1991 IEEE).

**TABLE 4.2 Three Possible Actions Performed by the Controller**

| Cases | $b_{out}$ | $b_{in}$ | Action Performed by the Controller |
|---|---|---|---|
| (a) $X_{0-13} \leq Z_{0-13} < Q_{0-13}$ | 1 | 0 | Module $i$ shifts its contents to the left, and $Q_{0-23} = Z_{0-23}$ |
| (b) $Z_{0-13} < X_{0-13} \leq Q_{0-13}$ | 1 | 1 | Both Modules $i$ and $(i-1)$ shift their contents left, and $Q_{0-23} = X_{0-23}$ |
| (c) $X_{0-13} \leq Q_{0-13} \leq Z_{0-13}$ | 0 | 0 | Retain the $Q_{0-23}$ |

the DT/DS ranging from 0 to 4095. By cascading multiple Sequencer chips in series or in parallel, a larger cell pool (e.g., a few thousand cells) or a larger DT/DS value can be supported.

Since every module is identical, let us examine the operations of an arbitrary module, say Module $i$. When a new pair of the DT/DS and the address field, denoted by $Z_{0-23}$, is to be inserted into the sequencer, it is first broadcast to every module. By comparing the DT/DS values ($Q_{0-13}$) of Module ($i-1$) and Module $i$, and the new broadcast value ($Z_{0-13}$), the controller generates signals, $cp$, $cx$, $cz$, and $clk$, to shift the broadcast value ($Z_{0-23}$) into the 24-bit register in Module $i$, shift Module ($i-1$)s $Q_{0-23}$ to the register, or retain the register's original value. Table 4.2 lists these three possible actions performed by the controller, where $X_{0-13}$ is the Module ($i-1$)s $Q_{0-13}$. The $b_{out}$ is the borrow-out of ($Z_{0-13} - Q_{0-13}$), and the $b_{in}$ is the borrow-out of ($Z_{0-13} - X_{0-13}$). Since the smaller DT/DS is always on the right of the larger one, the case where $Q_{0-13} \leq Z_{0-13} < X_{0-13}$, or $b_{out}b_{in} = 01$, will not happen.

When a cell with the smallest DT/DS value is to be transmitted, its corresponding address will be shifted out from the sequencer chip, and the data of all registers will be shifted one position to the right. For instance, the $Q_{0-23}$ in Module $i$ will be shifted to the register in Module ($i-1$). Figure 4.40 shows the connection of signals between two cascaded sequencer chips.

Note that the $P^l_{0-23}$ of the left sequencer chip is connected to all 1s; $X^r_{0-23}$ and $b^l_{in}$ of the right sequencer chip are all connected to 0s. The superscripts of $l$ and $r$ indicate, respectively, the module at the left-most and the right-most of the sequencer chip. At the initialization, all the registers inside the chip are loaded with the largest DT/DS values, that is, all 1s, so that new arrival cells with DT/DS values between 0 and $2^{14} - 1$ can be

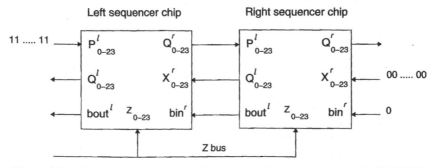

**Figure 4.40** Interconnection signals of two cascaded sequencer chips (©1991 IEEE).

inserted into the sequencer. The initialization is done by asserting the *init* and *srck* signals and setting $Z_{0-23}$ to $11 \ldots 11$.

## 4.6 BUFFER MANAGEMENT

The Internet is based on a connectionless end-to-end service with the advantages of flexibility and robustness. However, careful design is required to provide good service under heavy load situation. In fact, lack of attention to the dynamics of packet forwarding can result in severe service degradation or 'Internet meltdown.' This phenomenon was first observed during the early growth phase of the Internet in mid 1980s [26], and is technically called 'congestion collapse.'

The original fix for Internet meltdown was provided by Van Jacobson. Beginning in 1986, Jacobson developed the congestion avoidance mechanisms that are now implemented in TCP [27, 28]. These mechanisms operate in the hosts to make TCP connections to 'back off' during congestion. We say that TCP flows are 'responsive' to congestion signals (i.e., packets being dropped) from the network. It is primarily these TCP congestion avoidance algorithms that prevent today's Internet from congestion collapse.

However, that is not the end of the story. Considerable research has been done on Internet dynamics since 1988. It has become clear that the TCP congestion avoidance mechanisms [29], while necessary and powerful, are not sufficient to provide good service in all circumstances. Basically, there is a limit to how much control can be accomplished from the edges of the network. Beside packet scheduling algorithms, buffer management mechanisms are needed in the routers to complement the endpoint congestion avoidance mechanisms. Below we present some examples of the buffer management in the Internet.

### 4.6.1 Tail Drop

The traditional technique for managing router queue lengths is tail drop (TD), which sets a maximum length (in terms of packets) for each queue, accepts packets for the queue until the maximum length is reached (i.e., we say the queue is full), and then drops subsequent incoming packets until the queue decreases because a packet from the queue has been transmitted.

Tail drop is very simple but it has two important drawbacks. First, in some situations tail drop allows a single connection or a few flows to monopolize queue space, preventing other connections from getting room in the queue. This 'lock-out' phenomenon is often the result of synchronization or other timing effects.

Second, tail drop allows queues to maintain a full (or, almost full) status for long periods of time, since tail drop signals congestion (via a packet drop) only when the queue has become full. It is important to reduce the steady-state queue size for queue management, because even though TCP constrains a flow's window size, packets often arrive at routers in bursts [30]. If the queue is full or almost full, an arriving burst will cause multiple packets to be dropped. This can result in a global synchronization of flows throttling back, followed by a sustained period of lowered link utilization, reducing overall throughput.

The point of buffering in the network is to absorb data bursts and to transmit them during the ensuing bursts of silence [31]. This is essential to permit the transmission of bursty data. According to [31], queue limits should not reflect the steady state queues we want maintained in the network; instead, they should reflect the size of bursts we need to absorb.

### 4.6.2 Drop on Full

Besides tail drop, there are two alternative drop on full disciplines: *random drop on full* or *drop front on full*. Under the random drop on full discipline, a router drops a randomly selected packet from the queue when the queue is full and a new packet arrives. While, under the drop front on full discipline [32], the router drops the packet at the front of the queue when the queue is full and a new packet arrives. This facilitates TCP with faster response to network congestion, resulting in a higher throughput. Both of these solve the lock-out problem, but neither solves the full-queues problem described above.

### 4.6.3 Random Early Detection (RED)

In the current Internet, dropped packets serve as a critical mechanism of congestion notification to end nodes. The solution to the full-queues problem is for routers to drop packets before a queue becomes full, so that end nodes can respond to congestion before buffers overflow. This proactive approach is called 'active queue management' according to [31]. Random Early Detection (RED) [33] drops arriving packets probabilistically. The probability of drop increases as the estimated average queue size grows. Thus, if the queue has been mostly empty in the 'recent past,' RED will not tend to drop packets unless the queue overflows. On the other hand, if the queue has recently been relatively full, indicating persistent congestion, newly arriving packets are more likely to be dropped [31, 33].

The RED algorithm itself consists of two main parts: estimation of the average queue size and the decision of whether or not to drop an incoming packet. The RED calculates the average queue size $avg$, using a low-pass filter with an exponential weighted moving average. The average queue size is compared to two thresholds, a minimum threshold $min_{th}$ and a maximum threshold $max_{th}$. When the average queue size is less than the minimum threshold, no packets are marked. When the average queue size is greater than the maximum threshold, every arriving packet is marked. If marked packets are in fact dropped, or if all source nodes are cooperative, this ensures that the average queue size does not significantly exceed the maximum threshold.

When the average queue size is between the minimum and the maximum threshold, each arriving packet is marked with probability $p_a$, where $p_a$ is a function of the average queue size $avg$. Each time a packet is marked, the probability that a packet is marked from a particular connection is roughly proportional to that connection's share of the bandwidth at the router. The general RED algorithm is given in Figure 4.41.

The RED router has two separate algorithms. The algorithm for computing the average queue size determines the degree of burstiness that will be allowed in the router queue. The algorithm for calculating the packet-marking probability determines how frequently the router marks packets, given the current level of congestion. The goal is for the router to mark packets at fairly evenly spaced intervals to avoid biases and global synchronization, and to mark packets sufficiently frequently to control the average queue size.

The detailed algorithm for the RED is given in Figure 4.42. The router calculates $avg$ at each packet arrival using

$$avg \leftarrow avg + w \cdot (q - avg)$$

```
for each packet arrival
calculate the average queue size avg
if min_th ≤ avg < max_th
     calculate probability p_a
     with probability p_a:
          mark the arriving packet
else if max_th ≤ avg
     mark the arriving packet
else
     admit the arriving packet in the buffer.
```

**Figure 4.41**  General algorithm for RED routers.

When the queue is empty (the idle period), it considers this period by estimating the number $m$ of small packets that *could* have been transmitted during this idle period,

$$avg \leftarrow (1 - w)^m avg,$$

where $m$ is equal to the queue idle time ($time - q\_time$) divided by the small packet transmission time ($s$), as shown in Figure 4.42. That is, after the idle period, the router computes the average queue size as if $m$ packets had arrived to an empty queue during that period.

As avg varies from $min_{th}$ to $max_{th}$, the packet-marking probability (or drop probability) $p_b$ varies linearly from 0 to $P_{max}$:

$$p_b \leftarrow P_{max}(avg - min_{th})/(max_{th} - min_{th}),$$

as illustrated in Figure 4.43.

The final packet-marking probability $p_a$ increases slowly as the count (the number of packets) increases since the last marked packet:

$$p_a \leftarrow p_b/(1 - count \cdot p_b),$$

which ensures that the router does not wait too long before marking a packet. The larger the count, the higher the marking probability. The router marks each packet that arrives at the router when the average queue size *avg* exceeds $max_{th}$.

One option for the RED router is to measure the queue in bytes rather than in packets. With this option, the average queue size accurately reflects the average delay at the router. When this option is used, the algorithm would be modified to ensure that the probability that a packet is marked is proportional to the packet size in bytes:

$$p_b \leftarrow P_{max}(avg - min_{th})/(max_{th} - min_{th})$$

$$p_b \leftarrow p_b \cdot \text{PacketSize}/\text{MaximumPacketSize}$$

$$p_a \leftarrow p_b/(1 - count \cdot p_b)$$

In this case, a large FTP packet is more likely to be marked than is a small TELNET packet.

The queue weight $w$ is determined by the size and duration of bursts in queue size that are allowed at the router. The minimum and maximum thresholds $min_{th}$ and $max_{th}$ are determined by the desired average queue size. The average queue size that makes the

**Saved Variables:**

| | |
|---|---|
| $avg$: | average queue size |
| $q\_time$: | start of the queue idle time |
| $count$: | number of packets since last dropped packet |

**Fixed Parameters:**

| | |
|---|---|
| $w$: | queue weight |
| $min_{th}$: | minimum queue length threshold |
| $max_{th}$: | maximum queue length threshold |
| $P_{max}$: | maximum value for $p_b$ |
| $s$: | typical transmission time (of a small packet) |

**Others:**

| | |
|---|---|
| $q$: | current queue size |
| $p_a$: | current packet-marking probability |
| $time$: | current time |

Initialization:
    $count \leftarrow -1$
    $avg \leftarrow 0$
for each packet arrival
    calculate the new average queue size $avg$:
        if the queue is non-empty
            $avg \leftarrow avg + w \cdot (q - avg)$
        else
            $m = (time - q\_time)/s$
            $avg \leftarrow (1 - w)^m avg$
    if $min_{th} \leq avg < max_{th}$
        increment $count$
        calculate probability $p_a$:
            $p_b \leftarrow P_{max}(avg - min_{th})/(max_{th} - min_{th})$
            $p_a \leftarrow p_b/(1 - count \cdot p_b)$
        with probability $p_a$:
            mark the arriving packet
            $count \leftarrow 0$
    else if $max_{th} \leq avg$
        mark the arriving packet
        $count \leftarrow 0$
    else $count \leftarrow -1$
when queue becomes empty
    $q\_time \leftarrow time$

**Figure 4.42**   Detailed algorithm for RED routers.

desired tradeoffs (such as the tradeoff between maximizing throughput and minimizing delay) depends on network characteristics [33].

The RED mechanism relies on *random* dropping decisions when the buffer content exceeds a given threshold, so that heavy flows experience a larger number of dropped packets in case of congestion. Hence, the RED aims at penalizing flows in proportion to the amount of traffic they contribute, and prevents any of them from grabbing a disproportionate amount of resources.

The probability that a packet from a particular flow is dropped is roughly proportional to the flow's share of the link bandwidth. Thus, a flow that is utilizing a larger share of the link

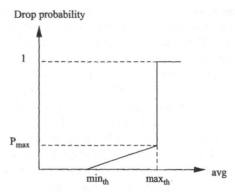

**Figure 4.43**   RED algorithm.

bandwidth is forced to reduce its rate rather quickly. One of the main advantages of RED is that it does not require per flow state to be maintained in the router. As a result, RED is relatively simple to implement and can be used in conjunction with the simple first-in-first-out (FIFO) scheduler to reduce congestion in the network. This can be of significance in the Internet backbone, where there may be hundreds of thousands of flows on a given link.

RED effectively controls the average queue size while still accommodating bursts of packets without loss. RED's use of randomness breaks up synchronized processes that lead to lock-out phenomena. There have been several implementations of RED in routers, and papers have been published reporting on experience with these implementations [34–36]. For example, weighted RED (WRED) [34] combines the capabilities of the RED algorithm with IP precedence (a three-bit field in the IP packet header). This combination provides for preferential traffic handling for high-priority packets. It can selectively discard lower-priority traffic when the router interface starts to get congested, and can provide differentiated performance characteristics for different classes of service. All available empirical evidence shows that the deployment of active queue management mechanisms in the Internet would have substantial performance benefits [31].

### 4.6.4   Differential Dropping: RIO

RIO stands for RED routers with In/Out bit [37, 38]. It is designed to support Assured Service in the Differentiated Services Internet [5]. The general approach of this service mechanism is to define a *service allocation profile* for each user, and to design a mechanism (e.g., RIO) in the router that favors traffic that is within those service allocation profiles. The basic idea is to monitor the traffic of each user as it enters the network, and tag packets as either In or Out of their service allocation profiles, then at each congested router, preferentially drop packets that are tagged as being Out. The idea of using In/Out is the same as used with the cell loss priority (CLP) bit in ATM networks.

Inside the network, at the routers, there is no separation of traffic from different users into different flows or queues. The packets of all users are aggregated into one queue, just as they are today. Different users can have very different profiles, which will result in different users having different quantities of In packets in the service queue. A router can treat these packets as a single common pool. This attribute of the scheme makes it very easy to implement.

RIO uses the same mechanism as RED, but is configured with two sets of parameters, one for In packets and the other for Out packets. By choosing the parameters for respective algorithms differently, RIO is able to discriminate against Out packets in times of congestion and preferentially drop Out packets.

In particular, upon each packet arrival at the router, the router checks whether the packet is tagged as In or Out. If it is an In packet, the router calculates $avg_{in}$, the average queue size for the In packets; if it is an Out packet, the router calculates $avg_{total}$, the average queue size for all (both In and Out) arriving packets. The probability of dropping an In packet depends on $avg_{in}$, and the probability of dropping an Out packet depends on $avg_{total}$.

As shown in Figure 4.44, there are three parameters for each of the twin algorithms. The three parameters, $min_{in}$, $max_{in}$, and $P_{max_{in}}$, define the normal operation $[0, min_{in})$, congestion avoidance $[min_{in}, max_{in})$, and congestion control $[max_{in}, \infty)$ phases for In packets. Similarly, $min_{out}$, $max_{out}$, and $P_{max_{out}}$ define the corresponding phases for Out packets.

The discrimination against Out packets in RIO is created by carefully choosing the parameters. First, by choosing $min_{out} < min_{in}$ the RIO router drops Out packets much earlier than it drops In packets. Second, in the congestion avoidance phase, it drops Out packets with a larger probability, by setting $P_{max_{out}} > P_{max_{in}}$. Third, it goes into congestion control phase for the Out packets much earlier than for the In packets, by choosing $max_{out} \ll max_{in}$. In essence, RIO drops Out packets first when it detects incipient congestion, and drops all Out packets if the congestion persists. Only when the router is flooded with In packets, as a last resort, it drops In packets in the hope of controlling congestion. In a well-provisioned network, this should never happen. If it does, it is a clear indication that the network is underprovisioned.

Figure 4.45 shows the RIO algorithm. By using $avg\_total$ to determine the probability of dropping an Out packet, routers can maintain short queue length and high throughput no matter what kind of traffic mix it has. The Out packets represent opportunistic traffic, and there is no valid indication of what amount of Out packets is proper. Simply using the average Out packet queue size to control the dropping of Out packets would not cover the case where the total queue is growing due to arriving In packets.

### 4.6.5 Fair Random Early Detection (FRED)

As pointed out in [39], RED does not always ensure all flows a fair share of bandwidth. In fact, RED is unfair to low speed TCP flows. This is because RED randomly drops

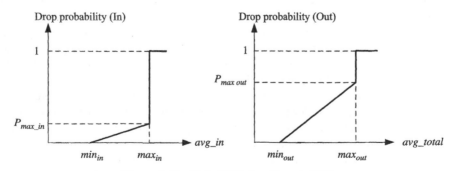

**Figure 4.44** Twin RED algorithms in RIO.

```
For each packet arrival
    if it is an In packet
        calculate the average In queue size avg_in;
    else calculate the average queue size avg_total;

If it is an In packet
    if min_in ≤ avg_in < max_in
        calculate probability P_in;
        with probability P_in drop this packet;
    else if max_in ≤ avg_in
        drop this packet.

If it is an Out packet
    if min_out ≤ avg_total < max_out
        calculate probability P_out;
        with probability P_out drop this packet;
    else if max_out ≤ avg_total
        drop this packet.
```

**Figure 4.45**   RIO algorithm.

packets when the maximum threshold is crossed and it is possible that one of these packets belongs to a flow that is currently using less than its fair share of bandwidth. Since TCP reacts rather strongly to packet loss, the lost packet will force further reduction in the congestion window resulting in an even lower rate. The fair random early detection (FRED) mechanism, presented in [39] as a modification to RED, intends to reduce some of its unfairness. Basically, FRED generates selective feedback to a filtered set of connections that have a large number of packets queued.

In brief, FRED acts just like RED, but with the following additions. FRED introduces the parameters $min_q$ and $max_q$, which are the minimum and maximum number of packets each flow should be allowed to buffer. FRED introduces the global variable $avgcq$, an estimate of the average per-flow buffer count; flows with fewer than $avgcq$ packets queued are favored over flows with more. FRED maintains a count of buffered packets $qlen$ for each flow that currently has any packets buffered. FRED maintains a variable *strike* for each flow, which counts the number of times the flow has failed to respond to congestion notification; FRED penalizes flows with high *strike* values.

FRED allows each connection to buffer $min_q$ packets without loss. All additional packets are subject to RED's random drop. An incoming packet is always accepted if the connection has fewer than $min_q$ packets buffered and the average buffer size is less than $max_{th}$. Normally, a TCP connection sends no more than three packets back-to-back: two because of delayed ACK, and one more due to a window increase. Therefore, $min_q$ is set to two to four packets.

When the number of active connections is small ($N \ll (min_{th}/min_q)$), FRED allows each connection to buffer $min_q$ number of packets without dropping. It also dynamically raises $min_q$ to the average per-connection queue length ($avgcq$). For simplicity, it calculates this value by dividing the average queue length ($avg$) by the current number of active connections. A connection is active when it has packets buffered, and is inactive otherwise.

FRED never lets a flow buffer more than $max_q$ packets, and counts the number of times each flow tries to exceed $max_q$ in the per-flow *strike* variable. Flows with high *strike* values are not allowed to queue more than $avgcq$ packets; that is, they are not allowed to use more packets than the average flow. This allows adaptive flows to send bursts of packets, but prevents nonadaptive flaws from consistently monopolizing the buffer space.

The original RED estimates the average queue length at each packet arrival. In FRED, the averaging is done at arrival and departure. Therefore, the sampling frequency is the maximum of the input and output rate, which helps reflect the queue variation accurately. In addition, FRED does not modify the average if the incoming packet is dropped unless the instantaneous queue length is zero. Without this change, the same queue length could be sampled multiple times when the input rate is substantially higher than the output link rate. This change also prevents an abusive user from defeating the purpose of the low pass filter, even if all his/her packets are dropped. Interested readers are referred to [39] for further details of the FRED algorithm.

### 4.6.6 Stabilized Random Early Detection (SRED)

Similar to RED, stabilized RED (SRED) [40] preemptively discards packets with a load-dependent probability when a buffer in a router seems congested. SRED has an additional feature, that, over a wide range of load levels, helps it stabilize its buffer occupation at a level independent of the number of active connections. SRED does this by estimating the number of active connections or flows. This estimate is obtained without collecting or analyzing state information on individual flows, as FRED does [39].

The main idea is to compare, whenever a packet arrives at some buffer, the arriving packet with a randomly chosen packet that recently preceded it into the buffer. When the two packets are of the same flow, we declare a *hit*. The sequence of hits is used in two ways, and with two different objectives in mind:

- To estimate the number of active flows.
- To find candidates for misbehaving flow.

The definition of *hit* can be flexible. The strongest plausible requirement is to declare a *hit* only when the two packets indeed are of the same flow: same destination and source addresses, same destination and source port numbers, and same protocol identifiers. Alternatively, one could use a more lax definition of *hit*, for example only the same source address. We may also choose not to check for a hit for every arriving packet. Instead, we can test for hits for only a random or deterministic subsequence of arriving packets. Also, we can compare the arriving packet with not one, but with some $K > 1$ randomly chosen packets from the recent past. That would give information of the type '$J$ out of $K$' hits, which can be used to more accurately estimate the number of flows.

Rather than maintaining per-flow state, a small cache is used to store a list of $M$ recently seen flows, with the following extra information for each flow in the list: a *Count* and a *time stamp*. The list is called *zombie list* according to [40] and the flows in the list *zombies*.

The zombie list starts out empty. As packets arrive, as long as the list is not full, for every arriving packet, the packet flow identifier (source address, destination address, etc.) is added to the list, the *Count* of that zombie is set to zero, and its time stamp is set to the arrival time of the packet.

Once the zombie list is full, it works as follows: Whenever a packet arrives, it is compared with a randomly chosen zombie in the zombie list.

*Hit.* If the arriving packet's flow matches the zombie we declare a *hit*. In that case, the *Count* of the zombie is increased by one, and the time stamp is reset to the arrival time of the packet in the buffer.

*No hit.* If the two are not of the same flow, we declare a *no hit*. In that case, with probability $p$ the flow identifier of the packet is overwritten over the zombie chosen for comparison. The *Count* of the zombie is set to zero, and the time stamp is set to the arrival time at the buffer. With probability $1 - p$ there is no change to the zombie list.

Irrespective of whether there was a hit or not, the packet may be dropped if the buffer occupancy is such that the system is in random drop mode. The drop probability may depend on whether there was a hit or not.

Define $P(t)$ to be an estimate for the hit frequency around the time of the arrival of the $t$th packet at the buffer. For the $t$th packet, let

$$h(t) = \begin{cases} 0 & \text{if no hit,} \\ 1 & \text{if hit,} \end{cases} \qquad (4.23)$$

and let

$$P(t) = (1 - \alpha)P(t - 1) + \alpha h(t), \qquad (4.24)$$

with $0 < \alpha < 1$. It has been shown in [40] that $P(t)^{-1}$ is a good estimate for the effective number of active flows in the time shortly before the arrival of packet $t$.

To reduce comparison overhead, it is allowable to update $P(t)$ not after every packet, but say after every $L$ packets or at predetermined epochs. If $H$ hits are got out of $L$ packets, a possible update rule is

$$P(\text{new}) = (1 - L\alpha)P(\text{old}) + \alpha H. \qquad (4.25)$$

As long as $0 \leq L\alpha \ll 1$, this has practically the same effect as updating after every packet [40].

Let us denote the packet drop probability function by $p_z$. According to [40], a function $q(x)$ is defined as follows:

$$q(x) = \begin{cases} p_{\max} & \text{if } \dfrac{B}{3} \leq x < B, \\[2mm] \dfrac{p_{\max}}{4} & \text{if } \dfrac{B}{6} \leq x < \dfrac{B}{3}, \\[2mm] 0 & \text{if } 0 \leq x < \dfrac{B}{6}, \end{cases} \qquad (4.26)$$

where $B$ is the buffer size, $x$ is the backlog, and $p_{\max}$ is a parameter ranging between 0 and 1. The range of interest for $p_{\max}$ is $(0.09, 0.15)$ according to [40]. Higher values for $p_{\max}$ merely serve to drive too many TCP flows into time-out, while much lower values allow relatively large congestion windows.

When packet $t$ arrives at the buffer, SRED first updates $P(t)$ from Eq. (4.24). If at the arrival instant the buffer contains $x$ bytes, SRED drops the packet with probability $p_z$ which equals

$$p_z = q(x) \times \min\left\{1, \frac{1}{[\beta P(t)]^2}\right\} \times \left[1 + \frac{h(t)}{P(t)}\right], \qquad (4.27)$$

where $\beta$ is a parameter with the suggested value 256 according to [40].

Note that, unlike RED, SRED does not compute average queue length (this operation can easily be added if needed). In [40], it has been shown that using an averaged buffer occupation does not improve performance. The motivation for choosing (4.26) and (4.27) is multifold. First, the buffer occupancy can vary considerably because of widely varying round-trip times, flows using different maximum segment sizes (MSSs), and transients caused by new flows before they reach the equilibrium of TCP flow and congestion control window. By making the drop probability depend on the buffer occupancy, which is the role of $q$ in (4.27), SRED ensures that the drop probability increases when the buffer occupancy increases, even when the estimate $P(t)$ remains the same.

The ratio 4 in Eq. (4.26) is chosen such that TCP connections reach the new equilibrium after a single packet loss. When $0 \leq P(t) < 1/\beta$, SRED uses $p_z = q$ according to Eq. (4.27). This is for two reasons. First, if the drop probability becomes too large, TCP flows spend much or most of their time in time-out. So further increasing $p_z$ is not sensible. Second, when $P(t)$ becomes small (when hits are rare), estimating $P(t)$ becomes unreliable.

SRED uses hits directly in the dropping probabilities, as indicated by the last term $[1 + (h(t)/P(t))]$ in (4.27). This is based on the idea that misbehaving flows are likely to generate more hits. There are two reasons. First, misbehaving flows by definition have more packet arrivals than other flows and so trigger more comparisons. Second, they are more likely to be present in the zombie list. This increases the drop probability for overactive flows and can also reduce TCP's bias in favor of flows with short RTTs. Interested readers are referred to [40] for further details on the SRED algorithm.

### 4.6.7 Longest Queue Drop (LQD)

Motivated by the fact that if connections are given equal weights, then connections that use the link more (get a higher share of the bandwidth unused by other connections) tend to have longer queues, longest queue drop (LQD) was proposed in [41] for buffer management. Biasing the packet drops such that connections with longer queues have higher drop rates should make the bandwidth sharing more fair. In addition, the LQD policy offers some flow isolation and protection since if one connection misbehaves consistently, only this connection experiences an increased loss rate.

The LQD requires searching through the backlogged queues to determine which is the longest queue. Ref. [41] proposes a variant of LQD that is particularly easy to implement, approximated longest queue drop (ALQD). A register holds the length and identity of the longest queue as determined at the previous queuing operation (queue, dequeue, drop). On every queuing event (including enqueuing and dequeuing), the current queue length is compared with the longest queue identified in the register. If it is the same queue, the queue length in the register is adjusted. If the current queue is longer, its identity and length are now stored in the register. A similar scheme called Quasi-Pushout is proposed in [42]. Below we briefly introduce the ALQD algorithm and present an implementation architecture.

```
for i = 0 to N − 1
/* N is the number of queues. Each queue may correspond to each port of a switch */
{
    if (queue i has an arriving packet) {
        if (data memory full) {
            push out HOL packet of current Qmax;
            decrement length of current Qmax by length of the dropped packet;
        }
        store cell-by-cell the incoming packet;
        increment length of queue i by length of the incoming packet;
        if (current Qmax is shorter than queue i)
            assign queue i as the new Qmax;
    }
    if (queue j has a departing packet) {
        send out the packet;
        decrement its queue length by length of the outgoing packet;
    }
    if (current Qmax is shorter than queue j)
        assign queue j as the new Qmax;
}
```

**Figure 4.46**    ALQD scheme.

Instead of sorting out the real longest queue among $N$ flow queues, the ALQD [41] tracks the quasi-longest queue ($Q_{max}$) by using three comparisons only. One is on the arrival of a packet: the queue length of the destined queue is increased and compared with that of the $Q_{max}$. The other two are on the departure or dropping of a packet: the queue length of the selected queue is decreased and compared with that of the $Q_{max}$. If the new length of the destined/selected queue is greater than that of the $Q_{max}$, the flow identifier (FID) and length of the $Q_{max}$ are replaced with that of the particular queue. That is, the destined/selected queue becomes the new $Q_{max}$.

The ALQD drops the HOL packet of the currently longest queue when the data memory is full, because dropping from the front can trigger TCP's fast retransmit/recovery feature faster and, hence, increase throughput [41]. Figure 4.46 shows the ALQD algorithm.

Since packets are of variable length, they are divided into a number of fixed-length segments (or cells) to fully use the data memory in routers. The above algorithm actually checks on each packet arrival whether the data memory is full. Therefore, dropping a packet will guarantee sufficient memory space for the incoming cell. It is not necessary to double check the memory status after dropping a packet. A packet arrival event is defined as when its last cell has arrived at the system. Similarly, a packet departure event is when its last cell has left the system. The queue length updates are performed on packet arrival/departure/dropping events.

ALQD requires only $O(1)$ complexity in time and space. However, its state does not reflect exactly the state of the system. So optimal behavior at all times cannot be ensured especially when scheduling weights vary over a very wide range. A scenario could be constructed where ALQD cannot free enough memory and some incoming packets would have to be dropped, thereby temporarily breaching the strict flow isolation property of LQD. However, the degradation is such that it makes the complexity-performance tradeoff worthwhile [41].

## REFERENCES

[1] S. Shenker and J. Wroclawski, *Network element service specification template*, RFC 2216 (Informational), Sept. 1997. [Online]. Available at: http://www.ietf.org/rfc/rfc2216.txt

[2] "Data link provider interface (DLPI)," The Open Group, Jan. 2000.

[3] H. J. Lee, M. S. Kim, W. K. Hong, and G. H. Lee, "QoS parameters to network performance metrics mapping for SLA monitoring," *KNOM Review*, vol. 5, no. 2 (Dec. 2002).

[4] Z. Wang, *Internet QoS: Architectures and Mechanisms for Quality of Service*, Morgan Kaufmann, San Francisco, California, 2001.

[5] S. Blake, D. Black, M. Carlson, E. Davies, Z. Wang, and W. Weiss, *An architecture for differentiated service*, RFC 2475 (Informational), Dec. 1998, updated by RFC 3260. [Online]. Available at: http://www.ietf.org/rfc/rfc2475.txt

[6] Cisco. [Online]. Available at: http://www.cisco.com/univercd/cc/td/doc/product/software/ios120/12cgcr/qos_c/qcpart4/qcpolts.htm

[7] S. Shenker and J. Wroclawski, *General characterization parameters for integrated service network elements*, RFC 2215 (Proposed Standard), Sept. 1997. [Online]. Available at: http://www.ietf.org/rfc/rfc2215.txt

[8] D. Bertsekas and R. Gallager, *Data Networks*, 2nd ed., Prentice-Hall, Englewood Cliff, NJ, 1992.

[9] N. McKeown, *Packet switch architectures class*. [Online]. Available at: http://klamath.stanford.edu/~nickm

[10] P. Marbach, "Priority service and max-min fairness," *IEEE/ACM Transactions on Networking*, vol. 11, no. 5, pp. 733–746 (Oct. 2003).

[11] M. Shreedhar and G. Varghese, "Efficient fair queueing using deficit round-robin," *IEEE/ACM Transactions on Networking*, vol. 4, issue 3, pp. 375–385 (June 1996).

[12] A. Parekh and R. Gallager, "A generalized processor sharing approach to flow control in integrated services networks: the single node case," *IEEE/ACM Transactions on Networking*, vol. 1, issue 2, pp. 344–357 (June 1993).

[13] A. Parekh and R. Gallager, "A generalized processor sharing approach to flow control in integrated services networks: the multiple node case," *IEEE/ACM Transactions on Networking*, vol. 2, issue 2, pp. 137–150 (Apr. 1994).

[14] D. Stiliadis, "Traffic scheduling in packet-switched networks: analysis, design, and implementation," Ph.D. Dissertation, University of California, Santa Cruz, June 1996.

[15] J. Bennett, D. C. Stephens, and H. Zhang, "High speed, scalable, and accurate implementation of fair queueing algorithms in ATM networks," in *Proc. IEEE ICNP'97*, Atlanta, Georgia, pp. 7–14 (1997).

[16] L. Zhang, "Virtual clock: a new traffic control algorithm for packet switching networks," in *Proc. ACM SIGCOMM*, Philadelphia, Pennysylvania, pp. 19–29 (Sept. 1990).

[17] S. J. Golestani, "A self-clocked fair queueing scheme for broadband applications," in *Proc. IEEE INFOCOM*, Toronto, Canada, pp. 636–646 (June 1994).

[18] D. Stiliadis and A. Varma, "Latency-rate servers: a general model for analysis of traffic scheduling algorithms," in *Proc. IEEE INFOCOM*, San Francisco, California, vol. 1, pp. 111–119 (Mar. 1996).

[19] J. C. Bennett and H. Zhang, "$WF^2Q$: worst-case fair weighted fair queueing," in *Proc. IEEE INFOCOM*, San Francisco, California, vol. 1, pp. 120–128 (Mar. 1996).

[20] D. Stiliadis and A. Varma, "A general methodology for design efficient traffic scheduling and shaping algortihms," in *Proc. IEEE INFOCOM'97*, Kobe, Japan, vol. 1, pp. 326–335 (Apr. 1997).

[21] D. Stiliadis and A. Varma, "Efficient fair queueing algorithms for packet-switched networks," *IEEE/ACM Transactions on Networking*, vol. 6, issue 2, pp. 175–185 (Apr. 1998).

[22] J. Bennett and H. Zhang, "Hierarchical packet fair queuing algorithms," *IEEE/ACM Transactions on Networking*, vol. 5, no. 5, pp. 675–689 (Oct. 1997).

[23] S. Suri, G. Varghese, and G. Chandranmenon, "Leap forward virtual clock: a new fair queueing scheme with guaranteed delays and throughput fairness," in *Proc. IEEE INFOCOM*, Kobe, Japan, vol. 2, pp. 557–565 (Apr. 1997).

[24] H. Chao, "A novel architecture for queue management in the ATM network," *IEEE Journal on Selected Areas in Communications*, vol. 9, issue 7, pp. 1110–1118 (Sept. 1991).

[25] H. Chao and N. Uzun, "A VLSI sequencer chip for ATM traffic shaper and queue manager," *IEEE Journal of Solid-State Circuits*, vol. 27, no. 11, pp. 1634–1643 (Nov. 1992).

[26] J. Nagle, *Congestion control in IP/TCP internetworks*, RFC 896, Jan. 1984. [Online]. Available at: http://www.ietf.org/rfc/rfc896.txt

[27] V. Jacobson, "Congestion avoidance and control," in *Proc. ACM SIGCOMM '88*, Stanford, California, vol. 18, no. 4, pp. 314–329 (Aug. 1988).

[28] R. Braden, *Requirements for Internet Hosts – Communication Layers*, RFC 1122 (Standard), Oct. 1989. [Online.] Available at: http://www.ietf.org/rfc/rfc1122.txt

[29] W. Stevens, *TCP slow start, congestion avoidance, fast retransmit, and fast recovery algorithms*, RFC 2001 (Proposed Standard), Jan. 1997, obsoleted by RFC 2581. [Online]. Available at: http://www.ietf.org/rfc/rfc2001.txt

[30] W. Leland, M. Taqqu, W. Willinger, and D. Wilson, "On the self-similar nature of ethernet traffic (Extended Version)," *IEEE/ACM Transactions on Networking*, vol. 2, issue 1, pp. 1–15 (Feb. 1994).

[31] B. Braden, D. Clark, J. Crowcroft, B. Davie, S. Deering, D. Estrin, S. Floyd, V. Jacobson, G. Minshall, C. Partridge, L. Peterson, K. Ramakrishnan, S. Shenker, J. Wroclawski, and L. Zhang, *Recommendations on queue management and congestion avoidance in the Internet*, RFC 2309 (Informational), Apr. 1998. [Online]. Available at: http://www.ietf.org/rfc/rfc2309.txt

[32] T. V. Lakshman, A. Neidhardt, and T. Ott, "The drop from front strategy in TCP over ATM and its interworking with other control features," in *Proc. IEEE INFOCOM*, San Francisco, California, pp. 1242–1250 (Mar. 1996).

[33] S. Floyd and V. Jacobson, "Random early detection gateways for congestion avoidance," *IEEE/ACM Transactions on Networking*, vol. 2, no. 4, pp. 397–413 (Aug. 1993).

[34] *Quality of Service (QoS) Networking*, Cisco Systems, June 1999, white paper.

[35] C. Villamizar and C. Song, "High performance TCP in ANSNET," *Computer Communications Review*, vol. 24, issue 5, pp. 45–60 (Oct. 1994).

[36] M. Gaynor, *Proactive packet dropping methods for TCP gateways*, Oct. 1996. [Online]. Available at: http://www.eecs.harvard.edu/~gaynor/final.ps

[37] D. Clark and J. Wroclawski, "An approach to service allocation in the internet," July 1997, Internet Draft: draft-diff-svc-alloc-00.txt

[38] K. Nichols, V. Jacobson, and L. Zhang, "A two-bit differentiated services architecture for the internet," Nov. 1997, Internet Draft: draft-nichols-diff-svc-arch-00.txt

[39] D. Lin and R. Morris, "Dynamics of random early detection," in *Proc. SIGCOMM*, Cannes, France, pp. 127–137 (Sept. 1997).

[40] T. Ott, T. Lakshman, and L. Wong, "SRED: stabilized RED," in *Proc. IEEE INFOCOM*, New York, NY, vol. 3, pp. 1346–1355 (Mar. 1999).

[41] B. Suter, T. V. Lakshman, D. Stiliadis, and A. K. Choudhury, "Design considerations for supporting TCP with per-flow queueing," in *Proc. IEEE INFOCOM*, San Francisco, California, vol. 1, pp. 299–306 (Mar. 1998).

[42] Y. S. Lin and C. B. Shung, "Quasi-pushout cell discarding," *IEEE Communications Letters*, vol. 1, issue 5, pp. 146–148 (Sept. 1997).

# CHAPTER 5

# BASICS OF PACKET SWITCHING

An Internet Protocol (IP) router is a vital network node in today's packet switching network. It consists of multiple input/output ports. Packets from different places arrive at the input ports of the IP router. They are delivered to appropriate output ports by a switch fabric according to a forwarding table, which is updated by routing protocols. In the packet switch network, packets from various input ports may destine for the same output port simultaneously, resulting in output port contention. How to arbitrate and schedule packets when contention arises is an important and challenging issue in designing a high-performance scalable packet switch.

Traditional telephony networks use circuit switching techniques to establish connections. In the circuit switching scheme, there is usually a centralized processor that determines all the connections between input and output ports. Each connection lasts for an average of 3 minutes. For an $N \times N$ switch, there are at most $N$ connections simultaneously and the time required to make each connection is 180 seconds divided by $N$. For instance, if $N$ is 1000, the time to make a connection is at most 180 ms, which is quite relaxed for most of switch fabrics using current technology, such as CMOS crosspoint switch chips. However, for IP routers, the time needed to configure the input–output connections is much more stringent, and it is normally based on a fixed-length time slot. For instance, it could be as small as 64 bytes to cope with the smallest packet length of 40 bytes. For a 10 Gbit/s line, the slot time is about 50 ns. As the line bit rate increases and the number of the switch ports increases, the time needed for each connection is further reduced. As a result, it is impractical to employ centralized connection processors to establish connections between the inputs and the outputs.

Thus, for IP routers, we do not use a centralized connection processor to establish connections. But rather, a self-routing scheme is used to establish input–output connections in a distributed manner. In other words, the switch fabric has intelligence to route packets to proper

*High Performance Switches and Routers*, by H. Jonathan Chao and Bin Liu
Copyright © 2007 John Wiley & Sons, Inc.

output ports, based on the physical output port addresses attached in front of each packet. One of switch fabrics that have self-routing capability is, for instance, the banyan switch.

In addition to routing packets in the IP router, another important function is to resolve the output port contention when more than one packet is destined for the same output port at the same time. There are several contention-resolution schemes that have been proposed since the first packet switch architecture was proposed in early 1980s. One way to resolve the contention is to allow all packets that are destined for the same output port to arrive at the output port simultaneously. Since only one packet can be transmitted via the output link at a time, the remaining packets are queued at the output port. A switch with such architecture is called the output-buffered switch. For such a scheme, there is a need to operate the switch fabric and the memory at $N$ times of the line speed, where $N$ is the switch size. As the line speed or the switch port number increases, this scheme becomes practically impossible to implement. However, if all packets are not allowed to go to the same output port at a time, a scheduling scheme (or called arbitration scheme) is required to arbitrate the packets that are destined for the same output port. Packets that lose contention have to wait at the input buffer. A switch with such architecture is called the input-buffered switch.

The way of handling output contention will impact the switch performance, complexity, and implementation cost. Some schemes are implemented in a centralized manner and some in a distributed manner. The latter usually allows the switch to be scaled in both line rate and switch size while the former is for a smaller size switch and is usually less complex. In addition to scheduling packets at the inputs when resolving output port contention, packet scheduling is also implemented at the output of the switch. It schedules packet transmission order according to their priorities and/or allocated bandwidth to meet each connection's delay/throughput (i.e., quality of service) requirements. Packet scheduling to achieve quality of service requirements is discussed extensively in Chapter 4.

## 5.1  FUNDAMENTAL SWITCHING CONCEPT

Before discussing switching principles and architectures, some basic concepts in packet switching are first presented.

*Switching and Routing.*  The basic goals for switching and routing are the same, both try to transfer information from one part to another. However, routing normally represents a large-scale perspective, where information is exchanged between two nodes that can be separated by a large distance in the network. While switching normally refers to the information exchanged within a network node. Moreover, routing usually needs the cooperation of other network nodes, and is based on a routing protocol, while switching is only a function of a single device, and is based on a forwarding table, switching architectures, and scheduling algorithms. Figures 5.1 and 5.2 illustrate examples for switching and routing.

*Unicast and Multicast.*  Majority of network connections are point-to-point, which is called unicast. As a result, traffic that enters an input port of a switch fabric is only destined for an output port. However, for applications of video/audio conferences and data broadcasting, traffic from one source is sent to several different destinations. To support multicast, extra switching mechanism is required to copy data from one input port to multiple output ports. The multicast in a switch fabric is illustrated in Figure 5.3.

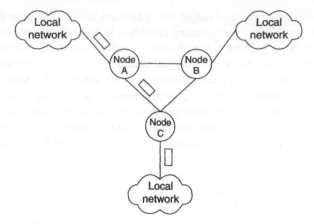

**Figure 5.1**  Typical routing example.

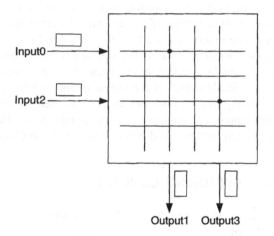

**Figure 5.2**  Typical switching example.

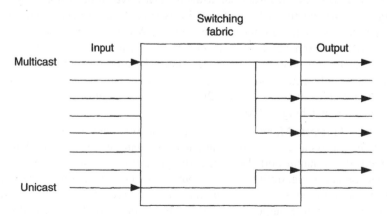

**Figure 5.3**  Multicast in switching fabric.

*Throughput and Speedup.* The throughput of a switch fabric is defined as the ratio of the average aggregated output rate to the average aggregated input rate when all the input ports carry 100% traffic at line rate. It is a positive value no more than one.

A speedup of $k$ means that the internal forwarding rate of the switch fabric is $k$ times the input line rate. So when a speedup exceeds one, buffers must be used at output ports. Speedup allows a switch fabric to forward more than one packet at the same time slot to the output port to alleviate output port contention, resulting in a higher throughput.

*Blocking and Output Contention.* Here we refer to blocking and output contention in space-division switching, since in time-division switching, traffic is multiplexed to avoid blocking.

In space-division switching, the main issue is the matching of input–output ports. Nonblocking means that when there is a request generated between an idle input port and an idle output port, a connection can always be set up. Note that an idle port refers to a port not connected nor requested. On the other hand, blocking means that it is possible that no connection can be set up between the idle input/output pair. Figure 5.4 shows an internal blocking in a three-stage Clos switch, when the idle input port 9 requests the idle output port 4 or 6, a connection cannot be set up because of internal blocking. Another example is shown in Figure 5.5, in a delta network, input port 0 is requesting output port 5 and input port 2 is requesting output port 4, but both need the same output port in the second stage to set up connections, which causes internal blocking. A typical nonblocking switch architecture is a crossbar switch.

Another problem that degrades the throughput of a switching fabric is the output contention. It is not because of the design of switching architecture, but due to the nature of bursty IP traffic. If more than one input port requests the same output port, only one can be granted, so the others have to wait. This is depicted in Figure 5.6. The output contention greatly affects the overall utilization of the switching fabric.

*Cell-mode Switching and Packet-mode Switching.* In ATM networks, information is packed into fixed-size cells. So in an ATM switch, scheduling takes place per cell

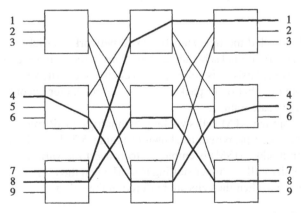

**Figure 5.4** Internal blocking in a Clos network caused by a new connection between input 9 and output 4 or 6.

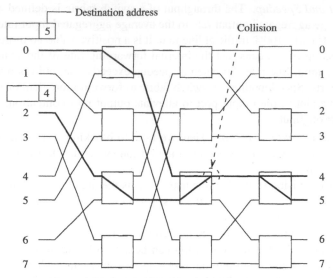

**Figure 5.5** Internal blocking in a delta network.

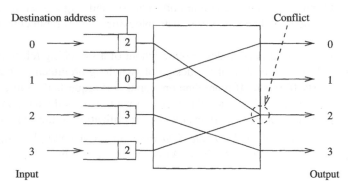

**Figure 5.6** Output port contention.

time, which is called the time slot. But in IP networks, variable-length packets are adopted, and so traditional scheduling algorithms in the switching fabric of IP routers operate per packet basis. It is called pure packet-mode switching. However, because of the random distribution of packet lengths, the scheduler becomes too complex to design in large-scale routers.

To implement the ATM cell switching technology in IP routers, a popular architecture [1] has been proposed, as shown in Figure 5.7. In each input port, an input segmentation module (ISM) is employed to convert the variable-size IP packet into several fixed-size cells.[1] Proper stuffing is used when the remaining packet is shorter than a whole cell. Then the cells are buffered in the cell queues (CQs), for example,

---

[1]Cell is defined to be a fixed-length data unit used in the switch fabric. It consists of a cell header, used for routing in the switch fabric and payload. It needs not necessarily to be an ATM cell.

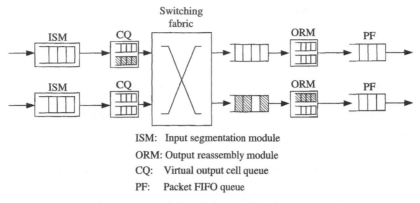

ISM:  Input segmentation module
ORM:  Output reassembly module
CQ:   Virtual output cell queue
PF:   Packet FIFO queue

**Figure 5.7**   Input queuing cell switch with segmentation and reassembly.

virtual output queues (VOQs), each associated with each output. More details about VOQs can be found in Chapter 7. Specific scheduling algorithms are implemented in selecting cells out of VOQs and switching them to correct output port. The output reassembly module (ORM) is required in each output port to reassemble cells of the same packet together. After the ORM, a packet FIFO (PF) is used to buffer the reassembled packets when the ORM has a speedup. This switching strategy is called cell-mode switching in IP routers.

Recent studies by Marsan et al. [2] and Ganjali et al. [3] have presented another scheduling strategy, packet-mode switching. A packet is divided into fixed-size cells like in cell-mode, but cells of the same packet are scheduled contiguously, not independently. The advantages of packet-mode switching are that the reassembly of packets become much easier. It also benefits from lower average packet delay as compared to cell-mode scheduling when the variance of packet length distribution is small.

## 5.2 SWITCH FABRIC CLASSIFICATION

The switch fabrics can be classified based on their switching techniques into two groups: time-division switching (TDS) and space-division switching (SDS). TDS is further divided into shared-memory type and shared-medium type. SDS is further divided into single-path switches and multiple-path switches, which are in turn further divided into several other types, as illustrated in Figure 5.8.

### 5.2.1 Time-Division Switching

Cells from different inputs are multiplexed and forwarded through a data path connecting all inputs and outputs. Typical time-division switching structures are the shared-memory switch (see Chapter 6) and the shared-medium switch. The time-division switching structure is limited by the internal communication bandwidth that should reach the aggregated forwarding bandwidth of all the input ports. However, this class of switch provides an advantage. Since every cell flows across the single communication structure, it can be easily extended to support multicast/broadcast operations.

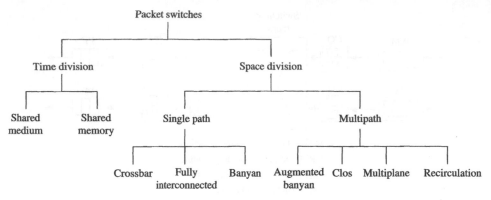

**Figure 5.8** Classification of switching architecture.

In a shared-medium switch, shown in Figure 5.9, cells arriving at input ports are time-division multiplexed into a common high-speed medium, such as a bus or a ring, of bandwidth equal to $N$ times the input line rate. An address filter (AF) and an output FIFO buffer are used in each output line that connects to the shared medium. The AF examines the header of each incoming cell and then accepts only the cells destined for itself. In this way, the multiplexed incoming cells are demultiplexed into correct output ports. Due to the separate FIFO buffer in each output port, the memory utilization of shared-medium switch is lower than the shared-memory structure. For a shared-medium switch, the switch size is limited by the memory read/write access time, within which $N$ incoming and 1 outgoing cells in a time slot need to be accessed. Suppose the time for a cell slot is $T_{cell}$ and the memory access time is $T_{mem}$, the number of switch size $N$ can be calculated using the following equation:

$$(N + 1) \leq \frac{T_{cell}}{T_{mem}}$$

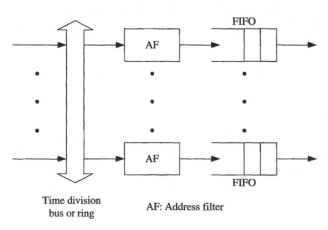

**Figure 5.9** Shared-medium switching architecture.

For example, the cell slot time for a 64-byte packet at a 10 G interface is

$$T_{cell} = \frac{Packetsize}{throughput} = (64 \times 8)/(10 \times 10^9) = 51.2\,ns.$$

If $T_{mem} = 4$ ns, a total of $\lfloor(51.2/4) - 1\rfloor = 11$ ports can be supported. In a shared-memory switch (see Chapter 6), same as shared-medium switches, cells from all the input ports are time-division multiplexed into the central logic. However, they are not forwarded immediately and flood to all the outputs as in the shared-medium structure. Instead, cells are buffered in a central memory, and then scheduled to the demultiplexer where cells destined for different output ports are separated. The shared memory structure is better in memory utilization than the separate FIFO structure in the shared-medium structure, but requires twice memory speed.

### 5.2.2  Space-Division Switching

The space-division switching (SDS) stands for the structure where multiple data paths are available between the input and the output ports and cells of the different input-output connections can be forwarded concurrently, when no blocking is present. The total switching capacity is then the product of the bandwidth of each path and the number of paths that can transmit cells simultaneously. However, in practice, the capacity of the switch is restricted by physical implementation constraints such as the device pin count and backplane connections.

The SDS switches are classified based on the number of available paths between any input–output pair. In single-path switches, only one path exists for any input-output pair, while in multiple-path switches there is more than one. The former has simpler routing control than the latter, but the latter has better connection flexibility and fault tolerance.

***Single-Path Switches.*** In Figure 5.8, single path switches are classified into crossbar-based switches, fully interconnected switches, and banyan-based switches.

*Crossbar Switch.* A $4 \times 4$ crossbar switch is shown in Figure 5.10, where horizontal lines represent the inputs to the switch, and vertical lines represent the outputs. Basically, an $N \times N$ crossbar switch consists of a two-dimensional array of $N^2$ cross-points, each corresponding to an input–output pair. Each crosspoint has two possible states: cross (default) and bar. A connection between input port $i$ and output port $j$ is established by setting the $(i, j)$th crosspoint switch to the bar state while letting other crosspoints along the connection remain in the cross state. The bar state of a crosspoint can be triggered individually by each incoming cell when its destination matches with the output address. No global information about other cells and their destinations is required. This property is called the self-routing property, by which the control complexity is significantly reduced in the switching fabric as the control function is distributed among all crosspoints. The crossbar switch allows the transferring of up to $N$ cells with different input ports and different output destinations in the same time slot.

Crossbar switches have three attractive properties: internally nonblocking, simple in architecture, and modular. However, its number of the crosspoints grows as a function of $N^2$. If constructing larger multistage switch with small crossbar switch modules, the complexity can be improved to $O(N \log N)$. There is no internal blocking in a crossbar switch. As shown in Figure 5.11, there are four requests, input port 1 to

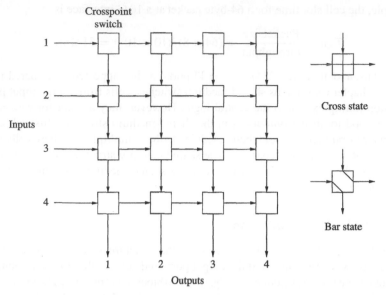

**Figure 5.10**   4 × 4 crossbar switch.

output port 3, input port 2 to output port 4, input port 3 to output 1 and input port 4 to output 3. Except the last request, the first three requests can be switched at the same time without internal blocking. However, there is a contention between the first and the last request marked by a dotted circle in Figure 5.11.

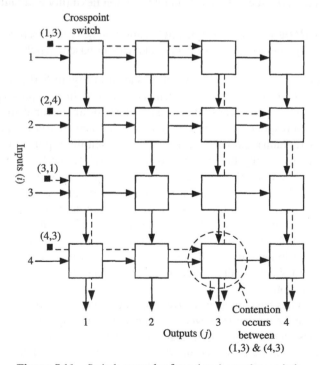

**Figure 5.11**   Switch examples for a 4 × 4 crossbar switch.

There are several possible locations for the buffers in a crossbar switch, such as (1) at the crosspoints in the switch fabric, (2) at the inputs of the switch, and (3) at the inputs and outputs of the switch. Each one has its advantages and disadvantages; they are detailed in Section 5.3.

*Fully interconnected switches.* Another kind of single-path space-division switches are the fully interconnected switches. In a fully interconnected switch, the complete connectivity between inputs and outputs is usually accomplished by means of $N$ separate broadcast buses from every input port to all output ports, as shown in Figure 5.12. $N$ separate buffers are required in such a switch, one at each output port. However, if each of these $N$ output buffers in the fully interconnected switch is partitioned and dedicated to each input line, yielding $N^2$ dedicated buffers, it becomes topologically identical with the crosspoint-buffered switch and thus provides exactly the same performance and implementation complexity.

The fully interconnected switch operates in a similar manner to the shared medium switch. A cell from any input port is broadcast to every output port. The difference is that multiple cells from several input ports can be simultaneously broadcasted to every output port. Therefore, separate cell filters and dedicated buffers, one for each output port, are required to filter out the misdelivered cells and to temporarily store the properly destined cells.

Moreover, the fully interconnected switch is different from the shared medium switch in that the speed-up requirement caused by a sequential transmission over the shared medium is replaced by space overhead of the total $N^2$ separate broadcast buses. This is considered a disadvantage of the switch type. The advantages of the fully interconnected switch lie in its simple and nonblocking structure, similar to the crossbar-based switch.

*Banyan-based switches.* The banyan-based switches are also the single-path space-division switches. They are a family of self-routing switches constructed from $2 \times 2$ switching elements with a single path between any input–output pair. As shown in Figure 5.13, there are three isomorphic topologies: *delta*, *omega*, and

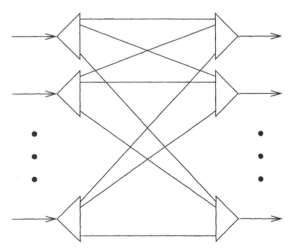

**Figure 5.12**   A fully interconnected switch.

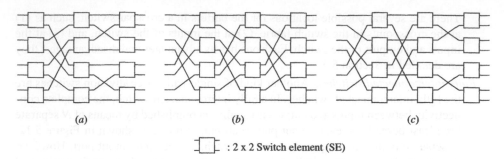

: 2 x 2 Switch element (SE)

**Figure 5.13** Three different topologies of banyan-based switches (*a*) Delta network; (*b*) Omega network; (*c*) Banyan network.

*banyan* networks, belonging to banyan-based family. All of them offer an equivalent performance. The detailed description of banyan switches is in Section 5.4.

*Multiple-Path Switches.* Multiple path switches are classified as *augmented banyan* switches, *Clos* switches, *multiplane switches*, and *recirculation* switches, as shown in Figure 5.14.

*Augmented Banyan Switches.* In a regular $N \times N$ banyan switch, cells pass through $\log N$ stages of switching elements before reaching their destinations. The augmented banyan switch, as illustrated in Figure 5.14*a*, refers to the banyan switch that has more stages than the regular banyan switch. In the regular banyan type switch, once a cell is deflected to an incorrect link and thus deviates from a predetermined unique path, the cell is not guaranteed to reach its requested output. Here, in the augmented banyan switch, deflected cells are provided more chances to be routed to their destinations

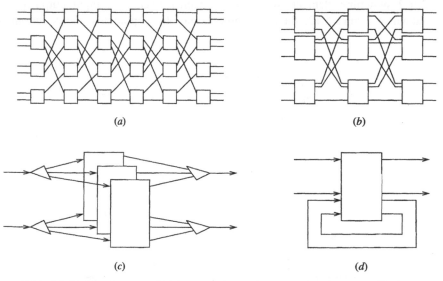

**Figure 5.14** Multiple-path space-division switches (*a*) Augmented Banyan; (*b*) 3-stage clos; (*c*) Multiplane; (*d*) Recirculation.

again by using later augmented stages. When the deflected cells do not reach their destinations after the last stage, they will be discarded.

The advantage of the augmented banyan switch is that by adding augmented stages, the cell loss rate is reduced. The performance of the switch is improved. The disadvantage of this switch type is its complicated routing scheme. Cells are examined at every augmented stage to determine whether they have arrived at their requested output ports. If so, they will be sent to the output interface module. Otherwise, they are routed to the next stage and will be examined again. Another disadvantage is that the number of augmented stages needs to be sufficiently large to satisfy desired performance. Adding each augmented stage to the switch causes increased hardware complexity. The tandem banyan switch [4] and dual shuffle exchange switch [5] are examples of the augmented banyan switches.

*Three-Stage Clos Switches.* The structure of a three-stage Clos switch, as shown in Figure 5.14*b*, consists of three stages of switch modules. The first stage is used to distribute traffic, and in the middle stage, several parallel switch modules are built to provide multiple paths through the switches, and at last in the third stage cells from different switch modules of the middle stage are switched to the correct output ports. More details are described in Section 5.4.

*Multiplane Switches.* Figure 5.14*c* shows a multiplane switch. They refer to the switches that have multiple, usually identical, switch planes. Multiplane switches are mainly proposed as a way to improve system throughput. By using some mechanisms to distribute the incoming traffic loading, cell collisions within the switches can be reduced. Additionally, more than one cell can be transmitted to the same output port by using each switch plane so the output lines are not necessary to operate at a faster speed than that of the input lines. Another advantage of the multiplane switches is that they are used as a means of achieving reliability since the loss of a complete switch plane will reduce the capacity but not the connectivity of the switches. The parallel banyan switch and the Sunshine switch [6] are examples of the multiplane switches.

*Recirculation Switches.* Recirculation switches, as shown in Figure 5.14*d*, are designed to handle the output port contention problem. By recirculating the cells that did not make it to their output ports during the current time slot back to the input ports via a set of recirculation paths, the cell loss rate can be reduced. This results in system throughput improvement. The disadvantage of the recirculation switches is that they require a larger size switch to accommodate the recirculation ports. Also, recirculation may cause out-of-sequence errors. Some mechanisms are needed to preserve the cell sequence among the cells in the same connection. The representative recirculation switches are the Starlite switch [7] and the Sunshine switch [6].

## 5.3  BUFFERING STRATEGY IN SWITCHING FABRICS

Since the burst arrival of traffic are likely to contend for the output ports and/or internal links, buffers are required to temporarily store cells that lose the contention. Various buffering strategies are described below.

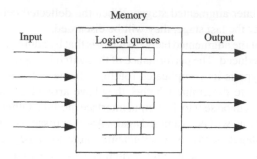

**Figure 5.15**    Shared-memory queuing structure.

### 5.3.1 Shared-Memory Queuing

The shared-memory queuing structure is shown by Figure 5.15, where a memory unit is used to store cells from all input ports. The memory contains $N$ logical queues, one per output port, and each queue stores the cells destined for the corresponding output. It is thus said the memory is shared by all the output ports and the utilization of memory is maximized. However, the disadvantage is that in each time slot the memory must accommodate $N$ concurrent write accesses and $N$ concurrent read accesses, which limits the switch to a small size. Details are described in Chapter 6.

### 5.3.2 Output Queuing (OQ)

Another queuing strategy shown in Figure 5.16 is output queuing. Under this structure, cells are immediately forwarded to the destined output ports once they arrive at the inputs. Since the arrival rate of each output port is larger than the output line rate, buffers are needed at the output ports. The output queuing structure benefits from better QoS control ability, as the destining cells are always available at the output ports to be scheduled based on their priority levels, allocated bandwidth, and QoS requirements. However, this structure suffers from memory speed constraint and thus switch size limitation. This is because there can be up to $N$ cells from different input ports destined for the same output port at the same cell time. The memory utilization is not as good as the shared-memory queuing's.

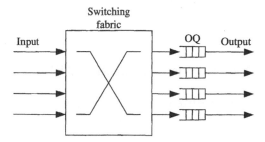

**Figure 5.16**    Output queuing structure.

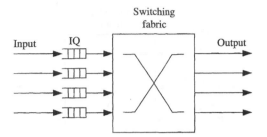

**Figure 5.17**    Input queuing structure.

### 5.3.3    Input Queuing

Due to the switch size limitation of the output queuing structure, the input queuing structure has attracted much more attention in recent years. As shown in Figure 5.17, pure input queuing has one FIFO queue per input port to buffer cells. A scheduling algorithm is required to match input ports with output ports in each time slot, as only one cell heading to an output port can be forwarded per time slot. One problem of input queuing is the so-called head-of-line (HOL) blocking. For instance, in Figure 5.18 input port 0 cannot send its head-of-line cell to output port 2 because of losing output contention to input port 3. However, the cell queued at input port 0 behind the HOL cell cannot be transmitted even if the destined output port 1 is idle. This severely degrades the switch throughput. It is proved that under uniform traffic arrival, the throughput of an input buffered switch is at most 58.6 percent [8, 9]. Several solutions such as channel grouping and windowing were proposed to increase the throughput.

### 5.3.4    Virtual Output Queuing (VOQ)

To eliminate HOL blocking, the virtual output queuing (VOQ) structure has been widely used. In Figure 5.19, same as the input queuing structure, cells are buffered at input ports. But the input buffer is divided into $N$ logical queues, called VOQ, storing the cells destined for the associated output port. The HOL cell of each VOQ is scheduled in current cell time, comparing to the input queuing structure, only one HOL cell of each input can be forwarded. However, since the logical queue number is $N$ times the input queuing structure, scheduling algorithm is much more sophisticated. It was a very hot research topic, and many scheduling algorithms have been proposed [1, 10–13]. The main function is to

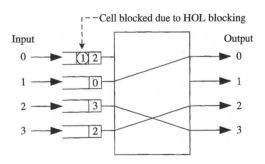

**Figure 5.18**    HOL blocking in input queuing structure.

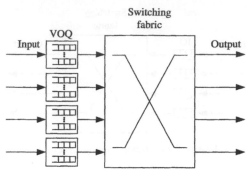

**Figure 5.19**    VOQ structure.

select an input–output matching from an $N \times N$ request matrix. Both delay/throughput performance and implementation complexity must be considered. More details can be found in Chapter 7.

### 5.3.5    Combined Input and Output Queuing

Another way to alleviate HOL blocking is to allow each output port to receive more than one cell in each time slot. That is to have the switch fabric operate $S$ times of the line rate, where $1 < S < N$. Since the switch fabric operates faster than line rate, buffers must be placed at input and output ports to cope with the speed discrepancy between the line rate and the switch fabric speed.

In the original combined input and output queuing space (CIOQ) structure shown in Figure 5.20, each input and output port has a FIFO queue. It is proved that with a speedup of four, the CIOQ switch can achieve 99 percent throughput under independent uniform input traffic [14, 15].

An improved CIOQ structure [16, 17], shown in Figure 5.21, has $N$ VOQ queues in the input buffer, while each output port still has a single FIFO queue. It is proved that under a slightly constrained traffic, this CIOQ structure can emulate a FIFO output queue (FIFO-OQ) switch with a speedup of 2 with bounded delay difference [18]. Note that the FIFO-OQ switch provides the best delay/throughput. More details can be found in Chapter 7.

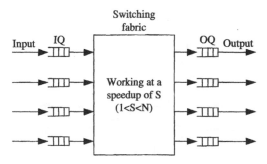

**Figure 5.20**    Combined input and output queuing structure with FIFO queue.

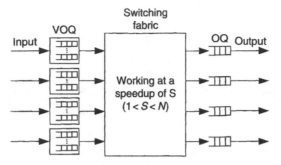

**Figure 5.21**    Combined input and output queuing structure with VOQ.

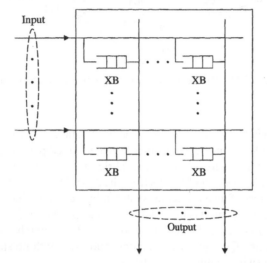

**Figure 5.22**    Crosspoint buffered crossbar structure.

### 5.3.6  Crosspoint Queuing

For a crossbar switch fabric, a buffer can be placed at each crosspoint, as shown in Figure 5.22. Incoming cells are first placed in the corresponding crosspoint buffer (XB), waiting to be transmitted to the output ports. An arbitrator of each output selects a cell among the XBs on the same column based on some scheduling scheme, for example, round-robin. This switch can achieve the same performance as the OQ switches because of no HOL blocking. However, since there are $N^2$ discrete buffers, the sharing effect is very poor. With limited chip space, only a few cells can be implemented. As a result, this switch usually combines VOQs at each input. Details can be found in Chapter 11.

### 5.4  MULTIPLANE SWITCHING AND MULTISTAGE SWITCHING

A large-scale switch is usually built with multiple switch modules (either in chips or boards) interconnected in a different structures. They are partitioned into single-stage or multistage switches.

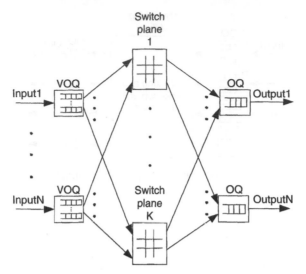

**Figure 5.23** Parallel packet switching structure with crossbar.

*Parallel Packet Switch.* Figure 5.23 shows a single-stage switch fabric with multiple identical switch modules connected in parallel, which is called parallel packet switch (PPS) [19–21]. As a cell stream enters the switching fabric, it is distributed to $K$ parallel planes. The challenging issue is how to find $K$ cells from the $N$ VOQs in each time slot such that the throughput is maximized. Since the center switch fabric does not have buffers, there shall be no cell out of order concern. It is proved that given a speedup of 2, the PPS structure can emulate a first-come-first-serve (FCFS) output-queued (OQ) switch; given a speedup of 3, the PPS can emulate any QoS queuing discipline, and even with no speedup, the PPS can mimic the FCFS OQ switch within a delay bound.

However, since the PPS use single-stage switch fabric, it cannot support large port count, while multi-stage switching can [22, 23]. The multistage switch structures connect the input and output ports in multiple stages and can be divided into two categories. One is the fully connected multistage network, where in every two adjacent stages, each module in the first stage connects to every module in the next stage. The other is the partially connected multistage network, where each module in the first stage only connects to a subset of the modules in the next stage.

*Banyan-Based Switch.* An example of the partially connected multistage network is the banyan network as shown in Figure 5.24. A typical example of the fully connected multistage structure is the Clos switch structure, as shown in Figure 5.25.

An $N \times N$ banyan network consists of $\log_b N$ stages of $b \times b$ switching elements. Each stage has multiple $b \times b$ switching elements whose inputs and outputs are labeled 0 to $b - 1$. The interstage connection patterns are such that only one path exists between any input of the first stage and any output of the last stage.

The banyan network has self-routing capability. When a cell enters in one of the input ports, it uses the output address as the routing information when traversing all the stages. For example, in Figure 5.24, a cell in input port 1 destined for output port 2, ('010') is

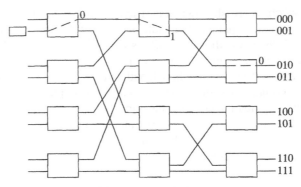

**Figure 5.24**   Banyan switching structure.

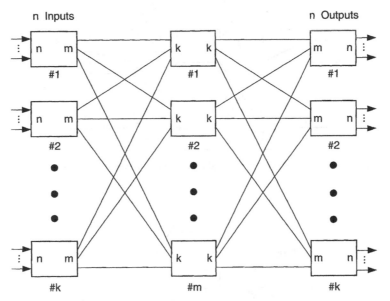

**Figure 5.25**   Clos switching structure.

rounded to the top link (0) of the first switch element, to the down link (1) of the second switch element, and to the top link (0) of the third switch element.

The banyan-based switch provides several advantages. It has fewer switch elements than the crossbar-based and the fully interconnected switch, $O(N \log N)$ versus $O(N^2)$. Self-routing property is also an attractive feature in that no control mechanism is needed for routing cells. Routing information is contained within each cell and it is used while the cell is routed along the path.

However, the main drawback of the banyan-based switch is that it is an internally blocking switch. Its performance degrades rapidly as the size of the switch increases. The performance may be improved if layer switching elements are employed (i.e., $b > 2$). This leads to the class of *delta-based* switches.

*Clos-Network Switch.* A crossbar switch is strictly *nonblocking* in that a path is always available to connect an idle input port to an idle output port. This is not always true for the Clos switch. Figure 5.26 shows a three-stage Clos switch with $N = 9$, $n = 3$, and $m = 3$. The bold lines indicate the existing connections. It can be seen that input port 9 cannot be connected to either output port 4 or 6, even though both of these output lines are idle. However, by rearranging the existing connections, the new connection request can be accommodated. Thus, the Clos network is rearrangably nonblocking.

By increasing the value of $m$ (the number of middle-stage switch modules), the probability of blocking is reduced. To find the value of $m$ needed for a strictly nonblocking three-stage switch, let us refer to Figure 5.27.

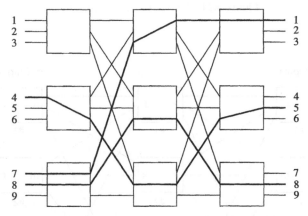

**Figure 5.26**   Example of internal blocking in a three-stage Clos switch.

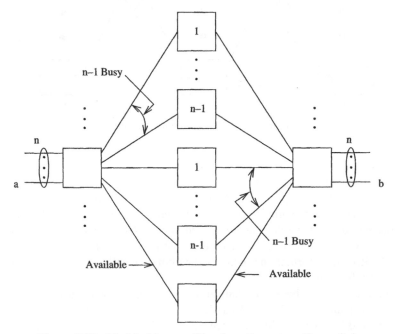

**Figure 5.27**   Nonblocking condition for a three-stage Clos switch.

We wish to establish a path from input port $a$ to output port $b$. The worst case situation for blocking occurs if all of the remaining $n - 1$ input lines and $n - 1$ output lines are busy and are connected to different middle-stage switch modules. Thus a total of $(n - 1) + (n - 1) = 2n - 2$ middle-stage switch modules are unavailable for creating a path from $a$ to $b$. However, if one more middle-stage switch module exists, an appropriate link must be available for the connection. Thus, a three-stage Clos switch will be nonblocking if

$$m \geq (2n - 2) + 1 = 2n - 1$$

The total number of crosspoints $N_x$ in a three-stage Clos switch when it is symmetric (i.e., $m = k$) is

$$N_x = 2Nm + m \left(\frac{N}{n}\right)^2$$

Substituting $m = 2n - 1$ into $N_x$, we obtain

$$N_x = 2N(2n - 1) + (2n - 1)\left(\frac{N}{n}\right)^2$$

for a nonblocking switch. For a large switch size, $n$ is large. We can approximate

$$N_x \simeq 2N(2n) + 2n \left(\frac{N}{n}\right)^2 = 4Nn + 2\left(\frac{N^2}{n}\right)$$

To optimize the number of crosspoints, differentiate $N_x$ with respect to $n$ and set the result to 0. The result will be $n \simeq (N/2)^{1/2}$. Substituting into $N_x$,

$$N_x = 4\sqrt{2}N^{3/2} = O(N^{3/2})$$

The three-stage Clos switch provides an advantage in that it reduces the hardware complexity from $O(N^2)$ in the case of the crossbar switch to $O(N^{3/2})$ while the switch could be designed to be nonblocking. Furthermore, it also provides more reliability since there is more than one possible path through the switch to connect any input port to any output port. The main disadvantage of this switch type is that some fast and intelligent mechanism is needed to rearrange the connections in every time slot so that internal blocking can be avoided. This would be the bottleneck when the switch size becomes large. In practice, it is difficult to avoid the internal blocking although the switch itself is nonblocking. Once the contention on the internal links occurs, the throughput is degraded. This can be improved by either increasing the number of internal links between switch modules or increasing the bandwidth of internal links so that more than one cell from the input module that are destined to the same third-stage module can be routed.

## 5.5 PERFORMANCE OF BASIC SWITCHES

This section describes performance of three basic switches: input-buffered, output-buffered, and completely shared-buffer.

### 5.5.1 Traffic Model

***Bernoulli Arrival Process and Random Traffic.*** Cells arrive at each input in a slot-by-slot manner. Under Bernoulli arrival process, the probability that there is a cell arriving in each time slot is identical and is independent of any other slot. This probability is referred as the offered load of the input. If each cell is equally likely to be destined for any output, the traffic becomes uniformly distributed among the switch.

Consider the FIFO service discipline at each input. Only the HOL cells contend for access to the switch outputs. If every cell is destined for a different output, the switch fabric allows each to pass through to its respective output. If $k$ HOL cells are destined for the same output, one is allowed to pass through the switch, and the other $k - 1$ must wait until the next time slot. While one cell is waiting its turn for access to an output, other cells may be queued behind it and blocked from possibly reaching idle outputs. A Markov model can be established to evaluate the saturated throughput when $N$ is small.[2] When $N$ is large, the slot-by-slot number of HOL cells destined for a particular output becomes a Poisson process. As described in Section 5.5.2, the HOL blocking limits the maximum throughput to 0.586 when $N \to \infty$.

***On–Off Model and Bursty Traffic.*** In the bursty traffic model, each input alternates between active and idle periods of geometrically distributed duration. Figure 5.28 considers an on–off source model in which an arrival process to an input port alternates between on (active) and off (idle) periods. A traffic source continues sending cells in every time slot during the on period, but stops sending cells in the idle period. The duration of the active period called a burst is determined by a random variable $X \in \{1, 2, \ldots\}$, which is assumed to be geometrically distributed with a mean of $\beta$ cells (i.e., the mean burst length). Similarly, the duration of the off period is determined by a random variable $Y \in \{0, 1, 2, \ldots\}$, which is also assumed to be geometrically distributed with a mean of $\alpha$ cells. Define $q$ as the probability of starting a new burst (on period) in each time slot, and $p$ as the probability of terminating a burst. Cells arriving at an input port are assumed to be destined for the same output. Thus, the probability that the on period lasts for a duration of $i$ time slots is

$$\Pr\{X = i\} = p(1 - p)^{i-1}, \quad i \geq 1$$

and we have the mean burst length

$$\beta = E[X] = \sum_{i=1}^{\infty} i \Pr\{X = i\} = 1/p.$$

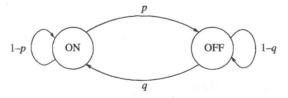

**Figure 5.28**   On–off source model.

---

[2]Consider the state as the different destination combinations among the HOL cells.

The probability that an off period lasts for $j$ time slots is

$$\Pr\{Y = j\} = q(1 - q)^{j-1}, \quad j \geq 0$$

and we have

$$\alpha = E[Y] = \sum_{j=0}^{\infty} j \Pr\{Y = j\} = (1 - q)/q.$$

The offered load $\rho$ is the portion of time that a time slot is active:

$$\rho = \frac{1/p}{1/p + \sum_{j=0}^{\infty} jq(1-q)^j} = \frac{q}{q + p - pq}.$$

### 5.5.2 Input-Buffered Switches

We consider first-in-first-out (FIFO) buffers in evaluating the performance of input queuing. We assume that only the cells at the head of the buffers can contend for their destined outputs. If there are more than one cell contending the same output, only one of them is allowed to pass through the switch and the others have to wait until the next time slot. When a head-of-line (HOL) cell loses contention, at the same moment it may also block some cells behind it to reach idle outputs. As a result, the maximum throughput of the switch is limited and cannot be 100 percent.

To determine the maximum throughput, we assume that all the input queues are saturated. That is, there are always cells waiting in each input buffer, and whenever a cell is transmitted through the switch, a new cell immediately replaces it at the head of the input queue. If there are $k$ cells waiting at the heads of input queues addressed to the same output, one of them will be selected at random to pass through the switch. In other words, each of the head-of-line (HOL) cells has equal probability $(1/k)$ of being selected.

Consider all $N$ cells at the heads of input buffers at time slot $m$. Depending on the destinations, they can be classified into $N$ groups. Some groups may have more than one cell, and some may have none. For those which have at least a cell, one of the cells will be selected to pass through the switch, and the remaining cells have to stay until the next time slot. Denote $B_m^i$ as the number of remaining cells destined for output $i$ in the $m$th time slot, and $B^i$ the random variable in the steady state [8, 9]. Also denote $A_m^i$ as the number of cells moving to the heads of the input queues during the $m$th time slot and destined for output $i$, and $A^i$ the corresponding steady-state random variable. Note that a cell can only move to the head of an input queue if the HOL cell in the previous time slot was removed from that queue for transmission to an output. Hence, the state transition of $B_m^i$ can be represented by:

$$B_m^i = \max\left(0, B_{m-1}^i + A_m^i - 1\right). \tag{5.1}$$

We assume that each new cell arrival to the head of an input queue has the equal probability $1/N$ of being destined for any given output. As a result, $A_m^i$ has the following binomial distribution:

$$\Pr\left[A_m^i = k\right] = \binom{F_{m-1}}{k}(1/N)^k(1 - 1/N)^{F_{m-1}-k},$$

$$k = 0, 1, \ldots, F_{m-1}, \tag{5.2}$$

where

$$F_{m-1} \stackrel{\triangle}{=} N - \sum_{i=1}^{N} B_{m-1}^{i}. \tag{5.3}$$

$F_{m-1}$ represents the total number of cells transmitted through the switch during the $(m-1)$st time slot, which in saturation is equal to the total number of input queues which have a new cell moving into the HOL position in the $m$th time slot. That is,

$$F_{m-1} = \sum_{i=1}^{N} A_{m}^{i}. \tag{5.4}$$

When $N \to \infty$, $A_m^i$ has a Poisson distribution with rate $\rho_m^i = F_{m-1}/N$. In steady state, $A_m^i \to A^i$ also has a Poisson distribution. The rate is $\rho_0 = \overline{F}/N$, where $\overline{F}$ is the average of the number of cells passing through the switch, and $\rho_0$ is the utilization of output lines (i.e., the normalized switch throughput). The state transition of $B^i$ is driven by the Markov process same as the $M/D/1$ queues in the steady state. Using the results for the mean steady-state queue size for an $M/D/1$ queue, for $N \to \infty$ we have

$$\overline{B^i} = \frac{\rho_0^2}{2(1-\rho_0)}. \tag{5.5}$$

In the steady state, (5.3) becomes

$$\overline{F} = N - \sum_{i=1}^{N} \overline{B^i}. \tag{5.6}$$

By symmetricity, $\overline{B^i}$ is equal for all $i$. In particular,

$$\overline{B^i} = \frac{1}{N} \sum_{i=1}^{N} \overline{B^i} = 1 - \frac{\overline{F}}{N} = 1 - \rho_0. \tag{5.7}$$

It follows from (5.5) and (5.7) that $\rho_0 = \left(2 - \sqrt{2}\right) = 0.586$.

When $N$ is finite and small, the switch throughput can be calculated by modeling the system as a Markov chain. The numerical results are given in Table 5.1. Note that the throughput rapidly converges to 0.586 as $N$ increases.

The results also imply that, if the input rate is greater than 0.586, the switch will become saturated, and the throughput will be 0.586. If the input rate is less than 0.586, the throughput will be 100 percent, and every cell will get through the switch after some delay. To characterize the delay, a discrete-time $Geom/G/1$ queuing model can be used to obtain an exact formula of the expected waiting time for $N \to \infty$.

The result is based on the following two assumptions: (1) The arrival process to each input queue is a Bernoulli process. That is, the probability that a cell arrives in each time slot is identical and independent of any other slot. We denote this probability as $p$, and call it the offered load. (2) Each cell is equally likely to be destined for any one output. The 'service time' for a cell at the head of line consists of the waiting time until it gets

TABLE 5.1    The Maximum Throughput Achievable
Using Input Queuing with FIFO Buffers

| N | Throughput |
|---|---|
| 1 | 1.0000 |
| 2 | 0.7500 |
| 3 | 0.6825 |
| 4 | 0.6553 |
| 5 | 0.6399 |
| 6 | 0.6302 |
| 7 | 0.6234 |
| 8 | 0.6184 |
| $\infty$ | 0.586 |

selected, plus one time slot for its transmission through the switch. As $N \to \infty$, and in the steady state, the number of cells arriving to the heads of input queues, and addressed to a particular output (say $j$) has the Poisson distribution with rate $p$. Hence, the service time distribution for the discrete-time $Geom/G/1$ model is the delay distribution of another queuing system: a discrete-time $M/D/1$ queue with customers served in random order.

Using standard results for a discrete-time $Geom/G/1$ queue, we obtain the mean cell waiting time for input queuing with FIFO buffers

$$\overline{W} = \frac{p\overline{S(S-1)}}{2(1-p\overline{S})} + \overline{S} - 1, \tag{5.8}$$

where $S$ is the random variable of the service time obtained from the $M/D/1$ model. The mean cell waiting time for input queuing with FIFO buffers is computed and shown in Figure 5.29 for $N \to \infty$.

### 5.5.3   Output-Buffered Switches

With output queuing, cells are only buffered at outputs, at each of which a separate FIFO is maintained. Consider a particular (i.e., tagged) output queue. Define the random variable $A$ as the number of cell arrivals destined for the tagged output in a given time slot. In [8, 9], based on the same assumptions as in Section 5.5.2 on the arrivals, we have

$$a_k \triangleq \Pr[A = k] = \binom{N}{k} (p/N)^k (1 - p/N)^{N-k}, \qquad k = 0, 1, 2, \dots. \tag{5.9}$$

When $N \to \infty$, (5.9) becomes

$$a_k \triangleq \Pr[A = k] = \frac{p^k e^{-p}}{k!}$$
$$k = 0, 1, 2, \dots, N = \infty \tag{5.10}$$

Denote $Q_m$ as the number of cells in the tagged queue at the end of the $m$th time slot, $A_m$ the number of cell arrivals during the $m$th time slot, and $b$ the capacity of the output buffer,

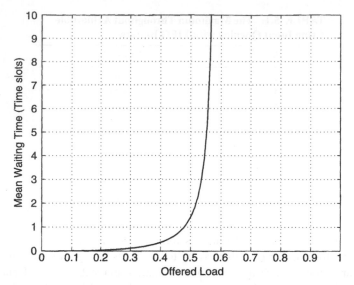

**Figure 5.29** The mean waiting time for input queuing with FIFO buffers for the limiting case for $N = \infty$.

we have

$$Q_m = \min\{\max\left(0, Q_{m-1} + A_m - 1\right), b\}. \tag{5.11}$$

If $Q_{m-1} = 0$ and $A_m > 0$, there is no cell waiting at the beginning of the $m$th time slot, but we have $A_m$ cells arriving. We assume that one of the arriving cells is immediately transmitted during the $m$th time slot; that is, a cell goes through the switch without any delay.

For finite $N$ and finite $b$, this can be modeled as a finite-state, discrete-time Markov chain with state transition probabilities $P_{ij} \triangleq \Pr[Q_m = j \mid Q_{m-1} = i]$ in the following:

$$P_{ij} = \begin{cases} a_0 + 1 & i = 0, \, j = 0 \\ a_0 & 1 \le i \le b, \, j = i - 1 \\ a_{j-i+1} & 1 \le j \le b - 1, \, 0 \le i \le j \\ \displaystyle\sum_{m=j-i+1}^{N} a_m & j = b, \, 0 \le i \le j \\ 0 & \text{otherwise} \end{cases} \tag{5.12}$$

where $a_k$ is given by (5.9) and (5.10) for a finite $N$ and $N \to \infty$, respectively. The steady-state queue size can be obtained recursively from the following Markov chain balance equations:

$$\begin{cases} q_1 \triangleq \Pr[Q = 1] = \dfrac{(1 - a_0 - a_1)}{a_0} \cdot q_0 \\ q_n \triangleq \Pr[Q = n] = \dfrac{(1 - a_1)}{a_0} \cdot q_{n-1} - \displaystyle\sum_{k=2}^{n} \dfrac{a_k}{a_0} \cdot q_{n-k}, \quad 2 \le n \le b, \end{cases}$$

where

$$q_0 \triangleq \Pr[Q = 0] = \frac{1}{1 + \sum_{n=1}^{b} q_n/q_0}.$$

No cell will be transmitted on the tagged output line during the $m$th time slot if, and only if, $Q_{m-1} = 0$ and $A_m = 0$. Therefore, the switch throughput $\rho_0$ is represented as:

$$\rho_0 = 1 - q_0 a_0.$$

A cell will be lost if, when emerging from the switch fabric, it finds the output buffer already containing $b$ cells. The cell loss probability can be calculated as follows:

$$\Pr[\text{cell loss}] = 1 - \frac{\rho_0}{p},$$

where $p$ is the offered load.

Figures 5.30$a$ and 5.30$b$ show the cell loss probability for output queuing as a function of the output buffer size $b$ for various switch size $N$ and offered loads $p = 0.8$ and 0.9. At the 80 percent offered load, a buffer size of $b = 28$ is good enough to keep the cell loss probability below $10^{-6}$ for arbitrarily large $N$. The $N \to \infty$ curve can be a close upper bound for finite $N > 32$. Figure 5.31 shows the cell loss performance when $N \to \infty$ against the output buffer size $b$ for offered loads $p$ varying from 0.70 to 0.95.

Output queuing achieves the optimal throughput-delay performance. Cells are delayed unless it is unavoidable when two or more cells arriving on different inputs are destined for the same output. With Little's result, the mean waiting time $\overline{W}$ can be obtained as follows:

$$\overline{W} = \frac{\overline{Q}}{\rho_0} = \frac{\sum_{n=1}^{b} n q_n}{1 - q_0 a_0}.$$

Figure 5.32 shows the numerical results for the mean waiting time as a function of the offered load $p$ for $N \to \infty$ and various values of the output buffer size $b$. When $N \to \infty$ and $b \to \infty$, the mean waiting time is obtained from the $M/D/1$ queue as follows:

$$\overline{W} = \frac{p}{2(1-p)}.$$

### 5.5.4  Completely Shared-Buffered Switches

With completely buffer sharing, all cells are stored in a common buffer shared by all inputs and outputs. One can expect that it will need less buffer to achieve a given cell loss probability, due to the statistical nature of cell arrivals. Output queuing can be maintained logically with linked lists, so that no cells will be blocked from reaching idle outputs, and

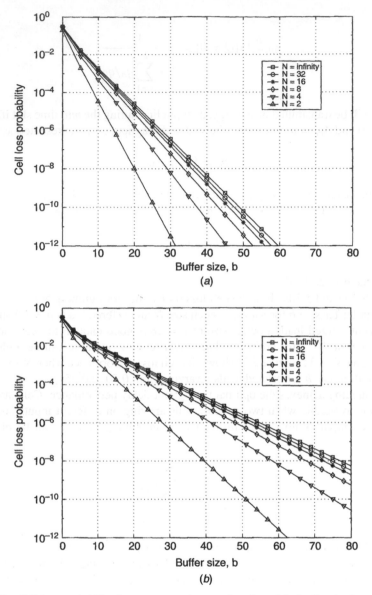

**Figure 5.30** Cell loss probability for output queuing as a function of the buffer size $b$ and the switch size $N$, for offered loads (a) $p = 0.8$ and (b) $p = 0.9$.

we still can achieve the optimal throughput-delay performance as with dedicated output queuing.

In the following, we will take a look on how it improves the cell loss performance. Denote $Q_m^i$ as the number of cells destined for output $i$ in the buffer at the end of the $m$th time slot. The total number of cells in the shared buffer at the end of the $m$th time slot is $\sum_{i=1}^{N} Q_m^i$. If the buffer size is infinite, then

$$Q_m^i = \max\left\{0, Q_{m-1}^i + A_m^i - 1\right\}, \tag{5.13}$$

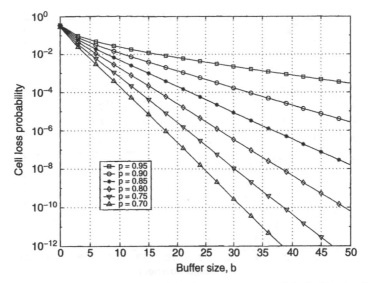

**Figure 5.31** Cell loss probability for output queuing as a function of the buffer size $b$ and offered loads varying from $p = 0.70$ to $p = 0.95$, for the limiting case of $N = \infty$.

where $A_m^i$ is the number of cells addressed to output $i$ that arrive during the $m$th time slot.

With a finite buffer size, cell arrivals may fill up the shared buffer and the resulting buffer overflow makes (5.13) only an approximation. However, we are only interested in the region of low cell loss probability (e.g., less than $10^{-6}$), in which this approximation is still good.

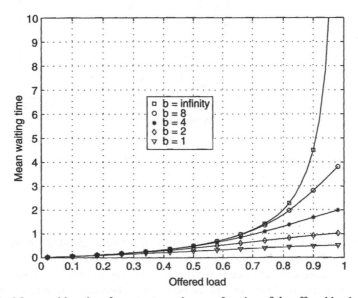

**Figure 5.32** Mean waiting time for output queuing as a function of the offered load $p$, for $N = \infty$ and output FIFO sizes varying from $b = 1$ to $b = \infty$.

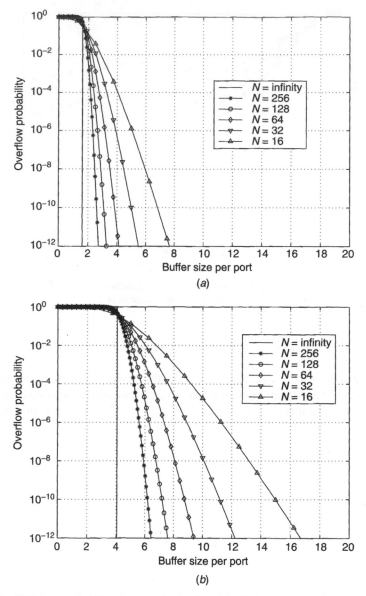

**Figure 5.33**   Cell loss probability for completely shared buffering as a function of the buffer size per output $b$ and the switch size $N$, for offered loads (a) $p = 0.8$ and (b) $p = 0.9$.

When $N$ is finite, $A^i$, which is the number of cell arrivals destined for output $i$ in the steady state, is not independent of $A^j$ ($j \neq i$). This is because, at most $N$ cells arrive to the switch, and a large number of cells arriving for one output implies a small number for the remaining outputs. As $N$ goes to infinity, however, $A^i$ becomes an independent Poisson random variable (with mean value $p$). Then, $Q^i$, which is the number of cells in the buffer that are destined for output $i$ in the steady state also becomes independent of $Q_j$ ($j \neq i$). We will use the Poisson and independence assumption for finite $N$. These the approximations are good for $N \geq 16$.

Therefore we model the steady-state distribution of $\sum_{i=1}^{N} Q^i$, the number of cells in the buffer, as the $N$ fold convolution of $N$ $M/D/1$ queues. With the assumption of an infinite buffer size, we then approximate the cell loss probability by the overflow probability $\Pr\left[\sum_{i=1}^{N} Q^i \geq Nb\right]$. Figure 5.33a and 5.33b show the numerical results.

## REFERENCES

[1] F. A. Marsan, A. Bianco, P. Giaccone, E. Leonardi, and E. Neri, "Packet scheduling in input-queued cell-based switches," in *Proc. IEEE INFOCOM'01*, Anchorage, Alaska, vol. 2, pp. 1085–1094 (Apr. 2001).

[2] F. A. Marsan, A. Bianco, P. Giaccone, E. Leonardi, and F. Neri, "Packet-mode scheduling in input-queued cell-based switches," *IEEE/ACM Transactions on Networking*, vol. 10, no. 5, pp. 666–678 (Oct. 2002).

[3] Y. Ganjali, A. Keshavarzian, and D. Shah, "Input queued switches: cell switching vs. packet switching," in *Proc. IEEE INFOCOM'03*, San Francisco, California, vol. 3, pp. 1651–1658 (Mar. 2003).

[4] F. A. Tobagi, T. K. Kwok, and F. M. Chiussi, "Architecture, performance and implementation of the tandem banyan fast packet switch," *IEEE Journal on Selected Areas in Communications*, vol. 9, no. 8, pp. 1173–1193 (Oct. 1991).

[5] S. C. Liew and T. T. Lee, "$N \log N$ dual shuffle-exchange network with error-correcting routing," in *Proc. IEEE ICC'92*, vol. 1, Chicago, Illinois, pp. 1173–1193 (June 1992).

[6] J. N. Giacopelli, J. J. Hickey, W. S. Marcus, W. D. Sincoskie, and M. Littlewood, "Sunshine: a high-performance self-routing broadband packet switch architecture," *IEEE Journal on Selected Areas in Communications*, vol. 9, no. 8, pp. 1289–1298 (Oct. 1991).

[7] A. Huang and S. Knauer, "STARLITE: a wideband digital switch," in *Proc. IEEE GLOBECOM'84*, Atlanta, Georgia, pp. 121–125 (Dec. 1984).

[8] M. J. Karol, M. Hluchyj, and S. Morgan, "Input vs. output queuing on a space-division packet switch," *IEEE Transactions on Communications*, vol. 35, no. 12, pp. 1347–1356 (Dec. 1987).

[9] M. J. Karol, M. Hluchyj, and S. Morgan, "Input vs. output queuing on a space-division packet switch," *IEEE Transactions on Communications*, vol. 35, issue 12 (Dec. 1987).

[10] N. McKeown, "Scheduling algorithms for input-queued cell switches," Ph.D. Thesis, UC Berkeley, May 1995.

[11] N. McKeown, "iSLIP: a scheduling algorithm for input-queued switches," *IEEE/ACM Transactions on Networking*, vol. 7, no. 2, pp. 188–201 (Apr. 1999).

[12] H. J. Chao, "Saturn: a terabit packet switch using Dual Round-Robin," *IEEE Communications Magazine*, vol. 38, issue 12, pp. 78–84 (Dec. 2000).

[13] D. N. Serpanos and P. I. Antoniadis, "FIRM: a class of distributed scheduling algorithms for high-speed ATM switches with multiple input queues," in *Proc. IEEE INFOCOM'00*, Tel Aviv, Israel, pp. 548–554 (Mar. 2000).

[14] A. L. Gupta and N. D. Georganas, "Analysis of a packet switch with input and output buffers and speed constraints," in *Proc. IEEE INFOCOM'91*, Bal Harbour, Florida, vol. 2, pp. 694–700 (Apr. 1991).

[15] J. S.-C. Chen and T. E. Stern, "Throughput analysis, optimal buffer allocation, and traffic imbalance study of a generic nonblocking packet switch," *IEEE Journal on Selected Areas in Communications*, vol. 9, no. 3, pp. 439–449 (Apr. 1991).

[16] S. T. Chuang, A. Goel, N. McKeown, and B. Prabhakar, "Matching output queueing with a combined input/output-queued switch," *IEEE Journal on Selected Areas in Communications*, vol. 17, no. 6, pp. 1030–1039 (June 1999).

[17] B. Prabhakar and N. McKeown, "On the speedup required for combined input and output queued switching," *Automatica*, vol. 35, no. 12 (Dec. 1999).

[18] S. Iyer and N. McKeown, "Using constraint sets to achieve delay bounds in CIOQ switches," *IEEE Communications Letters*, vol. 7, no. 6, pp. 275–277 (June 2003).

[19] S. Iyer, A. Awadallah, and N. McKeown, "Analysis of a packet switch with memories running slower than the line-rate," in *Proc. IEEE INFOCOM'00*, Tel Aviv, Israel, vol. 2, pp. 529–537 (Mar. 2000).

[20] S. Iyer and N. McKeown, "Making parallel packet switches practical," in *Proc. IEEE INFOCOM'01*, Anchorage, Alaska, vol. 3, pp. 1680–1687 (Apr. 2001).

[21] S. Iyer and N. McKeown, "Analysis of the parallel packet switch architecture," *IEEE/ACM Transactions on Networking*, vol. 11, no. 2, pp. 314–324 (Apr. 2003).

[22] H. J. Chao, Z. Jing, and S. Y. Liew, "Matching algorithms for three-stage bufferless Clos network switches," *IEEE Communications Magazine*, vol. 41, no. 10, pp. 46–54 (Oct. 2003).

[23] A. Jajszczyk, "Nonblocking, repackable, and rearrangeable Clos networks: fifty years of the theory evolution," *IEEE Communications Magazine*, vol. 41, no. 10, pp. 28–33 (Oct. 2003).

# CHAPTER 6

# SHARED-MEMORY SWITCHES

In shared-memory switches, all input and output ports have access to a common memory. In every cell time slot, all input ports can store incoming cells and all output ports can retrieve their outgoing cells (if any). A shared-memory switch works essentially as an output-buffered switches, and thereby achieving optimal throughput and delay performance. Furthermore, for a given cell loss rate, a shared memory switch using centralized memory management requires less amount of buffers than other switches. However, the switch size is limited by the memory read/write access time, within which $N$ incoming and $N$ outgoing cells in a time slot need to be accessed. As shown in the formula given below, the memory access cycle must be shorter than $1/(2N)$ of the cell slot, which is the ratio of the cell length and the link speed:

$$\text{Memory access cycle} \leq \frac{\text{cell length}}{2 \cdot N \cdot \text{link speed}}$$

For instance, with a cell slot of 2.83 μs (53-byte cells at the line rate of 149.76 Mbit/s, or 155.52 Mbit/s × 26/27) and with a memory cycle time of 10 ns, the switch size is limited to 141.

Several commercial ATM switch chip sets based on the shared memory architecture provide several tens Gbit/s capacity. Some people may argue that the memory density doubles every 18 months and memory saving by the shared-memory architecture is not that significant. However, since the memory used in the ATM switch requires high speed (e.g., 5–10 ns cycle time), they are expensive. Thus, reducing the total buffer size can considerably reduce the implementation cost. Some vendors' shared-memory switch chip sets can have the capability of integrating with other space switches to build a large-capacity switch (e.g., a few hundred Gbit/s). Although shared-memory switch has the advantage of saving buffer size, the buffer can be occupied by one or a few output ports that are congested

*High Performance Switches and Routers*, by H. Jonathan Chao and Bin Liu
Copyright © 2007 John Wiley & Sons, Inc.

and leaves no room to other cells destined for other output ports. Thus, there is normally a cap for the buffer size that can be used by any output port.

The following sections discuss different approaches to organizing the shared memory and necessary control logics, respectively. The basic idea of the shared-memory switch is to use logical queues to link the cells destined for the same output port. Section 6.1 describes this basic concept and the structure of the logical queues, and the pointer processing associated with writing and reading cells to and from the shared memory. Section 6.2 describes a different approach to implementing the shared-memory switch by using the content addressable memory (CAM) instead of the random access memory (RAM) as in most approaches. Although CAM is not as cost-effective and **as** fast as RAM, the idea of using CAM to implement the shared-memory switch is interesting because CAM approach eliminates the need of maintaining the logical queues. Since the switch size is limited by memory chip's speed constraint, several approaches have been proposed to increase the switch size, such as the space-time-space approach in Section 6.3, parallel shared memory switches in 6.4.3 and multistage shared memory switches in Section 6.4. Section 6.5 describes several shared-memory switch architectures to accommodate the multicasting capability.

## 6.1  LINKED LIST APPROACH

Figure 6.1 illustrates the concept of the shared-memory switch architecture. Cells arriving on all input lines are time-division multiplexed into a single stream, which is then converted to a parallel word stream and fed to the common memory for storage. Internally to the memory, cells are organized into separate logical queues, one for each output lines. Cells destined for the same output port are linked together in the same logical queue. On the other hand, an output stream of cells is formed by retrieving the head-of-line (HOL) cells from the output queues sequentially, one per queue; the output stream is then time-division demultiplexed, and cells are transmitted on the output lines. Each logical queue is confined by two pointers, the head pointer (HP) and the tail pointer (TP). The former points to the first cell of a logical queue, while the latter points to the last cell of a logical queue or to a vacant location to which the next arriving cell will be stored.

Figure 6.2 depicts a linked-list based shared-memory switch where a logical queue is maintained for each output to link all cells in the memory destined for the output. Each logical queue is essentially operated as a FIFO queue.

The switch operation is as follows. Incoming cells are time-division multiplexed to two synchronized streams: a stream of data cells to the memory, and a stream of the

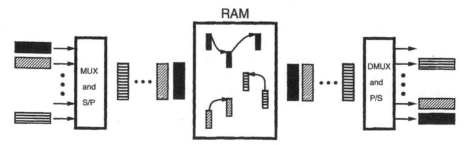

**Figure 6.1**   Logical queues in a shared-memory switch.

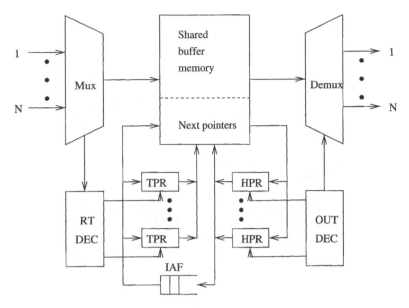

**Figure 6.2**    Basic structure of a linked list based shared-memory switch.

corresponding headers to the route decoder (RT DEC) for maintaining logical queues. The RT DEC then decodes the header stream one by one, accesses the corresponding tail pointer register (TPR), and triggers the WRITE process of the logical queue. An idle address of the cell memory is simultaneously read from an idle address FIFO (IAF) that holds all vacant cell locations of the shared memory.[1] This is the next address pointer in the cell memory as the address for storing the next arriving cell. This address is also put into the corresponding TPR to update the logical queue. Figure 6.3 shows two logical queues, where next pointers (NPs) are used to link the cells in the same logical queue. TPR 0 and HPR 0 (head pointer register) correspond to output port #0, where $(n - 1)$ cells are linked together. TPR 1 and HPR 1 correspond to output port #1, The end of each logical queue indicates the address into which the next cell to the output will be written.

The READ process of the switch is the reverse of the WRITE process. The cells pointed by the HPRs (heads of each logical queue) are read out of the memory one by one. The resulting cell stream is demultiplexed into the outputs of the switch. The addresses of the leaving cells then become idle, and will be put into the IAF.

Figure 6.4 illustrates an example of adding and deleting a cell from a logical queue. In this example, the TP points to a vacant location to which the next arriving cell will be stored. When a cell arrives, it is stored in the cell memory at a vacant location pointed by

---

[1] Since FIFO chips are more expensive than memory chips, an alternative to implement the IAF is to store vacant cells' addresses in memory chips, rather than in FIFO chips, and link the addresses in a logical queue. However, this approach requires more memory access cycles in each cell slot than using FIFO chips approach and thus can only support a smaller switch size.

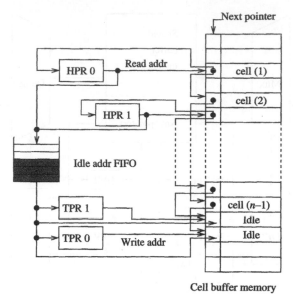

**Figure 6.3**   Two linked-list logical queues.

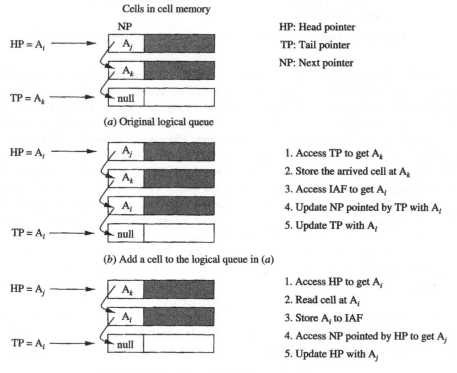

Cells in cell memory

HP: Head pointer
TP: Tail pointer
NP: Next pointer

(a) Original logical queue

1. Access TP to get $A_k$
2. Store the arrived cell at $A_k$
3. Access IAF to get $A_l$
4. Update NP pointed by TP with $A_l$
5. Update TP with $A_l$

(b) Add a cell to the logical queue in (a)

1. Access HP to get $A_i$
2. Read cell at $A_i$
3. Store $A_i$ to IAF
4. Access NP pointed by HP to get $A_j$
5. Update HP with $A_j$

(c) Delete HOL cell from the logical queue in (b)

**Figure 6.4**   Adding and deleting a cell in a logical queue for the tail pointer pointing to a vacant location.

the TP ($A_k$ in Figure 6.4a). An empty location is obtained from the IAF (e.g., $A_l$). The NP field pointed by the TP is changed from null to the next arriving cell's address ($A_l$ in Figure 6.4b). After that, the TP is replaced by the next arriving cell's address ($A_l$). When a cell is to be transmitted, the HOL cell of the logical queue pointed by the HP ($A_i$ in Figure 6.4b) is accessed for transmission. A cell to which the NP points ($A_j$ in Figure 6.4b) becomes the HOL cell. As a result, the HP is updated with the new HOL cell's address ($A_j$ in Figure 6.4c). Meanwhile, the vacant location ($A_i$) is put into in the IAF for use by future arriving cells.

Figure 6.5 illustrates an example of adding and deleting a cell in a logical queue for the tail pointer pointing to the last cell of the queue. The writing procedures are different in Figures 6.4 and 6.5, while the reading procedures are identical. While the approach in Figure 6.4 may have an advantage of better applying parallelism for pointer processing, it wastes one cell buffer for each logical queue. For a practical shared memory switch with 32 or 64 ports, the wasted buffer space is negligible compared with the total buffer size of several tens of thousands. However, if the logical queues are arranged on a per connection basis (e.g., in packet fair queueing scheduling), the wasted buffer space can be quite large as the number of connections can be several tens of thousand. As a result, the approach in Figure 6.5 will be a better choice in this situation.

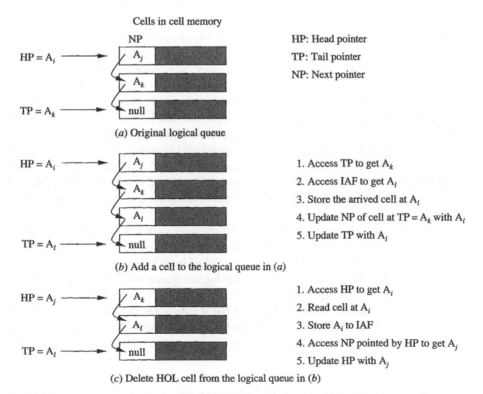

**Figure 6.5** Adding and deleting a cell in a logical queue for the tail pointer pointing to the last cell of the queue.

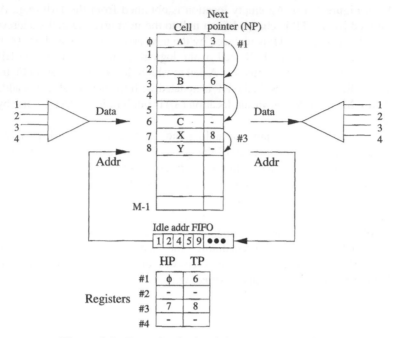

**Figure 6.6**  Example of a 4 × 4 shared-memory switch.

As shown in Figures 6.4 and 6.5, each write and read operation requires five memory access cycles.[2] For an $N \times N$ switch, the number of memory access cycles in each time slot is $10N$. For a time slot of $2.83\,\mu s$ and a memory cycle time of $10\,ns$, the maximum number of switch ports is 28, which is much smaller than the number when considering only the time constraint on the data path (e.g., it was shown at the beginning of the chapter that using the same memory technology, the switch size can be 141. That is because we did not consider the time spent on updating the pointers of the logical queues). As a result, pipeline and parallelism techniques are usually employed to reduce the required memory cycles in each time slot. For instance, the pointer updating and cell storage/access can be executed simultaneously. Or, the pointer registers can be stored inside a pointer processor instead of at an external memory, thus reducing the access time and increasing parallelism of pointer operations.

Figure 6.6 shows an example of a 4 × 4 shared-memory switch. In this example, the TP points to the last cell of a logical queue. Cells A, B, and C destined for output port #1 form a logical queue with HP = 0 and TP = 6 and are linked by NPs shown in the figure. Cells X and Y destined for output port #3 form another logical queue with HP = 7 and TP = 8. Assuming a new cell D destined for output #1 arrives, it will be written to memory location 1 (this address is provided by the IAF). Both the NP at location 6 and TP1 are updated with value 1. When a cell from output #1 is to be read for transmission, HP1 is first accessed to locate the HOL cell (cell A at location 0). Once it is transmitted, HP1 is updated with the NP at location 0, which is 3.

[2]Here, we assume the entire cell can be written to the shared memory in one memory cycle. In real implementation, cells are usually written to the memory in multiple cycles. The number of cycles depends on the memory bus width and the cell size.

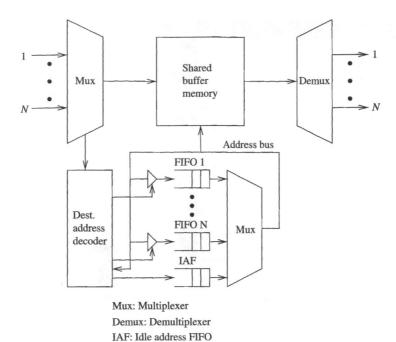

Mux: Multiplexer
Demux: Demultiplexer
IAF: Idle address FIFO

**Figure 6.7**    Using FIFOs to maintain the logical queues.

Alternatively, the logical queues can be organized with dedicated FIFO queues, one for each output port [1]. The switch architecture is shown in Figure 6.7. The performance is the same as using linked lists. The necessary amount of buffering is higher due to the buffering required for the FIFO queues, but the implementation is simpler and the multicasting and priority control easier to implement. For instance, when an incoming cell is broadcast to all output ports, it requires at least $N$ pointer updates in Figure 6.2, while in Figure 6.7 the new address of the incoming cell can be written to all FIFO queues at the same time. The size of each FIFO in Figure 6.7 is $M \times \log M$ while the size of each pointer register in Figure 6.2 is only $\log M$, where $M$ is the number of cells that can be stored in the shared memory. This approach provides better reliability than the linked-list approach (Fig. 6.2) in that if the cell address stored in FIFO is corrupted due to hardware failure, only one cell is affected. However, in the linked-list approach, if the pointer in the linked list is corrupted, cells in the remaining list will be either routed to an incorrect output port, or never be accessed.

## 6.2    CONTENT ADDRESSABLE MEMORY APPROACH

In the CAM-based switch [2], the shared-buffer RAM is replaced by a CAM/RAM structure, where the RAM stores the cell and the CAM stores a tag used to reference the cell. This approach eliminates the need of maintaining the logical queues. A cell can be uniquely identified by its output port number and a sequence number, and these together constitute the tag. A cell is read by searching for the desired tag. Figure 6.8 shows the switch architecture. Write circuits serve input ports and read circuits serve output ports, both on a round-robin

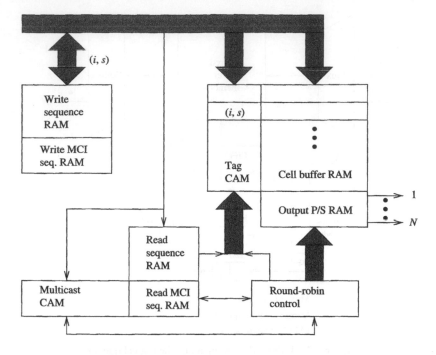

Tag: (Output address, sequence number), e.g., $(i, s)$
MCI: Multicast connection identifier

**Figure 6.8**  Basic architecture of a CAM-based shared-memory switch.

basis as follows:

For a **write**:

(1) Read the write sequence number $WS[i]$ from the write sequence RAM (WS-RAM) (corresponding to the destination port $i$), and use this value ($s$) for the cell's tag **i, s**.
(2) Search the tag CAM for the first empty location **emp**.
(3) Write the cell into the buffer (**B[emp]** = cell), and **i, s** into the associated tag.
(4) Increment the sequence number $s$ by one and update $WS[i]$ with $(s + 1)$.

For a **read**:

(1) Read the read sequence number RS[j] from the read sequence RAM (RS-RAM) (corresponding to the destination port $j$), say $t$.
(2) Search for the tag with the value **j, t**.
(3) Read the cell in the buffer associated with the tag with the value **j, t**.
(4) Increment the sequence number $t$ by one and update $RS[i]$ with $(t + 1)$.

This technique replaces link storage indirectly with content-addressable tag storage, and read/write pointers/registers with sequence numbers. A single extra 'valid' bit to identify if buffer is empty is added to each tag, effectively replacing the idle address FIFO (IAF) and its pointers. No address decoder is required in the CAM/RAM buffer. Moreover, since

**TABLE 6.1  Comparison of Linked List and CAM-Access**

|  | Linked List | CAM-Access |
|---|---|---|
| Cell storage | RAM | CAM/RAM |
| (decode/encode) | (decode) | (neither) |
| bits | $256 \times 424 = 108{,}544$ | $256 \times 424 = 108{,}544$ |
| Look-up | Link:RAM | Tag:CAM |
| bits | $256 \times 8 = 2048$ | $256 \times (4+7) = 2{,}816$ |
| Write and read reference | Address registers | Sequence number registers |
| (queue length checking) | (additional counters) | (compare $W$ and $R$ numbers) |
| bits | $2 \times 16 \times 8 = 256$ | $2 \times 16 \times 7 = 224$ |
| Idle address storage | IAF | CAM valid bit |
| (additional overhead) | (pointer maintenance, | (none) |
|  | extra memory block) |  |
| bits | $256 \times 8 = 2048$ | $256 \times 1 = 256$ |
| Total bits | 112,896 | 111,840 |

Sample switch size is $16 \times 16$ with $2^8 = 256$ cell buffer capacity; seven-bit sequence numbers are used.

the CAM does not output the address of tag matches ('hits'), it requires no address encoder (usually a source of CAM area overhead). Both linked list address registers and CAM-access sequence number registers must be initialized to known values on power-up. If it is necessary to monitor the length of each queue, additional counters are required for the linked list case while sequence numbers can simply be subtracted in the CAM-access case. Table 6.1 summarizes this comparison, and provides bit counts for an example single-chip configuration. Although the number of bits in the linked list and CAM-access approaches are comparable, the latter is less attractive due to the slower speed and higher implementation cost for the CAM chip.

## 6.3  SPACE-TIME-SPACE APPROACH

Figure 6.9 depicts an $8 \times 8$ example to show the basic configuration of the space-time-space (STS)-type shared-memory switch [3]. Separate buffer memories are shared among all input and output ports via crosspoint space-division switches. The multiplexing and demultiplexing stages in the traditional shared-memory switch are replaced with crosspoint space switches, thus the resulting structure is referred to STS-type. Since there is no time-division multiplexing, the required memory access speed may be drastically reduced.

The WRITE process is as follows. The destination of each incoming cell is inspected in a header detector, and is forwarded to the control block that controls the input-side space switch and thus the connection between the input ports and the buffer memories. As the number of shared-buffer memories (SBMs) is equal to or greater than the number of input ports, each incoming cell can surely be written into an SBM as far as no SBM is full. In order to realize the buffer sharing effectively, cells are written to the least occupied SBM first and the most occupied SBM last. When a cell is written into an SBM, its position (the SBM number and the address of the cell in the SBM) is queued in the address queue. The read address selector picks out the first address from each address queue and controls the output-side space switch to connect the picked cells (SBMs) with the corresponding output

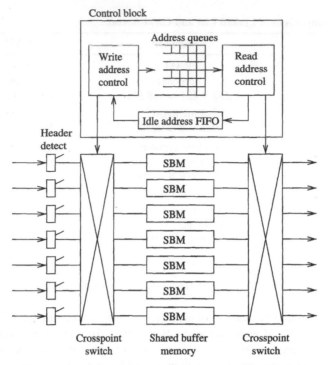

**Figure 6.9** Basic configuration of STS-type shared-memory ATM switch.

ports. It may occur that two or more cells picked for different output ports are from the same SBM. An example is shown in Figure 6.10. Thus, to increase switch's throughput it requires some kind of internal speedup to allow more than one cell to be read out from an SBM in every cell slot. Another disadvantage of this switch is the requirement of searching for the least occupied SBM (may need multiple searches in a time slot), which may cause a system bottleneck when the number of SBMs is large.

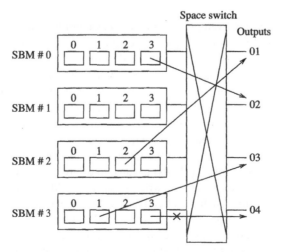

**Figure 6.10** Blocking in STS-type shared-memory switch.

## 6.4 SCALING THE SHARED-MEMORY SWITCHES

Since single shared memory switch is hard to scale to much larger capacity, it is a feasible approach to connect multiple shared memory blocks together in a multi-stage topology. The most common multi-stage topology is the three-stage Clos network (Fig. 6.11). There, the blocks in adjacent stages are fully connected.

In practical, several switch architectures are proposed which interconnected small-scale shared-memory switch modules with a multi-stage network to build a large-scale switch. Among them are Washington University Gigabit Switch [4], Concentrator-based Growable Switch Architecture [5], Multinet switch [6], Siemens switch [7], and Alcatel switch [8].

### 6.4.1 Washington University Gigabit Switch

Turner proposed an ATM switch architecture called the Washington University Gigabit Switch (WUGS) [4]. The overall architecture is shown in Figure 6.12. It consists of three main components; the input port processors (IPPs), the output port processors (OPPs), and

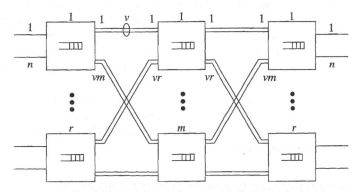

**Figure 6.11**   Three-stage switching fabric of shared-memory blocks.

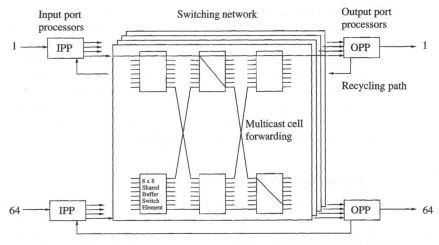

**Figure 6.12**   Washington university gigabit switch (WUGS) (©1997 IEEE).

the central switching network. The IPP receives cells from the incoming links, buffers them while awaiting transmission through the central switching network and performs the virtual path/circuit translation required to route cells to their proper outputs. The OPP resequences cells received from the switching network and queues them while they await transmission on the outgoing link. This resequencing operation increases the delay and implementation complexity. Each OPP is connected to its corresponding IPP, providing the ability to recycle cells belonging to multicast connections. The central switching network is made up of switching elements (SEs) with eight inputs and eight outputs and a common buffer to resolve local contention. The SEs switch cells to the proper output using information contained in the cell header or distribute cells dynamically to provide load balancing. Adjacent switch elements employ a simple hardware flow control mechanism to regulate the flow of cells between successive stages, eliminating the possibility of cell loss within the switching network.

The switching network uses a Benes network topology. The Benes network extends to arbitrarily large configurations by the way of a recursive expansion. Figure 6.12 shows a 64 port Benes network. A 512 port network can be constructed by taking eight copies of the 64 port network and adding the first and fifth stage on either side, with 64 switch elements a copy. Output $j$ of the $i$th switch element in the first stage is then connected to input $i$ of the $j$th 64 port network. Similarly, output $j$ of the $i$th 64-port network is connected to input $i$ of the $j$th switch element in the fifth stage. Repeating in this way, any large size network can be obtained. For $N = 8^k$, the Benes network constructed using eight port switch elements has $(2k - 1)$ stages. Since $k = \log_8 N$, the number of switch elements scales in proportion to $N \log_8 N$, which is the best possible scaling characteristic. In [4], it is shown that when dynamic load distribution is performed in the first $(k - 1)$ stages of the Benes network, the load on the internal data paths of the switching network cannot exceed the load on the external ports; that is, the network achieves ideal load balancing. This is true for both point-to-point and multipoint traffic.

### 6.4.2 Concentrator-Based Growable Switch Architecture

A concentrator-based growable switch architecture is shown in Figure 6.13 [5]. The $8 \times 8$ output ATM switches (with the shared-memory structure) are each preceded by an $N \times 8$ concentrator. The $N \times 8$ concentrator is preceded by a front-end broadcast network (i.e., a memoryless cell distribution network). The concentrators are preceded by address filters that only accept cells that are destined to its group of dedicated outputs. The valid cells in each concentrator are then buffered for a FIFO operation. In other words, each concentrator is an $N$-input eight-output FIFO buffer. The actual ATM cell switching is performed in the ATM Output Switch. Obviously, this is increasingly challenging as $N$ becomes large. For instance, a $512 \times 8$ concentrator can be built using a column of eight $64 \times 8$ concentrators followed by another $64 \times 8$ concentrator. At 2.5 Gbit/s per port, a $64 \times 64$ switch has a capacity of 160 Gbit/s, and a $512 \times 512$ switch has a capacity of 1.28 Tbit/s.

### 6.4.3 Parallel Shared-Memory Switches

A parallel shared-memory structure is given in Figure 6.14 [9]. $N$ input ports are divided into $\lceil N/n \rceil$ groups, with each group of $n$ input ports. There are in total $\lceil N/n \rceil^2$ shared-memory switch modules, each with $n$ ports, connected in parallel. $\lceil N/n \rceil^2$ switch modules are divided into $\lceil N/n \rceil$ groups with $\lceil N/n \rceil$ blocks in each group (as the dotted area in

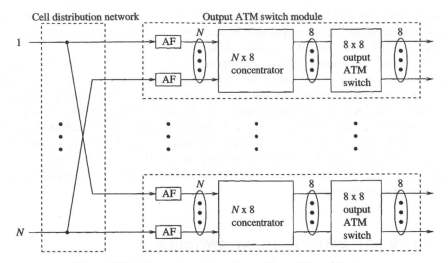

**Figure 6.13**   Concentrator-based growable switch architecture.

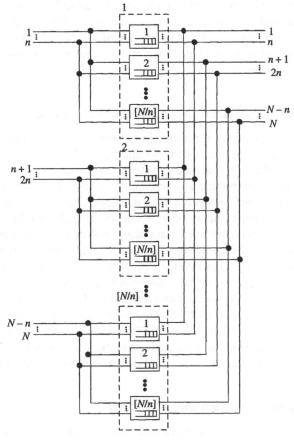

**Figure 6.14**   Switching fabric with parallel shared-memory switches.

Fig. 6.14). Each group of $n$ input ports are connected to each of $\lceil N/n \rceil$ switch modules, as shown in the figure. At the output side, each output group ($n$ ports) is connected to the outputs of $\lceil N/n \rceil$ switch modules, as shown in the figure.

In this parallel architecture, arrival packets are stored in one of its connected shared-memory switch modules that contain the output port that the packets are destined for. For instance, packets from the $i$th input port group destined for $j$th output port group are stored in the $j$th switch module in $i$th shared memory group. As a result, incoming traffic is partitioned into $\lceil N/n \rceil^2$ groups and each is handled by a switch module. This parallel switch architecture allows each shared-memory switch module operating $\lceil N/n \rceil$ times slower than a single $N \times N$ shared-memory switch. However, more buffer capacity is required to guarantee the same cell loss rate of a single $N \times N$ shared-memory switch due to less sharing efficiency.

## 6.5   MULTICAST SHARED-MEMORY SWITCHES

Of the various ATM switch architectures, the shared-memory switch provides superior benefits compared to others. Since its memory space is shared among its switch ports, it achieves high buffer utilization efficiency. Under conditions of identical memory size, the cell-loss probability of the shared-memory switches is smaller than output-buffered switches. Additionally, multicast operations can be easily supported by this switch architecture. In this section, some classes of multicast shared-memory switches are described along with their advantages and disadvantages.

### 6.5.1   Shared-Memory Switch with a Multicast Logical Queue

The simplest way to implement multicasting in a shared-memory switch is to link all multicasting cells in a logical queue as shown in Figure 6.15. The advantage of this approach is the number of logical queues that need to be updated in every cell slot is minimized. The multicast routing table stores routing information, such as a bit-map of output ports to which the multicast cells are routed. In this example, multicast cells always have higher priority than unicast cells. It is called strict priority, where unicast cells will be served only when the multicast logical queue is empty or the multicast HOL cell is not destined for the output port for which multicast cells are destined. Of course, there can be other service policies between unicast and multicast cells than the strict priority. For instance, they can be served in a round-robin manner, or a weighted round-robin manner with the weight depending on, for example, the ratio of unicast and multicast traffic load. However, the major disadvantage of this approach is there may be HOL blocking for the multicast logical queue when the schemes other than the strict priority are used. This is because when the multicast HOL cell is blocked because of yielding its turn to unicast cells, it may block other multicast cells that are behind it which could otherwise have been transmitted to some idle outputs.

### 6.5.2   Shared-Memory Switch with Cell Copy

In this approach, a multicast cell is replicated into multiple copies for all its multicast connections by a cell-copy circuit located before the routing switch. Bianchini and Kim [10] proposed a nonblocking cell-copy circuit for multicast purposes in an ATM switch.

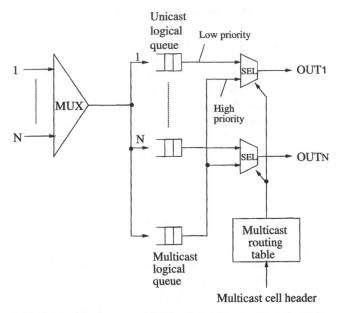

**Figure 6.15**  A shared-memory ATM switch with a multicast logical queue.

Each copy is stored in the SBM. The address for each copy is queued in output address queues (AQs).

Figure 6.16 shows an example of a shared-memory switch with a cell-copy circuit. A multicast cell arrives and is replicated into three copies for output ports 0, 1, and 3. These three

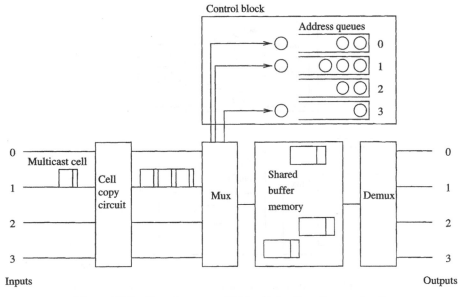

**Figure 6.16**  Shared-memory ATM switch with cell-copy circuit.

copies of the cell are stored at different locations of the shared buffer memory. Meanwhile, their addresses are stored at corresponding address queues. In this scheme, after replicating the multicast cell, each copy is treated the same way as a unicast cell. It provides fairness among cells. The major disadvantage of this approach is that, in the worst case, $N$ cells might be replicated to $N^2$ cells. Thus, the number of replicated cells to the SBM in each switch cycle could be $O(N^2)$. Since only at most $N$ cells could be transmitted, this would result in storing $O(N^2)$ cells in each cycle. For a finite memory space, it would result in considerable cell loss. The replication of multicast cells would also require $O(N^2)$ cells to be written to the SBM, which will further limit the switch size from the memory speed. Moreover, adding the cell-copy circuit in the switch increases hardware complexity.

### 6.5.3  Shared-Memory Switch with Address Copy

Saito et al. [11] have proposed a scheme that required less memory for the same cell loss probability. A similar architecture was also proposed by Schultz and Gulak [12] in the same year. In these schemes, an address-copy circuit is used in the controller. When a multicast cell arrives, only a single copy is stored in the shared buffer memory (SBM). Its address is copied by the address-copy circuit and queued into multiple address queues, as shown in Figure 6.17. The multicast cell will be read multiple times to different output ports. Once completed, the cell's address becomes available for the next arriving cells.

In this architecture, multicast cell counters (MCCs) are required to hold the number of copies of each multicast cell. The MCC values are loaded as new cells (unicast or multicast). They are decreased by one each time a copy of a cell is read out from the SBM.

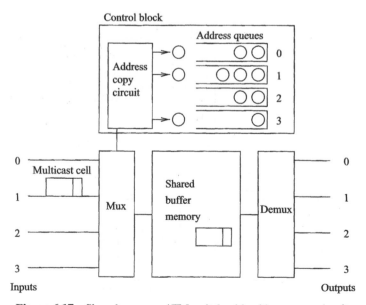

**Figure 6.17**   Shared-memory ATM switch with address-copy circuit.

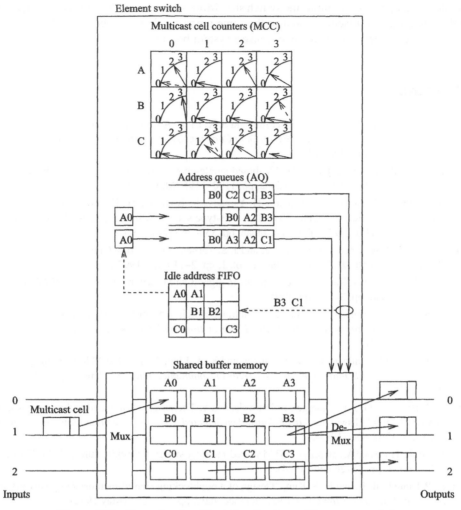

**Figure 6.18**  Example of multicast function in an address-copy switch.

Figure 6.18 illustrates an example of a 3 × 3 ATM switch. In this example, a multicast cell arriving at input port 1 is destined for output ports 1 and 2. The multicast cell is written into A0 in the SBM, and its address is provided by an Idle Address FIFO (IAF). Other vacant cells' addresses stored in the IAF are A1, B1, B2, C0, and C3. A0 is copied and queued in the Address Queues 1 and 2. At the same time, the MCC of A0 is set to two. Another multicast cell stored at B3 is destined for output ports 0 and 1. As it is transmitted to both output ports 0 and 1, the associated MCC becomes zero and the address B3 is released to the IAF. Within the same time slot, the cell stored at C1 is read to output port 2. Since it still has one copy to be sent to output port 0, its address C1 is not released until it is transmitted to output port 0.

Although in each time slot the maximum number of cells to be written into the buffer is $N$, the number of replications of cell addresses for incoming cells could be $O(N^2)$ in the broadcast case, which still limits the switch size. More specifically, since the address queues or the MCCs are in practice stored in the same memory, there can be up to $N^2$ memory accesses in each cell slot, which may cause a system bottleneck for a large $N$.

## REFERENCES

[1] H. Lee, K. H. Kook, C. S. Rim, K. P. Jun, and S. K. Lim, "A limited shared output buffer switch for ATM," in *Proc. Fourth Int. Conf. on Data Commun. Syst. and their Performance*, Barcelona, Spain, pp. 163–179 (June 1990).

[2] K. J. Schultz and P. G. Gulak, "CAM-based single-chip shared buffer ATM switch," in *Proc. IEEE ICC'94*, New Orleans, Louisiana, pp. 1190–1195 (May 1994).

[3] K. Oshima, H. Yamanaka, H. Saito, H. Yamada, S. Kohama, H. Kondoh, and Y. Matsuda, "A new ATM switch architecture based on STS-type shared buffering and its LSI implementation," in *Proc. IEICE'92*, Yokohama, Japan, pp. 359–363 (Mar. 1992).

[4] T. Cheney, J. A. Fingerhut, M. Flucke, and J. S. Turner, "Design of a Gigabit ATM switch," in *Proc. IEEE INFOCOM'97*, Kobe, Japan, vol. 1, pp. 2–11 (Apr. 1997).

[5] K. Y. Eng and M. J. Karol, "State of the art in gigabit ATM switching," in *Proc. IEEE BSS'95*, Poznan, Poland, pp. 3–20 (Apr. 1995).

[6] H. S. Kim, "Design and performance of multinet switch: a multistage ATM switch architecture with partially shared buffers," *IEEE/ACM Transactions on Networking*, vol. 2, no. 6, pp. 571–580 (Dec. 1994).

[7] W. Fischer, O. Fundneider, E. H. Goeldner, and K. A. Lutz, "A scalable ATM switching system architecture," *IEEE Journal on Selected Areas in Communications*, vol. 9, no. 8, pp. 1299–1307 (Oct. 1991).

[8] T. R. Banniza, G. J. Eilenberger, B. Pauwels, and Y. Therasse, "Design and technology aspects of VLSI's for ATM switches," *IEEE Journal on Selected Areas in Communications*, vol. 9, no. 8, pp. 1255–1264 (Oct. 1991).

[9] J. Garcia-Haro and A. Jajszczyk, "ATM shared-memory switching architectures," *IEEE Network*, vol. 8, no. 4, pp. 18–26 (July 1994).

[10] R. P. Bianchini, Jr. and H. S. Kim, "Design of a nonblocking shared-memory copy network for ATM," in *Proc. IEEE INFOCOM'92*, Florence, Italy, pp. 876–885 (May 1992).

[11] H. Saito, H. Yamanaka, H. Yamada, M. Tuzuki, H. Kondoh, Y. Matsuda, and K. Oshima, "Multicast function and its LSI implementation in a shared multibuffer ATM switch," in *Proc. IEEE INFOCOM'94*, Toronto, Canada, vol. 1, pp. 315–322 (June 1994).

[12] T. H. Lee and S. J. Liu, "Multicasting in a shared buffer memory switch," in *Proc. IEEE TENCON'93*, Beijing, People's Republic of China, pp. 209–212 (Oct. 1993).

# CHAPTER 7

# INPUT-BUFFERED SWITCHES

Fixed-length switching technology is widely accepted as an efficient approach to achieving high switching efficiency for high-speed packet switches. Variable-length IP packets are segmented into fixed-length "cells" at inputs and are reassembled at the outputs. When high-speed packet switches were constructed for the first time, they used, either internal shared buffer or input buffer and suffered the problem of throughput limitation. As a result, historically most research focused on the output buffering architecture. Since the initial demand for switch capacity was in the range of a few hundred Mbit/s to a few Gbit/s, output buffered switches seemed to be a good choice because of their high throughput/delay performance and memory utilization (for shared memory switches). In the first few years of deploying ATM switches, output buffered switches (including shared memory switches) dominated the market. However, as the demand for large-capacity switches increased rapidly (either line rates or the switch port number increased), the speed requirement for the memory had to increase accordingly. This limits the capacity of output buffered switches. Although output buffered switches have optimal delay-throughput performance for all traffic distributions, the $N$-times speed-up for the memory operation speed limits the scalability of this architecture. Therefore, in order to build larger-scale and higher-speed switches, people now have focused on input-buffered, or combined-input-output-buffered switches with advanced scheduling and routing techniques, which are the main subjects of this chapter.

Input buffered switches are desirable for high-speed switching, since the internal operation speed is only moderately higher than the input line speed. But there are two problems: (1) throughput limitation due to the head-of-line (HOL) blocking (throughput limited to 58.6 percent for FIFO buffering), and (2) the need of arbitrating cells due to output port contention. The first problem can be circumvented by moderately increasing the switch fabric's operation speed or the number of routing paths to each output port (i.e., allowing multiple cells arriving at the output port at the same time slot). The second problem

*High Performance Switches and Routers*, by H. Jonathan Chao and Bin Liu
Copyright © 2007 John Wiley & Sons, Inc.

is resolved by novel, fast arbitration (i.e., scheduling) schemes that are described in this chapter. According to Moore's Law, memory density doubles every 18 months. But the memory speed increases at a much slower rate. For instance, the memory speed is 4 ns for state-of-the-art CMOS static RAM compared to 5 ns one or two years ago. On the other hand, the speed of logic circuits has increased at a much higher rate than that of memory. Recently, much research has been devoted to devising faster scheduling schemes to arbitrate cells from input ports to output ports.

Some scheduling schemes even consider per-flow scheduling at the input ports to meet the delay/throughput requirements for each flow, which of course greatly increases implementation complexity and cost. Scheduling cells on a per-flow basis at input ports is much more difficult than at output ports. For example, at an output port, cells (or packets) can be time-stamped with values based on their allocated bandwidth and transmitted in an ascending order of their time stamp values. However, at an input port, scheduling cells must take output port contention into account. Thus, it makes the problem so complicated that so far no feasible scheme has been devised.

## 7.1 SCHEDULING IN VOQ-BASED SWITCHES

The basic input buffer switch model is shown in Figure 7.1. A FIFO queue is implemented in front of each input of the switch fabric, and is used to store incoming packets. They are then scheduled to transmit to the switch fabric. Because of the HOL blocking, Section 5.3 shows that the overall throughput of the input buffer structure is limited to 58.6 percent under uniform traffic, and even worse under non-uniform traffic.

Because of the throughput limitation from the FIFO queue structure, virtual output queue (VOQ) structure, as shown in Figure 7.2, has been widely used to eliminate the HOL blocking and thus improves the system throughout. In each input buffer, there are $N$ FIFO queues ($N$ is the switch size), each corresponding to an output port, or $N^2$ FIFO queues in total. In other words, packets/cells arriving at input port $i$ and destined for output port $j$ are stored in $VOQ_{i,j}$ (i.e., $Q_{i,j}$ in Fig. 7.2). The HOL cell of each VOQ can be scheduled for transmission in every time slot. However, there will be at most one cell among the $N$ VOQs being selected for transmission.

The cell arrival to input port $i$ is a stochastic process $A_i(t)$. Within each time slot, there is at most one arrived at each input port. The cell that arrived at input port $i$ and destined to output $j$ is put into queue $Q_{ij}$. At time slot $t$, the queue length of $Q_{ij}$ is denoted as $L_{ij}(t)$.

$A_{ij}(t)$ denotes the arrival process from input $i$ to output $j$ with an arrival rate of $\lambda_{ij}$, and $A(t) = \{A_{ij}(t), 1 \le i \le N \text{ and } 1 \le j \le N\}$. If the arrivals to each input and each output are

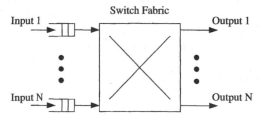

**Figure 7.1** Input-buffered switch model with FIFO queues.

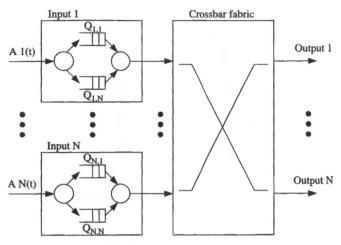

**Figure 7.2**   Input-buffered structure with virtual output queues.

admissible, that is,

$$\sum_{i=1}^{N} \lambda_{ij} < 1, \; \forall j \quad \text{and} \quad \sum_{j=1}^{N} \lambda_{ij} < 1, \; \forall i$$

then the set $A(t)$ is admissible. Otherwise, it is not admissible. The arrival rate matrix is denoted as $\Lambda = [\lambda_{ij}]$.

Let the service matrix $S(t) = [s_{ij}(t)]_{N \times N}$ represent the matchings at time slot $t$ with each element:

$$s_{ij}(t) = \begin{cases} 1, & \text{if a cell is transfered from } i \text{ to } j \\ 0, & \text{otherwise} \end{cases}$$

A cell arrival that is an independent process satisfies the following two conditions: (1) Cell arrivals to each input port are independent and identically distributed; (2) The arrivals to an input port are independent from other input ports. If the arrival rates are equal, and the destinations are uniformly distributed among all output ports, then the arrival distribution is said to be uniform.

Throughput and delay are used to evaluate a switch's performance. Throughput is defined to be the average number of cells transmitted in a time slot, and delay is defined to be the time experienced by a cell from arrival to departure. A switch is defined to be stable, if the expected queue length is bounded, that is,

$$E\left[\sum_{ij} L_{ij}\right] < \infty, \; \forall t.$$

If a switch is stable under any independent and admissible input traffic, then the switch can achieve 100 percent throughput.

Sophisticated scheduling algorithms are required to schedule cells to the switch fabric in each time slot. These scheduling algorithms can be modeled as a bipartite graph matching

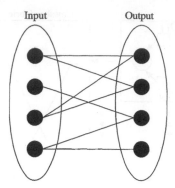

**Figure 7.3**   Bipartite graph matching example.

problem. In Figure 7.3, $N$ nodes on the left stand for the $N$ input ports, while the $N$ nodes on the right stand for $N$ output ports. The edge between an input port and an output port denotes that there are requests for cells to be transferred between them. A scheduler is responsible for selecting a set of the edges (also called matches) from at most $N^2$ edges, where each input is connected to at most one output and each output is connected to at most one input. A matching example is shown in Figure 7.4 where the dotted lines represent the requests that are not granted. A matching of input–output can be represented as a permutation matrix $M = (M_{i,j}), i,j \leq N$, where $M_{i,j} = 1$ if input $i$ is matched to output $j$ in the matching.

To select a proper scheduling algorithm, several factors must be considered:

*Efficiency.* The algorithm should achieve high throughput and low delay. In other words, select a set of matches with more edges in each time slot.

*Fairness.* The algorithm should avoid the starvation of each VOQ.

*Stability.* The expected occupancy of each VOQ should remain finite for any admissible traffic pattern.

*Implementation Complexity.* The algorithm should be easy for hardware implementation. High implementing complexity will cause long scheduling time, which further limits the line speed of the switch.

With the above design objectives, many scheduling algorithms have been proposed. We will examine some of these algorithms in detail.

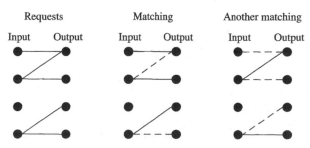

**Figure 7.4**   Matching example.

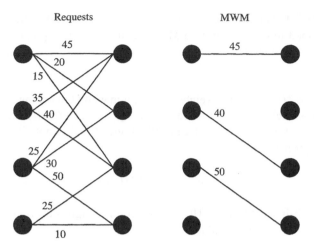

**Figure 7.5**   Maximum weight match example.

## 7.2  MAXIMUM MATCHING

### 7.2.1  Maximum Weight Matching

In a bipartite graph, we define $w_{i,j}$ as the weight of edge $e_{i,j}$, from input $i$ to output $j$. Weight of a VOQ refers usually, but not restricted to, the length (number of packets in backlog) of the VOQ. The maximum weight matching (MWM) $M$ for a bipartite graph is one that maximizes $\sum_{e_{(i,j)} \in M} w_{i,j}$. Figure 7.5 shows an example of a maximum weight match.

**Theorem 1:** A maximum weight matching algorithm achieves 100 percent throughput under any admissible traffic [1, 2].

MWM can be solved in time $O(N^3)$ [3], which is, too large for a high-speed packet switch. By carefully selecting the weight of each edge, or using approximations of MWM, we can reduce the complexity of computing maximum weight matches.

LQF (longest queue first) and OCF (oldest cell first) [1] are two MWM algorithms that were proposed early on. LQF uses the queue length $L_{ij}(t)$ as the weight $w_{ij}(t)$ and OCF uses the HOL cell's waiting time as the weight $w_{ij}(t)$. Under admissible traffic, these two algorithms can achieve 100 percent throughput. Under inadmissible traffic, starvation can occur for LQF, but not for OCQ. In order to reduce the complexity of LQF, the LPF (longest port first) algorithm is proposed [4] with weight $w_{ij}(t)$ defined to be the port occupancy:

$$w_{ij}(t) = \begin{cases} R_i(t) + C_j(t), & L_{ij}(t) > 0 \\ 0, & \text{otherwise} \end{cases}$$

where $R_i(t) = \sum_{j=1}^{N} L_{ij}(t)$, $C_j(t) = \sum_{i=1}^{N} L_{ij}(t)$. Since the weight of LPF is not equal to the queue length, it has the advantage of both maximum size matching (MSM) and MWM.

### 7.2.2  Approximate MWM

In the work of Shah and Kopikare [5], a class of approximations to MWM, 1-APRX, was proposed and defined as follows. Let the weight of a schedule obtained by a scheduling algorithm $B$ be $W^B$. Let the weight of the maximum weight match for the same switch state be $W^*$. $B$ is defined to be a 1-APRX to MWM, if the following property is always true: $W^B \geq W^* - f(W^*)$, where $f(\cdot)$ is a sub-linear function, that is, $\lim_{x \to \infty} [f(x)/x] = 0$ for any switch state.

**Theorem 2:** Let $W^*(t)$ denote the weight of maximum weight matching scheduling at time $t$, with respect to switch state $Q(t)$ (where $Q(t) = [Q_{i,j}(t)]$ and $Q_{i,j}(t)$ denotes the number of cells in $VOQ_{i,j}$). Let $B$ be a 1-APRX to MWM and $W^B(t)$ denote its weight at time $t$. Further, $B$ has a property that,

$$W^B(t) \geq W^*(t) - f(W^*(t)), \qquad \forall t, \tag{7.1}$$

where $f(\cdot)$ is a sub-linear function. Then the scheduling algorithm $B$ is stable under any admissible Bernoulli i.i.d. input traffic.

Theorem 2 can be used to prove the stability of some matching algorithms that are not MWM and with lower complexity. Examples are the de-randomized matching algorithm with memory in Section 7.5.2 and the Exhaustive Service Matching with Hamiltonian Walk in Section 7.4.4.

### 7.2.3 Maximum Size Matching

Maximum size matching (MSM) finds the match containing the maximum number of edges. Obviously, maximum size matching is a special case of the maximum weight matching when the weight of each edge is 1. The time complexity of MSM is $O(N^{2.5})$ in survey [6]. Figure 7.6 shows an example of a maximum size match.

It has been shown by simulation that MSM delivers 100 percent throughput when the traffic is permissible uniform [7]. However, under admissible nonuniform traffic, it can lead to instability and unfairness, and under impermissible distribution, it can lead to starvation for some ports [1].

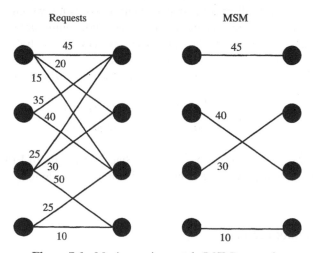

**Figure 7.6** Maximum size match (MSM) example.

## 7.3 MAXIMAL MATCHING

A maximal matching algorithm leads to a maximal match by adding connections incrementally, without removing connections made earlier in the matching process. In a maximal match, if a nonempty input is not matched to any output, all destination outputs of the cells waiting in this input must have been matched to other inputs. Figure 7.7 shows an example of a maximal match. Generally speaking, a maximal match has fewer matched edges than a maximum size match, but is simpler to implement.

Maximal matching algorithms have lower implementation complexity than MWM. However, simulation results show that maximal matching achieves 100 percent throughput under uniform traffic, but not under nonuniform traffic. Speedup is needed to guarantee 100 percent throughput when a maximal matching algorithm is used. A switch with a speedup of $s$ can transfer up to $s$ cells from each input and up to $s$ cells to each output within a time slot. An output-queued switch has a speedup of $N$ and an input-queued switch has a speedup of 1. Usually, when $1 < s < N$, the switch is called a combined input- and output-queued (CIOQ) switch, since cells need to be buffered at the inputs before switching as well as at the outputs after switching.

**Theorem 3:** Under any admissible traffic, a CIOQ switch using any maximal matching algorithm achieves 100 percent throughput for any speedup $s \geq 2$ [8, 9].

One way to implement maximal matching is to use iterative matching algorithms that use multiple iterations to converge on a maximal match. In each iteration, at least one more connection is added to the match before a maximal match is achieved. Therefore, a maximal match can always be found within $N$ iterations. Some multiple iteration matching algorithms converge faster and require fewer iterations, for example, $\log_2 N$. The main difference between various iterative matching algorithms is the rationale for selection of input ports to grant, and output ports to accept, when scheduling.

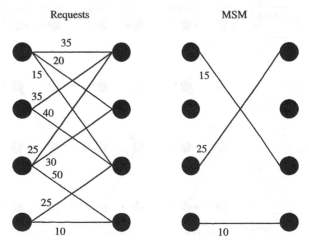

**Figure 7.7**   Maximal match example.

### 7.3.1    Parallel Iterative Matching (PIM)

The PIM scheme [10] uses random selection to solve the contention between inputs and outputs. Input cells are first queued in VOQs. Each iteration consists of three steps. There can be up to $N$ iterations in each time slot. Initially, all inputs and outputs are unmatched and only those inputs and outputs that are not matched at the end of an iteration will be eligible to participate in the next matching iteration. The three steps in each iteration operate in parallel on each input and output as follows.

Step 1: *Request.* Each unmatched input sends a request to every output for which it has a queued cell.

Step 2: *Grant.* If an unmatched output receives multiple requests, it grants one by randomly selecting a request over all requests. Each request has an equal probability of being granted.

Step 3: *Accept.* If an input receives multiple grants, it selects one to accept in a fair manner and notifies the output.

Figure 7.8 shows an example of PIM in the first iteration. In step 1, input 1 requests output 1 and 2, input 3 requests output 2 and 4, input 4 requests output 4. In step 2, output 1 grants the only request from input 1, output 2 randomly chooses input 3 to grant, and output 4 chooses input 3. In the last step 3, input 1 accepts the only grant from output 1 and input 3 randomly chooses output 2 to accept.

It has been shown that each iteration resolves, on average, at least 25 percent of the remaining unresolved requests. Thus, the algorithm converges at $O(\log N)$ iterations, where $N$ denotes the number of ports. No memory or state is used to keep track of how recently a connection was made in the past since, at the beginning of a cell time slot, the match begins over, independently of the matches that were made in previous cell time slots. On the other hand, PIM does not perform well for a single iteration. The throughput of PIM for one iteration is about 63 percent under uniform traffic. The reason is as follows:

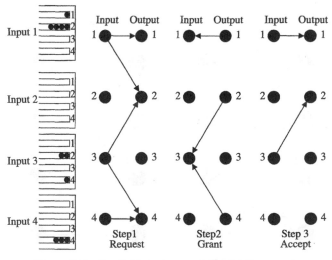

**Figure 7.8**    Parallel iterative matching (PIM) example.

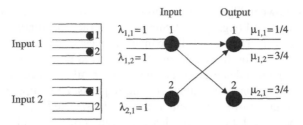

**Figure 7.9** Example of unfairness in PIM under heavy, oversubscribed load with more than one iteration.

Assume that each VOQ of an $N \times N$ switch is nonempty. With PIM, each output will receive $N$ requests, one from each input. The probability that an output selects a particular input to grant is $1/N$, so that the probability that an input is not selected by an output is $1 - (1/N)$. If an input is granted by at least one output, this input will randomly select one of them to accept and be matched. In other words, if an input does not receive any grant, it will not be matched. This will happen when none of the outputs selects this input to grant, with a probability of $[1 - (1/N)]^N$, or $1/e$ as $N \to \infty$. Therefore, the throughput tends to $1 - (1/e) \simeq 0.63$ as $N \to \infty$.

Thus, under uniform traffic, PIM achieves 63 percent and 100 percent throughput for 1 and $N$ iterations, respectively. Despite the 100 percent throughput PIM achieves with $N$ iterations. When the switch is oversubscribed, PIM can lead to unfairness between connections [11]. Figure 7.9 shows such a situation. In the figure, input port 1 has cells to output port 1 and 2 in every time slot and similarly input port 2 has cells to output port 1. Under PIM, input port 1 will only accept output port 1 for a quarter of the time since output port 1 should first grant input port 1 and then input port 1 should accept output port 1. However, since no input port competes with input port 1 at output port 2, input port 1 will accept output port 2 during the other three quarters of the time. This results in unfairness between traffic from input port 1 to output port 1 and from input port 1 to output port 2. Moreover, implementing a random function at high speed can be expensive.

### 7.3.2 Iterative Round-Robin Matching (*i*RRM)

The *i*RRM scheme [12] works similar to PIM, but uses the round-robin schedulers instead of random selection at both inputs and outputs. Each scheduler maintains a pointer pointing at the port that has the highest priority. Such a pointer is named accept pointer $a_i$ at input $i$ and grant pointer $g_j$ at output $j$. The steps for this algorithm are as follows:

Step 1: *Request.* Each unmatched input sends a request to every output for which it has a queued cell.

Step 2: *Grant.* If an unmatched output receives any requests, it chooses the one that appears next in a round-robin schedule starting from the highest priority element. The output notifies each input whether or not its request was granted. The pointer $g_i$ is incremented (module $N$) to one location beyond the granted input.

Step 3: *Accept.* If an input receives multiple grants, it accepts the one that appears next in its round-robin schedule starting from the highest priority element. Similarly, the pointer $a_j$ is incremented (module $N$) to one location beyond the accepted output.

An example is shown in Figure 7.10. In this example, we assume that the initial value of each grant pointer is input 1 (e.g., $g_i = 1$). Similarly, each accept pointer is initially pointing to output 1 (e.g., $a_j = 1$). During step 1, the inputs request transmission to all outputs that they have a cell destined for. In step 2, among all received requests, each grant scheduler selects the requesting input that is nearest to the one currently pointed to. Output 1 chooses input 1, output 2 chooses input 1, output 3 has no requests, and output 4 chooses input 3. Then, each grant pointer moves one position beyond the selected one. In this case, $g_1 = 2$, $g_2 = 2$, $g_3 = 1$, and $g_4 = 4$. In step 3, each accept pointer decides which grant is accepted in a similar way as the grant pointers did. In this example, input 1 accepts output 1, and input 3 accepts output 4; then $a_1 = 2$, $a_2 = 1$, $a_3 = 1$, and $a_4 = 1$. Notice that the pointer $a_3$ accepted the grant issued by output 4, so the pointer returns to position 1.

Although *i*RRM brings good fairness by using a round-robin policy, it actually does not achieve much higher throughput than PIM under 1 iteration. This is predominantly due to the output pointer update mechanism. Considering the situation when input port $i$ with accept pointer pointing to $j$ has cells for all output ports, and the grant pointers in all output point to $i$, with one iteration, only one cell will be transferred in the system from input port $i$ to output port $j$. It is worse that all output pointers are updated to $i + 1$ identically. This phenomenon in *i*RRM is called output synchronization. It significantly degrades the throughput of *i*RRM. An example is given in Figure 7.11. The $2 \times 2$ switch with one iteration *i*RRM will only achieve 50 percent throughput under heavy load.

### 7.3.3 Iterative Round-Robin with SLIP (*i*SLIP)

As illustrated in the above section, although easily implemented in hardware, the *i*RRM, in some cases, suffers from output synchronization. An enhanced scheme (*i*SLIP) was presented in the work of McNeown [11].

The steps for this scheme are as follows:

Step 1: *Request.* Each unmatched input sends a request to every output for which it has a queued cell.

Step 2: *Grant.* If an unmatched output receives multiple requests, it chooses the one that appears next in a fixed, round-robin schedule starting from the highest priority element. The output notifies each input whether or not its request was granted. The grant pointer $g_i$ is incremented (module $N$) to one location beyond the granted input if and only if the grant is accepted in step 3 of the first iteration.

Step 3: *Accept.* If an input receives multiple grants, it accepts the one that appears next in a fixed, round-robin schedule starting from the highest priority element. The pointer $a_j$ is incremented (modulo $N$) to one location beyond the accepted output. The accept pointers $a_i$ are only updated in the first iteration.

The main difference compared to *i*RRM is that in *i*SLIP, the grant pointers update their positions only if their grants are accepted. Also, the output grant pointer and input accept pointer will only be updated during the first iteration, since if the pointers are updated in each iteration, some connection may be starved indefinitely. Figure 7.12 shows an example. It depicts a request graph in the first time slot. Assume that the accept pointer of input port 1 points to output port 1, and the grant pointer of output 2 points to input port 1. During the first iteration of that time slot, the input port 1 will accept output port 1, and in the second iteration, output port 2 will grant input port 2, since input port 1 has been connected.

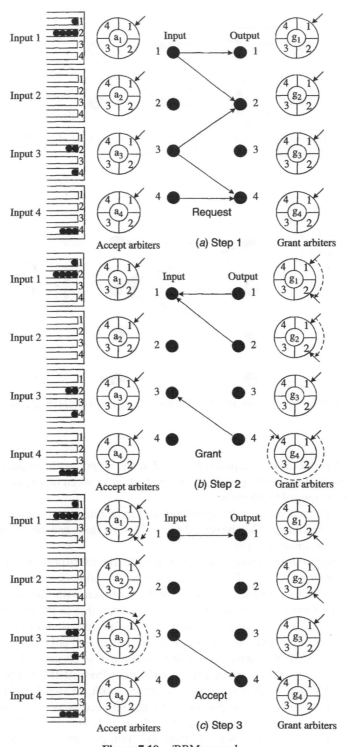

**Figure 7.10**  *i*RRM example.

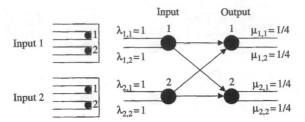

**Figure 7.11**    Synchronization of output arbiters leads to a throughput of just 50 percent in *i*RRM under heavy, oversubscribed load with more than one iteration.

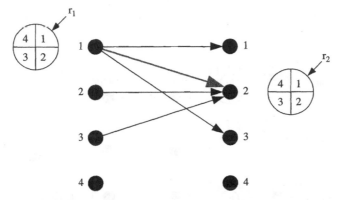

**Figure 7.12**    Request graph when *i*SLIP will cause starvation if pointers are updated in every iteration.

When the input port 2 finally accepts output port 2, the grant pointer in output port 2 will be updated beyond input port 1 to port 3. So the connection between input port 1 and output port 2 may be postponed indefinitely.

However, in this scheme of updating pointer only in first iteration, starvation is avoided because every requesting pair will be served within 2$N$ time slots, and the newest connected pair is assigned the lowest priority.

Because of the round-robin motion of the pointers, the algorithm provides a fair allocation of bandwidth among all flows. This scheme contains 2$N$ arbiters, where each arbiter is implementable with low complexity. The throughput offered with this algorithm is 100 percent under uniform traffic for any number of iterations due to the desynchronization effect (see Section 7.3.5). A matching example of this scheme is shown in Figure 7.13. Considering the example from the *i*RRM discussion, initially all pointers $a_j$ and $g_i$ are set to 1. In step 2 of *i*SLIP, the output accepts the request that is closer to the pointed input in a clockwise direction; however, in a manner different from *i*RRM, the pointers $g_i$ are not updated in this step. They wait for the acceptance result. In step 3, the inputs accept the grant that is closer to the one pointed to by $a_i$. The accept pointers change to one position beyond the accepted one, $a_1 = 2$, $a_2 = 1$, $a_3 = 1$, and $a_4 = 1$. Then, after the accept pointers decide which grant is accepted, the grant pointers change to one position beyond the accepted grant (i.e., a non-accepted grant produces no change in a grant pointer position). The new values for these pointers are $g_1 = 2$, $g_2 = 1$, $g_3 = 1$, and $g_4 = 4$. In the

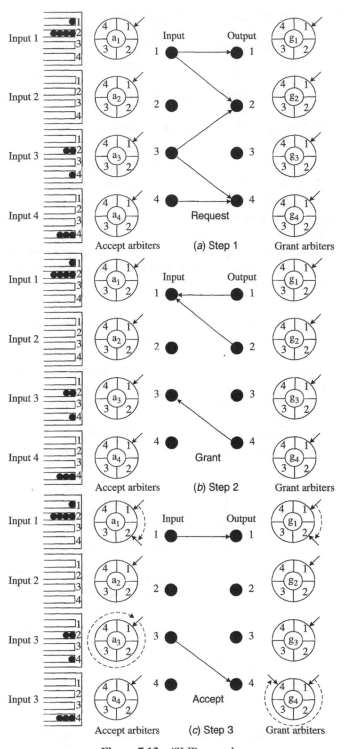

**Figure 7.13** *i*SLIP example.

following iterations, only the unmatched input and outputs are considered and the pointers are not modified (i.e., updating occurs in the first iteration only).

*i*SLIP can achieve 100 percent throughput with a single iteration under uniform Bernoulli independent and identically distributed (i.i.d.) arrival traffic [13, 14]. This is because, within a finite time, the pointer of each output arbiter will point to an input different from all other output pointers, so that every input will have one cell to be served in every time slot. We will show this by using a ball game.

Under heavy traffic, the *i*SLIP scheduling algorithm reduces to the following rules:

- In any time slot, each input sends requests to every output.
- At any output, if the pointer points to $k$ in a time slot, this output grants the request from the $k$th input. If the grant is selected to be accepted by the $k$th input arbiter, in the next time slot the pointer points to $(k + 1) \mod N$; if it is not selected, in the next time slot the pointer will be still at $k$.
- At any input $k$, if only one output arbiter pointer points to $k$, this output will be selected by input $k$; if there are $m(m > 1)$ output arbiter pointers pointing to input $k$, one of them will be selected.

We define a vector $X_i = (x_{1,i}, \ldots, x_{k,i}, \ldots, x_{N,i})$ to express the state of input arbiters; in time slot $i$, there are $x_{k,i}$ output arbiter pointers pointing to input $k$, $k = 1, \ldots, N$, $0 \leq x_{k,i} \leq N$, $\sum_{k=1}^{N} x_{k,i} = N$.

If at time slot $i$, $x_{k,i} = 1$, $k = 1, \ldots, N$, which indicates that each input is pointed by an output arbiter pointer, then the throughput is 100 percent in this time slot. We will now proceed to show $X_i = (1, 1, \ldots, 1)$ for all $i \geq N - 1$. Thus a throughput of 100 percent can be sustained indefinitely after $N - 1$ time slots.

To simplify the notation, we will drop the mod $N$, that is, $(k + l) \mod N$ will be represented by $k + l$. Using the *i*SLIP arbitration rules to the vector $X_i$, we get:

$$
x_{k,i+1} = \begin{cases}
0 & x_{k,i} \leq 1, x_{k-1,i} = 0 \\
x_{k,i} - 1 & x_{k,i} > 1, x_{k-1,i} = 0 \\
1 & x_{k,i} \leq 1, x_{k-1,i} > 0 \\
x_{k,i} & x_{k,i} > 1, x_{k-1,i} > 0
\end{cases} \tag{7.2}
$$

By cyclically shifting $X_i$ to the left by one slot every slot time, we get another vector $Y_i = (y_{1,i}, \ldots, y_{k,i}, \ldots, y_{N,i})$. This $Y_i$ is defined as follows: in time slot 0,

$$
Y_0 = X_0 \tag{7.3}
$$

that is, $y_{k,0} = x_{k,0}$, $k = 1, \ldots, N$, and in time slot $m \geq 0$,

$$
y_{k,m} = x_{k+m,m}, \quad k = 1, \ldots, N \tag{7.4}
$$

At any time slot, $y_{k,i}$ represents the state of one input arbiter. If, and only if, in time slot $i$, $y_{k,i} = 1$ for all $k = 1, \ldots, N$, then $x_{k,i}$ also equals to 1 for all $k$. Therefore it is sufficient to show that $Y_i = (1, 1, \ldots, 1)$ for all $i \geq N - 1$ to prove the 100 percent throughput of *i*SLIP under uniform traffic.

According to (7.2), (7.3), and (7.4), we get

$$
y_{k,i+1} = \begin{cases} 0 & y_{k+1,i} \leq 1, y_{k,i} = 0 \quad (\textit{condition 1}) \\ y_{k+1,i} - 1 & y_{k+1,i} > 1, y_{k,i} = 0 \quad (\textit{condition 2}) \\ 1 & y_{k+1,i} \leq 1, y_{k,i} > 0 \quad (\textit{condition 3}) \\ y_{k+1,i} & y_{k+1,i} > 1, y_{k,i} > 0 \quad (\textit{condition 4}) \end{cases}
\tag{7.5}
$$

From (7.5), by considering the third and fourth conditions, we can conclude that whenever $y_k$ is larger than 0, it will always be larger than 0 after that. According to this conclusion, if in time slot $i$, $y_{k,i} = 1$ for all $k = 1, \ldots, N$, then for any time slot $j > i$, all $y_{k,j}$ will always be larger than 0. Since there are $N$ inputs and $N$ outputs, and $\sum_{k=1}^{N} y_k = N$, after time slot $i$, $y_k = 1, k = 1, \ldots, N$, which indicates that $x_k = 1$ for all $k$ and the throughput will always be 100 percent. We will next prove that with any initial state $Y_0$, in a finite number of time slots $M$, where $M$ is no more than $N - 1$, we will always have $y_{k,M} = 1, k = 1, \ldots, N$.

The state vector $Y$ and its state transitions can be expressed as a game shown in Figure 7.14. In the game, we have $N$ balls placed in $N$ boxes. In time slot $i$, there are $y_{k,i}$ balls in the $k$th box, $k = 1, \ldots, N$. We will show that no matter how many balls there are in each box at the beginning, after at most $N - 1$ time slots, every box will always contain exactly one ball.

The rule that determines the movement of the balls in the boxes is as follows:

In time slot $i$, if box $k$ is occupied and has $m$ balls, $m > 0$, then in time slot $i + 1$, one of the $m$ balls will stay in box $k$ and the others, if any, will move to box $k - 1$. Since all the balls are identical, without losing generality we will require that the ball that arrived at box $k$ earliest will stay in and occupy box $k$, and the others, if any, will move to box $k - 1$. If more than one ball arrives at an empty box, one of them is picked arbitrarily to stay there. Thus if a ball is put into an empty box, it stays there indefinitely.

Figure 7.14 shows an example of the movement of balls. In the figure, black balls are those that occupy a box permanently and white balls keep moving until they find an empty box and occupy it, at which point they turn black. We will prove that each of the $N$ balls will find a box to occupy permanently in no more than $N - 1$ time slots, so that every box will always have one ball in it.

We will now show that the game corresponds to the state transitions of $Y_i$ as defined in (7.5). By following the rules above, and by knowing how many balls there are in box $k$ and box $k + 1$ in time slot $i$ ($y_{k,i}$ and $y_{k+1,i}$), we can get the number of balls in box $k$ in time slot $i + 1$ ($y_{k,i+1}$), which is identical with (7.5):

*Condition 1.* If in time slot $i$, box $k$ is empty and box $k + 1$ has at most one ball, then in time slot $i + 1$, box $k$ is still empty.

*Condition 2.* If in time slot $i$, box $k$ is empty and box $k + 1$ has $j$ balls, $j > 1$, then in time slot $i + 1$, one of these $j$ balls stays in box $k + 1$ and box $k$ will have the other $j - 1$ balls.

*Condition 3.* If in time slot $i$, box $k$ has $j$ balls, $j > 1$, and box $k + 1$ has at most one ball, then in time slot $i + 1$, no ball will move from box $k + 1$ to box $k$, and only one ball (which permanently occupies box $k$) will stay in box $k$.

*Condition 4.* If in time slot $i$, there are $m$ balls in box $k$ and $j$ balls in box $k + 1$, $m > 1$ and $j > 1$, then in time slot $i + 1$, one of the $m$ balls (which permanently occupies box $k$) stays in box $k$ and others move to box $k - 1$, one of the $j$ balls (which permanently occupies box $k + 1$) stays in box $k + 1$ and $j - 1$ balls move to box $k$; box $k$ will then have $j$ balls.

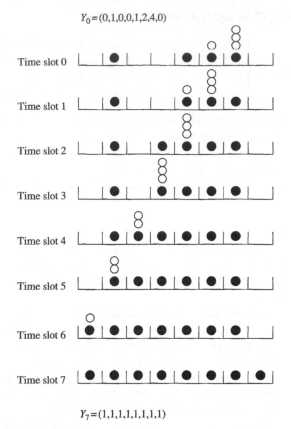

$Y_0 = (0,1,0,0,1,2,4,0)$

Time slot 0

Time slot 1

Time slot 2

Time slot 3

Time slot 4

Time slot 5

Time slot 6

Time slot 7

$Y_7 = (1,1,1,1,1,1,1,1)$

**Figure 7.14** States of the system in 8 time slots when $N = 8$ and with the initial state $Y_0 = (0, 1, 0, 0, 1, 2, 4, 0)$.

In time slot 0, if a solitary ball occupies a box, it means that it has already found its final box. What we need to show is that if a ball does not occupy a box in time slot 0, it will find its box within $N - 1$ time slots.

Suppose in time slot 0, box $k$ is occupied and there is a white ball (named ball B) in it; then, in the next time slot, ball B must move to box $k - 1$. We will next use a proof by contradiction. Assume that until time slot $N - 1$, ball B still cannot find its own box to occupy; this means it has moved in every time slot and traveled $N - 1$ boxes, all of which were occupied. Since box $k$ is already occupied, all $N$ boxes are occupied by $N$ balls. With ball B, there will be a total of $N + 1$ balls in the system, which is impossible. So the assumption is wrong and ball B will find a box to occupy within $N - 1$ time slots.

Therefore, we conclude that any ball can find a box to occupy within $N - 1$ time slots, and from time slot $N - 1$, each box has one ball in it. Thus $Y_i, y_{k,i} = 1, k = 1, \ldots, N, i \geq N - 1$, for any $Y_0$, which indicates that after time slot $N - 1$, each output arbiter pointer will point to a different input, and will continue to do so indefinitely. This guarantees a throughput of 100 percent.

### 7.3.4  FIRM

Similar to *i*RRM and *i*SLIP, FIRM [15] also implements the round-robin scheduler to update input accept and output grant pointers. The only difference in this scheme lies in that the output grant pointers update their positions to the one beyond the granted input port if the grant is accepted in step 3, and update to the granted input port if the grant is not accepted in step 3. The steps for one iteration of this scheme are as follows:

Step 1: *Request.* Each unmatched input sends a request to every output for which it has a queued cell.

Step 2: *Grant.* If an unmatched output receives multiple requests, it chooses the one that appears next in a fixed, round-robin schedule starting from the highest priority element. The output notifies each input whether or not its request was granted. The grant pointer $g_i$ is incremented (modulo $N$) to one location beyond the granted input if the grant is accepted in step 3. It is placed to the granted input if the grant is not accepted in step 3.

Step 3: *Accept.* If an input receives multiple grants, it accepts the one that appears next in a fixed, round-robin schedule starting from the highest priority element. The pointer $a_j$ is incremented (modulo $N$) to one location beyond the accepted output. The accept pointers $a_i$ are only updated in the first iteration.

Compared to *i*SLIP, FIRM is fairer as it approximates first come first serve (FCFS) closer to the improved update scheme of the output grant pointer. An example is shown in Figures 7.15 and 7.16.

In the cycle 0 of the example given in Figure 7.15, input 2 has queued cells for outputs 2 and 4, while input 3 has queued cells for outputs 1 and 3. No cells are queued in inputs 1 and 4. Initially, all pointers $a_j$ and $g_i$ are set as shown in Figure 7.15*a*. In step 1, input 2 sends requests to outputs 2 and 4 while input 3 sends requests to outputs 1 and 3. In step 2, the outputs grant the request that is closest to the pointed input by the grant pointer in the clockwise direction. So, input 2 receives grants from outputs 2 and 4; and input 3 receives grants from outputs 1 and 3. In step 3, the inputs accept the grant that is closest to the pointed output by the accept pointer. Hence, input 2 accepts the grant from output 4 and input 3 accepts the grant from output 3. As a result, $a_2$ and $a_3$ are updated and now point to outputs 1 and 4, respectively, ($a_1$ and $a_4$ are not updated). However, in a manner different from *i*SLIP, the grant pointers of outputs 3 and 4 are updated to inputs 4 and 3, respectively, since their grants were accepted and those of outputs 1 and 2 are updated to inputs 3 and 2, respectively, since their grants were not accepted. This completes cycle 0 of FIRM.

Figure 7.16 shows the situation at the beginning of cycle 1. New cells arrive from input 2 to output 1. Due to the difference in updating the output grant pointer in cycle 0, FIRM will grant input 2 in output 2 and input 3 in output 1, the two granted cells are both old cells that arrived in cycle 0. This example shows that FIRM is better in performing FCFS of arriving cells and is fairer, compared to *i*SLIP and *i*RRM.

### 7.3.5  Dual Round-Robin Matching (DRRM)

The DRRM scheme [16, 17] works similar to *i*SLIP, using the round-robin selection instead of random selection. But it starts the round-robin selection at inputs and only sends one

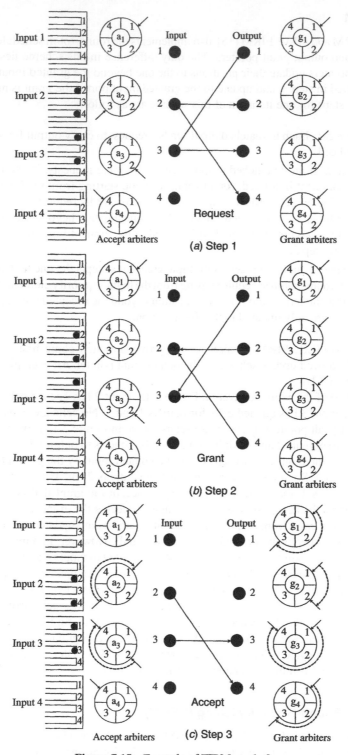

**Figure 7.15**     Example of FIRM–cycle 0.

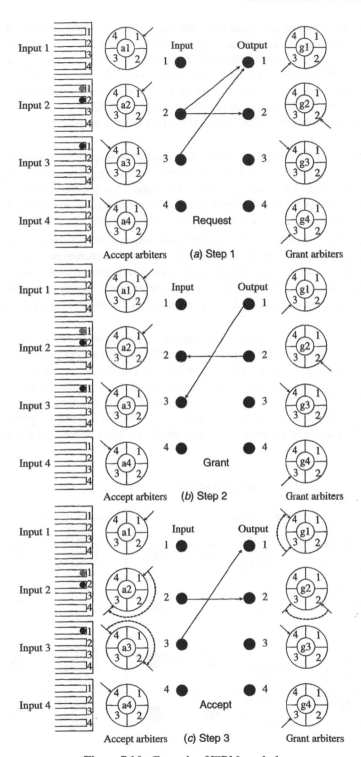

**Figure 7.16** Example of FIRM–cycle 1.

request from each non-empty input port. An input arbiter is used to select a non-empty VOQ according to the round-robin service discipline. After the selection, each input sends a request, if any, to the destined output arbiter. An output arbiter receives up to $N$ requests. It chooses one of them based on the round-robin service discipline, and sends a grant to the winner input port. Because of the two sets of independent round-robin arbiters, this arbitration scheme is called dual round-robin matching (DRRM).

The dual round-robin matching (DRRM) has two steps in a cycle:

Step 1: *Request.* Each input sends an output request corresponding to the first nonempty VOQ in a fixed round-robin order, starting from the current position of the pointer in the input arbiter. The pointer remains unchanged if the selected output is not granted in step 2. The pointer of the input arbiter is incremented by one location beyond the selected output if and only if the request is granted in step 2.

Step 2: *Grant.* If an output receives one or more requests, it chooses the one that appears next in a fixed round-robin scheduling starting from the current position of the pointer in the output arbiter. The output notifies each requesting input whether or not its request was granted. The pointer of the output arbiter is incremented to one location beyond the granted input. If there are no requests, the pointer remains where it is.

Because each input sends at most one request and receives at most one grant in each time slot, it is not necessary for input ports to conduct a third accept phase.

Figure 7.17 shows an example of the DRRM algorithm. In the request phase, each input chooses a VOQ and sends a request to an output arbiter. Assume input 1 has cells destined for both outputs 1 and 2. Since its round-robin pointer $r_1$ is pointing to 1, input arbiter 1 sends a request to output 1 and finally updates its pointer to 2 when its grant is accepted by output 1. Let us consider output 3 in the grant phase. Since its round-robin pointer $g_3$ is

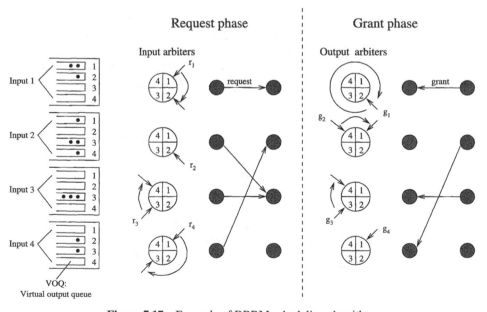

**Figure 7.17**   Example of DRRM scheduling algorithm.

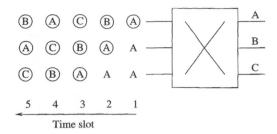

Ⓑ    Indicate that the cell is granted to output B in the time slot.

**Figure 7.18**  Desynchronization effect of DRRM under the fully loaded situation.

pointing to 3, output arbiter 3 grants input 3 and updates its pointer to 4. Similar to *i*SLIP, DRRM also has the desynchronization effect. The input arbiters granted in different time slots have different pointer values, and each of them requests a different output, resulting in desynchronization. However, the DRRM scheme requires less time to perform arbitration and is easier to implement. This is because less information exchange is needed between input arbiters and output arbiters. In other words, DRRM saves initial transmission time required to send requests from inputs to outputs in *i*SLIP.

Consider the fully loaded situation in which every VOQ always has cells. Figure 7.18 shows the HOL cells chosen from each input port in different time slots. In time slot 1, each input port chooses a cell destined for output A. Among those three cells, only one (the first one in this example) is granted and the other two have to wait at the HOL. The round-robin pointer of the first input advances to point to output B in time slot 2, and a cell destined for B is chosen and then granted because there are no contenders. The other two inputs have their HOL cells unchanged, both destined for output A. Only one of them (the one from the second input) is granted and the other has to wait until the third time slot. At that time, the round-robin pointers among the three inputs have been desynchronized and point to C, B, and A, respectively. As a result, all three cells chosen are granted.

Figure 7.19 shows the tail probability under FIFO+RR (FIFO for input selection and RR for round-robin arbitration), DRRM, and *i*SLIP arbitration schemes. The switch size is 256 and the average burst length is 10 cell slots (with the ON–OFF model). The performances of DRRM and *i*SLIP are comparable at speedup of 2, while all three schemes have almost the same performance as speedup $s \geq 3$.

### 7.3.6  Pipelined Maximal Matching

Maximal matching is widely adopted in the scheduling of input buffered switches, either with one cycle matching or multiple iterative matching. However, the computing complexity of maximal matching is, too high to complete within a single time slot when the switch size increases or the line rate becomes high.

In the work of Oki et al. [18], a scheduling algorithm called pipelined maximal matching (PMM) based on pipeline was proposed to resolve the problem. The PMM scheme relaxes the computation time for maximal matching to more than one time slot. As shown in Figure 7.20, the PMM scheduler consists of $N^2$ request counters (RC) and $K$ subschedulers. Each subscheduler has $N^2$ request subcounters (RSC). As shown in Figure 7.21, each

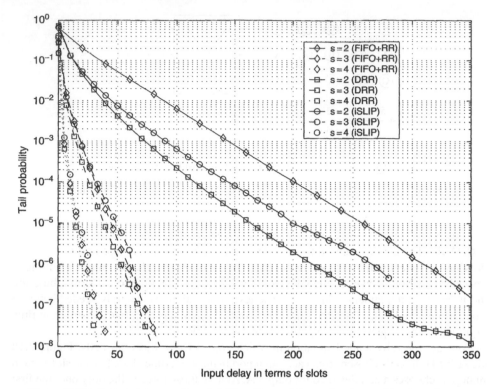

**Figure 7.19** Comparison on tail probability of input delay under three arbitration schemes.

subscheduler operates the maximal matching in a pipelined manner and takes $K$ time slots to complete the matching. After each time slot, one of the $K$ subschedulers finishes a matching, which is used in the next time slot. DRRM is implemented in the subscheduler to achieve a maximal matching. Since $K$ time slots are provided for one scheduling, multiple iterative DRRM (*i*DRRM) can be adopted.

Before a detailed description of PMM, several notations are first defined: $RC(i, j)$ denotes the request counter associated with $VOQ(i, j)$. $C(i, j)$ keeps the value of $RC(i, j)$, which is the number of accumulated requests associated with $VOQ(i, j)$ that have not been sent to any subscheduler. $RSC(i, j, k)$ denotes the request subcounter in the $k$th subscheduler that is associated with $VOQ(i, j)$, and $SC(i, j, k)$ keeps its value. The $SC(i, j, k)$ is the number of remaining requests that are dispatched from $RC(i, j)$ and not transferred yet. Each $SC(i, j, k)$ is limited to $SC_{max}$. It is found that when $SC_{max} = 1$, the delay performance is best. At initial time, each $C(i, j)$ and $SC(i, j, k)$ are set to zero. PMM operates as follows.

*Phase 1.* When a new cell enters $VOQ(i, j)$, the counter value of $RC(i, j)$ is increased as $C(i, j) = C(i, j) + 1$.

*Phase 2.* At the beginning of every time slot $t$, if $C(i, j) > 0$ and $SC(i, j, k) < SC_{max}$, where $k = t \bmod K$, then $C(i, j) = C(i, j) - 1$ and $SC(i, j, k) = SC(i, j, k) + 1$. Otherwise, $C(i, j)$ and $SC(i, j, k)$ are not changed.

*Phase 3.* At $Kl + k \leq t < K(l + 1) + k$, where $l$ is an integer, subscheduler $k$ operates the maximal matching according to the adopted algorithm.

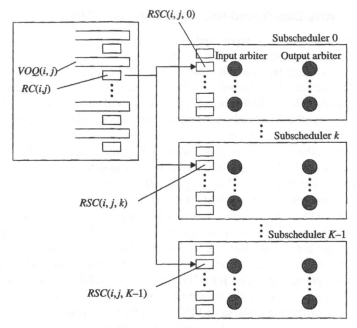

**Figure 7.20**  Structure of the PMM scheduler.

*Phase 4.* By the end of every time slot $t$, subscheduler $k$, where $k = (t - (K - 1))$ mod $K$, completes the matching. When input–output pair $(i, j)$ is matched, $SC(i, j, k) = SC(i, j, k) - 1$. The HOL cell in $VOQ(i, j)$ is sent to output $j$ at the next time slot. This ensures that cells from the same VOQ are transmitted in sequence, since only the HOL cell of each VOQ can be transferred when any request is granted.

Since the scheduling timing constraint has been relaxed, each subscheduler is now allowed to take several time slots to complete a maximal matching. By implementing the iterative DRRM, PMM can approximate the performance of $i$DRRM, providing 100 percent throughput under uniform traffic and fairness for best-effort traffic. Besides, cell order of the same VOQ is preserved.

Apart from PMM, other algorithms based on pipeline have been proposed, such as the Round-Robin Greedy Scheduling (RRGS) [19], but PMM is better in providing fairness and scalability.

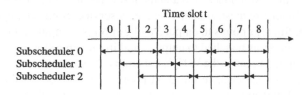

**Figure 7.21**  Timing diagram of PMM with three subscheduler.

### 7.3.7 Exhaustive Dual Round-Robin Matching (EDRRM)

In most scheduling algorithms, inputs and outputs are matched in each time slot. This is similar to the limited service policy with a limit of 1 [20] in a polling system. In order to improve the performance under non-uniform and burst traffic, some improved scheduling methods modify the limit-1 service policy to the limit-$\infty$ policy so that whenever an input is matched to an output, all cells in the corresponding VOQ will be transferred in the following time slots before any other VOQ at the same input can be served. This is called the exhaustive service policy [20] in polling systems.

Combining the exhaustive service policy with DRRM, the exhaustive DRRM (EDRRM) [21] was proposed. In EDRRM, the input pointer is not updated until the current VOQ is exhausted. Besides the exhaustive scheduling, EDRRM has two other differences compared to DRRM. First, the pointer in the output arbiter always points to the latest matched input and does not update its location after a service because the output has no idea if the currently served VOQ will become empty after this service. Second, in EDRRM, if an input sends a request to an output but gets no grant, the input will update its pointer of input arbiter to the next location beyond the requested output, while in DRRM, this pointer will remain where it is until it gets a grant. The reason for this is because in EDRRM, if an input cannot get a grant from an output, it means that the output is most likely being matched with another input for all the cells waiting in the same VOQ. Therefore, it is better to update the pointer of input arbiter to search for another free output, rather than to wait for this busy one. The detailed description of EDRRM is shown below.

Step 1: *Request.* Each input moves its pointer to the first nonempty VOQ in a fixed round-robin order, starting from the current position of the pointer in the input arbiter, and sends a request to the output corresponding to this VOQ. The pointer of the input arbiter is incremented by one location beyond the selected output if the request is not granted in step 2, or if the request is granted and after one cell is served, this VOQ becomes empty. Otherwise, if there are remaining cells in this VOQ after sending one cell, the pointer remains at this nonempty VOQ.

Step 2: *Grant.* If an output receives one or more requests, it chooses the one that appears next in a fixed round-robin scheduling starting from the current position of the pointer in the output arbiter. The pointer is moved to this position. The output notifies each requesting input whether or not its request was granted. The pointer of the output arbiter remains at the granted input. If there are no requests, the pointer remains where it is.

Figure 7.22 shows an example of the EDRRM arbitration algorithm, where $r_1$, $r_2$, $r_3$, and $r_4$ are arbiter pointers for inputs 1, 2, 3, and 4, and $g_1$, $g_2$, $g_3$, and $g_4$ are arbiter pointers for outputs 1, 2, 3, and 4. At the beginning of the time slot, $r_1$ points to output 1 while $g_1$ does not point to input 1, which means that in the last time slot, input 1 was not matched to output 1, and now input 1 requests output 1 for a new service. Similarly, $r_2$ requests output 3 for a new service. Since $r_3$ points to output 3 and $g_3$ points to input 3, it is possible that in the last time slot input 3 was matched to output 3 and in this time slot output 3 will transfer the next cell from input 3 because the VOQ is not empty. Input 4 and output 2 have a similar situation as input 3 and output 3. In the grant phase, output 1 grants the only request it receives from input 1 and updates $g_1$ to 1, output 2 grants a request from input 4 and output 3 grants a request from input 3. The request from input 2 to output 3 is not granted, so $r_2$

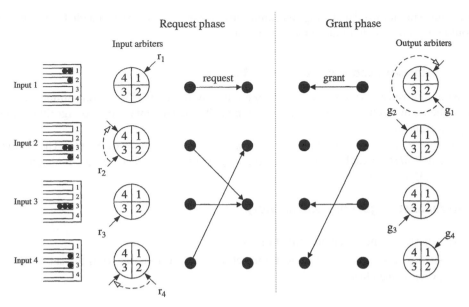

**Figure 7.22**    Example of EDRRM scheduling algorithm.

moves to 4. By the end of this time slot, the first VOQ of input 1 and the third VOQ of input 3 are still nonempty so that $r_1$ and $r_3$ are not updated. $r_4$ is updated to 3 because the second VOQ of input 4 has become empty.

## 7.4  RANDOMIZED MATCHING ALGORITHMS

Determining the maximum weight matching essentially involves a search procedure, which can take many iterations and be time-consuming. Since the goal is to design high-performance schedulers for high aggregate bandwidth switches, algorithms that involve, too many iterations are unattractive [22].

In this section, we will introduce several randomized matching algorithms using memory or arrivals. The usage of memory and arrivals are based on two observations:

*Using memory.*  In each time slot, there can be at most one cell that arrives at each input, and at most one cell that departs from each input. Therefore, the queue length of each VOQ does not change much during successive time slots. If we use the queue length as the weight of a connection, it is quite possible that a heavy connection will continue to be heavy over a few time slots. With this observation, matching algorithms with memory use the match (or part of the match) in the previous time slot as a candidate of the new match.

*Using arrivals.*  Since the increase of the queue length is based on the arrivals, it might be helpful to use the knowledge of recent arrivals in finding a match.

Since the decision is not based upon the complete knowledge of a large state space, but upon a few random samples of the state, the decision process can be significantly simplified.

By using a randomized matching algorithm, we may not find "the best" match, but the match could be good enough to make the switch stable.

### 7.4.1 Randomized Algorithm with Memory

The randomized algorithm with memory presented by Tassiulas [23] is a very simple matching scheme that achieves 100 percent throughput. The disadvantage of this algorithm is its high average delay.

At time $t$, let $Q(t) = [q_{ij}]_{N \times N}$, where $q_{ij}$ is the queue length of $VOQ_{ij}$. The weight of a match $M(t)$, which is the sum of the lengths of all matched VOQs, is denoted by $W(t) = \langle M(t), Q(t) \rangle$.

***Randomized Algorithm with Memory***

1. Let $S(t)$ be the schedule used at time $t$.
2. At time $t + 1$, uniformly select a match $R(t + 1)$ at random from the set of all $N!$ possible matches.
3. Let

$$S(t + 1) = \arg \max_{S \in \{S(t), R(t+1)\}} \langle S, Q(t + 1) \rangle. \tag{7.6}$$

The function of arg selects the $S$ that makes $\langle S, Q(t + 1) \rangle$ achieve its maximum in the above equation.

**Theorem 4:** The randomized algorithm with memory is stable under any Bernoulli i.i.d. admissible arrival traffic [23].

### 7.4.2 De-randomized Algorithm with Memory

In [21], a matching algorithm was presented to de-randomize the randomized algorithm with memory by using Hamiltonian walk.

A Hamiltonian walk is a walk which visits every vertex of a graph exactly once. For a $N \times N$ switch, the total number of possible matches is $N!$. If those matches are mapped on to a graph with $N!$ vertices so that each vertex corresponds to a match, a Hamiltonian walk on the graph visits each vertex exactly once every $N!$ time slots. The vertex that is visited at time $t$ is denoted by $H(t)$. The complexity of generating $H(t + 1)$ from $H(t)$ is $O(1)$ [24].

***De-randomized Algorithm with Memory***

1. Let $S(t)$ be the match used at time $t$.
2. At time $t + 1$, let $R(t + 1) = H(t)$, the match visited by the Hamiltonian walk.
3. Let

$$S(t + 1) = \arg \max_{S \in \{S(t), R(t+1)\}} \langle S, Q(t + 1) \rangle. \tag{7.7}$$

**Theorem 5:** An input-queued switch using the de-randomized algorithm with memory is stable under all admissible Bernoulli i.i.d. input traffic [22].

### 7.4.3 Variant Randomize Matching Algorithms

The fact that matching algorithms with simple ideas, such as randomized and de-randomized algorithms with memory, achieve 100 percent throughput as MWM does shows an important insight. That is, to achieve 100 percent throughput, it is not necessary to find "the best" match in each time slot. However, "better" matches do lead to better delay performance. Simulation results show that the randomized and de-randomized algorithms with memory have very high delay. In order to improve the delay performance, extra work is needed to find "better" matches. In [22], three algorithms with much better delay performance and higher complexity were proved to be stable.

**APSARA.** The APSARA algorithm [25] employs the following two ideas:

1. Use of memory.
2. Exploring neighbors in parallel. The neighbors are defined so that it is easy to compute them using hardware parallelism.

In APSARA, the "neighbors" of the current match are considered as candidates of the match in the next time slot. A match $S'$ is defined as a neighbor of a match $S$ if, and only if, there are two input–output pairs in $S$, say input $i_1$ to output $j_1$ and input $i_2$ to output $j_2$, switching their connections so that in $S'$ input $i_1$ connects to output $j_2$ and $i_2$ connects to output $j_1$. All other input–output pairs are the same under $S$ and $S'$. We denote the set of all the neighbors of a match $S$ as $N(S)$. As shown in Figure 7.23 [22], the matching $S$ for a $3 \times 3$ switch and its three neighbors $S1$, $S2$, and $S3$ are given below: $S = (1, 2, 3), S1 = (2, 1, 3), S2 = (1, 3, 2),$ and $S3 = (3, 2, 1)$.

Let $S(t)$ be the matching determined by APSARA at time $t$. Let $H(t + 1)$ be the match corresponding to the Hamiltonian walk at time $t + 1$. At time $t + 1$, APSARA does

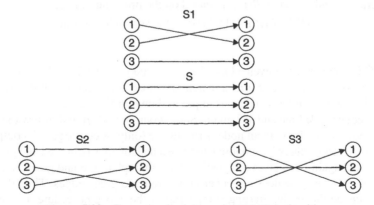

**Figure 7.23** Example of neighbors in APSARA algorithms.

the following:

1. Determine $N(S(t))$ and $H(t)$.
2. Let $M(t+1) = N(S(t)) \cup H(t+1) \cup S(t)$. Compute the weight $\langle S', Q(t+1)\rangle$ for all $S' \in M(t+1)$.
3. Determine the match at $t+1$ by

$$S(t+1) = \arg \max_{S' \in M(t+1)} \langle S', Q(t+1)\rangle. \tag{7.8}$$

APSARA requires the computation of the weight of neighbors. Each such computation is easy to implement. However, computing the weights of all $\binom{N}{2}$ neighbors requires a lot of space in hardware for large values of $N$. To overcome this, two variations were considered in the work of Giaccone et al. [22] by reducing the number of neighbors considered in each time slot.

*LAURA.* There are three main features in the design of LAURA [25]:

1. Use of memory.
2. Nonuniform random sampling.
3. A merging procedure for weight augmentation.

Most of a matching's weight is typically contained in a few edges. Thus, it is more important to choose edges at random than it is to choose matchings at random. Equally, it is more important to remember the few good edges of the matching at time $t$ for use in time $t+1$ than it is to remember the entire matching at time $t$ [26].

The randomized and de-randomized algorithms with memory provide poor delay performance because they carry matches between time slots via memory. When the weight of a heavy match resides in a few heavy edges, it is more important to remember the heavy edges rather than the whole match. This observation motivates LAURA, which iteratively augments the weight of the current match by combining its heavy edges with the heavy edges of a randomly chosen match.

Let $S(t)$ be the match used by LAURA at time $t$. At time $t+1$ LAURA does the following:

1. Generate a random match $R(t+1)$ based on the procedure in [22].
2. Use $S(t+1) = MERGE(R(t+1), S(t))$ as the schedule for time $t+1$.

*The MERGE Procedure.* Given a bipartite graph and two matches $M1$ and $M2$ for this graph, the MERGE procedure returns a match $M$ whose edges belong either, to $M1$ or to $M2$. MERGE works as follows and an example is shown in Figure 7.24.

Color the edges of $M1$ red and $M2$ green. Start at output node $j_1$ and follow the red edge to an input node, say $i_1$. From input node $i_1$ follow the (only) green edge to its output node, say $j_2$. If $j_2 = j_1$, stop. Otherwise, continue to trace a path of alternating red and green edges until $j_1$ is visited again. This gives a "cycle" in the subgraph of red and green edges.

Suppose the above cycle does not cover all the red and green edges. Then there exists an output $j$ outside this cycle. Starting from $j$, repeat the above procedure to find another cycle. In this fashion, find all cycles of red and green edges. Suppose there are $m$ cycles,

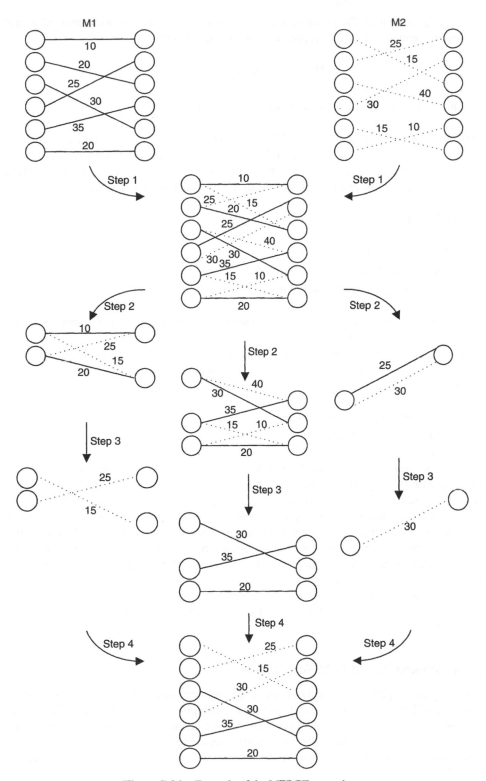

**Figure 7.24**    Example of the MERGE procedure.

$C_1, \ldots, C_m$ at the end. Then each cycle, $C_i$, contains two matches: $G_i$ with green edges and $R_i$ with red edges. The MERGE procedure returns the match

$$M = \cup_{i=1}^{m} \arg \max_{S \in \{G_i, R_i\}} \langle S, Q(t) \rangle. \tag{7.9}$$

The complexity of the MERGE procedure is $O(N)$.

**SERENA.** SERENA is a variant of LAURA that uses packet arrival times as a source of randomness. The basic version of LAURA merges the past schedule with a randomly generated matching. In contrast, SERENA considers the edges that received arrivals in the previous time slot and merges them with the past matching to obtain a higher-weight matching [26].

SERENA [25] is based on the following ideas:

1. Use of memory.
2. Exploiting the randomness of arrivals.
3. A merging procedure, involving new arrivals.

In SERENA, in order to provide information about recent traffic load, arrival patterns are used to generate a new match.

Let $S(t)$ be the match used by SERENA at time $t$. Let $A(t+1) = [A_{ij}(t+1)]$ denote the arrival graph, where $A_{ij}(t+1) = 1$ indicates arrival at input $i$ destined to output $j$. At time $t+1$:

1. Turn $A(t+1)$ into a full match.
2. Use $S(t+1) = MERGE(S(t), A(t+1))$ as the schedule.

In the second step, the MERGE procedure combines two full matches (with $N$ connections each) into a new match. However, it is possible that $A(t+1)$ is not a match when more than one input has arrivals destined to one output. Therefore, it is necessary to convert $A(t+1)$ into a match in the first step as follows. If an output has more than one arrival edge, pick the edge with the highest weight and discard the remaining edges. At the end of this process, each output is matched with at most one input. After that, if $A(t+1)$ is not a full match, simply connect the remaining input–output pairs by adding edges in a round-robin fashion, without considering their weights.

The complexity of SERENA is $O(N)$. In the work of Giaccone et al. [22], the authors preferred SERENA against APSARA and LAURA because of its good performance and low implementation complexity.

### 7.4.4 Polling Based Matching Algorithms

A polling model [20] is a system of multiple queues accessed in a cyclic order by a single server. A polling system can have different service disciplines, such as the exhaustive service and the limited service. When the server switches to a queue, it serves some customers with a limited service discipline, while it serves all other customers with an exhaustive service discipline. Usually, the exhaustive service discipline is more efficient than other service disciplines.

Exhaustive service match with Hamiltonian walk (EMHW), presented in the work of Li [14] and Li et al. [27], is a class of matching algorithms inspired by exhaustive service polling systems. In an exhaustive service matching algorithm, when an input is matched to an output, all the packets waiting in the corresponding VOQ will be served continuously before any other VOQ related to the input and the output can be served. EMHW achieves stability and low packet delay with low implementation complexity.

EMHW is defined as follows:

1. Let $S(t)$ be the schedule used at time $t$.
2. At time $t + 1$, generate a match $Z(t + 1)$ by means of the exhaustive service matching algorithm, based on the previous schedule $S(t)$, and $H(t + 1)$, the match visited by a Hamiltonian walk.
3. Let

$$S(t + 1) = \arg \max_{S \in \{Z(t+1), H(t+1)\}} \langle S, Q(t + 1) \rangle. \tag{7.10}$$

**Theorem 6.** An EMHW is stable under any admissible Bernoulli i.i.d. input traffic [14, 27].

The stability of EMHW is achieved due to two efforts. Unlike most other matching algorithms, which try to find efficient matches in each time slot, exhaustive service matching achieves efficiency by minimizing the matching overhead over multiple time slots. Cells forwarded to outputs are held in reassembly buffers that can only leave the switch when all cells belonging to the same packet are received so that the packet is reassembled. The total delay a packet suffers, from the time it arrives at the input to the time it departs at the output, includes the cell delay incurred traversing the switch and the time needed for packet reassembly. In exhaustive service matching, since all the cells belonging to the same packet are transferred to the output continuously, the packet delay is significantly reduced. The stability of EMHW is guaranteed by introducing matches generated by a Hamiltonian walk. This lower bounds the weight of matches, hence guaranteeing stability.

**HE-*iSLIP*.** Exhaustive schemes can be used in conjunction with existing matching algorithms, such as *i*SLIP. The time complexity of exhaustive service *i*SLIP with Hamiltonian walk (HE-*i*SLIP), which belongs to the class of stable algorithm EMHW, is as low as $O(\log N)$. Simulation results show that HE-*i*SLIP achieves very good packet delay performance.

In EMHW, an input (output) is busy if it is matched to an output (input), otherwise it is free. For exhaustive service *i*SLIP (E-*i*SLIP), at the beginning of each time slot, each input (output), which was busy (i.e., matched) in the previous time slot, checks its state by checking the corresponding VOQ. If the VOQ has just been emptied, the input (output) changes its state to free and increments its pointer to one location beyond the matched output (input). Otherwise, the input (output) keeps its state as busy and does not update its pointer. A detailed description of the three step E-*i*SLIP algorithm follows:

Step 1: *Request.* Each free input sends a request to every output for which it has a queued cell. Each busy input sends a request to the matched output.

Step 2: *Grant*. If an output (either free or busy) receives any requests, it chooses one of them in a fixed round-robin order starting from the current position of the pointer. The output notifies each input whether or not its request was granted. Note that the output pointer points to the granted input if the grant is accepted in Step 3.

Step 3: *Accept*. If an input receives any grant, it sets its state to busy, and accepts one of the multiple grants in a fixed round-robin order starting from the current position of the pointer. The input pointer then points to the matched output.

In E-$i$SLIP, free outputs only get requests from free inputs, and free inputs only get grants from free outputs.

Figure 7.25 shows an example of E-$i$SLIP in a time slot. By the end of the last time slot, input 1 is matched to output 2, and input 4 is matched to output 1. At the beginning of the current time slot, none of their corresponding VOQs was empty, and the other inputs and outputs were free. Therefore, input 1 and input 4 only send one request each, to output 2 and output 4, respectively. Input 2 and input 3 send requests for non-empty VOQs, to outputs 1 and 3, and outputs 3 and 4, respectively. Outputs 1 and 2 grant inputs to which they are matched, and inputs 1 and 4 accept their grants. Output 3 gets two requests. It grants input 3 according to the status of its round robin pointer (not shown). Output 4 only gets one request from input 3, and it grants the request. Input 3 receives two grants, and it accepts output 3 according to the status of its round robin pointer (again, not shown). Input 3 and output 3 are matched and change their state to busy. At the beginning of the next time slot, if input 1 does not have a new arrival to output 2, the corresponding VOQ will be empty and input 1 and output 2 will set their states to free.

HE-$i$SLIP does the following in each time slot $t + 1$:

1. Run E-$i$SLIP, which generates a match $Z(t + 1)$ based on the previous match $S(t)$ and updates the pointer and the state of each input and output.

2. Generate a match $H(t + 1)$ by Hamiltonian walk.

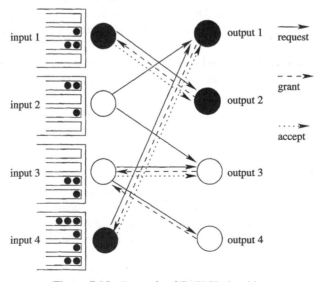

**Figure 7.25**   Example of E-$i$SLIP algorithm.

3. Compare the weights of $Z(t+1)$ and $H(t+1)$. If the weight of $H(t+1)$ is larger, set $S(t+1) = H(t+1)$. For each matched input (output), set its state to busy, and update its pointer to the output (input) with which it is matched. Unmatched inputs and outputs set their states to free and do not update their pointers. If the weight of $Z(t+1)$ is larger, simply set $S(t+1) = Z(t+1)$. No further pointer or state updating is needed since it has been done in the first step.

**Cell Delay Performance Analysis.** The cell delay performance of E-$i$SLIP under uniform traffic can be analyzed by using an exhaustive random polling system model [28]. The expression of the average cell delay $E(T)$ is as follows:

$$E(T) = \frac{1}{2}\left[\frac{\delta^2}{r} + \frac{\sigma^2}{(1-N\mu)\mu} + \frac{Nr(1-\mu)}{1-N\mu} + \frac{(N-1)r}{1-N\mu}\right] \quad (7.11)$$

where $\mu$ is the arrival rate for a VOQ, $\sigma^2$ is the variance of the arrival process for a VOQ, and $r = E(S)$, $\delta^2 = E(S^2) - E^2(S)$. Here $S$ is the switch-over time, the time taken for the server to switch from one VOQ after service completion to another VOQ for a new service period. The expressions of $E(S)$ and $E(S^2)$ are as below. The details can be found in the work of Li [14] and Li et al. [29].

$$E(S) = \sum_{n=1}^{\infty} n(1-Q_S)^n Q_S = \frac{1-Q_S}{Q_S}. \quad (7.12)$$

and

$$E(S^2) = \sum_{n=1}^{\infty} n^2(1-Q_S)^n Q_S = \frac{1-Q_S}{Q_S}\left[\frac{2(1-Q_S)}{Q_S} + 1\right], \quad (7.13)$$

where

$$Q_S = \sum_{m=1}^{N}\binom{N-1}{m-1}\rho^{N-m}(1-\rho)^{m-1}[1-(1-\rho)^m]\sum_{i=0}^{m-1}\binom{m-1}{i}(1-w)^{m-i-1}w^i\frac{1}{i+1}$$

$$= 1 - \sum_{m=1}^{N}\binom{N-1}{m-1}\rho^{N-m}(1-\rho)^{m-1}(1-w)^m \quad (7.14)$$

and

$$w = \frac{1}{m}\left[1-(1-\rho)^m\right]. \quad (7.15)$$

When $N$ is large,

$$E(T) \to E(S)\frac{N}{1-\rho}. \quad (7.16)$$

Numerical results show that for all $\rho < 1$, the average switch-over time, $E(S)$, is around 0.58 time slots when $N$ is large. Therefore, for a fixed $\rho$, $E(T)$ is linear in $N$ when $N$ is large.

### 7.4.5 Simulated Performance

In this section, we will show some simulation results under uniform and nonuniform arrival traffic for the delay performance of a 32 by 32 VOQ switch with benchmark stable algorithms, MWM, $i$SLIP, the de-randomized matching algorithm, SERENA and HE-$i$SLIP with implementation complexity $O(N^3)$, $O(\log N)$, $O(\log N)$, $O(N)$ and $O(\log N)$, respectively.

In fixed-length switches, variable-length IP packets are segmented into fixed-length cells at the inputs, and the cells are placed in the corresponding VOQ. When a cell is transferred to its destination output, it will stay in a buffer and wait for the other cells of the same packet. After the complete reception of all the cells of the same packet, these cells will be reassembled into a packet. The delay a packet suffers before it is reassembled into a packet and delivered to its destination includes the cell delay, and the waiting time at the output reassembly buffer, which is often ignored by many researchers. For a more realistic evaluation of switch performance, we consider the following average delays in our simulation.

*Cell delay.* The delay a cell suffers from the time it enters the system to the time it is transferred from the input to its destined output.

*Reassembly delay.* The delay a cell suffers from the time it is transferred to it destined output to the time it is reassembled and departs the system.

*Packet delay.* As in [30], the packet delay of a packet is measured from the time when the last cell of a packet enters the system to the time it departs.

***Under Uniform Traffic.*** Three different packet patterns are considered in this section, as follows:

*Pattern 1.* The packet length is fixed with a size of 1 cell. This also allows for comparison with the cell delay used in many papers.

*Pattern 2.* The packet length is fixed with a size of 10 cells.

*Pattern 3.* Based on the Internet traffic measurements by Claffy et al. [31], where 60 percent of the packets are 44 bytes, 20 percent are 552 bytes, and the rest are 1500 bytes. In the simulation, the packet size distribution is defined as follows: the size of 60 percent of the packets is 1 cell, the size of 20 percent of the packets is 13 cells, and the size of other 20 percent packets is 34 cells. This assumes a cell payload of 44 bytes. The average packet size is 10 cells.

Simulation results under packet patterns 1, 2, and 3 are shown in Figures 7.26, 7.27, and 7.28, respectively.

The packet delay of the de-randomized matching algorithm is always much higher than 10,000 cell time slots and are therefore not shown in the figures. We can see that under uniform traffic, the packet delay of HE-$i$SLIP is always lower than $i$SLIP and SERENA. In the figures, SERENA has the highest packet delay when the traffic load is low to moderately high. Under heavy load, $i$SLIP has the highest packet delay. MWM has a higher packet delay than HE-$i$SLIP for packet patterns 2 and 3.

As shown in Figure 7.26, MWM has the lowest delay when the packet size is 1 cell, but has higher packet delay than HE-$i$SLIP when the average packet size is $>1$, as shown in Figures 7.27 and 7.28. Figures 7.29 and 7.30 explain why this happens. The cell delay

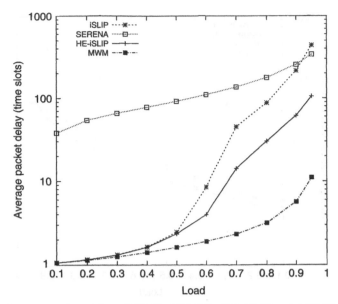

**Figure 7.26** Average packet delay of *i*SLIP, SERENA, HE-*i*SLIP and MWM under uniform traffic when the packet length is 1 cell.

of MWM is always lower than HE-*i*SLIP, but its reassembly delay is much higher. In HE-*i*SLIP, the cells in the same packet are usually transferred continuously. The only exception is when the match generated by Hamiltonian walk is picked because of its larger weight. However, this does not happen very often. Therefore, the reassembly delay of HE-*i*SLIP is always close to half of the packet length.

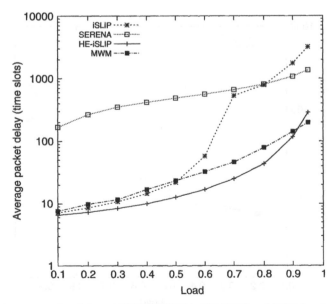

**Figure 7.27** Average packet delay of *i*SLIP, SERENA, HE-*i*SLIP and MWM under uniform traffic when the packet length is 10 cells.

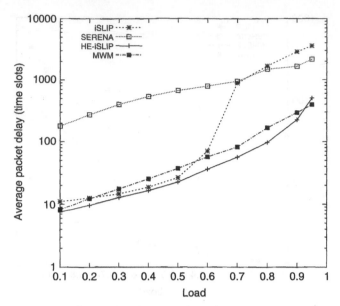

**Figure 7.28** Average packet delay of *i*SLIP, SERENA, HE-*i*SLIP and MWM under uniform traffic with variable packet length.

***Performance Under Nonuniform Traffic.*** Two typical nonuniform traffic patterns, diagonal and hotspot, are considered in this section. The packet length is assumed to be 1 cell in the simulation. *i*SLIP is not included in the performance comparison since it is not stable under nonuniform traffic.

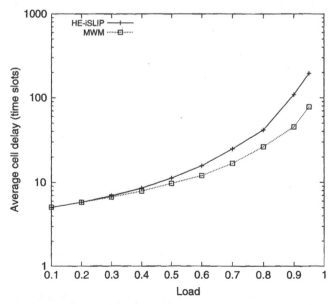

**Figure 7.29** Average cell delay of HE-*i*SLIP and MWM under uniform traffic when the packet length is 10 cells.

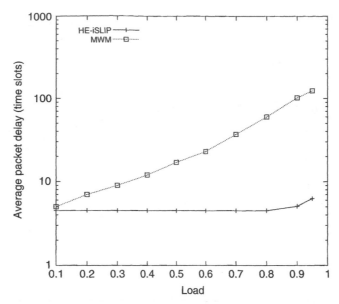

**Figure 7.30**  Average reassembly delay of HE-$i$SLIP and MWM under uniform traffic with variable packet length.

With the diagonal traffic pattern [21, 30], the arrival rate for each input is the same. For input $i$ a fraction $f$ of arrivals are destined to output $i$, and other arrivals are destined to output $(i + 1) \mod N$.

Table 7.1 shows the average delays, under diagonal traffic, of the de-randomized matching algorithms, SERENA, HE-$i$SLIP and MWM, respectively. The arrival rate to each input is 0.85. MWM has the best delay performance under diagonal traffic. The delay of SERENA is lower than HE-$i$SLIP when $f$ is large and similar to HE-$i$SLIP when $f$ is small. The delay of the de-randomized matching algorithm is much higher than those of other schemes.

In the hotspot traffic pattern, the arrival rate for each input is identical. For input $i$, a fraction $p$, $1/N \leq p < 1$, of arrivals are destined to output $i$, and other arrivals are uniformly destined to other outputs [21, 29]. Figure 7.31 shows the average delay of HE-$i$SLIP and SERENA for a $32 \times 32$ switch for different values of $p$ when the arrival rate is 0.95 and the packet size is 1 cell. The delay for the de-randomized algorithm with memory is, too high and therefore not shown in the figure. The simulation results show that HE-$i$SLIP always has a lower delay than SERENA, but higher delay than MWM.

Compared to HE-$i$SLIP, the delay of SERENA is lower under diagonal traffic but higher under the hotspot traffic pattern. This can be explained by the fact that SERENA takes

**TABLE 7.1  Average Delay of a 32 × 32 Switch Under Diagonal Traffic Pattern**

| $f$ | 0.1 | 0.2 | 0.3 | 0.4 | 0.5 |
|---|---|---|---|---|---|
| De-randomized | 1164 | 425.4 | 532.1 | 369.2 | 371.9 |
| SERENA | 3.945 | 6.606 | 8.570 | 9.517 | 10.08 |
| HE-$i$SLIP | 3.167 | 8.502 | 30.54 | 56.22 | 86.13 |
| MWM | 1.848 | 2.532 | 3.115 | 3.337 | 3.440 |

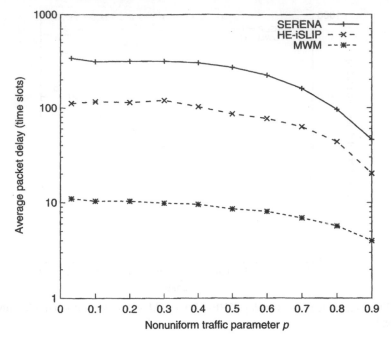

**Figure 7.31**    Average packet delay of SERENA, HE-*i*SLIP and MWM under the hotspot traffic pattern.

the arrival pattern at each time slot into account to generate the new match. However, if there is more than one arrival destined to the same output, only one of them, which is randomly selected, can be considered. Under diagonal traffic, only two inputs can have traffic to a given output. This makes it relatively easy for a new match to adapt to the arrival pattern. Indeed, SERENA is particularly suitable for a traffic pattern with which each output is always fed by only a few inputs. When traffic pattern is such that many inputs feed a given output, the SERENA algorithm is less effective, as in the hotspot or uniform traffic pattern case, since arrivals in a given slot give less indication of a good match.

## 7.5    FRAME-BASED MATCHING

By taking advantage of the tremendous transmission and switching capacity of optical fibers, many researchers have explored the possibility of building optical switching fabrics while packet processing and storage are still handed by electronics. As compared to electronic switch fabrics, a pair of E/O & O/E converters can be saved in optical switch fabrics, thus reducing the system cost.

Packet scheduling in optical switch fabrics is quite different from that in electronic switch fabrics as shown in Figure 7.32. In an electronic switch fabric, the switch fabric is reconfigured without any delay. Cells can be transferred back-to-back, and packet scheduling has to be completed before the switch configuration. But in an optical switch fabric, the switch reconfiguration is much slower, and is not negligible. During the switch

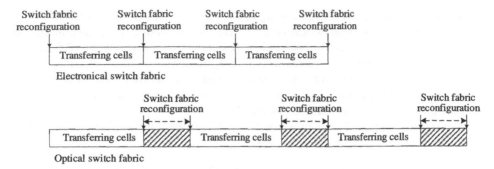

**Figure 7.32**  Comparison of operations between an electronic and optical switch fabric.

fabric reconfiguration, no data can be transferred. These reconfiguration overheads range from milliseconds for bubble and free-space MEMS (Microelectromechanical Systems) switches, to 10 μs for MEMS wavelength switches, and 10 ns for opto-electronic switch techniques [32].

Taking into account the non-zero reconfiguration overheads, a different framework for packet scheduling in optical switches has been studied. Instead of scheduling at every time slot, multiple cells are merged together to form a large frame and scheduled and switched as a group, so as to reduce the switching overhead. This type of scheduling algorithms is called frame-based matching algorithms. The following questions are then raised: How many cells should we schedule and switch together? How can we schedule full frames and partially filled frames? What is the performance difference between traditional algorithms and frame-based matching algorithms? Frame-based matching has the following advantages:

1. Low overhead. For a 40 Gbps interface, a typical cell size (64 byte) only lasts 12.8 ns. If the reconfiguration overhead is 20 ns, the switch utilization is only about 40 percent. But if 100 cells form a frame and are switched together, the switch utilization is improved to 98 percent.

2. The time required for scheduling frames is much more relaxed and more complex but higher performance scheduling algorithms can be explored in frame-based matching. With the above example, the scheduling time can be extended from 12.8 ns to 128 ns.

Research on frame-based matching is also important for electronic switch fabrics. As the line speed increases from 10 Gbps to 40 Gbps to 100 Gbps or more, the cell slot becomes smaller and smaller, and frame-based matching can be used to eliminate the constraints with the price of a larger delay.

In the following, we introduce some work related to frame-based matching including reducing the reconfiguration frequency, fixed-size frame-based matching, and asynchronous variable-size frame-based matching.

### 7.5.1  Reducing the Reconfiguration Frequency

The objective of frame-based matching is to lower the bandwidth waste by reducing the reconfiguration frequency. The algorithms presented in [32] can exactly emulate an unconstrained (zero overhead) switch in a switch with reconfiguration overhead, such as an optical switch. That is, any scheduling algorithms designed for an unconstrained switch can be exactly emulated in an optical switch fabric. The emulation is executed in the following steps. First, in an unconstrained switch, acknowledged requests within $T$ time slots are accumulated. Second, in the switch with reconfiguration overhead, an algorithm is executed, and a set of $N_s$ switch schedules are generated to acknowledge the same batch of requests. Finally, at each output port, packets are reordered to exactly emulate the same departure process in the unconstrained switch.

For instance, suppose $T = 5$ in a $2 \times 2$ switch and the unconstrained switch fabric configurations in consecutive $T$ time slots are

$$\begin{bmatrix} 1 & 0 \\ 0 & 1 \end{bmatrix}, \begin{bmatrix} 0 & 1 \\ 1 & 0 \end{bmatrix}, \begin{bmatrix} 1 & 0 \\ 0 & 1 \end{bmatrix}, \begin{bmatrix} 0 & 1 \\ 1 & 0 \end{bmatrix} \quad \text{and} \quad \begin{bmatrix} 1 & 0 \\ 0 & 1 \end{bmatrix}.$$

In another way, we can keep the switch fabric configuration

$$\begin{bmatrix} 1 & 0 \\ 0 & 1 \end{bmatrix}$$

for three time slots, and then

$$\begin{bmatrix} 0 & 1 \\ 1 & 0 \end{bmatrix}$$

for two time slots. The two types of configuration can transfer the same cells over the five time slots from inputs to corresponding outputs, but the second type only requires one reconfiguration of the switch fabric. Obviously, in a $2 \times 2$ switch, some combinations of the two basic switch configurations

$$\begin{bmatrix} 1 & 0 \\ 0 & 1 \end{bmatrix} \quad \text{and} \quad \begin{bmatrix} 0 & 1 \\ 1 & 0 \end{bmatrix}$$

can achieve the same scheduling results for any given $T$. Then what is the minimum $N_s$ in a $N \times N$ switch?

**Exact Covering.** The problem of emulation is identical to the "cover" problem in math.

*Cover*: Matrix $A$ is covered by a set of switch configurations $P(1), \ldots, P(N_s)$ and corresponding weights $\phi(1), \ldots, \phi(N_s)$ if

$$\sum_{k=1}^{N_s} \phi(k) p_{i,j}(k) \geq a_{i,j}, \qquad \forall i, \quad j \in \{1, \ldots, N\},$$

where $a_{i,j}$ and $p_{i,j}(k)$ are elements of matrix $A$ and $P(k)$, respectively, and $\phi(k)$ is the weight of a switch configuration matrix $P(k)$. $P(k)$ is a $N \times N$-permutation matrix, which means each element of $P(k)$ is, either 0 or 1, and there is only one 1 in each row and each column.

In the case of equality for all $i$ and $j$, the switch configurations exactly cover $A$.

For a given $N \times N$ switch fabric, if all the requests are cumulated to form a matrix $C(T)$, where $C(T)$ is a matrix whose rows and columns sum to $T$. The number of necessary and sufficient switch configurations $N_s$ that can exactly cover any $C(T)$ is $N^2 - 2N + 2$.

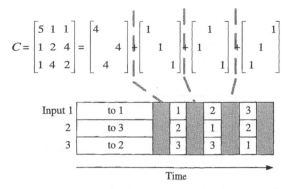

**Figure 7.33** Example of exact covering $\{T = 7\}$.

Figure 7.33 shows an example of exact covering with $T = 7$. The matrix $C$ is exactly covered with four switch configurations. The switch configuration

$$\begin{bmatrix} 1 & 0 & 0 \\ 0 & 0 & 1 \\ 0 & 1 & 0 \end{bmatrix}$$

is kept for four time slots and others are one time slot.

Complex algorithms that achieve an exact covering are typical and can be found in the work of Inukai [33] and Chang et al. [34]. They perform $O(N^2)$ maximum size matchings, and the complexity of each maximum size matching is $O(N^{2.5})$, so the complexity of exact covering is $O(N^{4.5})$.

In the exact covering, there are no empty time slots during transferring cells. Thus the required speedup to compensate for empty slots speedup $S_{min} = 1$, and the total speedup of the switch fabric $S = T/[T - \delta(N^2 - 2N + 2)]$, where $\delta$ is the switch reconfiguration overhead in time slots.

**Minimum Switching.** Exact covering provides a bound where $S_{min} = 1$, but $O(N^2)$ switch configurations are needed. Whereas, the minimum switching configurations that can cover any arbitrary matrix $C$ is $N$. These $N$ permutation matrixes do not have any 1s in the same row and the same column.

Obviously, if none of the elements of $C$ is zero, any switching configurations that are less than $N$ cannot cover $C$. For example, the matrix

$$\begin{bmatrix} 2 & 2 \\ 2 & 2 \end{bmatrix}$$

cannot be covered with less than two different switch configurations.

For the same matrix shown in Figure 7.33, it can be covered with three configurations as shown in Figure 7.34. These switch configurations do not exactly cover matrix $C$, and there are empty time slots, so the speedup is required to compensate these empty time slots. To transmit a general cumulative schedule matrix $C(T)$ in $N$ switch configurations, $S_{min}$ must be at least $\Omega(\log N)$ for $T > N$. At the same time, to cover a general cumulative schedule matrix $C(T)$ with $N$ switch configurations, $S_{min} = 4T(4 + \log_2 N)$ is sufficient.

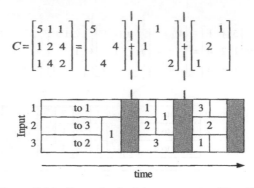

**Figure 7.34**  Example of minimum covering $\{T = 9\}$.

The algorithm with $N$ configurations is also proposed in the work of Towles and Dally [32]. The algorithm is mainly made of $N$ maximum size matchings and thus the total time complexity is $O(N^{3.5})$.

***DOUBLE.***  As described in the previous section, using the minimal number of switchings requires a speedup of at least $\log N$. In this section, we show that by allowing $2N$ switchings, the minimum speedup $S_{\min}$ can be reduced to approximately two. Most importantly, the minimum speedup is no longer a function of $N$. This approach has the advantage of the EXACT algorithm, a small constant speedup, combined with a number of switchings that grows linearly with $N$.

DOUBLE [35] algorithm works as follows:

Step 1.  *Split C.*  Define and $N \times N$ matrix $A$ such that $a_{i,j} = \lfloor c_{i,j}/(T/N) \rfloor$.

Step 2.  *Color A.*  Construct the bipartite multigraph $G_A$ from $A$ (the number of edges between vertices is equal to the value of the corresponding entry of $A$). Find a minimal edge-coloring of $A$. Set $i \leftarrow 1$.

Step 3.  *Schedule coarse.*  For a specific color in the edge-coloring of $G_A$, construct a switch configuration $P(i)$ from the edges assigned that color. Set $\phi(i) \leftarrow \lceil T/N \rceil$ and $i \leftarrow i + 1$. Repeat step 3 for each of the colors in $G_A$.

Step 4.  *Schedule fine.*  Find any $N$ nonoverlapping switch schedules $P(N + 1), \ldots,$ $P(2N)$ and set $\phi(N + 1), \ldots, \phi(2N)$ to $\lceil T/N \rceil$.

DOUBLE works by separating $C$ into coarse and fine matrices and devotes $N$ configurations to each. The algorithm first generates the coarse matrix $A$ by dividing the elements of $C$ by $T/N$ and taking the floor. The rows and columns of $A$ sum to at most $N$, thus the corresponding bipartite multigraph can be edge-colored in $N$ colors. Each subset of edges assigned to a particular color forms a matching, which is weighted by $\lceil T/N \rceil$. The fine matrix for $C$ does not need to be explicitly computed because its elements are guaranteed to be less than $\lceil T/N \rceil$. Thus, any $N$ configurations that collectively represent every entry of $C$, each weighted by $\lceil T/N \rceil$, can be used to cover the fine portion.

An example execution of DOUBLE is shown in Figure 7.35. The algorithm begins by creating the coarse matrix $A$ by dividing each element in $C$ by $T/N$ and taking the floor. So, in the example, entry (1,1) of $A$ contains $\lfloor 16/(T/N) \rfloor = 16/(16/4) = 4$. The resulting matrix $A$ has row and column sums $\leq 4$, ensuring that it can be edge colored with four colors

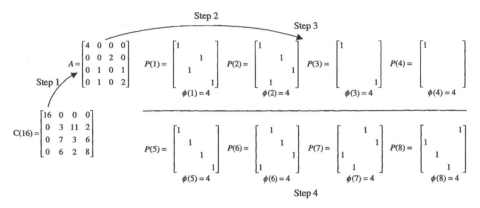

**Figure 7.35** Example of DOUBLE $\{N = 4, T = 16\}$.

(step 2). Then, the edges assigned to each color are converted to schedules in step 3. For example, $P(1)$ corresponds to the subset of edges assigned to color 1 during step 2. Also, some of the schedules may not be complete permutations because the row and column sums of $A$ are less than $N$, such as $P(3)$ and $P(4)$, but it is still guaranteed that all the elements of $A$ are covered. In general, step 3 creates at most $N$ matchings with weight $\lceil T/N \rceil$, for a total weight of approximately $T$.

Step 4 picks four nonoverlapping schedules, $P(5)$ through $P(8)$, and each is assigned a weight of $\lceil T/N \rceil = 4$. In general, step 4 creates the same total weight as step 3: approximately $T$. Therefore, the total weight to schedule $C(T)$ using DOUBLE is approximately $2T$ and $S_{\min} = 2$.

In brief, exact covering generates $N_s = N^2 - 2N + 2$ schedules for every $T$ time slots, and no speedup is required. The complexity of exact covering is $O(N^{4.5})$. Minimum switching generates only $N$ schedules to cover the batch of requests, but requires a speedup of $\Omega (\log N)$. The complexity of minimum switching is $O(N^{3.5})$. DOUBLE generates $N_s = 2N$ schedules for every $T$ time slots and a speedup of two is required. The DOUBLE algorithm produces schedules with these properties in $O(N^2 \log N)$ time using the edge-coloring algorithm of [36]. When the port number $N$ and the reconfiguration overhead $\delta$ are large, the delay of exact covering will not be accepted. When the bandwidth is expensive, the $\Omega (\log N)$ speedup of minimum switching will cause, too much bandwidth waste. DOUBLE will be a better tradeoff between delay and bandwidth for a large range of $N$ and $T$.

### 7.5.2 Fixed Size Synchronous Frame-Based Matching

Li et al. [37] have described a fixed-size synchronous frame-based matching scheme, where every $K$ time slots are grouped into a frame. When $K = 1$, the frame-based matching becomes the cell-based matching. In a frame-based matching, we can assume $K \gg 1$. The matching is computed for each frame and the switch fabric is only updated on frame boundaries. Since the time to compute the new matching set is not limited to one time slot, more complex scheduling can be executed in frame-based matching.

Figure 7.36 shows the working process of the synchronous frame-based matching. Each matching for the next frame is computed in $m$ time slots and the result is available at the end of each frame. Then, at the beginning of the next frame, $L$ time slots are needed to reconfigure the switch fabric. In the following $K - L$ time slots, valid packets are switched from matched

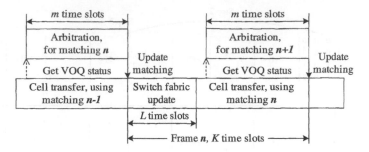

**Figure 7.36**  Fixed-size synchronous frame-based matching scheme.

input ports to output ports. $L$ time slots overhead are introduced by reconfiguration in each frame. At least $K/(K - L)$ speedup is required to compensate the bandwidth during the reconfiguration. In the following, three kinds of fixed-size synchronous frame-based matching schemes are studied.

***Frame-Based Maximum Weight Matching.*** In the cell-based scheduling, maximum weight matching (MWM) has been proved to be stable for any admissible traffic that satisfies the strong law of large numbers (SLLN). Naturally, MWM may be used in frame-based matching. But in frame-based matching, we cannot achieve maximum weight at each time slot. Instead, as shown in Figure 7.36, we can compute a matching that achieves the maximum weight at the time slot of getting VOQ status. The frame-based MWM is still stable under any admissible Bernoulli i.i.d. traffic.

The complexity of MWM is $O(N^3)$, which is not practically implemented even with the relaxed timing available under frame-based matching.

***Frame-Based Maximal Weight Matching.*** Maximal weight matching algorithm is proposed to approximate MWM with less complexity. The most straightforward maximal weight matching algorithm is to sort all $N^2$ VOQs by their weight and always select the VOQs with the largest weight for service. Ties can be broken randomly. The complexity of this sorting operation is $O(N^2 \log N)$. Sorting VOQs in a distributed manner at each input line card can further reduce the time complexity. The details of this algorithm are as follows.

Step 1: At $m$ time slots before a new frame starts, get weights for all VOQs. At each input, sort all $N$ VOQs by their weights in decreasing order. Let $h = N$.

Step 2: Consider the $h$ VOQs at the top of the $h$ sorted lists, and select the one with the largest weight and match the corresponding input and output. Delete the sorted list of the corresponding input and all VOQs destined to the corresponding output.

Step 3: $h = h - 1$. If $h > 0$, go to step 2.

Step 4: Update the matching set at the boundary of a new frame.

The complexity of step 1 is $O(\log N)$. Step 2 also takes $O(\log N)$ steps, and at most $N$ executions are needed. So the total time complexity is $O(N \log N)$.

Figure 7.37 shows an example of frame-based maximal weight matching where the port number is four. During iteration 1, the weight of $L(1, 2)$ is the maximum, so the match

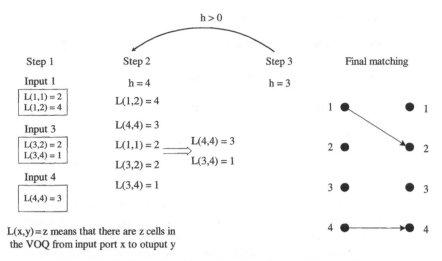

$L(x,y)=z$ means that there are z cells in
the VOQ from input port x to otuput y

**Figure 7.37**    Example of frame-based maximal weight matching.

between input port 1 and output 2 is established. Then $L(1, 2)$, $L(1, 1)$, and $L(3, 2)$ are removed, and only $L(4, 4)$ and $L(3, 4)$ are left in the following iterations.

***Frame-Based Multiple Iteration Weighted Matching.*** In a cell-based electronic switch, practical matching schemes, such as PIM, iSLIP, and DRRM, use multiple iterations to converge on a maximal size matching. Similarly, multiple iterative weighted matching scheme, such as longest queue first ($i$LQF) and oldest queue first ($i$OQF), converge on a maximal weight matching within $\log N$ iterations.

In an optical switch, a frame-based multiple iteration weighted matching can be used to converge on a frame-based maximal weight matching. Simulation results show that by using $\log N$ iterations, the schedule can achieve almost the same performance as that of a frame-based maximal weight matching. A frame-based multiple iterative weighted matching scheme works as the following in every iteration.

Step 1: Each unmatched input sends requests for all nonempty VOQs along with their weights.

Step 2: If an unmatched output receives any request, it selects the request with the largest weight and sends a grant to the corresponding input. Ties are broken randomly.

Step 3: If an unmatched input receives multiple grants, it accepts the grant corresponding to the largest weight. Ties are broken randomly. The corresponding input and output port are set to be matched and excluded from the following iterations.

Figure 7.38 shows an example of frame-based multiple iteration weighted matching. The value upon each edge is the weight from an input to the corresponding output. Each output grants an input with the highest weight, and each input accepts an output with the highest weight.

The complexity of one iteration is $O(\log N)$, and $\log N$ iterations are needed to converge the frame-based maximal weight matching. Therefore, the complexity of this scheme is as low as $O(\log^2 N)$. Moreover, this algorithm can be implemented in a distributed manner and is more practical.

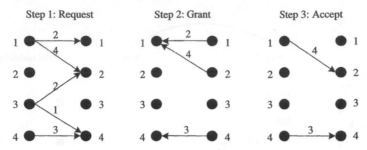

**Figure 7.38**  Example of frame-based maximal weight matching.

When the configuration time $L$ is set to 0, our simulation results show that the throughput of a frame-based MWM algorithm under uniform traffic is 100 percent, and is close to 100 percent under all non-uniform traffic patterns considered by Li et al. [21] except the diagonal traffic pattern. According to previous studies, the diagonal traffic pattern is an extremely unbalanced nonuniform pattern, in which for an input $i$, a ratio $p$ of arrivals is destined to output $i$, and $1 - p$ to output $(i + 1)$ mod $N$. Switches usually have worse performance under diagonal traffic than under other more balanced traffic patterns. The throughput of frame-based maximal weight matching under diagonal traffic is always higher than 88 percent. Moreover, the simulated throughput performance of the frame-based multiple iteration weighted matching is almost the same as that of the frame-based maximal weight matching.

Delay performance is measured in time slots, where one time slot is the time to transfer one fixed-size packet. The performance of frame-based multiple iteration weighted matching is quite close to the performance of the frame-based maximal weight matching. Figure 7.39 shows the average delay of the frame-based maximal weight matching for different switch sizes when the reconfiguration time $L$ is 0 or 10, and the frame length $K$ is 50 time slots. We can infer that under light load, the average delay with nonzero $L$ is close to the sum of $L$ and the average delay when $L$ is zero. Note that the average delay is close to $NK/2$. This result is consistent with the intuition that under a moderate load regime, the arriving packet has to wait for $N/2$ frames before its own VOQ is served. Therefore, when $K$ becomes large, the measured delay will increase linearly. For example, when $K = 200$, the corresponding delay is about four times than shown in Figure 7.39.

If a cell slot time is 100 ns, a delay of 1400 time slots is about 140 µs. Therefore, a future reduction in switch reconfiguration time to 10 µs will make it feasible. Given a switch size $N$, reconfiguration time $L$ and the required delay, the corresponding frame size can then be determined.

### 7.5.3  Asynchronous Variable-Size Frame-Based Matching

In fixed-size synchronous frame-based matching schemes, the switch fabric is updated for each frame instead of each time slot to reduce the reconfiguration frequency. However, if only part of the connections is reconfigured when necessary and others keep transferring cells, which is corresponding to asynchronous frame matching, the overhead can be reduced further, especially under heavy offered load. This variation is feasible. For instance, MEMS-based optical switches can reconfigure a subset of input and output ports while the other input-output ports continue to switch packets. Exhaustive service matching and limited

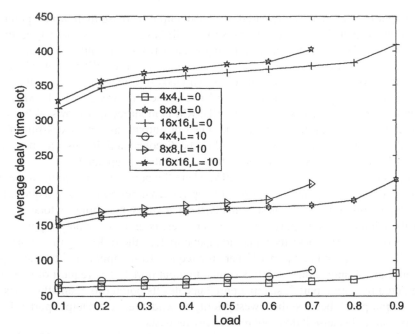

**Figure 7.39** Average delay of frame-based maximal weight matching switch under uniform traffic when $K = 50$.

service matching algorithms [21] can be extended for asynchronous variable-size frame matching [37]. Under uniform traffic, we can expect that exhaustive service matching and limited service matching will lead to similar performance. Under nonuniform traffic, limited service matching can avoid unfairness and instability.

For an optical switch, exhaustive service dual round-robin matching (EDRRM) can be modified so that arbitration will only be done when necessary. In the original EDRRM, arbitration is done by input arbiters and output arbiters based on the round-robin service discipline. When an output is matched to an input, this output is locked by the input. When the VOQ under service is emptied, the corresponding input sends a message to the

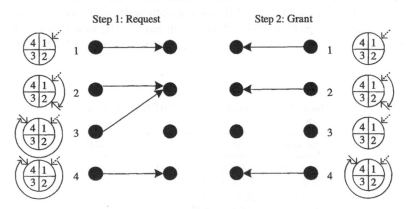

**Figure 7.40** Example of EDRRM with four ports.

locked output to release it. The released input and output increase their arbiter pointers by one location, so that the VOQ just being served will have the lowest priority in the next arbitration. A locked output cannot grant any request from other inputs. An input sends requests to outputs if and only if it is not matched to any output. When a match is found, only this new connection will be updated which leads to a reconfiguration time, and all other connections stay uninterrupted. In order to reduce the frequency of switch fabric reconfigurations, in frame-based matching EDRRM is modified as follows. When a VOQ is completely served and the corresponding input or output has not successfully found a new match, the connection for this VOQ will not be disconnected. In this way, new arrivals to this VOQ can still be transferred before the switch fabric is updated.

Figure 7.40 shows an example of EDRRM where the port number is four. At the beginning, all the pointers are pointing at port 1. In step 1, each input port sends a request. In step 2, each output port grants the requests. Finally, there are three matchings in total. Input port 1 locks its pointer to output port 1 because its request is granted by output port 1. At the same time, output port 1 locks its pointer to input port 1. In the following time slots, output port 1 will always grant input port 1 if there is a request from input port 1 to output port 1. Input port 2 and 4 update their pointers similar to input port 1. The request of input port 3 is not granted by output port 2, so input port 3 updates its pointer to 4, and thus makes the VOQ to output port 3 become the lowest priority to send a request. Output port 3 does not update its pointer because it does not receive any requests.

To further reduce the bandwidth overhead, one possible variation of EDRRM is to start searching for the next matching when the number of cells waiting in the VOQ under service drops below a threshold. Additionally, since the arbitration time is not necessarily limited to one time slot, a higher complex matching scheme can be used to improve the performance and this will be a future topic of research.

When the reconfiguration time $L$ is larger than zero in an optical switch, throughput is expected to degrade. Simulated throughput with different values of non-zero $L$ and different switch size is shown in Table 7.2. It shows that throughput is relatively insensitive to $L$. The throughput can be improved by an appropriate speedup.

When the reconfiguration overhead $L > 0$, the variable frame schemes have better delay performance than fixed frame schemes under low and moderate loads. This is due to the fact that under low loads, fixed frames are often not filled, which leads to unnecessary additional delay. In variable-size frame-based matching schemes, the frame size adapts to the load of each VOQ, which means most frames are accumulated to be fully filled.

The delay performance of an optical EDRRM switch under uniform traffic can be analyzed by using an exhaustive random polling system model. The model can be applied to predict the performance of switches with, too large size to be simulated. The performance

**TABLE 7.2  Throughput of an EDRRM Optical Switch**

| $L$ (time slots) | 0 | 10 | 100 | 1000 |
|---|---|---|---|---|
| $4 \times 4$ switch | 0.9926 | 0.9913 | 0.9760 | 0.8946 |
| $8 \times 8$ switch | 0.9408 | 0.9399 | 0.99383 | 0.9232 |
| $16 \times 16$ switch | 0.9680 | 0.9673 | 0.9587 | 0.9279 |
| $32 \times 32$ switch | 0.9794 | 0.9768 | 0.9636 | 0.9153 |

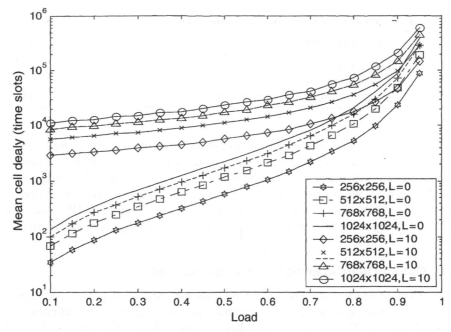

**Figure 7.41**    Average cell delay of the EDRRM with large switch size and varied $L$ under uniform traffic.

analysis with $L$ is a straightforward extension of the analysis without introducing $L$ in [29]. When $N$ goes to infinity, the average switch over time and the average delay converge to a limit for $\rho < 1$.

$$\lim_{N \to \infty} E(S) = \frac{1 - e^{-\rho}}{1 - e^{-(1-\rho)(1-e^{-\rho})}} - 1 + L,$$

and

$$E(T) \to E(S)\frac{N - \rho}{1 - \rho} + \frac{2 - \rho}{2(1 - \rho)} \approx E(S)\frac{N}{1 - \rho}.$$

Figure 7.41 shows the calculated average delay $E(T)$ of four switches of large size when the reconfiguration time $L$ is 0 and 10. Compared with switches with zero configuration overhead, the delay is approximately increased by $LN/(1 - \rho)$. For instance, when $N = 256$, $L = 10$, and $\rho = 0.1$, the additional delay caused by non-zero $L$ is about 2844 time slots. The delay can be lowered with a speedup to compensate the configuration overhead.

## 7.6  STABLE MATCHING WITH SPEEDUP

The stable matching problem is a bipartite matching, proposed by Gale and Shapley [38]. An existing algorithm to solve the problem is GSA (Gale-Shapley algorithm) with a lower complexity bound of $O(N^2)$ [39]. In the input-buffered matching algorithms, GSA tries to find stable input–output port matching by using predefined input port priority lists and

TABLE 7.3  **Comparison of Stable Marriage Algorithms**

| Algorithm | Input Preference List | Output Preference List | Speedup | Complexity |
|---|---|---|---|---|
| MUCFA | Urgent value | Urgent value | 4 | $\omega(N^2)$ |
| CCF | Output occupancy | Urgent value | 2 | $O(N)$ |
| LOOFA | Output occupancy | Arrival time | 2 | $O(N)$ |

output port priority lists, which are mainly used to solve input and output port contention. A match is considered to be stable, when all the matched input and output ports cannot find a better matching with a higher priority from those unmatched input and output ports.

In this section, we discuss three stable matching algorithms: most-urgent-cell-first algorithm (MUCFA), critical cell first (CCF), last-in-highest-priority (LIHP), and lowest-output-occupancy-cell-first (LOOFA). Table 7.3 summarizes the operations and complexity.

### 7.6.1  Output-Queuing Emulation with Speedup of 4

The most urgent cell first algorithm (MUCFA) scheme [40] schedules cells according to the "urgency". A shadow switch with output queuing is considered in the definition of the "urgency" of a cell. The urgency is also called the time to leave (TL), which indicates the time from the present that the cell will depart from the OQ switch. This value is calculated when a cell arrives. Since the buffers of the output-queued switch are FIFO, the urgency of a cell at any time equals the number of cells ahead of it in the output buffer at that time. It gets decremented after every time slot. Each output has the record of the urgency value of every cell destined for it. The algorithm is run as follows:

1. At the beginning of each phase, each output sends a request for the most urgent cell (i.e., the one with the smallest TL) to the corresponding input.
2. If an input receives more than one request, then it will grant to that output whose cell has the smallest urgency number. If there is a tie between two or more outputs, a supporting scheme is used. For example, the output with the smallest port number wins, or the winner is selected in a round-robin fashion.
3. Outputs that lose contention will send a request for their next most urgent cell.
4. The above steps run iteratively until no more matching is possible. Then cells are transferred and MUCFA goes to the next phase.

An example is shown in Figure 7.42. Each number represents a queued cell, and the number itself indicates the urgency of the cell. Each input maintains three VOQs, one for each output. Part (a) shows the initial state of the first matching phase. Output 1 sends a request to input 1 since the HOL cell in $VOQ_{1,1}$ is the most urgent for it. Output 2 sends a request to input 1 since the HOL cell in $VOQ_{1,2}$ is the most urgent for it. Output 3 sends a request to input 3 since the HOL cell in $VOQ_{3,3}$ is the most urgent for it. Part (b) illustrates matching results of the first phase, where cells from $VOQ_{1,1}$, $VOQ_{2,2}$, and $VOQ_{3,3}$ are transferred. Part (c) shows the initial state of the second phase, while part (d) gives the matching results of the second phase, in which HOL cells from $VOQ_{1,2}$ and $VOQ_{3,3}$ are matched.

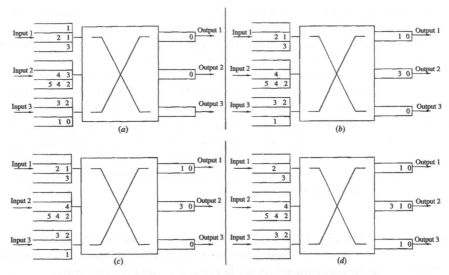

**Figure 7.42**  An example of two phases of MUCFA.

It has been shown that, under an internal speedup of 4, a switch with virtual-output queuing and MUCFA scheduling can behave identically to an output-queued switch, regardless of the nature of the arrival traffic.

### 7.6.2  Output-Queuing Emulation with Speedup of 2

This category of algorithms is based on an implementation of priority lists for each arbiter to select a matching pair [41]. The input priority list is formed by positioning each arriving cell at a particular place in the input queue. The relative ordering among other queued cells remains unchanged. This kind of queue is called a push-in queue. Some metrics are used for each arriving cell to determine the location. Furthermore, if cells are removed from the queue in an arbitrary order, we call it a push-in arbitrary out (PIAO) queue. If the cell at the head of queue is always removed next, we call it a push-in first out (PIFO) queue.

The algorithms described in this section also assume a shadow output-queued switch, based on which the following terms are defined:

1. Time to leave – $TL(c)$ is the time slot in which cell $c$ would leave the shadow OQ switch. Of course, $TL(c)$ is also the time slot in which cell $c$ must leave from the real switch for the identical behavior to be achieved.

2. Output cushion – $OC(c)$ is the number of cells waiting in the output buffer at cell $c$'s output port that have a lower TL value than cell $c$. If a cell has a small (or zero) output cushion, then it is urgent to be delivered to its output so that it can depart when its TL is reached. Conversely, if a cell has a large output cushion, it may be temporarily set aside while more urgent cells are delivered to their outputs. Since the switch is work-conserving, a cell's output cushion is decremented after every time slot. A cell's output cushion increases only when a newly arriving cell is destined for the same output and has a more urgent TL.

3. Input thread – $IT(c)$ is the number of cells ahead of cell $c$ in its input priority list. $IT(c)$ represents the number of cells currently at the input that have to be transferred to their outputs more urgently than cell $c$. A cell's input thread is decremented only when a cell ahead of it is transferred from the input, and is possibly incremented when a new cell arrives. It would be undesirable for a cell to simultaneously have a large input thread and a small output cushion – the cells ahead of it at the input may prevent it from reaching its output before its TL. This motivates the definition of slackness.

4. Slackness – $L(c)$ equals the output cushion of cell $c$ minus its input thread, that is, $L(c) = OC(c) - IT(c)$. Slackness is a measure of how large a cell's output cushion is with respect to its input thread. If a cell's slackness is small, then it is urgent to be transferred to its output. Conversely, if a cell has a large slackness, then it may be kept at the input for a while.

***Critical Cell First (CCF).*** CCF is a scheme for inserting cells in input queues that are PIFO queues. An arriving cell is inserted as far from the head of its input queue as possible such that the input thread of the cell is not larger than its output cushion (i.e., a positive slackness). Suppose that cell $c$ arrives at input port P. Let $x$ be the number of cells waiting in the output buffer at cell $c$'s output port. Those cells have a lower TL value than cell $c$ or the output cushion $OC(c)$ of $c$. Insert cell $c$ into $(x + 1)$th position from the front of the input queue at P. As shown in Figure 7.43, each cell is represented by its destined output port and the time to leave. For example, cell (B,4) is destined for output B and has a TL value equal to 4. Part ($a$) shows the initial state of the input queues. Part ($b$) shows the insertion of two incoming cells (C,4) and (B,4) to ports Y and Z, respectively. Cell (C,4) is inserted at the third place of port Y and cell (B,4) at the second place of port Z. Hence, upon arrival, both cells have zero slackness. If the size of the priority list is less than $x$ cells, then place $c$ at the end of the input priority list. In this case, cell $c$ has a positive slackness. Therefore, every cell has a non-negative slackness on arrival.

***Last in Highest Priority (LIHP).*** LIHP is also a scheme for inserting cells at input queues. It was proposed mainly to show and demonstrate the sufficient speedup to make an input–output queued switch emulate an output-queued switch. LIHP places a newly arriving

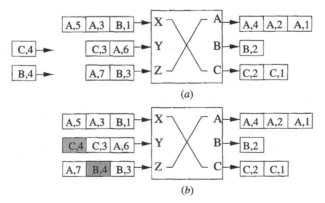

(a)

(b)

**Figure 7.43** Example of CCF priority placement.

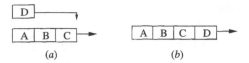

**Figure 7.44** Example of placement for LIHP. (*a*) Initial state; (*b*) New incoming cell is placed at the highest priority position..

cell right at the front of the input priority list, providing a zero input thread ($IT(c) = 0$) for the arriving cell. See Figure 7.44 for an example. The scheduling in every arbitration phase is a stable matching based on the time to leave value and the position in its input priority list of each queued cell.

The necessary and sufficient speedup is $2 - 1/N$ for a $N \times N$ input-and-output queued switch to exactly emulate a $N \times N$ output-queued switch with FIFO service discipline.

The necessary condition can be shown by the example as shown below. Since the speedup $2 - (1/N)$ represents a non-integral distribution of arbitration phases per slot between one and two, we first describe how scheduling phases are distributed. A speedup of $2 - (1/N)$ corresponds to having a truncated time slot out of every $N$ time slots; the truncated time slot has just one scheduling phase, whereas the other $N - 1$ time slots have two scheduling phases each. Figure 7.45 shows the difference between one-phased and two-phased time slots. We assume that the scheduling algorithm does not know in advance whether a time slot is truncated.

Recall that a cell is represented as a tuple $(P, TL)$, where $P$ represents which output port the cell is destined to and $TL$ represents the time to leave for the cell. For example, the cell $(C,7)$ must be scheduled for port $C$ before the end of time slot 7.

The input traffic pattern that provides the lower bound for an $N \times N$ input–output queued switch is given as follows. The traffic pattern $N$ spans time slots, the last of which is truncated:

1. In the first time slot, all input ports receive cells destined for the same output port, $P_1$.
2. In the second time slot, the input port that had the lowest time to leave in the previous time slot does not receive any more cells. In addition, the rest of the input ports receive cells destined for the same output port, $P_2$.

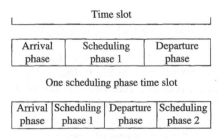

**Figure 7.45** One scheduling phase and two scheduling-phase time slots.

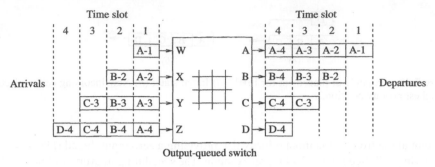

**Figure 7.46** Lower bound input traffic pattern for a 4 × 4 switch.

3. In the $i$th time slot, the input ports that had the lowest time to leave in each of the $i-1$ previous time slots do not receive any more cells. In addition, the rest of the input ports must receive cells destined for the same output port, $P_i$.

One can repeat the traffic pattern just mentioned as many times as is required to create arbitrarily long traffic patterns. Figure 7.46 shows the above sequence of cells for a 4 × 4 switch. The departure events from the output-queued switch are depicted on the right, and the arrival events are on the left. For simplicity, we present the proof of our lower bound on this 4 × 4 switch instead of a general $N \times N$ switch.

Figure 7.47 shows the only possible schedule for transferring these cells across in seven phases. Of the four time slots, the last one is truncated, giving a total of seven phases. Cell A-1 must leave the input side during the first phase, since the input–output queued switch does not know whether the first time slot is truncated. Similarly, cells B-2, C-3, and D-4 must leave during the third, fifth, and seventh phases, respectively (see Fig. 7.47$a$). Cell A-2 must leave the input side by the end of the third phase. However, it cannot leave during the first or the third phase because of contention. Therefore, it must depart during the second phase. Similarly, cells B-3 and C-4 must depart during the fourth and sixth phases, respectively (see Fig. 7.47$b$). Continuing this elimination process (see Fig. 7.47$c$ and $d$), there is only one possible scheduling order. For this input traffic pattern, the switch needs all seven phases in four time slots, which corresponds to a minimum speedup of 7/4 (or $2 - 1/4$). The proof of the general case for a $N \times N$ switch is a straightforward extension of the 4 × 4 example.

### 7.6.3 Lowest Output Occupancy Cell First (LOOFA)

The LOOFA is a work-conserving scheduling algorithm [42]. It provides 100 percent throughput and a cell delay bound for feasible traffic, using a speedup of 2. An input-and-output queued architecture is considered. Two versions of this scheme were presented: the greedy and the best-first. This scheme considers three different parameters associated with a cell, say cell $c$, to perform a match: the number of cells in its destined output queue or output occupancy $OCC(c)$, the time stamp of a cell or cell age $TS(c)$, and the smallest port number to break ties. Under the speedup of 2, each time slot has two phases. During each phase, the greedy version of this algorithm works as follows (see Figure 7.48 for

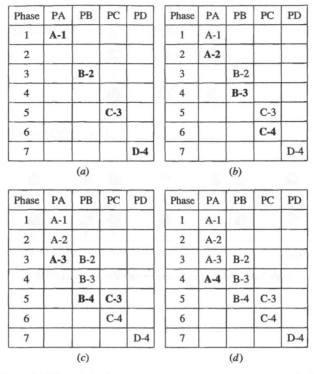

| Phase | PA | PB | PC | PD |
|---|---|---|---|---|
| 1 | A-1 | | | |
| 2 | | | | |
| 3 | | B-2 | | |
| 4 | | | | |
| 5 | | | C-3 | |
| 6 | | | | |
| 7 | | | | D-4 |

(a)

| Phase | PA | PB | PC | PD |
|---|---|---|---|---|
| 1 | A-1 | | | |
| 2 | A-2 | | | |
| 3 | | B-2 | | |
| 4 | | B-3 | | |
| 5 | | | C-3 | |
| 6 | | | C-4 | |
| 7 | | | | D-4 |

(b)

| Phase | PA | PB | PC | PD |
|---|---|---|---|---|
| 1 | A-1 | | | |
| 2 | A-2 | | | |
| 3 | A-3 | B-2 | | |
| 4 | | B-3 | | |
| 5 | | B-4 | C-3 | |
| 6 | | | C-4 | |
| 7 | | | | D-4 |

(c)

| Phase | PA | PB | PC | PD |
|---|---|---|---|---|
| 1 | A-1 | | | |
| 2 | A-2 | | | |
| 3 | A-3 | B-2 | | |
| 4 | A-4 | B-3 | | |
| 5 | | B-4 | C-3 | |
| 6 | | | C-4 | |
| 7 | | | | D-4 |

(d)

**Figure 7.47** Scheduling order for the lower bound input traffic pattern in Figure 7.46.

an example):

1. Initially, all inputs and outputs are unmatched.
2. Each unmatched input selects an active VOQ (i.e., a VOQ that has at least one cell queued) going to the unmatched output with the lowest occupancy, and sends a request to that output. Ties are broken by selecting the smallest output port number. See part (a) in Figure 7.48.
3. Each output, on receiving requests from multiple inputs, selecting the one with the smallest $OCC$ and sends the grant to that input. Ties are broken by selecting the smallest port number.
4. Return to step 2 until no more connections can be made.

An example of the greedy version is shown in Figure 7.48. The tuple "$x, y$" in the VOQ represents the output occupancy $OCC(c)$ and the timestamp $TS(c)$ of cell $c$, respectively. In the upper part of the figure, the arrows indicate the destination for all different cells at the input ports. The gray arrows in the lower part of the figure indicate the exchange of requests and grants. The black arrows indicate the final match. Part (a) shows that each input sends a request to the output with the lowest occupancy. Output 2 receives two requests, one from A and the other from B, while output 3 receives a request from input C. Part (b) illustrates that, between the two requests, output 2 chooses input A, the one with lower $TS$. Output 3 chooses the only request, input C.

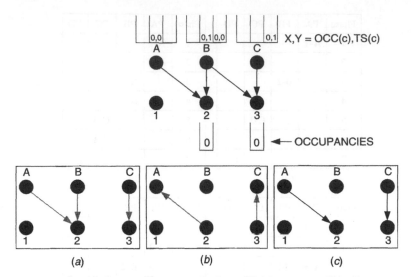

**Figure 7.48**   Matching example with the greedy LOOFA.

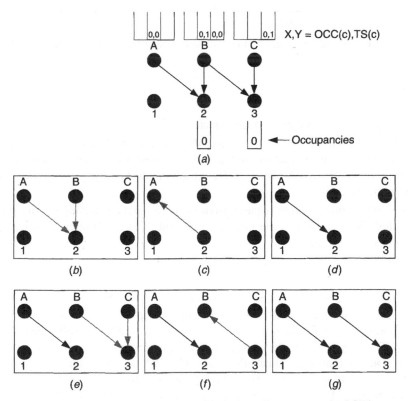

**Figure 7.49**   Matching example with the best-first version of LOOFA.

The best-first version works as follows:

1. Initially, all inputs and outputs are unmatched.
2. Among all unmatched outputs, the output with the lowest occupancy is selected. Ties are broken by selecting the smallest output port number. All inputs that have a cell destined for the selected output send a request to it.
3. The output selects the cell request input with the smallest time stamp and sends the grant to the input. Ties are broken by selecting the smaller input port number.
4. Return to step 2 until no more connections can be made (or $N$ iterations are completed).

Figure 7.49 shows a matching example with the best-first version example. The selection of the output with the lowest $OCC(c)$ results in a tie. Outputs 2 and 3 have the lowest $OCC$. This tie is broken by selecting output 2 since this port number is the smaller number. Therefore, inputs A and B send a request to this output as shown in part ($b$), while part ($c$) illustrates that output 2 grants the oldest cell, input A. Part ($d$) shows the matching result after the first iteration. The second iteration begins in part ($e$) when output 3 is chosen as the unmatched output port with the lowest $OCC$ with requests from inputs B and C. Input B is chosen in part ($f$) for its lowest $TS(c)$. Part ($g$) depicts the final match.

Both algorithms achieve a maximal matching, with the greedy version achieving it in less iterations. On the other hand, it has been proven that, when combined with the oldest-cell-first input selection scheme, the best-first version provides delay bounds for rate-controlled input traffic under a speedup of 2. Denote $D_a$ and $D_o$ as the arbitration delay and the output queuing delay of any cell. It can be shown that $D_a \leq 4N/(S-1)$ and $D_o \leq 2N$ cell slots, where $S$ is the speedup factor.

## REFERENCES

[1] N. McKeown, A. Mekkittikul, V. Anantharam, and J. Walrand, "Achieving 100% throughput in an input-queued switch," *IEEE Transactions on Communications*, vol. 47, no. 8, pp. 1260–1267 (Aug. 1999).

[2] L. Tassiulas and A. Ephremides, "Stability properties of constrained queueing systems and scheduling policies for maximum throughput in multihop radio networks," *IEEE Transactions on Automatic control*, vol. 37, no. 12, pp. 1936–1949 (Dec. 1992).

[3] R. E. Tarjan, "Data structures and network algorithms," in *Proc. Society for Industrial and Applied Mathematics*, Pennsylvania (Nov. 1983).

[4] A. Mekkittikul and N. Mckeown, "A practical scheduling algorithm to achieve 100% throughput in input-queued switches," *INFOCOM'98*, San Francisco, California, pp. 792–799 (Mar. 1998).

[5] D. Shah and M. Kopikare, "Delay bounds for approximate maximum weight matching algorithms for input queued switches," in *Proc. IEEE INFOCOM'02*, New York, pp. 1024–1031 (June 2002).

[6] J. E. Hopcroft and R. M. Karp, "An $n^{\frac{5}{2}}$ algorithm for maximum matchings in bipartite graphs," SIAM, J. Comput., vol. 2, no. 4, pp. 225–231 (Dec. 1973).

[7] N. McKeown, "Scheduling algorithms for input-queued cell switches," Ph.D. thesis, UC Berkeley, May 1995.

[8] J. G. Dai and B. Prabhakar, "The throughput of data switches with and without speedup," in *Proc. IEEE INFOCOM'00*, Tel Aviv, Israel, pp. 556–564 (Mar. 2000).

[9] E. Leonardi, M. Mellia, F. Neri, and M. A. Marsan, "On the stability of input-queued switches with speed-up," *IEEE/ACM Transactions on Networking*, vol. 9, no. 1, pp. 104–118 (Feb. 2001).

[10] T. E. Anderson, S. S. Owicki, J. B. Saxe, and C. P. Thacker, "High speed switch scheduling for local area networks," *ACM Transactions on Computer Systems*, vol. 11, no. 4, pp. 319–352 (Nov. 1993).

[11] N. McKeown, "The iSLIP scheduling algorithm for input-queued switches," *IEEE/ACM Transactions on Networking*, vol. 7, no. 2, pp. 188–201 (Apr. 1999).

[12] N. McKeown, P. Varaiya, and J. Warland, "Scheduling cells in an input-queued switch," *IEE Electronics Letters*, vol. 29, issue 25, pp. 2174–2175 (Dec. 1993).

[13] Y. Li, S. Panwar, and H. J. Chao, "On the performance of a dual round-robin switch," in *Proc. IEEE INFOCOM 2001*, Anchorage, Alaska, vol. 3, pp. 1688–1697 (Apr. 2001).

[14] Y. Li, "Design and analysis of schedulers for high speed input queued switches," Ph.D. Dissertation, Polytechnic University, Brooklyn, New York, Jan. 2004.

[15] D. N. Serpanos and P. I. Antoniadis, "FIRM: a class of distributed scheduling algorithms for high-speed ATM switches with multiple input queues," in *Proc. IEEE INFOCOM'00*, Tel Aviv, Israel, pp. 548–554 (Mar. 2000).

[16] H. J. Chao and J. S. Park, "Centralized contention resolution schemes for a large-capacity optical ATM switch," in *Proc. IEEE ATM Workshop*, Fairfax, Virginia (May 1998).

[17] H. J. Chao, "Satur: A terabit packet switch using dual round-robin," *IEEE Communications Magazine*, vol. 38, no. 12, pp. 78–84 (Dec. 2000).

[18] E. Oki, R. Rojas-Cessa, and H. J. Chao, "A pipeline-based maximal-sized matching scheme for high-speed input-buffered switches," *IEICE Transactions on Communications*, vol. E85-B, no. 7, pp. 1302–1311 (July 2002).

[19] A. Smiljanic, R. Fan, and G. Ramamurthy, "RRGS-round-robin greedy scheduling for electronic/optical terabit switches," in *Proc. IEEE GLOBECOM'99*, Rio de Janeireo, Brazil, pp. 1244–1250 (Dec. 1999).

[20] H. Takagi, "Queueing analysis of polling models: an update," in *Stochastic Analysis of Computer and Communication Systems*. Elsevier Science Inc., New York; pp. 267–318, 1990.

[21] Y. Li, S. Panwar, and H. J. Chao, "The dual round-robin matching switch with exhaustive service," in *Proc. High Performace Switching and Routing (HPSR) 2002*, Kobe, Japan (May 2002).

[22] P. Giaccone, B. Prabhakar, and D. Shah, "Towards simple, high-performance schedulers for high-aggregate bandwidth switches," in *Proc. IEEE INFOCOM'02*, New York, vol. 3, pp. 1160–1169 (2002).

[23] L. Tassiulas, "Linear complexity algorithms for maximum throughput in radio networks and input queued switches," in *Proc. IEEE INFOCOM'98*, San Francisco, California, vol. 2, pp. 533–539 (Mar. 1998).

[24] A. Nijenhuis and H. Wilf, *Combinatorial Algorithms: for Computers and Calculators*. Academic Press, Orlando, Florida, 1978.

[25] P. Giaccone, B. Prabhakar, and D. Shah, "Randomized scheduling algorithms for high-aggregate bandwidth switches," *IEEE Journal on Selected Areas in Communications*, vol. 21, no. 4, pp. 546–559 (May 2003).

[26] D. Shah, P. Giaccone, and B. Prabhakar, "Efficient randomized algorithms for input-queued switch scheduling," *IEEE Micro*, vol. 22, no. 1, pp. 10–18 (Jan. 2002).

[27] Y. Li, S. Panwar, and H. J. Chao, "Exhaustive service matching algorithms for input queued switches," in *Proc. Workshop on High Performance Switching and Routing (HPSR 2004)*, Phoenix, Arizona (Apr. 2004).

[28] L. Kleinrock and H. Levy, "The analysis of random polling systems," *Operations Research*, vol. 36, no. 5, pp. 716–732 (Sept. 1988).

[29] Y. Li, S. Panwar, and H. J. Chao, "Performance analysis of a dual round robin matching switch with exhaustive service," in *Proc. IEEE GLOBECOM'02*, Taipei, Taiwan, vol. 3, pp. 2292–2297 (Nov. 2002).

[30] F. A. Marsan, A. Bianco, P. Giaccone, E. Leonardi, and E. Neri, "Packet scheduling in input-queued cell-based switches," in *Proc. IEEE INFOCOM'01*, Anchorage, Alaska, vol. 2, pp. 1085–1094 (Apr. 2001).

[31] K. Claffy, G. Miller, and K. Thompson, "The nature of the beast: recent traffic measurements from an Internet backbone," in *Proc. INET'98*, Geneva, Switzerland, pp. 21–24 (July 1998).

[32] B. Towles and W. Dally, "Guaranteed scheduling for switches with configuration overhead," in *Proc. IEEE INFOCOM'02*, New York, vol. 1, pp. 342–351 (June 2002).

[33] T. Inukai, "An efficient SS/TDMA time slot assignment algorithm," *IEEE Transactions on Communications*, vol. 27, no. 10, pp. 1449–1455 (Oct. 1979).

[34] C. S. Chang, W. J. Chen, and H. Y. Huang, "Birkhoff–von Neumann input buffered crossbar switches," in *Proc. IEEE INFOCOM'00*, Tel Aviv, Israel, pp. 1614–1623 (Mar. 2000).

[35] B. Towles and W. J. Dally, "Guaranteed scheduling for switches with configuration overhead," *IEEE/ACM Transactions on Networking*, vol. 11, no. 5, pp. 835–847 (Oct. 2003).

[36] R. Cole and J. Hopcroft, "On edge coloring bipartite graph," *SIAM Journal on Computing*, vol. 11, no. 3, pp. 540–546 (1982).

[37] Y. Li, S. Panwar, and H. J. Chao, "Frame-based matching algorithms for optical switches," in *Proc. IEEE Workshop on High Performance Switching and Routing (HPSR 2003)*, Torino, Italy, pp. 97–102 (June 2003).

[38] D. Gale and L. S. Shapley, "College admission and the stability of marriage," *American Mathematical Monthly*, vol. 69, no. 1, pp. 9–15 (1962).

[39] D. Gusfield and R. Irving, *The Stable Marriage Problem: Structure and Algorithms*. The MIT Press, Cambridge, Massachusetts, 1989.

[40] B. Prabhakar and N. McKeown, "On the speedup required for combined input and output queued switching," *Automatica*, vol. 35, issue 12, pp. 1909–1920 (Dec. 1999).

[41] S. T. Chuang, A. Goel, N. McKeown, and B. Prabhakar, "Matching output queuing with a combined input/output-queued switch," *IEEE Journal on Selected Areas in Communications*, vol. 17, no. 6, pp. 1030–1039 (June 1999).

[42] P. Krishna, N. Patel, A. Charny, and R. Simcoe, "On the speedup required for work-conversing crossbar switches," *IEEE Journal on Selected Areas in Communications*, vol. 17, no. 6, pp. 1057–1066 (June 1999).

# CHAPTER 8

# BANYAN-BASED SWITCHES

The very early theoretical work on multistage interconnection networks (MIN) was done in the context of circuit-switched telephone networks [1, 2]. The aim was to design a nonblocking multistage switch with a number of crosspoints less than a single-stage crossbar switch. After many such networks were studied and introduced for interconnecting multiple processors and memories in parallel computer systems, several types of them such as banyan and shuffle-exchange networks were proposed [3–5] as a switching fabric because several cells could be routed in parallel and the switching function could be implemented regularly in hardware.

In this chapter, we describe the banyan-family of switches, which have attracted many researchers for more than two decades now to build interconnection networks. Section 8.1 classifies banyan-family switch architectures into different categories based on their nature and property. Section 8.2 describes Batcher-sorting network switch architecture. Section 8.3 introduces output-contention resolution algorithms in banyan-family switches. Section 8.4 describes the Sunshine switch which extends the Batcher-banyan switching architecture. Section 8.5 describes some work on deflection routing over banyan-family networks. Section 8.6 introduces a self-route copy network where the nonblocking property of the banyan network is generalized to support multicasting.

## 8.1 BANYAN NETWORKS

The banyan class of interconnection networks was originally defined by Goke and Lipovski [6]. It has the property that there is exactly one path from any input to any output. Figure 8.1 shows four networks belonging to this class: the shuffle-exchange network (also called the omega network), the reverse shuffle-exchange network, the banyan network, and the baseline network.

*High Performance Switches and Routers*, by H. Jonathan Chao and Bin Liu
Copyright © 2007 John Wiley & Sons, Inc.

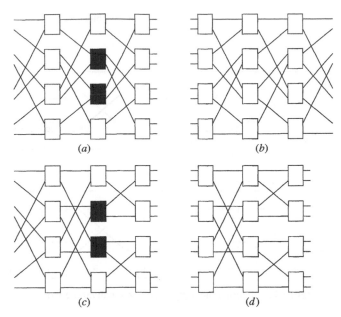

**Figure 8.1** Four different banyan networks: (*a*) shuffle-exchange (omega) network; (*b*) reverse shuffle-exchange network; (*c*) banyan network; (*d*) baseline network. We can see that (*a*) and (*c*) are isomorphic by interchanging two shaded nodes in the figures.

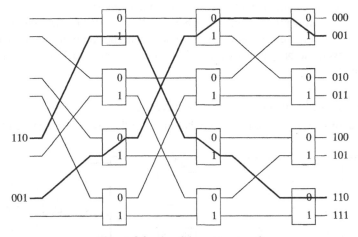

**Figure 8.2**  8 × 8 banyan network.

The common principal properties of these networks are: (1) they consist of $n = \log_2 N$ stages and $N/2$ nodes per stage;[1] (2) they have the self-routing property such that the unique $n$-bit destination address can be used to route a cell from any input to any output, each bit for a stage; and (3) their regularity and interconnection pattern are very attractive for VLSI implementation. Figure 8.2 shows a routing example in an 8 × 8 banyan network where the bold lines indicate the routing paths. On the right-hand side, the address of each output destination is labeled as a string of $n$ bits, $b_1 \cdots b_n$. A cell's destination address is encoded

---

[1]A regular $N \times N$ network can also be constructed from identical $b \times b$ switching nodes in $k$ stages where $N = b^k$.

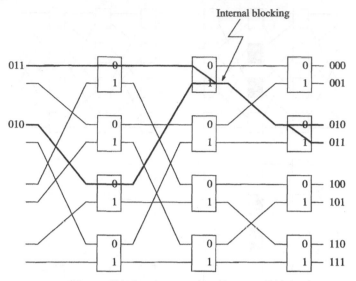

**Figure 8.3** Internal blocking in an 8 × 8 banyan network.

into the header of the cell. In the first stage, the most significant bit $b_1$ is examined. If it is a 0, the cell will be forwarded to the upper outgoing link; if it is a 1, the cell will be forwarded to the lower outgoing link. In the next stage, the next most significant bit $b_2$ will be examined and the routing is performed in the same manner.

The internal blocking refers to the case where a cell is lost due to the contention on a link inside the network. Figure 8.3 shows an example of internal blocking in an 8 × 8 banyan network. However, the banyan network will be internally nonblocking if both conditions below are satisfied:

- There is no idle input between any two active inputs;
- Output addresses of the cells are in either an ascending order or a descending order.

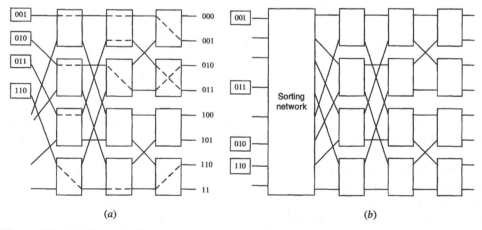

**Figure 8.4** (a) Example showing the banyan network is nonblocking for sorted inputs. (b) Nonblocking sort-banyan network.

See Figure 8.4. Consider the banyan network to be preceded by a network that concentrates the cells and sorts the cells according to their output destinations. The overall sort-banyan network will be internally nonblocking.

## 8.2 BATCHER-SORTING NETWORK

A sorting network is formed by a series of merge networks of different sizes. Figure 8.5$a$ shows an $8 \times 8$ Batcher-sorting network [7] consisting of merge networks of three different sizes. A merge network (see Figure 8.5$b$) is built by $2 \times 2$ sorting elements in stages, and the pattern of exchange connections between each pair of adjacent stages is the same as in

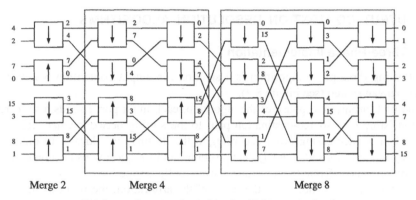

Merge 2          Merge 4                    Merge 8

- Batcher sorting network consists of multiple merge networks.

-Total numbers of stages= $(1 + 2 + \cdots + \log_2 N) = (\log_2 N)(1 + \log_2 N)/2$

(*a*)

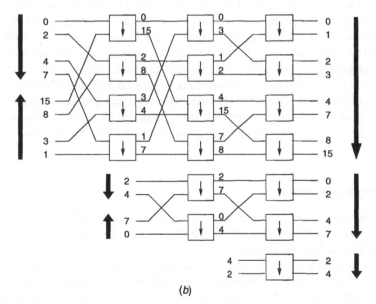

(*b*)

**Figure 8.5** Basic structure of a Batcher-sorting network. (*a*) Batcher-sorting network; (*b*) Corresponding merge networks.

a banyan network. We can observe that, if the order of the destinations of the first half input cells is ascending and that of the second half is descending, then the merge network will sort the cells into an ascending list at the outputs. An $8 \times 8$ sorting network will be formed if an $8 \times 8$ merge network is preceded by two $4 \times 4$ merge networks and four $2 \times 2$ merge (sorting) elements. A completely random list of eight input cells will be first sorted into four sorted lists of two cells, then two sorted lists of four cells, and finally a sorted list of eight cells.

A $N \times N$ merge network consists of $\log_2 N$ stages and $N \log_2 N/2$ elements. A sorting network has $1 + 2 + \cdots + \log_2 N = \log_2 N(\log_2 N + 1)/2$ stages and $N \log_2 N (\log_2 N + 1)/4$ elements. Figure 8.6 shows a $64 \times 64$ Batcher-banyan switch network, where the last six stages of switch elements belong to the banyan network.

## 8.3  OUTPUT CONTENTION RESOLUTION ALGORITHMS

### 8.3.1  Three-Phase Implementation

The following three-phase algorithm is a solution for output contention resolution in a Batcher-banyan switch (see Figure 8.7).

In the first (arbitration) phase of the algorithm, each input port $i$ sends a short request only, consisting of a source-destination pair, to the sorting network where the requests are sorted in nondecreasing order according to the destination address. In other words, conflicting requests are sorted at adjacent positions, and a request wins the contention only if its destination is different from the one above it in the sorted list.

As the input ports do not know the result of the arbitration, the requests that won the arbitration must send an acknowledgment to the input ports via an interconnection network in the second phase (the so-called acknowledgment phase). The feedback network in Figure 8.7b consists of $N$ fixed connections, each from an output of the Batcher network to the corresponding input of the Batcher network. Each acknowledgment carries the source that has won the contention back to an input of the Batcher network. These acknowledgments (sources) are routed through the entire Batcher-banyan network at distinct outputs according to the source address. When these acknowledgments are feedbacked to the inputs through an identical fixed network, each input port knows if it has won the contention. The input ports that finally receive an acknowledgment are guaranteed conflict-free output.

These input ports then transmit the full cell in the third and final phase (see Figure 8.7c) through the same Batcher-banyan network. Input ports that fail to receive an acknowledgment retain the cell in a buffer for the retry in the next time slot when the three-phase cycle is repeated.

### 8.3.2  Ring Reservation

A Batcher-banyan cell switch design with ring reservation is shown in Figure 8.8 [8]. The switch comprises the Batcher-banyan switch fabric, several switch interfaces, and a ring head-end (RHE) and timing generator.

A switch interface supports ring reservation and provides input cells buffering, synchronization of cells sent to the switch fabric, and output cells buffering. Cells entering the switch are buffered in a FIFO until they can participate in the reservation procedure. When an output is successfully reserved, the cell is delivered to the switch fabric at the beginning of the next cell cycle, and the next queued cell can begin to participate in the

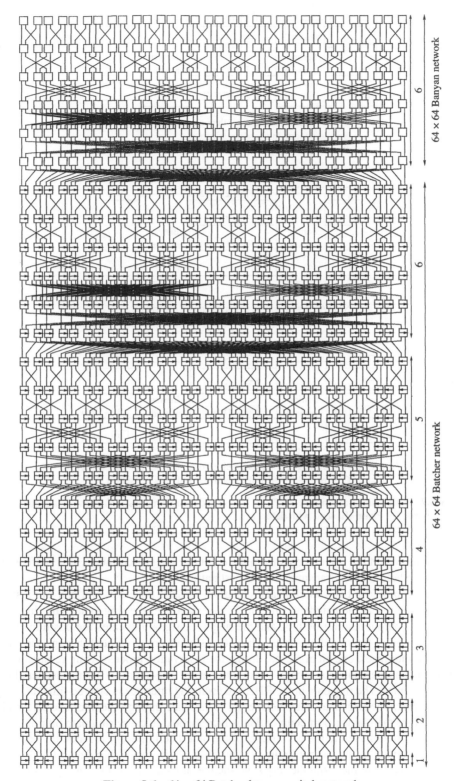

**Figure 8.6**   64 × 64 Batcher-banyan switch network.

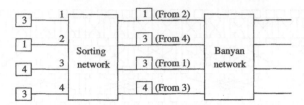

(*a*)    - Send source-destination pair through sorting network
         - Sort destination in non-decreasing order
         - Purge adjacent requests with same destination

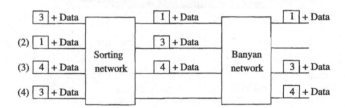

(*b*)    - Send ACK with source to ports winning contention
         - Route ACK through Batcher-banyan network

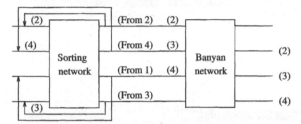

(*c*)    - Acknowledged ports send cells through Batcher-banyan network
         - Cells not acknowledged are buffered and retry in the next slot

**Figure 8.7** Three-phase algorithm. (*a*) Phase I: send and resolve request; (*b*) Phase II: acknowledge winning ports; (*c*) Phase III: send with data.

reservations. When the cell emerges from the output of the switch fabric, it is buffered in the interface before being transmitted to its destination.

The RHE provides two switch synchronization signals: bit clock and cell cycle start; and three ring reservation signals: ring clock, ring data, and the ring sync. The ring data is a series of output reservation bits, and the ring sync signal indicates the position of the first output port in the ring data series. These two signals are circulated through the RHE and switch interfaces, one bit at a time, during the reservation process. Ring reservation is performed at the beginning of each cell cycle after every ring interface has the header of the oldest cell copies. The ring data in the RHE and each ring interface is cleared (idle) at every cell cycle start. The ring data series then begins to circulate through the interface bit-by-bit. Each interface maintains a port counter that is incremented in every ring data bit time. The port counter is compared to the destination of the oldest cell in every bit time indicating if the cell is destined for the output in the next bit time. During each ring data bit time, each switch interface examines both the ring sync and the ring data bit. If the ring sync signal is

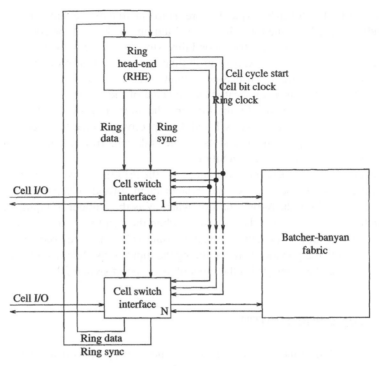

**Figure 8.8**  Batcher-banyan switch with ring reservation.

true, which means the next ring data bit corresponds to the first output, then the port counter is reset in the next bit time. If the destination of the cell matches with the port counter and the ring data bit is idle, the switch interface writes 'busy' on the ring to show that the output has been occupied in the next switch cycle. If the ring data bit is already BUSY, or if the port counter does not match the destination of the oldest cell, the ring data bit is left unchanged. Since each interface makes no more than one reservation per switch cycle, no collisions can take place in the switch fabric. While the ring reservation is being performed, the cells reserved in the previous switch cycle are transmitted to the switch fabric.

As shown in Fig. 8.9, at the first time slot, the output port addresses of cells from input ports 1 and 5 are matched, some checks are used to indicate that the cells can be sent to

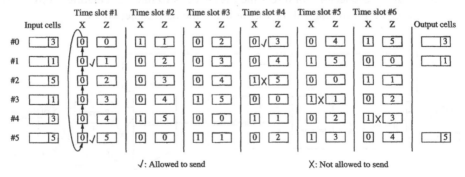

**Figure 8.9**  Implementation of the ring reservation scheme.

these output ports. The token bits $x_1$ and $x_5$ are set to one to indicate that output ports 1 and 5 are already reserved. All the token bits are shifted up one bit and the counter values are also modulo-increased by one for the second time slot. There are no matches found at the second and the third time slots. At the fourth time slot, the output port addresses of cells from input ports 0 and 2 are matched. Since output port 5 is already reserved for the cell in the previous time slot, which is indicated by the value of the token bit $x_2$, the cell at input port 2 cannot be sent. Similarly, for the fifth and the sixth time slots, cells at input ports 3 and 4 cannot be sent to output ports 1 and 3, respectively, since those output ports are already reserved in the previous time slots. At the end, cells from the input ports that are checked are the ones winning the contention.

In this example, since there are six input ports, the arbitration cycle can be completed within six time slots. This scheme uses the serial mechanism and, in general, the arbitration cycle can be done within the $N$-bit time slot, where $N$ is the number of input/output ports of the switch. This will become the bottleneck when the number of ports of the switch is large. However, by arbitrarily setting the appropriate values for the counters prior to the arbitration, this scheme provides fairness among the input ports. Another advantage of this scheme is that it can be employed at the input of any type of switch fabric.

## 8.4 THE SUNSHINE SWITCH

Sunshine switch [9] uses the combination of a Batcher-sorting network and parallel banyan routing networks to provide more than one path to each destination. Figure 8.10 shows a block diagram of the architecture. The $k$ parallel banyan routing networks provide $k$ independent paths to each output. If more than $k$ cells request a particular output during a time slot, then some excess cells are overflowed into a shared recirculating queue and then resubmitted to the switch at dedicated input ports. The recirculating queue consists of $T$ parallel loops and $T$ dedicated inputs to the Batcher-sorting network. Each recirculating loop can hold one cell. A delay block is put within the loops to align recirculated cells with those new arrivals from the input port controllers (IPCs) in the next time slot. During each time slot, the Batcher network sorts newly arrived and recirculated cells in the order of destination address and priority. This enables the trap network to resolve output port contention by selecting the $k$ highest priority cells for each destination address. Since there are $k$ parallel banyan networks, each output can accept $k$ cells in a time slot. When there are more than $k$ cells destined for an output, the excess will enter the recirculating queue. The concentrator and the selector will direct the excess cells to the recirculating loops, while those cells selected for routing will be forwarded to the banyan networks.

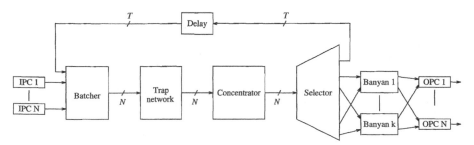

**Figure 8.10**   Block diagram of the Sunshine switch.

Each cell is inserted with a control header at the input port controller. The header format is shown in Figure 8.11. It contains two control fields: a routing field and a priority field, both are ordered starting with the most significant bit. In the routing field, the first bit is a cell activity bit to indicate if the cell contains valid information ($A = 1$), or the cell is empty ($A = 0$). Then the destination address (DA) field identifying the desired output port follows. The priority field consists of the quality of service (QoS) indicator and the internal switch priority (SP). The QoS field distinguishes cells from higher priority services such as circuit emulation, from lower priority services such as connectionless service, and ensures higher priority cells to be routed before lower priority cells when conflicts arise. The SP field is used internally by the switch to indicate the number of time slots that a cell has been delayed, and gives higher priority to recirculate cells. This guarantees that cells from a given source will be routed in sequence.

When the cells are sorted, they are arranged in ascending order of destination address. The priority field, where a higher numerical value represents a higher priority level, appears as an extension of the routing field. This causes cells destined for the same output to be arranged in the descending order of priority. In the trap network, the address of every cell is compared with that of the cell $k$ positions above. If a cell has the same address as the cell $k$ positions above, which indicates that there are at least $k$ cells with higher priority, then the cell is marked to be recirculated, and its routing field is interchanged with the priority field because the priority field is more concerned with the following concentration sorting network than the recirculation loss. Otherwise, the cell is one of the $k$ (or less) highest priority cells for the address, and is set to be routed.

In the Batcher concentration network, there are two groups of cells, one group of cells to be routed and the other to be recirculated, each is sorted into a contiguous list, respectively. Then the group of cells to be routed forms a list in ascending order of the destination address, to avoid subsequent internal blocking in the banyan networks. The group of cells to be recirculated is sorted into a separate contiguous list according to the priority. If the recirculating queue overflows, the cells with lower priorities are more likely to be dropped than those with higher priorities.

Cells are then directed to the selector that differentiates two groups of cells towards $k$ banyan networks and to $T$ recirculators, respectively. Cells that enter the recirculators will have their routing and priority fields interchanged back into the original format. Their priority, SP, is incremented as the cell has been recirculated.

The outputs of the selectors are spread among the $k$ banyan networks by connecting every $k$th output to the same banyan network. This ensures every two cells destined for the same output are separated into different banyan networks. The cells in each banyan network still constitute a contiguous list destined for distinct outputs, which satisfies the

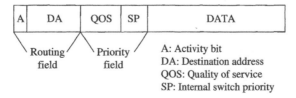

**Figure 8.11**   Header format.

nonblocking condition in a banyan network. Every cell then reaches the desired output of a banyan network, and all corresponding outputs are grouped together to an output queue in the output port controller (OPC).

## 8.5 DEFLECTION ROUTING

### 8.5.1 Tandem Banyan Switch

Figure 8.12 shows the tandem banyan switching fabric (TBSF) [10]. It consists of multiple banyan networks in series. While two cells contend at any node in a banyan network, one of them will just be deflected to the wrong output of the node and finally arrive at an incorrect destination of the banyan network. The deflected cell is then forwarded to the next banyan network. This process continues again and again until the cell reaches the desired output or it gets out of the last banyan network at an undesired output and is regarded as lost. Each output of every banyan network is connected to the corresponding output buffer. A cell is marked misrouted when it gets deflected in a banyan network to distinguish from those properly routed cells and to avoid affecting their routing at later stages within the network. At outputs of each banyan network, the cells that have reached their respective destinations are extracted from the fabric and placed in output port buffers. Note that the load of successive banyan networks decreases and so does the likelihood of conflicts. With a sufficiently large number of banyan networks, it is possible to reduce the cell loss to desired levels. Numerical results show that each additional banyan network improves the cell loss probability by one order of magnitude.

The operation of the TBSF is described as follows. A switching header is appended to each cell when it enters the switching fabric, and it comprises the following four fields:

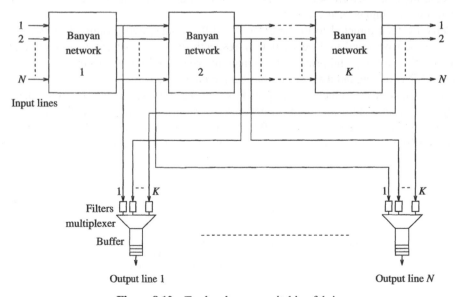

**Figure 8.12** Tandem banyan switching fabric.

- *Activity Bit a*: It indicates whether the slot contains a cell ($a = 1$), or is empty ($a = 0$).
- *Conflict Bit c*: It indicates whether the cell has already been misrouted at some previous stage of the present network ($c = 1$), or not ($c = 0$).
- *Priority Field P*: It is optional and is used if multiple priority is supported over the switch.
- *Address Field D*: It contains the destination address, $d_1, d_2, \ldots, d_n$ ($n = \log_2 N$).

The state of a switching element at stage $s$ of a banyan network is primarily determined by three bits in each header of the two input cells; namely, $a$, $c$, and $d_s$. If multiple priority is supported, then the switch state also depends on the priority field $P$. The algorithm is as follows, where the bits are indexed by 1 and 2 corresponding to the two input cells.

1. If $a_1 = a_2 = 0$, then no action is taken, that is, leaves the switch in the present state;
2. If $a_1 = 1$ and $a_2 = 0$, then set the switch according to $d_{s1}$;
3. If $a_1 = 0$ and $a_2 = 1$, then set the switch according to $d_{s2}$;
4. If $a_1 = a_2 = 1$, then
    (a) If $c_1 = c_2 = 1$, then no action is taken;
    (b) If $c_1 = 0$ and $c_2 = 1$, then set the switch according to $d_{s1}$;
    (c) If $c_1 = 1$ and $c_2 = 0$, then set the switch according to $d_{s2}$;
    (d) If $c_1 = c_2 = 0$, then
        i. If $P_1 > P_2$, then set the switch according to $d_{s1}$;
        ii. If $P_1 < P_2$, then set the switch according to $d_{s2}$;
        iii. If $P_1 = P_2$, then set the switch according to either $d_{s1}$ or $d_{s2}$.
        iv. If one of the cells has been misrouted, then set its conflict bit to 1.

In order to minimize the number of bits to be buffered at each stage to perform the above algorithm, thus to minimize the latency incurred at each stage, the address bit is placed in the first position of the address field. This can be done by cyclically shifting the address field by one bit at each stage. It is then possible to keep the latency at each stage, as low as 3 bit times without considering multiple-priority support, and it is constant over all stages.

It is simple to differentiate successful cells and deflected cells at outputs of each banyan network with the conflict bit: if $c = 0$, then the cell has been properly routed; if $c = 1$, then the cell has been misrouted. A cell with $c = 0$ is accepted by the output buffer, and is rejected by the next banyan network by setting the activity bit in that slot to 0. Conversely, a cell with $c = 1$ is ignored by the output buffer, but is accepted by the following banyan network with its conflict bit reset to 0 for further routing.

All cells entering the tandem banyan switch fabric in the same time slot must be bit-synchronized throughout the entire fabric. If ignoring the propagation delay, the delay for each cell in a banyan network is constant and is equal to $n$ times the processing delay at a switching element, or the time difference between two cells emerging from adjacent banyan networks. In order to have all cells from different banyan networks arriving at an output buffer at the same time, an appropriate delay element can be placed between each output and each banyan network.

In addition, the output buffer memory should have an output bandwidth equal to $V$ bit/s and an input bandwidth equal to $KV$ bit/s to accommodate as many as $K$ cells arriving in the same slot.

### 8.5.2 Shuffle-Exchange Network with Deflection Routing

Liew and Lee [11] considered an $N \times N$ shuffle-exchange network (SN) with $n = \log_2 N$ stages, each consisting of $(N/2)2 \times 2$ switch elements. Figure 8.13 shows an $8 \times 8$ SN. Switch nodes in each stage are labeled by an $(n-1)$-bit binary number from top to bottom. The upper input (output) of a node is labeled with a 0, and the lower input (output) is labeled with a 1. A cell will be forwarded to output 0(1) at stage $i$ if the $i$th most significant bit of its destination address is 0(1). The interconnection between two consecutive stages is called 'shuffle exchange'. The output $a_n$ of node $X = (a_1a_2 \cdots a_{n-1})$ is connected to the input $a_1$ of node $Y = (a_2a_3 \cdots a_n)$ of the subsequent stage. The link between node $X$ and node $Y$ is labeled as $\langle a_n, a_1 \rangle$. The path of a cell from input to output is completely determined by the source address $S = s_1 \cdots s_n$ and the destination address $D = d_1 \cdots d_n$. It can be expressed symbolically as follows:

$$S = s_1 \cdots s_n$$

$$\xrightarrow{\langle -, s_1 \rangle} \quad (s_2 \cdots s_n) \xrightarrow{\langle d_1, s_2 \rangle} (s_3 \cdots s_n d_1)$$

$$\xrightarrow{\langle d_2, s_3 \rangle} \quad \cdots \xrightarrow{\langle d_{i-1}, s_i \rangle} (s_{i+1} \cdots s_n d_1 \cdots d_{i-1})$$

$$\xrightarrow{\langle d_i, s_{i+1} \rangle} \quad \cdots \xrightarrow{\langle d_{n-1}, s_n \rangle} (d_1 \cdots d_{n-1})$$

$$\xrightarrow{\langle d_n, 0 \rangle} \quad d_1 \cdots d_n = D.$$

The node sequence along the path is embedded in the binary string $s_2 \cdots s_n d_1 \cdots d_{n-1}$, represented by an $(n-1)$-bit window moving one bit per stage from left to right.

The state of a cell traveling in the SN can be represented by a two-tuple $(R, X)$, where $R$ is its current routing tag and $X$ is the label of the node that the cell resides. At the first stage, the cell is in state $(d_n \cdots d_1, s_2 \cdots s_n)$. The state transition is determined by the self-routing

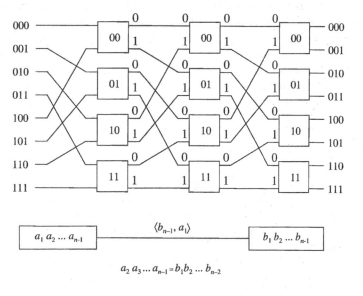

**Figure 8.13** 8 x 8 shuffle-exchange network.

algorithm as follows:

$$(r_1 \cdots r_k, x_1 x_2 \cdots x_{n-1}) \xRightarrow{\text{exchange}} (r_1 \cdots r_{k-1}, x_1 x_2 \cdots x_{n-1})$$

$$\text{input label } x_n \qquad\qquad\qquad \text{output label } r_k$$

$$\xRightarrow[\langle r_k, x_1 \rangle]{\text{shuffle}} (r_1 \cdots r_{k-1}, x_2 \cdots x_{n-1} r_k).$$

Notice that the routing bit used in the switching node is removed from the routing tag after each stage, before the node label is shuffled to the next stage. Finally, the cell will reach the state $(d_n d_1 \cdots d_{n-1})$, from which the following $2 \times 2$ element will switch the cell to the destination.

When a contention occurs at a switch node, one of cells will be successfully routed while the other one will be deflected to the wrong output. As a result, only the non-deflected cells can reach their desired outputs eventually. The deflected cells can restart routing (with routing tag reset to $d_n \cdots d_1$) again at the deflection point, and if the SN is extended to consist of more than $n$ stages, those deflected cells could reach the destination at later stages. As some cells will reach their destinations after fewer numbers of stages than others, a multiplexer is needed to collect cells that reach physical links of the same logical address at different stages. A cell will eventually reach its destination address with good probability provided that the number of stages $L$ is sufficiently large. If it cannot reach the destination after $L$ stages, it is considered lost.

### 8.5.3  Dual Shuffle-Exchange Network with Error-Correcting Routing

The error-correcting SN is highly inefficient, especially when $n$ is large. This is because routing of the cell must be restarted from the beginning whenever it is deflected. This is illustrated by the state-transition diagram in Figure 8.14a, where the state is the distance or the number of stages away from destination. A desired network should be one with the state-transition diagram shown in Figure 8.14b, in which the penalty is only one step backward.

An example is the dual shuffle-exchange network that consists of a shuffle exchange network and an unshuffle-exchange network (USN) [11]. An $8 \times 8$ USN is shown in Figure 8.15.

It is the mirror image of the SN. Routing in successive stages is based on the least significant bit through the most significant bit. Using a numbering scheme similar to that in

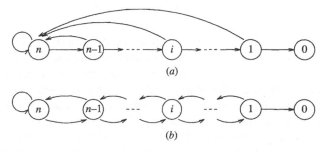

(a)

(b)

**Figure 8.14**  (a) State-transition diagram of a cell in the shuffle-exchange network, where the distance from destination is the state; (b) One-step penalty state transition diagram.

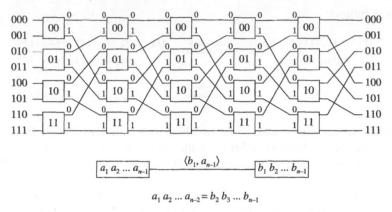

**Figure 8.15**    $8 \times 8$ unshuffle-exchange network with five stages.

SN, the path of a cell with source address $S = s_1 \cdots s_n$ and destination address $D = d_1 \cdots d_n$ can be expressed by

$$S = s_1 \cdots s_n$$

$$\xrightarrow{\langle -, s_n \rangle} \quad (s_1 \cdots s_{n-1}) \quad \xrightarrow{\langle d_n, s_{n-1} \rangle} \quad (d_n s_1 \cdots s_{n-2})$$

$$\xrightarrow{\langle d_{n-1}, s_{n-2} \rangle} \quad \cdots \quad \xrightarrow{\langle d_{i+2}, s_{i+1} \rangle} (d_{i+2} \cdots d_n s_1 \cdots s_i)$$

$$\xrightarrow{\langle d_{i+1}, s_i \rangle} \quad \cdots \quad \xrightarrow{\langle d_2, s_1 \rangle} \quad (d_2 \cdots d_n)$$

$$\xrightarrow{\langle d_1, 0 \rangle} \quad d_1 \cdots d_n \quad = D.$$

An $(n-1)$-bit window sliding on the binary string $d_2 \cdots d_n s_1 \cdots s_{n-1}$ one bit per stage from right to left exactly gives the sequence of nodes along the routing path. The initial state of the cell is $(d_1 \cdots d_n, s_1 \cdots s_{n-1})$, and the state transition is given by

$$(r_1 \cdots r_k, x_1 x_2 \cdots x_{n-1}) \quad \xrightarrow{exchange} \quad (r_1 \cdots r_{k-1}, x_1 x_2 \cdots x_{n-1})$$
$$\text{input label } x_n \qquad\qquad\qquad \text{output label } r_k$$

$$\xrightarrow[\langle r_k, x_{n-1} \rangle]{unshuffle} \quad (r_1 \cdots r_{k-1}, r_k x_1 \cdots x_{n-2})$$

At the last stage, the cell is in state $(-d_1 d_2 \cdots d_n)$, reaches its destination.

Suppose a USN is overlaid on top of a SN, and each node in the USN is combined with its corresponding node in SN such that a cell at any of the four inputs of the node can access any of the outputs of the node. The shuffle and the unshuffle interconnections between adjacent stages (nodes) compensate each other, so that the error caused by deflection in the SN can be corrected in the USN in only one step. See Figure 8.16, where cell $A$ enters a SN from input 010 to output 101, and cell $B$, from input 100 to output 100. They collide at the second stage when they both arrive at node 01 and request for output 0. Suppose cell $B$ wins the contention and cell $A$ is deflected to node 11 in the third stage. Imagine cell $A$ is

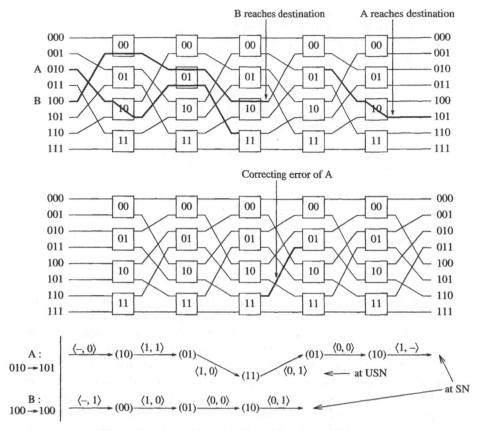

**Figure 8.16** Deflection error in SN is corrected with USN.

moved to the companion node 11 in the corresponding USN, and is switched to output 0. Then it returns at reach node 01, the same node (label) when error occurred, in two stages. At this point, the deflection error has been corrected and cell $A$ can continue on its normal path in the SN. Intuitively, any incorrect routing operation is undone in the SN by a reverse routing operation in the USN.

The above procedure can be formulated more rigorously as follows. Consider a cell in state $(r_1 \cdots r_k, x_1 \cdots x_{n-1})$, the cell should be sent out on link $\langle r_k, x_1 \rangle$ in the SN. Suppose it is deflected to link $\langle \bar{r}_k, x_1 \rangle$ instead and reaches node $(x_2 \cdots x_{n-1} \bar{r}_k)$ in the next stage. The error correction starts by attaching the bit $x_1$ to the routing tag instead of removing the bit $r_k$, so that the state of the cell will be $(r_1 \cdots r_k x_1, x_2 \cdots x_{n-1} \bar{r}_k)$ in the next stage. Then the cell is moved to the companion node in the USN to correct the error. If the cell is successively routed this time, it will be sent out on link $\langle x_1, \bar{r}_k \rangle$ and return to the previous state $(r_1 \cdots r_k, x_1 \cdots x_{n-1})$. Similarly, an error occurring in the USN can also be fixed in one step with the SN. In general, a cell in the SN may also be deflected to a link in the USN and vice versa, and consecutive deflections can occur. A simple algorithm to take these considerations into account is described in the following.

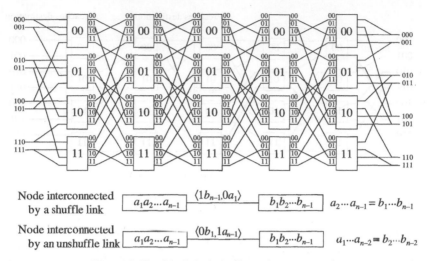

**Figure 8.17**   $8 \times 8$ dual-shuffle exchange network.

First of all, the companion $2 \times 2$ switch elements in the SN and in the USN are merged to form $4 \times 4$ switch elements to allow cells to be switched between the SN and the USN. Figure 8.17 shows a dual shuffle-exchange network built with $4 \times 4$ switch elements. A new labeling scheme is used. The four inputs (outputs) of a switch node are labeled by 00, 01, 10, 11 from top to bottom. Outputs 00 and 01 are connected to the next stage according to an unshuffling pattern, while outputs 10 and 11 are connected to the next stage according to a shuffling pattern. On the other hand, inputs 00 and 01 are connected to the previous stage according to a shuffling pattern, while inputs 10 and 11 are connected to the previous stage according to an unshuffling pattern. A link with label $\langle 1a, 0b \rangle$ is an unshuffle link and a link with label $\langle 0a, 1b \rangle$ is a shuffle link. Two nodes $(a_1 \cdots a_{n-1})$ and $(b_1 \cdots b_{n-1})$ are connected by an unshuffle link $\langle 0b_1, 1a_{n-1} \rangle$ if $a_1 \cdots a_{n-2} = b_2 \cdots b_{n-1}$, and by a shuffle link $\langle 1b_{n-1}, 0a_1 \rangle$ if $a_2 \cdots a_{n-1} = b_1 \cdots b_{n-2}$.

Since each switch node has four outputs, two routing bits are required to specify the desired output of a cell at each stage. A cell with destination $D = d_1 \cdots d_n$ can be either routed through the USN or the SN. Accordingly, the initial routing tag of a cell is set to either $0d_1 \cdots 0d_n$ (USN) or $1d_n \cdots 1d_1$ (SN), respectively.

The state of a cell at any particular time is denoted by $(c_1 r_1 \cdots c_k r_k, x_1 \cdots x_{n-1})$. There are two possible regular transitions at a switch node; the cell will be sent out on an unshuffle link if $c_k = 0$ and a shuffle link if $c_k = 1$. The corresponding state transitions are given by

$$(c_1 r_1 \cdots c_k r_k, x_1 \cdots x_{n-1}) \longrightarrow \begin{cases} \xrightarrow{\langle 0 r_k, 1 x_{n-1} \rangle} & (c_1 r_1 \cdots c_{k-1} r_{k-1}, r_k x_1 \cdots x_{n-2}) \\ & \text{if } c_k = 0 \\ \xrightarrow{\langle 1 r_k, 0 x_1 \rangle} & (c_1 r_1 \cdots c_{k-1} r_{k-1}, x_2 \cdots x_{n-1} r_k) \\ & \text{if } c_k = 1 \end{cases}$$

Without deflections, it is easy to see that a cell with the initial routing set to $0d_1 \cdots 0d_n$ ($1d_n \cdots 1d_1$) will stay in the USN (SN) links throughput the routing process until it reaches the desired destination at one of the USN (SN) links.

The routing direction is given as follows:

1. If output $c_k r_k$ is available and $k = 1$, the cell has reached its destination; output the cell before the next shuffle if $c = 1$, and after the next unshuffle if $c = 0$.
2. If output $c_k r_k$ is available and $k > 1$, remove the two least significant bits from the routing tag and send the cell to the next stage.
3. If output $c_k r_k$ is unavailable and $k < n$, choose any other available outputs, attach the corresponding 2 bits for error-correcting to the routing tag and send the cell to the next stage.
4. If output $c_k r_k$ is unavailable and $k = n$, reset the routing tag to its original value, either $0d_1 \cdots 0d_n$ or $1d_n \cdots 1d_1$; this prevents the length of the routing tag from growing in an unbounded fashion.

Figure 8.18 illustrates the complete error-correcting algorithm. For any node with label $(x_1 \cdots x_{n-1})$, the error correcting tag of outputs 00 and 01 is $1x_{n-1}$, and the error-correcting tag of outputs 10 and 11 is $0x$. In either case, the error-correcting tag is just the second component $\bar{c}x$ in the link label $\langle cr, \bar{c}x \rangle$, where $x = x_{c+\bar{c}(n-1)}$, which is either $x_1$ or $x_{n-1}$ depending on $c = 1$ (SN) or $c = 0$ (USN). Therefore, a cell deflected to link $\langle cr, \bar{c}x \rangle$ will return to its previous state via link $\langle \bar{c}x, cr \rangle$ in the next stage. This point is illustrated in Figure 8.19 by the same example given in Figure 8.16.

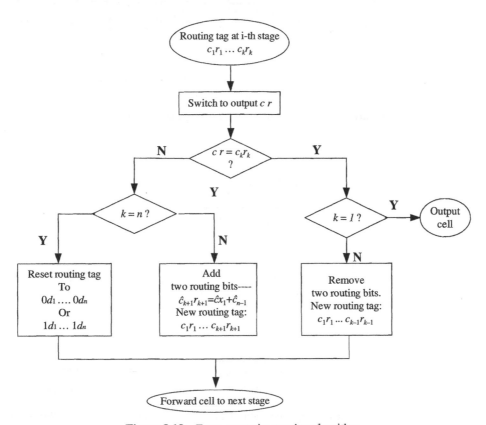

**Figure 8.18**    Error-correcting routing algorithm.

This algorithm can implicitly handle successive deflections as shown by the finite-state machine representation of the algorithm in Figure 8.20. The state transitions when deflection occurred are given by

$$(c_1r_1 \cdots c_kr_k, x_1 \cdots x_{n-1}) \longrightarrow \begin{cases} \xRightarrow{\langle 0r, 1x_{n-1} \rangle} & (c_1r_1 \cdots c_kr_k 1 x_{n-1}, rx_1 \cdots x_{n-2}) \\ & \text{if } c_kr_k \neq 0r \\ \xRightarrow{\langle 1r, 0x_1 \rangle} & (c_1r_1 \cdots c_kr_k 0 x_1, x_2 \cdots x_{n-1}r) \\ & \text{if } c_kr_k \neq 1r \end{cases}$$

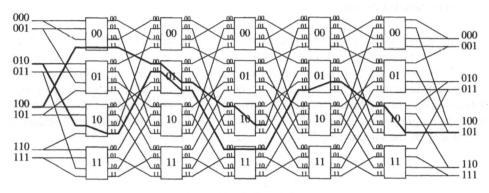

State transition of cells A and B

$$\overset{\text{error}}{\qquad} \quad \overset{\text{error correction}}{\qquad}$$

A: $010 \rightarrow (111011, 10) \rightarrow (1110, 01) \rightarrow (111000, 11) \rightarrow (1110, 01) \rightarrow (11, 10) \rightarrow 101$

B: $100 \rightarrow (101011, 00) \rightarrow (1010, 01) \rightarrow (10, 10) \rightarrow 100$

**Figure 8.19** Example of error-correcting routing in DSN.

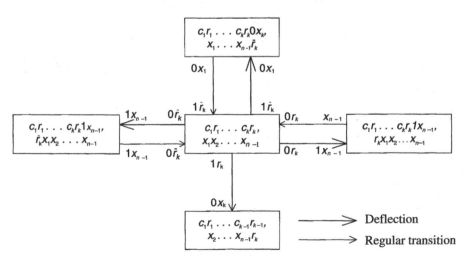

**Figure 8.20** Finite-state machine representation of the error-correcting routing algorithm when $c_k = 1$.

## 8.6  MULTICAST COPY NETWORKS

Figure 8.21 illustrates a serial combination of a copy network and a point-to-point switch for supporting point-to-multipoint communications [12]. The copy network replicates cells from various inputs simultaneously, and then copies of broadcast cells are routed to the final destination by the point-to-point switch.

A copy network consists of the following components and its basic structure is shown in Figure 8.22.

- Running adder network (RAN) generates running sums of the copy numbers, specified in the headers of input cells.
- Dummy address encoder (DAE) takes adjacent running sums to form a new header for each cell.

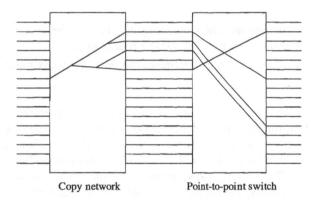

Copy network            Point-to-point switch

**Figure 8.21**  Multicast cell switch consists of a copy network and a point-to-point switch.

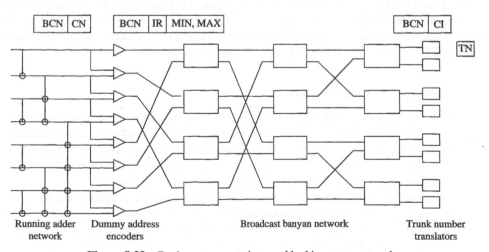

Running adder network    Dummy address encoders    Broadcast banyan network    Trunk number translators

**Figure 8.22**  Basic components in a nonblocking copy network.

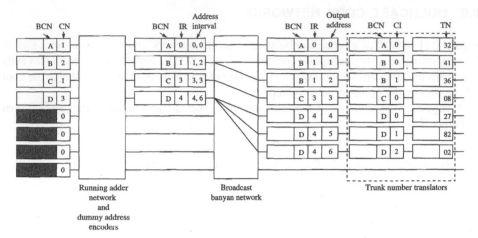

**Figure 8.23** Header translations in the copy network.

- Broadcast banyan network (BBN) is a banyan network with broadcast switch nodes capable of replicating cells based on two-bit header information.
- Trunk number translator (TNT) determines the outgoing trunk number for each cell copy.

The multicasting mechanism of the copy network lies in the header translations illustrated in Figure 8.23. First, the number of copies (CNs) specified in the cell headers are added up recursively over the running adder network. Based on the resulting sums, the dummy address encoders form new headers with two fields: a dummy address interval and an index reference (IR). The dummy address interval is formed by the adjacent running sums, namely, the minimum (MIN) and the maximum (MAX). The index reference is set equal to the minimum of the address interval, and is used later by the trunk number translators to determine the copy index (CI). The broadcast banyan network replicates cells according to a Boolean interval splitting algorithm based on the address interval in the new header. When a copy finally appears at the desired output, the TNT computes its copy index from the output address and the index reference. The broadcast channel number (BCN) and the copy index form a unique identifier into a trunk number (TN), which is added to the cell header and used to route the cell to its final destination.

### 8.6.1 Broadcast Banyan Network

***Generalized Self-Routing Algorithm.*** A broadcast banyan network is a banyan network with switch nodes that are capable of replicating cells. A cell arriving at each node can be either routed to one of the output links, or it can be replicated and sent out on both links. There are three possibilities and the uncertainty of making a decision is $\log_2 3 = 1.585$, which means that the minimum header information for a node is 2 bits.

Figure 8.24 illustrates a generalization of the 1-bit self-routing algorithm to the multi-bit case for a set of arbitrary $N$-bit destination addresses. When a cell arrives at a node in stage $k$, the cell routing is determined by the $k$th bits of all destination addresses in the header. If they are all '0' or all '1', then the cell will be sent out on link 0 or link 1, respectively. Otherwise, the cell and its copy are sent out on both links and the destination addresses in

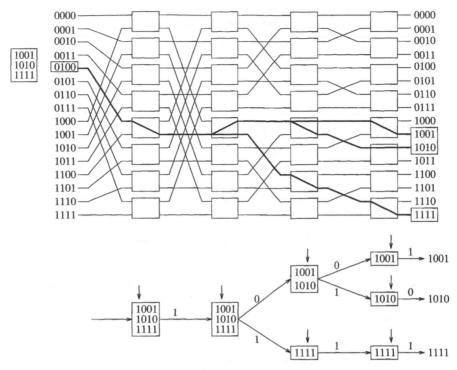

**Figure 8.24** Input–output tree generated by generalized self-routing algorithm.

the header are modified correspondingly to the two cell copies: the header of the cell copy sent out on link 0 or link 1, contains those addresses in the original header with the $k$th bit equal to 0 or 1, respectively.

Several problems may arise in implementing the generalized self-routing algorithm. First, a cell header contains a variable number of addresses and the switch nodes have to read all of them. Second, the cell header modification depends on the entire set of addresses, which is a processing burden on switch nodes. Finally, the set of paths from any input to a set of outputs forms a tree in the network. The trees generated by an arbitrary set of input cells are not link-independent in general and the network is obviously blocking due to the irregularity of the set of actual destination addresses in the header of each cell. However, fictitious addresses instead of actual addresses can be used in the copy network, where cells are replicated but need not be routed to the actual destinations. The fictitious addresses for each cell may then be arranged to be contiguous such that an address interval consisting of the MIN and the MAX can represent the whole set of fictitious addresses. The address intervals of input cells can be specified to be monotonic to satisfy the nonblocking condition for the broadcast banyan network described below.

***Boolean Interval Splitting Algorithm.*** An address interval is a set of contiguous $N$-bit binary numbers, which can be represented by two numbers, namely, the minimum and the maximum. Suppose that a node at stage $k$ receives a cell with the header containing an address interval specified by the two binary numbers: $\min(k-1) = m_1 \cdots m_N$ and $\max(k-1) = M_1 \cdots M_N$, where the argument $(k-1)$ denotes stage $(k-1)$ from where

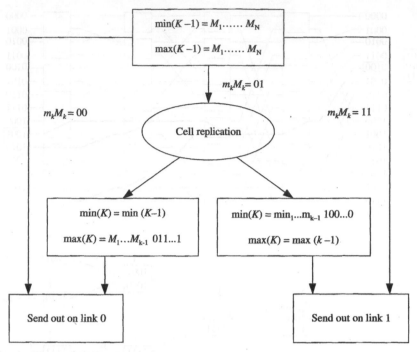

**Figure 8.25**  Switch node logic at stage $k$ of a broadcast banyan network.

the cell came to stage $k$. The generalized self-routing algorithm gives the direction for cell routing as follows, and as illustrated in Figure 8.25.

- If $m_k = M_k = 0$ or $m_k = M_k = 1$, then send the cell out on link 0 or 1, respectively.
- If $m_k = 0$ and $M_k = 1$, then replicate the cell, modify the headers of both copies (according to the scheme described below) and send each copy out on the corresponding link.

The modification of a cell header is simply splitting the original address interval into two subintervals, as expressed in the following recursion. For the cell sent out on link 0,

$$\begin{cases} \min(k) = \min(k-1) = m_1 \cdots m_N \\ \max(k) = M_1 \cdots M_{k-1} 01 \cdots 1, \end{cases}$$

and for the cell sent out on link 1,

$$\begin{cases} \min(k) = m_1 \cdots m_{k-1} 10 \cdots 0 \\ \max(k) = \max(k-1) = M_1 \cdots M_N. \end{cases}$$

Figure 8.26 illustrates the Boolean interval splitting algorithm. From the rules it is realized that $m_i = M_i, i = 1, \ldots, k-1$ holds for every cell that arrives at stage $k$. The event $m_k = 1$ and $M_k = 0$ will never occur.

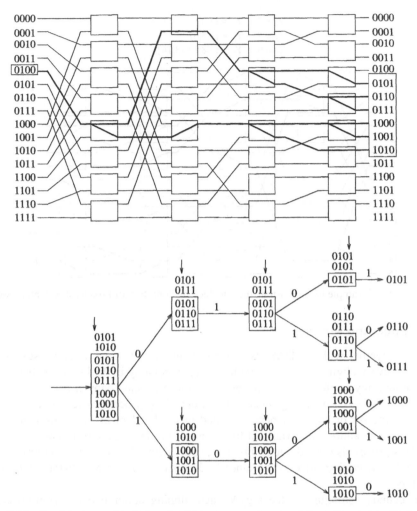

**Figure 8.26** Boolean interval splitting algorithm generates the tree while replicating a cell according to the address intervals.

### Nonblocking Condition of Broadcast Banyan Networks.

A broadcast banyan network is nonblocking if the active inputs $x_1, \ldots, x_k$ and the corresponding sets of outputs $Y_1, \ldots, Y_k$ satisfy the following:

(1) (Monotone): $Y_1 < Y_2 < \cdots < Y_k$, or $Y_1 > Y_2 > \cdots > Y_k$.

(2) (Concentration): Any input between two active inputs is also active.

The above inequality $Y_i < Y_j$ means that every output address in $Y_i$ is less than any output address in $Y_j$. Figure 8.27 illustrates a nonblocking example with active inputs $x_1 = 7$, $x_2 = 8$, $x_3 = 9$, and corresponding outputs $Y_1 = \{1, 3\}$, $Y_2 = \{4, 5, 6\}$, $Y_3 = \{7, 8, 10, 13, 14\}$.

$$x_1 = 7 \quad Y_1 = \{1,3\}$$
$$x_2 = 8 \quad Y_2 = \{4,5,6\}$$
$$x_3 = 9 \quad Y_3 = \{7,8,10,13,14\}$$

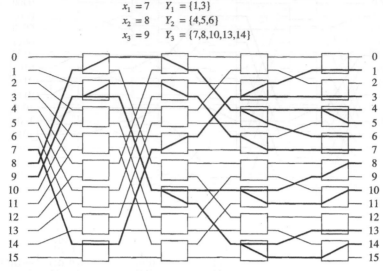

**Figure 8.27** Example to demonstrate the nonblocking condition of broadcast banyan network.

## 8.6.2 Encoding Process

The RAN together with the DAEs is used to arrange the destination addresses for each cell so that every eligible cell can be replicated appropriately in the broadcast banyan network without any conflicts. Cell replications in the broadcast banyan network are aided by two processes, an encoding process and a decoding process. The encoding process transforms the set of copy numbers, specified in the headers of incoming cells, into a set of monotone address intervals that form the cell headers in the broadcast banyan network. This process is carried out by a running adder network and a set of dummy address encoders. The decoding process determines the destinations of copies with the trunk number translators.

The recursive structure of the $\log_2 N$-stage running adder network is illustrated in Figure 8.28. The adder network consists of $(N/2)\log_2 N$ adders, each with two inputs and two outputs where a vertical line denotes a pass. The east output is the sum of both the west and the north inputs, while the south output just propagates the north input down. The running sums of CNs are then generated at each port after $\log_2 N$ stages, before the dummy address encoders form the new headers from adjacent running sums. The new header consists of two fields: one is the dummy address interval represented by two $\log_2 N$-bit binary numbers (the minimum and the maximum), and the other contains an index reference that is equal to the minimum of the address interval. Note that the length of each interval is equal to the corresponding copy number in both addressing schemes.

Denote $S_i$ as the $i$th running sum, the sequence of dummy address intervals will be generated as follows:

$$(0, S_0 - 1), (S_0, S_1 - 1), \ldots, (S_{N-2}, S_{N-1} - 1),$$

where the address is allocated beginning with 0. As shown in the previous section, this sequence satisfies the nonblocking condition over the broadcast banyan network.

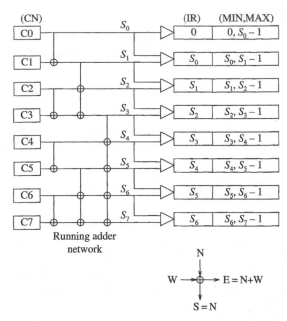

**Figure 8.28**  Running adder network and dummy address encoders.

### 8.6.3 Concentration

To satisfy the nonblocking condition of the broadcast banyan network, idle inputs between active inputs must be eliminated. This function should be performed before cells enter the broadcast banyan network, for example, prior to the BBN or right after the DAE in Figure 8.22. A reverse banyan network is thus used to concentrate active inputs into a contiguous list. As illustrated in Figure 8.29, the routing address in the reverse banyan network is determined by the running sums over activity bits to produce a set of continuous monotonic addresses.

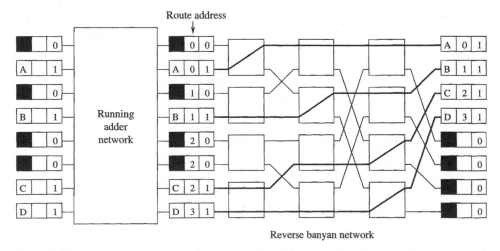

**Figure 8.29**  Input concentrator consists of a running adder network and a reverse banyan network.

### 8.6.4  Decoding Process

When a cell emerges from the broadcast banyan network, the address interval in its header contains only one address, that is, according to Boolean interval splitting algorithm,

$$\min(\log_2 N) = \max(\log_2 N) = \text{output address}.$$

The cell copies belonging to the same broadcast channel should be distinguished by copy index, which is determined at the output of broadcast banyan network (see Figure 8.30) by,

$$\text{copy index} = \text{output address} - \text{index reference}.$$

Recall that the index reference is initially set equal to the minimum of address interval.

A trunk number translator is used to assign the actual address to each cell copy so that it will be routed to its final destination in the succeeding point-to-point switch. Trunk number assignment can be accomplished by a simple table lookup identifier (searching key) that consists of the broadcast channel number (BCN) and the copy index (CI) associated with each cell. When a TNT receives a cell copy, it first converts the output address and IR into CI, and then replaces the BCN and CI with the corresponding trunk number in the translation table. The translation process is illustrated in Figure 8.31.

### 8.6.5  Overflow and Call Splitting

Overflow will occur in the RAN of the copy network when the total number of copy requests exceeds the capacity of the copy network. If partial service (also called call splitting) is not allowed in cell replication and a cell must generate all its copies in a time slot, then the throughput may be degraded when overflow occurs. As illustrated in Figure 8.32, overflow occurs at port 3 and only five cell copies are allowed although more than eight requests are available.

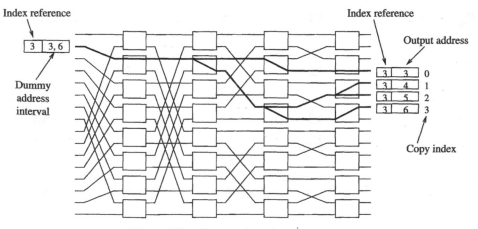

**Figure 8.30**  Computation of copy indexes.

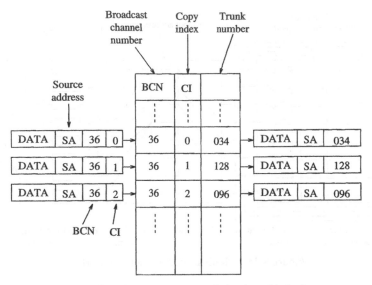

**Figure 8.31**    Trunk number translation by table lookup.

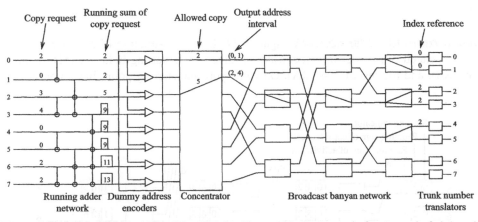

**Figure 8.32**    8 × 8 nonblocking copy network without call-splitting: only five instead of eight cell copies are allowed in this time slot.

### 8.6.6    Overflow and Input Fairness

Overflow will also introduce unfairness among incoming cells, because the starting point of the RAN is fixed. Since the calculation of running sum always starts from input port 0 in every time slot, lower numbered input ports have higher service priorities than the higher numbered ports.

This unfairness problem will be solved if the RAN is re-designed to calculate the running sums cyclically starting from any input port, and the starting point of computing the running sums in every time slot is determined adaptively by the overflow condition in the previous time slot. A cyclic RAN (CRAN) is illustrated in Figure 8.33. The current starting point is port 3, and call-splitting is performed at port 6 and the new starting point in the next slot

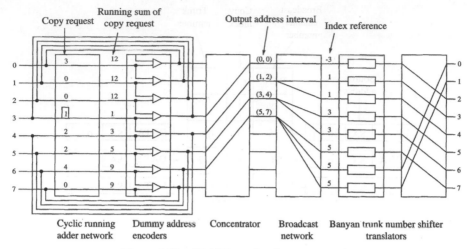

**Figure 8.33** CRAN in an 8 × 8 copy network.

will be port 6. The negative index reference −3, provided by the DAE, implies that the copy request from port 3 is a residual one, and three copies have been generated in the previous time slot.

***Cyclic running adder network*** Figure 8.34 shows the structure of an 8 × 8 CRAN. The associated cell header format consists of three fields: starting indicator (SI), running sum (RS), and routing address (RA). Only one port, the starting point, has a nonzero SI

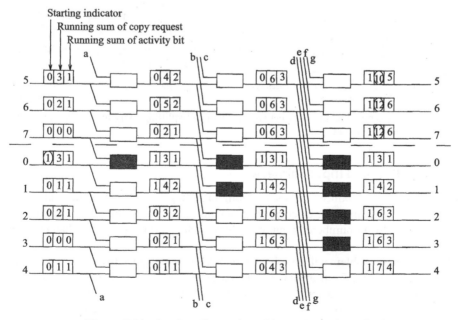

**Figure 8.34** 8 × 8 cyclic running adder network (CRAN).

initially. The RS field is initially set equal to the number of copies requested by the input cell. The RA field is initially set equal to 1 if the port is active, otherwise it is set to 0. At the output of the running adder network, the RA field will carry the running sum over activity bits, to be used as the routing address in the following concentrator.

A set of cyclic passing paths is implemented in each stage of CRAN so that recursive computation of running sums can be done cyclically. In order to emulate the actual running sums computation from a starting point, however, some passing paths should be virtually cut as illustrated in Figure 8.34, which is equivalent to the shaded nodes ignoring their links while computing the running sums. These nodes are preceded by a cell header with the SI field equal to 1, as it is propagated from the starting point over the CRAN. The header modification in a node is summarized in Figure 8.35.

The next starting point will remain the same unless overflow occurs, in which case, the first port facing the overflow will be the next starting point. If we denote the starting point as port 0, and number other ports from 1 to $N - 1$ in a cyclic manner, then the SI bit that indicates the next starting point is updated with adjacent RS fields at each port as follows:

$$SI_0 = \begin{cases} 1 & \text{if } RS_{N-1} \leq N \\ 0 & \text{otherwise} \end{cases}$$

and

$$SI_i = \begin{cases} 1 & \text{if } RS_{i-1} \leq N \text{ and } RS_i > N \\ 0 & \text{otherwise,} \end{cases}$$

where $i = 1, 2, \ldots, N - 1$.

In order to support call-splitting, every input port should know how many copies are served in each time slot. This piece of information is called starting copy number (SCN). A set of feedback loops is then established to send this information back to input ports after it is determined with adjacent running sums as follows:

$$SCN_0 = RS_0,$$

and

$$SCN_i = \begin{cases} \min(N - RS_{i-1}, RS_i - RS_{i-1}) & \text{if } RS_{i-1} < N \\ 0 & \text{otherwise} \end{cases}$$

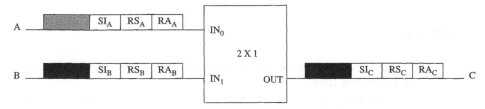

**Figure 8.35**  Operation of a node in CRAN.

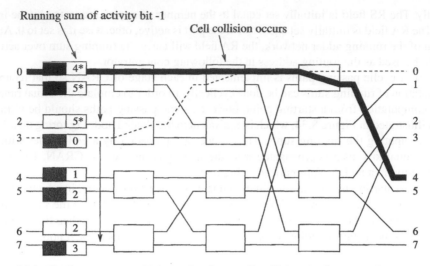

**Figure 8.36** Cyclic monotone addresses give rise to cell collisions in the reverse banyan network. Port 2 and port 6 are idle.

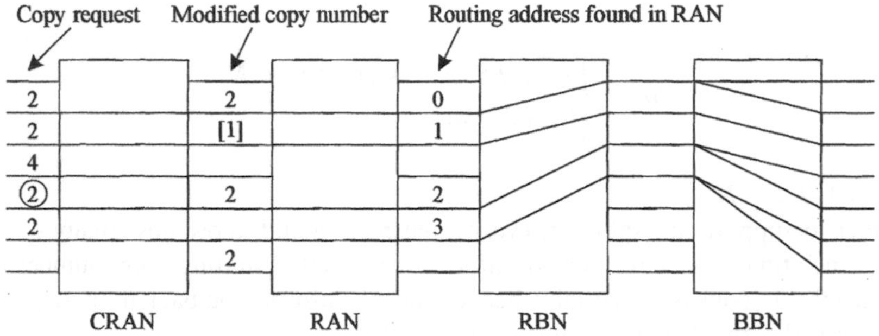

**Figure 8.37** Additional RAN is used to concentrate active cells. The starting point is marked by encircling its copy request.

***Concentration.*** The starting point in a CRAN may not be port 0, and the resulting sequence of routing addresses in the reverse banyan network (RBN) may not be continuous monotone. As illustrated in Figure 8.36, internal collisions may occur in the RBN.

This problem can be solved if an additional RAN with fixed starting point (port 0) is added in front of the RBN. As shown in Figure 8.37, this additional RAN will recalculate the running sums of RAs so that the resulting sequence of RAs becomes continuous monotone.

## REFERENCES

[1] C. Clos, "A study of non-blocking switching network," *Bell System Technical Journal*, vol. 32, no. 2, pp. 404–426 (Mar. 1953).

[2] V. E. Benes, "Optimal rearrangeable multistage connecting networks," *Bell System Technical Journal*, vol. 43, pp. 1641–1656 (July 1964).

[3] J. S. Turner and L. F. Wyatt, "A packet network architecture for integrated services," in *Proc. Globecom'83*, San Diego, California, pp. 2.1.1–2.1.6 (Nov. 1983).

[4] J. J. Kulzer and W. A. Montgomery, "Statistical switching architecture for future services," in *Proc. ISS'84*, Florence, Italy, pp. 22A.4.1–22A.4.6 (May 1984).

[5] J. S. Turner, "Design of a broadcast packet switching network," *IEEE Transaction on Communications*, vol. 36, pp. 734–743 (June 1998).

[6] L. R. Goke and G. J. Lipovski, "Banyan networks for partitioning multiprocessor systems," in *Proc. 1st Annu. Int. Symp. Comput. Architecture*, Gainesville, Florida, pp. 21–28 (Dec. 1973).

[7] K. E. Batcher, "Sorting networks and their application," in *Proc. Spring Joint Comput. Conf. AFIPS*, Washington, DC, pp. 307–314 (1968).

[8] B. Bingham and H. Bussey, "Reservation-based contention resolution mechanism for Batcher-banyan packet switches," *Electronic Letters*, vol. 24, no. 13, pp. 772–773 (June 1988).

[9] J. N. Giacopelli, J. J. Hickey, W. S. Marcus, W. D. Sincoskie, and M. Littlewood, "Sunshine: a high-performance self-routing broadband packet switch architecture," *IEEE Journal on Selected Areas in Communications*, vol. 9, no. 8, pp. 1289–1298 (Oct. 1991).

[10] F. A. Tobagi and T. Kwok, "The tandem banyan switching fabric: a simple high-performance fast packet switch," in *Proc. IEEE INFOCOM'91*, Bal Harbour, Florida, pp. 1245–1253 (Apr. 1991).

[11] S. C. Liew and T. T. Lee, "$N \log N$ dual shuffle-exchange network with error-correcting routing," *IEEE Transactions on Communications*, vol. 42, no. 2, pp. 754–766 (Feb. 1994).

[12] T. T. Lee, "Nonblocking copy networks for multicast packet switching," *IEEE Journal on Selected Areas in Communications*, vol. 6, no. 9, pp. 1455–1467 (Dec. 1988).

# CHAPTER 9

# KNOCKOUT-BASED SWITCHES

As shown in Chapter 5, output buffer switches (including the shared-memory switches) provide the best throughput/delay performance. The problem of the output buffered switches is that their capacity is limited by the memory speed. Consider the case of an ATM switch with 100 ports: What is the probability of all 100 cells arriving at the same output port at the same time slot? If the probability is very low, why do we need to have the output buffer to receive all 100 cells at the same slot? A group of researchers at Bell Labs in the late 1980s tried to resolve this problem by limiting the number of cells that can arrive at an output port in each time slot and thus the speed requirement of the memory at the output ports is no longer a constraint to the switch system. Excessive cells are discarded by the switch fabric. The concept is called the 'knockout principle'. The question is how many cells should be delivered to the output port in each time slot. If too many, memory speed may be a bottleneck. If too few, the cell loss rate in the switch fabric may be too high to be acceptable. For a given cell loss rate, this number can be determined. The number is found to be 12 for a cell loss rate of $10^{-10}$, independent of the switch size.

The result seems very encouraging in a way that the memory speed is no longer a bottleneck for the output buffered switch. However, there are no commercial switches implemented with the knockout principle. This is because the results that are obtained assume that input traffic distribution from different inputs are uncorrelated, which may be unrealistic in the real world. In addition, people are not comfortable with the fact that cells are discarded by the switch fabric. Usually, cells are discarded when the buffer is filled or exceeds some predetermined thresholds.

Although the knockout principle has not been used in real switching systems, its concept has attracted many researchers in the past and various architectures based on this concept have been proposed. Some of them are discussed in this chapter. Section 9.1 describes the knockout principle and an implementation and architecture of a knockout switch. Section 9.2

*High Performance Switches and Routers*, by H. Jonathan Chao and Bin Liu
Copyright © 2007 John Wiley & Sons, Inc.

describes a useful and powerful concept, channel grouping, to save the routing links in the switch fabric. A generalized knockout principle that extends the original knockout principle by integrating the channel grouping concept is described. Section 9.3 describes a two-stage multicast output-buffered switch that is based on the generalized knockout principle. Section 9.4 is an appendix that shows the derivation of some equations used in this chapter.

## 9.1  SINGLE-STAGE KNOCKOUT SWITCH

### 9.1.1  Basic Architecture

The knockout switch [1] is illustrated as in Figure 9.1. It is composed of a completely broadcasting interconnection fabric and $N$ buses interfaces. The interconnection fabric for the knockout switch has two basic characteristics: (1) each input has a separate broadcast bus, and (2) each output has access to all broadcast buses and thus all input cells.

With each input having a direct path to every output, no switch blocking occurs within the interconnection fabric. The only congestion in the switch takes place at the interface to each output where cells can arrive simultaneously on different inputs destined for the same output. The switch architecture is modular in a way that the $N$ broadcast buses can reside on an equipment backplane with the circuitry for each of the $N$ input/output pairs placed on a single plug-in circuit card.

Figure 9.2 illustrates the architecture of the bus interface associated with each output of the switch. The bus interface has three major components. At the top there are a row of $N$ cell filters where the address of every cell is examined, with cells addressed to the output allowed to pass on to the concentrator and all others blocked. The concentrator then achieves an $N$ to $L$ ($L \ll N$) concentration of the input lines, and up to $L$ cells in each time slot will emerge at the outputs of the concentrator. These $L$ concentrator outputs then enter a shared buffer that is composed of a barrel shifter and $L$ separate FIFO buffers. The shared buffer allows complete sharing of the $L$ FIFO buffers and provides the equivalent of a single queue with $L$ inputs and one output, each operated under a FIFO queuing discipline. The operation of the barrel shifter is shown in Figure 9.3. At time $T$, cells A, B, C arrive and are stored in the top three FIFO buffers. At time $(T + 1)$, cells D to J arrive and begin to

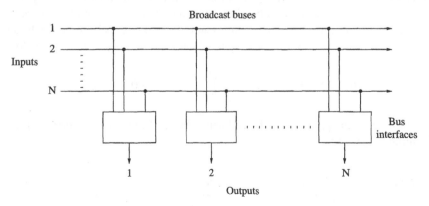

**Figure 9.1**    Knockout switch interconnection fabric.

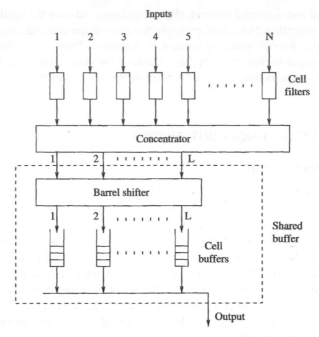

**Figure 9.2** Knockout switch bus interface (©1987 IEEE).

be stored in the 4th FIFO in a round robin manner. The number of positions that the barrel shifter shifts is equal to the sum of the arriving cells mod $L$.

### 9.1.2 Knockout Concentration Principle

All cells passing through the cell filters enter the concentrator, with an $N$ to $L$ concentration. If there are $k \leq L$ cells arriving in a time slot for a given output, these $k$ cells will emerge from the concentrator on outputs 1 to $k$ after leaving the concentrator. If $k > L$, then all $L$ outputs of the concentrator will have cells and $k - L$ cells will be dropped (i.e., lost) within the concentrator.

The cell loss probability is evaluated as follows. It is assumed that, in every time slot, there is a fixed and independent probability $\rho$ that a cell arrives at an input. Every cell is equally likely to be destined for each output. Denote $P_k$ as the probability of $k$ cells arriving in a time slot all destined for the same output, which is binomially distributed as follows:

$$P_k = \binom{N}{k} \left(\frac{\rho}{N}\right)^k \left(1 - \frac{\rho}{N}\right)^{N-k} \qquad k = 0, 1, \ldots, N. \tag{9.1}$$

It then follows that the probability of a cell being dropped in a concentrator with $N$ inputs and $L$ outputs is given by

$$\Pr[\text{cell loss}] = \frac{1}{\rho} \sum_{k=L+1}^{N} (k-L)P_k = \frac{1}{\rho} \sum_{k=L+1}^{N} (k-L)\binom{N}{k} \cdot \left(\frac{\rho}{N}\right)^k \left(1 - \frac{\rho}{N}\right)^{N-k}. \tag{9.2}$$

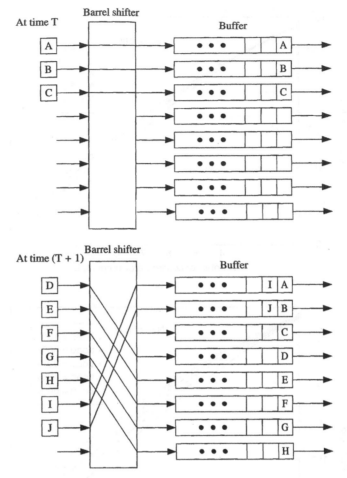

**Figure 9.3**   Operation of a barrel shifter.

Taking the limit as $N \rightarrow \infty$, and with some manipulations,

$$\Pr [\text{cell loss}] = \left[ 1 - \frac{L}{\rho} \right] \left[ 1 - \sum_{k=0}^{L} \frac{\rho^k e^{-\rho}}{k!} \right] + \frac{\rho^L e^{-\rho}}{L!} \qquad (9.3)$$

Using (9.2) and (9.3), Figure 9.4*a* shows a plot of the cell loss probability versus $L$, the number of outputs on the concentrator, for $\rho = 0.9$ and $N = 16, 32, 64, \infty$. Note that a concentrator with only eight outputs achieves a cell loss probability less than $10^{-6}$ for an arbitrately large $N$. This is comparable to the probability of losing a 500-bit cell from transmission errors with a bit error rate of $10^{-9}$. Also note from Figure 9.4*a* that each additional output added to the concentrator beyond eight results in an order of magnitude decrease in the cell loss probability. Hence, independent of the number of inputs $N$, a concentrator with 12 outputs will have a cell loss probability $<10^{-10}$. Figure 9.4*b* illustrates, for $N \rightarrow \infty$, that the required number of concentrator outputs is not particularly sensitive to

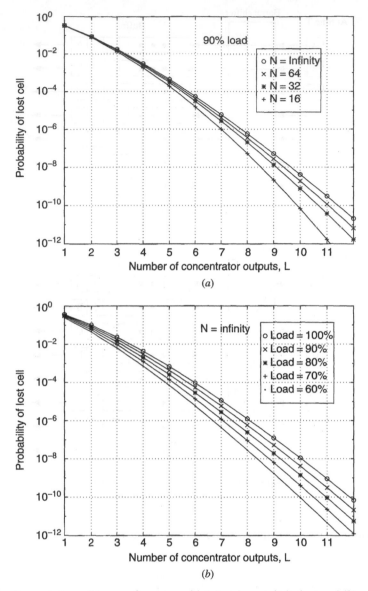

**Figure 9.4**   Concentrator cell loss performance with (*a*) various switch sizes and (*b*) various loads.

the load on the switch, up to and including a load of 100 percent. It is also important to note that, assuming independent cell arrivals on each input, the simple, homogeneous model used in the analysis corresponds to the worst case, making the cell loss probability performance results shown in Figure 9.4 upper bounds on any set of heterogeneous arrival statistics [2].

### 9.1.3   Construction of the Concentrator

The basic building block of the concentrator is a simple $2 \times 2$ contention switch shown in Figure 9.5*a*. The two inputs contend for the 'winner' output according to their activity bits.

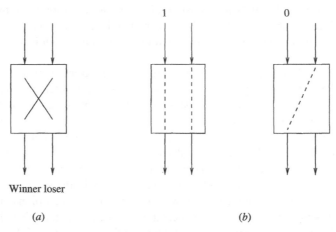

**Figure 9.5** (a) $2 \times 2$ contention switch; (b) States of $2 \times 2$ contention switch.

If only one input has an arriving cell (indicated by an activity bit $= 1$), it is routed to the winner (left) output. If both inputs have arriving cells, one input is routed to the winner output and the other input is routed to the loser output. If both inputs have no arriving cells, we do not care except that the activity bit for both should remain at logic 0 at the switch outputs.

The above requirements are met by a switch with the two states shown in Figure 9.5b. The switch examines the activity bit of the left input only. If the activity bit is a '1', the left input is routed to the winner output and the right input is routed to the loser output. If the activity bit is a '0', the right input is routed to the winner output, and no path is provided through the switch for the left input. Such a switch can be realized with as few as 16 gates, and having a latency of at most one bit. Note that priority is given to the cell on the left input to the $2 \times 2$ switch element. To avoid this, the switch element can be designed so that it alternates between selecting the left and right inputs as winners when there is a cell arriving on both inputs in the same time slot. However, suppose the priority structure of the $2 \times 2$ switch element were maintained and (as described below) the concentrator were designed so that one input, say the $N$th, always received the lowest priority for exiting a concentrator output. The cell loss probability for this worst case input, as $N \to \infty$, is given by

$$\Pr[\text{cell loss for the worst case input}] = 1 - \sum_{k=0}^{L-1} \frac{\rho^k e^{-\rho}}{k!}. \tag{9.4}$$

The above equation is obtained by considering there are $k$ cells destined for the same output port from the first $N - 1$ inputs, where

$$P_k = \binom{N-1}{k} \left(\frac{\rho}{N-1}\right)^k \left(1 - \frac{\rho}{N-1}\right)^{N-1-k} \qquad k = 0, 1, \ldots, N-1. \tag{9.5}$$

As $N \to \infty$, $P_k = \rho^k e^{-\rho}/k!$. Cells at the $N$th input will be transmitted to the output if the number of cells from the first $(N - 1)$ inputs destined for the same output port are less than or equal to $(L - 1)$. The entire summation in (9.4) is the probability that the cell from the $N$th input will not be lost. Comparing the results of (9.4) to the cell loss probability averaged over all inputs, as given by (9.3) and shown in Figure 9.4*b*, it is found that the worst case cell loss probability is about a factor of 10 greater than the average. This greater cell loss probability, however, can be easily compensated for by adding an additional output to the concentrator.

Figure 9.6 shows the design of an 8-input 4-output concentrator composed of these simple $2 \times 2$ switch elements and single-input/single-output 1-bit delay elements (marked $D$). At the input to the concentrator (upper left side of Fig. 9.6), the $N$ outputs from the cell filters are paired and enter a row of $N/2$ switch elements. One may view this first stage of switching as the first round of a tournament with $N$ players, where the winner of each match emerges from the left side of the $2 \times 2$ switch element and the loser emerges from the right side. The $N/2$ winners from the first round advance to the second round where they compete in pairs as before using a row of $N/4$ switch elements. The winners in the second round advance to the third round, and this continues until two compete for the championship: that is, for the right to exit as the first output of the concentrator. Note that if there is at least one cell arriving on an input to the concentrator, a cell will exit the first output of the concentrator.

A tournament with only a single tree-structured competition leading to a single winner is sometimes referred to as a single knockout tournament: lose one match and you are knocked out of the tournament. In a double knockout tournament, the $N - 1$ losers from the first section of competition compete in a second section, which produces a second place finisher (i.e., a second output for the concentrator) and $N - 2$ losers. As Figure 9.6 illustrates, the losers from the first section can begin competing in the second section before

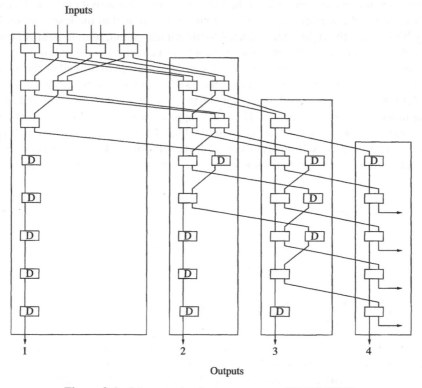

Figure 9.6    8-input to 4-output concentrator (©1987 IEEE).

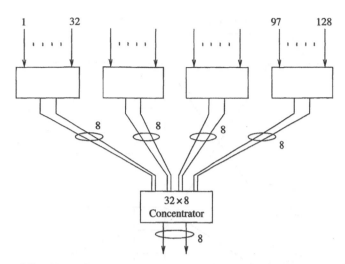

**Figure 9.7**    128-to-8 concentrator constructed from 32-to-8 concentrator chips.

the competition is finished in the first. Whenever there are an odd number of players in a round, one player must wait and compete in a later round in the section. In the concentrator, a simple delay element serves this function.

For a concentrator with $N$ inputs and $L$ outputs, there are $L$ sections of competition, one for each output. A cell entering the concentrator is given $L$ opportunities to exit through a concentrator output. In other words, a cell losing $L$ times is knocked out of the competition and is discarded by the concentrator. In all cases, however, some cells are lost only if more than $L$ cells arrive in any one time slot. As we have seen, for $L \geq 8$, this is a low probability event.

For $N \gg L$, each section of the concentrator contains approximately $N$ switch elements for a total concentrator complexity of $16NL$ gates. For $N = 32$ and $L = 8$, this corresponds to a relatively modest 4000 gates. Once a concentrator micro-circuit is fabricated, Figure 9.7 illustrates how several identical chips can be interconnected to form a larger concentrator. The loss probability performance of the two-stage concentrator is the same as the single-stage concentrator. In general, a $K^J L$ input, $L$ output concentrator can be formed by interconnecting $J$ rows of $KL$-to-$L$ concentrator chips in a tree-like structure, with the $i$th row (counting from the bottom) containing $K^{i-1}$ chips. For the example illustrated in Figure 9.7, $L = 8$, $K = 4$, and $J = 2$.

## 9.2  CHANNEL GROUPING PRINCIPLE

The construction of a two-stage modular network is mostly based on the channel grouping principle [3] to separate the second stage from the first stage. With a group of outputs treated identically in the first stage, a cell destined for an output of this group can be routed to any output of the group before being forwarded to the desired output in the second stage. For instance, as shown in Figure 9.8, the cell at the top input destined for output 6 appears at the second input of the second group, while another input cell destined for output 0 appears at the first input of the first group. The first stage network routes cells to

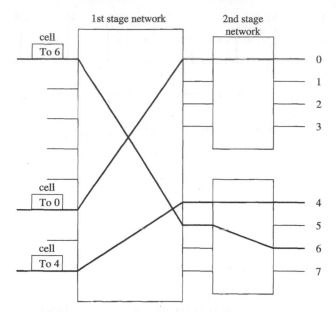

**Figure 9.8**    Illustration of channel grouping principle.

their proper output groups and the second stage network further routes cells to their proper output ports. This smoothes the problem of output contentions and thus achieves better performance/complexity tradeoff for the first-stage switch. More theoretic evaluations are provided as follows.

### 9.2.1    Maximum Throughput

This section focuses on the switch structure shown in Figure 9.9. An output group consists of $M$ output ports and corresponds to an output address for the 1st-stage network. A cell can access any of the $M$ corresponding output ports of the 1st-stage network. In any given time slot, at most $M$ cells can be cleared from a particular output group, one cell on each output port.

The maximum throughput of an input-buffered switch is limited by head-of-line blocking. The symmetric case (i.e., same number of input and output ports) is evaluated in [4] and the maximum throughput is 0.586. A similar approach could be taken for the asymmetric case to a point where the solution could be found by numerical analysis [5].

Table 9.1 lists the maximum throughput per input for various values of $M$ and $K/N$ [5]. The column in which $K/N = 1$ corresponds to special cases studied by Hluchyj and Karol [4] and Oie et al. [6]. For a given $M$, the maximum throughput increases with $K/N$ because the load on each output group decreases with $K/N$. For a given $K/N$, the maximum throughput increases with $M$ because each output group has more output ports for clearing cells.

Table 9.2 lists the maximum throughput as a function of the line expansion ratio (the ratio of the number of output ports to the number of input ports), $(K \times M)/N$. Notice that for a given line expansion ratio, the maximum throughput increases with $M$. Channel grouping has a stronger effect on throughput for smaller $(K \times M)/N$ than for larger $(K \times M)/N$.

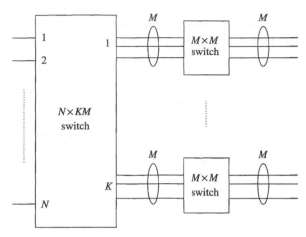

**Figure 9.9** Asymmetric switch with line expansion ratio, $(K \times M)/N$.

This is because for large $(K \times M)/N$, $M = 1$, the line expansion has already alleviated much of the throughput limitation due to head-of-line blocking.

### 9.2.2 Generalized Knockout Principle

This section generalizes the knockout concentration loss calculation to a group of outputs [7, 8]. Consider an $N \times N$ switch with two stages routing networks, as shown in Figure 9.10. A group of $M$ outputs at the 2nd-stage share $L \times M$ routing links from the 1st-stage network. The probability that an input cell is destined for this group of outputs is simply $M\rho/N$. If only up to $L \times M$ cells are allowed to pass through to the group of outputs, where $L$ is called the group expansion ratio, then

$$\Pr[\text{cell loss}] = \frac{1}{M\rho} \sum_{k=L \times M+1}^{N} (k - L \times M) \binom{N}{k} \left(\frac{M\rho}{N}\right)^k \cdot \left(1 - \frac{M\rho}{N}\right)^{N-k}. \quad (9.6)$$

**TABLE 9.1** **Maximum Throughput With $K/N$ kept Constant While $K, N \to \infty$**

| $M$ | $K/N$ | | | | | | | | |
|---|---|---|---|---|---|---|---|---|---|
| | 1/16 | 1/8 | 1/4 | 1/2 | 1 | 2 | 4 | 8 | 16 |
| 1 | 0.061 | 0.117 | 0.219 | 0.382 | 0.586 | 0.764 | 0.877 | 0.938 | 0.969 |
| 2 | 0.121 | 0.233 | 0.426 | 0.686 | 0.885 | 0.966 | 0.991 | 0.998 | 0.999 |
| 4 | 0.241 | 0.457 | 0.768 | 0.959 | 0.996 | 1.000 | 1.000 | 1.000 | |
| 8 | 0.476 | 0.831 | 0.991 | 1.000 | 1.000 | | | | |
| 16 | 0.878 | 0.999 | 1.000 | | | | | | |

**TABLE 9.2    Maximum Throughput With $(K \times M)/N$ kept Constant While $(K \times M), N \to \infty$**

|  | $(K \times M)/N$ | | | | | |
|---|---|---|---|---|---|---|
| $M$ | 1 | 2 | 4 | 8 | 16 | 32 |
| 1 | 0.586 | 0.764 | 0.877 | 0.938 | 0.969 | 0.984 |
| 2 | 0.686 | 0.885 | 0.966 | 0.991 | 0.998 | 0.999 |
| 4 | 0.768 | 0.959 | 0.996 | 1.000 | 1.000 | 1.000 |
| 8 | 0.831 | 0.991 | 1.000 | | | |
| 16 | 0.878 | 0.999 | | | | |
| 32 | 0.912 | 1.000 | | | | |
| 64 | 0.937 | | | | | |
| 128 | 0.955 | | | | | |
| 256 | 0.968 | | | | | |
| 512 | 0.978 | | | | | |
| 1024 | 0.984 | | | | | |

As $N \to \infty$,

$$\Pr[\text{cell loss}] = \left[1 - \frac{L}{\rho}\right]\left[1 - \sum_{k=0}^{L \times M} \frac{(M\rho)^k e^{-M\rho}}{k!}\right] + \frac{(M\rho)^{L \times M} e^{-M\rho}}{(L \times M)!}. \qquad (9.7)$$

The derivation of the above equation can be found in the appendix of this chapter. As an example, we set $M = 16$ and plot in Figure 9.11 the cell loss probability (9.7) as a function of $L \times M$ under various loads. Note that $L \times M = 33$ is large enough to keep the cell loss probability below $10^{-6}$ for a 90 percent load. In contrast, if the group outputs had been treated individually, the value of $L \times M$ would have been 128 ($8 \times 16$) for the same cell loss performance. The advantage from grouping outputs is shown in Figure 9.12 as the group expansion ratio $L$ versus a practical range of $M$ under different cell loss criteria. For a cell loss probability of $10^{-8}$, note that $L$ decreases rapidly from 8 down to less than 2.5 from group sizes $M$ larger than 16; a similar trend is evident for other cell loss probabilities.

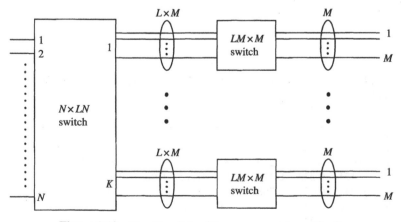

**Figure 9.10**    $N \times N$ switch with group expansion ratio, $L$.

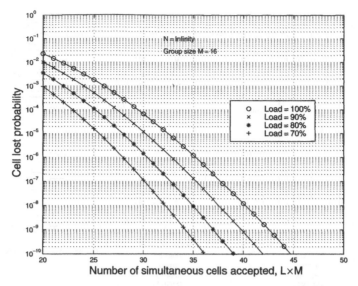

**Figure 9.11**   Cell loss probability when using the generalized knockout principle.

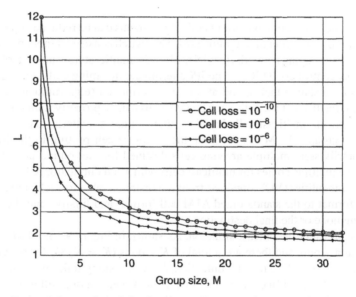

**Figure 9.12**   Ratio of the number of simultaneous cells accepted to group size for various cell loss probabilities.

## 9.3  TWO-STAGE MULTICAST OUTPUT-BUFFERED ATM SWITCH (MOBAS)

### 9.3.1  Two-Stage Configuration

Figure 9.13 shows a two-stage structure of the multicast output buffered ATM switch (MOBAS) that adopts the generalized knockout principle described above. As a result, the

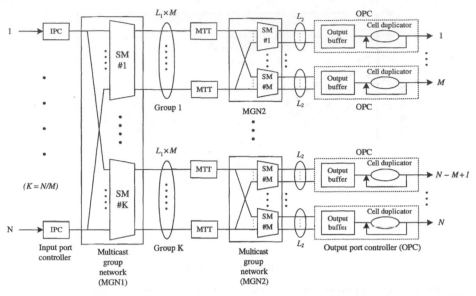

**Figure 9.13** Architecture of a multicast output buffered ATM switch (MOBAS) (©IEEE 1995).

complexity of interconnection wires and building elements can be reduced significantly, for example, by almost one order of magnitude [8]. The switch consists of input port controllers (IPCs), multicast grouping networks (MGN1, MGN2), multicast translation tables (MTTs), and output port controllers (OPCs). The IPCs terminate incoming cells, lookup necessary information in translation tables, and attach the information (e.g., multicast patterns and priority bits) to the front of the cells such that the cells can be properly routed in the MGNs. The MGNs replicate multicast cells based on their multicast patterns and send one copy to each output group. The MTTs facilitate the multicast cell routing in the MGN2. The OPCs temporarily store multiple arriving cells destined for that output port in an output buffer, generate multiple copies for multicast cells with a cell duplicator (CD), assign a new virtual channel identifier (VCI) obtained from a translation table to each copy, convert the internal cell format to the standardized ATM cell format, and finally send the cells to the next switching node or the final destination.

Let us first consider the unicast situation. As shown in Figure 9.13, all $M$ output ports are bundled in a group, and there are a total of $K$ groups ($K = N/M$) for a switch size of $N$ inputs and $N$ outputs. Due to cell contention, $L_1 \times M$ routing links are provided to each group of $M$ output ports. If there are more than $L_1 \times M$ cells in one cell time slot destined for the same output group, the excess cells will be discarded and lost. However, we can engineer $L_1$ (called the group expansion ratio) such that the probability of cell loss due to the competition for the $L_1 \times M$ links is lower than that due to the buffer overflow at the output port or bit errors occurring in the cell header. Performance study in Section 9.2.2 shows that the larger $M$ is, the smaller $L_1$ needs to be to achieve the same cell loss probability. For instance, for a group size of one output port, which is the case in the second stage (MGN2), $L_2$ needs to be at least 12 to have a cell loss probability of $10^{-10}$. But for a group size of 32 output ports, which is the case in the first stage (MGN1), $L_1$ just needs to be 2 to have the same cell loss probability. Cells from input ports are properly routed in MGN1 to one of the $K$ groups; they are then further routed to a proper output port through the MGN2. Up to $L_2$ cells can arrive simultaneously at each output port. An output buffer is used to store these cells and send out one cell at each cell time slot. Cells that originate from the same traffic source can be arbitrarily routed onto any of the $L_1 \times M$ routing links and their cell sequence is still retained.

Now let us consider a multicast situation where a cell is replicated into multiple copies in MGN1, MGN2, or both, and these copies are sent to multiple outputs. Figure 9.14 shows an example to illustrate how a cell is replicated in the MGNs and duplicated in the CD. Suppose a cell arrives at an input port $i$ and is to be multicast to four output ports: #1, #M, #(M + 1), and #N. The cell is first broadcast to all $K$ groups in MGN1, but only the groups, #1, #2, and #K accept the cell. Note that only one copy of the cell will appear in each group, and the replicated cell can appear at any of the $L_1 \times M$ links. The copy of the cell at the output of group #1 is again replicated into two copies at MGN2. There are, in total, four replicated cells that are created after the MGN2. When each replicated cell arrives at the OPC, it can be further duplicated into multiple copies by the CD as needed. Each duplicated copy at the OPC is updated with a new VCI obtained from a translation table at the OPC before it is sent to the network. For instance, two copies are generated at output port #1 and three copies at output port #(M + 1). The reason for using the CD is to reduce the output port buffer size by storing only one copy of the multicast cell at each output port instead of storing multiple copies that are generated from the same traffic source and multicast to multiple virtual circuits on an output port. Also note that since there are no buffers in both MGN1 and MGN2, the replicated cells from either MGN are aligned in time. However, the final duplicated cells at the output ports may not be aligned in time because they may have different queuing delays in the output buffers.

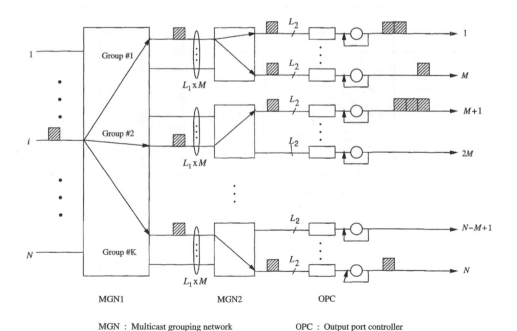

**Figure 9.14**   Example of replicating cells for a multicast connection in the MOBAS (©1995 IEEE).

### 9.3.2 Multicast Grouping Network (MGN)

Figure 9.15 shows a modular structure for the MGN at the first or the second stage. The MGN consists of $K$ switch modules for the first stage or $M$ for the second stage. Each switch module contains a switch element (SWE) array, a number of multicast pattern maskers (MPM), and an address broadcaster (AB). The AB generates dummy cells that have the same destination address as the output. This enables cell switching to be done in a distributed manner and permits the SWE not to store output group address information, which simplifies the circuit complexity of the SWE significantly and results in higher VLSI integration density. Since the structure and operation for MGN1 and MGN2 are identical, only MGN1 is described.

Each switch module in MGN1 has $N$ horizontal input lines and $L_1 \times M$ vertical routing links, where $M = N/K$. These routing links are shared by the cells that are destined for the same output group of a switch module. Each input line is connected to all switch modules, allowing a cell from each input line to be broadcast to all $K$ switch modules.

The routing information carried in front of each arriving cell is a multicast pattern, which is a bit map of all the outputs in the MGN. Each bit indicates if the cell is to be sent to the associated output group. For instance, let us consider a multicast switch with 1024 inputs and 1024 outputs and the number of groups in MGN1 and MGN2, $K$ and $M$, are both chosen to be 32. Thus, the multicast pattern in both MGN1 and MGN2 has 32 bits. For a unicast cell, the multicast pattern is basically a flattened output address (i.e., a decoded output address) in which only one bit is set to '1' and all the other 31 bits are set to '0'. For a multicast cell, there is more than one bit in the multicast pattern set to '1'. For instance, if

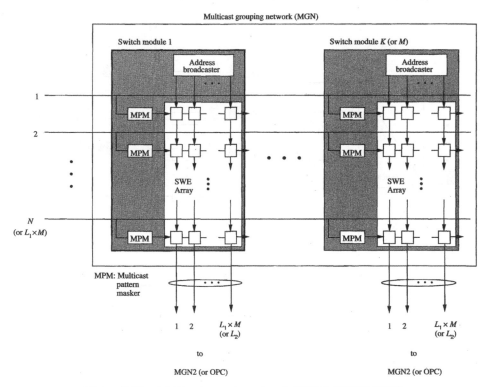

**Figure 9.15**  Multicast grouping network (MGN) (©1995 IEEE).

a cell, X, is multicast to switch modules $i$ and $j$, the $i$th and $j$th bits in the multicast pattern are set to '1'.

The MPM performs a logic AND function for the multicast pattern with a fixed 32-bit pattern in which only the $i$th bit, corresponding to switch module $i$, is set to '1' and all the other 31 bits are set to '0'. So, after cell X passes through the MPM in switch module $i$, its multicast pattern becomes a flattened output address where only the $i$th bit is set to '1'.

Each empty cell that is transmitted from the address broadcaster (AB) is attached, in the front, a flattened output address with only one bit set to '1'. For example, empty cells from the AB in switch module $i$ have only the $i$th bit set to '1' in their flattened address. Cells from horizontal inputs will be properly routed to different switch modules based on the result of matching their multicast patterns with empty cells' flattened addresses. For cell X, since its $i$th and $j$th bits in the multicast pattern are both set to '1', it matches with the flattened addresses of empty cells from the ABs in switch modules $i$ and $j$. Thus, cell X will be routed to the output of these two switch modules.

The SWE has two states, cross state and toggled state, as shown in Figure 9.16. The state of the SWE depends on the comparison result of the flattened addresses and the priority fields in cell headers. The priority is used for the cell contention resolution. Normally, the SWE is at cross state, that is, cells from the north side are routed to the south side, and cells from the west side are routed to the east side. When the flattened address of the cell from the west ($FA_w$) is matched with the flattened address of the cell from the north ($FA_n$), and when the west's priority level ($P_w$) is higher than the north's ($P_n$), the SWE's state is toggled; the cell from the west side is routed to the south side, and the cell from the north is routed to the east. In other words, any unmatched or lower-priority (including the same priority) cells from the west side are always routed to the east side. Each SWE introduces a 1-bit delay as the bit stream of cells passes it in either direction. Cells from MPMs and AB

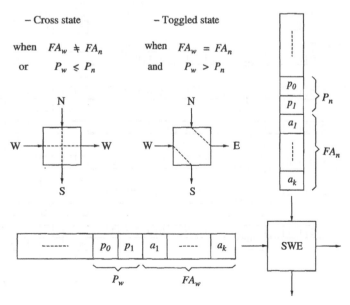

**Figure 9.16** Switching condition of the switch element (SWE).

are skewed by one bit before they are sent to each SWE array, due to the timing alignment requirement.

Figure 9.17 shows an example of how cells are routed in a switch module. Cells U, V, W, X, Y, and Z arrive at inputs 1 to 6, respectively, and are to be routed in switch module #3. In the cell header, there is a 3-bit multicast pattern ($m_3$ $m_2$ $m_1$) and a 2-bit priority filed ($p_1$ $p_0$). If a cell is to be sent to an output of this switch module, its $m_3$ bit will be set to '1'. Among these six cells, cells U, V, and X are for unicast where only one bit in the multicast pattern is set to '1'. The other three cells are for multicast, where more than one bit in the multicast pattern is set to '1'. It is assumed that a smaller priority value has a higher priority level. For instance, cell Z has the highest priority level ('00') and empty cells transmitted from the address broadcaster have the lowest priority level ('11'). The MPM performs a logic AND function for each cell's multicast pattern with a fixed pattern of '100'. For instance, after cell W passes through the MPM, its multicast pattern ('110') becomes '100' ($a_3$ $a_2$ $a_1$), which has only one bit set to '1' and is denoted as a flattened address. When cells are routed in the SWE array, their routing paths are determined by the state of SWEs, which are controlled according to the rules in Figure 9.16. Since cells V and X are not destined for this group, the SWEs they pass remain in a cross state. Consequently, they are routed to the right side of the module and are discarded. Since there are only three routing links

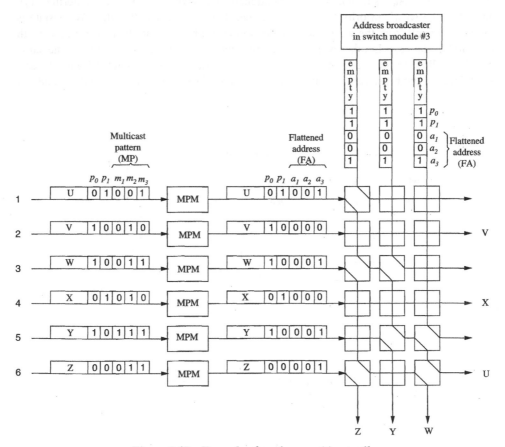

**Figure 9.17**    Example of routing a multicast cell.

in this example, while there are four cells destined to this switch module, the one with the lowest priority (i.e., cell U) loses the contention to the other three and is discarded.

Since the crossbar structure inherits the characteristics of identical and short interconnection wires between switch elements, the timing alignment for the signals at each SWE is much easier than that of other types of interconnection network, such as the binary network, the Clos network, and so on. The unequal length of the interconnection wires increases the difficulty of synchronizing the signals, and, consequently limits the switch fabric's size, such as the Batcher-banyan switch. The SWEs in the switch modules only communicate locally with their neighbors, as do the chips that contain a two-dimensional SWE array. The switch chips do not need to drive long wires to other chips on the same printed circuit board. Note that synchronization of data signals at each SWE is only required in each individual switch module but not in the entire switch fabric.

## 9.4  APPENDIX

Let us consider an ATM switch shown in Figure 9.10 and assume that cells arrive independently from different input ports and are uniformly delivered to all output ports. The variables used are defined as follows.

$N$  Number of a switch's input ports or output ports.

$M$  Number of output ports that are in the same group.

$L$  Group expansion ratio.

$\rho$  Offered load of each input port, or the average number of cells that arrive at the input port in each cell time slot.

$\rho/N$  Average number of cells from each input port destined for an output port in each cell time slot.

$\rho M/N$  Number of cells from each input port destined for an output group in each cell time slot.

$P_k$  Probability of $k$ cells arriving at an output group in each cell time slot.

$\lambda$  Average number of cells from all input ports that are destined for an output group in each cell time slot.

$\lambda'$  Average number for cells from all input ports that have arrived at an output group in each cell time slot.

The $P_k$ is given by the following binomial probability,

$$P_k = \binom{N}{k}\left(\frac{\rho M}{N}\right)^k\left(1 - \frac{\rho M}{N}\right)^{N-k} \qquad k = 0, 1, \ldots, N.$$

$$\lambda = \sum_{k=1}^{N}(kP_k) = N\left(\frac{\rho M}{N}\right) = \rho M$$

$$\lambda' = \sum_{k=1}^{LM} kP_k + \sum_{k=LM+1}^{N}(LM)\,P_k$$

$$= \lambda - \sum_{k=LM+1}^{N} kP_k + \sum_{k=LM+1}^{N} (LM)P_k$$

$$= \lambda - \sum_{k=LM+1}^{N} (k - LM)P_k.$$

Since, at most $L \times M$ cells are sent to each output group in each cell time slot, the excess cells will be discarded and lost. The cell loss probability is:

$$P(\text{cell loss}) = \frac{\lambda - \lambda'}{\lambda}$$

$$= \frac{1}{\lambda} \sum_{k=LM+1}^{N} (k - LM)P_k$$

$$= \frac{1}{\rho M} \sum_{k=LM+1}^{N} (k - LM)$$

$$\cdot \binom{N}{k} \left(\frac{\rho M}{N}\right)^k \left(1 - \frac{\rho M}{N}\right)^{N-k}. \tag{9.8}$$

As $N \to \infty$,

$$P_k = \frac{(\rho M)^k e^{-\rho M}}{k!}$$

$$P(\text{cell loss}) = \frac{1}{\rho M} \sum_{k=LM+1}^{\infty} (k - LM) \frac{(\rho M)^k e^{-\rho M}}{k!}$$

$$= \sum_{k=LM+1}^{\infty} \frac{(k - LM)}{\rho M} \frac{(\rho M)^k e^{-\rho M}}{k!}$$

$$= \sum_{k=LM+1}^{\infty} \frac{(\rho M)^{k-1} e^{-\rho M}}{(k-1)!}$$

$$- \frac{L}{\rho} \sum_{k=LM+1}^{\infty} \frac{(\rho M)^k e^{-\rho M}}{k!}$$

$$= \sum_{k=LM}^{\infty} \frac{(\rho M)^k e^{-\rho M}}{k!} - \frac{L}{\rho} \sum_{k=LM+1}^{\infty} \frac{(\rho M)^k e^{-\rho M}}{k!}$$

$$= \frac{(\rho M)^{LM} e^{-\rho M}}{(LM)!} + \sum_{k=LM+1}^{\infty} \frac{(\rho M)^k e^{-\rho M}}{k!}$$

$$- \frac{L}{\rho} \sum_{k=LM+1}^{\infty} \frac{(\rho M)^k e^{-\rho M}}{k!}$$

$$= \left(1 - \frac{L}{\rho}\right) \left( \sum_{k=LM+1}^{\infty} \frac{(\rho M)^k e^{-\rho M}}{k!} \right)$$

$$+ \frac{(\rho M)^{LM} e^{-\rho M}}{(LM)!}$$

$$= \left(1 - \frac{L}{\rho}\right) \left( 1 - \sum_{k=0}^{LM} \frac{(\rho M)^k e^{-\rho M}}{k!} \right)$$

$$+ \frac{(\rho M)^{LM} e^{-\rho M}}{(LM)!} \tag{9.9}$$

## REFERENCES

[1] Y.-S. Yeh, M. G. Hluchyj, and A. S. Acampora, "The knockout switch: A simple, modular architecture for high-performance packet switching," *IEEE Journal on Selected Areas in Communications*, vol. 5, no. 8, pp. 1274–1283 (Oct. 1987).

[2] W. Hoeffding, "On the distribution of the number of successes in independent trials," *Ann. Math. Statist.*, vol. 27, pp. 713–721 (1956).

[3] A. Pattavina, "Multichannel bandwidth allocation in a broadband packet switch," *IEEE Journal on Selected Areas in Communications*, vol. 6, no. 9, pp. 1489–1499 (Dec. 1988).

[4] M. G. Hluchyj and M. J. Karol, "Queueing in high-performance packet switching," *IEEE Journal on Selected Areas in Communications*, vol. 6, no. 9, pp. 1587–1597 (Dec. 1988).

[5] S. C. Liew and K. W. Lu, "Performance analysis of asymmetric packet switch modules with channel grouping," in *Proc. IEEE INFOCOM'90*, San Francisco, California, pp. 668–676 (June 1990).

[6] Y. Oie, M. Murata, K. Kubota, and H. Miyahara, "Effect of speedup in nonblocking packet switch," in *Proc. ICC'89*, Boston, Massachusetts, pp. 410–415 (June 1989).

[7] K. Y. Eng, M. J. Karol, and Y.-S. Yeh, "A growable packet (ATM) switch architecture: Design principles and applications," *IEEE Transactions on Communications*, vol. 40, no. 2, pp. 423–430 (Feb. 1992).

[8] H. J. Chao, "A recursive modular terabit/second ATM switch," *IEEE Journal on Selected Areas in Communications*, vol. 9, no. 8, pp. 1161–1172 (Oct. 1991).

# CHAPTER 10

# THE ABACUS SWITCH

The switches based on the knockout concept suffer from cell loss due to the lack of routing links in the switch fabric, for example, the concentrator in the knockout switch or the multicast grouping network (MGN) in the MOBAS (see Chapter 9). Although we can engineer the group expansion ratio ($L$) to achieve a satisfactory cell loss probability, say $10^{-10}$, it is based on the assumption that the traffic from different input ports is uncorrelated and input traffic is uniformly distributed to all output ports. The latter assumption gives the worst case cell loss probability, while the former assumption may not be realistic for applications such as Internet Web services. There may be a lot of traffic destined for the same popular site at the same time, resulting in a so-called hot-spot situation and an unacceptable cell loss probability. In order to reduce the cell loss rate, excessive cells can be stored at the input buffers, which results in the switch having buffers at the input and output ports. The switch to be discussed in this chapter belongs to this category.

We describe a switch that has a similar architecture to that of the MOBAS but does not discard cells in the switch fabric. When the head-of-line (HOL) cells of the input ports are sent to the switch fabric, they are held at the input ports until they have been successfully transmitted to the desired output port. The switch fabric is a crossbar structure, where switch elements, with the capability of routing cells and resolving contention based on cells' priority levels, are arranged in a two-dimensional array and is similar to an abacus. That's why the switch is called the Abacus switch. The challenging issue of designing an input–output buffered switch is to design a fast and scalable arbitration scheme.

The arbitration algorithm proposed in the Abacus switch takes advantage of the capability that the switch element can resolve contention for the routing links based on their priority levels. As a result, with some extra feedback lines and logic circuits at the input ports, the arbitration scheme can be implemented without adding much complexity and cost. The switch uses a new arbitration scheme to resolve the contention among the HOL cells.

*High Performance Switches and Routers*, by H. Jonathan Chao and Bin Liu
Copyright © 2007 John Wiley & Sons, Inc.

The arbitration is done in a distributed manner and thus enables the switch to grow to a large size.

Section 10.1 describes the basic architecture of the Abacus switch. Section 10.2 presents the new arbitration scheme that is implemented in a distributed manner. Section 10.3 depicts the implementation of an input controller and how it resolves contention resolution. Section 10.4 discusses the performance of the Abacus in throughput, delay, and loss. Section 10.5 shows a key component, the ATM routing and concentration (ARC) chip used to implement the Abacus switch. Section 10.6 describes three approaches to scale the Abacus switch to 1-Tbit/s capacity. Section 10.7 shows how the Abacus switch can also route switch packets through the switch fabric.

## 10.1  BASIC ARCHITECTURE

The Abacus switch [1] is a scalable multicast architecture with input and output buffering. It uses input buffers to temporarily store cells that lost contention to other inputs and thus eliminates the possibility of discarding cells due to the loss of contention in the switch fabric, as is the case with MOBAS. Figure 10.1 shows the architecture of the Abacus switch. It consists of input port controllers (IPCs), a MGN, multicast translation tables (MTTs), small switch modules (SSMs), and output port controllers (OPCs). The architecture is very similar to that of the MOBAS with the exception that the MGN2 in the MOBAS is replaced with the SSM and the Abacus switch has feedback lines from the RMs to the IPCs to facilitate output port contention resolution (see Section 10.2 for details). The RM (routing module) in the Abacus switch is exactly the same as the SM in the MOBAS and the term 'RM' will be used from now on. If the group size, $M$, is carefully chosen in a way that the second stage switch network's capacity is within 20 Gbit/s, it will be more cost-effective to implement the MGN2 in the MOBAS with a shared-memory switch module. For instance, for $M = 32$,

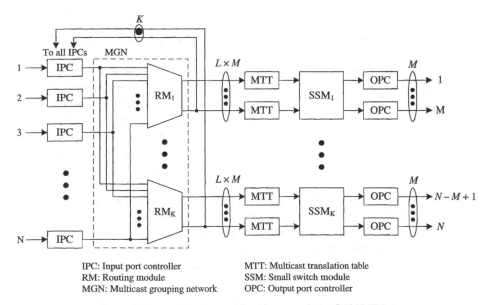

IPC: Input port controller          MTT: Multicast translation table
RM: Routing module                  SSM: Small switch module
MGN: Multicast grouping network     OPC: Output port controller

**Figure 10.1**  Architecture of the Abacus switch (©1997 IEEE).

$L = 2$, and line rate $= 155.52$ Mbit/s, the SSM's capacity is 10 Gbit/s. The IPC performs similar functions as those in the MOBAS, except that it also assists in resolving contention among cells that are destined for the same output group and buffering those cells losing contention.

The switch performs cell replication and cell routing simultaneously. Cell replication is achieved by broadcasting incoming cells to all RMs, which then selectively route cells to their output links. Cell routing is performed distributedly by an array of switch elements (SWEs). The concept of channel grouping described in Section 9.2 is applied to construct the MGN in order to reduce hardware complexity, where all $M$ output ports are bundled in a group. For a switch size of $N$ input ports and $N$ output ports, there are $K$ output groups ($K = N/M$). The MGN consists of $K$ routing modules; each providing $L \times M$ routing links to each output group. $L$ is defined as the group expansion ratio: the ratio of required routing links to the group size. Cells from the same virtual connection can be arbitrarily routed to any one of the $L \times M$ routing links and their sequence integrity will be maintained. Based on an arbitration mechanism to be described in Section 10.2, up to $L \times M$ cells from $N$ IPCs can be chosen in each RM. Cells that lose contention are temporarily stored in an input buffer and will retry in the next time slot. On the other hand, cells that are successfully routed through RMs will be further routed to proper output port(s) through the SSMs.

The group expansion ratio $L$ is engineered in such a way that the required maximum throughput in a switch fabric can be achieved. Performance study shows that the larger $M$ is, the smaller $L$ is required to be to achieve the same maximum throughput. For instance, for a group size $M$ of 16 and input traffic with an average burst length of 15 cells, $L$ has to be at least 1.25 to achieve a maximum throughput of 0.96. But, for a group size $M$ of 32 and the same input traffic characteristic, $L$ can be as low as 1.125 to achieve the same throughput. Since cell loss does not occur within the Abacus switch (unlike the MOBAS), $L$ is chosen to achieve sufficiently large maximum throughput and low delay in the input buffers, but not for cell loss rate as in the MOBAS. Its value can be slightly smaller than the one in the MOBAS (e.g., for $M = 32$, $L$ is 2 for a cell loss rate of $10^{-10}$).

Each RM in the MGN contains a two-dimensional array of switch elements and an address broadcaster (AB), as shown in Figure 10.2. It is similar to Figure 9.15 except that each RM provides a feedback line to all IPCs. The multicast pattern maskers (MPMs) are not shown here for simplicity.

Figure 10.3 shows routing information for a multicast ATM switch with $N = 256$ and $M = 16$, which consists of several fields, multicast pattern (MP), priority field (P), and a broadcast channel number (BCN). A MP is a bit map of all the output groups and is used in the MGN for routing cells to multiple output groups. Each bit indicates if the cell is to be sent to the associated output group. For instance, if the $i$th bit in the MP is set to '1', the cell is to be sent to the $i$th output group. The MP has $K$ bits for an MGN that has $K$ output groups (16 in this example). For a unicast call, its multicast pattern is basically a flattened output address (i.e., a decoded output address) in which only one bit is set to '1' and all other $(K - 1)$ bits are set to '0'. For a multicast call, there is more than one bit set to '1' in the MP, corresponding to the output groups for which the cell is destined.

A priority field (P), used to assist contention resolution, can be flexibly set to any value to achieve a desired service preference. For instance, the priority field may consist of an activity bit (A), a connection priority (C), a buffer state priority (Q), a retry priority (R), and an input port priority (S). Let us assume the smaller the priority value, the higher the priority level. The activity bit (A) indicates the validity of the cell. The activity bit (A) is set to '0' if the cell is valid and set to '1' otherwise. The connection priority (C) indicates the

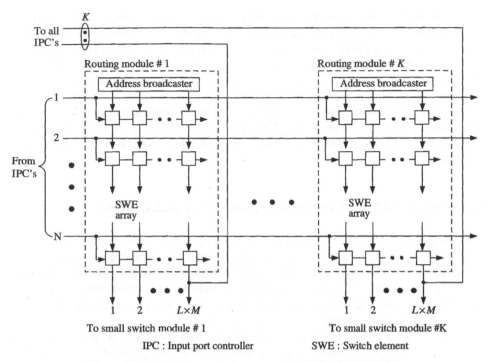

**Figure 10.2**   Multicast grouping network (MGN) (©1997 IEEE).

priority of the virtual connection, which can be determined during the call setup or service provisioning. The buffer state priority (Q) provides a sharing effect among $N$ input buffers by allowing the HOL cell in an almost-overflowed buffer (e.g., exceeding a predetermined threshold) to be transmitted sooner so that the overall cell loss probability is reduced. The retry priority (R) provides a global first-come-first-served (FCFS) discipline, allowing

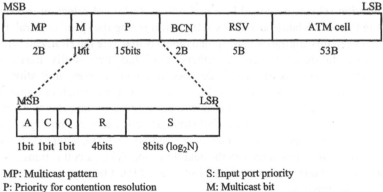

MP: Multicast pattern
P: Priority for contention resolution
A: Activity bit
C: Connection priority
Q: Buffer state priority
R: Retry priority

S: Input port priority
M: Multicast bit
BCN: Broadcast channel number
RSV: Reserved field for future growth
MSB: Most significant bit
LSB: Least significant bit

**Figure 10.3**   Routing information used by Abacus switch with $N = 256$, $M = 16$.

a cell's priority level to move up by one whenever it loses contention once. The retry priority (R) can initially be set to '1111' and decreased by one whenever losing contention once. In order to achieve fairness among input ports, the priority levels of the HOL cells at the input ports dynamically change at each time slot. The input port priority (S) can initially be set to its input port address with $\log_2 N$ bits and decreased by one at every time slot, thus achieving round-robin fairness.

The BCN in Figure 10.3 will be used to find a new multicast pattern in the MTT, allowing the copied cell to be further duplicated in the SSM. The BCN will also be used by the OPC to find a new virtual path identifier/virtual channel identifier (VPI/VCI) for each copy of the replicated cell.

## 10.2 MULTICAST CONTENTION RESOLUTION ALGORITHM

Here, we describe a novel algorithm that resolves output port contention among the input ports in a fair manner. It can also perform call splitting for multicasting and thus improves the system throughput. The output port contention resolution is often implemented by a device called an arbiter. Most proposed arbiters can only handle unicast calls (i.e., point-to-point communication) and $N$-to-1 selection, for example: three phase [2], ring reservation [3], and centralized contention resolution device [4].

Implementing an arbiter capable of handling call splitting and $N$-to-multiple selection is much more challenging in terms of timing constraint. At the beginning of the cell time slot, the arbiter receives $N$ multicast patterns, one from each input port, and returns acknowledgment to those input ports whose HOL cells have won contention. These cells are then allowed to transmit to the switch fabric. Let us consider these $N$ multicast patterns, each with $K$ bits, being stacked up and there are $K$ columns with $N$ bits in each column. Each column associates with each output group. The arbiter's job is to select up to, for example, $L \times M$ bits that are set to '1' from each column and repeat the operation for $K$ times, which must be finished in one cell time slot. In other words, the arbitration's timing complexity is in the order of $O(N \times K)$. The arbiter may become the system's bottleneck when $N$ or $K$ is large.

The arbitration scheme described here performs $N$-to-$L \times M$ selection in a distributed manner using the switch fabric and all IPCs, thus eliminating the speed constraint. Another difference between this arbitration scheme and others is that here the HOL cell is repeatedly sent to the switch fabric to compete with others until it has successfully transmitted to all necessary output groups that the cell is destined for. Unlike other arbitration schemes, the scheme described here does not wait for an acknowledgment before transmitting the cell. When a cell is routed in a switch fabric without waiting for an acknowledgment, two situations are possible. It could be successfully routed to all necessary output groups, or only routed to a subset of the output groups (including an empty set). The latter case is considered a failure, and the HOL cell will retry in the next time slot. When a cell is transmitted to the switch fabric, since it does not know if it will succeed, it must be stored in a one-cell buffer for possible retransmission.

Now the question is how the IPC knows whether or not its HOL cell has been successfully transmitted to all necessary output groups. In the Abacus switch, the RMs are responsible for returning the routing results to the IPC. One possible way is to let each RM inform the IPCs of the identification (e.g., the broadcast channel number) of the cells that have been successfully routed. However, since a cell could be routed to multiple output groups (for instance, up to $K$ output groups for a broadcast situation), one IPC may receive up to $K$ acknowledgments from $K$ RMs. The complexity of returning the identification of every successfully routed copy to all IPCs is too high to be practical for a large-scale switch. A scheme that significantly simplifies the complexity of the acknowledgment operation is described in the following.

The RM cannot only route cells to proper output groups, but also, based on cells' priority levels, choose up to $L \times M$ cells that are destined for the same output group. The HOL cell of each input port is assigned a unique priority level. After cells are routed through an RM, they are sorted at the output links of the RM according to their priority levels from left to right in a descending order (see Fig. 10.2). The cell that appears at the rightmost output link has the lowest priority level among the cells that have been routed through this RM. This lowest priority information is broadcast to all IPCs. Each IPC will then compare the local priority level ($LP$) of the HOL cell with a feedback priority, say $FP_j$, to determine if the HOL cell has been routed through the $RM_j$. Note that there are $K$ feedback priorities, $FP_1, \ldots, FP_K$. If the feedback priority level ($FP_j$) is lower than or equal to the local priority level ($LP$), the IPC determines that its HOL cell has reached one of the output links of the $RM_j$. Otherwise, the HOL cell must have been discarded in the $RM_j$ due to loss of contention and will be retransmitted in the next time slot. Since there are $K$ RMs in total, there will be $K$ lines broadcast from $K$ RMs to all IPCs, each carrying the lowest priority information in its output group.

The priority assigned to the HOL cells will be dynamically changed according to some arbitration policies, such as random, round-robin, state-dependent, or delay-dependent [5]. The random scheme randomly chooses the HOL cells of input ports for transmission; the drawback being a large delay variation. The round-robin scheme chooses HOL cells from input ports in a round-robin fashion by dynamically changing the scanning point from the top to the bottom input port (e.g., S field in Fig. 10.3). The state-dependent scheme chooses the HOL cell in the longest input queue such that input queue lengths are maintained nearly equal, achieving the input buffers sharing effect (e.g., Q field in Fig. 10.3). The delay-dependent scheme performs like a global FIFO, where the oldest HOL cell has the highest priority to be transmitted to the output (e.g., R field in Fig. 10.3). Since the arbitration is performed in a distributed manner by $K$ RMs and in parallel by IPCs, any of the above policies, or a combination of them, can be implemented by arbitrarily assigning a proper priority level to the HOL cell.

At the beginning of the time slot, each IPC sends its HOL cell to the MGN. Meanwhile, the HOL cell is temporarily stored in a one-cell sized buffer during its transmission. After cells have traversed through the RMs, priority information, $FP_1$ to $FP_K$ (the priority of the right most link of each RM), is fed back to every IPC. Each IPC will then compare the feedback priority level $FP_j, j = 1, 2, \ldots, K$, with its local priority level, $LP$. Three situations can happen: (a) $MP_j = 1$ and $LP \leq FP_j$ (recall that the smaller the priority value, the higher the priority level), which means the HOL cell is destined for the $j$th output group and has been successfully routed through the $j$th RM. The $MP_j$ bit is then set to '0'; (b) $MP_j = 1$ and $LP > FP_j$, which means the HOL cell is destined for the $j$th output group but discarded in the $j$th RM. The $MP_j$ bit remains '1'; (c) $MP_j = 0$, the $j$th bit of the HOL cell's multicast pattern can be equal to '0', which means the HOL cell is not destined for the $j$th output group. Then, the $MP_j$ bit remains '0'.

After all $MP_j$ bits ($j = 1, 2, \ldots, K$) have been updated according to one of the above three scenarios, a signal indicating whether the HOL cell should be retransmitted, 'resend', will be asserted to '1' if one or more bits in the multicast pattern remains '1'. The resend

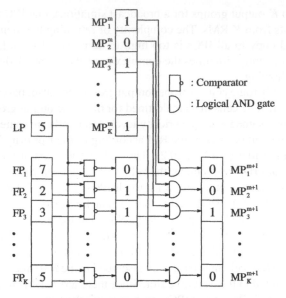

MP$_j^m$: Multicast pattern at the m-th time slot
MP$_j^{m+1}$: Multicast pattern at the (m+1)-th time slot
LP: Local priority level of the HOL cell
FP$_j$: Feedback priority level from j-th routing module

**Figure 10.4** Example of modifying a multicast pattern (MP) (©1997 IEEE).

signal is initially set to '0'. If multicast pattern bits are all '0', meaning the HOL cell has been successfully transmitted to all the necessary output groups, the resend signal will be disasserted. The IPC will then clear the HOL cell in the one-cell buffer and transmit the next cell in the input buffer in the next time slot (if any).

Figure 10.4 gives an example of how a multicast pattern is modified. Let us assume at the beginning of the $m$th time slot, the HOL cell is destined for three output groups: #1, #3, #$K$. Therefore, the multicast pattern at the $m$th time slot, $MP^m$, has three bits set to '1'. Let us also assume the local priority value ($LP$) of the HOL cell is 5 and the feedback priority values from #1, #2, #3, and #$K$ are 7, 2, 3, and 5, respectively, as shown in Figure 10.4. The result of comparing $LP$ with $FP$s is '0110...00', which is then logically ANDed with the $MP^m$ and produces a new multicast pattern, '0010...00', for the next time slot ($MP^{m+1}$). Since only the $MP_3^{m+1}$ is set to '1', the IPC determines that the HOL cell has been successfully routed to RMs #1 and #$K$ but discarded in RM #3 and will retransmit in the next time slot.

## 10.3 IMPLEMENTATION OF INPUT PORT CONTROLLER

Figure 10.5 shows a block diagram of the IPC. For easy explanation, let us assume the switch has 256 input ports and 256 output ports and every 16 output ports are in one group. A major difference between this IPC and traditional ones is the addition of the multicast contention resolution unit (MCRU), shown in a dashed box. It determines, by comparing

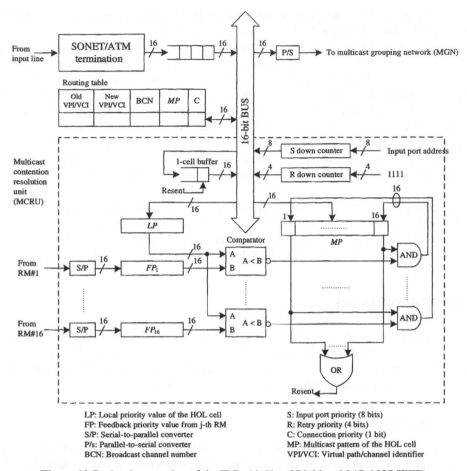

**Figure 10.5** Implementation of the IPC with $N = 256, M = 16$ (© 1997 IEEE).

$K$ feedback priorities with the local priority of the HOL cell, whether or not the HOL cell has been successfully routed to all necessary output groups.

Let us start from the left where the input line from the SONET/ATM network is terminated. Cells with 16 bits wide are written into an input buffer. The HOL cell's VPI/VCI is used to extract the necessary information from a routing table. This information includes a new VPI/VCI for unicast connections, a BCN for multicast connections, which uniquely identifies each multicast call in the entire switch, MP for routing cells in the MGN, and the connection priority (C). This information is then combined with a priority field to form the routing information, as shown in Figure 10.3.

As the cell is transmitted to the MGN through a parallel-to-serial (P/S) converter, the cell is also stored temporarily in a one-cell buffer. If the cell fails to successfully route through the RMs, it will be retransmitted in the next cell cycle. During retransmission, it is written back to the one-cell buffer in case it fails to route through again. The S down counter is initially loaded with the input address and decremented by one at each cell clock. The R down counter is initially set to all '1's and decreased by one every time the HOL cell fails to transmit successfully. When the R-counter reaches zero, it will remain at zero until the HOL cell has been cleared and a new cell becomes the HOL cell.

$K$ feedback priority signals, $FP_1$ to $FP_K$, are converted to 16-bit wide signals by the serial-to-parallel (S/P) converters and latched at the 16-bit registers. They are simultaneously compared with the HOL cell's local priority (LP) by $K$ comparators. Recall that the larger the priority value, the lower the priority level is. If the value of the $FP_j$ is larger than or equal to the local priority value (LP), the $j$th comparator's output is asserted low, which will then reset the $MP_j$ bit to zero regardless of what its value was ('0' or '1'). After the resetting operation, if any one of the $MP_j$ bits is still '1', indicating that at least one HOL cell did not get through the RM in the current cycle, the 'resend' signal will be asserted high and the HOL cell will be retransmitted in the next cell cycle with the modified multicast pattern.

As shown in Figure 10.5, there are $K$ sets of S/P, $FP$ register, and comparator. As a switch size increases, the number of output groups, $K$, also increases. However, if the time permits, only one set of this hardware is required by time-division multiplexing the operation of comparing the local priority value, $LP$, with $K$ feedback priority values.

## 10.4  PERFORMANCE

This section discusses the performance analysis of the Abacus switch. Both simulation and analytical results are shown to compare with each other. Simulation results are obtained with a 95 percent confidence interval, not greater than 10 percent for the cell loss probability or 5 percent for the maximum throughput and average cell delay.

### 10.4.1  Maximum Throughput

The maximum throughput of an ATM switch employing input queuing is defined by the maximum utilization at the output port. An input-buffered switch's HOL blocking problem can be alleviated by speeding-up the switch fabric's operation rate or increasing the number of routing links with an expansion ratio $L$. Several other factors also affect the maximum throughput. For instance, the larger the switch size ($N$) or burstiness ($\beta$), the smaller the maximum throughput ($\rho_{max}$) will be. However, the larger the group expansion ratio ($L$) or group size ($M$) is, the larger the maximum throughput will be.

Karol et al. [6] have shown that the maximum throughput of an input-buffered ATM switch is 58.6 percent for $M = 1, L = 1, N \to \infty$, with random traffic. Oie et al. [7] have obtained the maximum throughput of an input–output-buffered ATM switch for $M = 1$, an arbitrary group expansion ratio or speed-up factor $L$, and an infinite $N$ with random traffic. Pattavina [8] has shown, through computer simulations, the maximum throughput of an input–output-buffered ATM switch using the channel grouping concept for an arbitrary group size $M, L = 1$, and an infinite $N$ with random traffic. Liew and Lu [9] have shown the maximum throughput of an asymmetric input–output-buffered switch module for arbitrary $M$ and $L$, and $N \to \infty$ with bursty traffic.

Figure 10.6 shows that the maximum throughput is monotonically increasing with the group size. For $M = 1$, the switch becomes an input-buffered switch, and its maximum throughput $\rho_{max}$ is 0.586 for uniform random traffic ($\beta = 1$), and $\rho_{max} = 0.5$ for completely bursty traffic ($\beta \to \infty$). For $M = N$, the switch becomes a completely shared memory switch such as that proposed by Kozaki et al. [10]. Although it can achieve 100 percent

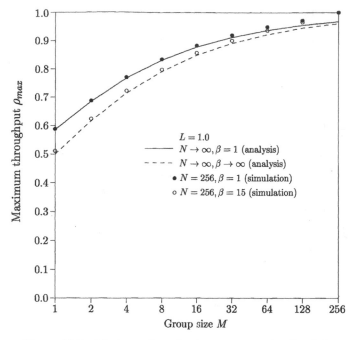

**Figure 10.6** Maximum throughput versus group size, $L = 1.0$.

throughput, it is impractical to implement a large-scale switch using such an architecture. Therefore, choosing $M$ between 1 and $N$ is a compromise between the throughput and the implementation complexity.

Figures 10.7 and 10.8 compare theoretical values and simulation values of the maximum throughput with different group expansion ratios $(L)$ for $M = 1$ and $M = 16$, respectively. The theoretical values can be obtained from Liew and Lu's analysis [9].

A HOL virtual queue is defined as the queue that consists of cells at the head of line of input buffers destined for a tagged output group. For uniform random traffic, the average number of cells $E[C]$ in the HOL virtual queue becomes

$$E[C] = \frac{\rho_o[2(L \times M) - \rho_o] - (L \times M)(L \times M - 1)}{2(L \times M - \rho_o)} + \sum_{k=1}^{L \times M - 1} \frac{1}{1 - z_k} \qquad (10.1)$$

where $z_0 = 1$ and $z_k$ $(k = 1, \ldots, L \times M - 1)$ are the roots of $z^{L \times M}/A(z) = [p + (1 - p)z]^{L \times M}$ and $A(z) = e^{-p\rho_o(1-z)}$. For completely bursty traffic, $E[C]$ becomes

$$E[C] = \frac{\sum_{k=0}^{L \times M - 1} k(L \times M - k)c_k + \rho_o}{L \times M - \rho_o} \qquad (10.2)$$

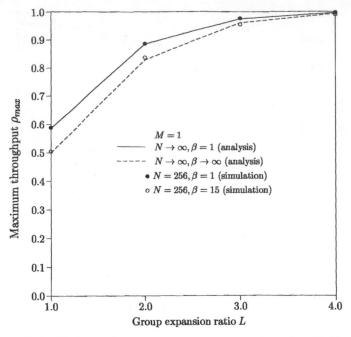

**Figure 10.7** Maximum throughput versus group expansion ratio with $M = 1$.

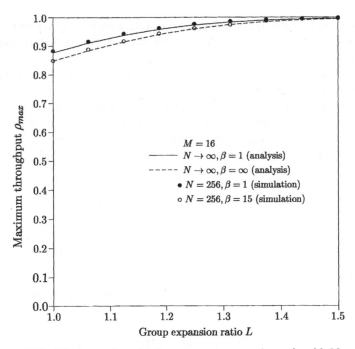

**Figure 10.8** Maximum throughput versus group expansion ratio with $M = 16$.

where

$$c_k = \begin{cases} \rho_o^k c_0/k! & \text{if } k < L \times M \\ \rho_o^k c_0/[(L \times M)!(L \times M)^{k-L \times M}] & \text{if } k \geq L \times M \end{cases}$$

$$c_0 = \frac{L \times M - \rho_o}{\sum_{k=0}^{L \times M - 1}(L \times M - k)\rho_o^k/k!}.$$

The maximum throughput of the proposed ATM switch can be obtained by considering the total number of backlogged cells in all $K$ HOL virtual queues to be $N$. This means under a saturation condition, there is always a HOL cell at each input queue. Since it is assumed that cells are to be uniformly distributed over all output groups, we obtain

$$E[C] = N/K = M. \tag{10.3}$$

The maximum throughput can be obtained by equating (10.1) and (10.3) for random traffic, and equating (10.2) and (10.3) for bursty traffic, respectively. If $\rho_o^*$ satisfies both equations, the maximum throughput at each input, $\rho_{max}$, is related to $\rho_o^*$ by $\rho_{max} = \rho_o^*/M$.

For a given $M$, the maximum throughput increases with $L$ because there are more routing links available between input ports and output groups. However, since a larger $L$ means higher hardware complexity, the value of $L$ should be selected prudently such that both hardware complexity and the maximum throughput are acceptable. For instance, for a group size $M$ of 16 (for input traffic with an average burst length of 15 cells), $L$ has to be at least 1.25 to achieve a maximum throughput of 0.95. But for a group size $M$ of 32 and the same input traffic characteristic, $L$ will be at least 1.125 to achieve the same throughput. Both analytical results and simulation results show that the impact of input traffic's burstiness on the maximum throughput is very small. For example, the maximum throughput for uniform random traffic with $M = 16$ and $L = 1.25$ is 97.35 percent, and for completely bursty traffic is 96.03 percent, only 1.32 percent difference. The discrepancy between theoretical and simulation results comes from the assumption of switch size $N$ and $\beta$. In theoretical analysis, it is assumed that $N \to \infty$, $\beta \to \infty$, but in simulation it is assumed that $N = 256$, $\beta = 15$. As these two numbers increase, the discrepancy reduces.

### 10.4.2 Average Delay

A cell may experience two kinds of delay while traversing through the Abacus switch: input-buffer delay and output-buffer delay. In theoretical analysis, the buffer size is assumed to be infinite. But in simulations, it is assumed that the maximum possible size for the input buffers and output buffers that can be sustained in computer simulations: $B_i = 1024$ and $B_o = 256$, respectively. Here, $B_i$ is the input buffer size and $B_o$ is the normalized output buffer size (i.e., the size of a physical buffer 4096 divided by $M$, 16). Although finite buffers may cause cell loss, it is small enough to be neglected when evaluating average delay.

Let us assume each input buffer receives a cell per time slot with a probability $\lambda$, and transmits a cell with a probability $\mu$. The probability $\mu$ is equal to 1.0 if there is no HOL blocking. But, as the probability of HOL blocking increases, $\mu$ will decrease. If $\lambda > \mu$, then the input buffer will rapidly saturate, and the delay at the input buffer will be infinite. The analytical results for uniform random traffic can be obtained from the analysis of Chang et al. [11],

$$E[T] = \frac{1 - \lambda}{\mu - \lambda}, \tag{10.4}$$

where $\lambda = \rho_i$, $\mu = \rho_i/E[C]$, and $E[C]$ is a function of $M$, $L$, $\rho_i$, and $\beta$ as $N \to \infty$, which can be obtained from (10.1) or (10.2).

Note that the input buffer's average delay is very small when the input offered load is less than the maximum saturation throughput. This results from small HOL blocking probability before the saturated throughput. It also shows that the impact of the burstiness of input traffic on the input buffer's average delay is very small when the traffic load is below the maximum throughput.

Figure 10.9 compares the average delay at the input and output buffers. Note that the input buffer's average delay is much smaller than the output buffer's average delay at traffic load less than the saturated throughput. For example, for an input offered load $\rho_i$ of 0.8 and an average burst length $\beta$ of 15, the output buffer's average delay $T_o$ is 58.8 cell times, but the input buffer's average delay $T_i$ is only 0.1 cell time.

Figure 10.10 shows simulation results of the input buffer's average delay versus the expanded throughput $\rho_j$ for both unicast and multicast traffic. It is assumed that the number of replicated cells is distributed geometrically with an average of $c$. The expanded throughput $\rho_j$ is measured at the inputs of the SSM and normalized to each output port. Note that multicast traffic has a lower delay than unicast traffic because a multicast cell can be sent to multiple destinations in a time slot while a unicast cell can be sent to only one destination in a time slot. For example, assume that an input port $i$ has 10 unicast cells and the other input port $j$ has a multicast cell with a fanout of 10. Input port $i$ will take at least 10 time

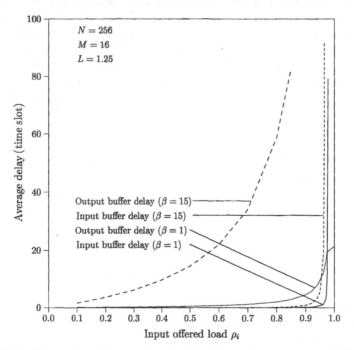

**Figure 10.9** Comparison of average input buffer delay and average output buffer delay.

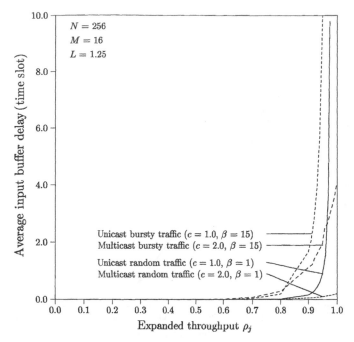

**Figure 10.10** Average input buffer delay versus expanded throughput for unicast and multicast traffic (simulation).

slots to transmit the 10 unicast cells while input port $j$ can possibly transmit the multicast cell in one time slot.

### 10.4.3 Cell Loss Probability

As suggested in the work of Pattavina and Bruzzi [12], there can be two buffer control schemes for an input–output-buffered switch: the queue loss (QL) scheme and the back-pressure (BP) scheme. In the QL scheme, cell loss can occur at both input and output buffers. In the BP scheme, by means of backward throttling, the number of cells actually switched to each output group is limited not only to the group expansion ratio ($L \times M$) but also to the current storage capability in the corresponding output buffer. For example, if the free buffer space in the corresponding output buffer is less than $L \times M$, only the number of cells corresponding to the free space are transmitted, and all other HOL cells destined for that output group remain at their respective input buffer. The Abacus switch can easily implement the backpressure scheme by forcing the AB in Figure 10.2 to send the dummy cells with the highest priority level, which will automatically block the input cells from using those routing links. Furthermore, the number of blocked links can be dynamically changed based on the output buffer's congestion situation.

Here, we only consider the QL scheme (cell loss at both input and output buffers). In the Abacus switch, cell loss can occur at input and output buffers, but not in the MGN. Figure 10.11 shows input buffer overflow probabilities with different average burst lengths, $\beta$. For uniform random traffic, an input buffer with a capacity of a few cells is sufficient to maintain the buffer overflow probability to be less than $10^{-6}$. As the average burst length increases, so does the cell loss probability. For an average burst length $\beta$ of 15, the required

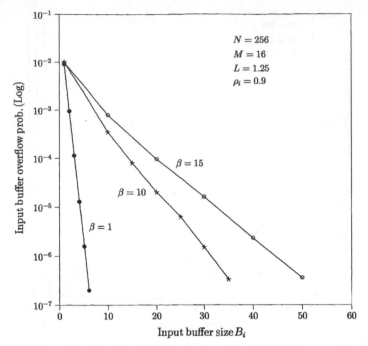

**Figure 10.11**   Input buffer overflow probability versus input buffer size (simulation).

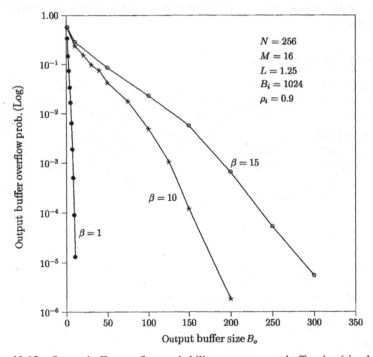

**Figure 10.12**   Output buffer overflow probability versus output buffer size (simulation).

input buffer size can be a few tens of cells for the buffer overflow probability of $10^{-6}$. By extrapolating the simulation result, the input buffer size is about 100 cells for $10^{-10}$ cell loss rate.

Figure 10.12 shows the output buffer overflow probabilities with different average burst lengths. Here, $B_o$ is the normalized buffer size for each output. It is shown that the required output buffer size is much larger than the input buffer size for the same cell loss probability.

## 10.5 ATM ROUTING AND CONCENTRATION (ARC) CHIP

An ASIC (Application Specific Integrated Circuit) has been implemented based on the Abacus switch architecture. Figure 10.13 shows the ARC chip's block diagram. Each block's function and design are explained briefly in the following sections. Details can be found in the work of Chao and Uzun [13]. The ARC chip contains $32 \times 32$ SWEs, which are partioned into eight SWE arrays, each with $32 \times 4$ SWEs. A set of input data signals, $w[0:31]$, comes from the IPCs. Another set of input data signals, $n[0:31]$, either comes from the output, $s[0:31]$, of the chips on the above row, or is tied to high for the chips on the first row (in the multicast case). A set of the output signals, $s[0:31]$, either go to the north input of the chips one row below or go to the output buffer.

$x_0$ signal is broadcast to all SWEs to initialize each SWE to a cross state, where the west input passes to the east and the north input passes to the south. $x_1$ signal specifies the address bit(s) used for routing cells, while $x_2$ signal specifies the priority field. Other $x$ output signals propagate along with cells to the adjacent chips on the east or south side.

$m[0:1]$ signals are used to configure the chip into four different group sizes as shown in Table 10.1: (1) eight groups, each with four output links; (2) four groups, each with eight output links; (3) two groups, each with 16 output links; and (4) one group with 32 output links. The $m[2]$ signal is used to configure the chip to either unicast or multicast application. For the unicast case, $m[2]$ is set to 0, while for the multicast case, $m[2]$ is set to 1.

As shown in Figure 10.14, the SWEs are arranged in a cross-bar structure, where signals only communicate between adjacent SWEs, easing the synchronization problem. ATM cells are propagated in the SWE array similar to a wave propagating diagonally toward the bottom right corner. The $x_1$ and $x_2$ signals are applied from the top left of the SWE array, and each

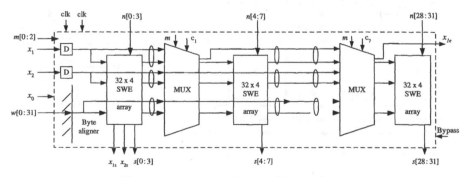

**Figure 10.13**  Block diagram of the ARC chip.

**TABLE 10.1    Truth Table for Different Operation Modes**

| m1 | m0 | Operation |
|----|----|-----------|
| 0  | 0  | 8 groups with 4 links per group |
| 0  | 1  | 4 groups with 8 links per group |
| 1  | 0  | 2 groups with 16 links per group |
| 1  | 1  | 1 group with 32 links per group |

$m2 = 1$ multicast, $m2 = 0$ unicast.

SWE distributes the $x_1$ and $x_2$ signals to its east and south neighbors. This requires the same phase to the signal arriving at each SWE. $x_1$ and $x_2$ signals are passed to the neighbor SWEs (east and south) after one clock cycle delay, as are data signals ($w$ and $n$). The $x_0$ signal is broadcast to all SWEs (not shown in Fig. 10.14) to precharge an internal node in the SWE in every cell cycle. The $x_{1e}$ output signal is used to identify the address bit position of the cells in the first SWE array of the next adjacent chip.

The timing diagram of the SWE input signals and its two possible states are shown in Figure 10.15. Two bit-aligned cells, one from the west and one from the north, are applied to the SWE along with the $dx_1$ and $dx_2$ signals, which determine the address and priority fields of the input cells. The SWE has two states: cross and toggle. Initially, the SWE is initialized to a cross state by the $dx_0$ signal, that is, cells from the north side are routed to the south side, and cells from the west side are routed to the east side. When the address of the cell from the west ($dw_a$) is matched with the address of the cell from the north ($dn_a$), and when the west's priority level ($dw_p$) is higher than the north's ($dn_p$), the SWEs are toggled. The cell from the west side is then routed to the south side, and the cell from the north is routed to the east. Otherwise, the SWE remains at the cross state.

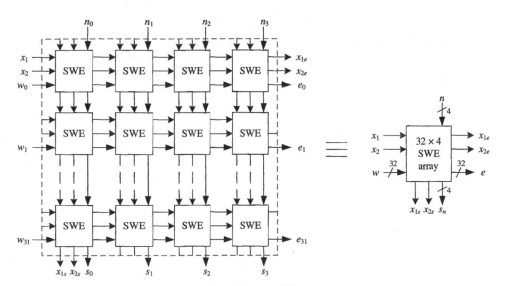

**Figure 10.14**    $32 \times 4$ SWE array.

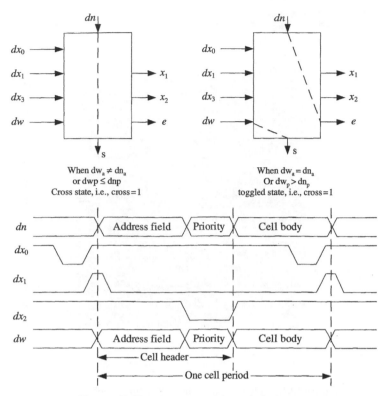

**Figure 10.15** Two states of the switch element.

The $32 \times 32$ ARC chip has been designed and fabricated using $0.8\,\mu m$ CMOS technology with a die size of $6.6 \times 6.6$ mm. Note that this chip is pad limited. The chip has been tested successfully up to 240 MHz and its characteristics are summarized in Table 10.2. Its photograph is shown in Figure 10.16.

**TABLE 10.2   Chip Summary**

| | |
|---|---|
| Process technology | $0.8$-$\mu m$ CMOS, triple metal |
| Number of switching elements | $32 \times 32$ |
| Configurable group size | 4, 8, 16, or 32 output links |
| Pin count | 145 |
| Package | Ceramic PGA |
| Number of transistors | 81,000 |
| Die size | $6.6 \times 6.6\,mm^2$ |
| Clock signals | Pseudo ECL |
| Interface signals | TTL/CMOS inputs, CMOS outputs |
| Maximum clock speed | 240 MHz |
| Worst-case power dissipation | 2.8 W at 240 MHz |

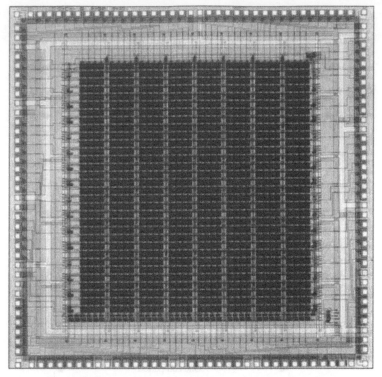

**Figure 10.16**   Photograph of the ARC chip (©1997 IEEE).

## 10.6   ENHANCED ABACUS SWITCH

This section discusses three approaches of implementing the MGN in Figure 10.1 to scale-up the Abacus switch to a larger-size. As described in Section 10.2, the time for routing cells through an RM and feeding back the lowest priority information from the RM to all IPCs must be less than one cell slot time. The feedback information is used to determine whether or not the cell has been successfully routed to the destined output group(s). If not, the cell will continue retrying until it has reached all the desired output groups. Since each SWE in an RM introduces a 1-bit delay as the signal passes it in either direction, the number of SWEs between the uppermost link and the rightmost link of an RM should be less than the number of bits in a cell. In other words, $N + L \times M - 1 < 424$ (see Section 10.2). For example, if we choose $M = 16, L = 1.25$, the equation becomes $N + 1.25 \times 16 - 1 < 424$. The maximum value of $N$ is 405, which is not large enough for a large-capacity switch.

### 10.6.1   Memoryless Multi-Stage Concentration Network

One way to scale up the Abacus switch is to reduce the time spent on traversing cells from the uppermost link to the rightmost link in a RM (see Fig. 10.2). Let us call this time the 'routing delay'. In a single-stage Abacus switch, the routing delay is $N + L \times M - 1$, which limits the switch size because it grows with $N$.

To reduce the routing delay, the number of SWEs that a cell traverses in a RM must be minimized. If we divide a MGN into many small MGNs, the routing delay can be reduced. Figure 10.17 shows a two-stage memoryless multi-stage concentration network (MMCN) architecture that can implement a large-capacity Abacus switch. It consists of $N$ IPCs, $J$ ($=N/n$) MGNs, and $K$ ($=N/M$) concentration modules (CMs). Each MGN has $K$ RMs, and each RM has $n$ input links and $L \times M$ output links. Each CM has $J \times (L \times M)$ input links and $L \times M$ output links.

After cells are routed through the RMs, they need to be further concentrated at the CMs. Since cells that are routed to the CM always have correct output group addresses, we do not need to perform a routing function in the CM. In the CM, only the concentration function is performed by using the priority field in the routing information. The structure and implementation of the RM and the CM are identical, except the functions performed are slightly different.

Recall that each group of $M$ output ports requires $L \times M$ routing links to achieve a high delay/throughput performance. The output expansion ratio of the RM must be equal to or greater than that of the CM. If not, the multicast contention resolution algorithm does not work properly. For example, let us assume that $N = 1024$, $M = 16$, and $n = 128$. Consider the case that there are 16 links between a RM and a CM, while there are 20 links between

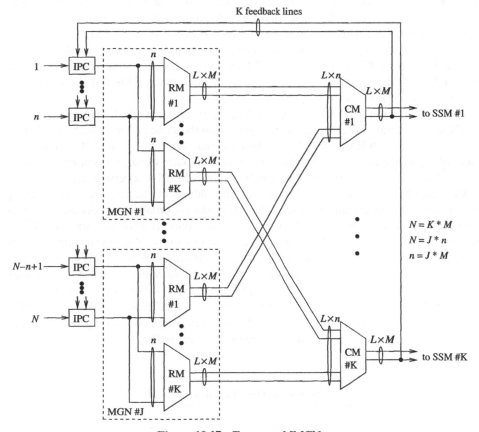

**Figure 10.17**   Two-stage MMCN.

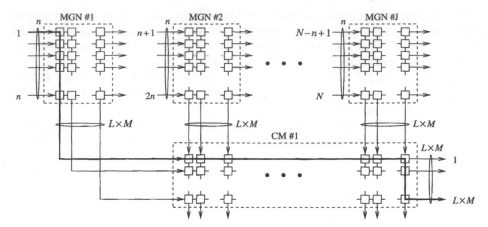

**Figure 10.18** Routing delay in a two-stage MMCN.

a CM and a SSM. If all 128 cells of MGN #1 are destined for output group #1 and no cells from other MGNs are destined for output group #1, the feedback priority of CM #1 will be the priority of the address broadcaster, which has the lowest priority level. Then, all 128 cells destined for output group #1 are cleared from the IPCs of MGN #1, even though only 20 cells can be accepted in the SSM. The other 108 cells will be lost. Therefore, the output expansion ratio of the RM must be equal to or greater than that of the CM.

Let us define $n$ as the module size. The number of input links of a RM is $n$, and the number of input links of the CM is $J \times (L \times M)$. By letting $n = J \times M$, the number of input links of the CM is on the same order with the number of input links of the RM because we can engineer $M$ such that $L$ is close to one.

In the MMCN, the feedback priorities (FPs) are extracted from the CMs and broadcast to all IPCs. To maintain the cell sequence integrity from the same connection, the cell behind the HOL cell at each IPC cannot be sent to the switch fabric until the HOL cell has been successfully transmitted to the desired output port(s). In other words, the routing delay must be less than one cell slot. This requirement limits the MMCN to a certain size.

Cells that have arrived at a CM must carry the address of the associated output group (either valid cells or dummy cells from the RM's address broadcaster). As a result, there is no need for using the AB in the CM to generate dummy cells to carry the address of the output group. Rather, the inputs that are reserved for the AB are substituted by the routing links of MGN #1. Thus, the routing delay of the two-stage MMCN is $n + (J - 1) \times (L \times M) + L \times M - 1$, as shown in Figure 10.18, which should be less than 424. Therefore, we have the following equations by replacing $J$ with $n/M$: $n + [(n/M) - 1] \times (L \times M) + L \times M - 1 < 424$. It can be simplified to $n < [425/(1 + L)]$. Thus, $N = J \times n = n^2/M < \{425^2/[M \times (1 + L)^2]\}$. Table 10.3 shows the minimum value of $L$ for a given $M$ to get a maximum throughput of 99 percent with random uniform traffic.

**TABLE 10.3  Minimum Value of $L$ for a Given $M$**

| $M$ | 1 | 2 | 4 | 8 | 16 | 32 |
|-----|---|---|------|------|------|-------|
| $L$ | 4 | 3 | 2.25 | 1.75 | 1.25 | 1.125 |

Clearly, the smaller the group size $M$, the larger the switch size $N$. The largest Abacus switch can be obtained by letting $M = 1$. But in this case ($M = 1$), the group expansion ratio ($L$) must be equal to or greater than four to have a satisfactory delay/throughput performance. Increasing the group size $M$ reduces the maximum switch size $N$, but also reduces the number of feedback links ($N^2/M$) and the number of SWEs ($LN^2 + L^2Nn$). Therefore, by engineering the group size properly, we can build a practical large-capacity Abacus switch. For example, if we choose $M = 16$ and $L = 1.25$, then the maximum module size $n$ is 188, and the maximum switch size $N$ is 2209. With the advanced CMOS technology (e.g., $0.25\,\mu$m), it is feasible to operate at the OC-12 rate (i.e., 622 Mbit/s). Thus, the MMCN is capable of providing more than 1 Tbit/s of capacity.

### 10.6.2  Buffered Multi-Stage Concentration Network

Figure 10.19 shows a two-stage buffered multi-stage concentration network (BMCN). As discussed in the previous section, the MMCN needs to have the feedback priority lines connected to all IPCs, which increases the interconnection complexity. This can be resolved by keeping RMs and CMs autonomous, where the feedback priorities (FPs) are extracted

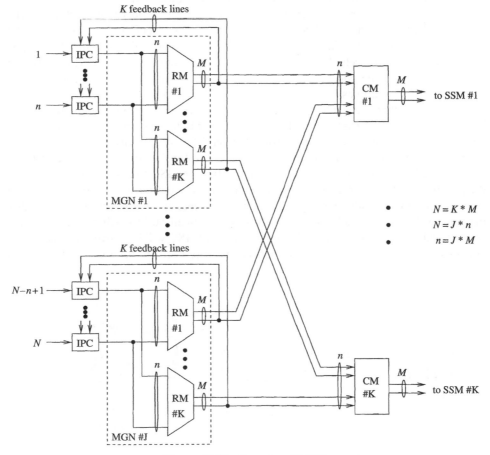

**Figure 10.19**  Two-stage BMCN.

from the RMs rather than from the CMs. However, buffers are required in the CMs since cells that successfully pass through the RMs and are cleared from input buffers may not pass through the CMs.

Figure 10.20 shows three ways of building the CM. Figure 10.20*a* uses a shared-memory structure similar to the MainStreet*Xpress* 36190 core services switch [14] and the concentrator-based growable switch architecture [15]. Its size is limited due to the memory speed constraint.

Figure 10.20*b* shows another way to implement the CM by using a two-dimensional SWE array and input buffers. One potential problem of having buffers at the input links of the CM is cell out-of-sequence. This is because after cells that belong to the same virtual connection are routed through a RM, they may be queued at different input buffers. Since the queue lengths in the buffers can be different, cells that arrive at the buffer with shorter queue lengths will be served earlier by the CM, resulting in cell out-of-sequence.

This out-of-sequence problem can be eliminated by time-division multiplexing cells from a RM ($M$ cells), storing them in an intermediate stage controller (ISC), and sending them sequentially to $M$ one-cell buffers, as shown in Figure 10.20*c*. The ISC has an internal FIFO buffer and logic circuits that handle feedback priorities as in the Abacus switch. This achieves a global FIFO effect and thus maintains the cells' sequence. Each ISC can receive up to $M$ cells and transmit up to $M$ cells during each cell time slot.

The key to maintaining cell sequence is to assign priority properly. At each ISC, cells are dispatched to the one-cell buffers whenever the one-cell buffers become empty and there are cells in the ISC. When a cell is dispatched to the one-cell buffer, the ISC assigns a priority value to the cell. The priority field is divided into two parts, port priority and sequence priority. The port priority field is more significant than the sequence priority. The port priority field has $\lceil \log_2 J \rceil$ bits for the $J$ ISCs in a CM, where $\lceil x \rceil$ denotes the smallest integer that is equal to or greater than $x$. The sequence priority field must have at least $\lceil \log_2 JM \rceil$ bits to ensure the cell sequence integrity to accommodate $L \times M$ priority levels, which will be explained in an example later. The port priority is updated in every arbitration cycle (i.e., in each cell slot time) in a round-robin fashion. The sequence priority is increased by one whenever a cell is dispatched from the ISC to a one-cell buffer. When the port priority has the highest priority level, the sequence priority is reset to zero at the beginning of the next arbitration cycle (assuming the smaller the priority value, the higher the priority level). This is because all cells in the one-cell buffers will be cleared at the current cycle. Using this dispatch algorithm, cells in the ISC will be delivered to the output port in sequence. The reason that the sequence priority needs to have $L \times M$ levels is to

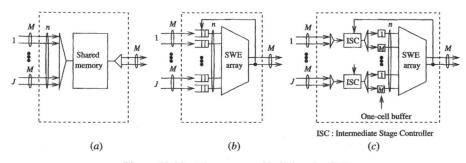

**Figure 10.20**   Three ways of building the CM.

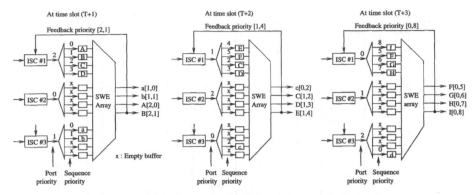

**Figure 10.21**    Example of priority assignment in the CM.

accommodate the maximum number of cells that can be transmitted from an ISC between two reset operations for the sequence priority.

Figure 10.21 shows an example of a cell's priority assignment scheme for $J = 3$ and $M = 4$. Port priority ($p$) and sequence priority ($q$) are represented by two numbers in [$p, q$], where $p = 0, 1, 2$, and $q = 0, 1, 2, \ldots, 11$. During each time slot, each ISC can receive up to four cells and transmit up to four cells. Let us consider the following case. ISC #1 receives four cells in every time slot, ISC #3 receives one cell in every time slot, and ISC #2 receives no cells.

The port priority is changed in every time slot in a round-robin fashion. In time slot $T$, ISC #1 has the highest port priority level, and ISC #3 has the lowest port priority level. In time slot ($T + 1$), ISC #2 has the highest port priority level, and ISC #1 has the lowest port priority level, and so on. ISC #3 has a higher port priority level than ISC #1 in time slots ($T + 1$) and ($T + 2$).

In time slot $T$, all four cells in the one-cell buffers of ISC #1 pass through the CM because they have the highest priority levels. In time slot ($T + 1$), ISC #3 transmits two cells (a and b) and ISC #1 transmits two cells (A and B). In time slot ($T + 2$), ISC #3 transmits one cell (c), while ISC #1 transmits three cells (C, D, and E). In time slot ($T + 3$), ISC #1 has the highest port priority ('0') and is able to transmit all its cells (F, G, H, and I). Once they are cleared from the one-cell buffers, ISC #1 resets its sequence priority to zero.

### 10.6.3  Resequencing Cells

As discussed before, the routing delay in the Abacus switch must be less than 424 bit times. If the routing delay is greater than 424, there are two possibilities. First, if a cell is held up in the input buffer longer than a cell slot time, the throughput of the switch fabric will be degraded. Second, if a cell next to the HOL cell is sent to the MGN before knowing if the HOL cell has been successfully transmitted to the desired output switch module(s), it may be ahead of the HOL cell that did not pass through the MGN. This cell out-of-sequence problem can be resolved with a resequencing buffer (RSQB) at the output port of the MGN.

For a switch size $N$ of 1024, output group size $M$ of 16, and group expansion ratio $L$ of 1.25, the maximum routing delay of the single stage Abacus switch is 1043 (i.e., $N + L \times M - 1$ as described previously). Therefore, an arbitration cycle is at least three cell time slots. If up to three cells are allowed to transmit during each arbitration cycle, the IPC must have three one-cell buffers arranged in parallel.

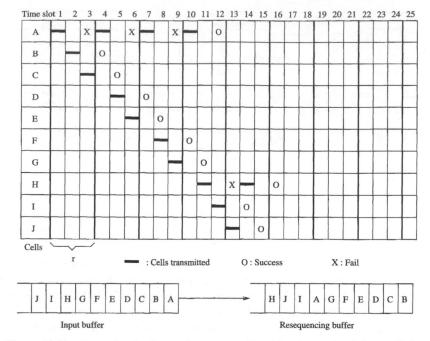

Figure 10.22 shows the cells A through J in a time-slot grid with transmitted/success/fail markings, followed by input buffer and resequencing buffer diagrams.

Cells — : Cells transmitted    O : Success    X : Fail

Input buffer: J I H G F E D C B A → Resequencing buffer: H J I A G F E D C B

**Figure 10.22** Example of cell out-of-sequence with arbitration cycle of three cell slots.

Figure 10.22 illustrates an example of the maximum degree of out-of-sequence. Assume cells A to J are stored in the same input buffer in sequence. In time slot 1, cell A is sent to the switch fabric. It takes three time slots to know if cell A has passed through the switch fabric successfully. In time slot 2, cell B is sent to the switch fabric, and in time slot 3, cell C is sent to the switch fabric. Before the end of time slot 3, the IPC knows that cell A has failed to pass the switch fabric, so cell A will be transmitted again in time slot 4. If cell A passes through the switch fabric successfully on the fourth try, up to six cells (cells B to G) can be ahead of the cell A. The cell arriving sequence in the RSQB is shown in Figure 10.22.

For this scheme to be practical, the size of the maximum degree of cell out-of-sequence and the size of the RSQB should be bounded. Let us consider the worst case. If all HOL cells of $N$ input ports are destined for the same output group and the tagged cell has the lowest port priority in time slot $T$, $L \times M$ highest priority cells will be routed in time slot $T$. In time slot $(T + 1)$, the priority level of the tagged cell will be incremented by one so that there can be at most $(N - L \times M - 1)$ cells whose priority levels are greater than that of the tagged cell. In time slot $(T + 2)$, there can be at most $(N - 2 \times L \times M - 1)$ cells whose priority levels are greater than that of the tagged cell, and so on.

The maximum degree of out-of-sequence can be obtained from the following. An arbitration cycle is equal to or greater than $r = \lceil N + L \times M - 1/424 \rceil$ cell time slots. A tagged cell succeeds in at most $s = \lceil N/L \times M \rceil$ tries. Therefore, in the worst case, the HOL cell passes through the switch fabric successfully in $(r \times s)$ time slots. Denote the maximum degree of out-of-sequence to be $t$; $t = r \times s$.

One way to implement the resequencing is to time stamp each cell with a value equal to the real time plus the maximum degree of cell out-of-sequence ($t$), when it is sent to the switch fabric. Let us call the time stamp the 'due time of the cell'. Cells at the RSQBs are

**TABLE 10.4  Maximum Degree of Cell Out-of-Sequence ($t$)**

| $N$ | $M$ | $L$ | $r$ | $s$ | $t$ |
|------|------|------|------|------|------|
| 1024 | 16 | 1.25 | 3 | 52 | 156 |
| 8192 | 16 | 1.25 | 20 | 410 | 8200 |

moved to the SSM when their due times are equal to the real time. This maintains the cell transmission sequence.

The drawbacks of this scheme are high implementation scomplexity of the RSQB and large cell transfer delay. Since a cell must wait in the RSQB until the real time reaches the due time of the cell, every cell experiences at least $t$ cell slot delay even if there is no contention. Table 10.4 shows the maximum degree of cell out-of-sequence for switch sizes of 1024 and 8192. For switch size 1024, the maximum degree of cell out-of-sequence is 156 cell slots, which corresponds to 441 μsec for the OC-3 line rate (i.e., $156 \times 2.83$ μsec).

## 10.6.4  Complexity Comparison

This section compares the complexity of the above three approaches for building a large-capacity Abacus switch and summarizes the results in Table 10.5. Here, the switch element in the RMs and CMs is a $2 \times 2$ crosspoint device. The number of inter-stage links is the number of links between the RMs and the CMs. The number of buffers is the number of ISCs. For the BMCN, the CMs have ISCs and one-cell buffers (Fig. 10.20$c$). The second and third parts of Table 10.5 give some numerical values of a 160 Gbit/s Abacus switch.

**TABLE 10.5  Complexity Comparison of Three Approaches for a 160 Gbit/s Abacus Switch**

|  | MMCN | BMCN | Resequencing |
|------|------|------|------|
| Number of switch elements | $LN^2 + L^2Nn$ | $N^2 + Nn$ | $LN^2$ |
| Number of inter-stage links | $JLN$ | $JN$ | 0 |
| Number of internal buffers | 0 | $JK$ | 0 |
| Number of MP bits | $K$ | $K$ | $K$ |
| Out-of-sequence delay | 0 | 0 | $\lceil (N + LM - 1)/424 \rceil \times \lceil N/(LM) \rceil$ |
| Routing delay in bits | $n + Ln - 1$ | $n + LM - 1$ | $N + LM - 1$ |
| Switch size $N$ | 1024 | 1024 | 1024 |
| Group size $M$ | 16 | 16 | 16 |
| Output exp. ratio $L$ | 1.25 | 1.25 | 1.25 |
| Module size $n$ | 128 | 128 | 128 |
| Number of switch elements | 1,515,520 | 1,179,648 | 1,310,720 |
| Number of inter-stage links | 10,240 | 8192 | 0 |
| Number of internal buffers | 0 | 512 | 0 |
| Number of MP bits | 64 | 64 | 64 |
| Out-of-sequence delay | 0 | 0 | 156 |
| Routing delay in bits | 287 | 147 | 1043 |

Here, it is assumed that the switch size $N$ is 1024, the input line speed is 155.52 Mbit/s, the group size $M$ is 16, the group expansion ratio $L$ is 1.25, and the module size $n$ is 128.

With respect to the MMCN, there are no internal buffers and no out-of-sequence cells. Its routing delay is less than 424 bit times. But the number of SWEs and inter-stage links is the highest among the three approaches.

For the BMCN, the routing delay is no longer a concern for a large-capacity Abacus switch. Its number of SWEs and inter-stage links is smaller than that of the MMCN. However, it may not be cost-effective when it is required to implement buffer management and cell scheduling in the intermediate-stage buffers to meet QoS requirements.

The last approach of resequencing out-of-sequence cells has no inter-stage links nor internal buffers. It requires a resequencing buffer at each output port. For a switch capacity of 160 Gbit/s, the delay caused by resequencing cells is at least 156 cell slot times.

## 10.7 ABACUS SWITCH FOR PACKET SWITCHING

The Abacus switch can also handle variable-length packets. To reserve cell[1] sequence in a packet, two cell scheduling schemes are used at the input buffers. The packet interleaving scheme transfers all cells in a packet consecutively, while the cell interleaving scheme transfers cells from different inputs and reassembles them at the output.

### 10.7.1 Packet Interleaving

A packet switch using the packet interleaving technique is shown in Figure 10.23. The switch consists of a memoryless nonblocking MGN, IPCs, and OPCs. Arriving cells are stored in an input buffer until the last cell of the packet arrives. When the last cell arrives, the packet is then eligible for transmission to output port(s).

In the packet interleaving scheme, all cells belonging to the same packet are transferred consecutively. That is, if the first cell in the packet wins the output port contention for a destination among the contending input ports, all the following cells of the packet will be transferred consecutively to the destination.

A packet interleaving switch can be easily implemented by the Abacus switch. Only the first cells of head-of-line (HOL) packets can contend for output ports. The contention among the first cells of HOL packets can be resolved by properly assigning priority fields to them. The priority field of a cell has $(1 + \log_2 N)$ bits. Among them, the $\log_2 N$-bit field is used to achieve fair contention by dynamically changing its value as in the Abacus switch. Prior to the contention resolution, the most-significant-bit (MSB) of the priority field is set to 1 (low priority). As soon as the first cell of an HOL packet wins the contention (known from the feedback priorities), the MSB of the priority field of all the following cells in the same packet is asserted to 0 (high priority). As soon as the last cell of the packet is successfully sent to the output, the MSB is set to 1 for the next packet. As a result, it is ensured that cells belonging to the same packet are transferred consecutively.

Figure 10.24 shows the average packet delay versus offered load for a packet switch with packet interleaving. In the simulations, it is assumed that the traffic source is an ON–OFF model. The packet size is assumed to have a truncated geometric distribution with an

---

[1]The cell discussed in this section is just a fixed-length segment of a packet and does not have to be 53 bytes like an ATM cell.

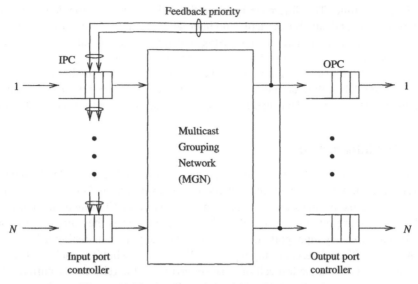

**Figure 10.23**    Packet switch with packet interleaving.

average packet size of 10 cells and the maximum packet size of 32 cells (to accommodate the maximum Ethernet frame size). The packet delay through the switch is defined as follows. When the last cell of a packet arrives at an input buffer, the packet is time-stamped with an arrival time. When the last cell of a packet leaves the output buffer, the packet is time-stamped

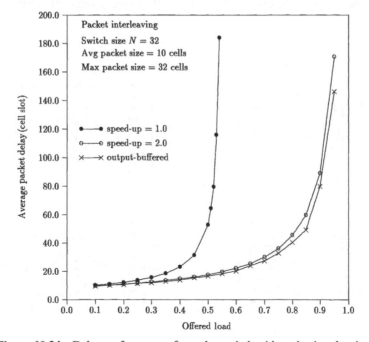

**Figure 10.24**    Delay performance of a packet switch with packet interleaving.

with a departure time. The difference between the arrival time and the departure time is defined as the packet delay. When there is no internal speedup ($S = 1$) in the switch fabric, the delay performance of the packet interleaving switch is very poor, mainly due to the HOL blocking. The delay/throughput performance is improved by increasing the speedup factor $S$ (e.g., $S = 2$). Note that the input buffer's average delay is much smaller than the output buffer's average delay. With an internal speedup of two, its output buffer's average delay dominates the total average delay and is very close to that of the output-buffered switch.

### 10.7.2 Cell Interleaving

A packet switch using a cell interleaving technique is shown in Figure 10.25. Arriving cells are stored in the input buffer until the last cell of a packet arrives. Once the last cell of a packet arrives, cells are transferred in the same way as in an ATM switch. That is, cells from different input ports can be interleaved with each other as they arrive at the output port. Cells have to carry input port numbers so that output ports can distinguish them from different packets. Therefore, each output port has $N$ reassembly buffers, each corresponding to each input port. When the last cell of a packet arrives at the reassembly buffer, all cells belonging to the packet are moved to the output buffer for transmission to the output link. In real implementation, only pointers are moved, not the cells. This architecture is similar to the one in [16] in the sense that they both use reassembly buffers at the outputs, but it is more scalable than the one in [16].

The operation speed of the Abacus switch fabric is limited to several hundred Mbit/s with state-of-the-art CMOS technology. To accommodate the line rate of a few Gbit/s (e.g., Gigabit Ethernet and OC-48), we can either use the bit-slice technique or the one shown in Figure 10.25, where the high-speed cell stream is distributed up to $m$ one-cell buffers at each input port. The way of dispatching cells from the IPC to the $m$ one-cell buffers is identical

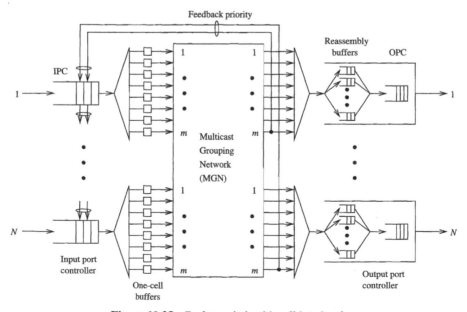

**Figure 10.25** Packet switch with cell interleaving.

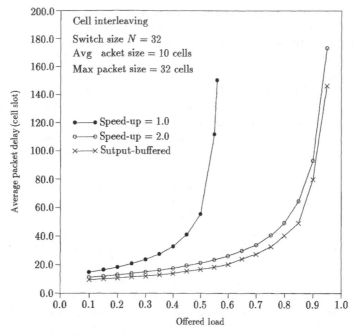

**Figure 10.26** Delay performance of a packet switch with cell interleaving.

to dispatching cells from the ISC to the $M$ one-cell buffers in Figure 10.20c. The advantage of using the technique in Figure 10.25 over the bit-slice technique is its smaller overhead bandwidth, since the latter shrinks the cell duration while keeping the same overhead for each cell.

Figure 10.26 shows the average packet delay versus offered load for a packet switch with cell interleaving. When there is no internal speedup ($S = 1$), the delay performance is poor. With an internal speedup $S$ of 2, the delay performance is close to that of an output-buffered packet switch. By comparing the delay performance between Figure 10.24 and Figure 10.26, we can see that the average delay performance is comparable. However, we believe that the delay variation of cell interleaving will be smaller than that of packet interleaving because of its finer granularity in switching.

## REFERENCES

[1] H. J. Chao, B. S. Choe, J. S. Park, and N. Uzun, "Design and implementation of Abacus switch: A scalable multicast ATM switch," *IEEE Journal on Selected Areas in Communications*, vol. 15, no. 5, pp. 830–843 (June 1997).

[2] J. Hui and E. Arthurs, "A broadband packet switch for integrated transport," *IEEE Journal on Selected Areas in Communications*, vol. 5, no. 8, pp. 1264–1273 (Oct. 1987).

[3] B. Bingham and H. Bussey, "Reservation-based contention resolution mechanism for Batcher-banyan packet switches," *Electronics Letters*, vol. 24, no. 13, pp. 772–773 (June 1988).

[4] A. Cisneros and C. A. Bracket, "A large ATM switch based on memory switches and optical star couplers," *IEEE Journal on Selected Areas in Communications*, vol. 9, no. 8, pp. 1348–1360 (Oct. 1991).

[5] R. Handel, M. N. Huber, and S. Schroder, *ATM networks: Concepts, Protocols, Applications*. Addison-Wesley Publishing Company, Reading, MA, 1994, Chapter 7.

[6] M. J. Karol, M. G. Hluchyj, and S. P. Morgan, "Input versus output queuing on a space-division packet switch," *IEEE Transactions on Communications*, vol. 35, pp. 1347–1356 (Dec. 1987).

[7] Y. Oie, M. Murata, K. Kubota, and H. Miyahara, "Effect of speedup in nonblocking packet switch," in *Proc. ICC'89*, Boston, Massachusetts, pp. 410–415 (June 1989).

[8] A. Pattavina, "Multichannel bandwidth allocation in a broadband packet switch," *IEEE Journal on Selected Areas in Communications*, vol. 6, no. 9, pp. 1489–1499 (Dec. 1988).

[9] S. C. Liew and K. W. Lu, "Comparison of buffering strategies for asymmetric packet switch modules," *IEEE Journal on Selected Areas in Communications*, vol. 9, no. 3, pp. 428–438 (Apr. 1991).

[10] T. Kozaki, N. Endo, Y. Sakurai, O. Matsubara, M. Mizukami, and K. Asano, "$32 \times 32$ shared buffer type ATM switch VLSI's for B-ISDN's," *IEEE Journal on Selected Areas in Communications*, vol. 9, no. 8, pp. 1239–1247 (Oct. 1991).

[11] C. Y. Chang, A. J. Paulraj, and T. Kailath, "A broadband packet switch architecture with input and output queuing," in *Proc. IEEE GLOBECOM'94*, San Francisco, California, pp. 448–452 (Nov. 1994).

[12] A. Pattavina and G. Bruzzi, "Analysis of input and output queuing for nonblocking ATM switches," *IEEE/ACM Transactions on Networking*, vol. 1, no. 3, pp. 314–328 (June 1993).

[13] H. J. Chao and N. Uzun, "An ATM routing and concentration chip for a scalable multicast ATM switch," *IEEE Journal of Solid-State Circuits*, vol. 32, no. 6, pp. 816–828 (June 1997).

[14] E. P. Rathgeb, W. Fischer, C. Hinterberger, E. Wallmeier, and R. Wille-Fier, "The Main-Street*xpress* core services node – a versatile ATM switch architecture for the full service network," *IEEE J. on Selected Areas in Communications*, vol. 15, no. 5, pp. 830–843 (June 1997).

[15] K. Y. Eng and M. J. Karol, "State-of-the-art in gigabit ATM switching," in *Proc. IEEE BSS'95*, Poznan, Poland, pp. 3–20 (Apr. 1995).

[16] I. Widjaja and A. I. Elwalid, "Performance issues in VC-merge capable switches for IP over ATM networks," in *Proc. INFOCOM'98*, San Francisco, California, pp. 372–380 (Mar. 1998).

# CHAPTER 11

# CROSSPOINT BUFFERED SWITCHES

The performance of packet switches are constrained by memory speed and the efficiency of the arbitration scheme used to select the cells that will traverse the switch at a given time. Output buffered (OB) switches use no arbitration at the inputs as the output buffers run at $N$ times faster than the speed of external links. Therefore, for a limited memory speed, the size of such switches is restricted to a small number of ports as link rates increase. On the other hand, the memory in input buffered (IB) switches runs at link-rate speeds, making these switches attractive. However, IB switches need to perform matching between input and outputs to resolve input and output contentions. Fast matching schemes for IB switches can be modeled as parallel matchings, where $N$ input and output arbiters perform the parallel selection and communication among them to decide the matching results. This communication adds overhead time to the matching process. The parallel matching process can be characterized by three phases: request, grant, and accept. Therefore, the resolution time would be the time spent in each of the selection phases plus the transmission delays for the exchange of request, grant, and accept information. As an example, a matching scheme must perform input or output arbitration within 6.4 ns in an IB switch with 40 Gbps (OC-768) ports and 64-byte cells, as input and output arbitrations may use up to half of a time slot, assuming that the transmission delays are decreased to a negligible value (e.g., the arbiters are implemented in a single chip, in a centralized way).

A solution to minimize the time overhead is to use buffers in the crosspoints of a crossbar fabric, or buffered crossbar. In a buffered crossbar switch, an input can avoid waiting for a matching to be completed before a cell is forwarded to the crossbar. However, the number of buffers grows in the same order as the number of crosspoints, $O(N^2)$, making implementation costly or infeasible for a large buffer size or a large number of ports. As VLSI technology has matured, buffered crossbars are considered feasible for a moderate size switch.

*High Performance Switches and Routers*, by H. Jonathan Chao and Bin Liu
Copyright © 2007 John Wiley & Sons, Inc.

The rest of this chapter is organized as follows. Section 11.1 introduces the basic combined input and crosspoint buffered (CIXB) switch structure. CIXB switches with virtual output queues (VOQs) at the input ports are discussed in Section 11.2. Sections 11.2.1 to 11.5 describe some variants of CIXB, namely CIXB-$k$ and CIXOB-$k$, and several scheduling schemes employed in these switches. More work related to crosspoint buffered switches can be found in References [1, 2].

## 11.1 COMBINED INPUT AND CROSSPOINT BUFFERED SWITCHES

A conventional crosspoint buffered switch is shown in Figure 11.1. It consists of a crossbar $N \times N$ switch fabric and buffers that are placed at each crosspoint. This switch and the memory operate at the line speed. When a cell arrives from an input port, it will enter the designated crosspoint buffer and wait to be scheduled to the output link. Although it has high throughput performance equivalent to that of output buffered switches, it is not feasible in implementation. The required number of buffers grows quadratically with $N$. Since crosspoint buffers are not shared among them, the total required buffer size is large, making it difficult to include the buffers on a chip.

To reduce the memory in the crosspoint buffer, CIXB switches were proposed [3], where large input buffers and small crosspoint buffers were adopted. The CIXB switch operates at the line rate, and its architecture is shown in Figure 11.2. When a cell arrives, it is first buffered at the input buffer, and transferred to the crosspoint buffer when it has a space. The number of crosspoint buffers and input buffers are $N^2$ and $N$, respectively. Different from the conventional crosspoint buffered switch, CIXB switches only need a small buffer at crosspoint. Thus, the total buffer size of the CIXB switch is much smaller than that of the conventional crosspoint buffered switch for the same switching performance.

Simulations show that the CIXB switch has superior traffic characteristics to the conventional crosspoint buffered switches. In the simulation, the switch size is assumed to be 32 and the input offered load is set to 0.8. Input buffer size is set to 8, 16, and 24

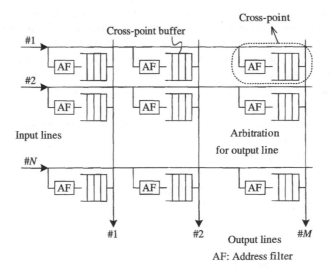

**Figure 11.1** Conventional crosspoint buffered switch.

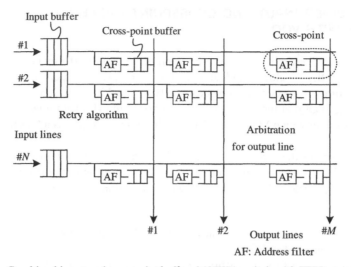

**Figure 11.2** Combined input and crosspoint buffered (CIXB) switch with FIFO queuing at inputs.

to 32 cells, respectively. A simple ring arbitration mechanism (i.e., round robin) is used to select cells from the crosspoint buffers on the same column. The simulation results in Figure 11.3 show the cell loss rates as a function of crosspoint buffer size. To achieve a cell loss rate of less than $10^{-8}$, the conventional crosspoint buffered switch needs 8-cell buffers at each crosspoint, and the CIXB switch needs only 4-cell buffers if 32-cell input buffers are used.

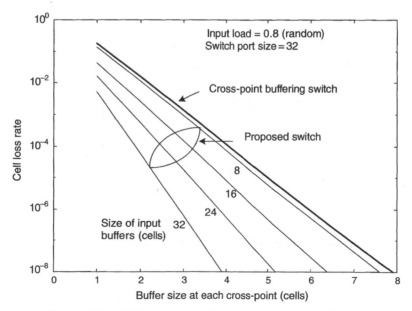

**Figure 11.3** Cell loss rates as a function of crosspoint buffer size.

## 11.2 COMBINED INPUT AND CROSSPOINT BUFFERED SWITCHES WITH VOQ

Although the CIXB switch can have a very high throughput performance, it suffers from head-of-line (HOL) blocking, and thus does not achieve 100 percent throughput. To overcome the throughput degradation due to the HOL blocking, a CIXB switch with virtual output queuing (VOQ) at the input ports was proposed in [4]. From now on, we will refer to a CIXB switch in which VOQ is used at each input port simply as a CIXB/VOQ or just CIXB switch.

Figure 11.4 shows the architecture of a CIXB switch. A crosspoint (XP) element in the crossbar (BX) that connects input port $i$ ($0 \leq i \leq N-1$) to output port $j$ ($0 \leq j \leq N-1$) is denoted as $XP_{i,j}$. The switch has the following major components:

*Input Buffers.* There are $N$ VOQs at each input. A VOQ at input $i$ that stores cells for output $j$ is denoted as $VOQ_{i,j}$.

*Crosspoint Buffer (XPB).* The XPB of $XP_{i,j}$ is denoted as $XPB_{i,j}$. The size of $XPB_{i,j}$ is $k$ cells. We call a CIXB switch with an XPB size $k$, CIXB-$k$.

*Flow Control.* A credit-based flow-control mechanism indicates input $i$ whether $XPB_{i,j}$ has room available for a cell or not. Each VOQ has a credit counter, where the maximum count is the number of cells that $XPB_{i,j}$ can hold. When the number of cells sent by $VOQ_{i,j}$ reaches the maximum count, $VOQ_{i,j}$ is considered not eligible for input arbitration and overflow on $XPB_{i,j}$ is avoided. The count is increased by one every time a cell is sent to $XPB_{i,j}$, and decreased by one every time that $XPB_{i,j}$ forwards a cell to output $j$. If $XPB_{i,j}$ has room for, at least, one cell, then $VOQ_{i,j}$ is considered eligible by the input arbiter.

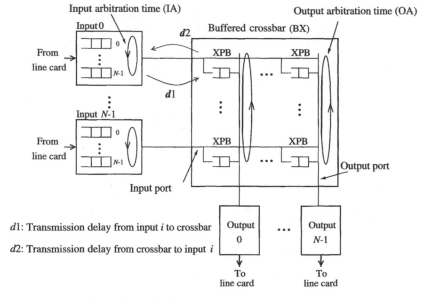

**Figure 11.4** CIXB switch model with VOQ at inputs.

*Input and Output Arbitration.* Round-robin arbitration is used at the input and output ports. An input arbiter selects an eligible $VOQ_{i,j}$ for sending a cell to $XPB(i,j)$. VOQ elegibility is determined by the flow-control mechanism. An output arbiter selects a non-empty $XPB_{i,j}$ for forwarding. Input and output arbitrations are performed separately, therefore, reducing cell selection complexity.

### 11.2.1 CIXB with One-Cell Crosspoint Buffers (CIXB-1)

Let us assume CIXB-1 has the following traffic model: All inputs have uniform traffic where each $VOQ_{i,j}$ receives cells at a rate $\rho_{i,j}$ such that $\sum_{i=0}^{N-1} \rho_{i,j} = 1.0$, $\sum_{j=0}^{N-1} \rho_{i,j} = 1.0$, and each $VOQ_{i,j}$ has a capacity $\sigma_{i,j}(t)$ such that $0 < \sigma_{i,j}(t) < \infty$ and $\sigma_{i,j}(t)$ is large. CIXB-1 reaches a state such that the number of cells entering the system equals the number of cells leaving it, defining 100 percent throughput. CIXB-1 has the following property:

**Property 1.** CIXB-1 achieves 100 percent throughput under uniform traffic [5].

For this property to be effective, we need to consider the round-trip time. Round-trip time $(RT)$ is defined as the sum of the delays of the input arbitration $(IA)$, the transmission of a cell from an input port to the crossbar $(d1)$, the output arbitration $(OA)$, and the transmission of the flow-control information back from the crossbar to the input port $(d2)$. Figure 11.4 shows an example of $RT$ for input 0 by showing the transmission delays for $d1$ and $d2$, and arbitration times, $IA$ and $OA$. Cell and data alignments are included in the transmission times. The condition for CIXB-1 to provide 100 percent throughput is such that, in general:

$$RT = d1 + OA + d2 + IA \leq k. \tag{11.1}$$

In other words, $RT$ time slots must be absorbed by the number of available cells in the XPB. The arbitration times $IA$ and $OA$ are constrained to $IA \leq 1$ and $OA \leq 1$.

As the cost of implementing memory in a chip is still considerable, although feasible with currently available VLSI technologies, it is important to minimize the XPB size within the implementation limits. A back-pressure flow control is expensive to consider with CIXB as the XPB size needs to be at least twice $RT$ ($k \geq 2RT$) to avoid underflow and, therefore, performance degradation. To evaluate this, consider the worst-case scenario: there is only a single flow in BX from input $i$ to output $j$. In this case, $XPB_{i,j}$ must have room available for all cells that can be transmitted to their outputs while the notification of back-pressure release travels back to input $i$ and a cell travels from input $i$ to $XPB_{i,j}$ (RT time), so that output port $j$ can continue forwarding cells from input port $i$. This is why the use of a credit-based flow control is more cost-effective in CIXB.

### 11.2.2 Throughput and Delay Performance

The performance of an IB switch using $i$SLIP scheduling, two combined input-crosspoint buffered switches, and an OB switch are studied by computer simulation. One of the CIXB switches is the CIXB-1 and the other uses a pre-determined permutation for input and output selections, where the permutation changes cyclically and in a fixed sequence, as time division multiplexing (TDM) works. TDM also uses one-cell XPB. $i$SLIP is used as the scheduling scheme in the IB switch, as $i$SLIP is based on round-robin selection. A comparison on the performance between IB and CIXB switches, where round-robin selection is used, is given. The comparison with the OB switch is used for the best possible performance. The traffic patterns studied in this section are uniform and non-uniform traffic with Bernoulli arrivals. Traffic with uniform distribution with bursty arrivals is also considered. Here, segmentation and re-assembly delays are not considered. Our simulation results are obtained with a 95 percent confidence interval.

***Uniform Traffic.*** The performance of various switches is compared here, including IB switches with 1SLIP and 4SLIP, CIXB-1, TDM, and OB switches under uniform traffic with Bernoulli and bursty arrivals (on–off modulated Markov process) for a switch size of $32 \times 32$. Note that 4 is almost the optimum number of iterations for $i$SLIP, as more iterations offer no significant measurable improvements [6]. Figure 11.5 shows that, under this traffic model, all switches provide 100 percent throughput. CIXB-1 provides an average delay close to OB. 1SLIP and TDM have similar average delay for high loads, and CIXB-1 delivers shorter average cell delay than 4SLIP and TDM. The reason why CIXB delivers this high performance is because at a given time slot, there could be more than one cell from input $i$ stored in crosspoints for different outputs that depart at the same time. Therefore, several cells from input $i$ could leave the switch in one time slot. In an IB switch, the number of cells that can traverse to an output port is one.

This small delay of CIXB-1 remains independent of the switch size according to results in the work of Rojas-Cessa et al. [7]. A low average cell delay is expected as it is similar to that of an OB switch.

Figure 11.6 shows the average delay performance of TDM, CIXB-1, and OB under on–off arrival uniform traffic. The traffic in this figure has an average burst length ($l$) of 1, 10, and 100 cells, where the burst length is exponentially distributed. The figure shows that CIXB-1 follows the throughput and average cell delay of an OB switch. TDM has a significantly larger delay than CIXB-1. Some differences can be noted between CIXB-1 and OB when the input load is close to 1.0.

***Nonuniform Traffic.*** $i$SLIP, TDM, and CIXB switches were evaluated under three traffic models with Bernoulli arrivals and nonuniform distributions: unbalanced [7], asymmetric [8], and Chang's models [9].

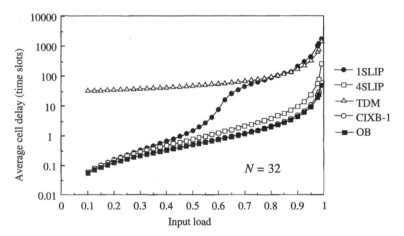

**Figure 11.5** Performance of CIXB, TDM, and OB under uniform traffic.

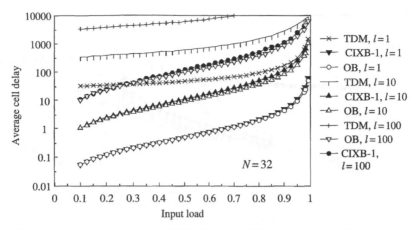

**Figure 11.6**  Performance of CIXB, TDM, and OB under bursty uniform traffic.

***Unbalanced Traffic.***  The unbalanced traffic model uses a probability $w$ as the fraction of input load directed to a single predetermined output, while the remaining load is directed to all outputs with a uniform distribution. Let us consider input port $s$, output port $d$, and the offered input load $\rho$ for each input port. The traffic load from input port $s$ to output port $d$, $\rho_{s,d}$ is given by $\rho_{s,d} = \rho\{w + [(1-w)/N]\}$ if $s = d$, and $\rho_{s,d} = \rho[(1-w)/N]$ otherwise, where $N$ is the switch size. Here, the aggregate offered load $\rho_d$ that goes to output $d$ from all input ports is given by $\rho_d = \sum_s \rho_{s,d} = \rho\{w + N \times [(1-w)/N]\} = \rho$. When $w = 0$, the offered traffic is uniform. On the other hand, when $w = 1$, the traffic is completely directional. This means that all the traffic of input port $s$ is destined for output port $d$ only, where $s = d$. Figure 11.7 shows $i$SLIP, CIXB-1, and TDM under unbalanced traffic for $0 \le w \le 1$, and observed the minimum throughput in terms of $w$ achieved by each switch. The throughput of $i$SLIP with 1 and 4 iterations are 64 percent and 80 percent, respectively. The throughput of CIXB-1 is 84 percent, higher than $i$SLIP. The throughput for TDM drops to almost 0 when $w = 1.0$, because of the predetermined connectivity that TDM provides, independently of the existing traffic. CIXB provides a higher throughput

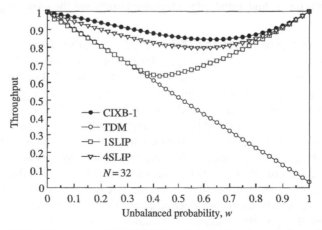

**Figure 11.7**  Througput of $i$SLIP, TDM, and CIXB-1 under unbalanced traffic.

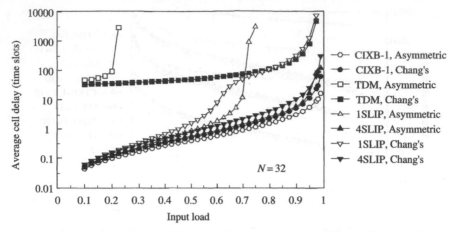

**Figure 11.8**   Delay performance of TDM and CIXB-1 under asymmetric and Chang's traffic models.

than IB switches with round-robin schemes [7] at the expense of having buffers in the crosspoints. These results clearly show the advantage of using a round-robin scheme and crosspoint buffers under unbalanced traffic.

***Chang's and Asymmetric Traffic.*** Chang's traffic model can be defined as $\rho = 0$ for $i = j$ and $\rho = 1/(N - 1)$, otherwise. The asymmetric traffic model can be defined as having different load for each input–output pair, such as $\rho_{i,(i+j) \bmod N} = a_j \rho$, where $a_0 = 0$, $a_1 = (r - 1)/(r^N - 1)$, $a_j = a_1 r^{j-1}$ $\forall j \neq 0$, and $\rho_{i,j}/\rho_{(i+1) \bmod N}$, $j = r$, $\forall i \neq 0$, $(i + 1) \bmod N \neq 0$, and $r = (100 : 1)^{-1/(N-2)}$. Figure 11.8 shows the average cell delay of $i$SLIP, TDM, and CIXB-1 under asymmetric and Chang's traffic models. $i$SLIP delivers close to 71 percent throughput under asymmetric traffic and close to 95 percent throughput under Chang's traffic. 4SLIP delivers close to 100 percent throughput under these two traffic patterns. TDM provides 20 percent throughput under asymmetric traffic, and close to 95 percent throughput under Chang's traffic. CIXB delivers 100 percent throughput and lower average cell delay than the other switches under both traffic models. These results show that having buffers in the crosspoints and round-robin arbitration improves the switching performance.

***Buffer and Switch Size Effect on CIXB-k.*** A $32 \times 32$ CIXB-$k$ for $k = \{1, 2, 8\}$ under uniform traffic was evaluated for the average delay performance and tail delay distribution. Because the similarity of the average cell delay in CIXB-1 and in OB switches, the value of $k$ in CIXB-$k$ produces non-measurable differences on the average delay performance under Bernoulli and bursty ($l = 10$) uniform traffic, as shown previously [7].

A more stringent test is performed by measuring the tail delay distribution of CIXB-$k$. Figure 11.9 shows that the tail delay distribution under Bernoulli uniform traffic, for different input loads, presents non-measurable differences for any $k$ value. This is because as long as the $k$ value complies with (11.1), the crosspoint buffers avoid underflow states. By providing a larger $k$, the number of cells leaving BX will not be larger as the optimum performance of the switch has already been reached. Therefore, the crosspoint buffer size can be kept as small as possible to minimize the amount of in-chip memory without having performance degradation.

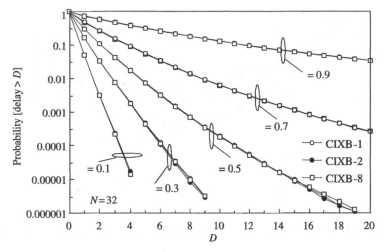

**Figure 11.9**   Tail delay distribution for different input loads and crosspoint buffer size $k$ under uniform traffic.

The effect of $k$ under non-uniform traffic is studied in a $32 \times 32$ CIXB-$k$, with $k$ values between 1 and 32. Figure 11.10 shows the effect of $k$ in CIXB under unbalanced traffic. This figure shows that the throughput of CIXB under non-uniform traffic is slightly improved when a larger $k$ is provided. When $k = N = 32$, the throughput barely reaches 99 percent. These results indicate that to achieve 100 percent throughput under this traffic pattern, a very large $k$ is needed. To provide a higher throughput under unbalanced traffic, a weighted round-robin scheme [6, 10] can be used. The weight of an input or output can be assigned by considering the queue occupancy or cell ages.

According to previous results, the high performance of CIXB is also independent of the switch size [7]. This result differs from the one that has been observed in IB switches.

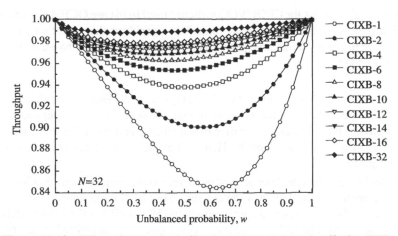

**Figure 11.10**   Effect of crosspoint buffer size under unbalanced traffic for CIXB-$k$.

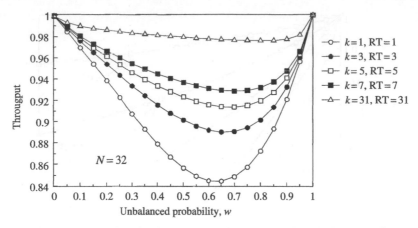

**Figure 11.11** Effect of buffer size and RT under unbalanced traffic in CIXB-$(k - RT)$.

### 11.2.3 Non-Negligible Round-Trip Times in CIXB-$k$

In the cases above, we assumed small round-trip times, such that (11.1) is satisfied with $k = 1$. Although the consideration of $k = 1$ is practical, the distance between the buffered crossbar and the port cards may be longer than one time slot. Therefore, $k$ needs to be increased to comply with (11.1).

In general, CIXB can be denoted as CIXB-$(k - RT)$, where $k \geq RT$, for non-negligible $RT$ values (i.e., $RT \geq 1$). We call this the general CIXB model. To observe the performance of a CIXB-$(k - RT)$ switch, we simulated a switch with different $k$ and $RT$ values for $k - RT = 0$ under unbalanced traffic. Figure 11.11 shows the throughput performance of CIXB-$(k - RT)$. The throughput performance is improved by larger $k$ values and slightly decreased by larger $RT$.

### 11.3 OCF_OCF: OLDEST CELL FIRST SCHEDULING

The scheduling algorithms for CIXB/VOQ switches used in [4] are OCF_OCF (oldest cell first), which selects a cell based on delay time. The algorithms that select a cell based on delay time have better cell delay time performance than the algorithms based on the simple ring arbitration [11].

*Output Scheduling.* The scheduler at output port $j$ selects the HOL cell with largest delay time. If more than one buffer is selected, then the scheduler at output port $j$ selects, from among these buffers, the buffer that queues a cell from the input port whose identifier is the smallest. Then the HOL cell at the selected buffer is transmitted to output port $j$.

*Input Scheduling.* The scheduler at input port $i$ selects the logical queue that has the cells and the smallest queue length of the crosspoint buffer. If more than one logical queue is selected, then the logical queue in which the HOL cell has the longest delay time will be selected. The HOL cell of the selected queue is transmitted to its crosspoint buffer.

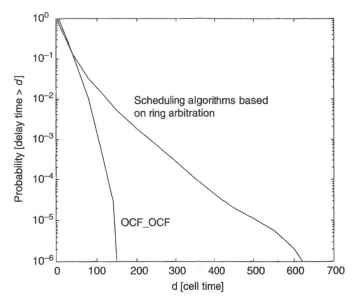

**Figure 11.12**    Probability of delay time in different scheduling algorithms.

To evaluate the performance of OCF_OCF, several simulations are performed. The traffic model used in simulations is assumed to be uniform, independent, identically distributed (i.i.d.).

The OCF_OCF is compared with a scheduling algorithm based on the ring arbitration. Figure 11.12 shows the probability of the delay time exceeding a certain time $d$. We assume that the offered load $\rho = 0.97$ and the buffer size at each crosspoint is one. It can be seen that the CIXB switch using the OCF_OCF has better cell delay time performance.

A CIXB switch using the OCF_OCF is compared with an input queued switch using the $i$-OCF algorithm [12] in terms of mean cell delay time in another simulation. With $i = 32$, it means the scheduling algorithm tries up to 32 times to find a conflict-free match between input and output ports. The buffer size at each input port in the CIXB switch and the input queued switch is infinite. The simulation results are shown in Figure 11.13, where CIXB_M1 and CIXB_M2 mean that the buffer size at each crosspoint in the CIXB switch is either one or two. A cell arriving at the CIXB switch must go through a buffer at an input port and a buffer at a crosspoint. The minimum cell delay time for the CIXB switch is two and that for the input-queued switch is one. From the figure, we can see that the mean cell delay time for the CIXB switch is larger than that for the input-queued switch at $\rho \leq 0.7$, and smaller when $\rho \geq 0.7$. This is because throughput of the CIXB switch is larger than that of the input-queued switch. It can also been seen that CIXB_M2 performs better than CIXB_M1.

A CIXB switch using OCF_OCF is also compared with a conventional crosspoint switch in terms of required buffer size. Here, it is assumed that the OCF algorithm is used as the scheduling algorithm for the crosspoint queued switch. Figure 11.14 shows the required buffer size per port for the CIXB switch and the conventional crosspoint queued switch with a cell loss ratio of under $10^{-9}$. It can been seen that the required buffer size for the CIXB switch is much less than that for the crosspoint queued switch, because the CIXB switch allows the input buffer to be shared by multiple output ports.

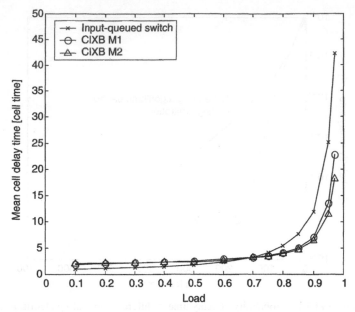

**Figure 11.13** Mean delay time: CIXB versus input-queued switch.

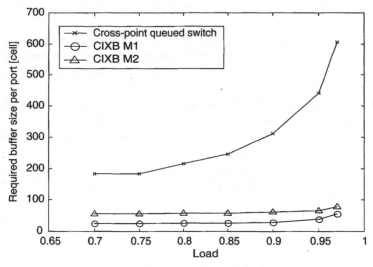

**Figure 11.14** Buffer size requirements.

## 11.4 LQF_RR: LONGEST QUEUE FIRST AND ROUND-ROBIN SCHEDULING IN CIXB-1

An $N \times N$ CIXB switch fabric with one buffer per crosspoint is cost-effective because the required memory speed is only twice the line rate for both the inputs and for the $N^2$ crosspoints. A scheduling algorithm in such a CIXB-1 switch, which uses longest queue first (LQF) scheduling for VOQs at the inputs and round-robin (RR) scheduling for the crosspoints, was presented by Javidi et al. [13]. Through fluid model techniques, it was shown that LQF_RR scheduling achieves 100 percent throughput for input traffic that satisfies the strong law of large numbers and has a load $\leq 1/N$ for any input/output pair.

Some definitions and notations are given below:

- $Z_{i,j}(n)$: The number of packets in $VOQ_{i,j}$ at the beginning of time slot $n$.
- $A_{i,j}(n)$: The cumulative number of packets that have arrived at $VOQ_{i,j}$ by time $n$.
- $D_{i,j}(n)$: The cumulative number of packets that have departed from $VOQ_{i,j}$ by time $n$.

Assume that the arrivals follow the strong law of large number; that is, with probability one,

$$\lim_{n \to \infty} \frac{A_{i,j}(n)}{n} = \lambda_{i,j} \qquad i, j = 1, \ldots, N, \tag{11.2}$$

where $\lambda_{i,j}$ is the arrival rate at $VOQ_{i,j}$.

By definition, a pair of input and output service algorithms is called "rate stable" if with probability one,

$$\lim_{n \to \infty} \frac{D_{i,j}(n)}{n} = \lambda_{i,j} \qquad i, j = 1, \ldots, N. \tag{11.3}$$

In [14], it has been proved that a switch operating under rate-stable service achieves 100 percent throughput.

**Theorem 1.** If $\lambda_{i,j} < 1/N$, a CIXB switch using the LQF_RR algorithm is rate stable.

Theorem 1 is proved using a fluid model for the switch. Its proof can be found by referring to the work of Javidi et al. [13].

## 11.5  MCBF: MOST CRITICAL BUFFER FIRST SCHEDULING

Up until to now, we have introduced several scheduling schemes for the CIXB switch, such as round-robin (RR_RR), OCF_OCF, and LQF_RR. For the input scheduling schemes such as LQF and OCF, the arbiter decisions are very time consuming due to the need for comparing a large number of values (i.e., queue length or cell age). In an attempt to reduce the arbitration complexity while keeping good performance, a scheduling scheme based on the shortest internal buffer first (SBF) at the input side and based on the longest internal buffer first (LBF) at the output side was proposed [15]. Most critical buffer first (MCBF) does not use any input state information, such as VOQ occupancies or VOQ head-of-line cells waiting time. The scheduling is based only on the internal buffers information.

Some notations are defined here to explain the MCBF scheduling.

- *Eligible VOQ (EVOQ)*: A $VOQ_{i,j}$ is said to be eligible (denoted $EVOQ_{i,j}$) for being scheduled in the input scheduling process if it is not empty and the internal buffer $XPB_{i,j}$ is not full.

- *LXPB$_i$* (the line of crosspoint buffers): The set of all the internal buffers *XPB$_{i,j}$* that correspond to the same input *i*.
- *NLB$_i$*: The number of cells held in *LXPB$_i$*.
- *CXPB$_j$* (the column of the crosspoint buffers): The set of internal buffers *XPB$_{i,j}$* that correspond to the same output *j*.
- *NCB$_j$*: The number of cells held in *CXPB$_j$*.

The operation of the MCBF is as follows:

*Input-Scheduling (SBF)*. For each input *i*: starting from the highest priority pointer's location, select the first EVOQ corresponding to min$_j${*NCB$_j$*} and send its HOL cell to the internal buffer *XPB$_{i,j}$*. Move the highest priority pointer to the location $j + 1$ (mod *N*).

*Output-Scheduling (LBF)*. For each output *j*: starting from the highest priority pointer's location, select the first *XPB$_{i,j}$* corresponding to max$_i${*NLB$_i$*} and send its HOL cell to the output. Move the highest priority pointer to the location $i + 1$ (mod *N*).

The MCBF scheme has two properties different from LQF and OCF schemes:

1. MCBF is almost stateless. It does its arbitration without any state information of the input VOQs.
2. MCBF maintains a load balancing among the internal buffers, that is, it keeps the outputs as busy as possible (work conserving).

The performance evaluation of MCBF, LQF_RR, and OCF_OCF were compared through two traffic models, bursty uniform and Bernoulli non-uniform, in a 32 × 32 CIXB switch.

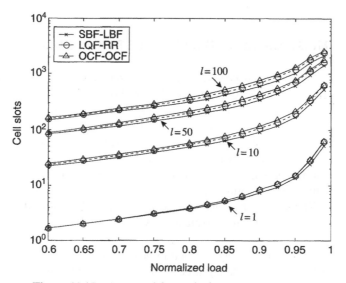

**Figure 11.15**   Average delay under bursty uniform traffic.

Figure 11.15 shows the average delay performance under bursty uniform traffic with average burst length ($l$) of 1, 10, 50, and 100 cells, respectively. Under heavy load, SBF_LBF has the smallest delay amongst all the schemes. At 99 percent load and burst length of 10, SBF_LBF has an average delay less than 80 percent that of LQF_RR. With an average burst length of 50 and at 99 percent load SBF_LBF has an average delay of 2523, while LQF_RR has 3014 and OCF_OCF has 3311.

## REFERENCES

[1] S.-T. Chuang, S. Iyer, and N. Mckeown, "Practical algorithm for performance guarantees in buffered crossbars," in *Proc. IEEE INFOCOM'05*, Miami, Florida, vol. 2, pp. 981–991 (Mar. 2005).

[2] G. Passas and M. Katevenis, "Packet mode scheduling in buffered crossbar (CICQ) switches," in *Proc. High Performance Switching and Routing (HPSR) 2006*, Poznan, Poland (June 2006).

[3] Y. Doi and N. Yamanaka, "A high-speed ATM switch with input and cross-point buffers," *IEICE Transactions on Communications*, vol. E76-B, no. 3, pp. 310–314 (Mar. 1993).

[4] M. Nabeshima, "Performance evaluation of a combined input- and crosspoint-queued switch," *IEICE Transactions on Communications*, vol. E83-B, no. 3, pp. 737–741 (Mar. 2000).

[5] Rojas-Cessa, E. Oki, and H. J. Chao, "CIXOB-$k$: Combined input-crosspoint-output buffered packet switch," in *Proc. IEEE GLOBECOM'01*, San Antonio, Texas, pp. 2654–2660 (Nov. 2001).

[6] N. McKeown, "$i$SLIP: a scheduling algorithm for input-queued switches," *IEEE/ACM Transactions on Networking*, vol. 7, no. 2, pp. 188–201 (Apr. 1999).

[7] R. Rojas-Cessa, E. Oki, Z. Jing, and H. J. Chao, "CIXB-1: combined input-one-cell-crosspoint buffered switch," in *Proc. IEEE Workshop on High Performance Switching and Routing*, Dallas, Texas, pp. 324–329 (May 2001).

[8] R. Schoenen, G. Post, and G. Sander, "Weighted arbitration algorithms with priorities for input-queued switches with 100% throughput," in *Proc. Broadband Switching Symposium'99*, Kingston, Canada, 1999. [Online]. Available at: http://www.schoenen-service.de/assets/papers/Schoenen99bssw.pdf

[9] C. S. Chang, D. S. Lee, and Y. S. Jou, "Load balanced Birkhoff–von Neumann switches," in *Proc. IEEE HPSR 2001*, Dallas, Texas, pp. 276–280 (May 2001).

[10] B. Li, M. Hamdi, and X.-R. Cao, "An efficient scheduling algorithm for input-queuing ATM switches," in *Proc. IEEE Broadband Switching Systems'97*, Taiwan, pp. 148–154 (Dec. 1997).

[11] E. Oki and N. Yamanaka, "A high-speed ATM switch based on scalable distributed arbitration," *IEICE Transactions Communications*, vol. E80-B, no. 9, pp. 1372–1376 (Sept. 1997).

[12] N. McKeown, "Scheduling algorithms for input-queued cell switches," Ph.D. Thesis, UC Berkeley, May 1995.

[13] T. Javidi, R. Magill, and T. Hrabik, "A high throughput scheduling algorithm for a buffered crossbar switch fabric," in *Proc. IEEE International Conference on Communications*, Helsinki, Finland, vol. 5, pp. 1586–1591 (June 2001).

[14] J. G. Dai and B. Prabhakar, "The throughput of data switches with and without speedup," in *Proc. IEEE INFOCOM'00*, Tel Aviv, Israel, pp. 556–564 (Mar. 2000).

[15] L. Mhamdi and M. Hamdi, "MCBF: a high-performance scheduling algorithm for buffered crossbar switches," *IEEE Communications Letters*, vol. 7, no. 9, pp. 451–553 (Sept. 2003).

# CHAPTER 12

# CLOS-NETWORK SWITCHES

In this chapter we consider an approach to building modular switches. The architecture is based on the Clos network (see Figure 12.1). Switch modules are arranged in three stages, and every module is interconnected with every other module in the adjacent stage via a unique link. Here, the three stages are referred to as the input stage, middle stage, and output stage. The modules in those stages are accordingly called input modules (IMs), central modules (CMs), and output modules (OMs). Each module is assumed to be non-blocking and could be, for example, the crossbar switches. Inputs are partitioned into groups of the same size, and the inputs in the same group are connected to an input module. Let $n$ be the number of inputs per group, and $k$ the number of input modules. The total number of inputs is given by $N = n \times k$. On the other hand, a mirror structure can be found on the output side. In the middle, there are $m$ $k \times k$ central modules, as each link on a central module is dedicated to either an IM or OM.

One could argue for only considering the two-stage interconnection network, in which every pair of modules of adjacent stages are interconnected with a dedicated link. In this case, only one cell can be transmitted between any pair of modules because there is just one path between them, causing a very high blocking probability. In a Clos network, however, two cells from an input module can take distinct paths via different central modules to get to the same output module. The central modules in the middle stage can be viewed as the routing resources shared by all input and output modules. One can expect that this will give a better tradeoff between the switch performance and complexity.

Because of this property, the Clos network was widely adopted in the traditional circuit-switched telephone network where a path is reserved in the network for each call. If a Clos network has enough central modules, a path can always be found for any call between an idle input and an idle output. Such a property is called nonblocking. Basically, there are two senses of nonblocking, strictly and rearrangeably. In a strictly nonblocking Clos network,

*High Performance Switches and Routers*, by H. Jonathan Chao and Bin Liu
Copyright © 2007 John Wiley & Sons, Inc.

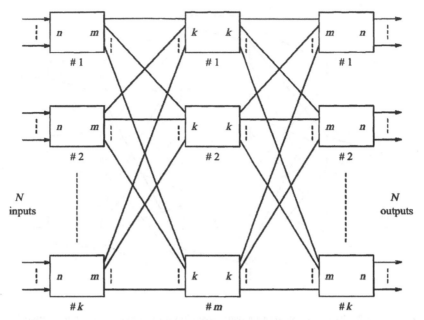

**Figure 12.1** A Clos-network switch.

every newly arriving call will find a path across the network without affecting the existing calls. With rearrangeably nonblocking, we may have to arrange paths for some existing calls in order to accommodate a new arrival.

This chapter will now focus on how the Clos network is used in packet switching. The rest of the chapter is organized as follows: first, we describe the basic routing properties in a Clos network and formulate the routing as a scheduling problem. Second, we discuss several scheduling schemes for the Clos network switch and classify them into three categories. First category is sequential optimal matching, which gives the maximum input–output matching at every timeslot at the cost of high complexity. In this category we also discuss two algorithms: The looping algorithm and $m$-matching algorithm [1]. The second category is semi-parallel matching, which provides the balance between performance and complexity, and we illustrate one algorithm, namely, the Euler partition algorithm [2]. The third category is parallel heuristic matching, which may not give the best matching but enjoys low complexity. We describe six algorithms: Karol's algorithm [3], the frame-base matching algorithm for the Clos network (f-MAC) [4], the concurrent matching algorithm for the Clos network (c-MAC) [4], the dual-level matching algorithm for the Clos network (d-MAC) [4], the random dispatching algorithm (Atlanta switch) [3], and the concurrent round-robin dispatching (CRRD) algorithm [3, 5].

## 12.1 ROUTING PROPERTY OF CLOS NETWORK SWITCHES

For the $N \times N$ switch shown in Figure 12.1, both the inputs and the outputs are divided into $k$ modules with $n$ lines each. The dimensions of the input and output modules are $n \times m$ and $m \times n$, respectively, and there are $m$ middle-stage modules, each of size $k \times k$.

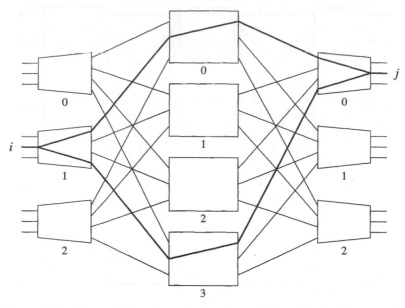

**Figure 12.2**   Two possible routing paths from input $i$ to input $j$ in the Clos network.

As illustrated in Figure 12.2, the routing constraints of the Clos network are briefly stated as follows:

1. Any central module can only be assigned to one input of each input module, and one output of each output module.
2. Input $i$ and output $j$ can be connected through any central module.
3. The number of alternate paths between input $i$ and output $j$ is equal to the number of central modules.

The routing problem is how to direct the input cells to the respective output modules without path conflicts. For every time slot, the traffic between input modules and output modules can be written as

$$T = \begin{pmatrix} t_{1,1} & t_{1,2} & \cdots & t_{1,k} \\ t_{2,1} & t_{2,2} & \cdots & t_{2,k} \\ \cdots & \cdots & \cdots & \cdots \\ t_{k,1} & t_{k,2} & \cdots & t_{k,k} \end{pmatrix}$$

where $t_{i,j}$ represents the number of cells arriving at the $i$th input module destined for the $j$th output module. The row sum is the total number of cells arriving at each input module, while the column sum is the number of cells destined for the output module, and they are denoted as

$$R_i = \sum_{j=1}^{k} t_{ij} \leq n \leq m, \qquad i = 1, 2, \ldots, k, \tag{12.1}$$

$$S_j = \sum_{i=1}^{k} t_{ij} \leq n, \qquad j = 1, 2, \ldots, k. \tag{12.2}$$

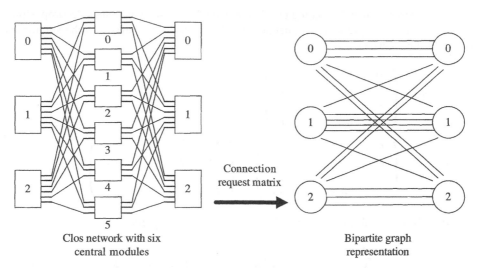

**Figure 12.3**    Bipartite graph representation of the Clos network routing problem.

The routing problem in the Clos network can be formulated as an edge coloring problem in a bipartite graph. With reference to Figure 12.3, a Clos network switch with six center modules and a given connection matrix can be transformed into a bipartite graph representation, where the numbers of lines connecting an input module and an output module is the number of requesting connections.

With the bipartite graph shown in Figure 12.3, the routing problem in the Clos network is transformed into an edge coloring problem in the graph. The aim is to use the minimum number of colors to color those lines in the bipartite graph such that there are no two colored lines the same for each module. Figure 12.4 is the solution of the edge coloring problem for the bipartite graph shown in Figure 12.3. Note that the lines with the same color indicate the routing in the Clos network via the same center module.

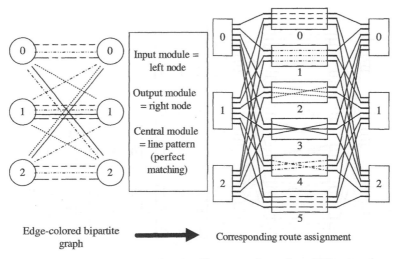

**Figure 12.4**    Edge coloring approach for the Clos network routing. Different edge colors are represented by different edge patterns.

Another way to solve the routing problem in the Clos network is matrix decomposition. This mathematical expression is to decompose the connection matrix into the summation of several sub-matrices

$$
T = \begin{pmatrix}
t_{1,1} & t_{1,2} & \cdots & t_{1,k} \\
t_{2,1} & t_{2,2} & \cdots & t_{2,k} \\
\cdots & \cdots & \cdots & \cdots \\
t_{k,1} & t_{k,2} & \cdots & t_{k,k}
\end{pmatrix}
$$

$$
= \begin{pmatrix}
a_{1,1} & a_{1,2} & \cdots & a_{1,k} \\
a_{2,1} & a_{2,2} & \cdots & a_{2,k} \\
\cdots & \cdots & \cdots & \cdots \\
a_{k,1} & a_{k,2} & \cdots & a_{k,k}
\end{pmatrix} + \begin{pmatrix}
b_{1,1} & b_{1,2} & \cdots & b_{1,k} \\
b_{2,1} & b_{2,2} & \cdots & b_{2,k} \\
\cdots & \cdots & \cdots & \cdots \\
b_{k,1} & b_{k,2} & \cdots & b_{k,k}
\end{pmatrix} + \cdots
$$

And each of the sub-matrices must have the following property:

$$
\sum_{j=1}^{k} a_{i,j} \leq 1, \qquad \sum_{j=1}^{k} b_{i,j} \leq 1, \qquad i = 1, 2, \ldots, k. \tag{12.3}
$$

and

$$
\sum_{i=1}^{k} a_{i,j} \leq 1, \qquad \sum_{i=1}^{k} b_{i,j} \leq 1, \qquad j = 1, 2, \ldots, k. \tag{12.4}
$$

Figure 12.5 illustrates the matrix decomposition approach in solving the routing problem in the Clos network for the same example given earlier in Figure 12.3.

In summary, the routing problem in Clos network can be interpreted as three equivalent questions:

1. How to assign central routes in a Clos network with $m$ central modules in order to accommodate a set of connection requests?

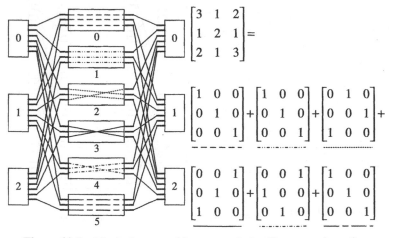

**Figure 12.5**  Matrix decomposition approach for Clos network routing.

2. How to edge-color a given bipartite graph with maximum degree $m$?

3. How to decompose a matrix with row/column sum $\leq m$ into $m$ matrices with row/column sum $\leq 1$?

In the following, we will discuss several well-known scheduling schemes for the Clos network in detail. They can be divided into three categories: (1) Sequential optimal matching; (2) Semi-parallel matching; (3) Parallel heuristic matching.

## 12.2  LOOPING ALGORITHM

Looping algorithm is a simple sequential optimal matching algorithm for the Clos network. The advantage of this algorithm is its simplicity and low complexity $O(N)$. Its disadvantage is that it only works for the $m = 2$ Clos network. In other words, the looping algorithm is only suitable for the Clos network with two center modules and input/output modules with a size of $2 \times 2$.

For a given input traffic matrix, the looping algorithm works as follows:

Step 1.  Start the looping algorithm from any arbitrary input port.

Step 2.  Find the desired output module that contains the destined output port via one of the center modules.

Step 3.  Loop back from the same output module in step 2, but with the alternative output port, and trace to the corresponding input port via the alternative center module from step 2.

Step 4.  Loop back from the same input module found in step 3, but with the alternative input port. Continue with steps 2–4.

Step 5.  If a close loop or an idle input/output is found, restart the looping algorithm from step 1.

An example to better illustrate the looping algorithm is as follows. Assume a Clos network switch with a total size of $8 \times 8$, consisting of four input modules and four output modules, each of which has a size of $2 \times 2$, and two center modules, each of which has a size of $4 \times 4$. For a given set of input/output connection requests, the looping algorithm

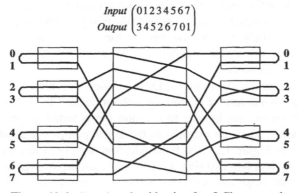

**Figure 12.6**    Looping algorithm in a $8 \times 8$ Clos network.

gives two sets of matching in Figure 12.6, one of them is maximum matching, while the other is not necessary.

We can trace a few steps of this example. Let us start with input 0: it desires output 3 and reaches output 3 via center module 0. Next we loop back from output 2 to input 3 via center module 1. Then input 2 takes its turn and finds output 5 via center module 0. Finally, we loop back from output 4 to input 1 via center module 1. Now we have a closed loop. The looping algorithm may restart with any of the remaining unassigned input ports. Eventually, we will complete all possible matches between the inputs and outputs.

Notice that, in the looping algorithm, each input–output pair takes turns to assign routes via the center module. Therefore, the total complexity of this algorithm is $O(N)$.

## 12.3   *m*-MATCHING ALGORITHM

The $m$-matching is another sequential optimal matching algorithm for the Clos network. The $m$-matching algorithm uses the bipartite graph as an approach to find perfect matching (only if the bipartite graph is regular). Thus, it does not have the switch size constraint.

As mentioned in the earlier section, the edge coloring problem tries to use the minimum amount of colors to color the bipartite graph such that there are no two identical colors from the same edge. The $m$-matching algorithm solves this edge coloring problem by assigning one color at a time. It assigns one color to the matching and removes the corresponding edges from the bipartite graph. Then it continues this process till all the edges are colored. Each color may take $O(N)$ steps to find a perfect matching from the bipartite graph. Thus with $m$ different colors, the $m$-matching algorithm has a time complexity of $O(mN)$.

The drawback of this matching algorithm is that it is incapable of handling irregular bipartite graphs. An irregular bipartite graph is the one that does not have an equal number of degrees from each node. In other words, each input module of the Clos network does not have an equal number of requests. In the case of the irregular bipartite graph, one may use maximum-size matching to transform an irregular bipartite graph into a regular one at the cost of increased complexity of $O(N^{2.5})$.

## 12.4   EULER PARTITION ALGORITHM

Both the looping algorithm and $m$-matching algorithm can give perfect matching for the Clos network. In other words, they always provide the best possible matching between input and output for a given traffic matrix. However, the former has a switch size constraint and the latter suffers high computation complexity. Next, we discuss a semi-parallel matching algorithm for the Clos network.

Similar to the $m$-matching algorithm, the Euler partition algorithm uses the edge coloring bipartite graph approach to resolve the routing problem in the Clos network. However, the Euler partition algorithm uses looping to partition the bipartite graph to achieve a fast edge coloring process. First, an example of the Euler partition algorithm. Refering to the bipartite graph in Figure 12.3, the Euler partition algorithm first uses two colors to divide the bipartite graph into two (Fig. 12.7). With reference to Figure 12.8, after Euler partition, one bipartite graph can be divided into two for further assignment. Note that the two partitioned bipartite graphs are independent of each other; thus the second iteration of the Euler partition algorithm can be done in a parallel manner. One thing to notice is that

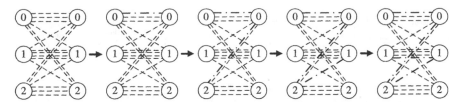

**Figure 12.7**   Euler partition algorithm, step 1.

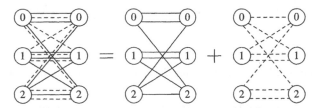

**Figure 12.8**   Euler partition algorithm, step 2.

the Euler partition algorithm is only efficient for an even degree bipartite graph. In the case of odd degree edges appearing in the bipartite graph, perfect matching to reduce the degree by 1 is used.

In summary, the Euler partition algorithm is a multi-iteration looping algorithm. Each iteration of the Euler partition algorithm consists of (1) in the case of an even degree bipartite graph, performing a Euler split to partition the graph into two; (2) in the case of an odd degree bipartite graph, performing perfect matching to reduce the degree by 1 and then performing Euler partition. As a result, the total complexity of the Euler partition algorithm is $O(N \log(m))$.

The Euler partition algorithm achieves the balance between performance and complexity. However, the Euler partition algorithm's complexity linearly increases with the switch size $N$. With an increase of link speed and switch size, it is neither scalable nor practical in today's high-speed networks. From here on, we will discuss six parallel heuristic algorithms for the Clos network. They might not achieve the perfect matching from timeslot to timeslot but they are ultrascalable and practical to implement in modern high-speed switches.

## 12.5   KAROL'S ALGORITHM

Karol's matching algorithm can assign central routes for cells in a heuristic manner and yet still achieve a good assignment result. Referring to Figure 12.1, let $i$ be the index of input modules (IMs) where $i \in 0, 1, 2, 3, \ldots, k - 1$. Let $j$ be the index of output modules (OMs) where $j \in 0, 1, 2, 3, \ldots, k - 1$ ($k$ is the number of center modules in the Clos network). In Karol's matching algorithm, each timeslot is divided into $k$ mini-slots. For $0 \leq t \leq k - 1$, in mini-slot $t$, IM $i$ communicate only with OM $j$ where $j = [(t + i) \text{ modulo } k]$. The purpose of this mini-slot matching is to attempt to find central-module routes for those cells from IM $i$ to OM $j$. After $k$ mini-slots, each IM–OM pair is matched up once and the entire central-module assignment is done in a distributed manner. Because of the unique switch architecture of the Clos-network switch, within each mini-slot central-module routes are independent among

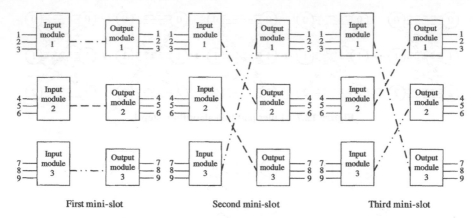

First mini-slot                     Second mini-slot                    Third mini-slot

**Figure 12.9**   Karol's matching algorithm in 3-stage Clos networks.

all IM–OM pairs, which enables each IM–OM pair to assign central-module routes freely without causing internal blocking. In order to achieve fairness among all traffic loads, the matching sequence of Karol's matching algorithm can be modified and done in a round robin fashion in such a way that for each set of traffic requests, the order of modules matching can be shifted among all matching pairs. For example, suppose that in the current timeslot, IM $i$ starts its mini-slot matching procedure from OM $j$. Then in the next timeslot, it may start from OM $[(j + 1)$ modulo $k]$, and so on and so forth. As a result, the complexity of Karol's algorithm is only $O(k)$.

An example of Karol's matching algorithm in the Clos network is given as follows. Let us consider a $9 \times 9$ Clos network switch, which has three IMs, three CMs, and three OMs. Therefore, it takes three mini-slots for all IMs to finish performing Karol's matching with all OMs. Figure 12.9 shows Karol's matching algorithm for these three mini-slots.

Further more, Karol's algorithm uses a vector for each input module and each output module to record the availability of the central modules. With reference to Figure 12.10, those vectors are matched up in pairs, each of which has one vector for an input module (e.g., $A_i$) and the other for an output module (e.g., $B_j$). Each IM/OM vector is composed of $m$ bits, and each bit corresponds to a CM. A "0" means that the link to the CM is available and "1" represents unavailable. For those pairs of modules that have a cell to dispatch between them, the two vectors will be compared to locate a "0," that is, an available link to a CM, if any.

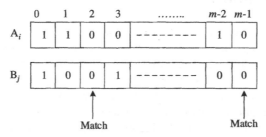

**Figure 12.10**   Vector representation of center route availability in Karol's algorithm. $A_i$ is a $m$-bit vector of $IM_i$; each bit indicates the availability of the link to the CM. $B_i$ is also a $m$-bit vector of $OM_j$; each bit indicates the availability of the link from the CM.

In the next three sections, a new class of matching algorithms, called MAC, for resolving scheduling problems in 3-stage Clos-network switches are presented. To relax the strict arbitration time constraint, MAC operates based on a frame of $r$ cells ($r > 1$).

## 12.6 FRAME-BASED MATCHING ALGORITHM FOR CLOS NETWORK (f-MAC)

Figure 12.11 shows the structure of a MAC packet switch, which consists of a packet scheduler (PS) and a 3-stage Clos-network switch fabric. The PS consists of $k$ scheduling input modules (SIMs) and $k$ scheduling output modules (SOMs), each of which corresponds to an input switch module (or output switch module) in the 3-stage Clos-network switch. A crosspoint switch with a reconfigured pattern is used to interconnect these SIMs and SOMs.

All incoming packets are first terminated at ingress line cards (ILCs), where they are segmented into cells (fixed length data units) and stored in a memory. The packet headers are extracted for IP address lookup, classification, and other functions such as traffic shaping/policing. Packets destined for the same output port are stored in the same virtual output queues (VOQs) in the ILCs. Multiple cells (e.g., $r$ cells) in the same VOQ form a frame that is sent to an output port once a grant signal is given by the PS. Let us define a cell time slot to be $T$, and the frame period $F = r \times T$, where $r$ is the frame size in number of cells. The ILCs send cell-arrival information to the PS. The PS then resolves contention, finds routing paths in the center stage, and sends grant signals to the ILCs in each extended frame period $F$. A large buffer with a re-assembly queue (RAQ) structure is used in the egress line card (ELC) to store the frames from the switch fabric and to re-assemble them into packets.

The first MAC algorithm to be discussed is the frame-based matching algorithm for Clos-network switch (f-MAC). The f-MAC includes two phases to solve the switching problems. It first resolves the contention of the frames from different input ports that are

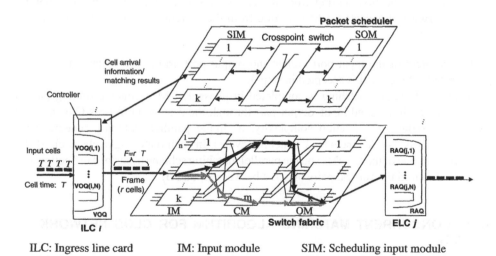

ILC: Ingress line card     IM: Input module        SIM: Scheduling input module
ELC: Egress line card      CM: Central module       SOM: Scheduling output module
VOQ: Virtual output queue  OM: Output module        RAQ: Re-assembly queue

**Figure 12.11**    Structure of a 3-stage Clos-network switch and a packet scheduler.

destined for the same output port. It then determines a routing path through the center stage (i.e., chooses a CM) for each matched input–output pair. Since there can be multiple possible paths (determined by the number of CMs) for each matched I/O, choosing a CM to reduce internal blocking and thus increase the throughput further complicates the scheduling algorithm design.

In the first phase, f-MAC is an extension of the exhaustive dual round-robin matching (EDRRM) scheme [6], by including the frame concept. Most iterative matching schemes, such as *i*SLIP [7] and DRRM [3], suffer from the problem of throughput degradation under unbalanced traffic distribution. The EDRRM scheme improves throughput by maintaining the existing matched pairs between the inputs and outputs so that the number of unmatched inputs and outputs is drastically reduced (especially at high load), thus reducing the inefficiency caused by not being able to find matches among those unmatched inputs and outputs. The f-MAC also modifies EDRRM slightly to further improve the throughput. One of the major problems of the exhaustive matching is that it may cause starvation in some inputs. One way to overcome this problem is to set a timer for each head-of-line (HOL) frame. When the timer expires, the request from the "expired" frame is given the highest preference.

In phase 1, f-MAC finds I/O matching and consists of three steps:

Step 1: *Request.* Each unmatched input sends a request to every output port arbiter for which it has a queued cell in the corresponding VOQ. The request is set at high priority if the queue length is above (or equal to) the threshold $r$; otherwise, the request is set at low priority. Each matched input only sends a high-priority request to its matched output.

Step 2: *Grant.* If each output port arbiter receives one or more high-priority requests, it chooses the first request to grant starting from the current position of the high-priority pointer. Otherwise, it grants the first low-priority request starting from the current position of the low-priority pointer.

Step 3: *Accept.* If each input port arbiter receives one or more high-priority grants, it accepts the first starting from the current position of the high-priority pointer. Otherwise, it accepts the first starting from the current position of the low-priority pointer.

The pointers of the input port arbiter and output port arbiter are updated to the next position only if the grant is accepted in step 3.

After input–output matching is completed in phase 1, f-MAC finds a routing path in phase 2 for each matched input–output pair through the 3-stage bufferless Clos-network switch. To reduce computation complexity, a simple parallel matching scheme [9] is adopted. That is, f-MAC includes $k$ matching cycles. In each matching cycle, each SIM is matched with one of the $k$ SOMs and the parallel matching scheme described in Section 12.5 is adopted to find the vertical pairs of zeros between $A_i$ and $B_j$.

## 12.7  CONCURRENT MATCHING ALGORITHM FOR CLOS NETWORK (c-MAC)

With the increase of switch sizes and port speeds, the hardware and interconnection complexity between input and output arbiters makes it very difficult to design the packet scheduler in a centralized way. This section presents a more scalable concurrent matching algorithm for Clos-network switches, called c-MAC. It is highly distributed such that the input–output matching and routing-path finding are concurrently performed by scheduling modules.

Figure 12.12 shows the architecture of the packet scheduler. It consists of $k$ SIMs and $k$ SOMs, each of which corresponds to an input switch module (or output switch module) in the 3-stage Clos-network switch (see Fig. 12.11). There are $n$ IPAs in each SIM. Each SIM consists of $n$ virtual output port arbiters (VOPAs), each of which corresponds to an output port in the corresponding OM. Each SIM has an input module arbiter (IMA), and each SOM has an output module arbiter (OMA). A crosspoint switch with a predetermined reconfigured pattern is used to interconnect these SIMs and SOMs. As shown in Figure 12.11, each ILC has $N$ VOQs, each corresponding to an ELC. A counter $C(i,j)$ in the PS is used to record the number of cells in the corresponding $VOQ(i,j)$.

The c-MAC scheme divides one frame period $f$ into $k$ matching cycles as shown in Figure 12.13. In each matching cycle, each SIM is matched with one of the $k$ SOMs. During each cycle, c-MAC includes two phases to find the input–output matches and routing paths, respectively.

At the beginning of each matching cycle, each SOM passes $m + 2n$ bits to the corresponding SIM, where the $m$ bits correspond to the state of $m$ input links of the corresponding OM; the $2n$ bits correspond to the state of $n$ output ports of the corresponding OM. There are four possible states for each output port: "00" when the output port is unmatched; "01" when the output port is matched with low priority in the last frame period; "10" when the output port is matched with high priority in the last frame period; "11" when the output port is matched in this frame period.

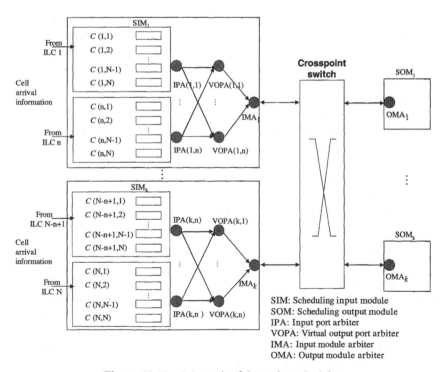

**Figure 12.12**   Schematic of the packet scheduler.

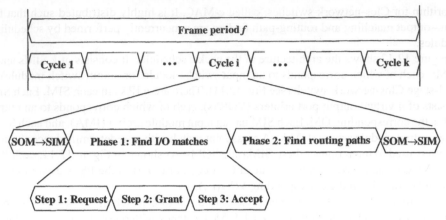

**Figure 12.13** Timing schematic of the c-MAC scheme.

It is assumed that the matching sequence between SIMs and SOMs is predetermined. For instance, in the first cycle, $SIM_i$ is matched with $SOM_j$, where $1 \leq i \leq k$ and $1 \leq j \leq k$. In the second cycle, $SIM_i$ is matched with $SOM_{(j \bmod k)+1}$. The procedure is repeated $k$ times. To achieve matching uniformity for all the SIMs, the beginning matching sequence between SIMs and SOMs is skewed one position at the beginning of each frame period.

Phase 1 finds I/O matching and consists of three steps as described below:

Step 1: *Request.* Each matched input port arbiter (IPA) only sends a high-priority request to its matched VOPA; each unmatched IPA (including the currently matched IPA but whose matched VOQ's queue length is less than a threshold $r$) sends a 2-bit request to every VOPA for which it has queued cells in the corresponding VOQ. ("00" means no request; "01" means low-priority request because queue length is less than $r$; "10" means high-priority request because queue length is larger than $r$; "11" means the highest priority because the waiting time of the HOL frame is larger than a threshold, $T_w$.) Note that, using the waiting time mechanism for the HOL frames prevents the starvation problem.

Step 2: *Grant.* Only the "available" VOPA performs the grant operation. A VOPA is defined to be "available," if its corresponding output port is
    (a) Unmatched; or
    (b) Matched in the last frame period with low priority (the VOPA receives at least one high-priority request at this frame period); or
    (c) VOPA is matched in the last frame period with high priority, but it receives the request from the matched IPA and its priority is becoming low-priority in this frame period.
If a VOPA is "available" and receives one or more high-priority requests, it grants the one that appears next in a fixed round-robin schedule starting from the current position of the high-priority pointer. If there are no high-priority requests, the output port arbiter grants one low-priority request in a fixed round-robin schedule starting from the current position of the low-priority pointer. The VOPA notifies each requesting IPA whether or not its request is granted.

Step 3: *Accept.* If the IPA receives one or more high-priority grants, it accepts the one that appears next in a fixed round-robin schedule starting from the current position of the high-priority pointer. If there are no high-priority grants, the input port arbiter accepts one low-priority request in a fixed round-robin schedule starting from the current position of the low-priority pointer. The input port arbiter notifies each VOPA whether or not its grant is accepted. Update of the pointers: The pointer of IPA and VOPA is updated to the chosen position only if the grant is accepted in Step 3 of phase 1 and also accepted in phase 2.

In phase 2, c-MAC adopts the parallel matching scheme [9] to find the routing paths for the matched I/O pairs as described in previous section.

## 12.8 DUAL-LEVEL MATCHING ALGORITHM FOR CLOS NETWORK (d-MAC)

In c-MAC, each pair of SIM–SOM needs to be matched once, regardless of the queuing status of the switch, yielding $k$ matching cycles for the arbitration in one frame period. This, however, results in a high time complexity that prevents the selection of a small frame size. To further reduce the scheduling time complexity and relax the arbitration time constraint, we have proposed a new dual-level matching algorithm for the Clos-network switch, call d-MAC, to determine the matching sequence between the SIMs and SOMs according to the queuing information of the switch.

The d-MAC scheme consists of two levels of matching, that is, module-level matching and port-level matching. The former is responsible for determining the SIM–SOM matching pattern according to the queuing status of the switch. The latter is responsible for determining the port-to-port matching and finding the internal routing path for the matched input–output pair, as the task of matching cycle in c-MAC.

For the module-level matching, the switching patterns of a number of, say $F$, frames can be determined simultaneously. These $F$ frames constitute a super-frame. We use the example shown in Figure 12.14 to illustrate the module-level matching steps of d-MAC as follows. With reference to Figure 12.14a, a traffic matrix is used to represent the queuing status of the switch, in which entry $(i, j)$ denotes the number of buffered cells that desire to be transmitted from $IM_i$ to $OM_j$. According to this traffic matrix, a request matrix can be obtained. Note that the request matrix gives the number of requests that can be sent from each SIM to each SOM. Then a scheduling algorithm can be employed to do arbitration among these requests, and this process produces a super-frame matrix, in which each entry represents the matching opportunities between each SIM and each SOM in one super-frame. With reference to Figure 12.14b, the super-frame matrix is further decomposed into the module-level matching matrices, where a module-level matching matrix represents the matching pattern of SIMs and SOMs in one matching cycle as shown in Figure 12.14c. The module-level matching is done after the module-level matching matrices are determined. With each of these matrices, the port-level matching can thereafter perform the task of matching cycle, that is, port-to-port matching and route assignment, for the given SIM–SOM pairs.

The module-level matching and port-level matching assignment can be performed in a pipelined manner as shown in Figure 12.15. As described above, each super-frame is composed of $F$ frames, and each frame consists of $r$ cells. Suppose that the number of matching cycles in each frame is set to be $k'$, where $k' \leq k$, the transmission time of $r$

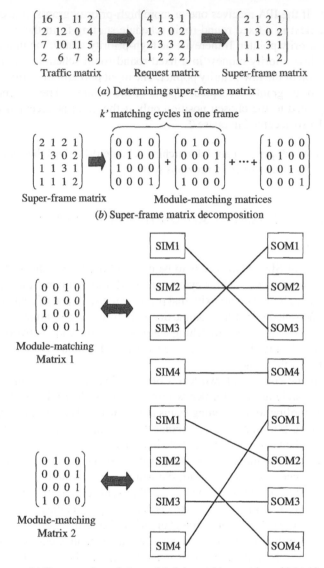

$$\begin{pmatrix} 16 & 1 & 11 & 2 \\ 2 & 12 & 0 & 4 \\ 7 & 10 & 11 & 5 \\ 2 & 6 & 7 & 8 \end{pmatrix} \implies \begin{pmatrix} 4 & 1 & 3 & 1 \\ 1 & 3 & 0 & 2 \\ 2 & 3 & 3 & 2 \\ 1 & 2 & 2 & 2 \end{pmatrix} \implies \begin{pmatrix} 2 & 1 & 2 & 1 \\ 1 & 3 & 0 & 2 \\ 1 & 1 & 3 & 1 \\ 1 & 1 & 1 & 2 \end{pmatrix}$$

  Traffic matrix        Request matrix    Super-frame matrix

(a) Determining super-frame matrix

$k'$ matching cycles in one frame

$$\begin{pmatrix} 2 & 1 & 2 & 1 \\ 1 & 3 & 0 & 2 \\ 1 & 1 & 3 & 1 \\ 1 & 1 & 1 & 2 \end{pmatrix} \implies \begin{pmatrix} 0 & 0 & 1 & 0 \\ 0 & 1 & 0 & 0 \\ 1 & 0 & 0 & 0 \\ 0 & 0 & 0 & 1 \end{pmatrix} + \begin{pmatrix} 0 & 1 & 0 & 0 \\ 0 & 0 & 0 & 1 \\ 0 & 0 & 0 & 1 \\ 1 & 0 & 0 & 0 \end{pmatrix} + \cdots + \begin{pmatrix} 1 & 0 & 0 & 0 \\ 0 & 1 & 0 & 0 \\ 0 & 0 & 1 & 0 \\ 0 & 0 & 0 & 1 \end{pmatrix}$$

  Super-frame matrix           Module-matching matrices

(b) Super-frame matrix decomposition

$$\begin{pmatrix} 0 & 0 & 1 & 0 \\ 0 & 1 & 0 & 0 \\ 1 & 0 & 0 & 0 \\ 0 & 0 & 0 & 1 \end{pmatrix}$$

Module-matching
Matrix 1

$$\begin{pmatrix} 0 & 1 & 0 & 0 \\ 0 & 0 & 0 & 1 \\ 0 & 0 & 0 & 1 \\ 1 & 0 & 0 & 0 \end{pmatrix}$$

Module-matching
Matrix 2

(c) Correspondence between Module-matching matrix and Matching
     pattern of SIMs/SOMs

**Figure 12.14**   Illustration of module-level matching of d-MAC ($k = 4$, $k' = 2$, $F = 3$).

cells must be greater than or equal to the arbitration time of $k'$ matching cycles. This is the constraint against selecting a small $r$. In each super-frame, there are a total of $F \times k'$ matching cycles. Thus $F$ sets of $k'$ module-matching matrices are to be determined for the next super-frame, while the scheduler is doing the port-level matching for the current super-frame.

The module-level matching algorithm is composed of two phases, that is, super-frame matching and super-frame decomposition.

The super-frame matching is to determine a super-frame matrix in accordance with the queuing status between the switch modules. Each entry in the super-frame matrix represents

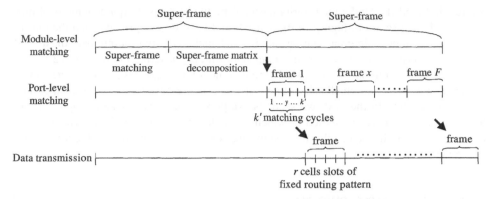

**Figure 12.15** Pipelined process of the d-MAC matching scheme.

the matching opportunities between each SIM and each SOM in one super-frame. A super-frame matrix is a $k \times k$ matrix with (i) no row/column sum greater than $F \times k'$, and (ii) no entry greater than $F$. To determine the super-frame matrix, the d-MAC scheme adopts an iterative request/grant/accept algorithm, modified from the $i$SLIP scheme.

The super-frame decomposition is to decompose the super-frame matrix into $F \times k'$ module-matching matrices. Each module-matching matrix records the matching status between the SIMs and SOMs in one matching cycle of the next super-frame. The matrix-decomposition problems can be solved by the edge-coloring algorithms. However, the optimal edge-coloring algorithms are not preferable here because of their high time complexity. Instead, we use a parallel matching heuristic [9] to decompose the super-frame matrix. This algorithm contains $k$ rounds. In each round, each SIM is communicating with one of $k$ SOMs. Each SIM/SOM maintains a two-tuple array that contains $F \times k'$ zero-one variables. Let $W_i(Z_j)$ be the array of $SIM_i(SOM_j)$

$$W_i(x, y) = \begin{cases} 0, & \text{if } SIM_i \text{ is unmatched in cycle } y \text{ of frame } x, \\ 1, & \text{if it has been matched in cycle } y \text{ of frame } x; \end{cases}$$

$$Z_i(x, y) = \begin{cases} 0, & \text{if } SIM_j \text{ is unmatched in cycle } y \text{ of frame } x, \\ 1, & \text{if it has been matched in cycle } y \text{ of frame } x; \end{cases}$$

where $1 \le x \le F$ and $1 \le y \le k'$.

When $SIM_i$ is communicating with $SOM_j$, the d-MAC scheme tries to find as many common zero entries in $W_i$ and $Z_j$ as possible to meet the number given by entry $(i, j)$ in the super-frame matrix. Note that no more than one "0" entry in the same frame can be assigned to the same SIM–SOM pair.

When the module-level matching is completed, the matching sequence between SIMs and SOMs (recorded in the module-matching matrices) is determined for the next super-frame. The port-level matching algorithm consists of $k'$ matching cycles in a frame. In each matching cycle, the port-level matching algorithm includes two steps: (i) the port-to-port matching assignment; (ii) the central module assignment.

To find the port-to-port matching for the corresponding pair of IM–OM, the d-MAC scheme adopts an iterative request/grant/accept algorithm, for example, $i$SLIP. To improve the matching efficiency, the d-MAC scheme also introduces high-priority and low-priority arbiters in the SIMs. Under the priority mechanism, the VOQs with queue lengths of more than $r$ cells will send out high-priority requests and have higher priority than the unfilled ones. To determine an internal routing path for each matched input–output pair, the d-MAC scheme adopts a heuristic parallel matching algorithm [6] described in Section 12.5.

In the above sections, we discussed various scheduling algorithms for bufferless Clos network switches in which all scheduling is done upon the packet entering the input modules of the switch. In the next two sections, we present other two scheduling algorithms for buffered Clos network switch in which the added buffer in the Clos network switch relaxes the scheduling so that the architecture and scheduling are more feasible for practical implementation.

## 12.9 THE ATLANTA SWITCH

The ATLANTA switch architecture has a three-stage multi-module memory/space/memory (MSM) arrangement. The MSM configuration uses buffers in the input and output stages, while the second stage is bufferless. A simple distributed self-routing algorithm is used to dispatch cells from the input to the output stage. Although cells are routed individually and multiple paths are provided from each input to each output, cell sequence is preserved due to its bufferless second stage. Selective backpressure is used from the output to the input buffers in the fabric, so the required buffers in the output stage are also relatively small.

The ATLANTA architecture provides support for multicast traffic. Cells belonging to a multicast virtual circuit are always replicated according to a minimum multicast tree, that is, they are replicated as far downstream as possible in the switch; this minimizes the amount of resources required to sustain the expansion in traffic volume internally to the switch due to multicasting. A single copy of a multicast cell is locally stored in each buffer, and replicated (if necessary) only when the cell is sent to the following stage in the switch or to its desired destinations.

In the following, we describe the operation of the MSM switch fabric with reference to the specific $40 \times 40$ configuration shown in Figure 12.16. The MSM configuration is based on three main principles:

- By using buffers in the first stage to store cells that cannot be routed to the output buffers at a given time, the number of paths necessary for nonblocking behavior can be greatly reduced.
- By using a bufferless center stage, cells belonging to the same virtual circuit can be routed individually without affecting cell sequence.
- By using selective backpressure from the output buffers to the input buffers, buffers can be located where they are most economical.

Under these design principles in the ATLANTA switch, the memory switch is used to implement the switching modules in the first and third stages, while crossbars are implemented in the second stage. Each module in the first and third stages must be connected to all crossbars. All interconnection lines between adjacent stages have the same rate as the input and output ports. To realize nonblocking in the MSM configuration, it is well known that its internal capacity must be higher than the aggregate capacity of the input ports. We call this "expansion." The required expansion is achieved by connecting fewer than eight ports to each input and output module. In the $40 \times 40$ configuration of Figure 12.16, five

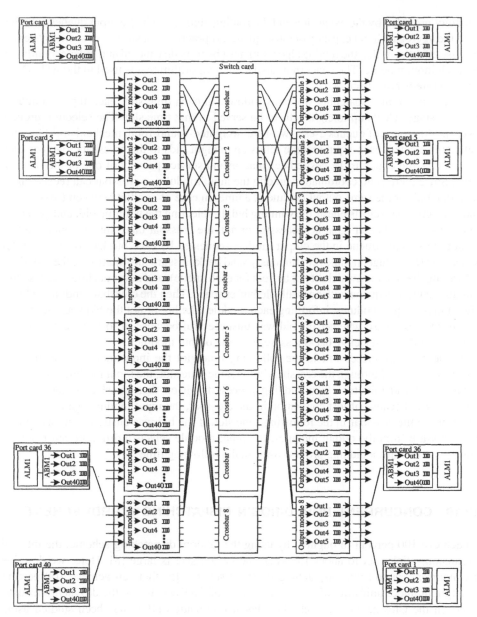

**Figure 12.16** Schematic configuration of a 40 × 40 multistage ATLANTA switch. (©1997 IEEE.)

ports are connected to each edge module for an expansion factor equal to 5 : 8. The expansion ratio is 1.6 (=8/5). Each module in the first stage maintains 40 groups of queues; each group corresponds to one of the output ports in the switch. Each module in the third stage manages a number of groups equal to the number of ports connected to that module (in this case five).

In order to minimize the required expansion, an efficient routing algorithm is necessary to route cells from the input to the output modules. Intuitively, the idea is that the fabric is nonblocking as long as the equivalent service capacity (i.e., the maximum switching capacity provided by the expansion and the routing algorithm) in the input queues is higher than the aggregate input capacity of those queues. A practical constraint for such a system to be cost-effective is that the routing algorithm must be fully distributed and independently run by each input module. The concurrent dispatching algorithm that is used in the ATLANTA architecture is now discussed.

The concurrent dispatching works as follows. In each time slot, each input module in the first stage selects up to eight cells to be served in that time slot. The selection process over the 40 groups of queues uses a two-level weighted-round-robin mechanism.[1] Once the cells are selected, each input module sends up to eight bids to the crossbars, one per each crossbar. A bid contains the desired destination and service priority of one of the selected cells. Since there is no coordination among the input modules, a crossbar can receive more than one bid for the same output module at a time. In case of conflict between two or more bids, the crossbar selects one as the winning bid. In selecting the winning bid, and generally in determining whether a bid is successful or not, the crossbar takes into account whether or not the specific queue in the output module requested by each bid has available buffer space (the third-stage modules continuously send backpressure information to the crossbars informing them of the availability of buffers for each queue), and never declares successful a bid that requests a queue with no available buffer space. Then the crossbar sends a feedback signal to the input modules, informing each module whether or not the bid was successful, and in the latter case whether the bid was unsuccessful because of lost contention in the crossbar or due to selective backpressure from the output modules.

If the bid was successful, in the following time slot the input module transmits the corresponding cell through the crossbar; in the same time slot, the input module also selects another cell and initiates a new bidding process for it on that crossbar. If the bid was unsuccessful because of lost contention in the crossbar, the input module again sends that same bid to the crossbar in the following time slot. If the bid was unsuccessful because of backpressure from the output modules, the input module selects a different cell from the buffer and initiates a bidding process for it in the following time slot.

## 12.10  CONCURRENT ROUND-ROBIN DISPATCHING (CRRD) SCHEME

To achieve 100 percent throughput by using the random dispatching scheme, the internal expansion ratio is set to about 1.6 when the switch size is large [8]. Here, we describe a concurrent round-robin dispatching (CRRD) scheme [5] that can achieve 100 percent throughput under uniform traffic. The basic idea of CRRD is to use the desynchronization effect in the Clos-network switch. The desynchronization effect has been studied using simple scheduling algorithms as $i$SLIP [7] and dual round-robin matching (DRRM) [6] in an input-queued crossbar switch. CRRD provides high switch throughput without expanding the internal bandwidth, while the implementation is simple because only simple round-robin arbiters are employed.

***Basic Architecture.*** Figure 12.17 shows the CRRD switch. The terminology used in this section is as follows:

---

[1] Cells in each group are further classified into several categories of different service priority.

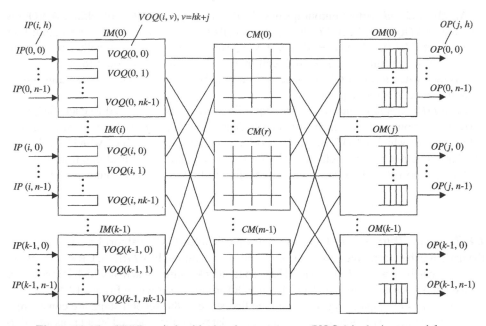

**Figure 12.17** CRRD switch with virtual output queues (VOQs) in the input modules.

| IM | Input module at the first stage. |
|---|---|
| CM | Central module at the second stage. |
| OM | Output module at the third stage. |
| $n$ | Number of input ports/output ports in each IM/OM, respectively. |
| $k$ | Number of IMs/OMs. |
| $m$ | Number of CMs. |
| $i$ | IM number, where $0 \le i \le k - 1$. |
| $j$ | OM number, where $0 \le j \le k - 1$. |
| $h$ | Input port (IP)/output port (OP) number in each IM/OM, respectively, where $0 \le h \le n - 1$. |
| $r$ | Central-module (CM) number, where $0 \le r \le m - 1$. |
| $IM(i)$ | $i$th IM. |
| $CM(r)$ | $r$th CM. |
| $OM(j)$ | $j$th OM. |
| $IP(i, h)$ | $h$th input port at $IM(i)$. |
| $OP(j, h)$ | $h$th output port at $OM(j)$. |
| $VOQ(i, v)$ | VOQ at $IM(i)$ that stores cells destined for $OP(j, h)$, where $v = hk + j$ and $0 \le v \le nk - 1$. |
| $G(i, j)$ | VOQ group at $IM(i)$ that consists of $n$ $VOQ(i, j, h)$s. |
| $L_i(i, r)$ | Output link at $IM(i)$ that is connected to $CM(r)$. |
| $L_c(r, j)$ | Output link at $CM(r)$ that is connected to $OM(j)$. |

The first stage consists of $k$ IMs, each of which has an $n \times m$ dimension. The second stage consists of $m$ bufferless CMs, each of which has a $k \times k$ dimension. The third stage consists of $k$ OMs, each of which has an $m \times n$ dimension.

An $IM(i)$ has $nk$ virtual output queues (VOQs) to eliminate HOL blocking. A VOQ is denoted as $VOQ(i, v)$. Each $VOQ(i, v)$ stores cells that go from $IM(i)$ to the output port $OP(j, h)$ at $OM(j)$, where $v = hk + j$. A VOQ can receive, at most, $n$ cells from $n$ input ports in each cell time slot. The HOL cell in each VOQ can be selected for transmission across the switch through $CM(r)$ in each time slot. This ensures that cells are transmitted from the same VOQ in sequence.

Each $IM(i)$ has $m$ output links. An output link $L_i(i, r)$, is connected to each $CM(r)$. A $CM(r)$ has $k$ output links, each of which is denoted as $L_c(r, j)$, and it is connected to $k$ OMs, each of which is $OM(j)$. An $OM(j)$ has $n$ output ports, each of which is $OP(j, h)$ and has an output buffer. Each output buffer receives at most $m$ cells at one time slot, and each output port at OM forwards one cell in a first-in-first-out (FIFO) manner to the output line.

**_CRRD Algorithm._** Figure 12.18 illustrates the detailed CRRD algorithm. To determine the matching between a request from $VOQ(i, v)$ and the output link $L_i(i, r)$, CRRD adopts an iterative matching within $IM(i)$. An IM has $m$ output link arbiters, each of which is associated with each output link, and each VOQ has a VOQ arbiter as shown in Figure 12.18.

Two phases of dispatching cells from the first stage to the second stage are considered. In phase 1, at most $m$ VOQs are selected as candidates and the selected VOQ is assigned to an IM output link. A request that is associated with this output link is sent from IM to CM. This matching between VOQs and output links is performed only within IM. In phase 2, each selected VOQ that is associated with each IM output link sends a request from IM to CM. CMs respond with the arbitration results to IMs so that the matching between IMs and CMs can be done.

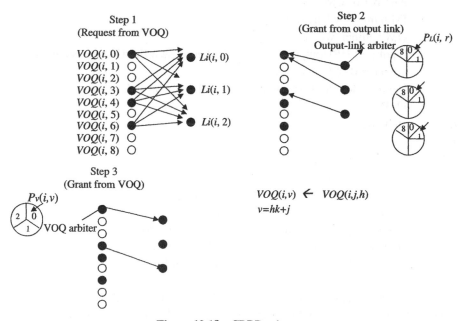

**Figure 12.18**    CRRD scheme.

*Phase 1. Matching within IM*

First iteration

Step 1: Each non-empty VOQ sends a request to every output-link arbiter, each of which is associated with $L_i(i, r)$, where $0 \leq i \leq k - 1$ and $0 \leq r \leq m - 1$.

Step 2: Each output link $L_i(i, r)$, where $0 \leq i \leq k - 1$ and $0 \leq r \leq m - 1$, independently searches a request among $nk$ non-empty VOQs. Each output-link arbiter associated with $L_i(i, r)$ has its own pointer $P_L(i, r)$, where $0 \leq i \leq k - 1$ and $0 \leq r \leq m - 1$. The output-link arbiter starts to search one non-empty VOQ request from the $P_L(i, r)$ in a round-robin fashion. Each output-link arbiter sends the grant to a requesting VOQ. Each VOQ has its own round-robin arbiter, and one pointer $P_v(i, v)$, where $0 \leq v \leq nk - 1$ to choose one output link. The VOQ arbiter starts to search one grant out of several grants that are given by the output-link arbiters from the position of $P_v(i, v)$.

Step 3: The VOQ that chooses one output link $L_i(i, r)$ by using the round-robin arbiter sends the grant to the selected output link. Note that the pointer $P_L(i, r)$ that is associated with each output link and $P_V(i, v)$ that is associated with each VOQ are updated to one position after the granted position, only if they are matched and the request is also granted by CM in phase 2.

*i*th iteration $(i > 1)$

Step 1: Each unmatched VOQ at the previous iterations sends a request to all the output-link arbiters again.

Steps 2 and 3: Follow the same procedure as in the first iteration.

*Phase 2. Matching between IM and CM*

Step 1: After phase 1 is completed, output link $L_i(i, r)$ sends the request to the CM. Then contention control in the CM is performed. Each $CM(r)$ has $k$ pointers $P_c(r, j)$, where $0 \leq r \leq m - 1$ and $0 \leq j \leq k - 1$, each of which corresponds to each $OM(j)$. The CM makes its arbitration using the pointer $P_c(r, j)$ in a round-robin fashion, and sends the grants to $L_i(i, r)$ of $IM(i)$. The pointer $P_c(r, j)$ is updated when the CM sends the grant to the IM.

Step 2: If the IM receives the grant from the CM, it sends a corresponding cell from that VOQ at the next time slot. Otherwise, the IM will not send a cell at the next time slot. The request that is not granted from the CM will be dispatched again at the next time slot because the pointers that are related to the ungranted requests are not updated.

The CRRD algorithm has to be completed within one time slot to provide the matching result every time slot.

Figure 12.18 shows an example of $n = m = k = 3$, where CRRD is operated at the first iteration in phase 1. At step 1, $VOQ(i, 0)$, $VOQ(i, 3)$, $VOQ(i, 4)$, and $VOQ(i, 6)$, which are non-empty VOQs, send requests to all the output-link arbiters. At step 2, output-link arbiters associated with $L_i(i, 0)$, $L_i(i, 1)$, and $L_i(i, 2)$, select $VOQ(i, 0)$, $VOQ(i, 0)$, and $VOQ(i, 3)$, respectively, according to their pointers' positions. At step 3, $VOQ(i, 0)$ receives two grants from both output-link arbiters of $L_i(i, 0)$ and $L_i(i, 1)$, selects $L_i(i, 0)$ by using its own VOQ arbiter, and sends a grant to the output-link arbiter of $L_i(i, 0)$. Since $VOQ(i, 3)$ receives one grant from an output-link arbiter $L_i(i, 2)$, it sends a grant to the output-link arbiter. With one

| | $T$ | 0 | 1 | 2 | 3 | 4 | 5 | 6 | 7 |
|---|---|---|---|---|---|---|---|---|---|
| $IM(0)$ | $P_V(0,0)$ | 0 | 1 | 0 | 0 | 0 | 1 | 0 | 0 |
| | $P_V(0,1)$ | 0 | 0 | 1 | 0 | 0 | 0 | 1 | 0 |
| | $P_V(0,2)$ | 0 | 0 | 0 | 1 | 0 | 0 | 0 | 1 |
| | $P_V(0,3)$ | 0 | 0 | 0 | 0 | 1 | 0 | 0 | 0 |
| $IM(1)$ | $P_V(1,0)$ | 0 | 0 | 1 | 0 | 0 | 0 | 1 | 0 |
| | $P_V(1,1)$ | 0 | 0 | 0 | 1 | 0 | 0 | 0 | 1 |
| | $P_V(1,2)$ | 0 | 0 | 0 | 0 | 1 | 0 | 0 | 0 |
| | $P_V(1,3)$ | 0 | 0 | 0 | 0 | 0 | 1 | 0 | 0 |
| $IM(0)$ | $P_L(0,0)$ | 0 | 1 | 2 | 3 | 0 | 1 | 2 | 3 |
| | $P_L(0,1)$ | 0 | 0 | 1 | 2 | 3 | 0 | 1 | 2 |
| $IM(1)$ | $P_L(1,0)$ | 0 | 0 | 1 | 2 | 3 | 0 | 1 | 2 |
| | $P_L(1,1)$ | 0 | 0 | 0 | 1 | 2 | 3 | 0 | 1 |
| $CM(0)$ | $P_c(0,0)$ | 0 | 1 | 0 | 1 | 0 | 1 | 0 | 1 |
| | $P_c(0,1)$ | 0 | 0 | 1 | 0 | 1 | 0 | 1 | 0 |
| $CM(1)$ | $P_c(1,0)$ | 0 | 0 | 1 | 0 | 1 | 0 | 1 | 0 |
| | $P_c(1,1)$ | 0 | 0 | 0 | 1 | 0 | 1 | 0 | 1 |

The request is granted by CM.

**Figure 12.19** Example of desynchronization effect in CRRD ($n = m = k = 2$).

iteration, $L_i(i, 1)$ cannot be matched with any non-empty VOQs. At the next iteration, the matching between unmatched non-empty VOQs and $L_i(i, 1)$ will be performed.

***Desynchronization Effect of CRRD.*** While the ATLANTA switch suffers contention at CM [8], CRRD decreases the contention at the CM because pointers $P_V(i, v)$, $P_L(i, r)$, and $P_c(r, j)$, are desynchronized.

By using a simple example, desynchronization of the pointers is demonstrated. Consider the example of $n = m = k = 2$ as shown in Figure 12.19. We can assume that every VOQ is always occupied with cells. Each VOQ sends a request to be selected as a candidate at every time slot. All the pointers are set to be $P_V(i, v) = 0$, $P_L(i, r) = 0$, and $P_c(r, j) = 0$ at the initial state. Only one iteration in phase 1 is considered here.

At time slot $T = 0$, since all the pointers are set to 0, only one VOQ in $IM(0)$, which is $VOQ(0, 0, 0)$, can send a cell with $L_i(0, 0)$ through $CM(0)$. The related pointers with the grant, $P_V(0, 0)$, $P_L(0, 0)$, and $P_c(0, 0)$, are updated from 0 to 1. At $T = 1$, three VOQs, which are $VOQ(0, 0, 0)$, $VOQ(0, 1, 0)$, and $VOQ(1, 0, 0)$, can send cells. The related pointers with the grants are updated. Four VOQs can send cells at $T = 2$. In this situation, 100 percent switch throughput is achieved. There is no contention at the CMs from $T = 2$ because the pointers are desynchronized.

## 12.11 THE PATH SWITCH

If we consider each input module and each output module as a node, a particular connection pattern in the middle stage of the Clos network can be represented by a regular bipartite multigraph with node degree $m$ as illustrated in Figure 12.20, where each central module corresponds to a group of $n$ edges, each connecting one distinct pair of input–output nodes (modules).

Suppose the routing algorithm of the Clos network is based on dynamic cell switching, and the amount of traffic from input module $I_i$ to output module $O_j$ is $\lambda_{ij}$ cells per time slot.

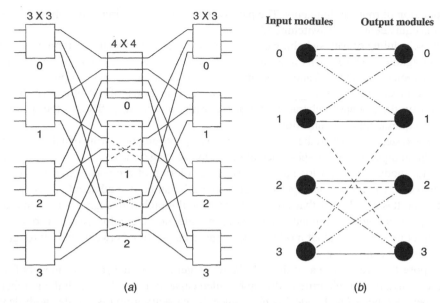

**Figure 12.20** Correspondence between the middle-stage route scheduling in a three-stage Clos network (*a*) and the edge-coloring of the equivalent regular bipartite multigraph (*b*). (©1997 IEEE.)

The connection pattern will change in every time slot according to arrival packets, and the routing will be calculated on a slot-by-slot basis. Let $e_{ij}(t)$ be the number of edges from $I_i$ to $O_j$ of the corresponding bipartite multigraph in time slot $t$. Then the capacity $C_{ij}$ of the virtual path between $I_i$ and $O_j$ must satisfy

$$C_{ij} = \lim_{T \to \infty} \frac{\sum_{t=1}^{T} e_{ij}(t)}{T} > \lambda_{ij}. \tag{12.5}$$

On the other hand, the routing of a circuit switched Clos network is fixed, and the connection pattern will be the same in every time slot. The capacity satisfies

$$C_{ij} = e_{ij}(t) = e_{ij} > \lambda_{ij}. \tag{12.6}$$

which implies that the peak bandwidth $C_{ij}$ is provided for each virtual circuit at call set-up time, and it does not take the statistical multiplexing into consideration at all. We conceived the idea of quasi-static routing, called path switching, using a finite number of different connection patterns in the middle stage repeatedly, as a compromise of the above two extreme schemes. For any given $\lambda_{ij}$, if $\sum_i \lambda_{ij} < n \le m$, and $\sum_j \lambda_{ij} < n \le m$, we can always find a finite number, $f$, of regular bipartite multigraphs such that

$$\frac{\sum_{t=1}^{f} e_{ij}(t)}{f} > \lambda_{ij}, \tag{12.7}$$

where $e_{ij}(t)$ is the number of edges from node $i$ to node $j$ in the $t$th bipartite multigraph. The capacity requirement (12.5) can be satisfied if the system provides connections repeatedly according to the coloring of these $f$ bipartite multigraphs, and these finite amounts of routing information can be stored in the local memory of each input module to avoid the slot-by-slot computation of route assignments. The path switching becomes circuit switching if $f = 1$, and it is equivalent to cell switching if $f \to \infty$.

The scheduling of path switching consists of two steps, the capacity assignment and the route assignment. The capacity assignment is to find the capacity $C_{ij} > \lambda_{ij}$ for each virtual path between input module $I_i$ and output module $O_j$; it can be carried out by optimizing some objective function subject to $\sum_i C_{ij} = \sum_j C_{ij} = m$. The choice of the objective function depends on the stochastic characteristic of the traffic on virtual paths and the quality of service requirements of connections.

The next step is to convert the capacity matrix, $[C_{ij}]$, into edge-coloring of a finite number, $f$, of regular bipartite multigraphs, each of them representing a particular connection pattern of central modules in the Clos network. An edge-coloring of a bipartite multigraph is to assign $m$ distinct colors to $m$ edges of each node such that no two adjacent edges have the same color. It is well-known that a regular bipartite multigraph with degree $m$ is $m$-colorable [10, 11]. Each color corresponds to a central module, and the color assigned to an edge from input module $i$ to output module $j$ represents a connection between them through the corresponding central module.

Suppose that we choose a sufficiently large integer $f$ such that $fC_{ij}$ are integers for all $i, j$, and form a regular bipartite multigraph, called capacity graph, in which the number of edges between node $i$ and node $j$ is $fC_{ij}$. Since the capacity graph is regular with degree $fm$, it can be edge-colored by $fm$ different colors [11]. Furthermore, it is easy to show that any edge-coloring of the the capacity graph with degree $fm$ is the superposition of the edge-coloring of $f$ regular bipartite multigraphs of degree $m$. Consider a particular color assignment $a \in \{0, 1, \ldots, fm - 1\}$ of an edge between input node $I_i$ and output node $O_j$ of the capacity graph. Let

$$a = r \cdot f + t, \qquad (12.8)$$

where $r \in \{0, 1, \ldots, m - 1\}$ and $t \in \{0, 1, \ldots, f - 1\}$ are the quotient and the remainder of dividing $a$ by $f$, respectively. The mapping $g(a) = (t, r)$ from the set $\{0, 1, \ldots, fm - 1\} \to \{0, 1, \ldots, f - 1\} \times \{0, 1, \ldots, m - 1\}$ is one-to-one and onto, that is

$$a = a' \iff t = t' \qquad \text{and} \qquad r = r'.$$

That is, the color assignment $a$, or equivalently the assignment pair $(t, r)$, of the edge between $I_i$ and $O_j$ indicates that the central module $r$ has been assigned to a route from $I_i$ to $O_j$ in the $t$th time-slot of every cycle. Adopting the convention in the TDMA system, each cycle will be called a frame and the period $f$ frame size. As illustrated by the example shown in Fig. 12.21, where $m = 3$ and frame size $f = 2$, the decomposition of the edge-coloring into assignment pairs guarantees that route assignments are either space interleaved or time interleaved. Thus, the relation (12.8) will be called the time-space interleaving principle.

### 12.11.1 Homogeneous Capacity and Route Assignment

For uniform traffic, where the distribution of traffic loading between input modules and output modules is homogeneous, the $fm$ edges of each node can be evenly divided into $k$ groups, where $k$ is the total number of input (output) modules. Each group contains $g = fm/k$ edges between any I/O pair, where the frame size $f$ should be chosen properly

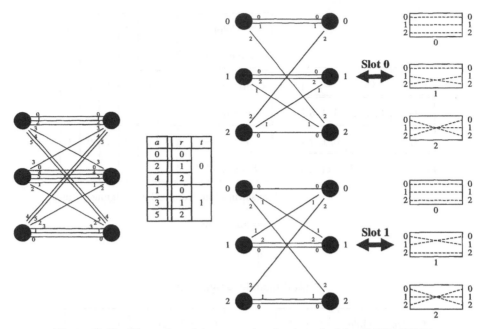

**Figure 12.21**    Illustration of time-space interleaving principle. (©1997 IEEE.)

to make the group size $g$ an integer. The edges of this capacity graph can be easily colored by the Latin Square given in Table 12.1, where each $A_i$, $0 \le i \le k - 1$, represents a set of distinct colors, for example,

$$A_0 = \{0, 1, \ldots, g - 1\}; \qquad A_1 = \{g, g + 1, \ldots, 2g - 1\}; \qquad \cdots$$

$$A_{k-1} = \{(k - 1)g, (k - 1)g + 1, \ldots, kg - 1\}.$$

Since each number in the set $\{0, 1, \ldots, fm - 1\}$ appears only once in any row or column in the table, it is a legitimate edge-coloring of the capacity graph. The assignment $a = (t, r)$ of an edge between the $I_i/O_j$ pair indicates that the central module $r$ will connect the input module $i$ to output module $j$ in the $t$th slot of every frame. As an example, for $m = 3$ and $k = 2$, we can choose $f = 2$ and thus $g = 3$.

Then, the groups of colors are $A_0 = \{0, 1, 2\}$ and $A_1 = \{3, 4, 5\}$, respectively. The procedure described above is illustrated in Figure 12.22, and the correspondence between the route assignments and the connection patterns in the middle stage is shown in Figure 12.23.

**TABLE 12.1    Latin Square Assignment**

|         | $O_0$     | $O_1$ | $O_2$ | $\cdots$ | $O_{k-1}$ |
|---------|-----------|-------|-------|----------|-----------|
| $I_0$   | $A_0$     | $A_1$ | $A_2$ | $\cdots$ | $A_{k-1}$ |
| $I_1$   | $A_{k-1}$ | $A_0$ | $A_1$ | $\cdots$ | $A_{k-2}$ |
| $\vdots$ | $\vdots$ | $\vdots$ | $\vdots$ | $\ddots$ | $\vdots$ |
| $I_{k-1}$ | $A_1$   | $A_2$ | $A_3$ | $\cdots$ | $A_0$     |

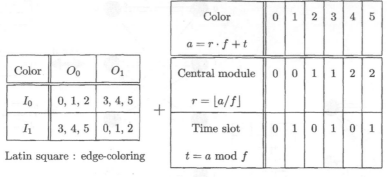

| Color $a = r \cdot f + t$ | 0 | 1 | 2 | 3 | 4 | 5 |
|---|---|---|---|---|---|---|
| Central module | 0 | 0 | 1 | 1 | 2 | 2 |
| $r = \lfloor a/f \rfloor$ | | | | | | |
| Time slot $t = a \bmod f$ | 0 | 1 | 0 | 1 | 0 | 1 |

| Color | $O_0$ | $O_1$ |
|---|---|---|
| $I_0$ | 0, 1, 2 | 3, 4, 5 |
| $I_1$ | 3, 4, 5 | 0, 1, 2 |

Latin square : edge-coloring

$+$

Transformation from color assignment into time-space pair

⇓

Central-module assignment

| Central module | $O_0$ | $O_1$ |
|---|---|---|
| $I_0$ | 0, 1 | 2 |
| $I_1$ | 2 | 0, 1 |

Time slot 0

| Central module | $O_0$ | $O_1$ |
|---|---|---|
| $I_0$ | 0 | 1, 2 |
| $I_1$ | 1, 2 | 0 |

Time slot 1

**Figure 12.22**   Route assignment by Latin Square for uniform traffic.

In the above example, since the number of central modules $m$ is greater than the number of input modules $k$, it is possible that more than one central module is assigned to some I/O pairs in one time slot. In the case that $m < k$, there are not enough central modules for all I/O pairs in one time slot assignment. Nevertheless, the total number of central modules assigned to every I/O pair within a frame should be the same, for uniform input traffic to fulfill the capacity requirement, and it is equal to $g = fm/k$. This point is illustrated in the following example. For $m = 4$ and $k = 6$, we choose $f = 3$ and $g = 2$. The same method will result in the connection patterns shown in Figure 12.24. It is easy to verify that the number of central modules (paths, edges) assigned for each I/O pair is equal to $g = 2$ per $f = 3$ slots.

### 12.11.2 Heterogeneous Capacity Assignment

The capacity assignment in a cross-path switch is virtual-path based. It depends on the traffic load on each virtual path to allocate the capacity and determine the route assignment. The Latin Square offers a legitimate capacity assignment with homogeneous traffic, but it may not be effective anymore with heterogeneous traffic with non-uniformly distributed traffic load over the virtual paths. A more general assignment method is therefore introduced and the procedure is illustrated in Figure 12.25. The assignment procedure has four steps, each of which will be explained along with an example in the following subsections.

| Central | Connected $I/O$ pairs at  time slot | |
|---------|-------------------------------|---|
| module  | 0                             | 1 |
| 0 | $I_0/O_0$, $I_1/O_1$ (BAR) | $I_0/O_0$, $I_1/O_1$ (BAR) |
| 1 | $I_0/O_0$, $I_1/O_1$ (BAR) | $I_0/O_1$, $I_1/O_0$ (CROSS) |
| 2 | $I_0/O_1$, $I_1/O_0$ (CROSS) | $I_0/O_1$, $I_1/O_0$ (CROSS) |

Connection pairs in central modules

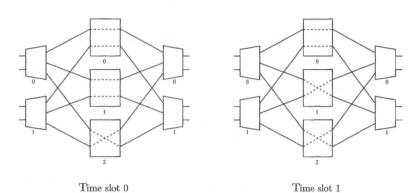

Time slot 0                              Time slot 1

**Figure 12.23**    Route scheduling in the middle-stage for uniform traffic. (©1997 IEEE.)

***Virtual Path Capacity Allocation* (*VPCA*).** This step is to allocate capacity to each virtual path based on the traffic loads. It can be formulated as an optimization problem with some traffic modeling.

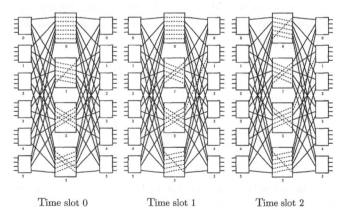

Time slot 0             Time slot 1             Time slot 2

**Figure 12.24**    Route scheduling in central modules for the second example of uniform traffic. (©1997 IEEE.)

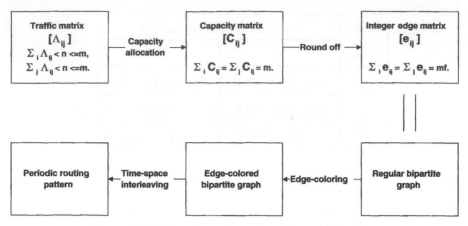

**Figure 12.25** Procedure of capacity and route assignment.

Consider the cross-path switch with parameters $n = 3$, $k = 3$, and $m = 4$. Suppose the traffic matrix is given by

$$\mathbf{T} = \begin{bmatrix} 1 & 1 & 1 \\ 2 & 1 & 0 \\ 0 & 1 & 1 \end{bmatrix}, \qquad (12.9)$$

the capacity assignment matrix calculated by the minimization of input-stage delay with $M/D/1$ model is

$$\mathbf{C} = \begin{bmatrix} 1.34 & 1.28 & 1.38 \\ 2.66 & 1.34 & 0 \\ 0 & 1.38 & 2.62 \end{bmatrix}. \qquad (12.10)$$

***The Round-Off Procedure.*** Some elements in the resulting capacity matrix may be non-integers. When they are rounded into integers that are required in the route assignment, round-off error arises. The concept of frame size is used to reduce the round-off error. Each element in the capacity matrix is multiplied by the frame size. Then the capacity per slot is translated into capacity per frame (see below). After that, we round the matrix into an integer matrix.

$$\mathbf{C} = \begin{bmatrix} 1.34 & 1.28 & 1.38 \\ 2.66 & 1.34 & 0 \\ 0 & 1.38 & 2.62 \end{bmatrix} \xrightarrow{\times f=3} \begin{bmatrix} 4.02 & 3.84 & 4.14 \\ 7.98 & 3.82 & 0 \\ 0 & 4.14 & 7.86 \end{bmatrix}$$

$$\xrightarrow{\text{rounding}} \begin{bmatrix} 4 & 4 & 4 \\ 8 & 4 & 0 \\ 0 & 4 & 8 \end{bmatrix} = \mathbf{E}. \qquad (12.11)$$

The round-off error is inversely proportional to $f$. That is, the error can be arbitrary small if the frame size is sufficiently large. However, since the amount of routing information stored in the memory is linearly proportional to $f$, the frame size is limited by the access speed and the memory space of input modules. In practice, the choice of frame size $f$ is a

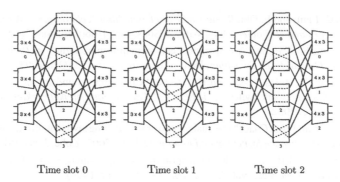

Time slot 0          Time slot 1          Time slot 2

**Figure 12.26**    Route Scheduling example (heterogenous traffic). (©1997 IEEE.)

compromise between the round-off error and the memory requirement. In general,

$$\mathbf{E} = \begin{bmatrix} e_{0,0} & e_{0,1} & \cdots & e_{0,k-1} \\ e_{1,0} & e_{1,1} & \cdots & e_{1,k-1} \\ \vdots & \vdots & \ddots & \vdots \\ e_{k-1,0} & e_{k-1,1} & \cdots & e_{k-1,k-1} \end{bmatrix} \simeq f \cdot \mathbf{C},$$

and

$$\sum_j e_{ij} = \sum_i e_{ij} = f \cdot m. \tag{12.12}$$

In the above matrix $\mathbf{E}$, each element $e_{ij}$ represents the number of the edges between the input module $i$ and output module $j$ in the $k \times k$ capacity graph, in which each node has a degree of $fm$.

**_Edge-Coloring._** The capacity graph can be colored by $fm$ colors, and each color represents one distinct time-space slot based on the time-space interleaving principle (12.8). Coloring can be found by complete matching, which is repeated recursively to reduce the degree of every node one-by-one. One general method to search for a complete matching is the so-called Hungarian algorithm or alternating-path algorithm [10, 12]. It is a sequential algorithm with the worst time complexity $O(k^2)$, or totally $O(fm \times k^2)$ because there are $fm$ matchings. If each of $fm$ and $k$ is a power of two, an efficient parallel algorithm proposed in [13] for conflict-free route scheduling in a three-stage Clos network with time complexity of $O(\log^2(fmk))$ can be used. Through the time-space interleaving, the middle-stage routing pattern is obtained in Figure 12.26.

## REFERENCES

[1] J. Hopcroft and R. Karp, "An $n$ 5/2 algorithm for maximum matchings in bipartite graphs," *SIAM Journal on Computing*, vol. 2, no. 4, pp. 225–231 (1973).

[2] R. Cole and J. Hopcroft, "On edge coloring bipartite graph," *SIAM Journal on Computing*, vol. 11, no. 3, pp. 540–546 (1982).

[3] H. J. Chao, C. Lam, and E. Oki, *Broadband Packet Switching Technologies – A Practical Guide to ATM Switches and IP Routers*. John Wiley & Sons, Inc., Hoboken, New Jercy, 2001.

[4] H. J. Chao and S. Y. Liew, "A new optical cell switching paradigm," in *Proc. International Workshop on Optical Burst Switching*, Dallas, Texas, pp. 120–132 (Oct. 2003).

[5] E. Oki, Z. Jing, R. Rojas-Cessa, and H. J. Chao, "Concurrent round-robin-based dispatching schemes for Clos-network switches," *IEEE/ACM Transactions on Networking*, vol. 10, no. 6, pp. 830–844 (Dec. 2002).

[6] Y. Li, S. Panwar, and H. J. Chao, "The dual round-robin matching switch with exhaustive service," in *Proc. High Performace Switching and Routing (HPSR) 2002*, Kobe, Japan (May 2002).

[7] N. McKeown, "*i*SLIP: a scheduling algorithm for input-queued switches," *IEEE/ACM Transactions on Networking*, vol. 7, no. 2, pp. 188–201 (Apr. 1999).

[8] F. M. Chiussi, J. G. Kneuer, and V. P. Kumar, "Low cost scalable switching solutions for broadband networking: the ATLANTA architecuture and chipset," *IEEE Communications Magazine*, vol. 35, issue 12, pp. 44–53 (Dec. 1997).

[9] M. Karol and C.-L. I, "Performance analysis of a growable architecture for broadband packet (ATM) switching," in *Proc. IEEE GLOBECOM'89*, Dallas, Texas, pp. 1173–1180 (Nov. 1989).

[10] F. T. Leighton, *Introduction to Parallel Algorithms and Architectures: Arrays · Trees · Hypercubes*. Morgan Kaufmann, San Francisco, California, 1992.

[11] R. J. Wilson, *Introduction to Graph Theory*. Academic Press, New York, 1972.

[12] R. J. McEliece, R. B. Ash, and C. Ash, *Introduction to Discrete Mathematics*. McGraw-Hill, New York, 1989.

[13] T. T. Lee and S. Y. Liew, "Parallel algorithm for benes networks," in *Proc. IEEE INFOCOM '96*, San Francisco, California (Mar. 1996).

# CHAPTER 13

# MULTI-PLANE MULTI-STAGE BUFFERED SWITCH

To keep pace with Internet traffic growth, researchers have been continually exploring new switch architectures with new electronic and optical device technologies to design a packet switch that is cost-effective and scalable to a very large capacity, for example, a few hundred tera bps or even a few peta bps [1].

Packet switches can be classified into single-stage switches and multi-stage switches. A single-stage switch fabric, such as a cross point switch, has only one path between each input–output port pair. Thus, it has no packet out-of-sequence problem and is relatively simple to design. However, due to the quadratic relationship between the switch size and the number of switching elements, it is not very scalable.

Multi-stage switch architectures, such as the Clos [2] or Benes networks, utilize multiple paths between each input–output pair with fewer switching elements allowing scalable and fault-tolerant designs. A multi-path switch fabric can be further classified into a memory-less switch fabric or a buffered switch fabric. A memory-less multi-path switch fabric has no packet out-of-sequence problem because the propagation delays through different paths are comparable. However, it requires the internal link to be resolved and output port contention by a centralized packet schedule with global information available, causing the control plane of the switch fabric to be unscalable in spite of a scalable data plane.

A buffered multi-path switch fabric does not require a centralized packet scheduler as contention is resolved between stages by using memories to temporarily store packets that lost contention for links or ports. Due to the nature of unbalanced incoming traffic, the queue lengths on the multiple paths between any input–output pair are very likely different. As a result, packets from the same flow may experience different delays while traversing different paths and cause packets to be out of sequence.

This chapter introduces ultra-scalable multi-plane multi-stage buffered switch architecture, called TrueWay, based on Clos-network. The Ciscos CRS-1 system [3] also uses a

*High Performance Switches and Routers*, by H. Jonathan Chao and Bin Liu
Copyright © 2007 John Wiley & Sons, Inc.

multi-plane multi-stage buffered switch based on Benes network. The more switch planes and stages, the more routing paths that exist between any input–output pair.

Thus, there are several challenging design issues related to designing the TrueWay switch:

- How to efficiently allocate and share the limited on-chip memories?
- How to intelligently schedule packets on multiple paths while maximizing the memory utilization and system performance?
- How to minimize link congestion and prevent buffer overflow (i.e., stage-to-stage flow control)?
- How to maintain packet order if they are delivered over multiple paths (i.e., port-to-port flow control)?

## 13.1  TRUEWAY SWITCH ARCHITECTURE

Figure 13.1 shows the TrueWay switch architecture [4]. The ingress traffic manager (TMI) distributes packets to different paths of different switch planes while the egress traffic manager (TME) collects packets traversing the switch fabric and buffers them to be transmitted to the network. The switch fabric consists of $p$ switch planes, each consisting of a three-stage Clos network. The study shows that a speedup of 1.6 provides very good performance. The switch can also support multiple priorities (e.g., $q = 2$).

The modules in the first, second, and third stages are denoted as input modules (IMs), center modules (CMs), and output modules (OMs). Each module can be logically considered a crosspoint buffered switch. The first stage of the switch plane consists of $k$ IMs, each with $n$ inputs and $m$ outputs. The second stage consists of $m$ CMs, each with $k$ inputs and $k$ outputs. The third stage consists of $k$ OMs, each with $m$ inputs and $n$ outputs.

Similar to conventional packet switches, each incoming packet is segmented into multiple fixed-length cells. The cells are then routed through the switch fabric independently and

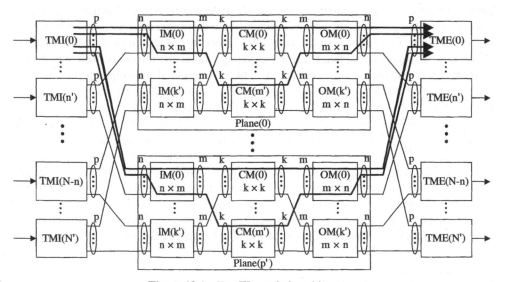

**Figure 13.1**    TrueWay switch architecture.

reassembled into packets using reassembly queues at the output ports. Cells are served using strict priority: Only when cells in the higher priority queues are completely served, can the cells in the lower priority queues be served.

### 13.1.1    Stages of the Switch

Each TMI has two types of queues, virtual output queue (VOQ) and virtual path queue (VPQ). Using two different queues at the TMI can avoid throughput degradation due to head-of-line (HOL) blocking. As shown in Figure 13.2, when a packet arrives at a TMI, it is segmented into cells and put into the corresponding VOQ. The packet in the VOQ, if a HOL packet, is moved to the VPQ depending on its Path ID (PID), and is used to determine the routing path consisting of the switch plane and CM numbers. Each output link of the TMI selects a VPQ and sends the HOL packet to the IM based on the scheduling scheme described later in this chapter.

Figure 13.3 illustrates the TME structure. When cells arrive at the TME, they are reassembled into a packet in the Reassembly Queue (RAQ). Once the RAQ has a complete packet, the pointers of the linked cells are moved from the RAQ to the class of service queue (CSQ). Since more than one RAQ may have a complete packet, packets can be served in a round-robin fashion to achieve fairness.

To avoid cell loss at the RAQ, TME sends flow control signals to the OM if the number of cells in the RAQ exceeds a threshold. Since the TME and OM are located at the same shelf, the round trip time (RTT) delay is small. Therefore, the RAQ size should only be greater than the largest packet size (e.g., 9 kB or 174 cells) plus the RTT delay (e.g., four cells) for 178 cells. Each cell is assumed to be 64 bytes with a payload of 52 bytes.

The term switch modules (SMs) refers to the IM, CM, or OM. Here, we assume $n = m = k$ to simplify the discussion. Each module has $n^2$ crosspoints and each crosspoint has $q$ queues, each of which corresponds to a priority level. Therefore, each SM has $n^2 \times q$

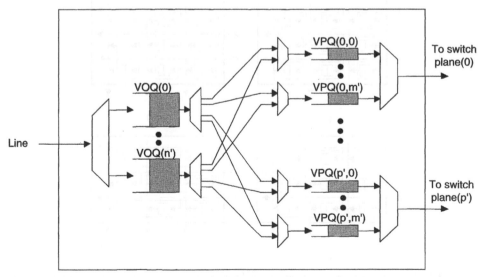

**Figure 13.2**    Ingress traffic manager (TMI) structure, where $n' = n - 1, m' = m - 1, p' = p - 1$.

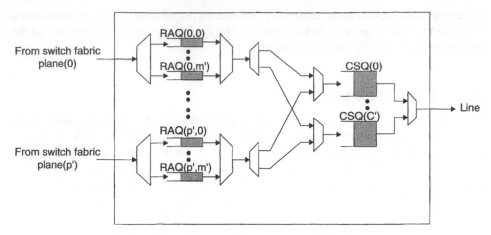

**Figure 13.3** Egress traffic manager (TME) structure.

queues. Each queue can receive and send one cell in each time slot. An incoming cell is stored in one of the queues according to its destination address and priority level.

Memory is the cost-consuming component of the high-speed switch. Thus, the efficient memory allocation will not only affect system performance, but also influence the cost of design. From the memory organization point-of-view, the SM can be crosspoint buffered, output-shared, all-shared, or input-shared memory as shown in Figure 13.4.

In the crosspoint buffered switch, each queue has its dedicated memory. Since there is no memory sharing, this approach requires the largest memory. In the output-shared architecture, all the vertical queues of each output are grouped together in a single output memory. With stage-to-stage flow control (to be described later), each queue needs to

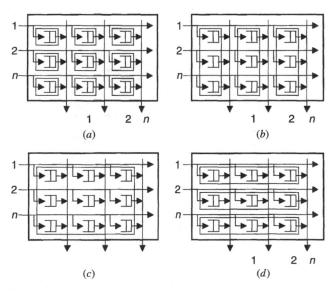

**Figure 13.4** Different memory organizations for the switch modules: (*a*) Crosspoint buffer memory; (*b*) Output-shared memory; (*c*) All-shared memory; (*d*) Input shared memory.

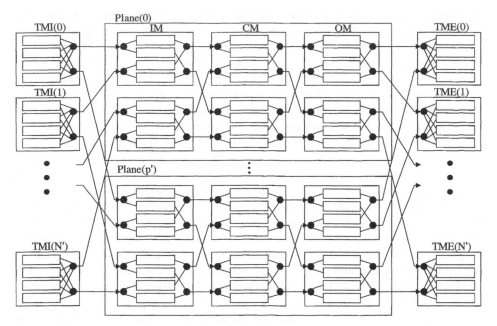

**Figure 13.5** Queue structure in the switch.

accommodate at least the RTT between stages. With a few cells of RTT and an SM size of 64, each output memory needs to hold more than a few hundred cells. As a result, the total memory size of each SM is required to be more than 10,000 cells, or close to 1 Mbits, which is too large for a switch chip.

In the all-shared memory SM, the queues are shared by the entire SM, which results in the following two problems. One is the bottleneck of memory speed. The memory in the all-shared memory SM has to write $n$ cells and read $n$ cells within a time slot, which is not feasible for high speed link rate. Another is the fairness of sharing. Under hot-spot traffic, cells destined for the hot-spot port can monopolize the buffer and the other cells destined for non-hot-spot ports can be blocked.

One way to mitigate the problems of the all-shared memory SM is to partition the memory into buffers to allow each buffer to be shared by $n$ queues, associated with the input link to make the flow control simple. Input-shared SM is a good choice because each buffer receives at most one cell per time slot. Although the buffer consists of $n$ queues, it is likely that most queues are empty. Therefore, the buffer size does not need to be equal to the sum of $n$ queues. The switch architecture showing SMs with input-shared queuing structure is illustrated in Figure 13.5.

## 13.2 PACKET SCHEDULING

In a typical multi-plane multi-stage switch, the number of reassembly queues is equal to the product of the number of inputs, the number of paths between any input–output pair, and the number of priorities. In this section, we discuss some packet interleaving schemes for the TrueWay switch to reduce the number of reassembly queues to the number of paths × the number of priorities, resulting in a reassembly buffer size independent of the switch size. The proposed schemes also offer high throughput and fairness, while maintaining cell integrity.

For the sake of simplicity, we assume each output link of the TMI, IM, CM, and OM has the same packet scheduling policy. A cell is transferred from a queue at the upstream side to a queue at the downstream side in the switch. The queue at the upstream side is called a source queue (SQ) and the queue at the downstream side is called a destination queue (DQ). Cells waiting at an SQ compete for the output link, since one link can send at most one cell in a timeslot. Scheduling schemes are employed to select which cell to send.

The straightforward way is to schedule cells in a round robin (RR) manner. It is called complete cell interleaving (CCI), which will give the best load balancing among possible paths and minimum cell transmission delays through the switch fabric. However, CCI requires a large number of RAQs, since at a given time, a DQ may have cells coming from various inputs over different paths, waiting to be reassembled. An example of a CCI algorithm in action is shown in Figure 13.6a. Although, all cells are transferred with a minimum delay, the requirement for separate RAQs, one for each input, is clear at DQ(X).

If packet boundaries are taken into account when scheduling (i.e., wait until a packet is completely sent before sending cells from another packet), this algorithm is called complete packet interleaving (CPI). The number of RAQs required is one per plane per priority, which is much less than the CCI scheme. The price paid here is the degraded throughput, since some output queues may be idle while waiting for the last cells of an incomplete packet

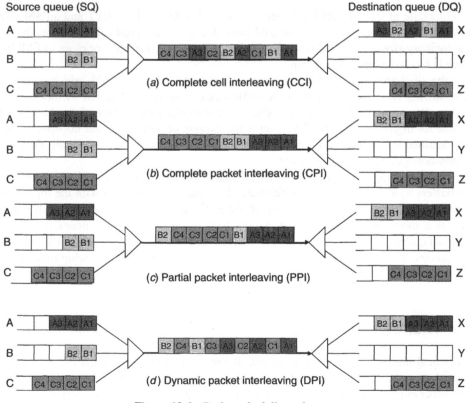

**Figure 13.6** Packet scheduling schemes.

to arrive, although there are cells destined for the idle output. Figure 13.6*b* illustrates the CPI. Unlike the CCI example of Figure 13.6*a*, here cells from different inputs arrive at the DQ(X) one after another (i.e., not intermingled), so there is no need to hold separate queues per input.

In addition to the degraded throughput, the packet-interleaving scheme also suffers from a possible deadlock situation. Let us assume that all but the last cell of packet $P_1$ is sent from the TMI to the TME. When the last cell of $P_1$ takes its turn, its transmission can be blocked because the buffer at the IM can be full of other cells coming from different VOQs. At the same time, the buffers at the IM can be full of fresh packets destined for the TME, to which the partial packet is destined. No fresh packets at the IM can be sent because they are partial packets. In the worst case, there can be a situation where all partial packets at the TMI are blocked due to the full buffers at the IM and all fresh packets at the IM are blocked because of the partial packets. Then all cells in the switch fabric are blocked, which results in a deadlock situation. In practice, the line cards have more memory than the switch fabric cards. So, the deadlock case generally occurs due to the lack of memory in switch modules. To avoid the deadlock situation, at least one cell space in the SM buffers should be reserved for all partial packets. Then any partial packet can forward a cell to the next stage and there will never be a deadlock situation.

In the following two subsections, we present two packet-interleaving algorithms, namely, partial packet interleaving and dynamic packet interleaving. These schemes allow high throughput while keeping the RAQ sizes comparably small. The deadlock situation is avoided by reserving at least one free memory space in the buffer for partial packets. Then any partial packet can forward a cell to the next stage, without causing deadlock. The details on how to reserve memory space to avoid deadlock is discussed in Section 13.3.

### 13.2.1  Partial Packet Interleaving (PPI)

The CCI scheme is attractive from the load-balancing point of view and the CPI scheme is attractive from the reassembly point of view. To take advantage of both the CCI scheme and the CPI scheme, we consider the partial packet interleaving (PPI) scheme, which stands between the CCI scheme and the CPI scheme.

PPI is similar to CPI. Once an SQ(A) starts sending a packet, it keeps sending the packet without moving to another SQ. However, unlike CPI, if SQ(A) becomes empty at some point before completing the transfer of this packet, other SQs with pending packets to other DQs will become eligible to send their packets. In this scheme, cells from packets destined to different DQs are allowed to be interleaved, but not those destined for the same DQ. Figure 13.6*c* illustrates the PPI. In this example, let us assume cell $C_1$ arrives at the SQ(C), after cell $B_1$ arrives at the SQ(B) but before the arrival of cell $B_2$. If the CPI algorithm is used, none of the cells of packet $P$ could be delivered until $B_2$ arrives (as in Fig. 13.6*b*), but PPI allows packet $C$ to use the link while it is idle (i.e., waiting for cell $B_2$) thus improving throughput. As a result, idle time is reduced so the throughput is improved, while the required number of RAQs is still comparable to the CPI scheme.

### 13.2.2  Dynamic Packet Interleaving (DPI)

In the PPI scheme, once an SQ(A) is selected, another SQ(B) can only be selected if the packet in SQ(A) is completed or SQ(A) becomes empty, whichever happens first. The dynamic packet interleaving scheme (DPI) moves to the next eligible SQ as soon as it sends

**TABLE 13.1    Number of RAQs Required at the TME for Different Scheduling Algorithms**

| Scheduling Scheme | Number of Reassembly Queues |
|---|---|
| CCI | $p \times q \times m \times n \times k$ |
| PPI or DPI | $p \times q \times m$ |
| CPI | $p \times q$ |

a cell from SQ(A). Figure 13.6*d* illustrates the operation of DPI. Assume that the SQs have a uniform arrival rate. Then in the CPI case, packets will be transferred one after another resulting in low throughput. In the PPI case, although the throughput will be similar to DPI, the load balancing for the following stage will be better for the DPI case. Thus, DPI is closer to the CCI scheme, in that it has a higher overall throughput. Fortunately, the number of RAQs is still the same as in the PPI scheme. Table 13.1 shows the number of RAQ requirements for each of the algorithms described above.

### 13.2.3    Head-of-Line (HOL) Blocking

As long as queues contain cells going to different destinations, HOL blocking (the blocking of a cell destined for an idle destination) is inevitable. For the TrueWay switch, the final destinations are the RAQs at the TMEs. In each OM, if each crosspoint has one queue per each RAQ, there will be no HOL blocking. For the CM, the immediate destinations are the queues at the OM. Since each crosspoint in the OM has as many queues as the total number of RAQs in the TMEs, the number of queues in each crosspoint of the CM increases very quickly. The effect is even more severe for the earlier stages (TMI and IM). In order to limit the number of queues in TMI and IM, HOL blocking should be allowed up to some extent to make the design feasible.

In the TMI, there are two kind of queues, VOQ and VPQ. The latter facilitates the cell distribution to different planes/CMs. The former keeps most cells of each flow (traffic of each input–output pair) and only sends one cell at a time to the VPQ, preventing the congested flow from sending too many cells and thus clogging the routing paths through the CMs.

## 13.3    STAGE-TO-STAGE FLOW CONTROL

It is a common practice to have a large memory at line cards and a small memory at switch fabric connection points. When a cell is transmitted over a link, the receiver should have free memory space to store the cell until it is transmitted to the next stage. Since the receiver has limited memory space, if the receiver memory becomes full, the sender must hold the cells until the receiver has free space. Therefore, a flow control mechanism has to be implemented to make sure there is no cell loss in the switch fabric. In this section, two well known flow control schemes: back-pressure and credit-based flow control (also known as N23), are first described, followed by a new flow control scheme dedicated to the TrueWay switch, called the DQ scheme.

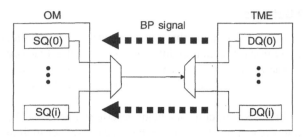

**Figure 13.7** Back-pressure scheme between OM and TME.

### 13.3.1 Back-Pressure

Back-pressure (BP) is one of the simplest and commonly used flow control schemes. It uses a back-pressure signal to make the senders aware of the buffer occupancy. With reference to Figure 13.7, one can simply implement the back-pressure flow control scheme by letting the receiver periodically send a one-bit signal to all senders to indicate the buffer status. A "0" indicates the buffer has enough space so that the senders can send cells to it freely, and a "1" indicates the buffer has exceeded a threshold, thus all senders should stop sending cells to it.

The BP is a simple flow control scheme, but it lacks fairness. For instance, if the buffer is consumed by a congested port, all other traffic suffers because the BP signal only indicates whether the buffer exceeds the threshold or not. Although the senders have packets destined for the non-hot-spot ports, they cannot go through the buffer.

### 13.3.2 Credit-Based Flow Control

Since the BP flow control scheme is unfair to all flows, we next describe a credit-based link-by-link flow control scheme N23 [5], which processes on a per virtual connection (VC) basis to maintain fairness among all flows.

The credit plays a major role in the credit-based flow control scheme. Each sender can only forward data cells over the link, when it holds enough credits given by the receiver. In other words, if there is no credit for a sender, the flow is unable to forward cells to the link. On the other hand, the receiver periodically sends credits to the sender indicating availability of buffer space for receiving data cells of the VC. After having received additional credits, the sender is eligible to forward more data cells of the VC to the receiver according to the received credit information. Each time the sender forwards a data cell of a VC, it decrements its current credit balance for the VC by one.

The receiver is eligible to send a credit cell to the sender each time after it has forwarded N2 data cells since the previous credit cell for the same VC was sent. Upon receiving a credit cell with a credit value of C for a VC, the sender is permitted to forward up to C–E data cells of the VC before the next successfully transmitted credit cell for the VC is received, where E is the number of data cells the sender has forwarded over the VC for the past time period of RTT. The subtraction takes care of in-flight cells from the sender to the receiver, which the receiver had not seen when the credit cell was sent. In other words, the current credit balance is equal to C–E. As long as the credit balance is greater than zero, the flow is able to forward data. The N2 value can be a design or engineering choice. The larger N2 is, the less the bandwidth overhead is, and the more buffer space each VC uses.

### 13.3.3 The DQ Scheme

The N23 is a fair-flow control scheme that considers each flow individually [5]; however, in the multi-plane multi-stage switch architecture, such as the TrueWay switch, per VC flow control is not practical due to the excessive amount of credit counters. Therefore, by adopting and modifying the N23 scheme, a new per DQ-based flow control, called the DQ scheme, is proposed.

Similar to the credit-based flow control scheme described above, the DQ scheme also uses credits to maintain traffic control. In the DQ scheme, each sender maintains two counters. They are the queue outstanding cell count (QOC) and the RTT Outstanding Counter (ROC). The QOC represents the sum of the cells left in the DQ and the cells on the link destined for the DQ. If the distance between the two SMs is far, the number of cells on the link can be large. The QOC needs to be updated according to the information provided by the DQ. One simple way to update the QOC is to have the DQ periodically send a credit update (CRT). On the other hand, the ROC counts the number of cells transmitted during the RTT just before the CRT is received. In addition to these two counters, a fixed value called maximum reserved cells (MRC) is set to warn the sender about the buffer occupancy. The MRC is an engineering parameter that will affect the performance of the TrueWay switch. In the performance analysis section, we show the effect of various MRC values on the TrueWay switch performance.

From the sender point of view, the eligibility of sending cells depends on the value of the QOC. As long as the value of the QOC is less than MRC, the sender is able to forward cells to the DQ. Whenever a cell is transmitted, the QOC is incremented by one. The QOC is updated whenever a credit update is received.

The receiver on the other side periodically sends a CRT to the sender, which contains the number of cells in the DQ. Then the QOC can be updated as the sum of the CRT and ROC (i.e., QOC = CRT + ROC). The summation counts the cells in transition while the CRT is delivered. When the QOC is updated, the ROC is reset to 0.

In the DQ scheme, the QOC update depends on the CRT, thus the delivery of the CRT becomes a crucial step. Next, we examine two possible ways to deliver the CRT, depending on the data sent as the CRT update. One way is to determine how many cells were transmitted from the DQ during the last credit update period. This scheme is vulnerable to CRT loss and cell loss. Once a cell or CRT is lost, it is difficult to resynchronize the QOC and the actual outstanding number of cells for the DQ. The other way is to determine how many cells are left in the DQ. In this scheme, the system becomes much more tolerant of cell loss or credit loss. Since the CRTs are sent periodically, if one CRT is lost, the preceding CRT is able to recover the queuing status easily.

To avoid the deadlock situation, at least one cell space in the SM buffers should be reserved for all partial packets. Then any partial packet can forward a cell to the next stage and there will never be a deadlock situation. For this purpose, we introduce a queue reserved cell (QRC) counter. The QRC is set to the MRC as soon as its first cell is sent. In other words, QRC should be equal to or less than the MRC. For example, if MRC = 8, the QRC is set to eight as soon as the beginning of packet (BOP) cell is granted and the QRC is set to 0 as soon as the end of packet (EOP) cell is granted. The QRC is decremented by one whenever the SQ sends a cell to the DQ.

If the QOC of the DQ is larger than the MRC, the QRC is set to 0. Although the QRC becomes 0, the SQ can send more cells to the DQ if the buffer has a free space. If the QOC is less than the MRC and the DQ flag (DQF) is equal to 1, the sum of QOC and QRC should always be equal to MRC. The DQF bit indicates if the DQ is taken or not. If the DQ is not taken (i.e., DQF = 0), there is no partial packet destined for the DQ and any BOP cell or single cell packet (SCP) cell can be sent to the DQ. If the DQ is taken (i.e., DQF = 1), there is a SQ that has a partial packet destined for that DQ and only that SQ can send a cell to the DQ. If the DQF is set to 1, a BOP cell or SCP cell should not be sent. If a BOP or SCP cell is sent, more than one packet is interleaved and packet integrity is not maintained in the DQ. To avoid this, no more than one packet is allowed to be interleaved for the DQ.

The buffer reserved cell (BRC) counter is the sum of the QRCs of all DQs in the buffer. By adding the QOC and BRC, the memory space is reserved for the partial packet. When the partial packet arrives at the SQ, although the sum of the BOC and BRC is equal to the buffer size, the cell is eligible for transmission if the QRC is greater than 0.

Figure 13.8 shows an example of the DQ scheme. Let us assume that only four DQs are active at a certain time. A DQ is considered to be active if it has an outstanding cell (i.e., QOC is greater than 0) or if there is a partial packet destined for the DQ. The QOC can have a value between 0 and 15. The total cell memory size is 32.

There are two partial packets (i.e., DQ(2) and DQ(3)). For DQ with a partial packet, only one SQ is eligible because the HOL cell of the SQ that sent a cell to the DQ should have a cell type of COP (Continue of Packet) or EOP and the DQF of the DQ should be set to 1. For the DQ without a partial packet, any BOP cell or SCP cell may be eligible. Since the sum of all QOCs and the BRC (i.e., 26) is less than the cell memory size (i.e., 32), there is room for a fresh packet. In the table part of Figure 13.8, "yes" means the cell is eligible and "no" means the cell is not eligible.

Figure 13.9 shows another example of the flow control mechanism. The DQ(3) has no outstanding cell but the last cell sent to the DQ was the BOP cell. Therefore, this DQ is considered to be active. Since the sum of QOCs and the BRC is equal to the cell memory size, there is no room for a fresh packet. The only eligible cell is one destined for DQ(3).

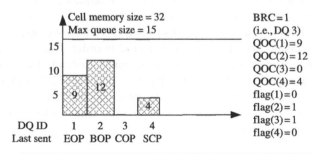

| | 1 | 2 | 3 | 4 |
|---|---|---|---|---|
| BOP | Yes | No | No | Yes |
| COP | No | Yes | Yes | No |
| EOP | No | Yes | Yes | No |
| SCP | Yes | No | No | Yes |

**Figure 13.8**  Example of DQ flow control.

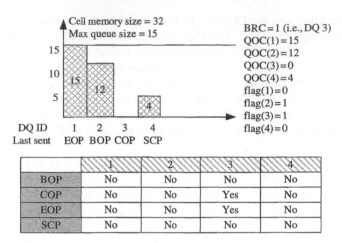

**Figure 13.9**   Example of flow control.

## 13.4   PORT-TO-PORT FLOW CONTROL

When building a packet switch, it is a common practice to segment each arriving packet into multiple fixed-length cells (e.g., 64 bytes), route them through the switch fabric, and reassemble them back into packets with the reassembly queues at the output ports. Although packets belonging to the same flow must be delivered in order, packets passing through different paths may experience different queuing delays and packets can be delivered out-of-sequence through the switch fabric. For example, packet A is sent to the switch fabric from the TMI before packet B is sent. However, packet B may arrive at the TME before packet A arrives at the TME because packet A experienced more delay in the switch fabric than packet B.

In this section, we present four schemes to tackle the packet out-of-sequence issue in the multi-plane multi-stage buffered switch. The schemes can be categorized into two approaches, namely a hashing method and a buffer re-sequencing method. In the first approach (hashing), it forces the cells belonging to the same flow to take the same path through the switch fabric. As a result, all cells from a given flow will experience the same amount of queuing delay. Thus packets are delivered in order. Along this approach, we present two hashing schemes: static hashing and dynamic hashing. The second approach allows packet out-of-sequence within the switch fabric. However, TME uses a resequencing buffer to resequence the cells back into order before delivering them to the next link. We introduce two practical resequencing techniques. They are time-stamp-based resequencing and window-based resequencing.

### 13.4.1   Static Hashing

With reference to Figure 13.10, the static hashing scheme simply eliminates the packet out-of-sequence problem by hashing flows into a flow group and sending all packets of the same flow group to the same path. If cells belonging to the same flow traverse through the same path [6] (i.e., the same switch plane and the same CM) until they have all left the switch fabric, then all packets will be delivered in order.

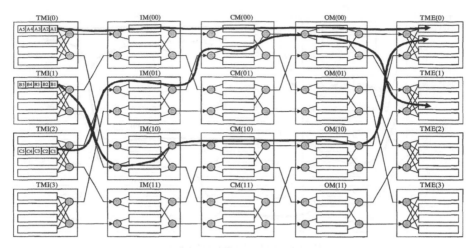

**Figure 13.10**    Static hashing.

As we know, in today's Internet, a core router may experience millions of packet flows; on the other hand, the TrueWay switch only has $p \times m$ paths between each input–output pair. Thus, it is impossible to assign a unique path to each individual packet flow traveling through the switch. As a result, the concept of flow group is introduced into the static hashing scheme. One simple way to hash flows into a flow group is to use CRC-16 (16-bit cyclic redundancy check). The static hashing scheme uses flow group ID (FGID) to distinguish each packet flow group. For instance, in the TrueWay switch with eight planes and 64 CMs, the total number of paths is 512, which is much smaller than the number of FGIDs (i.e., $216 = 65,536$ in the case of CRC-16). Therefore, the FGID must be mapped to the Path ID (PID).

One simple way to perform this mapping is to divide the FGID by the number of paths. The remainder is the PID. For example, if the FGID is 33,333 and the number of paths is 512, the PID becomes 53. Then all the packets with the FGID of 33,333 will be routed through the first plane (i.e., PLA = 0) and the 53rd CM (i.e., CMA = 53). This mapping is called static hashing. In summary, the static hashing allows TMIs to hash each incoming packet flow into flow groups and assign them into predetermined paths.

Load unbalancing is one problem of the static hashing scheme. This is mainly caused by different flow sizes (i.e., packet flows having different bandwidths). Even if the hashing achieves nearly even distribution of the packet flows to different routing paths, different flow sizes will cause the bandwidths on the routing paths to be uneven, and thus congestion on some of internal links.

### 13.4.2  Dynamic Hashing

To improve the load balancing problem, dynamic hashing is introduced where the input port maintains a count of outstanding packets in the switch fabric for each flow. If there is an outstanding packet in the switch fabric, all the following packets belonging to the flow must be sent to the same path with the previous packet. If not, they can be sent to any other path.

With reference to Figure 13.11, the TMI keeps track of the number of outstanding packets in the switch fabric using an outstanding packet counter (OPC). That is, the OPC indicates the outstanding number of packets in the switch fabric associated with the FGID

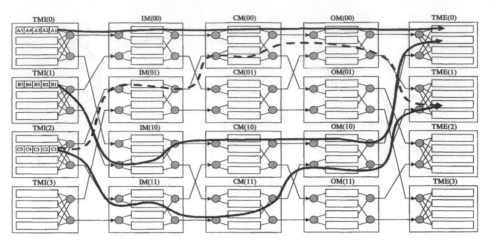

**Figure 13.11** Dynamic hashing.

from the TMI. The OPC is incremented by one whenever a new packet with the FGID is sent to the switch fabric and is decremented by one whenever the TMI receives a packet acknowledgment (PACK) with the FGID from the TME. The TME sends a PACK when it receives the last cell of the packet (i.e., EOP or SCP cell).

The TMI maintains two tables: a distribution table and a status table. The distribution table contains the PID and the OPC for each FGID. The TMI determines the PID of each flow using its flow ID (FID). The PID is identified by a switch fabric plane number and a CM number in the plane.

The PID in the distribution table is valid while the OPC is greater than 0. If the OPC reaches 0, a new PID can be assigned to the FGID. If the OPC becomes 0, the FGID can be assigned to a different path from the previous path without having a packet out-of-sequence problem. This could be helpful for path congestion because if the OPC is equal to 0, the packets of the flow do not need to take the previous path. This scheme is called dynamic hashing. The simulation shows that dynamic hashing performs better than static hashing under traffic distributions with large flows.

In the case of multiple scheduling priorities, it will provide separate paths for each scheduling priority. Then since there is no overlap between different scheduling priorities, the operation of dynamic hashing for a single scheduling priority case can be applied to the multiple scheduling priorities.

The dynamic hashing works as follows. The TMI checks the FGID of the packet. If the OPC of the FGID is greater than 0, the packet is assigned to the path on the distribution table. If not, the TMI chooses one of the multiple paths according to the congestion status of each path, which is provided by the status table. The status table maintains two flags. One flag is used to indicate if the path is not accessable due to a link failure or a chip failure. If this flag is set, no packets must be sent to the path. The other flag is used to indicate if the path is congested or not. To set this flag, the input port needs feedback information from the switch fabric. The TMI will choose one path among the paths whose congestion flag is set to 0.

The status table is used to find an uncongested path. Path selection is performed in two phases. In the first phase, the status table chooses the plane in a round-robin fashion, which has at least one path whose congestion flag is set to 0. In the second phase, the status table

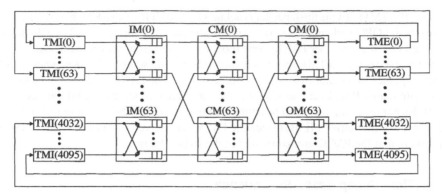

**Figure 13.12**    Packet acknowledgment in dynamic hashing.

chooses the CM, whose congestion flag is equal to 0. If the congestion flag is equal to 1, the path is considered congested. If it is equal to 0, the path is considered uncongested. If all congestion flags are equal to 0, the arbiter chooses one path in a round-robin manner among the CMs.

It is possible for packets of the same flow to take different paths as long as all the previous packets have left the switch fabric. This scheme achieves better load balancing than static hashing because the TMI assigns packets of the same flow to less congested paths. The static hashing scheme must assign packets to the pre-determined path even though the path is congested.

Next, we show how PACK can be efficiently delivered along with a data packet. The PACK can be delivered by the cell header. With reference to Figure 13.12, the PACK is sent to the neighboring TMI and the TMI sends the PACK to the switch fabric using the cell header. The PACK is sent through the same plane that the data cells go through. In the multi-plane multi-stage switch architecture, it is possible that multiple PACKs are generated at the same timeslot. Therefore, buffers for PACKs are inevitable in the multi-plane multi-stage switch. Although PACKs are delivered via the same switch fabric as the data packets, each IM, CM, and OM uses separate output FIFO queues to store PACKs in case of congestion. In other words, PACKs are queued separately from data packets at each switch module. Note that TMEs and TMIs do not require FIFOs to store the PACKs because they are able to process PACKs as soon as they arrive.

We use an example to show how PACKs are delivered in the multi-plane multi-stage switch. For instance, TMI(0) sends a packet to TME(4032). TMI(0) sends the last cell of the packet to TME(4032) and increments the OPC by one. TME(4032) receives the last cell of the packet, creates a PACK, and passes it to TMI(4032). Then TMI(4032) sends the PACK to IM(63). IM(63) chooses one of the CMs (e.g., CM(0)) for the PACK and stores it at the output buffer. Again, the output buffers at the IM, CM, and OM are FIFO. Therefore, if the buffer is not empty, it sends one PACK in each cell slot. CM(0) receives the PACK and stores it at the FIFO destined for OM(0) because the PACK is destined for TMI(0). Similarly, OM(0) receives the PACK and stores it at the FIFO destined for TME(0). TME(0) receives the PACK and passes it to TMI(0). Finally, TMI(0) receives the PACK and decrements the OPC by one.

Since the FIFOs at the IM, CM, and OM have a finite size, the PACK can be discarded due to the buffer overflow. To recover a lost PACK, the TMI sends a flush packet if the OPC is non-zero for a long time. If a flush packet is sent, the packets with the corresponding FID are held at the TMI until the flush packet is acknowledged. If the flush PACK is received, the TMI resets the OPC and chooses a new path for the packet with the FGID. To distinguish the flushed PACK from other PACKs, one more bit in the cell header must be used.

In the worst case, each TME receives up to $p$ PACKs and sends $p$ PACKs, where $p$ is the number of planes in the multi-plane multi-stage switch. The PACK will not be backlogged unless more than $p$ PACKs are destined for the same TMI. Since each TMI can receive up to $p$ PACKs per time slot, there can be contention in the switch fabric if more than $p$ PACKs are destined for the same TMI. But since the PACKs are served in a cell-interleaved mode, it is unlikely that the PACKs are congested in the switch fabric.

### 13.4.3   Time-Stamp-Based Resequence

The first technique to resequencing packets is to use a time-based sequence number (SN). With reference to Figure 13.13, each packet carries a SN based on the arrival time at the input port, and is resequenced at the TME before its departure. The time-stamp-based resequence is a very simple resequencing technique to implement; however, it has limitations on a large scale switch. First, in a large scale switch, the SN is large and results in a large overhead ratio, which can be too big to be practical. A high overhead ratio implies an increase in implementation cost or performance degradation due to reduced internal speedup. Second, since Internet traffic is very complicated and each packet may travel freely along any path in the time-stamp-based scheme, it is difficult to estimate the out-of-sequence degree. Even in the case where the degree of out-of-sequence is bounded, implementing the resequencing circuits increases the cost. With these two disadvantages, implementation of time-stamp based resequencing in a high performance switch is commonly discouraged.

### 13.4.4   Window-Based Resequence

The next resequencing technique we propose is called window-based resequencing. Similar to time-stamp-based resequencing, window-based resequencing uses a SN for each flow. The SN ranges from 0 to W-1, where W is the window size. Therefore, the number of cells in the switch fabric for a flow cannot exceed W. If there are $N$ input ports and $N$ output

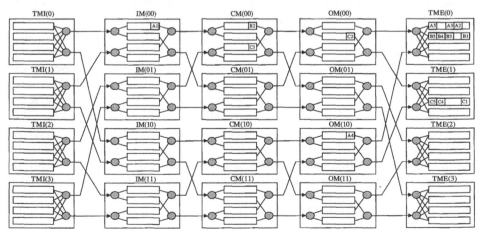

**Figure 13.13**   Time-stamp-based resequencing.

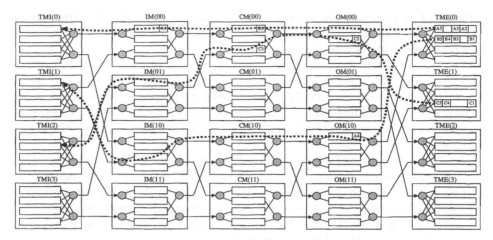

**Figure 13.14**    Window-based resequencing.

ports, the number of flows is $N^2$. Each input port has $N$ VOQs; each output port has $N$ virtual input queues (VIQs).

With reference to Figure 13.14, when an input port sends a cell to the switch fabric, it attaches an SN to the cell header. The SN is given by the VOQ manager. The VOQ manager maintains two pointers for each VOQ [the sequence head pointer (SEQ.head) and the sequence tail pointer (SEQ.tail)]. The SEQ.head is the SN to be attached to the cell sent from the input port. Right after a cell is sent, the SEQ.head is incremented by one.

When an output port receives a cell, it stores the cell in the VIQ according to its SN. The output port moves a cell from the VIQ to the reassembly queue (RAQ) only when the VIQ has a cell in order. Since the VIQ can receive cells out-of-order, it maintains a sequence pointer (SEQ.ptr). The SEQ.ptr indicates the SN for the VIQ to wait for. When a cell arrives at the TME with the SEQ.ptr, the cell is moved from the VIQ to the RAQ and the SEQ.ptr is incremented by one. If the SEQ.ptr is a multiple of $P$ (i.e., the number of switch planes), the output port sends an acknowledgment (ACK) packet with the SN of SEQ.ptr.

When an input port receives an ACK packet, it updates its SEQ.tail pointer. If the SN in the ACK packet is in the eligible range, the SEQ.tail is updated to the SN in the ACK packet. If the SN in the ACK packet is not in the eligible range, the SEQ.tail is not updated. The delivery of ACK packets can be implemented as those in the dynamic hashing algorithm described in Section 13.4.2.

The window-based resequencing scheme uses a sliding window technique. With reference to Figure 13.15, the TMI only allows $W$ unacknowledged packets for each flow in the switch fabric. Once TME acknowledges the number of successful packet transmissions, TMI releases the same amount of packets into the switch fabric. Thus, although packets may get out-of sequence within the switch fabric, the TME only needs $W$ length of resequencing buffer to sort the packets back in order.

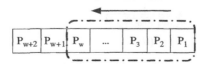

**Figure 13.15**    Sliding window technique in window-based resequencing.

Figure 13.16 summarizes the window-based resequencing algorithm. The three pointers (SEQ.head, SEQ.tail, and SEQ.ptr) are updated as already described. This ensures that the three pointers are always within the eligible range.

The question is how large the window size $W$ must be in order to get 100 percent throughput. $W$ must be equal to or greater than the round-trip time (RTT) in the unit of time slot, multiplied by the number of cells transmitted by the input port at each time slot, where the time slot is the time to transmit one cell. For example, if the RTT is 24 time slots and the number of cells transmitted by the input port in a time slot is eight, $W$ must be at least 192 cells long.

The RTT is composed of the propagation time between the input port and the output port, and the queuing time at the switch fabric. The propagation time is deterministic and fixed because it is proportional to the distance between the input port and the output port. If the switch fabric has a multi-stage architecture, the propagation time between the input port and the output port is the sum of the propagation times between the input port and IM, IM and CM, CM and OM, and OM and the output port.

For example, if the link speed is 2.5 Gbps and the cell size is 64 bytes (i.e., 512 bits), the time slot is 204.8 nsec. If the distance between IM and CM is 100 m, the propagation delay is 500 nsec (i.e., $100\,\text{m} \div 2 \times 10^8\,\text{m/s}$), which is equivalent to three time slots. Let us assume that the RTT between IM and CM is eight time slots and that between the input port and IM is four time slots. Then the propagation time between the input port and the output port is 24 time slots.

If the switch fabric is not congested, the queuing time at the switch fabric is negligible and the RTT is close to the propagation time. If the queuing time is less than eight time slots and the propagation time is 24 time slots, the RTT is less than 32 time slots and it is enough to set the window size $W$ to 256 cells. Note that the queuing time is the sum of the queuing delay of the forward direction from the input port to the output port for the delivery of the data cells, and that of the reverse direction from the output port to the input port for the delivery of the ACK packets.

If all input ports dispatch cells as evenly as possible to all possible paths, the queuing delay at the switch fabric will be minimized. One way to dispatch cells as evenly as possible

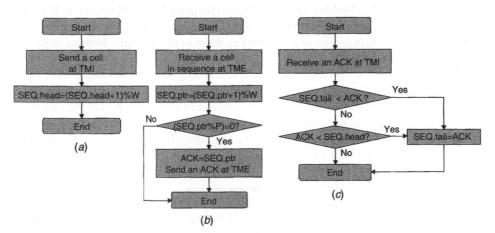

**Figure 13.16** Window-based resequencing flow diagram (*a*) Cell transmission at TMI; (*b*) Cell reception and ACK transmission at TME; (*c*) ACK reception at TMI.

to all possible paths is RR dispatching. That is, each input port maintains a path round-robin (RR) pointer per output port. If there is a valid cell at the head of the VOQ, the HOL cell of the VOQ is sent to the path in the path RR pointer and the path RR pointer is incremented by one.

## 13.5 PERFORMANCE ANALYSIS

This section provides performance results of the TrueWay switch architecture. The system parameters used in computer simulations evaluating the performance are as follows. There are eight planes and the IM, CM, and OM have 16 input links and 16 output links. There are 256 TMs. Each TM receives up to four cells per time slot and sends up to eight cells per time slot satisfying an internal speedup of 1.6.

The RTT between the TM and the IM/OM is assumed to be four time slots. The RTT between the IM/OM and CM is assumed to be eight time slots. The cell acknowledgment period is four time slots. The number of flows per TMI is 100,000. The VOQ size is 1024 cells and the cell memory size at the TMI is 262,144 cells. The RAQ size is 256 cells and the cell memory size at the TME is 4096 cells. The DQ size is 15 cells and the cell memory size at the SM is 32 cells.

It is assumed that all TMIs have the same traffic model. The simulation assumes a single priority level and a unicast destination. Each simulation generated about 20 million cells.

### 13.5.1 Random Uniform Traffic

Random uniform traffic is characterized as the traffic with the same length packets (e.g., one cell) with uniformly distributed destinations and similar flow bandwidth. The throughput performance of the proposed switch under random uniform traffic is always the same as the offered load, which is the expected result. The delay performance of the proposed switch under random uniform traffic is slightly larger than that of the output-buffered switch, as shown in Figure 13.17. This is because of the arbitration time and the distance between modules.

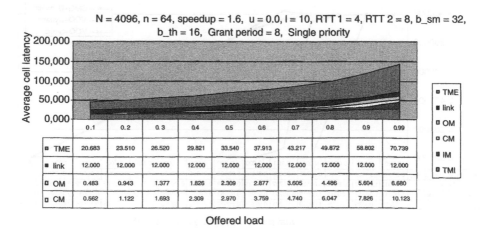

Figure 13.17 Delay performance under random uniform traffic.

### 13.5.2 Hot-Spot Traffic

The destinations of packets coming to the switch are independent of each other. Therefore, it is possible that a large portion of the traffic is destined for the same TME at the same time. The destination of a packet is determined by the non-uniform parameter $u$. If $u = 0.0$, the destination is uniform over all the TMEs. If $u = 1.0$, the destination is fixed to one hot-spot TME. In between these extremes, $u \times 100$ percent of the traffic has a fixed destination to one hot-spot TME and the other $(1 - u) \times 100$ percent of the traffic is uniformly distributed over all the TMEs. Figure 13.18 shows the maximum throughput versus the non-uniform parameter $u$ for various scheduling schemes.

### 13.5.3 Bursty Traffic

For this simulation, the average packet size is assumed to be 10 cells, with a maximum packet size of 192 cells. If the average packet size is smaller, the performance would be better. The average packet size in Internet traffic is about 280 bytes (i.e., five cells) and the maximum packet size is 9000 bytes (i.e., 161 cells).

Figure 13.19 shows the throughput performance of the PPI scheme and DPI scheme under bursty traffic. DPI1 is the DPI scheme with an MRC of 1 cell. DPI8 has an MRC of eight cells. It is observed that DPI8 performs best among the four schemes. Thus, our choice for the scheduling scheme is DPI8. It is also possible to let the MRC value be set externally.

### 13.5.4 Hashing Schemes

This section describes the performance of the TrueWay switch with two different hashing schemes. To analyze the performance of static hashing and dynamic hashing, a variety of traffic loading techniques are used to evaluate the impact on both hashing algorithms.

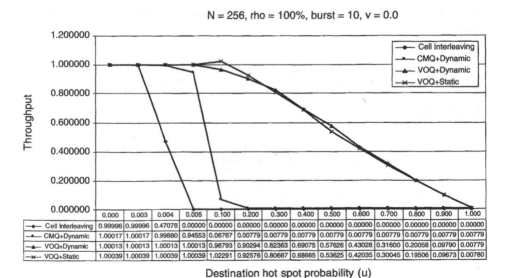

**Figure 13.18** Throughput performance under hot-spot traffic.

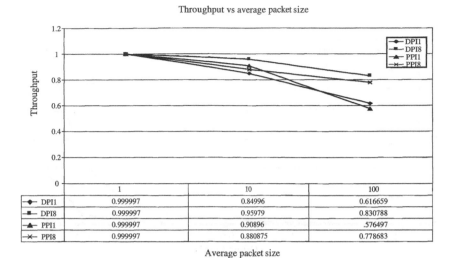

Figure 13.19    Performance under bursty traffic.

It is true that the flow bandwidth of Internet traffic has large variations. Some flows are a few kbps while some flows are a few Gbps. Assume that the port speed is 10 Gbps, the number of light flows is 100,000, and the number of heavy flows is 10. Let $v$ be the percentage of the heavy traffic. If $v = 0.0$, then all flows have the same bandwidth and the flow bandwidth is 100 kbps. If $v = 0.5$, the heavy flows have a bandwidth of 500 Mbps while the light flows have a bandwidth of 50 kbps. If $v = 1.0$, all flows will have the same bandwidth, 1 Gbps. Figure 13.20 shows the impact of flow bandwidth variation on the system throughput for static hashing and dynamic hashing. We can see that the dynamic

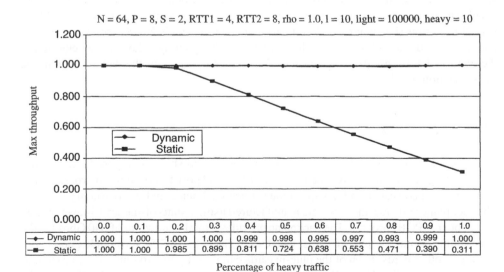

Figure 13.20    Throughput performance of static hashing and dynamic hashing.

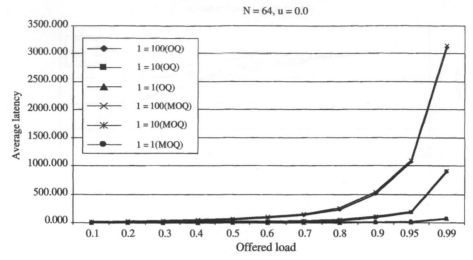

**Figure 13.21** Delay performance under bursty traffic.

hashing scheme is immune to any bandwidth variation, while the static hashing could not maintain 100 percent throughput under various traffic loading conditions.

### 13.5.5 Window-Based Resequencing Scheme

We set the window size $W$ to 256, which is analyzed in the earlier section that evaluates the TrueWay switch performance with the window-based resequencing scheme.

Figure 13.21 shows the delay performance of the proposed scheme under bursty traffic, compared with the optimal output-queued switch (OQ). The packet size is assumed to be geometrically distributed with the average packet size of $l$. Three sets of traffic patterns are shown ($l = 1$, $l = 10$, and $l = 100$). As in Figure 13.21, the delay in the switch fabric is very small. The worst-case average queuing delay observed in the switch fabric, VOQ, and VIQ was 21 time slots (i.e., approximately 4.3 µsec if one time slot is 204.8 nsec) when $l = 100$ and the offered load is 99 percent. This verifies that the queuing delay can be neglected in the window-based resequencing scheme. Thus the analysis about the window size in the earlier section is valid.

### 13.6 PROTOTYPE

A small-scale TrueWay switch on a chassis is prototyped, as shown in Figure 13.22, to evaluate various packet scheduling schemes, link-to-link and port-to-port flow control schemes. The prototype consists of a high-speed multi-trace backplane and up to 16 plug-in cards. The backplane and plug-in cards were manufactured using a state-of-the-art 14-layer printed circuit board (PCB) process. The backplane provides a total bandwidth of 640 Gbps for the inter-connection of the plug-in cards, where each card has 16 2.5-Gbps duplex ports connecting to other cards. Each of the plug-in cards can have up to two units, where each unit consists of one Xilinx Virtex-II 3000 FPGA, one Velio Octal 3.125 Gbps SerDes, and the necessary logic circuits.

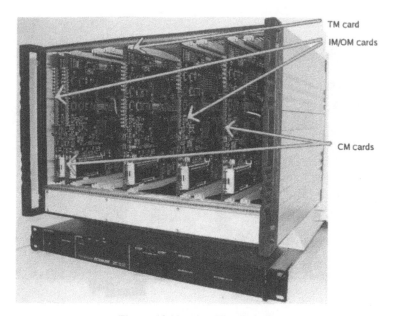

**Figure 13.22** TrueWay testbed.

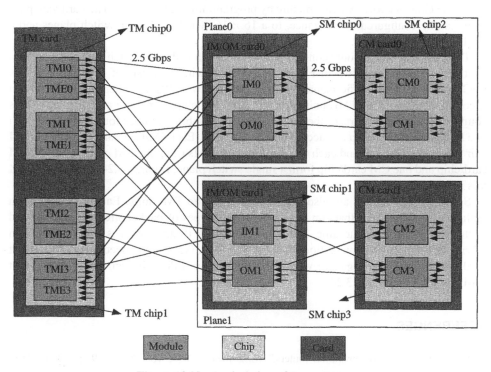

**Figure 13.23** Logical view of the prototype.

**Figure 13.24** Testbed card with two FPGAs (under heat sink) and two Velio Serdes chips.

The chassis provides a generic framework for testing different packet scheduling schemes under the Clos-network switch structure by programming FPGA chips. The hardware platform can be configured, for instance, to a $16 \times 16$ switch with four switch planes and a total capacity of 40 Gbps.

The current prototype only consists of a $4 \times 4$ switch with two switch planes for demonstration purposes, as shown in Figure 13.23. This switch consists of five cards and six FPGAs in total. The traffic manager (TM) card has two FPGAs, where each FPGA can accommodate two TMI/TME unit pairs (i.e., two TM chips), making a total of four TMs connecting to the four ports of the switch. The switch fabric includes four cards, each with one FPGA. One card/chip can accommodate two SMs. Each IM/OM card has one IM/OM pair (i.e., one SM chip) and each CM card has two CMs (i.e., one SM chip). One IM/OM card/chip and one CM card/chip form a single switch plane. Figure 13.24 shows a photo of this implementation.

Some testing features are also implemented into the TM chips. Each TM chip has a built-in traffic generator that can generate different types of packet streams to be applied to the switch. At the same time, TM chips also check if any packet is lost in the switch fabric. The Xilinx ISE Foundation toolkit with VHDL (very high-speed integrated circuit hardware description language) was used for the entire FPGA implementation. A 2-unit card is shown in Figure 13.24.

## REFERENCES

[1] H. J. Chao, "Next generation routers," *IEEE Proceedings*, vol. 90, no. 9, pp. 1518–1558 (Sept. 2002).

[2] C. Clos, "A study of non-blocking switching networks," *Bell System Technical Journal*, vol. 32, no. 3, pp. 406–424 (Mar. 1953).

[3] R. Sudan and W. Mukai, *Introduction to the Cisco CRS-1 Carrier Routing System*, Cisco Systems, Inc., San Jose, California (Jan. 1994).

[4] H. J. Chao, J. S. Park, S. Artan, S. Jiang, and G. Zhang, "TrueWay: A highly scalable multi-plane multi-stage buffered packet switch," in *Proc. IEEE Workshop on High Performance Switching and Routing*, Hong Kong, pp. 246–253 (May 2005).

[5] H. T. Kung, T. Blackwell, and A. Chapman, "Credit-based flow control for ATM networks: Credit update protocol, adaptive credit allocation, and statistical multiplexing," in *Proc. ACM SIGCOMM*, London, United Kingdom, pp. 101–115 (Aug. 1994).

[6] Y. C. Jung, C. K. Un, S. M. Ryu, and S. C. Lee, "Analysis of out-of-sequence problem and preventative schemes in parallel switch architecture for high-speed ATM network," *Proceedings of the IEEE*, vol. 141, no. 1, pp. 29–38 (Feb. 1994).

# CHAPTER 14

# LOAD-BALANCED SWITCHES

Internet traffic continues to grow rapidly, and to keep pace with demand, there has been a significant research effort into high-speed large-capacity packet switch architectures that consume less power yet outperform current switch architectures. Because of memory speed constraints, most proposed large-capacity packet switches use input buffering alone or in combination with other schemes, such as output buffering or cross-point buffering. The issue of how to schedule packets efficiently to achieve high throughput and low delay for a large-capacity switch has been one of the main research topics in the past few years. Although several practical scheduling schemes have been proposed or implemented, for example, *i*SLIP [1], DRRM [2], and others, most of them require a centralized packet scheduler, an increase in the interconnection complexity between the line cards and the packet scheduler, and a speedup for the switch fabric to compensate for some deficiencies in packet scheduling. Most practical packet-scheduling schemes cannot achieve 100 percent throughput especially under some traffic distributions.

Recently, a novel switch architecture, the load-balanced Birkhoff–von Neumann (LB-BvN) switch proposed by Chang et al. [3], overcame the above-mentioned problems and opened up a new avenue for designing large-capacity packet switches without using a packet scheduler, and for achieving 100 percent throughput under nearly all traffic distributions.

## 14.1 BIRKHOFF–VON NEUMANN SWITCH

Before introducing load-balanced Birkhoff–von Neumann switches, let us look into the traditional Birkhoff–von Neumann switch. With reference to Figure 14.1, the Birkhoff–von

*High Performance Switches and Routers*, by H. Jonathan Chao and Bin Liu
Copyright © 2007 John Wiley & Sons, Inc.

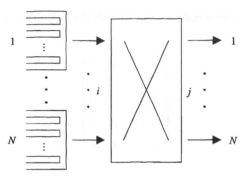

**Figure 14.1** Birkhoff–von Neumann switch.

Neumann switch is an input-buffered switch. It uses the virtual output queuing (VOQ) technique to solve the head-of-line (HOL) blocking problem.

The principle behind solving output port contention in the Birkhoff–von Neumann switch is to use the capacity decomposition approach described by Birkhoff [4] and von Neumann [5] to schedule the connection patterns. Let $\mathbf{r} = [r_{i,j}]$ be the rate matrix with $r_{i,j}$ being the rate allocated to the traffic from input $i$ to output $j$ for an $N \times N$ input-buffered switch with the following conditions:

$$\sum_{i=1}^{N} r_{i,j} \leq 1, \qquad j = 1, 2, \ldots, N, \tag{14.1}$$

and

$$\sum_{j=1}^{N} r_{i,j} \leq 1, \qquad i = 1, 2, \ldots, N. \tag{14.2}$$

Then, there exists a set of positive numbers $\phi_k$ and permutation matrices $\mathbf{P}_k$, $k = 1, 2, \ldots, K$, for some $K \leq N^2 - 2N + 2$ that satisfies

$$\mathbf{r} \leq \sum_{k=1}^{K} \phi_k \mathbf{P}_k, \tag{14.3}$$

and

$$\sum_{k=1}^{K} \phi_k = 1. \tag{14.4}$$

When such a decomposition is obtained, it is simply a case of scheduling the connection pattern $\mathbf{P}_k$ proportional to its weight $\phi_k$. For the details of the decomposition algorithm, refer to Chang et al. [6, 7].

For instance, a $4 \times 4$ input-buffered switch with the traffic rate matrix:

$$\begin{pmatrix} \frac{1}{3} & \frac{2}{3} & 0 & 0 \\ \frac{2}{3} & \frac{1}{3} & 0 & 0 \\ 0 & 0 & 1 & 0 \\ 0 & 0 & 0 & 1 \end{pmatrix}$$

Using the Birkhoff–von Neumann rate decomposition, we obtain the following two permutation matrices $P_1$ and $P_2$ with corresponding weight $\phi_1$ and $\phi_2$:

$$\frac{1}{3}\begin{pmatrix} 1 & 0 & 0 & 0 \\ 0 & 1 & 0 & 0 \\ 0 & 0 & 1 & 0 \\ 0 & 0 & 0 & 1 \end{pmatrix}, \quad \frac{2}{3}\begin{pmatrix} 0 & 1 & 0 & 0 \\ 1 & 0 & 0 & 0 \\ 0 & 0 & 1 & 0 \\ 0 & 0 & 0 & 1 \end{pmatrix}$$

With these two permutation matrices in hand, it is easy to schedule the connection pattern according to its weight. The connection pattern corresponding to this example is shown in Figure 14.2.

If the allocated bandwidth is larger than the arrival rate for each input–output pair, Chang [6, 7] has shown that the Birkhoff–von Neumann input-buffered switch can achieve 100 percent throughput without framing and internal speedup. However, the complexity of Birkhoff–von Neumann decomposition is as high as $O(N^{4.5})$, and the number of permutation matrices deduced from the Birkhoff–von Neumann decomposition algorithm is $O(N^2)$, which may not scale for switches with a large number of input/output ports.

Thus, the Birkhoff–von Neumann input-buffered switch has attractive system performance but suffers from computational complexity and scalability. However, let us consider a special case of an input-buffered switch, in which all inputs have uniform traffic distribution.

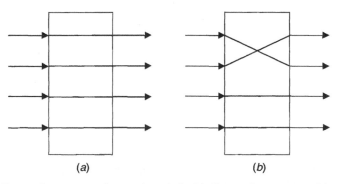

(a)                    (b)

**Figure 14.2**   Connection pattern of example switch. (*a*) Connection pattern with weight $1/3$; (*b*) Connection pattern with weight $2/3$.

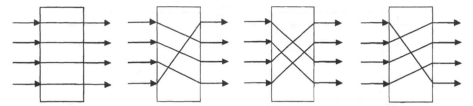

**Figure 14.3**    Connection patterns of a $4 \times 4$ input-buffered load-balanced switch.

We can easily construct a traffic rate matrix for such a $4 \times 4$ switch, as follows:

$$\begin{pmatrix} \frac{1}{4} & \frac{1}{4} & \frac{1}{4} & \frac{1}{4} \\ \frac{1}{4} & \frac{1}{4} & \frac{1}{4} & \frac{1}{4} \\ \frac{1}{4} & \frac{1}{4} & \frac{1}{4} & \frac{1}{4} \\ \frac{1}{4} & \frac{1}{4} & \frac{1}{4} & \frac{1}{4} \end{pmatrix};$$

and the permutation matrices and corresponding weights for this load-balanced switch are:

$$\begin{pmatrix} 1 & 0 & 0 & 0 \\ 0 & 1 & 0 & 0 \\ 0 & 0 & 1 & 0 \\ 0 & 0 & 0 & 1 \end{pmatrix}, \begin{pmatrix} 0 & 1 & 0 & 0 \\ 0 & 0 & 1 & 0 \\ 0 & 0 & 0 & 1 \\ 1 & 0 & 0 & 0 \end{pmatrix}, \begin{pmatrix} 0 & 0 & 1 & 0 \\ 0 & 0 & 0 & 1 \\ 1 & 0 & 0 & 0 \\ 0 & 1 & 0 & 0 \end{pmatrix}, \begin{pmatrix} 0 & 0 & 0 & 1 \\ 1 & 0 & 0 & 0 \\ 0 & 1 & 0 & 0 \\ 0 & 0 & 1 & 0 \end{pmatrix}.$$

The connection patterns according to these permutations are shown in Figure 14.3.

Notice that in an input-buffered switch with uniform traffic distribution, the Birkhoff–von Neumann decomposition gives us simply the periodic time division multiplexed (TDM) connection pattern. In other words, a deterministic TDM switch fabric can ensure a load-balanced switch to achieve 100 percent throughput with a scheduling complexity of $O(1)$. This is the motivation for designing a two-stage load-balanced Birkhoff–von Neumann switch.

## 14.2  LOAD-BALANCED BIRKHOFF–VON NEUMANN SWITCHES

This section presents the load-balanced Birkhoff–von Neumann switch architecture and its performance including throughput, delay, and buffer usage.

### 14.2.1  Load-Balanced Birkhoff–von Neumann Switch Architecture

With reference to Figure 14.4, the load-balanced Birkhoff–von Neumann (LB-BvN) switch consists of two crossbar switch stages and one set of VOQs between these stages. The first stage performs load balancing and the second stage performs switching. This switch does not need any schedulers since the connection patterns of the two switch stages are

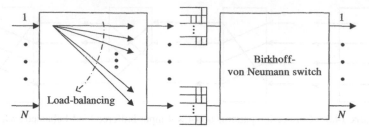

**Figure 14.4** LB-BvN switch.

deterministic and are repeated periodically. The connection patterns should be selected so that in every consecutive $N$ timeslot, each input should connect to each output exactly once with a duration of one timeslot.

The LB-BvN switch has the following advantages:

1. *Scalability.* On-line complexity of the scheduling algorithm of the switch is $O(1)$.

2. *Low Hardware Complexity.* Only two crossbar switch fabrics and buffers are required, and the two crossbar switch fabrics can be realized by the Banyan networks, due to deterministic and periodic connection patterns. Neither internal speedup nor rate estimation (as in the original Birkhoff–von Neumann switch) is needed in this switch.

3. *100 Percent Throughput.* Load-balanced Birkhoff–von Neumann switch achieves 100 percent throughput as an output-buffered switch for unicast and multicast traffic.

4. *Low Average Delay in Heavy Load and Bursty Traffic.* When input traffic is bursty, load balancing is very effective in reducing delay. The average delay of the load of the LB-BvN switch is proven to converge to that of an output-buffered switch under heavy load.

5. *Efficient Buffer Usage.* When both the LB-BvN switch and the corresponding output-buffered switch are allocated with the same finite amount of buffers at each port, the packet loss probability in the LB-BvN is much smaller than that in an output-buffered switch when the buffer is large.

### 14.2.2 Performance of Load-Balanced Birkhoff–von Neumann Switches

As mentioned in the earlier section, a single-stage input-buffered crossbar switch using deterministic sequence achieves 100 percent throughput for uniform Bernoulli i.i.d. (independent and identically distributed) traffic. In the LB-BvN switch, the first stage supplies the second stage with such a traffic distribution by performing load-balancing using deterministic connection patterns. Since the second-stage switch receives uniform Bernoulli i.i.d. traffic, the entire system can reach 100 percent throughput for nearly all input traffic patterns. A rigorous proof of the throughput for the LB-BvN switch and the conditions on input traffic requirements are given by Chang et al. [3].

With reference to Figure 14.5, the average delay of the LB-BvN switch is noticeably better than that of the single-stage Birkhoff–von Neumann switch, and converges to output-buffered switches at heavy load above 0.9.

This excellent average delay performance in the LB-BvN switch is due to the first-stage load-balancing switch. It efficiently reduces the burstiness of traffic from inputs to VOQs

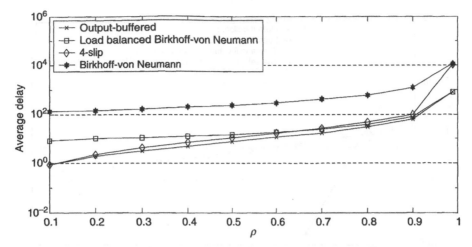

**Figure 14.5** Average delay under the uniform bursty traffic.

between two stages. As a result, the second-stage Birkhoff–von Neumann switch always receives uniform Bernoulli i.i.d. traffic. Hence, the average delay is significantly better than the single stage Birkhoff–von Neumann switch and has convergence with output-buffered switches at high traffic load. Figure 14.6 illustrates the effect of the first-stage load-balancing switch under uniform bursty traffic. Notice the traffic at each VOQ is indeed uniform Bernoulli i.i.d.

Chang et al. [3] mathematically compared the average delay between the output-buffered switch and the LB-BvN switch. As Table 14.1 shows, under heavy load bursty traffic ($\rho \to 1$), the average delays of both switches are similar.

In addition to 100 percent throughput and outstanding average delay, the LB-BvN switch is more efficient in buffer usage than the corresponding output-buffered switch. With reference to Figure 14.7, the decay rate of the tail distribution of queue length in the LB-BvN

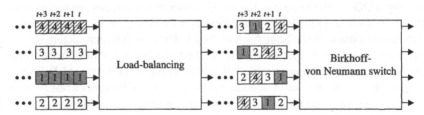

**Figure 14.6** Burst reduction in the uniform bursty traffic model.

**TABLE 14.1  Average Delay of Output-Buffered Switch and LB-BvN**

| Delay | Output-Buffered | Load-Balanced |
|---|---|---|
| i.i.d. | $(N-1) \cdot \rho/N \cdot 2(1-\rho)$ | $(N-1)/2(1-\rho)$ |
| Bursty | $(N-1) \cdot \rho/2(1-\rho)$ | $(N-1)/2(1-\rho)$ |

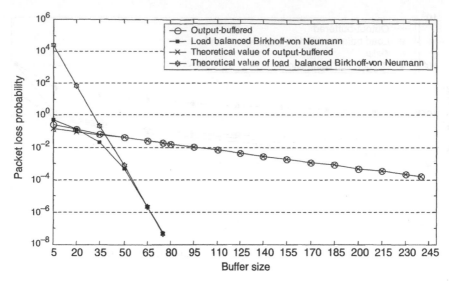

**Figure 14.7** Packet loss probability under uniform bursty traffic ($N = 16$, $\rho = 0.8$).

is much smaller than that of the corresponding output-buffered switch. This implies that if we allocate the same finite amount of buffer in each port of both switches, the LB-BvN switch has a much smaller packet loss probability than that of the output-buffered switch.

## 14.3 LOAD-BALANCED BIRKHOFF–VON NEUMANN SWITCHES WITH FIFO SERVICE

A flow is defined as all of the packets[1] going from one input $i$ to one output $k$ and is denoted as $S(i, k)$. Since the traffic at the input of the switch is not necessarily uniform, the number of packets from different flows can vary. This situation is reflected as the difference in queue lengths at the VOQs in the middle of the switch. Since those queues are served uniformly independent of their lengths, delays in addition to the queuing delay and out-of-sequence of packets are inevitable in the basic form of the LB-BvN switch architecture (Fig. 14.4).

The remainder of this chapter is dedicated to the techniques that have been proposed to solve the packet out-of-sequence problem that is inherent in the original LB-BvN switch. Why is this such a problem? Out-of-sequence packets make TCP trigger a fast recovery, and TCP's sliding window is reduced by half. This also reduces end-to-end throughput by half. Taking a closer look at how packets are transmitted out of sequence, we need to focus on the four flows $S(1, 4)$, $S(2, 3)$, $S(3, 1)$, and $S(4, 2)$ from Figure 14.6, each of which contains four packets (a, b, c, and d), and has an arrival order of a < b < c < d. Each diagram in Figure 14.8 represents the switching stage of the LB-BvN switch at different times within a single connection cycle.

At time $t$ in Figure 14.8a, four packets, 4a, 3a, 1a, and 2a, arrive at each of the four VOQs. Since there are no packets queued for the outputs determined by this connection pattern, no packets are transmitted.

---

[1] Packets and cells are interchangeable in the chapter.

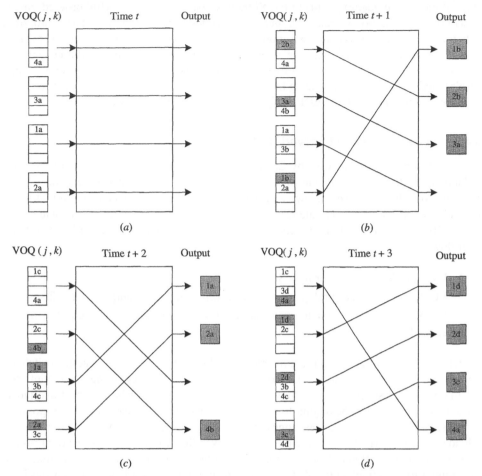

**Figure 14.8** LB-BvN switching stages. (*a*) LB-BvN Switching stage at time *t*; (*b*) LB-BvN Switch stage at time *t* + 1; (*c*) LB- BvN Switching stage at time *t* + 2; and (*d*) LB-BvN Switching stage at time *t* + 3.

At time *t* + 1, four more packets (2b, 4b, 3b, and 1b) arrive at the VOQs, as shown in Figure 14.8*b*. The new connection pattern allows three packets from the inputs to be transmitted. Already we can begin to notice the out-of-sequence problem since packets 1b and 2b have been transmitted while packets 1a and 2a, which arrived one time slot earlier, are still waiting in the buffers.

At time *t* + 2, four new packets arrive and the current connection pattern transmits three more packets. Notice that packet 1a arrives at output 1 while in the previous time slot packet 1b has already been transmitted, as shown in Figure 14.8*c*. At time *t* + 3, the last packets of each of the four flows arrive at the second-stage inputs as shown in Figure 14.8*d*. The connection pattern then repeats itself in a periodic fashion, allowing buffered packets to be transmitted when they are connected to their desired output ports.

Seven schemes, proposed to solve the problem of out-of-sequence packets in the LB-BvN switches, are now described: (1) FCFS (first come first served) based scheduling policy [8], (2) EDF (earliest deadline first) based scheduling policy [8], (3) EDF-3DQ (EDF using a three-dimensional queue) [9], (4) FFF (full frames first) [9], (5) FOFF (full ordered frames first) [10], (6) Mailbox switch [11], and (7) the Byte-Focal switch [12]. These proposed schemes can be categorized into two approaches. The second approach is to prevent packets from being received out-of-sequence at the outputs, for example, FFF and Mailbox switch. The second approach is to limit out-of-sequence packets to an upper bound, for example, $O(N^2)$, and then add a resequencing buffer (RB) at the output to reorder the packets. Such schemes include FCFS, EDF, EDF-3DQ, FOFF, and Byte-Focal switch.

### 14.3.1 First Come First Served (FCFS)

The FCFS scheme was proposed by Chang et al. [8], who are also the authors of the load-balancing Birkhoff–von Neumann switch. To tackle the out-of-sequence issue in the original LB-BvN switch, FCFS requires two additional buffers. With reference to Figure 14.9, the two additional buffers are: (1) the load-balancing buffer at every input of the switch, and (2) the RB at the output of the switch. The definitions of the terms used in Figure 14.9 are as follows:

1. FS$(i, k)$. Flow splitter for flow S$(i, k)$.
2. VCQ$(i, j)$. Virtual central queue at input $i$, corresponding to output $j$ of the first stage.
3. VOQ$(j, k)$. Virtual output queue at input $j$, corresponding to output $k$ of the second stage.

The operation of the switch is summarized as follows. Packets arriving at the switch are spread to virtual central queues (VCQs) for load balancing. This spreading is accomplished as follows. FCFS schemes have a flow-splitter for each flow at each input port that labels packets at each input as belonging to a particular flow S$(i, k)$. Since there are $N$ possible outputs, there are $N$ possible flows, one corresponding to each of the $N$ output ports. Next, a load balancer distributes all of the packets of a given flow to the $N$ VCQs in a round-robin manner (there is a different load balancer for each flow) [10]. For each flow splitter, there is a pointer to keep track of the VCQ$(i, j)$ that the previous packet from that flow has been sent to.

The first-stage switch follows a periodic deterministic pattern to connect an input $i$ to an output $j$ for one timeslot in each frame slot. A frame slot is defined as $N$ timeslots. At timeslot $t$, the connection pattern $(i, j)$ satisfies

$$i - 1 = (j - 1 + t) \bmod N, \tag{14.5}$$

where $t = 1, 2, \ldots, i = 1, 2, \ldots, N$, and $j = 1, 2, \ldots, N$.

The second-stage switch operates similar to the first one with a periodic deterministic pattern such that at time $t$, the connection pattern $(j, k)$ satisfies

$$k - 1 = (j - 1 + t) \bmod N, \tag{14.6}$$

where $t = 1, 2, \ldots, j = 1, 2, \ldots, N$, and $k = 1, 2, \ldots, N$.

FCFS has jitter control in front of the second-stage buffers as shown in Figure 14.10. Packets from the same flow are distributed evenly in the first stage and arrive at the jitter control stage. Since packets of the same flow may experience different delays in the first-stage buffer due to the different lengths of VCQs, jitter control is used to restore packets'

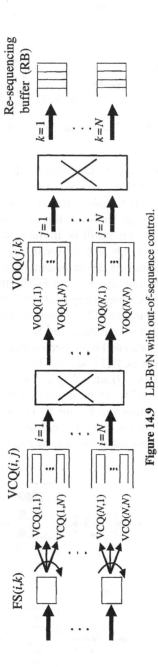

**Figure 14.9** LB-BvN with out-of-sequence control.

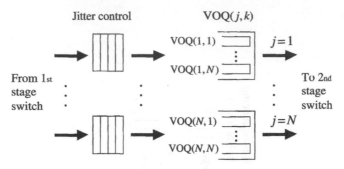

**Figure 14.10**    Second-stage buffers of FCFS.

arriving order at the second-stage buffer by imposing a delay, up to $N \times (N - 1)$ timeslots, to each packet before joining the VOQs. In other words, every packet will experience the same amount of delay, $N \times (N - 1)$ timeslots, from the time of their arrival at the VCQs to the time when they join the VOQs. However, this does not necessarily mean that their departures from the second-stage buffer will be in the same order as their arrivals. This is because they are likely to join VOQs with different lengths (although the difference is bounded by $N$ cells). As a result, packets are out-of-sequence when they arrive at the output buffers. A RB is required at the outputs. For the FCFS, the jitter control increases the implementation complexity and increases every packet's delay by $N \times (N - 1)$ timeslots.

The following example shows how the FCFS scheme resolves the packet out-of-sequence problem in the LB-BvN switch. Let us consider a flow $S(1, 1)$, which implies a packet stream from input 1 to output 1. Packets Pa and Pb are two consecutive packets from flow $S(1, 1)$ with sequence Pa $<$ Pb. As seen in the FCFS scheme described above in Figure 14.9, Pa and Pb split into two consecutive VCQ$(1, j)$ and VCQ$(1, j + 1)$ in a round-robin fashion upon their arrival. Without losing generality, let us assume Pa and Pb are queued at VCQ$(1, 1)$ and VCQ$(1, 2)$, respectively, as shown in Figure 14.11. Since the queue length of each VCQ$(i, j)$ is not uniform at all times, packets belonging to the same flow may depart from input VCQ$(i, j)$ in an uncoordinated fashion. In this case, Pb will depart VCQ$(1, 2)$

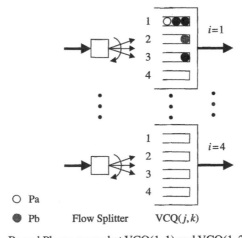

**Figure 14.11**    Pa and Pb are queued at VCQ$(1, 1)$ and VCQ$(1, 2)$, respectively.

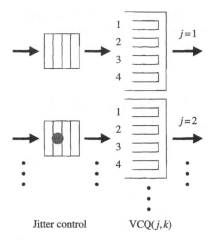

**Figure 14.12**    Pb is delayed in jitter control due to out-of-sequence caused by VCQ(*i*, *j*).

eight timeslots (two frame slots) earlier than Pa, which causes packet out-of-sequence problems. FCFS prevents this out-of-sequence problem by adding jitter control in front of VOQ(*j*, *k*). In this example, Pb is delayed in the jitter control stage by two frame slots (Fig. 14.12), so that it will enter VOQ(2, 1) at the same frame slot as Pa enters VOQ(1, 1). However, the queue lengths of VOQ(*j*, *k*) are not uniformly distributed from timeslot to timeslot either, as Figure 14.13 shows. Although the jitter-control stage resolves the out-of-sequence problem caused by input buffer VCQ(*i*, *j*), flow S(1, 1) may still experience the out-of-sequence problem due to VOQ(*j*, *k*). As a result, RBs are required at each output. The resequencing buffer reorders the packets so that packets of the same flow depart in the same order as they arrive. After resequencing, packets are stored in the output buffer until their transmission.

The FCFS scheme resolves the out-of-sequence problem in the original LB-BvN switch with the cost of: (1) two additional groups of buffers at inputs and outputs, respectively;

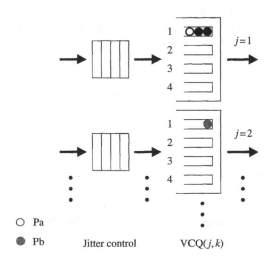

**Figure 14.13**    Pa and Pb are queued at VOQ(1, 1) and VOQ(2, 1) that have different queue lengths.

(2) additional average packet delay up to $N \times (N - 1)$ timeslots due to the jitter control; and (3) increased implementation complexity by adding jitter control and the resequencing buffer. With jitter control, the FCFS is able to bound the resequence delay to $N^2$ cell. Thus, the RB size is bounded to $N^2$ cells.

### 14.3.2 Earliest Deadline First (EDF) and EDF-3DQ

The earliest deadline first (EDF) is another scheduling policy scheme proposed by Chang et al. [8] to resolve the packet out-of-sequence issue in the original LB-BvN switch. The EDF uses the same switch architecture and switch operation as the FCFS. However, the EDF scheme eliminates jitter control. Instead, it assigns a deadline to every packet to determine its departure from the second-stage buffer, VOQ($j$, $k$). The deadline can be either the departure time of a corresponding output-buffered switch or simply the packet's arrival time. The packets in the second-stage buffer are served based on their deadline values. The earlier the deadline, the earlier the packet is served at the second-stage switch. Since packets arrive at VOQ($j$, $k$)s in an uncoordinated fashion, the HOL packet is not necessarily carrying the earliest deadline. Searching the smallest timestamp in each VOQ is prohibitively complex and costly. Moreover, each flow S($i$, $k$) may traverse different VOQ($j$, $k$)s to reach the output port ($k$). Different lengths of VOQ($j$, $k$) can still cause the mis-sequence problem. The EDF scheme requires a RB with a size of $2N^2 - 2N$ cells to reorder the cells.

EDF-3DQ [9] improves the EDF scheme by replacing the VOQs in the second-stage buffers with three-dimensional queues (3DQs). With reference to Figure 14.14, in the 3DQs structure, there is a different queue per ($i$, $j$, $k$); hence, there are a total of $N^3$ logical queues between first- and second-stage switches in EDF-3DQs. In the original VOQ structure, each VOQ($j$, $k$) contains packets from multiple flows destined for output port $k$. In the 3DQ structure, each VOQ($j$, $k$) has associated with it a total of $N$ queues labeled 3DQ($i$, $j$, $k$). Each of these $N$ queues contains packets of the same flow. There are a total of $N$ possible flows. Hence, there are $N$ queues for each VOQ($j$, $k$). For example, 3DQ(1, 1, 1) contains only packets of flow S(1, 1); 3DQ(2, 1, 1) only contains packets of flow S(2, 1). In the original VOQ structure, both of these flows may be placed in a single queue. So the objective of the 3DQ structure is to separate packets at each VOQ into their individual flows. With 3DQs, the earliest packet for ($j$, $k$) is always the HOL packet in its

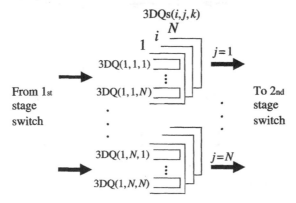

**Figure 14.14** Three-dimensional queues (3DQs) in EDF.

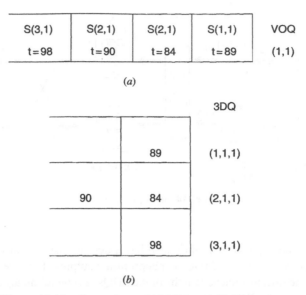

**Figure 14.15** Comparison of (a) VOQ and (b) 3DQ structure.

queue. As a result, we only need to compare $N$ HOL packets' timestamp to find the earliest deadline packet, instead of comparing $Q_{max}$ timestamps in the original EDF scheme, where $Q_{max}$ is one maximum queue length of the VOQ.

Figure 14.15 shows the effect of 3DQs in performing the EDF scheme. Figure 14.15a is an example of packet-queuing status in the original VOQ($j$, $k$) structure. It can be easily seen that to find the earliest deadline packet, all packets in the queue need to be compared. In contrast, Figure 14.15b is the queuing status of the same packets in Figure 14.15a, but in a 3DQ format. Notice that the HOL packet of each 3DQ($i$, $j$, $k$) always carries the earliest deadline. Therefore, to perform the EDF scheme, only a comparison of $N$ timestamps is needed.

Although EDF-3DQ relaxes the constraints of searching the smallest timestamp in the complete queue, it still requires a comparison of $N$ timestamps of $N$ HOL packets of the 3DQs in each timeslot, limiting the switch size or the line rate. Moreover, EDF-3DQ still requires the same size of RB at each output port as in EDF, $2N^2 - 2N$.

### 14.3.3 Full Frames First (FFF)

This scheme uses a frame-based approach, called full frames first (FFF) [9], to solve the out-of-sequence problem in the LB-BvN switch. The FFF scheme is different from the other schemes in the sense that it completely eliminates the out-of-sequence problem and thus requires no RB buffers at the outputs. With reference to Figure 14.16, the switch architecture of the FFF scheme is similar to those of FCFS and EDF, except that FFF has 3DQs between two switch fabrics instead of VOQs in FCFS and EDF. Most importantly, FFF does not require any RBs.

Similar to FCFS and EDF, each traffic flow $S(i, k)$ is split into $N$ VCQ($i$, $j$)s in a round-robin fashion upon their arrival at inputs. The first-stage switch fabric in FFF deterministically delivers packets from VCQ($i$, $j$)s to 3DQ($i$, $j$, $k$)s in a periodic manner.

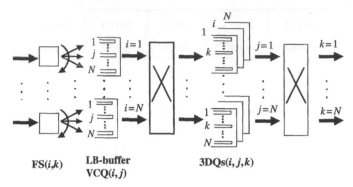

FS(*i,k*)    **LB-buffer**    3DQs(*i, j, k*)
VCQ(*i, j*)

**Figure 14.16**   FFF scheme.

Likewise, the second-stage switch fabric also has a deterministic connection pattern for switching packets from $3DQ(i, j, k)$s to their appropriate outputs. To prevent packet out-of-sequence due to the different queue lengths of the 3DQs, a scheduling algorithm is needed to serve packets from the 3DQs to the outputs.

In FFF, a candidate set of 3DQs for $(i, k)$ consists of packets from $(i, 1, k)$, $(i, 2, k)$, and $(i, N, k)$. It is important to remember that each $3DQ(i, j, k)$ contains packets from unique flows (packets from different flows will not be found in the same queue). Because of load balancing, a flow is uniformly distributed among all $N$ 3DQs. Assume that the last serviced packet in the candidate set came from $3DQ(i, j_{\text{last}}, k)$. Because of the properties of the load-balancer and 3DQs, it is known that the next in-order packet for the flow $S(i, k)$ will come from $3DQ(i, j_{(\text{last}+1)\bmod N}, k)$. Let $p_{ik}$ be the pointer to the $3DQ(i, j, k)$ of the next in-order packet: $p_{ik} = j_{(\text{last}+1)\bmod N}$. For instance, let Pa and Pb be two packets belonging to the same flow $S(1, 1)$ with sequence Pa < Pb. They will be queued at VCQ(1, 1) and VCQ(1, 2), respectively, upon their arrival at their inputs (Fig. 14.17a). Although Pa and Pb will transfer to 3DQs in different timeslots, one can expect they will be queued at $3DQ(1, 1, 1)$ and $3DQ(1, 2, 1)$, respectively. In other words, if Pa is from $3DQ(1, 1, 1)$, then the next in-order packet will necessarily be read from the $3DQ(1, 2, 1)$ with $p_{ik} = 1 + 1 = 2$, which is Pb in this example (Fig. 14.17b).

In FFF, a cycle is defined as $N$ consecutive timeslots; a frame for flow $(i, k)$ is defined as $f(i, k) = (i, p_{ik}, k), (i, p_{ik} + 1, k), \ldots, (i, N, k)$; and a frame is full if every $3DQ(i, j, k)$ for $j = p_{ik}, \ldots, N$ is non-empty. One can easily see that if the frame is full, then the second-stage switch fabric can continuously transfer in-order packets from $3DQ(i, p_{ik}, k)$ up until $3DQ(i, N, k)$. This is the key to preventing out-of-sequence packets in the FFF. Searching for full frames is performed once every cycle. An output reads all the packets in a full frame from one input, before moving on to read a full frame from the next input. Each output, $k$, uses a round-robin pointer $p_{ff}(k)$ to remember which input the last full frame came from, so that each output gives an opportunity to each input in turn to send a full frame to it. If there are no full frames, output $k$ serves the non-full frames in a round-robin manner by using a pointer $p_{nff}(k)$.

More precisely, the FFF scheme consists of three computation steps for each output port $k$ at the beginning of every cycle:

Step 1:  Determine which of the frames f($i, k$) is full.

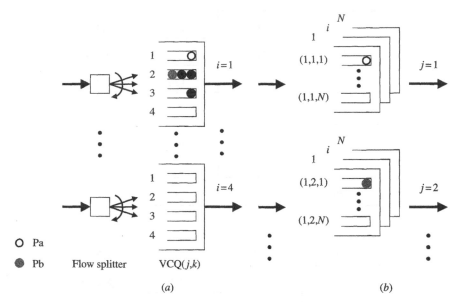

**Figure 14.17** Property of flow splitter and 3DQs. (*a*) Pa and Pb at input VCQ($j, k$); (*b*) Pa and Pb at 3DQ($i, j, k$).

Step 2:   Starting at $p_{ff}(k)$, find the first full frame and then update the full frame pointer $p_{ff}(k)$ to that input associated with the full frame.

Step 3:   If there is no full frame, starting at $p_{nff}(k)$, find the first non-full frame, then update the non-full frame pointer $p_{nff}(k)$ accordingly.

Next, we use an example to illustrate FFF in more detail. Let us assume a $3 \times 3$ LB-BvN switch with the FFF scheduling algorithm. At the beginning of a cycle, the 3DQs for output 1 are in the state shown in Figure 14.18. To better explain the algorithm, we rearrange the 3DQs so that all of the queues containing packets from a given input are adjacent to each other (Fig. 14.19). The numbers indicate the packet sequence number within its flow. Let us also assume that $p_{ff}(1) = p_{nff}(1) = 3$; and the frame pointer $p_{11}(1)$, $p_{21}(1) = 3$, and $p_{31}(1) = 1$.

At the first timeslot, FFF serves the first full frame for input 3 because of $p_{ff}(1) = 3$. The first full frame consists of $ff1 = 136, 137,$ and $138$. After serving this full frame, pointers are updated as $p_{ff}(1) = 1$ and $p_{31}(1) = 1$. In the next cycle, FFF serves the three packets from input 1 in frame $ff2 = 190, 191,$ and $192$, then updates $p_{11}(1) = 1$ and $p_{ff}(1) = 2$. According to the definition, $ff3 = 57$ is a full frame from input 2, though it only contains one packet. A frame is said to be full if and only if it is possible to transfer in-order cells from $(i, p_{ik}, k)$ up until $(i, N, k)$. The FFF serves it next and updates the pointers. After that, there is no full frame from input 3, but inputs 1 and 2 still have full frame. The FFF serves $ff4$ and $ff5$ in the next two cycles. Then, the pointers are updated as follows: $p_{ff}(1) = p_{nff}(1) = 3$, and $p_{11}(1) = p_{21}(1) = p_{31}(1) = 1$.

When there are no full frames left in the system, the FFF serves the non-full frames in round-robin order: $nff1$, $nff2$, and $nff3$. Pointers are updated to $p_{ff}(1) = p_{nff}(1) = 3$, $p_{11}(1) = 2$, $p_{21}(1) = 3$, and $p_{31}(1) = 3$. Note that packet 198 from input 1 will not be

| 196 | 193 | 190 | (1, 1, 1) |
|---|---|---|---|
| 61 | 58 | | (2, 1, 1) |
| 142 | 139 | 136 | (3, 1, 1) |

| | 194 | 191 | (1, 2, 1) |
|---|---|---|---|
| 62 | 59 | | (2, 2, 1) |
| 143 | 140 | 137 | (3, 2, 1) |

| 198 | 195 | 192 | (1, 3, 1) |
|---|---|---|---|
| | 60 | 57 | (2, 3, 1) |
| | | 138 | (3, 3, 1) |

**Figure 14.18**  Illustration of FFF algorithm in LB-BvN switch.

served due to missing packet 197. Similarly, packets 142 and 143 will not be served either, since $p_{31}(1) = 3$, the pointer is still waiting for packet 141.

The FFF features most of the benefits of the original LB-BvN switch with the benefit of the first in, first out (FIFO) service discipline. However, it requires complex 3DQs between

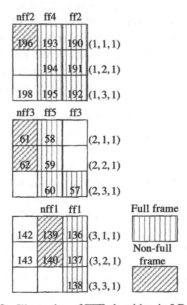

**Figure 14.19**  Illustration of FFF algorithm in LB-BvN switch.

two switch fabrics and a large amount of communication overhead flowing between the line cards to search for full frames.

### 14.3.4 Full Ordered Frames First (FOFF)

Full ordered frame first (FOFF) is another frame-based scheduling scheme to resolve the packet out-of-sequence problem in the LB-BvN switch [10]. Unlike FFF, FOFF allows packets to be out-of-sequence through the two switch stages. With reference to Figure 14.20, the switch architecture of the FOFF scheme consists of three groups of buffers and two deterministic TDM switch fabrics. The three groups of buffers are: (1) VOQ1($i$, $k$) at every input, each of which associates with output port $k$; (2) VOQ2($j$, $k$) between two switch fabrics, each of which associates with output port $k$; and (3) RB VCQ($j$, $k$) at outputs, each of which is dedicated to the inputs of the second switch fabric.

Packets are queued into VOQ1($i$, $k$) upon their arrival as they are in the traditional input-buffered switch. At the beginning of each frame slot (1 frame slot = $N$ timeslots), each input selects a VOQ1 that will send packets in the next frame slot. Full frames in different VOQ1s are first selected and served in a round-robin manner. If there are no full frames, partial frames are selected and served in a round-robin manner. When a partial frame is chosen to send in the next frame slot, there will be some bandwidth waste in the first-stage switch.

If at least one full frame from each input can be found in every frame slot, there will be no out-of-sequence problem. However, if an input can only send a partial frame, then because of the difference in the occupancies at the VOQ2s, packets will be out-of-sequence as they arrive at the output. But, this out-of-sequence is bounded. It has been proven that a re-sequence buffer of size $N^2$ at each output of the switch is enough to re-sequence the packets [10]. In other words, when there are $N^2 + 1$ packets in the RB, at least one of the HOL packets of the VCQs is a head-of-flow (HOF) packet and can be selected to transmit.

Partial frames can cause another problem in the FOFF besides the out-of-sequence problem. It can cause bandwidth waste in the first-stage switch and thus increase the average delay of packets. Figure 14.21 illustrates the bandwidth waste. Assume input 1 selects a partial frame to send in the next frame slot ($T_f = 2$), where the partial frame has $K$ packets, $K < N$. For simplicity, assume that input 1 sends its first packet of the frame to the first

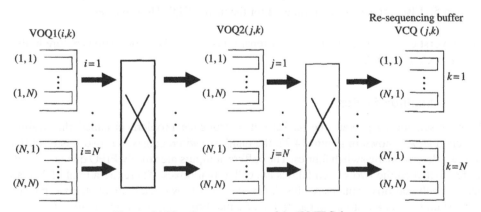

**Figure 14.20**  Queue structure of the FOFF Scheme.

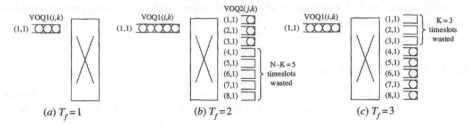

**Figure 14.21** Example of bandwidth waste for the first-stage switch in FOFF. $T_f$ shows the frame slot number. $N = 8$ timeslots are wasted to send one partial frame with $K = 3$ packets. Note that packets with circles constitute a full frame.

output of the first-stage switch (i.e., $j = 1$). At the end of this frame slot, input 1 sends $K$ packets and it wastes $N - K$ slots without sending any packets. In the next frame slot, a frame with $N - K$ packets at input 1 is defined as a full frame and is selected to transmit at $T_f = 3$. In $T_f = 3$, only $N - K$ packets can be sent, even if there are packets waiting in the same VOQ1, for example, VOQ1$(1, 1)$ in Figure 14.21c, wasting another $K$ timeslots. As a consequence, any partial frame will waste up to $N$ timeslots regardless of its partial frame size. Since the first stage is not work-conserving in terms of packets but only in terms of frames, no packets can be sent over the remaining timeslots for a partial frame. This increases the average delay.

The resequencing operation at the output could be quite challenging. It has been proven that there is at least one packet out of at most $N^2 + 1$ packets that is eligible to send. In each timeslot, we may need to search up to $N$ HOL packets of the VCQs before finding a HOF packet. A HOF packet of a flow is determined by comparing its sequence number with an expected sequence number for the flow. In each timeslot, each output performs the following operations to find a HOL packet:

Step 1: Determine which flow the HOL packet belongs to.

Step 2: Access the sequence number of the flow's HOF packet, for instance, from a table.

Step 3: Compare it with the HOL packet's sequence number.

Step 4: If matched, send the HOL packet and update to the flow's next sequence number.

Step 5: Else, repeat steps 1 through 4 for the next VCQ's HOL packet.

In the worst case, there could be up to $N$ repetitions of the above operations before finding a HOF packet to send.

### 14.3.5 Mailbox Switch

Another scheme to prevent the packet out-of-sequence problem is called the Mailbox switch [11]. As shown in Figure 14.22, the mailbox switch consists of two sets of buffers and two deterministic switch fabrics. The buffers at inputs are simply FIFO queues, and the buffers between the two switch fabrics are called mailboxes. There are a total of $N$ mailboxes. Each mailbox contains $N$ bins (indexed from 1 to $N$). Each bin contains $F$ packets. For instance, a packet stored in the $i$th bin of a mailbox is destined for the $i$th output port. Two switch fabrics have symmetric connection patterns over time such that at time $t$, input

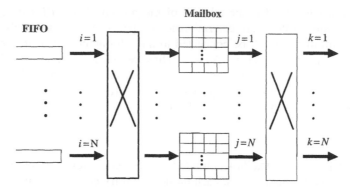

**Figure 14.22**   Mailbox switch architecture.

port $i$ is connected to output port $j$ if $(i + j) \bmod N = (t + 1) \bmod N$. From this condition, at time $t = 1$, input port 1 is connected to output port 1, input port 2 is connected to output port $N, \ldots$, and input port $N$ is connected to output port 2. Specifically, input port $i$ is connected to output port 1 at time $i$, output port 2 at time $i + 1, \ldots$, output port $N$ at time $i + N - 1$. Note that input port $i$ and output port $j$ are connected if and only if input port $j$ and output port $i$ are connected. Any switch fabric implementing such a connection pattern is referred to as a symmetric TDM switch. One can solve $j$ in $(i + j) \bmod N = (t + 1) \bmod N$ with the following function:

$$j = h(i, t) = [(t - i) \bmod N] + 1.$$

Thus, during the $t$th time slot, the $i$th input port is connected to the $h(i, t)$th output port of these two crossbar switch fabrics.

So, how do we solve the packet out-of-sequence problem? Since everything inside the switch is predetermined and periodic, the scheduled packet departure times can be fed back to inputs to compute the waiting time for the next packet so that packets can be scheduled in the order of their arrivals. This is possible because an input port of the first switch and the corresponding output port of the second switch are, in general, built on the same line card. The switch operation can be summarized as follows:

1. *Retrieve Mail.* At time $t$, the $k$th output port of the second switch is connected to the $h(k, t)$th mailbox. The packet in the first cell of the $k$th bin is transmitted to the $k$th output port. Packets in cells $2, 3, \ldots, F$ of the $k$th bin are moved forward to cells $1, 2, \ldots, F - 1$.

2. *Sending Mail.* Suppose that the HOL packet of the $i$th input port of the first switch is from flow $S(i, j)$. Note that the $i$th input port of the first switch is also connected to the $h(i, t)$th mailbox. To keep packets in sequence, this HOL packet is placed in the first empty cell of the $j$th bin of the $h(i, t)$th mailbox such that it will depart no earlier than $t + V_{i,j}(t)$. If no such empty cell can be found, the HOL packet is blocked and it remains the HOL packet of that FIFO.

3. *Updating Virtual Waiting Times.* All the flows that do not send packets at time $t$ decrease their virtual waiting time by 1, including flows that have blocked transmissions. To update the virtual waiting time for flow $S(i, j)$, suppose that the

HOL packet is placed in the $f$th cell of the $j$th bin of the $h(i, t)$th mailbox. As the connection patterns are deterministic and periodic, one can easily verify that the $h(i, t)$th mailbox will be connected to the $k$th output port of the second-stage switch at $t + ((k - j - 1) \bmod N) + 1$. Thus the departure time for this packet is $t + (f - 1)N + [(k - j - 1) \bmod N] + 1$. As such, the number of timeslots that have to pass at $t + 1$ for flow $(i, j)$ is $(f - 1)N + [(j - i - 1) \bmod N]$ and we have $V_{i,j}(t + 1) = (f - 1)N + [(j - i - 1) \bmod N]$.

Since the length of each mailbox is limited, and searching for an empty proper cell to place packets requires multiple tries, each unsuccessful try could result in backing off $N$ timeslots for the packet departure time. Such back-off not only affects the packet being placed, but also affects all the subsequent packets that belong to the same flow because the virtual waiting time of that flow is also increased by $N$ timeslots. To avoid such issues, it is better to limit the number of forward tries ($\delta$) that a cell can attempt, such that, after searching $\delta$ cells beyond the virtual waiting time, the packet just simply gives up on that timeslot. However, $\delta$ is a very vital parameter in the Mailbox switch. As shown in Figure 14.23, when $\delta$ is small, the system throughput is limited by the HOL blocking at the FIFO queues of the first switch. On the other hand, when $\delta$ is large, the throughput is limited by the stability of the virtual waiting times.

To achieve better throughput, one may also search for an empty cell with a limited number of backward tries $\delta_b$. By doing so, packets in the Mailbox switch might be out of sequence, but the resequencing delay is bounded. Figure 14.24 is the performance result of the Mailbox switch's limited forward tries and backward tries. We can see that the Mailbox switch can achieve a maximum throughput of 0.95.

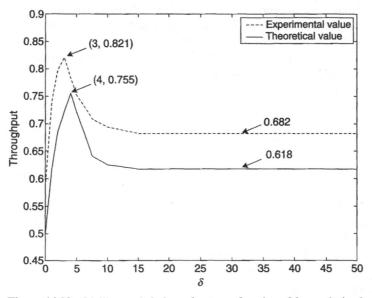

**Figure 14.23**   Mailbox switch throughput as a function of forward tries $\delta$.

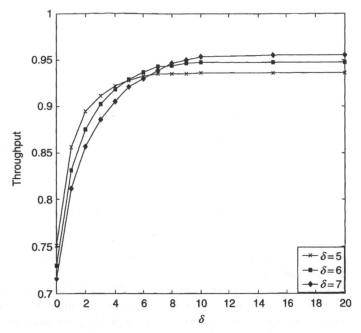

**Figure 14.24**   Maximum throughput as a function of $\delta_b$ in the mailbox switch.

### 14.3.6   Byte-Focal Switch

This section describes a practical load-balanced switch, called the Byte-Focal switch, which uses packet-by-packet scheduling to significantly improve the delay performance over switches of comparable complexity. It is called "Byte-Focal" to reflect the fact that packets of a flow (traffic from an input to an output) are spread to all line cards and brought to a focal point (the destined output). The Byte-Focal switch is simple to implement and highly scalable. It does not need a complex scheduling algorithm, or any communication between linecards, while achieving 100 percent throughput.

The Byte-Focal switch is based on packet-by-packet scheduling to maximize the bandwidth utilization of the first stage and thus improve the average delay performance. Figure 14.25 shows the Byte-Focal switch architecture. It consists of two deterministic switch fabrics and three stages of queues, namely, input queue $i$, center stage queue $j$, and output RB $k$, where $i, j, k = 1, 2, \ldots, N$. The deterministic switch fabrics operate the same way as the basic LB-BvN switch (Section 14.3.1), where both stages use a deterministic and periodic connection pattern.

There are two stages of VOQs in the Byte-Focal switch, VOQ1 and VOQ2 for the first- and second-stage switch, respectively. The flow $f_{ik}$ is defined as the packets arriving at the input port $i$ and destined to output port $k$. As shown in Figure 14.26, packets from $f_{ik}$ are placed in VOQ1$(i, k)$. Since at each time slot, the input port at the first stage is connected to the second stage cyclically, the packets in VOQ1$(i, k)$ are sent to the $N$ second-stage input ports in a round-robin manner and are placed in VOQ2$(1, k)$, VOQ2$(2, k)$, \ldots, VOQ2$(N, k)$ according to their final destination. The Byte-Focal switch guarantees that the cumulative number of packets sent to each second-stage input port for a given flow differs by at most one. The VOQ2 is then served by the second fixed, equal-rate switch. Since the packets, in

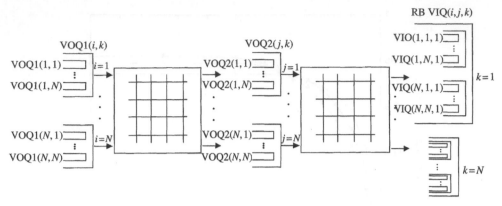

**Figure 14.25** The Byte-Focal switch architecture.

general, suffer different delays in the second stage, they arrive at the output out-of-order (see Fig. 14.26 for an example).

The Byte-Focal switch uses the virtual input queue (VIQ) structure for the RB. At each output, there are $N$ sets of VIQs where each set corresponds to an input port $i$. Within each VIQ set, there are $N$ logical queues with each queue corresponding to a second-stage input $j$. VIQ$(i, j, k)$ separates each flow not only by its input port $i$, but also by its second-stage queue $j$. Packets from input $i$ destined to output $k$ via second-stage input $j$ are stored in VIQ$(i, j, k)$. It is obvious that the packets in the same VIQ$(i, j, k)$ are in order.

The HOF packet is defined as the first packet of a given flow that has not yet left the switch, and the HOL packet as the first packet of a given VIQ$(i, j, k)$ queue. In each VIQ set, a pointer points to the VIQ$(i, j, k)$ at which the next expected HOF packet will arrive. Because of the service discipline of the first-stage switch, each input port evenly distributes packets in a round-robin order into the second-stage queue $j$. This guarantees that the HOF packet appears as a HOL packet of a VIQ set in a round-robin order. Therefore, at each time slot, if the HOF packet is at the output, it is served and the pointer moves to the next HOF packet location VIQ$(i, (j + 1) \bmod N, k)$.

Since there are $N$ flows per output, more than one HOF packet may be eligible for service in a given time slot. Therefore, in addition to the VIQ structure, there is a departure queue (DQ) with a length of at most $N$ entries that facilitates the round-robin service discipline. The DQ is simply a FIFO logical queue. It stores the indices of the VIQ sets, but only one from each VIQ set. When the HOF packet of VIQ set $i$ arrives, index $i$ joins the tail of the DQ. When a packet departs from the DQ, its index is removed from the head of the DQ and

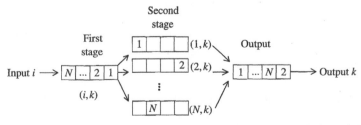

**Figure 14.26** Example flow of packets from VOQ1$(i, k)$ through the switch.

joins the tail of the DQ if its next HOF packet has arrived. The advantage of using the VIQ and the DQ structure is that the time complexity of finding and serving packets in sequence is $O(1)$. At each time slot, each VIQ set uses its pointer to check if the HOF packet has arrived, while the output port serves one packet from the head of the DQ.

As explained above, the VIQ structure ensures that the Byte-Focal switch will emit packets in order.

***First-Stage Scheduling.*** In the effort to improve the average delay performance, the scheduling scheme at the first stage plays a very important role in the Byte-Focal switch. The packets in VOQ1$(i, k)$ are cyclically distributed to the second stage. As a result, when the first-stage input port $i$ is connected to the second-stage input port $j$, only some of the VOQ1s at $i$ are eligible to send packets to $j$. As shown in Figure 14.27, this problem can be stated as follows:

Each VOQ1$(i,k)$ has a *J pointer* that keeps track of the last second-stage input to which a packet was transferred, and the next packet is always sent to the next second-stage input. As a HOL packet departs from a VOQ1$(i,k)$, its *J* pointer value increases by one mod $N$. When input $i$ is connected with $j$, each VOQ1$(i,k)$ whose *J* pointer value is equal to $j$ sends a request to the arbiter, and the arbiter selects one of them to serve.

The Byte-Focal switch performs the first-stage scheduling independently at each input port using locally available information. Thus, it does not need any communication between different linecards.

Let $P_{ik}(t)$ be the *J* pointer value for VOQ1$(i,k)$ at time $t$. Define a set $S_j(t) = \{$VOQ1$(i, k)|P_{ik}(t) = j\}$, then $S_j(t)$ is the set of VOQ1s that can send packets to the second-stage input $j$ at time $t$. Four ways of picking a VOQ1 to serve from the set $S_j(t)$ are considered next.

***Round-Robin.*** To achieve a small delay while maintaining fairness among all traffic flows, an efficient arbitration is necessary to schedule the departure of the HOL packets of the VOQ1s. One simple way to do the first-stage scheduling is to use the round-robin scheme. In round-robin arbitration, in the set $S_j(t)$, the arbiter at each input port selects one of them in round-robin order. This scheme is simple and easy to implement.

***Longest Queue First.*** Although the round-robin arbitration achieves fairness among all the traffic flows, under non-uniform traffic conditions, some congested VOQ1s could

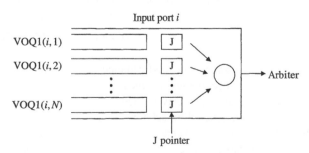

**Figure 14.27** Scheduling schemes at the first stage.

overflow and the system becomes unstable (see the simulation results in Fig. 14.29). To stabilize the system, high priority is given to the congested VOQ1s. The longest queue first (LQF) algorithm ensures that, at each time slot, the arbiter at each input port chooses to serve the longest queue from the set $S_j(t)$.

*Fixed Threshold Scheme.* The longest queue first scheme can achieve good performance. However, finding the longest queue can be time-consuming and is not practical for high-speed large-scale switches. It is easier to identify the congested VOQ1s by observing if their queue length exceeds a predetermined threshold (TH), $N$. Let $q_{ik}(t)$ be the length of the VOQ1$(i, k)$, and $q_{is}(t)$ be the length of the VOQ1$(i, s)$ being served. Define a subset $S'_j(t) = \{\text{VOQ1}(i, k) | \text{VOQ1}(i, k) \in S_j(t) \text{ and } q_{ik}(t) \geq TH\}$, then $S'_j(t)$ is the set of VOQ1s that have more than TH cells and can send cells to $j$. The fixed threshold algorithm is:

1. At each time slot, if $q_{is}(t) \geq TH$, continue to serve this queue.
2. If not, the arbiter picks in a round-robin manner among the queues in set $S'_j(t)$.
3. If $S'_j(t)$ is empty and $q_{is}(t) > 0$, then it keeps serving the queue corresponding to $q_{is}(t)$.
4. If $q_{is}(t) = 0$, pick in a round-robin manner among the queues in set $S_j(t)$.

*Dynamic Threshold Scheme.* As the switch size becomes large, setting the threshold to switch size $N$ causes large average delays. The reason is that the VOQ1 length has to reach a large value ($N$) before being identified as congested. Before reaching the threshold, it competes with other VOQ1s that have much smaller queue lengths. To better identify congested queues under different switch sizes and different traffic loadings, the dynamic threshold scheme is proposed. The dynamic threshold (TH) value is set to $Q(t)/N$, where $Q(t)$ is the total VOQ1 queue length at an input port at time $t$. $Q(t)/N$ is therefore the average VOQ1 queue length. The dynamic threshold scheme operates in the same way as the fixed threshold scheme except that the threshold is now set to the average queue length for that input.

In the simulation study, it is assumed that the switch size $N = 32$, unless otherwise noted. All inputs are equally loaded on a normalized scale $\rho \in (0, 1)$, and use the following traffic scenarios to test the performance of the Byte-Focal switch:

*Uniform i.i.d.*  $\lambda_{ij} = \rho/N$.

*Diagonal i.i.d.*  $\lambda_{ii} = \rho/2$, $\lambda_{ij} = \rho/2$, for $j = (i + 1) \bmod N$. This is a very skewed loading, since input $i$ has packets only for outputs $i$ and $(i + 1)$ *mod N*.

*Hot-spot.* $\lambda_{ii} = \rho/2$, $\lambda_{ij} = \rho/2(N - 1)$, for $i \neq j$. This type of traffic is more balanced than diagonal traffic, but obviously more unbalanced than uniform traffic.

Normally, for single-stage switches, the performance of a specific scheduling algorithm becomes worse as the loadings become less balanced.

This section compares the average delay induced by different algorithms. As seen in Figure 14.28, the frame-based scheduling scheme, FOFF, has a much larger delay. The reason is that FOFF wastes bandwidth whenever a partial frame is sent. At low traffic load, many frames will be sent as partial frames, resulting in considerable bandwidth wastage at the first stage. From the figure, it can be seen that at low load, the delay difference between

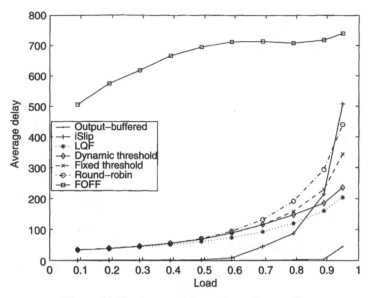

**Figure 14.28**   Average delay under uniform traffic.

FOFF and the Byte-Focal switch is quite large. The Byte-Focal switch performs packet-by-packet scheduling instead of frame-based scheduling, so it reduces the bandwidth wastage. At high traffic load, the Byte-Focal switch also achieves better performance than the FOFF. Compared to a single-stage algorithm, *i*Slip, when the loading is low, *i*Slip has a smaller average delay, but when the switch is heavily loaded, the Byte-Focal switch distributes the traffic evenly to the second stage, thus dramatically reducing the average delay.

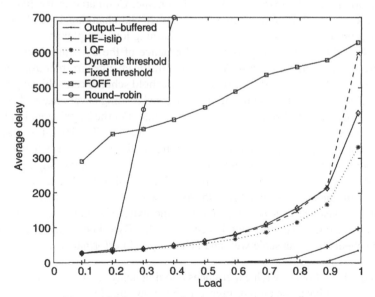

**Figure 14.29**   Average delay under hot-spot loading.

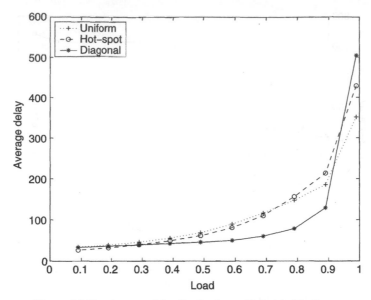

**Figure 14.30** Average delay for the dynamic threshold scheme.

Figure 14.29 shows the average delay of various schemes under hot-spot loading. Although the round-robin scheme is simple to implement, it is not stable under non-uniform loadings (as seen in the figure, the throughput is only about 30 percent). For reference, the performances of a typical single-stage switch, HE-$i$Slip [13] and the ouput-buffered switch are also provided. The LQF scheme has the best delay performance among the Byte-Focal switch schemes, but, unlike the fixed and dynamic threshold schemes, it is not practical due to its high implementation complexity. Figure 14.29 shows that the dynamic threshold scheme performance is comparable to the LQF scheme. Compared to the fixed threshold scheme, the dynamic threshold scheme can adapt to the changing input loadings, thus achieving a better delay performance, while maintaining low complexity.

Figure 14.30 shows the average delay performance of the dynamic threshold scheme under different input traffic scenarios. As the input traffic changes from uniform to hot-spot to diagonal (hence less balanced), the dynamic threshold scheme can achieve good performance, especially for the diagonal traffic. The diagonal loading is very skewed and difficult to schedule using the centralized scheduling architecture. For the Logdiagonal traffic matrix [14], the delay performance is comparable to hot-spot loading. The Byte-Focal switch performs load-balancing at the first stage, thus achieving good performance even under extreme non-uniform loadings. This greatly simplifies the traffic engineering design.

Figure 14.31 shows the average delays for the dynamic threshold scheme with different switch sizes with the load kept fixed at 0.95. As shown in the figure, under the input traffic models that are considered, the delay increases as the switch size increases, and the average delays are almost linear with the switch size. Since the Byte-Focal switch does not use a centralized scheduler, it can scale well and achieve good performance even for very large switch sizes.

A cell in the Byte-Focal switch experiences queuing delays at the first and second stage, and resequencing delay at the output. Figure 14.32 shows the three components of the total delay. As can be seen, the first-stage queuing delay and the second-stage queuing delay are

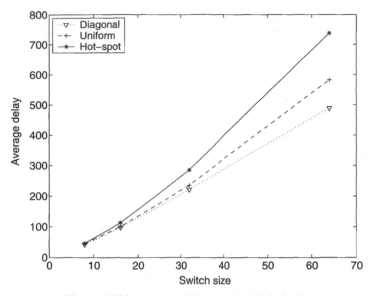

**Figure 14.31**  Average delay versus switch size $N$.

comparable, and the resequencing delay is much smaller compared to the other two delays. Figure 14.33 shows the resequencing delay increases as the switch size increases.

Since Internet traffic is bursty [15], let us consider the delay performance under bursty traffic. The burst length is set to be 10 cells. At a particular input port, after a burst, the probability that there is another burst arriving is $\mu$, and the probability that there is no

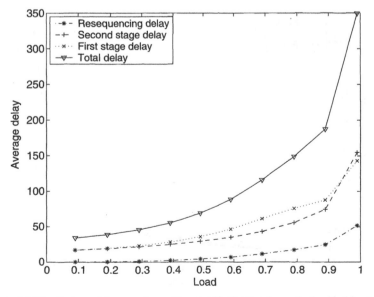

**Figure 14.32**  3-stage delays under uniform traffic for the dynamic threshold scheme.

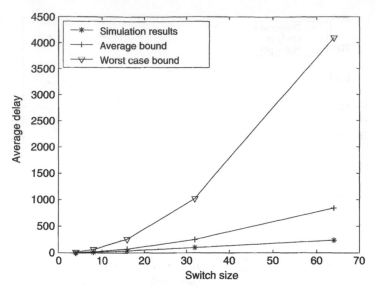

**Figure 14.33**    Resequencing delay with different switch size.

packet arriving corresponding to the next burst is $1 - \mu$. Then the loading to this input port is $\rho = 10\mu/(1 + 9\mu)$. Two scenarios are considered:

*Bursty 1.* Cells within the same burst are uniformly distributed to the $N$ output ports.

*Bursty 2.* Cells within the same burst are destined to the same destination; however, bursts are uniformly distributed over $N$ output ports.

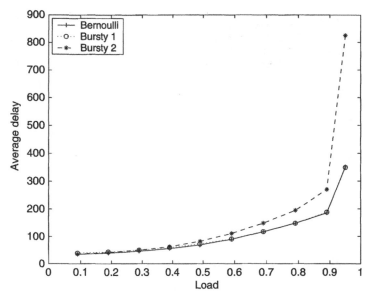

**Figure 14.34**    Average delay of the dynamic threshold scheme under bursty traffic.

Figure 14.34 shows the average delay of the Byte-Focal switch with the dynamic threshold scheme under the Bernoulli and bursty traffic models. It can be seen that the average delays under the Bernoulli and Bursty 1 traffic scenario are identical. In comparison with the single-stage switches, the Byte-Focal switch achieves considerable burst reduction. Therefore, it is very effective in reducing the average delay. From our simulations, the delay performance is worse for Bursty 2 as compared to Bursty 1 when the traffic load is high.

## REFERENCES

[1] N. McKeown, "*i*SLIP: a scheduling algorithm for input-queued switches," *IEEE/ACM Transactions on Networking*, vol. 7, no. 2, pp. 188–201 (Apr. 1999).

[2] H. J. Chao, "Saturn: a terabit packet switch using dual round-robin," *IEEE Communications magazine*, vol. 38, no. 12, pp. 78–84 (Dec. 2000).

[3] C. S. Chang, D. Lee, and Y. Jou, "Load balanced Birkhoff-von Neumann switches. Part I: One-stage buffering," *Computer Communications*, vol. 25, no. 6, pp. 611–622 (2002).

[4] G. Birkhoff, "Tres observaciones sobre el algebra lineal," *Univ. Nac. Tucum an Rev. Ser. A*, vol. 5, pp. 147–151 (1946).

[5] J. von Neumann, "A certain zero-sum two-person game equivalent to the optimal assignment problem," in *Contributions to the Theory of Games*. Princeton University Press, Princeton, NJ, vol. 2, pp. 5–12, 1982.

[6] C. Chang, W. Chen, and H. Huang, "On service guarantees for input buffered crossbar switches: a capacity decomposition approach by Birkhoff and von Neumann," in *Proc. IEEE IWQOS'99*, London, UK, pp. 79–86 (June 1999).

[7] C. S. Chang, W. J. Chen, and H. Y. Huang, "Birkhoff-von Neumann input buffered crossbar switches," in *Proc. IEEE INFOCOM'00*, Tel Aviv, Israel, pp. 1614–1623 (Mar. 2000).

[8] C. Chang, D. Lee, and Y. Jou, "Load balanced Birkhoff–von Neumann switche. Part II: Multistage buffering," *Computer Communications*, vol. 25, no. 6, pp. 623–634 (2002).

[9] I. Keslassy and N. McKeown, "Maintaining packet order in two-stage switches," in *Proc. IEEE INFOCOM'02*, New York, vol. 2, pp. 1032–1041 (June 2002).

[10] I. Keslassy, S. Chuang, K. Yu, D. Miller, M. Horowitz, O. Solgaard, and N. McKeown, "Scaling Internet routers using optics," in *Proc. ACM SIGCOMM*, Karlsruhe, Germany, pp. 189–200 (Aug. 2003).

[11] C. S. Chang, D. Lee, and Y. J. Shih, "Mailbox switch: A scalable two-stage switch architecture for conflict resolution of ordered packets," in *Proc. IEEE INFOCOM'04*, Hong Kong, vol. 3, pp. 1995–2006 (Mar. 2004).

[12] Y. Shen, S. Jiang, S. Panwar, and H. J. Chao, "Byte-Focal: a practical load balanced switch," in *Proc. IEEE Workshop on High Performance Switching and Routing* (HPSR'05), Hong Kong, pp. 6–12 (May 2005).

[13] Y. Li, S. Panwar, and H. J. Chao, "Exhaustive service matching algorithms for input queued switches," in *Proc. IEEE Workshop on High Performance Switching and Routing (HPSR 04)*, Phoenix, Arizona, pp. 253–258 (Apr. 2004).

[14] P. Giaccone, B. Prabhakar, and D. Shah, "Towards simple, high-performance schedulers for high-aggregate bandwidth switches," in *Proc. IEEE INFOCOM'02*, New York, vol. 3, pp. 1160–1169 (June 2002).

[15] W. Leland, M. Taqqu, W. Willinger, and D. Wilson, "On the self-similar nature of ethernet traffic (Extended Version)," *IEEE/ACM Transactions on Networking*, vol. 2, issue 1, pp. 1–15 (Feb. 1994).

# CHAPTER 15

# OPTICAL PACKET SWITCHES

Introduction of optical fibers to communication networks has caused a tremendous increase in the speed of data transmitted. The virtually unlimited bandwidth of optical fibers comes from the carrier frequency of nearly 200 THz [1]. Optical networking technology, such as add-drop multiplexers [2, 3], reconfigurable photonic switches [4], and wavelength multiplexing division (WDM), has progressed well and facilitated optical networking in the past few years [5, 6]. Especially, recent advances in dense wavelength multiplexing division (DWDM) technology have provided tremendous bandwidth in optical fiber communications [7]. However, the capability of switching and routing packets at this high bandwidth (e.g., 1 terabit/s) has lagged far behind the transmission capability. Building a large-capacity packet switching system using only electronic technology may potentially lead to a system bottleneck when interconnecting many electronic devices or modules, mainly caused by the enormous interconnection wires and the electromagnetic interference they would generate. With the advancement of optical devices technology, several packet switch architectures based on WDM technology have been proposed for large-capacity packet switches. Although today's optical packet switching technology is still very primitive and cannot compete with electronic switching technology, optical packet switches have great potential to scale-up their switching capacity as the technology of some key optical devices matures.

A photonic packet switch may require optical devices such as lasers, filters, couplers, memories, multiplexers, demultiplexers, and so on. At the present time, some optical devices are either very power-hungry or too slow in switching compared with electronic devices. However, it is possible to design high-capacity switches by the use of both electronic and optical technologies. In such switches, data transfer can be achieved through optical medium, and complicated functions such as contention resolution and routing control can be performed electronically. These switches are called hybrid switches. The hybrid

---

*High Performance Switches and Routers*, by H. Jonathan Chao and Bin Liu
Copyright © 2007 John Wiley & Sons, Inc.

switches that only convert a packet cell header into electronics for processing and controlling but leave the entire cell to be handled in the optical domain are called optically transparent.

The ongoing research into photonic packet switches is to develop faster and larger optical switches and new techniques that can be used to enhance the existing optical switch architectures. There are many issues to be considered when designing an optical packet switch, such as characteristics of the optical devices employed, scalability of the switch, power budget of the system, synchronization between electrical and incoming optical signals, performance of the switch under various traffic patterns, and so on. In addition, some of the techniques developed for optical packet switches could be applied to large scale packet switches where small electronic switch modules are interconnected by an optical interconnection network.

The techniques of space-division multiplexing (SDM), time-division multiplexing (TDM), and WDM have been used in designing optical switches. SDM requires a large number of binary switching elements. From the switch size and cost point of view, it is not an ideal approach for photonic switching. TDM is a more classical technique used in communications [8]. When it is applied to optical switching, complicated temporal compression and temporal expansion circuits are required. The throughput of such a switch is limited by the speed of the demultiplexer, which is actually controlled by electronics for the time being. WDM is made possible by the range of wavelengths on an optical fiber. WDM splits the optical bandwidth of a link into fixed, nonoverlapping spectral bands. Each band has a wavelength channel that can be used for a specific bit rate and transmission technique, independent of the choices for other channels.

In this chapter, we review several approaches to build a large-capacity packet switch and discuss their advantages and disadvantages. Depending on whether the contended packets are stored in the optical or in the electrical domain, these switch architectures are classified into opto-electronic packet switches (described in Section 15.1) and all optical packet switches (described in Section 15.4). Two opto-electronic packet switches are described in detail in Sections 15.2 and 15.3 to better understand switching operations and implementation complexity. Sections 15.5 and 15.6 describe optical packet switches using shared fiber delay lines for optical memory in single-stage and three-stage cases, respectively. In all the architectures presented here, switch control is achieved electronically since, for the time being, it is still complicated to realize logical operations optically. The capacity of electronic control units and the tuning speed of optical devices are the main performance-limiting factors in these architectures.

## 15.1 OPTO-ELECTRONIC PACKET SWITCHES

For the opto-electronic packet switches, optical switching networks are used for interconnection and transmission between electronic input and output modules. Logical control, contention resolution, and packet storage are handled electronically.

### 15.1.1 Hypass

HYPASS [9] in Figure 15.1 is an opto-electronic hybrid cell switch in which electronic components are used for memory and logic functions and optical components are used for routing and transporting data. In this figure, bold continuous lines represent optical paths, bold dashed lines represent serial data paths, dotted lines are tuning current paths, and thin continuous lines are control signal paths. The switch is composed of two networks: the

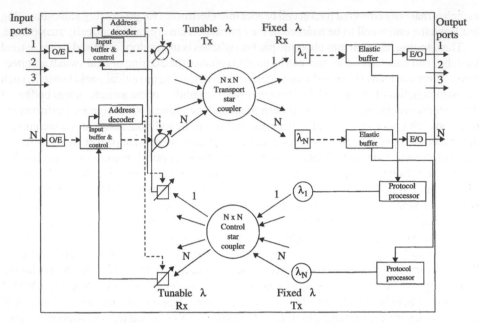

**Figure 15.1** Global diagram of the HYPASS implementation (© 1988 IEEE).

transport network and the control network. The architecture is based on the "broadcast and select" approach in both of the networks. There is a unique optical wavelength associated with each of the output ports. As shown in Figure 15.1, the transport network has tunable-wavelength laser transmitters at the input side, fixed-wavelength receivers at the output side, and an $N \times N$ star coupler that transfers the incoming data from inputs to outputs. In order to transfer control information from output ports to the input ports, a similar network is used.

When a cell arrives at an input port of the switch, it is first converted from optical to electronic and its destination address is obtained. Then, the cell is temporarily stored in the corresponding input buffer. The tunable wavelength laser transmitter of the corresponding input port is tuned to the wavelength of the requested output port. When a request-to-send signal (or poll) is received from the corresponding output port via the control network, the cell is transmitted through the transport network. The acknowledgment representing successful delivery of the cell is also transmitted through the control network. If there are multiple cells for the same output port, contention occurs. Power threshold detection or multiple bit detection on the cell preamble could be used to detect collision. The cells that do not get acknowledgments in a slot time are kept to retry later. In order to resolve contention and provide successful transmission of cells, the tree-polling algorithm (explained in [9]) is employed in the selection of inputs in the following cell slots. The cells that reach the output ports successfully are stored in the elastic buffers and transmitted over the optical fiber trunks after the necessary electrical to optical conversion.

The HYPASS architecture has advantages due to its parallel structure. However, since a slot time is based on the length of the polling step, transmission of a cell, and receipt of the acknowledgment, the time overhead for the electronic control and optical tuning operations are the factors that limit capacity. The switch does not have a multicasting capability due to the usage of fixed wavelength receivers at the output ports.

### 15.1.2  Star-Track

Star-Track [10] is another hybrid switch architecture. It is based on a two-phase contention resolution algorithm. It also supports multicasting. As shown in Figure 15.2, the switch is composed of two internal networks: an optical star transport network and an electronic control track surrounding the star network. The optical transport network has fixed wavelength optical transmitters at the input-ports side, and wavelength tunable optical receivers at the output-ports side. There is a unique wavelength associated with each input port. Input and output ports are connected through an optical star coupler. The output port conflicts are resolved by the ring reservation technique (see Section 8.3.2). The electronic control network that implements the ring-reservation technique is the major track linking input ports, output ports, and a token generator, sequentially.

Cells arriving at the input ports are stored in the input buffers after optical to electronic conversion. There are two control phases in a cell transmission cycle. In the first phase, input ports *write* their output port requests into the tokens circulating in the control network. The output ports *read* the tokens and tune their receivers to the appropriate input port wavelengths in the second phase. Then, the cell transmission starts over the star transport network. The transmission and control cycles are overlapped in time in order to increase throughput. Since each input has a unique wavelength and there is input–output port pair scheduling prior to transmission, cells are transmitted simultaneously without causing contention.

This architecture allows multicasting. However, the throughput of the switch may degrade as the number of multicasting connections increases due to output port collisions in the first phase. It is shown that this problem can be alleviated by call splitting (i.e., allowing a multicast call to be completed in multiple cell slots). This architecture can support different priority levels for the cell by adding minor tracks into the control network. However, in this case, the token should recirculate among the input ports more than once depending on

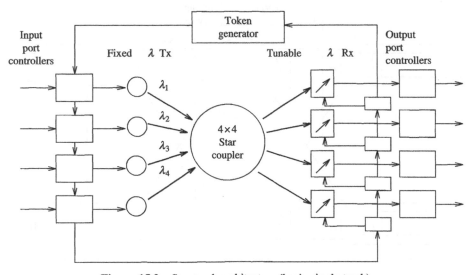

**Figure 15.2**   Star-track architecture (basic single track).

the number of priority levels. This will increase the length of the write phase and result in longer cell processing time.

The main drawback of the switch is the sequential processing of the token by input and output ports. As a result, the time taken for the token to travel through the entire ring increases as the size of the switch increases. In case of multiple priority levels, the recirculation period for the token becomes even longer. Here, head-of-line (HOL) blocking is another factor that degrades throughput.

### 15.1.3 Cisneros and Brackett

Cisneros and Brackett [11] proposed a large ATM switch architecture based on memory switch modules and optical star couplers. The architecture consists of input modules, output modules, optical star couplers, and a contention resolution device (CRD). Input and output modules are based on electronic shared memories. The architecture requires optical to electronic and electronic to optical conversions in some stages. Each output module has an associated unique wavelength. As shown in Figure 15.3, the input ports and output ports are grouped into size $n$, and each group is connected to $n \times m$ and $m \times n$ memory switches, respectively. The interconnection between the input and output modules is achieved by $k$ optical star couplers. There are $k$ tunable laser transmitters and $k$ fixed wavelength receivers connected to each optical star coupler. (In Fig. 15.3, optical transmitters and receivers are not shown in order to keep it simple). The cells transmitted through the switch are buffered at the input and output modules. In the proposed architecture, input and output lines transmit cells at the rate of 155.52 Mbit/s. The lines that interconnect the input modules to the optical stars and optical stars to the output modules run at 2.5 Gbit/s. The values of $n$, $k$, $N$, and $m$ are 128, 128, 16,384, and 8, respectively.

The internal routing header of a cell is composed of two fields. One specifies the output module and the other shows the port number in that specific output module. Each input

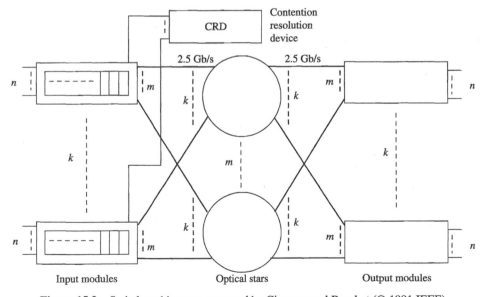

**Figure 15.3** Switch architecture proposed by Cisneros and Bracket (© 1991 IEEE).

module handles a single queue in which the incoming cells are kept in sequence. The input modules, the optical stars, and the output modules are connected as in a three-stage Clos network. However, the working principle is not the same as in the Clos network. Here, each input module sends the output module request of its HOL cell to the CRD. The CRD examines the requests and chooses one cell for each output module and responds. The cells that won the contention are routed through the first $k \times k$ optical star and their HOL pointers are advanced. This process is repeated for each optical star in a circular manner. Cells at the output modules are kept in sequence depending on which optical star they arrive in. In this architecture, all optical stars are kept busy if the CRD is $m$ times faster than a cell transfer time by the optical stars. The maximum amount of optical couplers is determined with respect to the time required to transfer a cell through an optical star and the time required to resolve contention by the CRD.

In the architecture, the time required for optical to electronic conversion, electronic to optical conversion, and tuning optical laser transmitters is not considered. All the calculations are mainly based on the time required to transfer a cell through an optical star. The output port contention resolution scheme is very complex and the electronic controller can become a bottleneck. The switch does not have multicast capability due to the fixed wavelength receivers. Moreover, the maximum throughput of the switch is limited to 58 percent because of the HOL blocking [12].

### 15.1.4  BNR (Bell-North Research) Switch

Munter et al. [13] introduced a high-capacity packet switch based on advanced electronic and optical technologies. The main components of the switch are input buffer modules, output buffer modules, a high-speed switching core, and a central control unit, as shown in Figure 15.4. The core switch contains a $16 \times 16$ cross-connect network using optical links running at 10 Gbit/s.

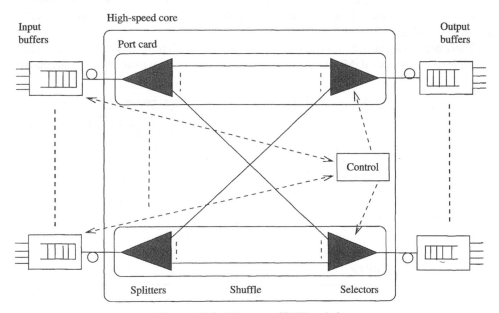

**Figure 15.4**  Diagram of BNR switch.

The central control unit receives requests from input buffer modules and returns grant messages. Each request message indicates the number of queued packets in the input buffer module, which is later used to determine the size of burst allowed to transmit to the switch fabric. A connection can only be made when both input and output ports are free. A control bus is used by the free input ports to broadcast their requests, and by the free output ports to return grant messages.

An arbitration frame consists of 16 packet time slots for a $16 \times 16$ core switch. In each slot, the corresponding output port polls all 16 inputs. For example, in time slot 1, output port 1 (if it is idle) will choose the input that has the longest queue destined for output port 1. If the input is busy, another input port that has the second longest queue will be examined. This operation repeats until a free input port is found. If a match is found (free input, free output, and outstanding request), a connection is made for the duration corresponding to the number of packets queued for this connection. So, the switch is a burst switch, not a packet switch. In time slot 2, output port 2 repeats the above operation. The switch capacity is limited by the speed of the central control unit. Packet streams can have a long waiting time in the input buffer modules under a high traffic load.

### 15.1.5  Wave-Mux Switch

Nakahira et al. [14] introduced a photonic asynchronous transfer mode (ATM) switch based on the input–output buffering principle. Basically, this switch consists of three kinds of modules: input group module (IGM), switching module (SWM), and output group module (OGM), as shown in Figure 15.5. They are connected by means of fiber optical lines. The inputs are divided into $p$ groups of size $n_1$ and each group is connected to an IGM. The cells arriving through optical lines are first converted to electronic signals by optical-to-electrical (O/E) converters and their header information is electrically processed at the header converter in IGMs. Both the header and payload of the arriving cell are processed and stored in an electronic random access memory (RAM). An optical sorter in each IGM is used to sort the cells with respect to their OGM requests and delivers them to SWM in a cell slot time.

There are $p$ optical switches in SWM. Each optical switch transmits optical wavelength multiplexed cells from IGM to OGM. In each cell time slot, these $p$ optical switches deliver

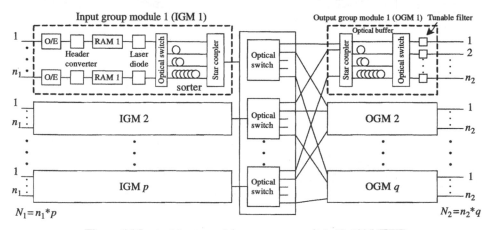

**Figure 15.5**  Architecture of the wave-mux switch (© 1995 IEEE).

at most $p$ trunks of wavelength multiplexed cells from the IGMs, which are destined for different OGMs. In each OGM, it is possible to have the cells with different wavelengths but with the same output port request. This is called output port contention and is solved by the use of an optical buffer. This optical buffer in the OGM is based on the fiber delay line principle. If no competing cells to the same output port are present in the optical buffer, the incoming wavelengths will be sent through the shortest optical fiber line. They are distributed to the tunable filters by an optical switch. Each tunable filter is then tuned to the wavelength of the requested output port.

The proposed optical switch architecture needs complex arbitration to solve the contention problem, not only for those cells in same IGM but for the cells in different IGMs as well. This will increase the complexity of control, thus limiting the switch size. In this switch, in order to avoid HOL blocking, cells destined for the same OGM can be read out of the RAM with the speed-up factor by two. There are many O/E and E/O converters required in the switching path, thus increasing implementation costs.

## 15.2  OPTOELECTRONIC PACKET SWITCH CASE STUDY I

Figure 15.6 shows a terabit IP router architecture with four major elements in the terabit IP router [15]: the optical interconnection network (OIN) supporting nonblocking and high-capacity switching, the ping-pong arbitration unit (PAU) resolving the output contention and controlling the switching devices, the router modules (RMs) performing IP packet forwarding, and the route controller (RC) constructing routing information for the RMs. There are two kinds of RM: input RM (IRM) and output RM (ORM). Both the IRMs and the ORMs implement IP packet buffering, route (table) lookup, packet filtering, and versatile interfaces, such as OC-3, OC12, OC-48, and Gigabit Ethernet. The interconnection between the RC and the RMs can be implemented with dedicated buses or through the OIN. Figure 15.6 simply illustrates the bus-based approach.

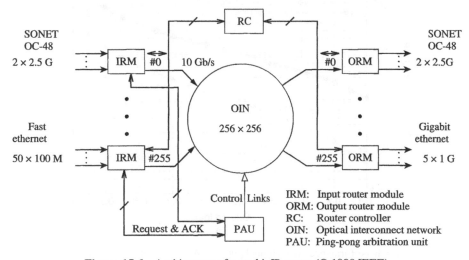

**Figure 15.6**   Architecture of a terabit IP router (© 1998 IEEE).

### 15.2.1  **Speedup**

The fixed-length segment switching technique is commonly adopted in high-capacity IP routers to achieve high-speed switching and better system performance.

Figure 15.7*a* suggests that a speedup factor of two is required to achieve nearly 100 percent throughput under bursty traffic with geometric distribution and an average burst size of 10 packet segments. Figure 15.7*b* shows the corresponding average delay. The total average delay of input and output queuing is very close to the theoretic bound of purely

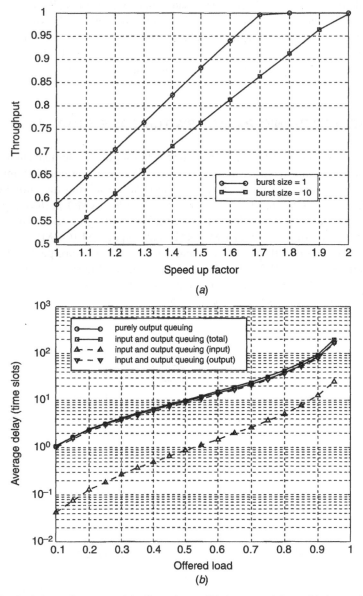

**Figure 15.7**  Switch performance: (*a*) Throughput; (*b*) Average delay with burst size = 10 and speedup factor = 2.

output queuing. The input delay is an order smaller than the total delay, hinting that an input queued switch with speedup 2, in the average sense, performs nearly as well as a purely output queued switch.

The speedup induces two more challenges: (1) doubling the switch transmission speed to 10 Gbit/s, and (2) halving the arbitration time constraint. The first challenge can be easily resolved with optical interconnection technology, while the second challenge can be resolved by the ping-pong arbitration (PPA) scheme described in Section 15.2.4.

### 15.2.2   Data Packet Flow

A data segment unit of 64 bytes is chosen to accommodate the shortest IP packets (40 bytes). Variable-length IP packets are segmented before being passed through the switch. Figure 15.8 depicts the flow of packets across the router. A simple round-robin packet scheduler is used at each input line interface (ILI) to arrange the packet arrivals from different interfaces (see also Fig. 15.6). It uses a first-in-first-out (FIFO) buffer per interface to store incoming packets. Since the output line speed of the scheduler is the sum of all interfaces, it can be shown that the maximum packet backlog at each input line FIFO is just twice that of the maximum IP packet size, the same large buffer can be chosen to avoid any packet loss.

The output packets of the scheduler enter the input switch interface (ISI) in which packet segmentation takes place. While a packet is being segmented, its IP header is first checked by the input packet filter (IPF) for network security and flow classification (i.e., inbound filtering), as shown in Figure 15.6. Afterwards, the header is sent to the input forwarding engine (IFE) for IP table lookup, deciding which ORM(s) the packet is destined for.

Data segments are stored in a FIFO waiting for arbitration before being forwarded through the OIN. The forwarding sequence is packet-by-packet, not cell-by-cell, for each ISI in order to simplify the reassembly. The input port number is added to each segment before it enters the OIN to ensure correct packet reassembly at the output ports.

Segments of a packet arriving at an output port may be interleaved with those from other input ports. While a packet is being reassembled, its IP header can be sent to the output packet filter (OPF) for outbound filtering and then to the output forwarding engine (OFE) for another IP route lookup deciding which outgoing interface(s) the packet should be destined for. The packets are then broadcast at the output line interface (OLI) to all desirable interfaces. Each interface can maintain two FIFOs supporting two priority traffic: real-time (RT) and non-real-time (NRT) packets.

### 15.2.3   Optical Interconnection Network (OIN)

Figure 15.9 shows the proposed $256 \times 256$ OIN, which can easily provide the multicast function due to its broadcast-and-select property. The OIN consists of two kinds of optical switching modules: input optical modules (IOMs) and output optical modules (OOMs). There are 16 of each kind in the OIN. Each IOM uses the same set of 16 different wavelengths $(\lambda_1 - \lambda_{16})$; each of the 16 input links at an IOM is assigned a distinct wavelength from the set, which carries packet segments under transmission. In each time slot, up to 16 packet segments at an IOM can be multiplexed by an arrayed-waveguide grating (AWG) router. The multiplexed signal is then broadcast to all 16 OOMs by a passive $1 \times 16$ splitter.

At each OOM, a $16 \times 16$ fully connected switching fabric performs the multicast switching function by properly controlling the semiconductor optical amplifier (SOA) gates. There

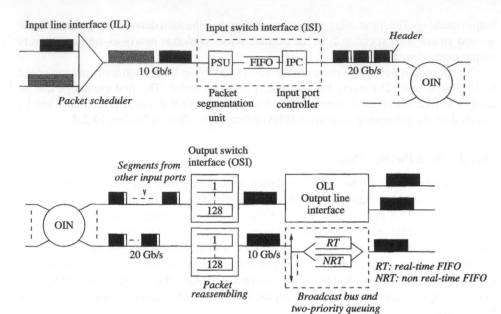

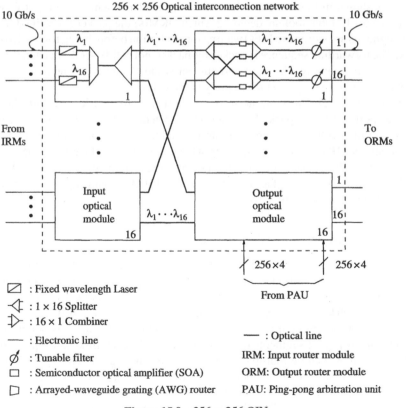

**Figure 15.8** Flow of packets across the router.

**Figure 15.9** 256 × 256 OIN.

are a total of 256 SOA gates in each OOM. At most 16 of them can be turned ON simultaneously. The tunable filter, controlled by the PAU, is used to dynamically choose one of the 16 wavelengths in every time slot. As illustrated in Figure 15.10, it is assumed that a packet segment from the $k$th input link of the $i$th IOM is destined for the $q$th and the 16th output links of the $j$th OOM, where $1 \leq i, j, k, q \leq 16$. These two multicast connections are established by turning on the SOA gates with index $(i, j, q)$ and $(i, j, 16)$ only (the others are turned off). The tunable filters at the $q$th and the 16th output links of the $j$th OOM are turned on with index $k$, which is provided by the PAU.

***Input Optical Module (IOM).*** The IOMs carry packets at 10 Gbit/s. At each IOM, distributed Bragg reflector (DBR) or distributed feedback (DFB) laser arrays can be used as the laser sources between 1525 nm and 1565 nm to match the gain bandwidth of commercially available erbium-doped fiber amplifiers (EDFAs). Each EDFA can amplify multiple wavelengths simultaneously. Each input link of an IOM is connected to a laser with fixed wavelength.

To improve the chirp performance, a DFB laser diode integrated with an external modulator (EM) operating at 10 Gbit/s has been fabricated [16]. To ensure output power levels and chirp performance, a SOA and EMs can be integrated with the DFB laser arrays [17]. This monolithically integrated WDM source is able to provide multi-wavelength capability and significantly reduce the cost per wavelength. In addition, it can also eliminate the

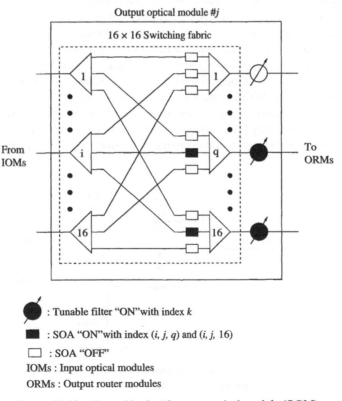

**Figure 15.10**    Control in the $j$th output optical module (OOM).

alignment of fibers to individual lasers, reduce component count and coupling loss between components, and increase the reliability.

**Output Optical Module (OOM).** Each 16 × 16 switching fabric should be capable of simultaneously connecting two or more IOMs to all tunable filters at an OOM. Thus, it needs to have broadcast capability and to be strictly nonblocking. As shown in Figure 15.10, a space switch can simply meet this requirement and can be constructed by using SOA gates.

In addition to their fast switching function (~1 ns), SOA gates can provide some gain to compensate the coupling loss and splitting loss caused by the splitters/combiners and the connection between discrete optical devices. Furthermore, SOA gates can be monolithically integrated with the passive couplers to enhance the reliability and loss performance between components.

**Tunable Filters.** Tunable filters are used to perform wavelength selection in the OIN. Three possible ways to implement the tunable filter are considered here.

*Type-I Tunable Filter.* A Type-I tunable filter, as shown in Figure 15.11, performs the wavelength selection in the electrical domain. Each output of a 16 × 16 switching fabric is connected to a 1 × 16 AWG router, which is made from high-index indium phosphide (InP) material and is capable of demultiplexing 16 wavelengths in the 1550 nm window. Figure 15.12 shows the connectivity of a 16 × 16 AWG router. For example, if the WDM signal enters the seventh input port of the AWG router, only the 14th wavelength ($\lambda_{14}$) will be sent out through the eighth output port. Each demultiplexed wavelength is detected through a high-speed signal detector. Each detector has a laser waveguide structure and can be monolithically integrated with the AWG router, thus increasing the reliability and reducing the packaging cost of the AWG router. Finally, a 16 × 1 electronic selector is used to select the desired signal from the 16 detectors. The selector is controlled by the 4-bit control signal from the PAU. An alternative electronic selector is an InP-based optoelectronic integrated circuits (OEIC) receiver array [18], which operates at 10 Gbit/s per channel and integrates 16 p-i-n photodiodes with heterojunction bipolar transistors (HBT) preamplifier.

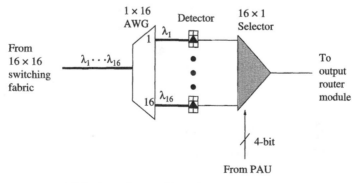

AWG : Arrayed-waveguide grating

PAU: Ping-pong arbitration unit

**Figure 15.11**  Type-I tunable filter.

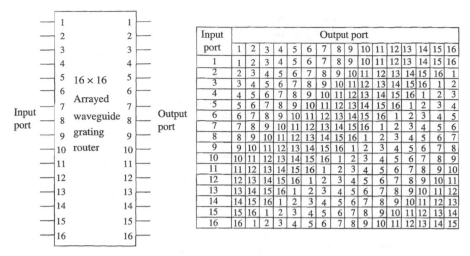

| Input port | Output port | | | | | | | | | | | | | | | |
|---|---|---|---|---|---|---|---|---|---|---|---|---|---|---|---|---|
| | 1 | 2 | 3 | 4 | 5 | 6 | 7 | 8 | 9 | 10 | 11 | 12 | 13 | 14 | 15 | 16 |
| 1 | 1 | 2 | 3 | 4 | 5 | 6 | 7 | 8 | 9 | 10 | 11 | 12 | 13 | 14 | 15 | 16 |
| 2 | 2 | 3 | 4 | 5 | 6 | 7 | 8 | 9 | 10 | 11 | 12 | 13 | 14 | 15 | 16 | 1 |
| 3 | 3 | 4 | 5 | 6 | 7 | 8 | 9 | 10 | 11 | 12 | 13 | 14 | 15 | 16 | 1 | 2 |
| 4 | 4 | 5 | 6 | 7 | 8 | 9 | 10 | 11 | 12 | 13 | 14 | 15 | 16 | 1 | 2 | 3 |
| 5 | 5 | 6 | 7 | 8 | 9 | 10 | 11 | 12 | 13 | 14 | 15 | 16 | 1 | 2 | 3 | 4 |
| 6 | 6 | 7 | 8 | 9 | 10 | 11 | 12 | 13 | 14 | 15 | 16 | 1 | 2 | 3 | 4 | 5 |
| 7 | 7 | 8 | 9 | 10 | 11 | 12 | 13 | 14 | 15 | 16 | 1 | 2 | 3 | 4 | 5 | 6 |
| 8 | 8 | 9 | 10 | 11 | 12 | 13 | 14 | 15 | 16 | 1 | 2 | 3 | 4 | 5 | 6 | 7 |
| 9 | 9 | 10 | 11 | 12 | 13 | 14 | 15 | 16 | 1 | 2 | 3 | 4 | 5 | 6 | 7 | 8 |
| 10 | 10 | 11 | 12 | 13 | 14 | 15 | 16 | 1 | 2 | 3 | 4 | 5 | 6 | 7 | 8 | 9 |
| 11 | 11 | 12 | 13 | 14 | 15 | 16 | 1 | 2 | 3 | 4 | 5 | 6 | 7 | 8 | 9 | 10 |
| 12 | 12 | 13 | 14 | 15 | 16 | 1 | 2 | 3 | 4 | 5 | 6 | 7 | 8 | 9 | 10 | 11 |
| 13 | 13 | 14 | 15 | 16 | 1 | 2 | 3 | 4 | 5 | 6 | 7 | 8 | 9 | 10 | 11 | 12 |
| 14 | 14 | 15 | 16 | 1 | 2 | 3 | 4 | 5 | 6 | 7 | 8 | 9 | 10 | 11 | 12 | 13 |
| 15 | 15 | 16 | 1 | 2 | 3 | 4 | 5 | 6 | 7 | 8 | 9 | 10 | 11 | 12 | 13 | 14 |
| 16 | 16 | 1 | 2 | 3 | 4 | 5 | 6 | 7 | 8 | 9 | 10 | 11 | 12 | 13 | 14 | 15 |

**Figure 15.12**   16 × 16 arrayed-waveguide grating (AWG) router connectivity.

*Type-II Tunable Filter.* A Type-II tunable filter, as shown in Figure 15.13, performs the wavelength selection optically. It has two AWGs. The first 1 × 16 AWG performs the demultiplexing function, while the second 16 × 1 AWG performs the multiplexing function. Only one of 16 wavelengths is selected by properly controlling the SOA gates. The selected wavelength passes through the second AWG and is then converted into an electronic signal by a detector. A planar lightwave circuit–planar lightwave circuit (PLC–PLC) direct attachment technique [19] can be used to construct this type of tunable filter and to integrate the AWG routers and the SOA gates. This hybrid integration of PLC and SOA gates can reduce the coupling loss and increase the reliability.

*Type-III Tunable Filter.* A Type-III tunable filter, as shown in Figure 15.14, performs the wavelength selection optically. Different from the Type-II filter, it uses only one 16 × 16 AWG router. Any one of the 16 wavelengths can be selected through its specific combination of SOA gates at input and output sides of AWG router [20]. Figure 15.15 shows a way to

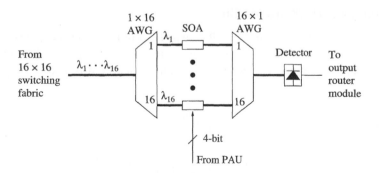

PAU: Ping-pong arbitration unit
AWG: Arrayed-waveguide grating
SOA: Semiconductor optical amplifier

**Figure 15.13**   Type-II tunable filter.

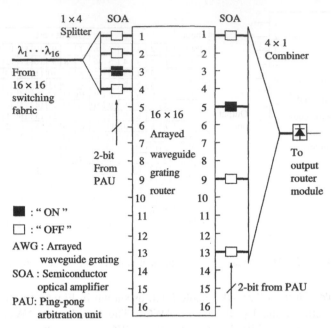

**Figure 15.14** Type-III tunable filter.

choose any one of the 16 wavelengths. The $16 \times 16$ AWG router will route a wavelength $\lambda_k$ from input port $x$ ($x = 1, 2, \ldots, 16$) to output port $y$ ($y = 1, 2, \ldots, 16$), where $k = (x + y - 1)$ modulo 16. For example, $\lambda_7$ will be selected as the output by turning on the third SOA gate at the input side and the fifth SOA gate at the output side of the AWG router, respectively. The quantity of SOA gates in the Type-III tunable filter is reduced by half; only eight SOA gates (four at the input and four at the output) are used instead of 16 SOA gates in the Type-II tunable filter. However, compared to Type-I and Type-II tunable filters, the Type-III tunable filter has more power loss caused by the $1 \times 4$ splitter and the $4 \times 1$ combiner.

### 15.2.4 Ping-Pong Arbitration Unit

As shown in Figure 15.6, a centralized PAU was used in the router [15]. The arbitration is pipelined with packet segment transmission in the OIN. In other words, while a HOL segment is being transmitted via the OIN, the segment next to it is also sending a request

| Input port | Output port | | | |
|---|---|---|---|---|
| | 1 | 5 | 9 | 13 |
| 1 | 1 | 5 | 9 | 13 |
| 2 | 2 | 6 | 10 | 14 |
| 3 | 3 | 7 | 11 | 15 |
| 4 | 4 | 8 | 12 | 16 |

**Figure 15.15** Connectivity of Type-III tunable filter.

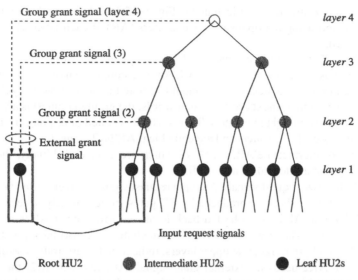

**Figure 15.16**   Tree-structured hierarchical arbitration (© 1999 IEEE).

to the arbitration unit. In order to minimize the delay of forwarding multicast request signals, 256 parallel arbiters are used, each of which is associated with one output and handles 256 input request signals. The 256 incoming multicast request signals must be handled simultaneously within one time slot, that is, 51.2 ns for 64-byte data segment sent at 10 Gbit/s.

***Principles of PPA.***   Consider an $N$-input packet switch. To resolve its output contention, a solution is to use an arbiter for each output to fairly select one among those incoming packets and send back a grant signal to the corresponding input. The arbitration procedure is as follows:

1. During every arbitration cycle, each input submits a one-bit request signal to each output (arbiter), indicating whether its packet, if any, is destined for the output.
2. Each output arbiter collects $N$ request signals, among which one input with active request is granted according to some priority order.
3. A grant signal is sent back to acknowledge the input.

Here, the second step that arbitrates one input among $N$ possible ones is considered.

A simple round robin scheme is generally adopted in an arbiter to ensure a fair arbitration among the inputs. Imagine there is a token circulating among the inputs in a certain ordering. The input that is granted by the arbiter is said to grasp the token, which represents the grant signal. The arbiter is responsible for moving the token among the inputs that have request signals. The traditional arbiters handle all inputs together and the arbitration time is proportional to the number of inputs. As a result, the switch size or capacity is limited given a fixed amount of arbitration time.

Here, it is suggested to divide the inputs into groups with each group having its own arbiter. The request information of each group is summarized as a group request signal. Further grouping can be applied recursively to all the group request signals at the current layer, forming a tree structure, as illustrated in Figure 15.16. Thus, an arbiter with $N$ inputs can be constructed using multiple small-size arbiters (AR) at each layer. Different group sizes can be used.

Assume $N = 2^k$. Figure 15.16 depicts a $k$-layer complete binary tree with a group size of two when $k = 4$. AR2 represents a 2-input AR. An AR2 contains an internal flag signal that indicates which input is favored. Once an input is granted in an arbitration cycle, the other input will be favored in the next cycle. In other words, the granted request is always chosen between left (input) and right alternately. That is why it is called ping-pong arbitration. The first layer consists of $2^{k-1}$ arbiters and are called leaf AR2s. The next $k - 2$ layers consist of arbiters called intermediate AR2s, $2^{k-i}$ of which are at layer $i$. Finally, the last layer consists of only one arbiter called a *root* AR2.

Every AR2 has two request signals. An input request signal at layer $i$ is the group request signal of $2^{i-1}$ inputs and can be produced by OR gates, either directly or recursively. The grant signal from an AR2 has to be fed back to all the lower-layer AR2s related to the corresponding input. Therefore, every leaf/intermediate AR2 also has an external grant signal that ANDs all grant signals at upper layers, indicating the arbitration results of upper layers. The root AR2 needs no external grant signal. At each leaf AR2, the local grant signals have to combine the upper-layer arbitration results (i.e., its external grant signal) and provide full information of whether the corresponding input is granted or not.

One important usage of the external grant signal is to govern the local flag signal update. If the external grant signal is invalid, which indicates that these two input requests as a whole are not granted at some upper layer(s), then the flag should be kept unchanged in order to preserve the original preference. As shown in Figure 15.16, the external grant signal of a leaf AR2 can be added at the final stage to allow other local logical operations to be finished while waiting for the grant signals from upper layers, which minimizes the total arbitration time.

Suppose $N$ inputs are served in the increasing order of their input numbers, that is, $1 \rightarrow 2 \rightarrow \cdots \rightarrow N \rightarrow 1$ under a round-robin scheme. Each AR2 by itself performs a round-robin service for its two inputs. The PPA, consisting of a tree of AR2s, is shown in Figure 15.16. It can serve the inputs in the order of $1 \rightarrow 3 \rightarrow 2 \rightarrow 4 \rightarrow 1$ when $N = 4$ for instance, which is still round-robin, if each input always has a packet to send and there is no conflict between all the input request signals. Its performance is shown by simulations as follows.

**Performance of PPA.** The performance of the PPA, FIFO + RR (FIFO for input queuing and round robin for arbitration), and output queuing is compared here. A speedup factor of two is used for PPA and FIFO + RR. Simulation results are obtained from a $32 \times 32$ switch under uniform traffic (the output address of each segment is equally distributed among all outputs), and bursty traffic (on–off geometric distribution) with an average burst length of 10 segments. The bursty traffic can be used as a packet traffic model with each burst representing a packet of multiple segments destined for the same output. The output address of each packet (burst) is also equally distributed among all outputs.

Figure 15.17 shows the throughput and total average delay of the switch under various arbitration schemes. It can be seen that the PPA performs comparably with the output queuing and the FIFO + RR. However, the output queuing is not scalable and the RR arbitration is slower than the PPA. The overall arbitration time of the PPA for an $N$-input switch is proportional to $\log_4 \lceil N/2 \rceil$ when every four inputs are grouped at each layer. For instance, the PPA can reduce the arbitration time of a $256 \times 256$ switch to 11 gates delay, less than 5 ns using the current CMOS technology.

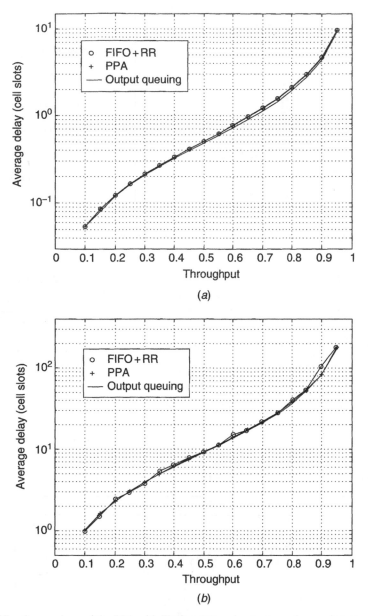

**Figure 15.17**   Comparison of the PPA with FIFO + RR and output queuing: switch throughput and total average delay for a speedup factor of two. (*a*) Uniform traffic; (*b*) Bursty traffic.

***Implementation of PPA.***   Multiple small arbiters can be recursively grouped together to form a large and multi-layer arbiter, as illustrated in Figure 15.16. Figure 15.18 depicts an *n*-input arbiter constructed by using *p* *q*-input arbiters (AR-q), from which the group request/grant signals are incorporated into a *p*-input arbiter (AR-p). Constructing a 256-input arbiter starting with the basic units, AR2s, is shown as follows.

Figure 15.19 shows a basic 2-input arbiter (AR2) and its logical circuits. The AR2 contains an internally feedbacked flag signal, denoted by $F_i$, that indicates which input is

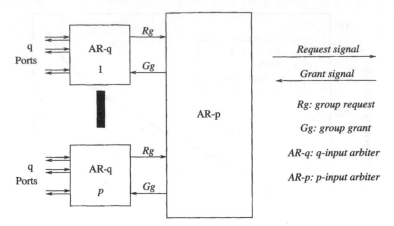

**Figure 15.18** Hierarchy of recursive arbitration with $n = pq$ inputs.

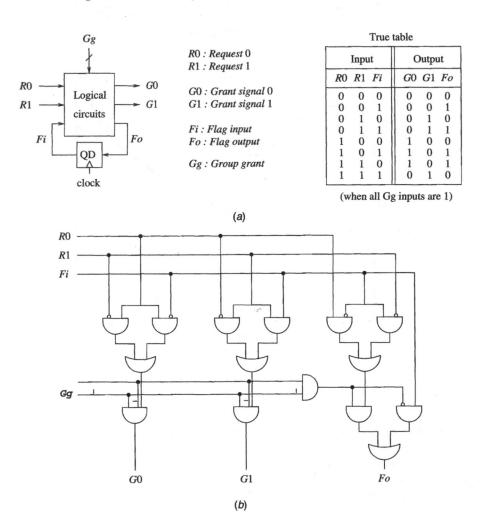

(a)

(b)

**Figure 15.19** (a) AR2 and its true table; (b) its logical circuits (© 1999 IEEE).

favored.[1] When all $G_g$ inputs are 1, indicating these two inputs requests ($R_0$ and $R_1$) as a whole are granted by all the upper layers, once an input is granted in an arbitration cycle, the other input will be favored in the next cycle, as shown by the true table in Figure 15.19a. This mechanism is maintained by producing an output flag signal, denoted by $F_o$, feedbacked to the input. Between $F_o$ and $F_i$, there is a D-flip-flop that functions as a register forwarding $F_0$ to $F_i$ at the beginning of each cell time slot. When at least one $G_g$ inputs is 0, indicating the group request of $R_0$ and $R_1$ is not granted at some upper layer(s), $G_0 = G_1 = 0$, $F_o = F_i$, that is, the flag is kept unchanged in order to preserve the original preference. As shown in Figure 15.19b, the local grant signals have to be ANDed with the grant signals from the upper layers to provide full information on whether the corresponding input is granted or not. $G_g$ inputs are added at the final stage to allow other local logical operations to be finished in order to minimize the total arbitration time.

A 4-input arbiter (AR4) module has four request signals, four output grant signals, one outgoing group request and one incoming group grant signal. Figure 15.20a depicts our design of an AR4 constructed by three AR2s (two leaf AR2s and one intermediate AR2; all have the same circuitry), two 2-input OR gates and one 4-input OR gate. Each leaf AR2 handles a pair of inputs and generates the local grant signals while allowing two external grant signals coming from the upper layers: one from the intermediate AR2 inside the AR4 and the other from outside AR4. These two signals directly join the AND gates at the final stage inside each leaf AR2 for minimizing the delay. Denote $R_{ij}$ and $G_{ij}$ as the group request signal and the group grant signal between input $i$ and input $j$. The intermediate AR2 handles the group requests ($R_{01}$ and $R_{23}$) and generates the grant signals ($G_{01}$ and $G_{23}$) to each leaf AR2, respectively. It contains only one grant signal that is from the upper layer for controlling the flag signal.

As shown in Figure 15.20b, 16-input arbiter (AR16) contains five AR4s in two layers: four at the lower layer handling the local input request signals and one at the higher layer handling the group request signals.

Figure 15.21 illustrates a 256-input arbiter (AR256) constructed using AR4s and its arbitration delay components. The path numbered from 1 to 11 shows the delay from the point when an input sends its request signal up until it receives the grant signal. The first four gate delays (1–4) account for the time taken for the input's request signal to pass though the four layers of AR4s and reach the root AR2, where one OR-gate delay is needed at each layer to generate the request signal (see Fig. 15.20a). The next three gate delays (5–7) account for the time that the root AR2 performs its arbitration (see Fig. 15.19b). The last four gate delays (8–11) account for the time that the grant signals at the upper layers take to pass down to the corresponding input. The total arbitration time of an AR256 is thus 11 gates delay. It then follows that the arbitration time ($T_n$) of an $n$-input arbiter using such implementation is

$$T_n = 2\log_4 \left\lceil \frac{n}{2} \right\rceil + 3. \tag{15.1}$$

**Priority PPA.** Among the packets contending for the same output, those from real-time sessions are more delay-sensitive than others from non-real-time sessions. Therefore, they should have a higher priority to be served first, and sessions (thus their packets) with various

---

[1]When the flag is low, $R_0$ is favored; when the flag is high, $R_1$ is favored.

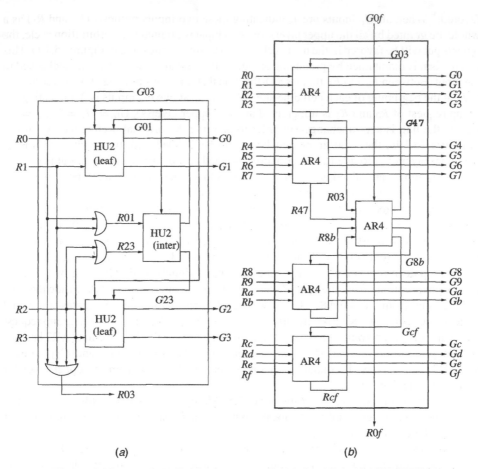

**Figure 15.20** (a) AR4; (b) AR16 constructed with five AR4s (© 1999 IEEE).

quality of service (QoS) requirements can be assigned different levels of service priority. It is shown how to enhance the PPA for handling priority as follows.

Two priority representations are used in our design for transferring efficiency and arbitration convenience, respectively. Suppose $p$ levels of priority are supported. An input has a total of $p + 1$ states, including the case of no request, which can be represented by using $\lceil \log_2(p + 1) \rceil$ bits. The inter-layer request information could be transferred either in serial using one line or in parallel using multiple lines, depending on the tradeoff chosen between delay and pin count complexity. The serial/parallel format transformation can be realized by using shift registers.

A group of $p$ lines is used in the second representation. At most, one of them is high indicating that there is one request at the corresponding level of priority. There will be no request if all output lines are low.

Our solution to multi-priority arbitration relies in a group of parallel single-priority arbiters to resolve the contention at each level of priority simultaneously. Multiple single-priority arbiters are necessary to maintain the arbitration states (states of the flip-flops) for each level of priority, which will be changed only when an input request at this priority

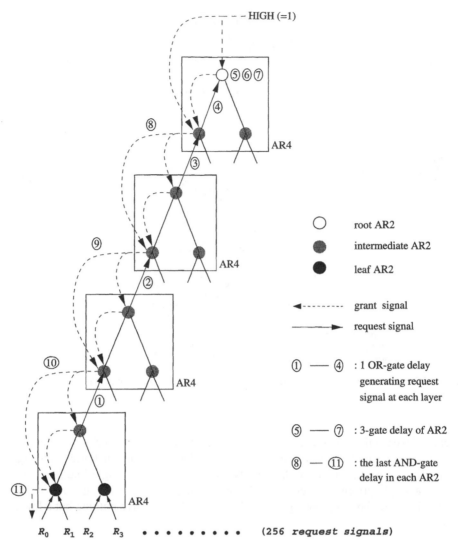

**Figure 15.21**    Decomposition of arbitration delay in an AR256 (© 1999 IEEE).

level is granted. A pre-processing phase and a post-processing phase are then added, as demonstrated in Figure 15.22, with a multi-priority arbiter, which handles 16 inputs and seven levels of priority. A decoder is used at each input to decode the three-line priority request into seven single lines, each representing the request in the corresponding level of priority and entering the corresponding arbiter for single-priority contention resolution. An OR gate is used at each output to combine all corresponding local grants from the single-priority arbiters to produce the final grants for each input.

Meanwhile, every single-priority arbiter generates a group request signal for the upper layer's arbitration; it receives a group grant signal later, which indicates if this group of requests (at the corresponding level of priority) is granted or not. A priority encoder collects all the group requests from the single-priority arbiters and indicates among them the highest priority with its three-line output. The outputs, in addition to being forwarded to

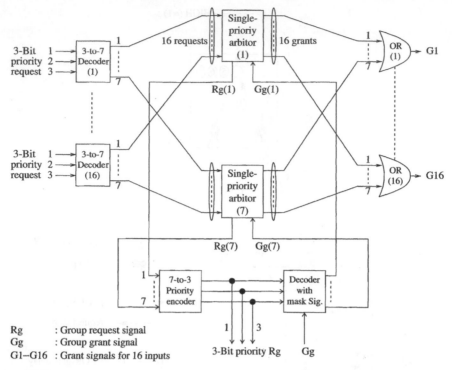

**Figure 15.22** Demonstration of priority handling with parallel arbitration: seven priority levels and 16 inputs.

the upper layer, will also be used to inhibit the arbiters with lower priority from producing any active grant. A decoder with its outputs masked by the upper-layer grant signal is used to decompose the output of the priority encoder into seven single-line grant signals, each for a single-priority arbiter. Only the arbiter at the corresponding level of priority receives the upper layer's grant signal, while all the others receive nothing but a low grant signal.

## 15.3 OPTOELECTRONIC PACKET SWITCH CASE STUDY II

### 15.3.1 Petabit Photonic Packet Switch Architecture

Figure 15.23 shows the system architecture of the proposed petabit photonic packet switch, called PetaStar. The basic building modules include the input and output port controllers (IPC and OPC), input grooming and output demultiplexing modules (IGM and ODM), a photonic switch fabric (PSF), centralized packet scheduler (PS), and a system clock distribution unit. The PSF is a three-stage Clos-network with columns of input switch modules (IMs), central switch modules (CMs), and output switch modules (OMs). The PS for the three-stage Clos-network switch can be found in Chapter 12. The incoming and outgoing line rates are assumed to be 10 Gbit/s. All incoming lines will first be terminated at line cards (not shown in the figure), where packets are segmented into cells (fixed length

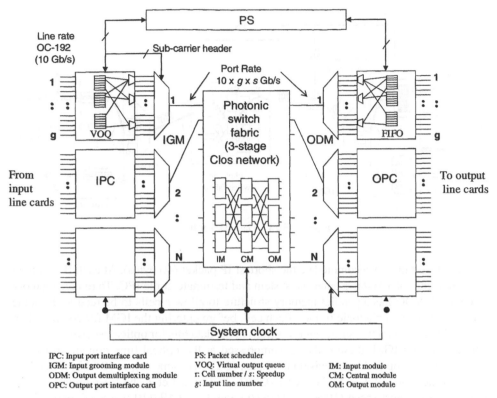

**Figure 15.23** System architecture of the PetaStar.

data units) and stored in a memory. The packet headers are extracted for IP address lookup.[2] All cell buffering is implemented electronically at the IPCs and OPCs, leaving the central PSF bufferless, that is, no photonic buffering is required in the system. As a result, the bit rate of each port can operate at a speed beyond the limits of the electronics. The port speed can be equal to or greater than (with a speedup) $g$ times the line rate, where $g$ is the grooming factor. Virtual output queues (VOQs) at IPCs, together with the PS, provide contention resolution for the packet switch. At the input end, the majority of incoming packets are stored in the ingress line cards, where packets are segmented and stored in its VOQs. Packets destined for the same output port are stored in the same VOQ. VOQs implemented at the IPC serve as the mirror of the VOQ memory structure in the line cards. As long as they can keep the cells flowing between the line card and IPC, the size of the VOQs at the IPC can be considerably smaller than its mirror part in the ingress line cards. Buffers at the OPC are used to store cells before they are sent out to the destined egress line cards. A large buffer with a virtual input queue (VIQ) structure implemented in the line card (not shown in Fig. 15.23) is used to store the egress cells from the PSF and to re-assemble them into packets.

Figure 15.24 shows how packets flow across the system. At the input, variable-length IP packets are first segmented into cells with a fixed length of 64 bytes (including some cell

---

[2]Functions such as classification and traffic shaping/policing are usually performed at the edge routers, but not at core routers.

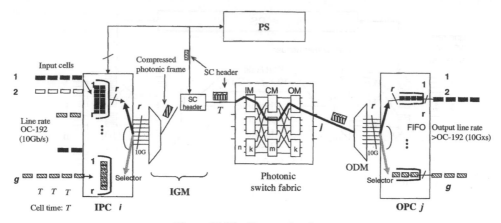

**Figure 15.24** Data packet flow.

overhead), suitable to accommodate the shortest IP packet (40 bytes). At each IPC, a total of $g$ input lines at 10 Gbit/s enter the system and terminate at the IPC. To reduce memory speed, each VOQ has a parallel memory structure to allow $r$ cells to be read at the same time ($r$ cells form a photonic frame). Each cell, before entering the IGM for compression, is scrambled to guarantee sufficient transitions in the data bits for optical receiver and clock recovery. In the IGM, these cells are compressed at the optical time domain to form a time-interleaved optical time division multiplex (OTDM) frame at $g \times 10$ Gbit/s. Let $T$ be the cell time slot and $T = 51.2$ ns for 10 Gbit/s line rate. Let $T_c$ be the compressed cell time slot at the port speed ($10 \times g \times s$ Gbit/s) and $T_c = 64B/(10 \times g \times s$ Gbit/s). Then the compressed photonic frame period $f = r \times T_c = r \times 64B/(10 \times g \times s$ Gbit/s). With $g = r$ and $s = 1$, the frame period $f$ is equal to the cell slot, $T$. Guardtime is added at the head of the frame to compensate for the phase misalignment of the photonic frames when passing through the PSF and to cover the transitions of optical devices.

At each stage of the photonic switching fabric, the corresponding sub-carrier header is extracted and processed to control the switching fabric. Since the PS has already resolved the contention, the photonic frame is able to find a path by selecting the proper output links at each stage in the switching fabric. Once the photonic frame arrives successfully at the designated output port, it is demultiplexed and converted back to $r$ cells at 10 Gbit/s in the electronic domain by the output demultiplexing module (ODM). The OPC then forwards the cells to their corresponding line cards based on the output line numbers (OLs).

As Figures 15.23 and 15.24 show, the optical signals run between the IGM and the ODM at a rate of $g \times 10$ Gbit/s, or 160 Gbit/s for $g = 16$. All optical devices/subsystems between them operate at $g \times 10$ Gbit/s. However, the electronic devices only operate at most 10 Gbit/s (with a speedup of 1), or even lower with parallel wires, for example, four SERDES signals, each at 2.5 Gbit/s (or 3.125 Gbit/s including 8B/10B coding).

Figure 15.25 illustrates the data structure at each stage of the switch. Before the data payload, two header fields that contain the OL in the destined output port and the input line number (IL) of the switch are added to each incoming cell (see Fig. 15.25$a$). The OL is used to deliver cells to the destined output lines when the photonic frame ($r$ cells) arrives at the OPC. A validity bit is inserted at the beginning of the cell to indicate if the cell is valid or not. The overhead bits introduced by OL and IL can be calculated as $\log_2(g)$ and $\log_2(g \times N)$, respectively. For example, for a petabit system with $N = 6400$ and $g = 16$, the cell header

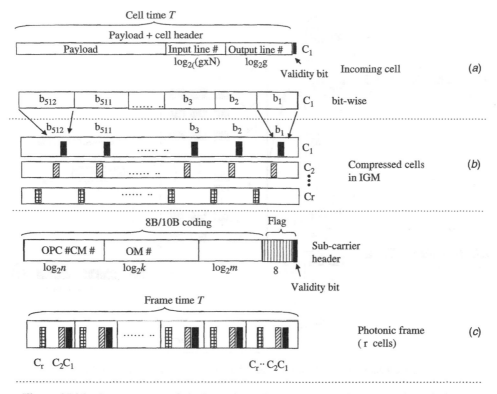

**Figure 15.25**   Data structure of: (*a*) Incoming cell; (*b*) Compressed cells; (*c*) Photonic frame.

length is 21 bits $(1 + 4 + 16)$. Bits in each cell are compressed and time-interleaved using OTDM techniques in the IGM to form the photonic frames that are ready to transmit through the PSF (see Fig. 15.25*b*). Each photonic frame goes along with an out-of-band sub-carrier (SC) header. Using the photonic frame as its carrier, the SC header is amplitude-modulated on the photonic frame at a much lower sub-carrier frequency. The estimated raw bandwidth required for the SC header is about 600 MHz. Standard multi-level coding schemes can be applied to further compress the SC bandwidth to 80 MHz or less, allowing the SC header to be carried around the DC frequency. The first field in the SC header is a flag containing a specific pattern for frame delineation since the photonic frames carrying the SC header do not precisely repeat in the time domain. The payload is 8B/10B coded for correctly finding the flag. Three fields are attached to the SC header to provide routing information at each stage of the PSF. The three fields include CM, OM, and OPC numbers with $\log_2(m)$, $\log_2(k)$, and $\log_2(n)$ bits of information, where $m$ and $k$ are the numbers of CM and OM, and $n$ is the number of outputs at each OM. At the beginning of the frame, a validity bit is added to indicate if the frame contains valid cells.

Figure 15.26 gives an example of how cells flow through the IPC. In this case, packets *A*, *B*, and *C* from input lines 1 and *g*, respectively, are destined for the same output port of the PSF (port 1). Packets *A* and *B* are heading towards output line 1 while packet *C* is headed towards output line *g* at the same OPC. Upon arriving at the IPC, each packet, already segmented into a number of fixed-size cells, is stored in the corresponding input line memory. In this example, packet *A* is segmented into 24 cells (cells $A_0$ to $A_{23}$), packet *B*

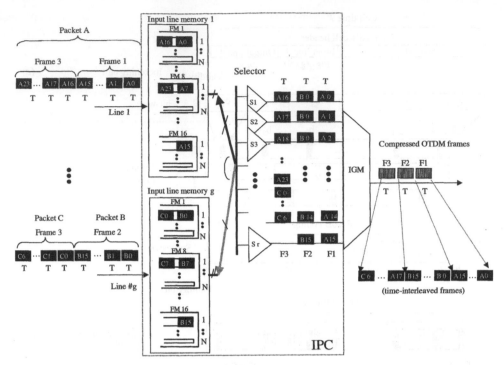

**Figure 15.26**    Example of illustrating how frames are formed in the PRC.

$B$ contains 16 cells (cells $B_0$ to $B_{15}$), and packet $C$ has eight cells (cells $C_0$ to $C_7$). All incoming cells are stored in the $r$ frame memories in a round-robin manner.

As soon as a cell arrives at the input line memory, a request is sent to the packet scheduler that tracks all of the incoming cells. The scheduler, based on a new hierarchical frame-based exhaustive matching scheme, sends back the grant signal if the transmission has been granted. As a result, 16 cells ($A_0$ to $A_{15}$) from input line memory 1 are selected at the first frame period to form frame number 1, followed by 16 cells ($B_0$ to $B_{15}$) from input line memory $g$ selected at the next frame period to form frame number 2. In this example, the remaining eight cells ($A_{16}$ to $A_{23}$) will be aggregated with another eight cells from $C$ packet ($C_0$ to $C_7$) to form frame number 3. The reason that packet $B$ is granted prior to the second half of packet $A$ is because packet $B$ has a filled frame and thus has a higher priority for transmission. At the IGM, cells are compressed into the time-interleaved photonic frames and are thus ready to be routed through the PSF.

Following the above example, Figure 15.27 shows how packets $A$, $B$, and $C$ are processed as they are demultiplexed at the OPC and reassembled at the egress line cards. Photonic frames containing the compressed cells are demultiplexed in the ODM and sent into $r$ parallel inputs to the selector array. According to the cell header, $A_0$ to $A_{15}$ go to the 16 FIFOs located in output line memory 1 at the first frame period. At the next frame period, $B_0$ to $B_{15}$ are sent to the same 16 FIFOs in output line memory 1. At the next frame period, photonic frame number 3 arrives at the OPC. The remaining part of packet $A$ is sent to input line memory 1, while cells from packet $C$ go to output line memory $g$. These cells are then read out from the FIFOs to the designated output line (output line 1 in this case) at a speed larger than 10 Gbit/s. The VIQs at the line card are used to reassemble packets $A$, $B$, and $C$.

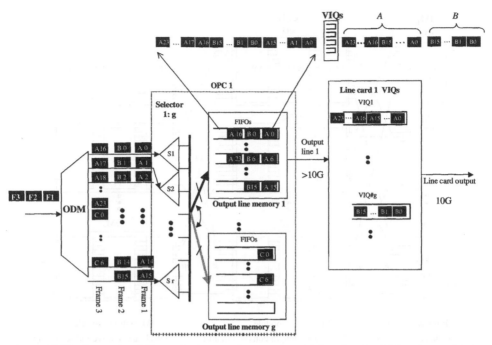

**Figure 15.27** Example of illustrating how packets are demultiplexed at the OPC and resembled at the egress line cards.

Synchronization can be challenging as the system scales. To achieve synchronization, a centralized frame clock will be supplied to each module in the system. Each switching action, including buffer reading and writing, switching of laser wavelength, and OTDM multiplexing and demultiplexing, will be synchronized according to the same frame clock signal with a frequency of, for example, 1/51.2 ns, or 19.5 MHz. The clock signal will be distributed among the modules using optical signals through fibers to provide a sharp stroke edge for triggering operations. A sinusoidal signal at 10 GHz will be distributed to each module as the base frequency for the synchronization. The sub-carrier provides a trigger signal at each switching stage. Upon detecting the sub-carrier signal in the sub-carrier unit (SCU), which indicates the arrival of a photonic frame at the input of the module, the SC processor will wait for a precise time delay before starting the switching operation. The time delay through the fiber connections will be chosen precisely so that it can accommodate the longest processing delay in the header process. We will study the minimum timing tolerance contributed by both photonic and electronics devices, as well as fiber length mismatch in the system, which will ultimately determine the guardtime between the photonic frames. For instance, with a frame period of 51.2 ns and 10 percent used for the guardtime overhead, the guardtime can be 5 ns, which is sufficiently large to compensate for the phase misalignment, fiber length mismatch, and optical device transitions.

### 15.3.2  Photonic Switch Fabric (PSF)

***Multistage PSF.***  Figure 15.28 shows the structure of the PSF. It consists of $k$ IMs, $m$ CMs, and $k$ OMs in a three-stage Clos network. The switch dimensions of the IM and OM are

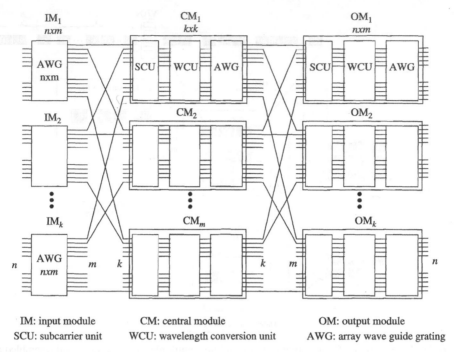

IM: input module    CM: central module    OM: output module
SCU: subcarrier unit    WCU: wavelength conversion unit    AWG: array wave guide grating

**Figure 15.28**    PSF architecture.

$n \times m$ while CM is $k \times k$. The IM at the first stage is a simple AWG device. The CMs and OMs consist of a SCU, a wavelength switching unit (WSU), and an AWG. A $6400 \times 6400$ switch can be realized using 80 wavelengths, that is, $n = m = k = 80$. With the port speed of 160 Gbit/s, total switch capacity reaches 1.024 petabit/s.

Based on the cyclic routing property of an $n \times n$ AWG router, full connectivity between the inputs and outputs of the IM can be established by arranging input wavelengths. By switching the laser wavelength at each of the $n$ inputs, the incoming optical signal that carries the photonic frame can emerge at any one of the $n$ outputs, resulting in an $n \times n$ non-blocking space switch. Since the AWG is a passive device, the reconfiguration of this space switch is solely determined by the active wavelength tuning of the input tunable laser. The wavelength switching can be reduced to a couple of nanoseconds by rapidly changing the control currents for multiple sessions in tunable semiconductor lasers [21–23].

An example of a wavelength routing table for an $8 \times 8$ AWG is shown in Figure 15.29. A wavelength routing table can be established to map the inputs and outputs on a specific wavelength plan. In general, the wavelength $\lambda_k$ from input $i$ $(i = 1, 2, \ldots, n)$ to output $j$ $(j = 1, 2, \ldots, n)$ can be calculated according to the following formula: $k = (i + j - 1)$ modulo $n$. For example, input (5) needs to switch to wavelength $\lambda_7$ to connect to output (3) for $n = 8$ as highlighted in the router table.

To cascade AWGs for multi-stage switching, CMs and OMs have to add wavelength conversion capability, where the incoming wavelengths from the previous stage are converted to new wavelengths. An all-optical technique is deployed to provide the necessary wavelength conversion without O/E conversion. Figure 15.30 illustrates the detailed design of the CM and OM. Three key elements used to implement the switch module are the SCU for header processing and recognition, the wavelength conversion unit (WCU) for performing

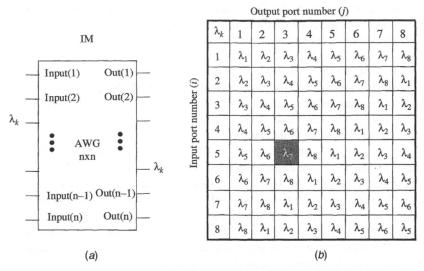

**Figure 15.29** Each input can use the wavelength assigned in the table to switch to any one of eight outputs. (*a*) IM based on an $n \times n$ AWG router; (*b*) Example of $8 \times 8$ wavelength routing table.

all-optical wavelength conversion, and the AWG as a space switch (the same as the one in the IM). The main function of the SCU is to process the SC header information for setting-up the switch path. The SC header information, which consists of 3 bytes, is readily available at each stage of the PSF as these bytes are carried out-of-band along with each photonic

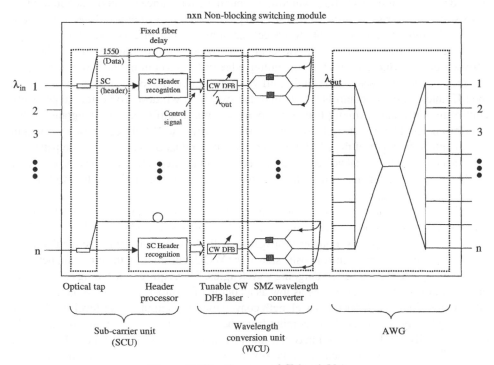

**Figure 15.30** Structure of CM and OM.

frame as shown in Figure 15.25c. Upon arriving at each module, a portion of the power from the photonic frame is stripped by an optical tap and fed into the SCU for sub-carrier demodulation. At the front end of the SCU, a low-bandwidth photo-detector and low-pass filter are able to recover the header information from the photonic frame. The SC header information is used to set the wavelength of the continuous-wave (CW) tunable laser in the WSU. On the data path, a fixed fiber delay is added to allow the SCU to have sufficient time to perform header recognition and processing. The total propagation time between the input and output links is properly controlled to guarantee that the frame arrives at each switch module within system timing tolerance.

Recently, wavelength conversion at the OTDM rate up to 168 Gbit/s was demonstrated that used a symmetric Mach-Zehnder (SMZ)-type all-optical switch [24, 25]. The strong refractive index change from the carrier-induced resonance nonlinearity in the SOAs, coupled with the differential interferometric effect, provides an excellent platform for high-speed signal processing. A similar device has also been demonstrated in demultiplexing an ultra-high bit rate OTDM signal at 250 Gbit/s, which shows its excellent high-speed capability. Therefore, we can consider using an array of such devices to accomplish the all-optical wavelength conversion at an ultra-high bit rate.

The basic structure of the WCU, based on a Mech-Zehnder (MZ) interferometer with in-line SOAs at each arm, is shown in Figure 15.31. The incoming signal with wavelength ($\lambda_{old}$) is split and injected into the signal inputs, entering the MZ interferometer from the opposite side of the switch. Figure 15.31b shows the operation of the wavelength conversion. A switching window at time domain can be set up (rising edge) by the femto-second ultrafast response induced by the signal pulses through the carrier resonance effect of SOAs. The fast response of the SOA resonance is in the femto-second regime, considerably shorter than the desired rise time of the switching window. Although the resonance effect of each individual SOA suffers from a slow tailing response (100 picoseconds), the delayed differential phase in the MZ interferometer is able to cancel the slow-trailing effects, resulting in a fast response on the trailing edge of the switching window. By controlling the differential time between the two SOAs accurately, the falling edge of the switching window can be set at the picosecond time scale. The timing offset between two SOAs located at each arm of the MZ interferometer controls the width of the switching window. To be able to precisely control the differential timing between two arms, a phase shifter is also integrated in the interferometer. The wavelength conversion occurs when a CW light at a new wavelength ($\lambda_{new}$) enters the input of the MZ interferometer. An ultrafast data stream whose pattern is the exact copy of the signal pulses at $\lambda_{old}$ is created with the new wavelength at the output of the MZ interferometer (marked switched output in the figure), completing the wavelength conversion from $\lambda_{old}$ to $\lambda_{new}$.

Using active elements (SOAs) in the WCU greatly increases the power budget while minimizing the possible coherent crosstalk in the multi-stage PSF. As shown in Figure 15.31a, the incoming signal pulses, counter-propagating with the CW light from the tunable DFB laser, eventually emerge at the opposite side of the WCU, eliminating the crosstalk between the incoming and the converted outgoing wavelengths. The required switching energy from the incoming signal pulses can be as low as a couple of femto-joules due to the large resonance non-linearity. After the wavelength conversion, the output power level for the new wavelength may reach mW-level coming from the CW laser. Therefore, an effective gain of 15 to 25 dB can be expected between the input and output optical signals through the WCU. This effective amplification is the key to the massive interconnected PSF maintaining effective power levels for the optical processing at each stage. The building modules

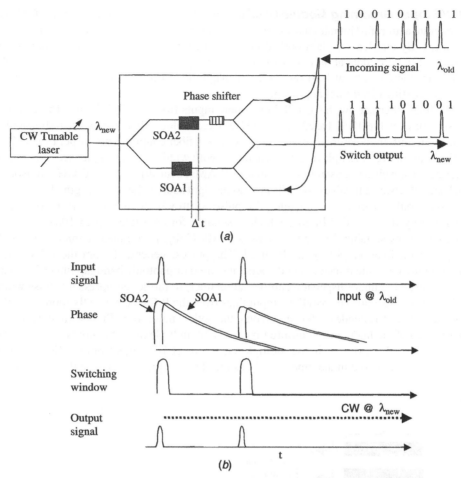

**Figure 15.31** (*a*) Wavelength conversion unit based on an SOA Mach-Zehnder interferometer with differential time delay between two arms. The input signal is $\lambda_{old}$ while the output signal is converted to a new wavelength ($\lambda_{new}$) determined by the CW tunable laser at the device input. (*b*) Timing diagram of the ultrafast wavelength conversion process.

used in the PSF have the potential to be monolithically integrated due to their similar architectures. There have already been attempts to build integrated SOAs in a waveguide structure on PLC technologies [26]. As shown in Figure 15.30, the components in the dashed lines are the best candidates for integration due to their similarity in architecture and design. This integration provides dramatic savings on the power budget and component cost.

To reach a total switch capacity of 1.024 petabit/s, the required bandwidth can be estimated to be 192 nm assuming 80 wavelengths at a 160-Gbit/s port speed, ultimately limiting the system scalability. It is necessary to apply techniques such as polarization multiplexing and the binary coding scheme to further reduce the total spectral width by a factor of two or more. The tuning range of laser and SOA also limits the scalability. However, we propose to use multiple components for tunable laser and SOAs, each of which is capable of tuning over a subset wavelength of the whole spectrum.

### OTDM Input Grooming Module (IGM).

*OTDM Input Grooming Module (IGM).* Optical time division multiplexing (OTDM) can operate at ultrafast bit rates that are beyond the current electronics limit, which is around 40 Gbit/s. By interleaving short optical pulses at the time domain, aggregated frames can be formed to carry data at bit rates of hundreds of gigabits per second. Using the OTDM technique, there can be at least one order of magnitude in bandwidth increase compared with the existing electronics approach.

The IGM interfaces with $r$ parallel electronic inputs from the IPC. Figure 15.32 shows the structure of the IGM based on the OTDM technology. It consists of a short-pulse generation unit, modulator array, and a passive $r \times r$ fiber coupler with proper time delays for time-interleaved multiplexing. Optical pulses with widths of several picoseconds can be generated using electro-absorption modulators (EAMs) over-driven by a 10-GHz sinusoidal clock signal. Using a tunable CW DFB laser as the light source, the wavelength of the output ultra-short pulses can also be tunable. The pulse width will be around 7–10 picoseconds generated by the cascaded EAMs, which is suitable for data rates up to 100 Gbit/s. To generate pulses suitable for higher bit rates (>100 Gbit/s), nonlinear compression with self-phase modulation (SPM) can be used. The pulses, generated from the EAMs, are injected into a nonlinear medium (a dispersion shifted or photonic bandgap fiber) followed by a compression fiber (dispersion compensation fiber) to further compress the pulse width to about 1 picosecond. The parallel $r$ input lines from the IPC electronically modulates the modulator array to encode the bit stream onto the optical pulse train. Precise time delays on each branch of the fiber coupler ensure time-division multiplexing of $r$ inputs. Through the parallel-to-serial conversion in the multiplexer, $r$ cells at 10 Gbit/s from the IPC are now effectively compressed in the time domain as the RZ-type photonic frame that operates at

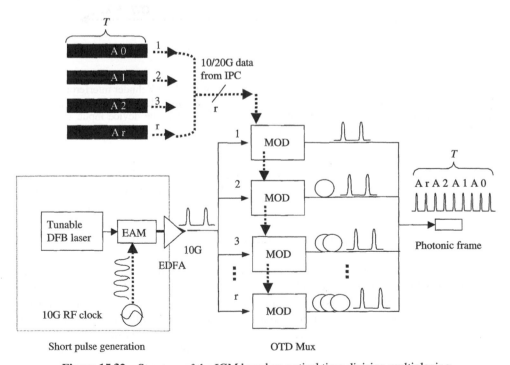

**Figure 15.32** Structure of the IGM based on optical time-division multiplexing.

$r \times 10$ Gbit/s in serial. The fiber coupler and time delays can be integrated using planar waveguide structures [26].

***OTDM Output Demultiplexing Module (ODM).*** At the receiving end of the system, the ODM demultiplexes photonic frames from the output of the PSF into $r$ parallel electronic signals at 10 Gbit/s. As Figure 15.33 shows, the ODM consists of a quarter-phase detector and quarter-phase shifter, an array of OTDM demultiplexers (DEMUX) based on EAMs, and the photo-detector (PD) array for O/E conversions. We have previously demonstrated ultrafast demultiplexing at 40, 80, 100, and 160 Gbit/s using cascaded EAMs as the gating device. As shown in the inset of Figure 15.33, the OTDM demultiplexer consists of two cascaded EAMs based on multiple quantum well devices [27, 28]. An SOA section is also integrated with the EAM to provide optical amplification at each stage. The optical transmission of the EAM, controlled by the driving electronic signal, responds highly nonlinearly and produces an ultra-short gating window in the time domain. Cascading the EAMs can further shorten the gating window compared to a single EAM. The incoming optical signal is split by a $1 \times r$ optical coupler into $r$ modulators located in the array structure. Each EAM is over-driven by a 10-GHz sinusoidal radiofrequency (RF) clock to create the gating window for performing demultiplexing. The RF driving signals supplied to adjacent modulators in the array structure are shifted by a time $\tau$, where $\tau$ is the bit interval inside the photonic frame. As a result, $r$ modulators are able to perform demultiplexing from $r \times 10$ Gbit/s down to 10 Gbit/s on consecutive time slots of the photonic frame.

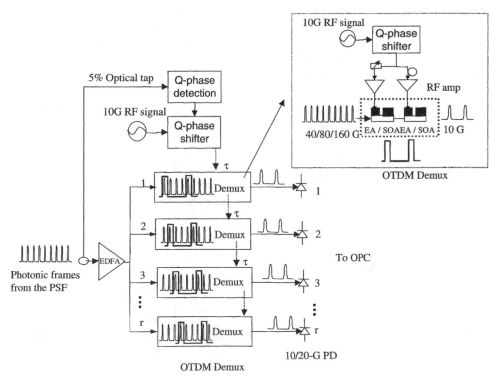

**Figure 15.33** Structure of the ODM. The OTDM demultiplexer, based on cascaded EAMs, is shown in the inset.

The incoming frames may inherit timing jitters induced by either slow thermal effects (fiber, device, and component thermal lengthening) or system timing errors. The result is a slow (compared to the bit rate) walk-off from the initial timing (phase). Since the frames are operating on a burst mode, traditional phase lock loop cannot be applied here. To track the slow varying jitters on the burst frames, we suggest a quarter-phase locking scheme using phase detection and a shifter.

A quarter-phase detector is shown in Figure 15.34. Four OTDM demultiplexers, based on EAM technology, are used as the phase detectors because of their high-speed gating capability. The driving RF sinusoidal signal for each modulator is now shifted by $(\frac{1}{4})\tau$. Depending on the phase (timing) of the incoming signal, one of the four demultiplexer outputs has the strongest signal intensity compared to the three other detectors. A $4:2$-bit decoder is then used to control the quarter-phase shifter to align the 10-GHz RF signal to the chosen phase. For example, assuming $EA_1$ aligns best with the incoming signal at one incident, output from $Q_0$ would be the strongest signal and would be picked up by the comparator. The clock that is supplied to the OTDM demux is then adjusted according to the detected phase.

The quarter-phase shifter, also shown in Figure 15.34, is used to rapidly shift the phase according to the detected phase. The quarter-phase shifter has been demonstrated using a digital RF switched delay lattice. The semiconductor switch is used to set the state at each stage. Depending on the total delay through the lattice, the output phase can be shifted by

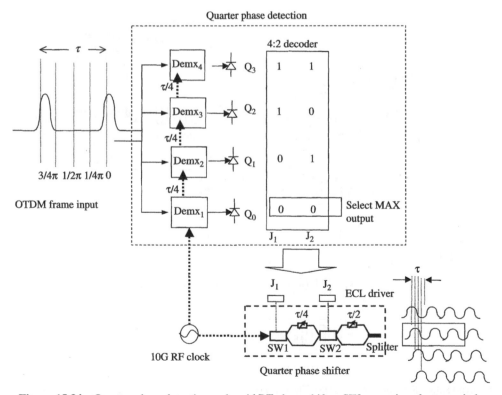

**Figure 15.34**    Quarter-phase detection and rapid RF phase shifter. SW = semiconductor switch.

changing the state at each lattice. The resulting clock is synchronized with the incoming packet with a timing error less than $\pm 1/8\tau$.

## 15.4  ALL OPTICAL PACKET SWITCHES

In optical packet switches, logical control and contention resolution are handled by an electronic controller and packets are carried and stored in optical memories. There are two kinds of optical memory used in the all optical packet switches; one is the traveling type based on fiber delay lines and the other is based on the fiber-loop type where packets, carried in different wavelengths, co-exist in the fiber loop.

### 15.4.1  The Staggering Switch

The staggering switch [29] is one of the optically transparent switches. The major components of the switch are splitter detectors, rearrangeable nonblocking switches, and a control unit. The switch architecture is based on two stages: the scheduling stage and the switching stage, as shown in Figure 15.35. These two stages could be considered as rearrangeably nonblocking networks. The scheduling stage and the switching stage are of size $N \times M$ and $M \times N$, respectively, where $M$ is less than $N$. These two stages are connected by a set of optical delay lines having unequal delay. The idea behind this architecture is to arrange incoming cells in the scheduling stage in such a way that there will be no output-port collision in the switching stage. This is achieved by holding the cells that cause output port collision on the delay lines. The delay on the delay line $d_i$ is equal to $i$ cell slots. The arrangement of incoming cells is accomplished electronically by the control unit according to the output port requests of incoming cells.

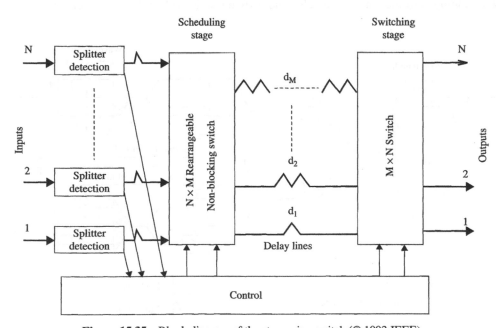

**Figure 15.35**   Block diagram of the staggering switch (© 1993 IEEE).

When a cell arrives at the switch, its header information is converted into electrical signal and sent to the control unit by the corresponding splitter detector. After evaluating the current destination requests considering the previous requests, the control unit sends the information related to the current schedule to the scheduling stage. The cell is routed through the scheduling stage with respect to the information sent by the control unit. Due to the statistical properties of the incoming cells, it is possible to lose some cells in the scheduling stage. After waiting for a certain period of time on the assigned delay line, the cell reaches the switching stage. No contention occurs in the switching stage due to the precautions taken by the control unit, and the cell reaches the requested output port. In this architecture, cells arriving at the same input port may arrive at output ports in the reverse order since they are assigned to different delay lines. Ordered delivery of cells at the output ports can be achieved by some additional operations in the control unit.

The main bottleneck in this switch architecture is the control unit. The proposed collision resolution algorithm is too complicated to handle large switch size or high input line rate. Some input buffers may be necessary in order to keep newly arriving cells while the control unit makes its arrangements.

### 15.4.2 ATMOS

Chiaroni et al. [30] proposed a $16 \times 16$ photonic ATM switching architecture for bit rates up to 10 Gbit/s. Basically, this switch consists of three main blocks: (1) the wavelength encoding block, (2) the buffering and time switching block, and (3) the wavelength selection block as shown in Figure 15.36. In the wavelength encoding block, there are $N$ wavelength converters – one per input. Each input is assigned a fixed wavelength by its wavelength converter. When a cell arrives, a small power of optical signal is tapped by a coupler and converted to electronic signal. There is a controller that processes this converted data and extracts the routing information for the cell. The arriving cells with different wavelengths are

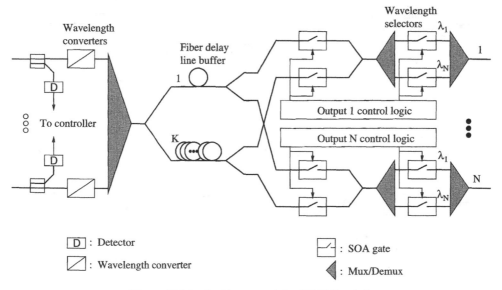

**Figure 15.36**  Architecture of the ATMOS switch.

wavelength-division multiplexed in the buffering and switching block by a multiplexer. The buffering and time switching block contains $K$ fiber delay lines to store the payloads of the incoming cells. There is also a space switch that is made of SOA gates. These gates are used to select the cells from the fiber delay lines and route them to the requested output ports. The wavelength selection block consists of multiplexer/demultiplexer and SOA gates in order to select a specific wavelength destined for an output port in a cell time slot. This switch can perform the multicast function by using the broadcast and select approach.

The cell contention problem is solved by the fiber delay lines. However, as this fiber delay line approach cannot provide the sharing property, a great number of delay lines are necessary to meet the cell loss requirement. The architecture is bulky in structure and the switch size is limited by the available number of wavelengths.

### 15.4.3 Duan's Switch

Duan et al. [31] introduced a $16 \times 16$ photonic ATM switching architecture, as shown in Figure 15.37, where each output port is assigned a fixed wavelength. This switch consists of three main blocks: wavelength encoding block, spatial switch block, and wavelength selection block. In the wavelength encoding block, there are $N$ wavelength converters, one per input and each being tuned to the destined output port. When a cell arrives, a small part of the wavelength is tapped by a coupler and sent to the electronic control unit, which processes the routing information of the cell. In a specific cell slot time, cells destined for different outputs are tuned to different wavelengths. These cells with different wavelengths are routed through the shortest path, which is selected by the SOA gates in the spatial switch. The spatial switch block contains $K$ fiber delay lines to store the payloads of the cells for contention resolution. Each fiber delay line can store up to $N$ different wavelengths. In the wavelength selection block, in each cell slot time, multiple wavelengths are broadcast to all output ports by a star coupler. There is a fixed wavelength filter at each output port. These

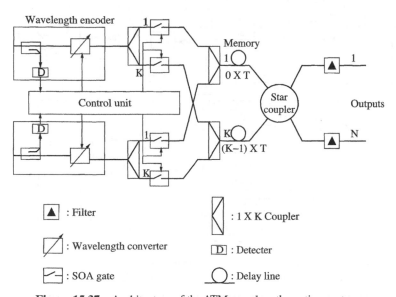

**Figure 15.37**  Architecture of the ATM wavelength routing system.

wavelength filters select the cells associated with their wavelengths and send them to the corresponding output ports.

This switch cannot perform multicast functions because of the fixed wavelength filters at the output ports. Furthermore, if there is more than one cell destined to the same output port, an arbitration mechanism is necessary in order to assign the incoming cells with the same wavelength to different fiber delay lines. Such a requirement increases the control complexity. In order to meet the cell loss requirement, more fiber delay lines are necessary. Moreover, the electronic controller always has to monitor the status of fiber delay lines to preserve the cell sequence.

### 15.4.4 3M Switch

Figure 15.38 shows the architecture of an enhanced $N \times N$ 3M switch, where incoming cells running at 2.5 Gbit/s are optically split into two paths. Cells on the top path remain in the optical domain and are routed through the optical switch plane. Cells on the bottom path are converted to the electronic domain, where their headers are extracted for processing (e.g., finding the output ports for which the cells are destined and finding new virtual path identifier/virtual channel identifier (VPI/VCI) values to replace the old VPI/VCI values). An electronic central controller, as shown in Figure 15.38, performs cell delineation, VCI-overwrite, cell synchronization, and routing. The first three functions are implemented in the photonic ATM front-end processor, while the last one is handled by a route controller that routes cells to proper output ports.

As shown in Figure 15.39, the cell format adopted in the system has 64 bytes with 5 bytes of header, 48 bytes of payload, and two guard time fields (with all ones), which are 6 and

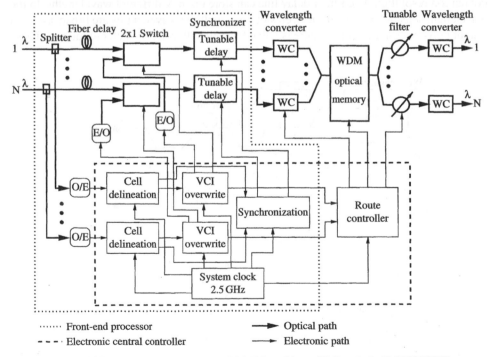

**Figure 15.38** Architecture of the WDM ATM multicast (3M) switch (© 2000 IEEE).

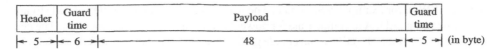

| Header | Guard time | Payload | Guard time |
|--------|-----------|---------|-----------|
| ← 5 → | ← 6 → | ← 48 → | ← 5 → (in byte) |

**Figure 15.39** Cell format adopted in the system.

5 bytes long, respectively. The guard times are used to accommodate the slow switching of optical devices, such as optical tunable filters. The lengths of the guard times between the cells, and between the cell header and the payload were arbitrarily chosen. Cells are transmitted back-to-back and not carried in synchronous optical network (SONET) frames. Not using SONET frames eliminates the possibility of having variable gaps between or within cells caused by the need to carry SONET transport and path overhead ranging from 1 to 49 bytes.

The incoming optical cells are first delayed by fiber lines, processed for their headers, and synchronized in the front-end processor before they are sent to the switch fabric. In the switch fabric, cells are converted to different wavelengths by wavelength converters (WCs) that are controlled by the route controller, which keeps track of the available wavelengths in the WDM optical shared memory. It is a fiber loop memory, as shown in Figure 15.40, and is used to store optical cells until they are ready to be transmitted to the next node. Using a 3-dB directional coupler, cells are coupled into the optical memory and co-exist with the existing cells. Accessing cells in the optical memory is done by controlling the $1 \times 2$ space

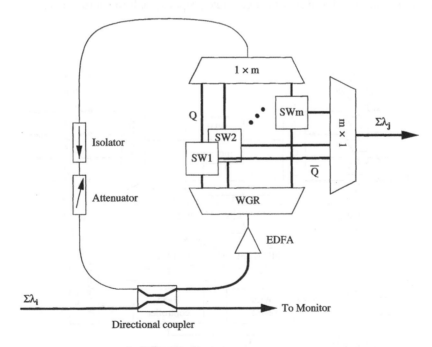

SW : Space switch (e.g., 1 × 2 SOA gate)
WGR : Waveguide grating router
EDFA : Erbium doped fiber amplifier

**Figure 15.40** Optical random access memory (© 2000 IEEE).

switches (SWs), for example, a SOA gate. The wavelengh-division multiplexed cell stream is amplified by an EDFA to compensate for power loss when looping in the memory. The cell stream is then demultiplexed by a waveguide grating router (WGR) into $m$ different channels, each carrying one cell. The maximum number of cells (i.e., wavelengths) simultaneously stored in this memory has been demonstrated to be 23 circulations at 2.5 Gbit/s. Cells read from the WDM optical shared memory are broadcast to all $N$ output ports by a $1 \times N$ splitter and selected by the destined output port (or ports, if multicast) through tunable filters that are tuned by the route controller on a per-cell basis. The final wavelength converter stage converts cells to their predetermined wavelengths. Other optical loop memory can be found in Refs. [32–36].

Figure 15.41 shows how the shared memory is controlled by a route controller. $R_1$–$R_4$ signals carry the output port addresses for which the cells are destined. An idle wavelength FIFO keeps track of available wavelengths in the memory. When up to four incoming cells arrive, free wavelengths are provided by the idle wavelength FIFO, and are used to convert incoming cells' wavelengths so they can be written to the loop memory at the same time. These wavelengths are stored in the FIFOs (FIFO 1–FIFO 4) according to the $R_1$–$R_4$ values. Since the 3M switch supports multicasting, the same wavelength can be written into multiple FIFOs. All the FIFOs (including the idle wavelength FIFO) have the same depth, storing up to $m$ wavelengths. While the wavelength values are written sequentially (up to four writes in each cell slot) to the FIFOs, the wavelengths of the HOL cells of the FIFOs are read simultaneously so that up to four cells can be read out simultaneously. They are, in turn, used to control the tunable filters to direct the cells to the proper output ports. The write controller and read controller generate proper signals to coordinate all functional blocks.

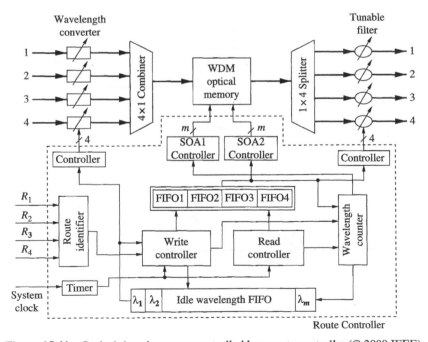

**Figure 15.41** Optical shared memory controlled by a route controller (© 2000 IEEE).

## 15.5  OPTICAL PACKET SWITCH WITH SHARED FIBER DELAY LINES SINGLE-STAGE CASE

### 15.5.1  Optical Cell Switch Architecture

To buffer cells, optical timeslot interchangers (OTSIs) have been widely employed [37]. An OTSI is a single-input-single-output optical (SISO) device that consists of a number of fibre delay lines (FDLs). Let $T_{\text{cell}}$ be the duration of each timeslot and $(F - 1)T_{\text{cell}}$ the maximum delay that can be imposed on a cell. Figures 15.42 and 15.43 depict a nonblocking OTSI and a blocking OTSI, respectively. An OTSI is said to be nonblocking if it can rearrange any positions of cells without internal blocking as long as there is no timeslot conflict. In some cases, internal blocking may occur in the OTSI even though there is no timeslot conflict; then the OTSI is said to be blocking. The implementation complexity of the nonblocking OTSI is very high; thus, in practice, the blocking OTSI is a more attractive solution for performing timeslot interchange.

With reference to Figure 15.44, a feedback-buffered optical-packet switch based on the AWG device has been proposed by Chia et al. [38]. In this switch architecture, the switching plane is combined with $N$ OTSIs, which are placed on the output side and are able to feed the delayed packets back to the input side of the switch. In the center, an AWG switch fabric is employed. Each inlet of the AWG switch fabric is associated with a tunable wavelength converter (TWC). The TWCs are needed because AWG devices switch optical signals according to their wavelengths. Those packets that lost contention are assigned delay

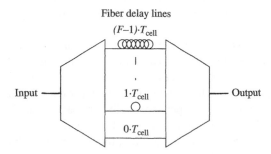

**Figure 15.42**   Nonblocking OTSI.

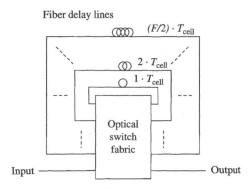

**Figure 15.43**   Blocking OTSI.

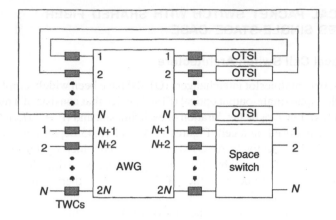

TWC : Tunable wavelength converter

OTSI: Optical timeslot interchanger

**Figure 15.44**    Optical buffered AWG packet switch.

values and switched to the proper OTSIs for buffering. Such a buffered switch is able to provide a low loss rate and low average delay. A major problem, however, is that TWCs are expensive. This problem can be resolved if other switching technologies, such as the micro-electro-mechanical system (MEMS) and SOA, are employed. Scheduling algorithms that can efficiently assign delay routes for optical packets by using blocking OTSIs have not yet received enough attention [38].

Time sliced optical burst switching (TSOBS) [37] is a variant of optical burst switching (OBS), in which burst contention is resolved in the time domain rather than in the wavelength domain, thus eliminating the necessity for wavelength conversion that occurs in the traditional OBS schemes [39, 40]. Ramamirtham and Turner [37] have also proposed an efficient scheduling algorithm for the per-input-OTSI optical switch. The architecture of the per-input-OTSI optical switch is given in Figure 15.45 where the OTSIs are the blocking ones as shown in Figure 15.43. In this algorithm, the existing schedule (switch configuration) is formulated as a directed graph, which gives all possible delay paths for data bursts. The assignment problem can thus be formulated as a searching problem in the directed graph. Nevertheless, there are two major problems with the per-input-OTSI switch. First, since an OTSI is employed and dedicated for each input port, the FDL requirement of the

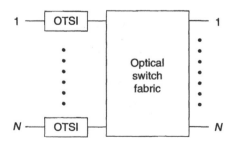

**Figure 15.45**    Per-input OTSI optical switch.

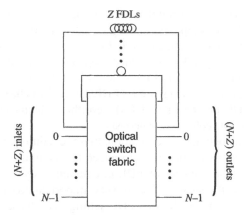

**Figure 15.46**   Single-stage shared-FDL optical switch.

entire switch is undesirably high. Second, as is the nature of an input-buffered switch, the switching schedule must resolve not only the output-port, but also the input-port contentions, thus limiting the overall performance of the switch.

In [41], Karol has proposed a single-stage shared-FDL switch for optical packet ATM switch. The structure of the single-stage shared-FDL switch is given in Figure 15.46. The switch contains a number of feedback FDLs that are shared among all input ports. Assume that there are $Z$ feedback FDLs, $N$ input ports, and $N$ output ports. Each FDL can delay cells by a fixed number of timeslots and any two FDLs may have the same or different delay values. The outputs (inputs) of FDLs and the inputs (outputs) of the switch are collectively called the inlets (outlets) of the switch fabric, yielding $N + Z$ inlets and $N + Z$ outlets.

To resolve contention, Karol has also proposed a non-reservation scheduling algorithm for the single-stage shared-FDL switch in which he assumed specifically that the delay values of the $Z$ FDLs are all different from $1 \ T_{cell}$ to $Z \ T_{cell}$. The algorithm is said to be non-reservation because there is no reservation (hence no departure time scheduling) for the cells that have lost in the contention and need to be buffered. That is, in each timeslot, cells can only be matched with the output ports for the current timeslot. For those buffered cells, there is no guarantee that they can obtain access to the desired output ports after coming out from the FDLs. Therefore, they may need to face another round of contention. Minimum reservation can be achieved by giving a higher priority to the cell that comes out from the longer FDL when resolving contention. However, since departure time is not scheduled in advance, the delay bound of Karol's algorithm can be very large and it may require a cell to be switched and recirculated many times. For example, the maximum number of recirculations required is ten in the simulation [41]. This is undesirable because the optical signal gets attenuated each time they are switched. Another issue of Karol's algorithm is that it is of high time complexity for scheduling cells, which is $O(Z^2)$, due to its sequential nature.

In the next section, we focus on the reservation scheduling algorithms in the single-stage shared-FDL switch. In contrast to the non-reservation scheduling algorithms, the reservation scheduling algorithms perform not only output port matching for the current timeslot, but also the FDL assignment for the entire journey of a delayed cell so that it can be scheduled to match with the desired output port in a future timeslot. The FDL assignment may involve one or more than one FDL circulation. If it is successful, the output port at the corresponding timeslot as well as the FDL path(s) along the journey are said to be reserved for the cell. However, if a cell that needs to be delayed fails to be scheduled to a future timeslot for the desired output port owing to FDL and/or output-port conflicts, it is discarded without entering the switch so that it does not occupy any resources. To achieve low cell loss rate, two new algorithms for scheduling cells in the single-stage shared-FDL optical switch have been proposed by Lieu et al. [42]. They are: (i) the sequential FDL assignment (SEFA) algorithm, which searches FDL routes for cells on a cell-by-cell basis; and (ii) the multi-cell FDL assignment (MUFA) algorithm, which uses sequential search to find FDL routes for multiple cells simultaneously.

In addition to FDL and output port reservation, these scheduling algorithms also exhibit flexible features that allow switch designers to select the maximum delay value, say $F - 1$ timeslots, and the maximum number of FDL circulations, say $K$ circulations, that can be imposed on a cell at the switch. This is very important from the traffic engineering point-of-view. Compared with Karol's FDL setting [41], these also allow two FDLs to have the same delay value, and assume that the delay values of FDLs are distributed among $2^0 T_{cell}, 2^1 T_{cell}, \ldots, 2(f - 1) T_{cell}$, where $f = \log_2 F$ for implementation. It is also worth noting that the single-stage shared-FDL switch and the proposed algorithms are also applicable for the circuit-based timeslot-wavelength division multiplexing (TWDM) networks [43–45] to perform timeslot interchange at a switching node so as to increase call admission rate.

### 15.5.2   Sequential FDL Assignment (SEFA) Algorithm

In SEFA [42], the FDL assignment is considered for a single cell at any given time. In practice, cells may arrive in the same timeslot. In that case, SEFA schedules these cells one after another. For forwarding cells, each shared-FDL switch maintains a configuration table. The configuration table is used to indicate the switching schedule of the switch, and it can be formulated into a slot transition diagram that includes all possible FDL routes for cells. The configuration table and the slot transition diagram are described as follows.

With reference to Figure 15.47, for $s \in$ outlets, $t \geq 0$, the entry of row $s$ and column $t$ in this table consists of two variables, $u(s, t)$ and $v(s, t)$, where $u(s, t) \in 0, 1$, and $v(s, t) \in$ inlets. Variable $u(s, t)$ is called the availability bit of outlet $s$ and it is a Boolean variable that indicates whether outlet $s$ is available in timeslot $t$. That is, if $u(s, t) = 1$, then outlet $s$ is idle in timeslot $t$; if $u(s, t) = 0$, then outlet $s$ is connected to inlet $v(s, t)$ in timeslot $t$. For the example given in Figure 15.47, $u(\text{output } p, t) = 0$ and $v(\text{output } p, t) = \text{input } 7$, indicates that output $p$ is busy in timeslot $t$ because it is scheduled to be connected to input 7. Note that the depth, that is, the number of columns, of the configuration table is $F$. The configuration table can be logically represented by a slot transition diagram, $G$, as shown in Figure 15.48.

In $G$, timeslot $t$ (i.e., column $t$ in the switch configuration table) is represented by a node with label $T(t)$. If FDL$a$ is available in timeslot $t$ (i.e., $u(\text{FDL}a, t) = 1$), it is represented by an arc from $T(t)$ to $T(t + Da)$, where $Da$ is the delay value of FDL $a$. With such a representation, an available FDL route from timeslot $t$ to timeslot $\tau$ is denoted by a path from $T(t)$ to $T(\tau)$ in $G$, where $\tau > t$. For example, path $T(t) \rightarrow$ FDL$a \rightarrow T(t + 2) \rightarrow$ FDL$c \rightarrow T(t + 6)$ in Figure 15.48 represents an available FDL route that can route a cell from timeslot $t$ to timeslot $t + 6$. Note that since different FDLs can have the same delay values, $G$ is a directed multigraph as shown in Figure 15.48.

For each node in $G$ to match the desired output port with the cell request, node $T(t)$ also keeps the availability status of all outputs in timeslot $t$, that is, $u(\text{output } p, t)$ for all $p$, $0 \leq p \leq (N - 1)$. Therefore, finding a valid FDL route starting from timeslot $t$ to a timeslot

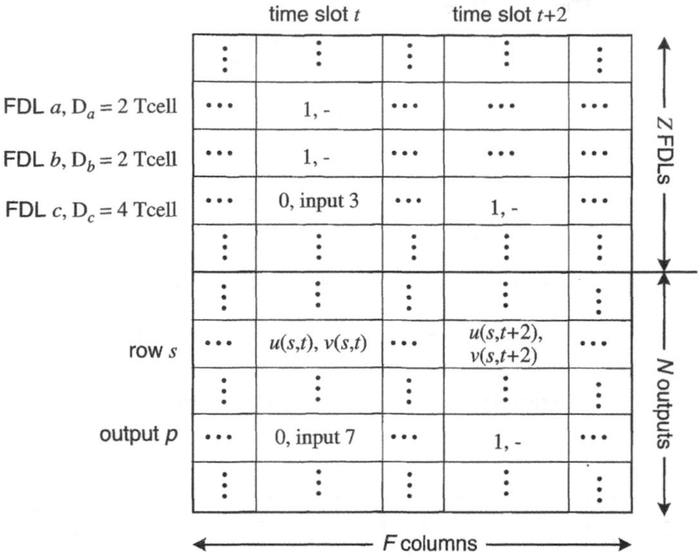

|  | time slot $t$ | | | time slot $t+2$ | |
|---|---|---|---|---|---|
| | $\vdots$ | $\vdots$ | $\vdots$ | $\vdots$ | $\vdots$ |
| FDL $a$, $D_a = 2$ Tcell | $\cdots$ | 1, - | $\cdots$ | $\cdots$ | $\cdots$ |
| FDL $b$, $D_b = 2$ Tcell | $\cdots$ | 1, - | $\cdots$ | $\cdots$ | $\cdots$ |
| FDL $c$, $D_c = 4$ Tcell | $\cdots$ | 0, input 3 | $\cdots$ | 1, - | $\cdots$ |
| | $\vdots$ | $\vdots$ | $\vdots$ | $\vdots$ | $\vdots$ |
| | $\vdots$ | $\vdots$ | $\vdots$ | $\vdots$ | $\vdots$ |
| row $s$ | $\cdots$ | $u(s,t)$, $v(s,t)$ | $\cdots$ | $u(s,t+2)$, $v(s,t+2)$ | $\cdots$ |
| | $\vdots$ | $\vdots$ | $\vdots$ | $\vdots$ | $\vdots$ |
| output $p$ | $\cdots$ | 0, input 7 | $\cdots$ | 1, - | $\cdots$ |
| | $\vdots$ | $\vdots$ | $\vdots$ | $\vdots$ | $\vdots$ |

*Z FDLs* / *N outputs* — *F columns*

**Figure 15.47**   Switch configuration table of optical cross connect (OCX).

in which output $p$ is available, is equivalent to finding a path in $G$ from $T(t)$ to any $T(\tau)$ in which $u$(output $p$, $\tau$) $= 1$. Note that if $u$(output $p, t$) $= 1$ in the beginning, the cell can be routed to output $p$ immediately in timeslot $t$ without passing through any FDL.

An example is given below. Consider a shared-FDL switch with two inputs, two outputs and two FDLs as shown in Figure 15.49. Suppose that some routes have been previously scheduled and the scheduled switch configurations for the next four time slots are given in Figure 15.50. These scheduled configurations are stored in a configuration table as shown in Figure 15.51, and this table can be further represented by a slot transition diagram as shown in Figure 15.52.

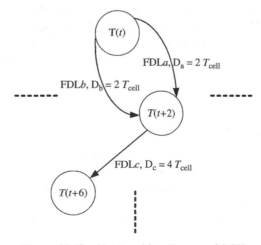

**Figure 15.48**   Slot transition diagram of OCX.

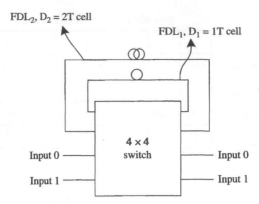

**Figure 15.49** $2 \times 2$ switch module, 2 FDLs.

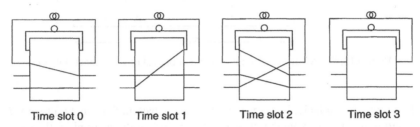

| Time slot 0 | Time slot 1 | Time slot 2 | Time slot 3 |

**Figure 15.50** Scheduled connections in the switch module ($F = 4$).

With the above existing configuration, suppose that a new cell arrives from input 0 in timeslot 0, requesting to be connected to output 0. Since output 0 is not available in timeslot 0 (i.e., $u$(output $0, 0) = 0$), we have to find an FDL assignment to route the new connection to any timeslot, say $\tau$, in which $u$(output $0, \tau) = 1$. With the slot transition diagram given in Figure 15.52, we can modify any search-based algorithms, such as the breadth-first search, for this objective. For the above example, two nonblocking FDL routes, $T(0) \to \text{FDL1} \to T(1) \to \text{FDL2} \to T(3)$ and $T(0) \to \text{FDL2} \to T(2) \to \text{FDL1} \to T(3)$ can be found, and both route the cell to $T(3)$ – the first timeslot in which output 0 is available.

Each time when a cell is passing through an FDL, regardless of the delay value of that FDL, it is said to be taking a delay operation (circulation). For example, both FDL routes given in the previous example impose two delay operations on the cell. Note that, a delay

| | time slot 0 | time slot 1 | time slot 2 | time slot 3 | |
|---|---|---|---|---|---|
| $\text{FDL}_1$, $D_1 = 1$ Tcell | 1, – | 0, input 1 | 1, – | 1, – | ------ |
| $\text{FDL}_2$, $D_2 = 2$ Tcell | 1, – | 1, – | 0, input 1 | 1, – | ------ |
| output 0 | 0, $\text{FDL}_2$ | 0, input 0 | 0, $\text{FDL}_1$ | 1, – | ------ |
| output 1 | 0, input 1 | 1, – | 0, input 0 | 0, input 1 | ------ |

**Figure 15.51** Configuration table of the example.

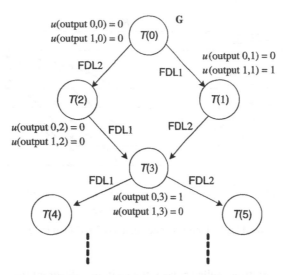

**Figure 15.52**   Slot transition diagram of the example.

operation is always followed by a switching operation. In practice, there may be a need to reduce the number of delay operations when scheduling FDL routes because optical signals are attenuated each time they are switched. Therefore, when multiple choices exist in which the desired output port is available, the selection criteria would be as follows:

1. Select the FDL route that involves the minimum number of delay operations.
2. If there are multiple valid FDL routes that involve the same minimum number of delay operations, we select the one with the smallest delay.
3. If there are multiple FDL routes involved in the same minimum number of delay operations and the same minimum delay value, one of them can be selected at random.

Theoretically, the size of the slot transition diagram can be infinitely large. However, one may limit the maximum number of delay operations (i.e., $K$ operations) and/or the maximum cell delay (i.e., $F - 1$ cell times) in SEFA for practical implementation. Under these constraints, if neither a direct connection nor a FDL route can be assigned to a cell for the desired output port, the cell is discarded immediately without entering the switch.

***SEFA Performance and Complexity.*** In the following, we provide the simulation results of SEFA for a $32 \times 32$ switch with 32 shared FDLs. Consider that the delay values of the 32 FDLs are distributed as evenly as possible between $1, 2, \ldots, 2^l, \ldots, F/2$ cell times, starting from 1. For instance, if $F = 128$, there are 5, 5, 5, 5, 4, 4, and 4 FDLs with delay values 1, 2, 4, 8, 16, 32, and 64 cell times, respectively. Compared with Karol's FDL length selection in [41], the reasons why an exponentially increasing length rather than linearly increasing length is chosen are as follows. (1) For those cells that need a large delay value for the desired output ports, we can delay them with only a few delay operations. (2) With fewer choices of FDL length, the size of slot transition diagram is smaller; hence the complexity of the algorithm can be reduced. The Bernoulli arrival process is assumed. Furthermore, when there is a cell arriving at an input port, it is equally likely to be destined for any one

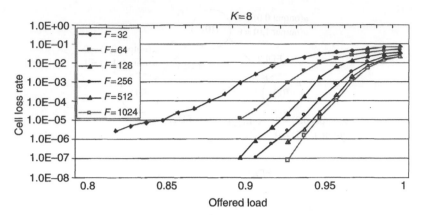

**Figure 15.53** Cell loss rate versus offered load (SEFA).

of the output ports. If multiple cells arrive at the switch at different input ports in the same timeslot, they are scheduled one after another sequentially.

Figure 15.53 shows the cell loss rate and the average cell delay, respectively, of cells with respect to the offered load under different $F$ values in SEFA, assuming $K = \infty$. From Figure 15.53, the larger the value of $F$, the smaller the cell loss rate. The reason is twofold. (1) The larger $F$ provides more alternative delay values for cells to search for timeslots in which the desired output ports are available. (2) An FDL with delay value $D$ can "buffer" up to $D$ cells; thus, according to the above setting of FDL delay values, the larger $F$ implies a larger buffer size for buffering cells. It is worth noting that when $F = 128$, the cell loss rate is $\sim 10^{-7}$ at a load of 0.9.

However, a large $F$ is not always preferable. With reference to Figure 15.54, the average cell delay increases as $F$ increases. The reason is that, in SEFA we always select the FDL route that involves the minimum number of delay operations when multiple choices are available. In the worst case, the FDL route with one delay operation having a delay value of $F/2$ will be selected rather than the FDL route with two delay operations but having a total delay value of only two. Thus it causes a larger cell delay. One possible way of resolving

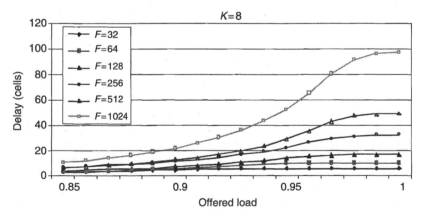

**Figure 15.54** Average cell delay versus offered load (SEFA).

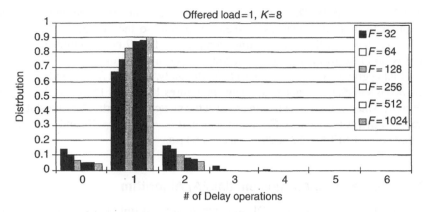

**Figure 15.55**    Distribution of the number of delay operations.

this problem is to search for the FDL routes in ascending order according to the total delay. However, this may result in more delay operations.

We also obtained the distribution of the number of delay operations under different $F$ values in SEFA, assuming $K = \infty$ and offered load $= 1$. Figure 15.55 shows that most cells passing through FDLs require less than four FDL delay operations. The reason is that, the more delay operations a FDL route involves, the more chance there is that it incurs FDL contention. Thus it can be assigned to a cell successfully with a lower probability. It is worth noting that, when $F \geq 128$, no cell is assigned a FDL route of four or more delay operations.

From the above observation, it may be conjectured that SEFA performs equally well when $K = 2$ and $K = \infty$, assuming $F \geq 128$. To verify this argument, Figure 15.56 shows the simulation result of cell loss rate with respect to the offered load under different settings of $K$, where $F$ is set to 128. Basically, when $K = 2$, $K = 3$, and $K = \infty$, respectively, the curves coincide with each other with slight differences, thus it verifies the above argument.

To find the time complexity of SEFA, we assume that the time needed for the SEFA scheduler to access a node in graph $G$ is $C_{se}$. For instance, $C_{se} = 5$ ns if the clock rate of

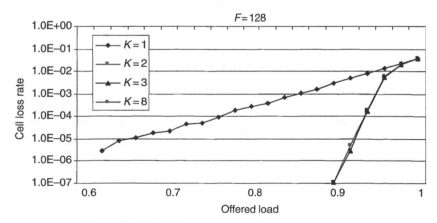

**Figure 15.56**    Cell loss rate under different settings of $K$.

the scheduler is 200 MHz. The scheduler in the worst case needs to search over all nodes in $G$ in order to find out a FDL assignment for a cell, so the number of nodes in $G$ is another factor that contributes to the time complexity. Let $Q$ be the number of nodes in $G$. There is no close-form solution to the value of $Q$ in terms of $F$ and $K$, but it can be observed that $Q$ grows exponentially with $K$. Fortunately, if we set $K = 2$ and $F = 128$, the performance is satisfactory enough as shown in Figures 15.53 and 15.54, (yielding $Q = 36$ only). Finally, since at most $N$ cells can arrive at the switch in a particular timeslot, the time complexity of SEFA is $N \times Q \times C_{se}$. For instance, if $N = 32$, $Q = 36$, and $C_{se} = 5$ ns, the time complexity of SEFA is $32 \times 29 \times 5\,\text{ns} = 4.64\,\mu\text{s}$.

### 15.5.3  Multi-Cell FDL Assignment (MUFA) Algorithm

In MUFA [46], we consider the FDL assignment for multiple cells simultaneously. To guarantee that the FDL routes with fewer delay operations are searched and assigned for cells earlier, the slot transition diagram is modified as follows.

With reference to Figure 15.57, in the modified slot-transition diagram, the node that represents the current timeslot is called node $T_0(0)$, where the subscript denotes the level of the node. $T_0(0)$ is the only level-0 node. Consider $1 \le k \le K$, where $K$ is the maximum number of delay operations for a cell. A node $T_k(t)$ is said to be a level-$k$ node, if any cell arriving at the switch at $T_0(0)$ can take $k$ delay operations to reach the node, where $t$ is the total delay value of the FDLs traversed. For example, $T_2(3)$ is a level-2 node because a cell can traverse two FDLs, with delay values 1 and 2 (total delay $= 3$), respectively, from $T_0(0)$ to $T_2(3)$. Note that for a delay value, there can be different nodes at different levels, such as $T_1(2)$ and $T_2(2)$ in Figure 15.57.

The parent of a level-$k$ node is a level-$(k - 1)$ node. A node can have multiple parents and/or multiple children. The link from a parent to a child is unique, and it indicates that there are FDLs that can delay cells from the parent to the child (delay value is $2^l$, where $0 \le l \le 6$ in this example), regardless of whether these FDLs are available in the parent node. However, the availability status of all output ports and FDLs at timeslot $t$ can be tracked with the availability bits that are kept locally at $T_k(t)$.

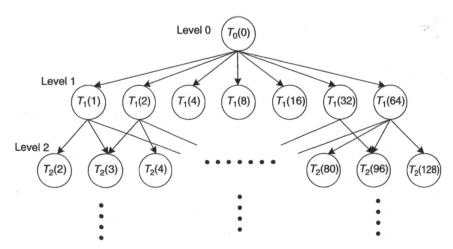

**Figure 15.57**  Modified slot transition diagram.

Let $OPA_j(t)$ denote the availability bit of output port $j$ and $FA_q(t)$ denote the availability bit of FDL $q$ in timeslot $t$, where $0 \leq j \leq N - 1$ and $0 \leq q \leq Z - 1$. That is, if $OPA_j(t) = 1$ ($FA_q(t) = 1$), then output port $j(FDL_q)$ is available in timeslot $t$; if $OPA_j(t) = 0$ ($FA_q(t) = 0$), then output port $j(FDL_q)$ is busy in timeslot $t$.

In any timeslot, the shared-FDL switch may receive up to $N$ requests. Upon receiving these requests, the switch controller activates the MUFA algorithm, which consists of $K + 1$ levels of assignment from level 0 to level $K$. The level 0 assignment has only one step, in which the algorithm attempts to assign direct connections for cells. The requests that have not been assigned connections (due to contention) are called the unfulfilled requests. Unfulfilled requests can be granted via FDL routes. This is done in the higher levels of assignment.

For $1 \leq k \leq K$, in the level-$k$ assignment, the MUFA algorithm tries to assign level-$k$ routes (routes from $T_0(0)$ to level-$k$ nodes) for the unfulfilled requests. With reference to Figure 15.58, the grant decisions of level-$k$ nodes for the unfulfilled requests are made by their parent node (which is a level-$(k - 1)$ node). Moreover, at any time, only one parent node performs the granting process. For example, during the level-1 granting process, node $T_0(0)$ is the parent of all level-1 nodes and it makes grant decisions for its children; during the level-2 granting process, each level-1 node acts as a parent node, one after another, from $T_1(1)$ to $T_1(64)$ to make grant decisions for their children (level-2 nodes), and so on. The granting process of a parent node is described as follows.

With reference to Figure 15.59, to make a granting decision, the parent node needs to collect three sets of data in addition to the FDL availability status of itself:

1. Output port availability status from all its children.
2. Available FDL routes from $T_0(0)$ (such information is kept at the ancestor nodes, updated in the end of each iteration, and is passed to the parent node in question when necessary).
3. Unfulfilled requests from the last processing node.

During the granting process, the parent node matches the unfulfilled requests with the output-port availabilities (OPAs) of its children in accordance with the number of available FDL routes from $T_0(0)$ to the child node. If multiple choices are available for an output port, the parent chooses the child node with the smallest delays for the corresponding requests. With reference to Figure 15.60, after the granting process, the parent node sends the updated

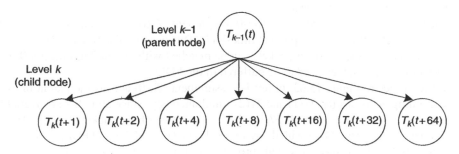

**Figure 15.58**  Parent node makes granting decisions for the child nodes.

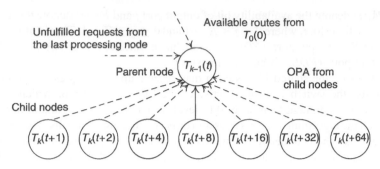

**Figure 15.59**    Before granting process at a parent node.

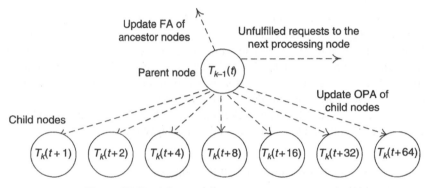

**Figure 15.60**    After granting process at a parent node.

OPAs back to the child nodes, updated FDL availabilities (FAs) back to the ancestors, and the unfulfilled requests to the next processing nodes. After level-$k$ granting is done (i.e., all level-$(k-1)$ nodes have acted as parent nodes), the algorithm proceeds to level-$(k+1)$ until $k = K$.

An example of MUFA is given below. Consider a shared-FDL switch with four inputs, four outputs and four FDLs that have delay values of 1, 1, 2, 2, respectively, as shown in Figure 15.61. Suppose that at timeslot 0, four packets arrive and they are all destined for output 3, where the packet from input $i$ to output $j$ is denoted by $(i, j)$. A modified slot-transition diagram can be constructed as shown in Figure 15.62. Note that this diagram is independent of the packet arrival.

To schedule the above packets, in level-0 assignment, $T_0(0)$ can grant one of the four packets (say packet $(0, 3)$) for output 3 at timeslot 0. This process also turns $OPA_3(0)$ from 1 to 0 in such a way that no other packets can be matched with output 3 at timeslot 0. For the other three packets, they need to be buffered in the FDLs.

With reference to Figure 15.63, in level-1 assignment, $T_0(0)$ acts as the parent of, and makes granting decisions for, $T_1(1)$ and $T_1(2)$ simultaneously. Since all FDLs are available at the time (i.e., $FA_q(0) = 1$ for all $FDL_q$, $1 \leq q \leq 4$), two of the packets [say $(1, 3)$ and $(2, 3)$] can be assigned the FDLs with delay values 1 and 2 (say FDL1 and FDL3), for output 3 in timeslots 1 and 2, respectively. This process also turns $FA_1(0)$, $FA_3(0)$, $OPA_3(1)$, and $OPA_3(2)$ from 1 to 0.

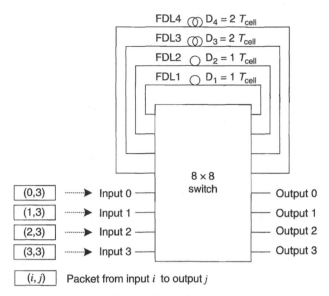

**Figure 15.61**   $4 \times 4$ switch module, 4 FDLs.

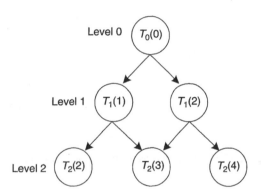

**Figure 15.62**   Modified slot-transition diagram for a $4 \times 4$ switch.

The remaining unfulfilled packet, $(3, 3)$, can be granted in level-2 assignment, in which $T_1(1)$ first acts as the parent of $T_2(2)$ and $T_2(3)$, and then $T_1(2)$ acts as the parent of $T_2(3)$ and $T_2(4)$. With reference to Figure 15.64, consider $T_1(1)$ acting as the parent of $T_2(2)$ and $T_2(3)$. From the top of $T_1(1)$, since there remains only one FDL (i.e., FDL2, where $FA_2(0) = 1$) that can shift a packet from $T_0(0)$ to $T_1(1)$, $T_1(1)$ can grant at most one packet for either $T_2(2)$ or $T_2(3)$. To the children of $T_1(1)$, output 3 at timeslot 2 has been assigned to another packet (i.e., $OPA_3(2) = 0$). Therefore, $T_1(1)$ can only grant packet $(3, 3)$ for output 3 at $T_2(3)$, and this consumes a FDL with delay value 2 (say FDL3) at timeslot 1. This process also turns $FA_2(0)$, $FA_3(1)$, and $OPA_3(3)$ from 1 to 0. The entire scheduling result of MUFA is given in Figure 15.65.

***MUFA Performance and Complexity.***  There are two possible phenomena that make MUFA and SEFA perform differently. (1) In MUFA, for a particular output port, it is

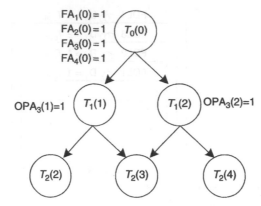

**Figure 15.63** $T_0(0)$ acts as the parent of $T_1(1)$ and $T_1(2)$.

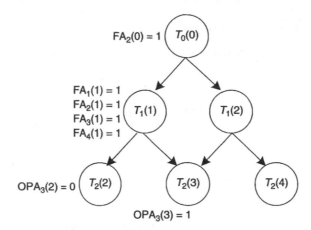

**Figure 15.64** $T_1(1)$ acts as the parent of $T_2(2)$ and $T_2(3)$.

guaranteed that the FDL routes with the fewer delay operations are assigned earlier. However, considering two FDL routes with the same number of delay operations, it is possible that the route with the larger delay is selected rather than the route with the smaller delay. This occurs when the former's parent node has a smaller index than that of the latter's parent node. For instance, with reference to Figure 15.57, the delay of the FDL route of $T_0(0) \rightarrow T_1(32) \rightarrow T_2(96)$ is larger than that of the FDL route of $T_0(0) \rightarrow T_1(64) \rightarrow T_2(80)$. Such a phenomenon does not occur in SEFA. (2) In SEFA, since cells that could be destined for different outputs are scheduled sequentially, it is possible that FDL routes with more delay operations are assigned to cells in the early time in such a way that they occupy the FDL resources and prevent the subsequent cells from finding FDL routes with fewer delay operations. In this case, FDL resources are less efficiently used in SEFA than MUFA. From Figures 15.66 and 15.67, phenomenon (1) makes SEFA perform better at a load < 0.95; phenomenon (2) makes MUFA perform better at a load > 0.95. Overall, the difference of performance between SEFA and MUFA is not significant.

To find the time complexity of MUFA, with reference to Figures 15.59 and 15.60, suppose that the time needed for a parent node to collect the necessary information is $C_{cl}$; the time

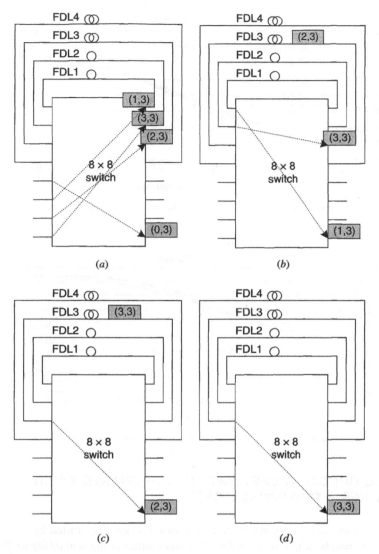

**Figure 15.65**   Scheduling result of MUFA. (*a*) Routing in Timeslot 0; (*b*) Routing in Timeslot 1; (*c*) Routing in Timeslot 2; (*d*) Routing in Timeslot 3.

needed for the parent node to grant unfulfilled requests is $C_{gr}$, where $C_{gr}$ includes a step of parallel AND operations (to match the unfulfilled requests with the available output ports at each child node) and $\log_2 F$ sequential steps of bit comparison (to grant the matches for each child node); the time needed for the parent node to pass the necessary information to the corresponding nodes is $C_{ps}$. Moreover, let $P$ be the number of nodes that act as parent nodes during the MUFA process. The time complexity of MUFA is $P \times (C_{cl} + C_{gr} + C_{ps})$. $P$ is a function of $K$ and $F$. For example, when $K = 2$ and $F = 128$, $P$ is equal to $1 + 7 = 8$. Let us assume $C_{cl} = C_{ps} = 5\,\text{ns}$, then $C_{gr} = (1 + \log_2 F) \times 5\,\text{ns} = 40\,\text{ns}$, and the time complexity is $8 \times 50\,\text{ns} = 400\,\text{ns}$.

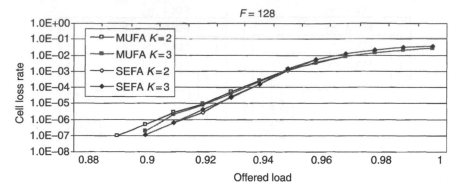

**Figure 15.66** Cell loss rate versus offered load (MUFA).

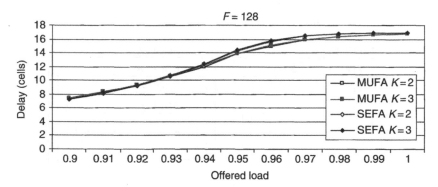

**Figure 15.67** Average cell delay versus offered load (MUFA).

## 15.6 ALL OPTICAL PACKET SWITCH WITH SHARED FIBER DELAY LINES – THREE-STAGE CASE

The scalability of the single-stage shared-FDL switch is greatly limited by the number of required cross points, which is $(N + Z)^2$. To further enhance the scalability of the optical-buffered switches, it is common to consider the multi-stage modular switch architecture due to its high scalability and low complexity nature. Among all multi-stage modular switch architectures, the Clos-network is the most practical and frequently used scheme and gives a balance of switch performance and hardware complexity.

A three-stage optical Clos-network switch (OCNS) contains $K$ $N \times M$ input modules (IMs), $K$ $M \times N$ output modules (OMs) and $M$ $K \times K$ center modules (CMs). Note that the size of the switch is $NK \times NK$. To buffer cells when contention occurs, FDLs can be placed at IMs, CMs, and/or OMs. However, different FDL placements can result in different scheduling complexity and performance. If the FDLs are only placed at OMs, cells are forced to be routed to the last stage as soon as they arrive at the switch. Since each OM can only accept up to $M$ cells at any given timeslot, excess cells will be discarded, which results in a high cell-loss rate. If the FDLs are only placed at CMs, global availability information is needed when scheduling a batch of incoming cells and thus this placement discourages distributed FDL scheduling schemes. As a result, the focus is on the OCNS in

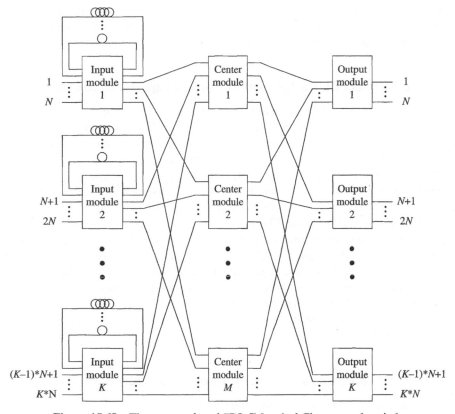

**Figure 15.68**   Three-stage shared-FDL-IM optical Clos-network switch.

which FDLs are only placed at IMs, as shown in Figure 15.68. We call this switch structure the three-stage shared-FDL-IM OCNS (SFI-OCNS). In the SFI-OCNS, cells can be delayed only at the first stage, while the second and third stages are used only for routing purposes; hence cells can be scheduled in a distributed manner. To give a fair comparison, we have studied the performance of different FDL placements. Our simulation results confirm that the SFI-OCNS has the lowest cell loss rate.

In addition to the departure schedule and FDL assignment, there is another issue in the three-stage SFI-OCNS: the central-route assignment. It is well-known that the number of CMs (i.e., $M$) in a three-stage Clos-network switch determines the non-blocking character-istic of the switch. If $M \geq 2N - 1$ [47], the switch is said to be strictly non-blocking because central routes can be arbitrarily assigned for the existing connections, yet none of the future connections will be blocked. However, given an $M$ smaller than $2N - 1$, the central routes must be assigned carefully; otherwise rearrangement may be necessary or internal blocking may occur. There are two kinds of central-route assignment algorithms for Clos-network switches: the optimized and the heuristic. Although the optimized algorithms can always find the optimal solution to the central-route assignment problem, they have a high time complexity. Therefore, in practice, heuristic algorithms are preferable for scalability at a cost of slight performance degradation.

It is challenging to devise efficient scheduling algorithms to assign departure times, FDL routes, and central routes for cells in the three-stage SFI-OCNS. SEFA and MUFA scheduling schemes in Sections 15.5.2 and 15.5.3, respectively, are extended for the SFI-OCNS. MUFAC is a practical algorithm to perform cell scheduling for the SFI-OCNSs due to its graceful scalability and distributed nature.

### 15.6.1   Sequential FDL Assignment for Three-Stage OCNS (SEFAC)

With reference to Figure 15.68, since each input module is a single-stage shared-FDL switch, it maintains its own slot transition diagram. In addition, the whole system has a bigger configuration table that keeps track of the availability of all outputs in each timeslot. Therefore, the output port and center-route availabilities are accessible by all input modules to perform scheduling algorithm. The FDL assignment and cell departure schedule are described in Section 15.6.2. Each input port takes turn to search for the earliest timeslot that satisfies the following three conditions: (i) that the destined output port is available in the timeslot, (ii) that there exists an FDL route on the corresponding input module that can move the cell from the current timeslot to the earliest timeslot, (iii) that a route between the IM and the destined OM is available at that timeslot. When all three conditions are met, the input port assigns the FDL routes, departure time, and randomly selects the center-route among all available center-routes. This searching process is performed one input port after another. In order to achieve fairness among all input ports, a round-robin mechanism can be included in the SEFAC algorithm in such a way that the priority of searching is rotated among all input modules.

### 15.6.2   Multi-Cell FDL Assignment for Three-Stage OCNS (MUFAC)

The three main tasks in the MUFAC algorithm are to:

1. Assign FDL routes in IMs.
2. Schedule cell departure times in correspondence with the output port availability.
3. Assign central-routes between IMs and OMs for multiple cells simultaneously.

In order to accomplish all three tasks, the original single-stage MUFA algorithm is enhanced and further incorporated with Karol's matching algorithm (Section 12.5).

***Karol's Matching Algorithm.***   An example of the matching sequence in Karol's matching algorithm in the OCNS is given as follows. Let us consider a $9 \times 9$ three-stage SFI-OCNS, which has three IMs, three CMs, and three OMs. Therefore, it takes three minislots for all the IMs to finish performing Karol's matching with all the OMs. Figure 15.69 illustrates such a matching sequence.

To find an available center-route in Karol's algorithm is quiet simple. Each IM–OM pair can be connected via $M$ CMs; a vector can be used for each input and output module to record the availability of the central modules. With reference to Figure 12.10, the $A_i$ vector records the available route from $IM_i$ to all CMs. Similarly, the $B_j$ vector records the available route between all CMs and $OM_j$. Each element in those vectors corresponds to each CM; a "0" means available and "1" represents unavailable. For those pairs of modules that have a cell to dispatch between them, the two vectors will be compared to locate an available central module if any.

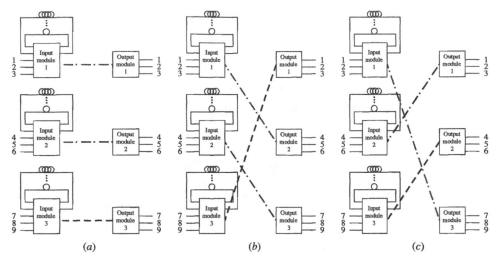

**Figure 15.69** Karol's matching algorithm in three-stage SFI-OCNS: (*a*) First Mini-slot; (*b*) Second Mini-slot; (*c*) Third Mini-slot.

***MUFAC.*** In MUFAC, each IM maintains its own transition diagram, and each level-k node $T_k(t)$ (as shown in Fig. 15.57) keeps the FDL availabilities of that IM for timeslot $t$. In addition, each OM keeps the corresponding output-port availabilities (OPAs), and each of the IMs and OMs keep the corresponding central-route availabilities (CRAs). With the transition diagram, nodes take turn to be the parent node from the level-0 node to each of the level-$(L - 1)$ nodes. Each of these turns is called an iteration.

Based on Karol's matching algorithm, an iteration is further divided into $K$ cycles. In each cycle, each IM is paired up with a particular OM, yielding $K$ IM–OM pairs, and only the cell requests for these IM–OM pairs will be handled. This is done by means of four phases, namely request, grant, accept, and update.

In the request phase, each IM works independently from the others, in which the parent node sends the unfulfilled requests to its child nodes so that they can execute the grant phase independently. At the same time, each child node also collects the OPAs from the paired OM for the corresponding timeslot so that it can grant the unfulfilled requests with the available output ports in the grant phase. After granting the unfulfilled requests, the child nodes pass their grant decisions back to the parent node. At the same time, the parent node collects the CRAs from its home IM and the paired OM. In the accept phase, the parent node makes the accept decision based on the following four criteria: (1) unfulfilled input requests; (2) availability of FDL on that IM for the corresponding timeslots; (3) availability of center-routes from that IM to the paired OM in the corresponding timeslots; and (4) when multiple grants occur, the parent accepts the grant with the earliest departure time. After the parent node makes the accept decision, it passes the decision to its child nodes for updating. In the update phase, the parent node updates the CRAs and FDL availabilities, while the child nodes update OPAs on the paired OM. This completes a cycle of MUFAC. Note that all these phases can be executed in a distributed manner. After $K$ cycles, a node is done with the role of the parent node, and the next node will take the role and run again the $K$ cycles. This process continues until the last parent node [a level-$(L - 1)$ node] is done with the iteration.

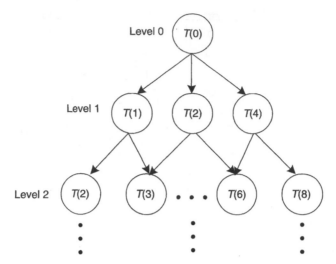

**Figure 15.70**   Slot transition diagram for a 9 × 9 OCNS.

A MUFAC example is given below. With reference to Figure 15.68, suppose that the switch just gets reset, so all output ports are available. We also assume the incoming cell requests from input 1 to input 9 are output ports 1, 4, 7, 1, 4, 7, 1, 4, 7, respectively. Each IM has a transition diagram as shown in Figure 15.70.

In the first iteration, MUFAC tries to assign direct connections for the cell requests. In this 9 × 9 three-stage OCNS, it requires three cycles to finish this task. Within each cycle, each IM consults with a different OM for current OPAs. In the first cycle, IM1 obtains OPAs and center-routes information from OM1. It finds out that output port 1 is available and assigns the direct connection. Similarly, IM2 and IM3 resolve output requests 4 and 7, respectively. In the second and third cycle, no more requests can be resolved because all desired output ports have been assigned in the first cycle. After three cycles, the assignment diagram for T0 nodes at each IM is shown in Figure 15.71.

In the second iteration, T0 becomes the parent of T1, T2, and T4. A four-step assignment process, namely, request, grant, accept, and update is performed three times in three cycles. In the first cycle, each IM does not have an unfulfilled request heading to the matched OM, so no assignment is made. In the second cycle, IM1 has a match with OM2 for output port 4 at T1; IM2 resolves output port 7 with OM3 at T1; and IM3 finds solution for output port 1 with OM1 at T1. In the third cycle, all remaining unfulfilled requests are resolved at T2. Figures 15.72 and 15.73 show the assignment diagram at T1 and T2 for each IM, respectively.

### 15.6.3   FDL Distribution in Three-Stage OCNS

The cell-loss performances of different FDL placement schemes for the three-stage OCNS are studied by using SEFAC in this subsection. We assume that the three-stage OCNS has 32 IMs, 32 OMs, 32 CMs, and each IM (OM) has 32 input ports (output ports). The overall switch size is 1024 × 1024. We consider five different cases of FDL placement scheme and compare their performances under uniform traffic. With reference to Figure 15.74, let Zin be the number of FDLs that are attached on each input module, and

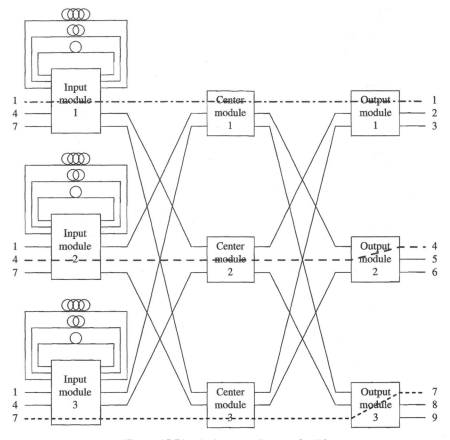

**Figure 15.71**  Assignment diagram for T0.

Zout be the number of FDLs that are attached on each output module. To give a fair comparison, we let Zin + Zout = 32. The cases studied are as follows: (*a*) Zin = 32, Zout = 0; (*b*) Zin = 24, Zout = 8; (*c*) Zin = 16, Zout = 16; (*d*) Zin = 8, Zout = 24; and (*e*) Zin = 0, Zout = 32.

As shown in Figure 15.75, placing all FDLs at the IMs achieves the best performance, while placing them all on the OMs results in the worst performance. To explain this, let us assume that there is no blocking in the middle stage and the entire switch is logically equivalent to a set of $K$ independent concentrator–knockout switches [48], each having the structure as shown in Figure 15.76. Since each IM has no buffer, incoming cells in the IMs are forced to go through the center stage to the OMs immediately upon their arrival at the switch. In the worst case scenario, all $K \times N$ input ports could have cells destined for the same OM. However, at any given timeslot, only up to $M$ cells can arrive at a given OM and the excess cells will be discarded by the CMs even before the cells reach the OM; this is the so-called knockout phenomenon. Therefore, the loss rate is the highest when all buffers are placed at the OMs. On the contrary, when FDLs are located at the IMs, cells can be buffered at the input stage and then directed to the corresponding OMs. Therefore, the performance is the best among all cases.

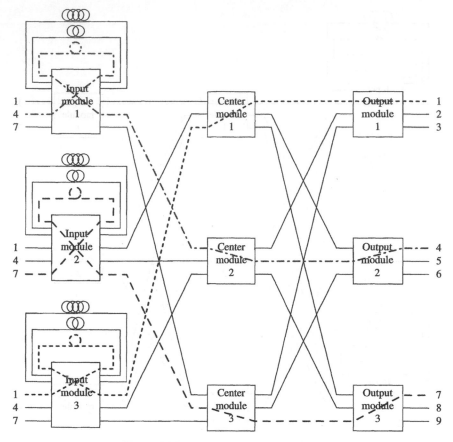

**Figure 15.72**    Assignment diagram for T1.

### 15.6.4  Performance Analysis of SEFAC and MUFAC

In our performance evaluation, we considered a $1024 \times 1024$ SFI-OCNS for both SEFAC and MUFAC. The SFI-OCNS consists of 32 IMs, 32 CMs, and 32 OMs, each module has 32 inputs and 32 outputs; we assume 32 FDLs are employed at each IM, and there are 5, 5, 5, 5, 4, 4, and 4 FDLs with delay values 1, 2, 4, 8, 16, 32, and 64 cell times, respectively. Furthermore, we limited the delay operation for each cell to 2 in both scheduling algorithms. In addition, we used a single stage $32 \times 32$ SEFA as a benchmark.

As shown in Figure 15.77, both three-stage SFI-OCNX FDL assignment algorithms can achieve $10^{-7}$ loss rate at 0.87 loads. There are two possible phenomena that make MUFAC and SEFAC perform differently. (1) In MUFAC, for a particular output port, we guarantee that the FDL routes with fewer delay operations are assigned earlier. However, considering two FDL routes with the same number of delay operations, it is possible that the route with the larger delay is selected rather than the route with the smaller delay. This occurs when the former's parent node has a smaller index than that of the latter's parent node. Such a phenomenon does not occur in SEFAC. (2) In SEFAC, since cells that could be destined for different outputs are scheduled sequentially, it is possible that FDL routes with the more delay operations are assigned to cells in the early time in such a way that

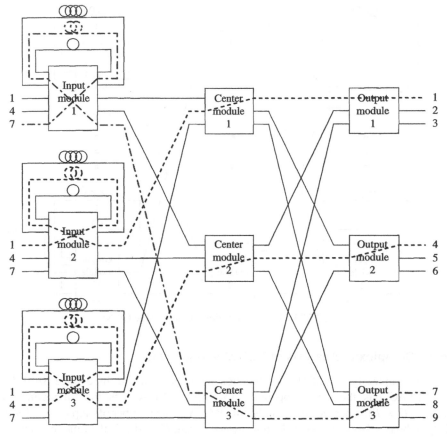

**Figure 15.73**   Assignment diagram for T2.

they occupy the FDL resources and prevent the subsequent cells from finding FDL routes with the fewer delay operations. In this case, FDL resources are less efficiently used in SEFAC than MUFAC. From Figure 15.77, phenomenon (1) makes SEFAC perform better at a load $<0.94$; phenomenon (2) makes MUFAC perform better at a load $>0.94$. Overall the performances of SEFAC and MUFAC for the SFI-OCNS are compatible.

Figure 15.78 shows the delay comparison of SEFAC and MUFAC, with SEFA as a benchmark. The plot shows that SEFAC and MUFAC have identical delay performance, and have an expected disadvantage as compared to SEFA at load 0.9 and above. This delay disadvantage is mainly the result of center-route limitation in the Clos-network switch architecture. Under light traffic loading, limited center-routes are more than the system's need; thus, the Clos-network switch architecture is transparent to FDL assignment. Therefore, SEFAC and MUFAC have compatible delay performance as compared to SEFA at light load. Under heavy traffic loading, center-route availabilities in the Clos-network switch architecture become a resource limitation; hence, SEFAC and MUFAC show delay disadvantages over SEFA at load 0.9 and above. On the other hand, as the offered load approaches 1, their difference becomes smaller. This may be due to the fact that the congestion mainly occurs at the FDL assignment in each switch module, rather than the route limitation through the CMs.

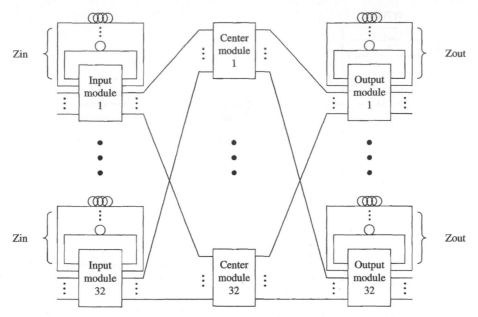

**Figure 15.74** FDL distribution in three-stage OCNS.

### 15.6.5 Complexity Analysis of SEFAC and MUFAC

The time complexity of SEFAC is a function of the size of the three-stage SFI-OCNS. Since SEFAC has the similar operation to SEFA, SEFAC has the time complexity $K \times N \times (Q \times T)$, where $K$ is the number of OMs, $N$ is the number of output ports for each OM, $Q$ is the number of nodes in the transition diagram $G$, and $T$ is the time for each input request to search one node in the transition diagram $G$ for output port and FDL availability. For instance, in a $1024 \times 1024$ SFI-OCNS, which has 32 IM, 32 CM, and 32 OM, each module has a size of $32 \times 32$, and each IM has 32 FDLs, then $K = 32$, $N = 32$. If we

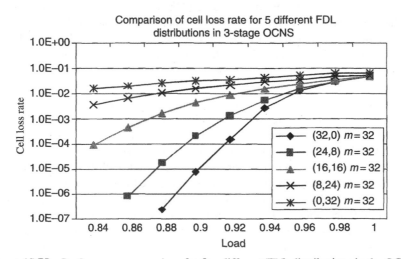

**Figure 15.75** Performance comparison for five different FDL distributions in the OCNS.

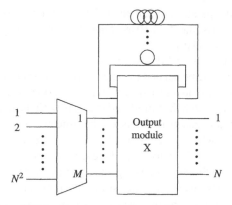

**Figure 15.76** Knockout principle at OM of the OCNS.

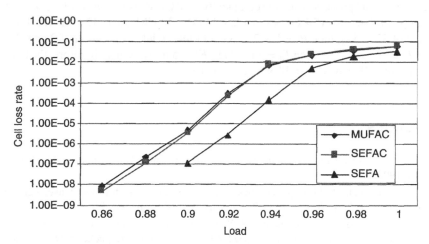

**Figure 15.77** Loss comparison of SEFAC and MUFAC.

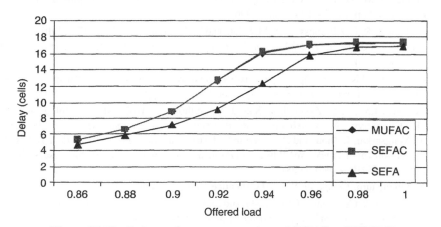

**Figure 15.78** Delay performance comparison of SEFAC and MUFAC.

limit the maximum delay operation to 2, then $Q$, the total number of nodes in the transition diagram $G$, is 36. Let us assume $T = 10$ ns. Thus, the total complexity of the SEFAC is $32 \times 32 \times (36 \times 10 \text{ ns}) = 369 \, \mu\text{s}$.

To find the time complexity of MUFAC, let us consider the complexity of MUFAC at each cycle first. Suppose the time needed for a parent node to send out an unfulfilled request is $T_r$; the time needed for child nodes to make a grant decision is $T_g$, which includes a step of parallel AND operations to match the unfulfilled requests with the available output ports; the time needed to find available center-routes is $T_c$; the time needed for parent nodes to make accepting decisions is $T_a$, where $T_a$ consists of $\log_2 F$ sequential steps of bit comparison (to grant the matches for each child node); and the time needed for all processing nodes to update information is $T_u$. Although requesting and updating are two different procedures in the MUFAC algorithm, these two tasks consist of only register accessing; so, they can be performed in parallel. Therefore, the time needed for these two tasks can be counted as one called $T_{r/u}$. Then the time for one cycle process is $T_g + T_a + T_{r/u}$. Moreover, let $K$ be the number of cycles in each process, and let $P$ be the number of nodes that act as parent nodes during the MUFAC process. The time complexity of MUFAC is $P \times K \times (T_g + T_a + T_{r/u})$. For example, a $1024 \times 1024$ OCNS that has 32 IMs, 32 CMs, and 32 OMs (each module has a size of $32 \times 32$), then $P = 1 + 7 = 8$ with limited delay operation of 2 and $K = 32$. Assume $T_g = T_{r/u} = 5$ ns, then $T_a = (1 + \log_2 F) \times 5 \text{ ns} = 40$ ns. Therefore, the total time complexity for MUFAC is $8 \times 32 \times 55 \text{ ns} = 14 \, \mu\text{s}$.

## REFERENCES

[1] P. E. Green, *Fiber Optic Communication Networks*. Prentice-Hall, Upper Saddle River, New Jercy, 1992.

[2] N. V. Srinivasan, "Add-drop multiplexers and cross-connects for multiwavelength optical networking," in *Proc. Tech. Dig., OFC'98*, San Jose, California, pp. 57–58 (Feb. 1998).

[3] C. K. Chan, F. Tong, L. K. Chen, and K. W. Cheung, "Demonstration of an add-drop network node with time slot access for high-speed WDMA dual bus/ring packet networks," in *Proc. Tech. Dig., OFC'98*, San Jose, California, pp. 62–64 (Feb. 1998).

[4] G. Chang, G. Ellinas, J. K. Gamelin, M. Z. Iqbal, and C. A. Brackett, "Multiwavelength reconfigurable WDM/ATM/SONET network testbed," *IEEE/OSA Journal of Lightwave Technology*, vol. 14, issue 6, pp. 1320–1340 (June 1996).

[5] R. E. Wanger, R. C. Alferness, A. A. M. Saleh, and M. S. Goodman, "MONET: Multiwavelength optical networking," *IEEE/OSA Journal of Lightwave Technology*, vol. 14, issue 6, pp. 1349–1355 (June 1996).

[6] S. Okamoto and K. Sato, "Optical path cross-connect systems for photonic transport networks," in *Proc. IEEE Global Telecommun. Conf.*, Houston, Texas, pp. 474–480 (Nov. 1993).

[7] A. K. Srivastava, J. L. Zyskind, Y. Sun, J. W. Sulhoff, C. Wolf, M. Zirngibl, R. Monnard, A. R. Charplyvy, A. A. Abramov, R. P. Espindola, T. A. Strasse, J. R. Pedrazzani, A. M. Vengsarkar, J. Zhou, and D. A. Ferrand, "1 Tb/s transmission of 100 WDM 10 Gb/s channels over 400 km of TrueWave$^{\text{TM}}$ fiber," in *Postdeadline Papers, OFC'98*, San Jose, California, pp. PD10-1–PD10-4 (Feb. 1998).

[8] A. S. Tanenbaum, *Computer Networks*. Prentice-Hall, New Jersey, 1981.

[9] E. Arthurs, M. S. Goodman, H. Kobrinski, and M. P. Vecchi, "HYPASS: an optoelectronic hybrid packet switching system," *IEEE Journal on Selected Areas in Communications*, vol. 6, no. 9, pp. 1500–1510 (Dec. 1988).

[10] T. T. Lee, M. S. Goodman, and E. Arthurs, "STAR-TRACK: a broadband optical multicast switch," *Bellcore Technical Memorandum Abstract*, 1989.

[11] A. Cisneros and C. A. Brackett, "A large ATM switch based on memory switches and optical star couplers," *IEEE Journal on Selected Areas in Communications*, vol. 9, no. 8, pp. 1348–1360 (Oct. 1991).

[12] M. J. Karol, M. G. Hluchyj, and S. P. Morgan, "Input versus output queueing on a space division packet switch," *IEEE Transactions on Communications*, vol. COM-35, no. 12, pp. 1347–1356 (Dec. 1987).

[13] E. Munter, L. Parker, and P. Kirkby, "A high-capacity ATM switch based on advanced electronic and optical technologies," *IEEE Communications Magazine*, vol. 33, issue 11, pp. 64–71 (Nov. 1995).

[14] Y. Nakahira, H. Inoue, and Y. Shiraishi, "Evaluation of photonic ATM switch architecture-proposal of a new switch architecture," in *Proc. International Switching Symposium*, Berlin, Germany, pp. 128–132 (1995).

[15] H. J. Chao and T.-S. Wang, "Design of an optical interconnection network for terabit IP router," in *Proc. IEEE LEOS'98*, Orlando, Florida, vol. 1, pp. 233–234 (Dec. 1998).

[16] D. Lesterlin, S. Artigaud, and H. Haisch, "Integrated laser/modulators for 10 Gbit/s system," in *Proc. 22nd European Conference on Optical Communication (ECOC'96)*, Olso, Norway, pp. 3.183–3.190 (Sep. 1996).

[17] M. G. Young, U. Koren, B. I. Milter, M. A. Newkirk, M. Chien, M. Zirngibl, C. Dragone, B. Tell, H. M. Presby, and G. Raybon, "A 16 × 1 wavelength division multiplexer with integrated distributed Bragg reflector laser and electroabsorption modulators," *IEEE Photonics Technology Letters*, vol. 5, no. 8, pp. 908–910 (Aug. 1993).

[18] K. C. Syao, K. Yang, X. Zhang, G. I. Haddad, and P. Bhattacharya, "16-channel monolithically integrated InP-based p-i-n/HBT photoreceiver array with 11-GHz channel bandwidth and low crosstalk," in *Proc. Optical Fiber Communication (OFC'97)*, Dallas, Texas, pp. 15–16 (Feb. 1997).

[19] I. Ogawa, F. Ebisawa, F. Hanawa, T. Hashimoto, M. Yanagisawa, K. Shuto, T. Ohyama, Y. Yamada, Y. Akahori, A. Himeno, K. Kato, N. Yoshimoto, and Y. Tohmon, "Lossless hybrid integrated 8-ch optical wavelength selector module using PLC platform and PLC-PLC direct attachment techniques," in *Proc. Optical Fiber Communication Conference (OFC'98)*, San Jose, California, pp. 1–4 (Feb. 1998).

[20] O. Ishida, H. Takahashi, and Y. Inoue, "Digitally tunable optical filters using arrayed-waveguide grating (AWG) multiplexers and optical switches," *IEEE/OSA Journal of Lightwave Technology*, vol. 15, no. 2, pp. 321–327 (1997).

[21] K. Yamakoshi, K. Nakai, N. Matsuura, E. Oki, R. Kawano, and N. Yamanaka, "5-Tbit/s frame-based ATM switching system using 2.5-Gbit/s/spl times/8 optical WDM," in *Proc. IEEE International Conference on Communications*, Helsinki, Finland, vol. 10, pp. 3117–3121 (June 2001).

[22] C. K. Chan, K. L. Sherman, and M. Zirngibl, "A fast 100-channel wavelength-tunable transmitter for optical packet switching," *IEEE Photonics Technology Letters*, vol. 13, issue 7, pp. 729–731 (July 2001).

[23] K. R. Tamura, Y. Inoue, K. Sato, T. Komukai, A. Sugita, and M. Nakazawa, "A discretely tunable mode-locked laser with 32 wavelengths and 100-GHz channel spacing using an arrayed waveguide grating," *IEEE Photonics Technology Letters*, vol. 13, issue 11, pp. 1227–1229 (Nov. 2001).

[24] S. Nakamura, Y. Ueno, and K. Tajima, "168-Gb/s all-optical wavelength conversion with a symmetric-Mach-Zehnder-type switch," *IEEE Photonics Technology Letters*, vol. 13, issue 10, pp. 1091–1093 (Oct. 2001).

[25] J. Leuthold, B. Mikkelsen, G. Raybon, C. H. Joyner, J. L. Pleumeekers, B. I. Miller, K. Dreyer, and R. Behringer, "All-optical wavelength conversion between 10 and 100 Gb/s with SOA delayed-interference configuration," *Optical and Quantum Electronic*, vol. 33, no. 7-10, pp. 939–952 (2001).

[26] H. Takara, S. Kawanishi, Y. Yamabayashi, Y. K. Tohmori, K. Takiguchi, Y. K. Magari, I. Ogawa, and A. Himeno, "Integrated optical-time division multiplexer based on planar lightwave circuit," *Electronics Letters*, vol. 35, issue 15, pp. 1263–1264 (1999).

[27] D. T. K. Tong, K.-L. Deng, B. Mikkelsen, G. Ranbon, K. F. Dreyer, and J. E. Johnson, "160 Gbit/s clock recovery using electroabsorption modulator-based phase-locked loop," *Electronics Letters*, vol. 36, no. 23, pp. 1951–1952 (2000).

[28] K.-L. Deng, D. T. K. Tong, C.-K. Chan, K. F. Dreyer, and J. E. Johnson, "Rapidly reconfigurable optical channel selector using RF digital phase shifter for ultra-fast OTDM networks," *Electronics Letters*, vol. 36, no. 20, pp. 1724–1725 (2000).

[29] Z. Hass, "The "staggering switch": an electrically controlled optical packet switch," *IEEE Journal of Lightwave Technology*, vol. 11, no. 5, pp. 925–936 (May 1993).

[30] D. Chiaroni, C. Chauzat, D. D. Bouard, and M. Sotom, "Sizeability analysis of a high-speed photonic packet switching architecture," in *Proc. 21st Eur. Conf. on Opt. Comm. (ECOC'95)*, Brussels, Belgium, pp. 793–796 (Sep. 1995).

[31] G. H. Duan, J. R. Fernandez, and J. Garabal, "Analysis of ATM wavelength routing systems by exploring their similitude with space division switching," in *Proc. IEEE International Conference on Communication*, Dallas, Texas, vol. 3, pp. 1783–1787 (June 1996).

[32] Y. Chai, J. H. Chen, F. S. Choa, J. P. Zhang, J. Y. Fan, and W. Lin, "Scalable and modularized optical random access memories for optical packet switching networks," in *Proc. CLEO'98*, San Francisco, California, pp. 397 (May 1998).

[33] Y. Chai, J. H. Chen, X. J. Zhao, J. P. Zhang, J. Y. Fan, F. S. Choa, and W. Lin, "Optical DRAMs using refreshable WDM loop memories," in *Proc. ECOC'98*, Madrid, Spain, pp. 171–172 (Sep. 1998).

[34] R. Langenhorst, M. Eiselt, W. Pieper, G. Groossleupt, R. Ludwig, L. Kuller, "Fiber loop optical buffer," *IEEE Journal of Lightwave Technology*, vol. 14, no. 3, pp. 324–335 (1996).

[35] G. Bendelli, M. Burzio, M. Calzavara, P. Cinato, P. Gambini, M. Puleo, E. Vezzoni, F. Delorme, and H. Nakajima, "Photonic ATM switch based on a multiwavelength fiber-loop buffer," in *Proc. OFC'95*, San Diego, California, pp. 141–142 (Feb. 1995).

[36] Y. Yamada, K. Sasayama, and K. Habara, "Transparent optical-loop memory for optical FDM packet buffering with differential receiver," in *Proc. ECOC'96*, Olsa, Norway, pp. 317–320 (Sept. 1996).

[37] J. Ramamirtham and J. Turner, "Time sliced optical burst switching," in *Proc. IEEE INFOCOM'03*, San Francisco, California, pp. 2030–2038 (Apr. 2003).

[38] M. C. Chia, D. K. Hunter, I. Andonovic, P. Ball, I. Wright, S. P. Ferguson, K. M. Guild, and M. J. O. Mahony, "Packet loss and delay performance of feedback and feed-forward arrayed-waveguide gratings-based optical packet switches with WDM inputs–outputs," *IEEE/OSA Journal of Lightwave Technology*, vol. 19, no. 9, pp. 1241–1254 (Sept. 2001).

[39] C. Qiao and M. Yoo, "Optical burst switching (OBS) – A new paradigm for an optical Internet," *Journal of High Speed Networks*, vol. 8, no. 1, pp. 69–84 (1999).

[40] I. Baldine, G. N. Rouskas, H. G. Perros, and D. Stevenson, "Jumpstart: a just-in-time signaling architecture for WDM burst-switched networks," *IEEE Communications Magazine*, vol. 40, no. 2, pp. 82–89 (Feb. 2002).

[41] M. J. Karol, "Shared-memory optical packet (ATM) switch," *Multigigabit Fiber Communications Systems*, vol. 2024, pp. 212–222 (July 1993).

[42] S. Y. Liew, G. Hu, and H. J. Chao, "Scheduling algorithms for shared fiber-delay-line optical packet switches. Part I: The single-stage case," *IEEE Journal of Lightwave Technology*, vol. 23, issue 4, pp. 1586–1600 (Apr. 2005).

[43] N. Huang, G. Liaw, and C. Wang, "A novel all-optical transport network with time-shared wavelength channels," *IEEE Journal on Selected Areas in Communications*, vol. 18, no. 10, pp. 1863–1875 (Oct. 2000).

[44] B. Wen and K. M. Sivalingam, "Routing, wavelength and time-slot assignment in time division multiplexed wavelength-routed optical WDM networks," in *Proc. IEEE INFOCOM'02*, New York, New York, vol. 3, pp. 1442–1450 (Apr. 2002).

[45] R. Srinivasan and A. K. Somani, "A generalized framework for analyzing time-space switched optical networks," in *Proc. IEEE INFOCOM'01*, Anchorage, Alaska, pp. 179–188 (Apr. 2001).

[46] S. Jiang, G. Hu, S. Y. Liew, and H. J. Chao, "Scheduling algorithms for shared fiber-delay-line optical packet switches, Part II: The 3-stage Clos-Network case," *IEEE Journal of Lightwave Technology*, vol. 23, issue 4, pp. 1601–1609 (Apr. 2005).

[47] C. Clos, "A study of non-blocking switching networks," *Bell System Technical Journal*, vol. 32, no. 3, pp. 406–424 (Mar. 1953).

[48] Y. S. Yeh, M. G. Hluchyj, and A. S. Acampora, "The knockout switch: a simple, modular architecture for high-performance switching," *IEEE Journal on Selected Areas in Communications*, vol. 5, no. 8, pp. 1274–1283 (Oct. 1987).

# CHAPTER 16

# HIGH-SPEED ROUTER CHIP SET

The previous chapters provide a general discussion of design issues for the next generation of routers, including IP address lookup, packet classification, traffic management, and packet switching techniques. This chapter describes several commercially-available chips that are destined for next-generation router implementation. These chips include: (1) network processors for various packet processing; (2) co-processors for route lookup and packet classification; (3) traffic managers; and (4) switch fabrics.

## 16.1 NETWORK PROCESSORS (NPs)

### 16.1.1 Overview

The first generation routers were based on software with general-purpose processors (GPP) performing both the data-plane and control-plane functionalities. It was easy to add new features and additional interfaces through system and software upgrading. This architecture was sufficient for bandwidth need during that period and still persists in today's low-end products, for example, Cisco 2500 Series routers.

With exponential increase of Internet traffic, however, processor-centric general-purpose computing architecture was unable to satisfy today's bandwidth demand, and application specific integrated circuits (ASICs) were introduced to cope with the problem. This brought about the advent of the second-generation routers, where performance-critical data-plane functionalities such as packet-forwarding are separated from other functions and performed by dedicated hardware [1]. Because of especially high performance of ASICs and the stability of middle-layer network protocols, hardware-based architecture has been widely adopted in many vendors' designs, including the Juniper M- and T-series.

*High Performance Switches and Routers*, by H. Jonathan Chao and Bin Liu
Copyright © 2007 John Wiley & Sons, Inc.

In order to meet various quality of service (QoS) requirement, routers with the ability to control latency and jitter for packet flows and assure guaranteed priorities, in cases of congestion, are required. Networks are also having to accommodate complicated protocols and applications such as IPv6, VoIP, IPsec, VPN, and so on. Moreover, digital subscriber line (DSL) and packet over SONET (POS) are added to legacy ATM (asynchronous transfer mode), IP, and Frame Relay. In order to meet these new transmission and switching demands, carriers needing a powerful and flexible solution offering a short time-to-market and long time-in-market solution, have turned to a new breed of packet processor – the network processor.

In spite of no official definition, a network processor is a programmable processor specific for network applications. As being the two architectures dominating the first two generations of routers, ASICs provide better performance but have higher costs, longer development cycles and less flexibility. GPPs, on the other hand, require too many cycles to perform the same task and thus cannot provide wire-speed processing. The focus of today's router vendors is to seek proper ways of combining the flexibility of GPPs with the performance of ASICs. Most mainstream vendors' products can be categorized as application specific instruction processors (ASIPs), that is, a programmable processor with an instruction set optimized for a particular application domain [2]. The network processing forum (NPF) was founded in 2001, aimed at speeding-up the standardizing process. A series of common specifications have been established since then, ranging from hardware interface, and application programming interface to benchmarks [3].

### 16.1.2 Design Issues for Network Processors

***Functional Requirements.*** The basic design methodology follows the "functional profiling to architecture exploration" procedure [4]. Network processors typically sit between the physical devices and the switch fabric along with the subsidiary static random access memory (SRAM), dynamic random access memory (DRAM), and in some cases, content addressable memory (CAM) and external co-processors, as shown in Figure 16.1. Network processors are dedicated to packet processing. Some network processors have to be able to

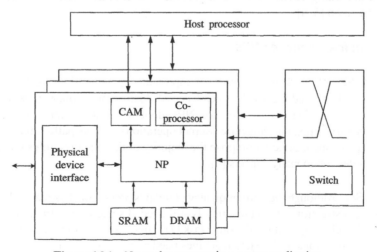

**Figure 16.1**  Network processor in a router application.

do general purpose processing with the absence of a host processor. Their tasks typically include:

*Media Access Control.*   Many network processors can handle the raw data stream coming from the physical links. Low-layer protocols like Ethernet framing and ATM cell processing will be realized directly in this kind of network processor.

*Packet Processing.*   Both header processing (such as field extraction) and payload processing (string searching and encryption), fall into this category.

*Packet Classification.*   Packet classification is the foundation for functions such as QoS, policing and traffic management. For example, a service provider may provide a tiered service where mission-critical traffic like E-commerce has a guaranteed delay of $<80$ ms, while all the other traffic is delivered with best effort. To enforce this policy, traffic must be identified and classified according to the QoS requirement, as it enters the service provider's network. Network processors can be used to perform this function.

*Policing and Traffic Management.*   Some vendors provide policing and traffic management functions in their network processor products. These operations are rather crucial to core routers and are related to QoS implementation.

Routers that are located at different locations on the Internet have different requirements of network processors. Core routers or backbone routers emphasize high-speed and high-throughput and should provide an advanced traffic management ability but do not need to offer feature-rich applications. Access routers only need limited traffic management capabilities, but huge processing power for the various applications running on them is desirable. The requirement for edge routers lies somewhere between the previous two. Furthermore, core routers typically have much larger routing tables than the other two. Therefore, it is obvious that this kind of router must be able to handle large amounts of looking-up operations with low latency. Interfaces needed by different kinds of routers are also different. An access router may be equipped with just a number of physical layer interfaces of a single type. On the other hand, the other two kinds of routers need to support many of the prevailing transmission formats, namely POS, Frame Relay, ATM, high-speed Ethernet, and so on [5, 6].

### Design Considerations for NPs

*Architecture Selection.*   Some obvious, but important, characteristics of network processing are the simplicity and the weak dependence of floating point operations, even in the higher-layer functionalities. Therefore, most NPs adopt the reduced instruction set computing (RISC)-like fixed-point architecture. Kernel operations such as pattern matching, table lookup, and queue management comprise the majority of the functionalities that affect the architecture selection in many aspects [4].

*Instruction Set.*   Although the core frequency of today's processors has reached 3 GHz, for most vendors, instruction set optimization is still needed since it can dramatically reduce the number of cycles required for the same task [7]. These tasks include: data transfer operations, bit-manipulations, finite state machines needed by protocols and services, and the routing/switching operations [8]. Some test benches aiming to facilitate this optimization are also devised to further exploit the program architecture [9]. Yet the optimized instruction set is a double-edged sword. Since many vendors have developed their own instruction set, corresponding software development becomes a key-point of success in the market with a lack of third-party support. If the original equipment manufacturers (OEMs) cannot obtain enough programming tools, there would be a long way for network processors to go from merely a hardware platform to a running engine in the router.

*Hardware Function Unit.* Special functional units are often provided for common networking operations that are usually cumbersome and error-prone to implement in software, yet easy to implement in hardware, such as cyclic redundancy check (CRC) and checksum operations. One type of these hardware function units is used for simple operations. The units produce one result within one pipeline stage of a processing element and typically cannot be shared among multiple processing elements.

Another extensively used form is a co-processor. As opposed to special functional units, co-processors often perform more complicated tasks and can be accessed by multiple processing elements. To achieve an actual increase in performance, co-processors must have the ability to work with other processing units simultaneously and collaboratively. They can be triggered by special instructions and can offload some complex functions from main processing units. Some network processor products have external co-processors, typically packet classification co-processors, security co-processors, and traffic managers [2].

*Parallelism.* Packet processing inherently has a large amount of data parallelism that can be exploited. Parallelism exists at both inter-packet and intra-packet levels. If we consider "packet flow", most processing is performed on a per packet basis with each packet going through similar but independent processing. This phenomenon is the main aspect of inter-packet parallelism. Moreover, within the many tasks to be performed on each packet, some of them are also independent of each other. That is what we call intra-packet parallelism. If we assign individual tasks for different packets into multiple threads, both of these two classes of parallelism can be viewed as thread-level parallelism (TLP). Instruction-level parallelism (ILP) refers to the phenomenon that part of instructions within one program can be executed simultaneously and still produce the right result. This is more fine-grained and more difficult to exploit, typically involving compiler cooperation and a multiple-issue mechanism for instructions [10]. While some control-plane processors still use traditional single-threaded processors, most mainstream NP manufacturers have developed various multi-threaded schemes making use of different levels of parallelism [11].

*Buffer and Memory.* Network processor design focuses on providing sufficient processing power to accomplish complex functionalities in addition to the elementary packet forwarding. However, even if processing capability was sufficient, the processor would not perform well without adequate memory bandwidth.

Under today's store-process-forward scheme, storage and buffer size dominates the efforts devoted to NP design. Packets might be buffered inside an NP waiting for processing elements to become available or might be stored inside or outside an NP before and after switching. A lookup table is also stored in memory on-chip or off-chip. What makes the design difficult is the tremendous memory bandwidth needed by both the packet processing and the lookup operation. In general, a packet will go through the memory interface up to four times in the ingress direction if deep packet processing is performed and involves being: (1) copied to proper buffers when received from the incoming port; (2) read out (header and some portions of the payload) for the purpose of classification, route lookup and/or modification; (3) copied back with the modified information; and (4) read out again for transmission. In some architectures the first two data transfers can be omitted with the help of internal buffers. It still leads to enormous memory bandwidth demands [12]. Given a 60 percent efficiency of DRAM utilization and an available double data rate synchronous dynamic random access memory (DDR SDRAM) speed of 266 MHz, several hundreds of pins are needed to satisfy the OC-48 line rate for the memory alone. One possible solution is on-chip, ultra-wide DRAM technology [13]. Some chip designers have followed this approach, for example, EZchip.

*Route-Lookup and Packet Classification Implementation.* Quite a few vendors have implemented lookup and classification operations in separate chips functioning as co-processors or as a component of a chip-set. These are the fundamental functions of both the basic forwarding-decision making and high-level services such as QoS and IP packet filtering. Most developers employ software solutions and some of them provide interfaces to ternary content addressable memory (TCAM) devices as an option. Researchers have made great efforts in the related fields, ranging from look-up table management to operation complexity, and from algorithms to implementations [12]. Manufacturers tend to use their own proprietary algorithms and solutions. In contrast to the complex software schemes or dedicated hardware search engines, TCAMs are easy to use and have the advantage of deterministic searching delay and high performance derived from the parallel and pipelined operation of TCAM devices. Its major weaknesses include high cost, large power consumption, and limited look-up width, which severely constrains its applications in long-item and/or high-volume classification tables, for example, the look-up table of the future IPv6 protocol with IP addresses of 128 bits [14].

*Software Support.* The prevalence of network processors heavily depends on third-party software and support to provide an easy-to-program environment. This in turn reduces time-to-market and increases time-in-market. The process is more difficult than that of other communication products because of the use of nonstandard application–optimized instruction set and the parallel architecture of network processors.

### 16.1.3  Architecture of Network Processors

Two major architectures of today's NP products are as follows: (1) "dedicated approach", where most of the necessary network processing (e.g., packet classification, header checking, and so on) is performed by specialized hardware or components with a highly optimized instruction set; (2) "brute force approach", where a multitude of RISC-based simplified processing elements (PEs) are integrated onto a single chip to exploit the parallelism of packet processing with only marginally specialized hardware support.

A typical architecture of a brute-force duplex/simplex network processor is shown in Figure 16.2. Let us examine the ingress packet flow, that is, port to switch direction. Packets are received by the physical layer (PHY) device interface and transmitted by the switch fabric interface. Before being processed by the processing elements array or being scheduled for transmission, they are buffered under the control of the buffer and memory management module. The two interface modules (PHY device interface and switch fabric interface) can also do some bit-manipulation operations for the implementation of layer 2 or upper layer functions such as frame header processing or CRC.

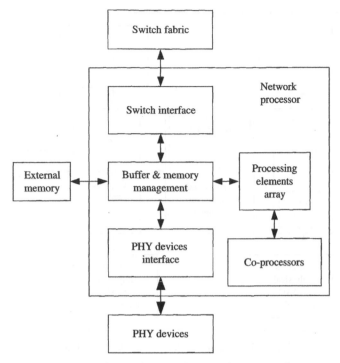

**Figure 16.2** Simple block diagram of a brute-force network processor.

In order to exploit the massive parallelism available in packet processing, especially the TLP, the processing unit may be constituted by a number of PEs with an optimized instruction set for network processing and a pipelined or even a super-pipelined architecture. Some implementations utilize very long instruction words (VLIW) or superscalar multiple-issue techniques to further exploit the ILP [15]. But the issue width of the instruction is often constrained to just two because of the limited ILP existing in integer non-scientific applications, that is, at most two instructions can be read out from instruction code memory and prepared for execution. Manufacturers like Intel and IBM use a network processor with a general-purpose processor core embedded in it, which is responsible for system initialization and part of packet processing workload, whereas others such as AMCC and Motorola just provide an external host central processing unit (CPU) interface.

### 16.1.4 Examples of Network Processors – Dedicated Approach

***IBM NP4GS3.*** The basic architecture is similar to that of Figure 16.2 but most network processing related functions are implemented in dedicated programmable coprocessors. NP4GS3 is a 2.5 Gbps duplex network processor. Its network interface can be configured either as Ethernet medium access control (MAC) or POS. The Ethernet mode can support up to four gigabit Ethernet or 40 fast Ethernet ports while the POS mode can support 16 OC-3c, four OC-12, four OC-12c, one OC-48, or one OC-48c POS framers. It has almost a symmetric architecture for the two packet flow directions that share the same embedded processor complex, as shown in Figure 16.3.

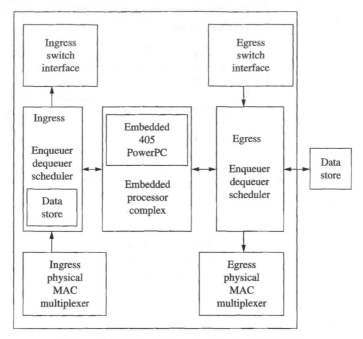

**Figure 16.3**   Simple function block of NP4GS3.

The physical MAC multiplexer moves the data between the physical layer devices and network processor, and keeps 36 Ethernet statistic counters per MAC, enabling support for many standard management information bases (MIBs) at wire speed. Ingress enqueuer/dequeuer/scheduler (EDS) buffers the incoming frames in the data store and extracts the frame header information for the embedded processor complex (EPC) to process. It also enqueues the frames to await transmission or discards them according to the processing results returned from the EPC with the help of hardware configured flow control mechanisms. Egress EDS is mainly responsible for frame reassembly and external buffer handling. The NP4GS3 provides two data-aligned synchronous link (DASL) ports at the switch side, which can also be used to cascade several NP4GS3s.

The NP4GS3 incorporates an embedded PowerPC subsystem that contains a 133 MHz PPC405 processor core with 16 KB of instruction cache and 16 KB of data cache. A peripheral component interconnect (PCI) bus is included to connect the NP4GS3 to an external host processor. EPC uses interrupts to communicate with PowerPC, appointing a particular DRAM location as a mailbox.

The processing core of the EPC consists of eight dyadic protocol processor units (DPPUs). Each DPPU incorporates two core language processors (CLPs), 10 shared coprocessors, two communication buses and one shared memory pool, as shown in Figure 16.4. CLPs execute the so-called picocode that is optimized for network applications. Each CLP can support two threads and the two threads can switchover with zero overhead. Although 32 independent threads can exist simultaneously, at any one time, only 16 of them are executed for frame forwarding, route table building, and network processor maintaining because each CLP has only one set of execution unit. Some hardware accelerators are shared among the DPPUs, facilitating the operations of thread allocation, packet protocol

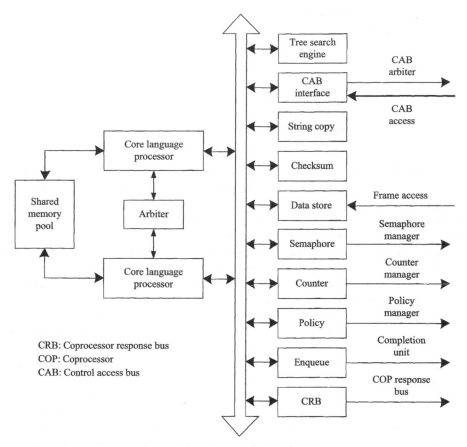

**Figure 16.4**   Function block of DPPU.

recognition, and packet order preservation. Of the ten co-processors, some act as the commonly seen checksum computing unit, string copier and tree search engine while the others provide interfaces to shared hardware assists. They include a policy manager that is used to determine the character of the incoming data stream, a counter manager that can contribute to the statistics, flow control and policy management, and a semaphore manager that assures the mutual exclusion access to a shared memory pool. These co-processors are called by a special kind of picocode and can work in parallel with each other and the CLPs.

The tree search engine (TSE) co-processor performs table search with the table maintained as Patricia trees. TSE supports three search modes: full match (FM) for layer 2 ARP address lookup, longest prefix match (LPM) for layer 3 IP address routing, and software managed table (SMT). Hardware supported geometric hash functions can yield lower collision rates than conventional bit-scrambling methods [16].

***Brute-Force Approach.*** Among the diversity of brute-force network processors, the main architectural difference lies in the multi-PE organization, that is, how multiple processing elements are organized into an array. Two basic organizations are parallel mode and pipeline mode. The former is widely adopted by most NP products while the latter often appears in some start-ups' design. Different variations can be made upon these two basic modes.

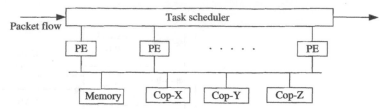

**Figure 16.5**    Parallel mode of PE organization.

*Example of Parallel Mode.* As is shown in Figure 16.5, a task scheduler is needed to assign incoming packets to available PEs. Processing elements of this type are typically not coupled very tightly and are usually identical. Interconnections among them and communication methods between them vary from different solutions. What functionalities each PE will perform are totally determined by the programmer.

Multi-threading is typically supported by each PE to exploit more TLP; thus, if one thread has been suspended waiting for the result of a co-processor, another one can get into the processing element and be executed. To take full advantage of this mechanism, hardware-facilitated thread-switching should be employed to hide latency.

Although this arrangement efficiently exploits both the inter-packet and intra-packet parallelism, when a programmer manually partitions the tasks among processing elements, extra burden is added to load balancing and this increases inter-PE communication overhead. So some programmers still stick to the "run to completion" programming model or just do very simple task partitioning.

Multi-threading also introduces new problems. Since the processing element is not dedicated to one packet, a new packet will be placed into a processing element when the suspended packet awaits its result to be returned from the co-processor. Thus deterministic packet processing performance cannot be determined and the packet order within the same flow may be distorted, which is usually unacceptable in a network node. This can be avoided by allocating packets of the same flow into the same thread. This method, however, will decrease the utilization when there are no available packets from other flows for a PE with suspended threads and new packets of the same flow keep coming in.

*AMCC nP7510.* AMCC nP7510 OC-192c network processor is capable of providing layer 2 and layer 3 cell/packet processing at wire speed for multi-service POS, ATM, and gigabit Ethernet systems. A simple functional block diagram is shown in Figure 16.6.

Two packet input/output (I/O) interface blocks connect nP7510 to the framer or switch fabric. In addition to the interface-specific functions, they also provide layer 2 functions such as AAL5 CRC and length checking, header sequence error checking, byte and cell length generation, OAM CRC checking and generation. The packet transform engine provides data paths and buffering between the framer interfaces. It performs special frame commands issued by the nPcores. These functions include add or delete information from a packet as it leaves the channel, or to create a new packet. The nP7510 contains six nPcores, which are microcontrollers with a network-optimized instruction set called network instruction set computing (NISC). Each nPcore can handle 24 tasks and up to 144 packets can be processed simultaneously. Incoming packets are allocated to the next available task in one of the microcontrollers, which is transparent to the microcode programmer. The nPcores also control the policy engine, which is a packet classification module differentiating among

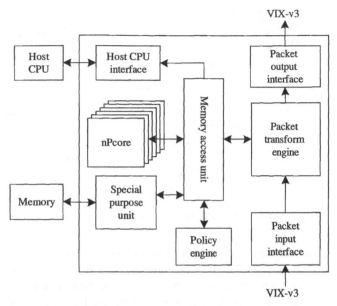

**Figure 16.6**   Block diagram of AMCC nP7510.

different kinds of packets/cells. It contains a $512 \times 68$-bit ternary policy database with a configurable number of entries, and entry width.

*Example of Pipeline Mode.*   As is shown in Figure 16.7, in pipelined mode the processing procedure is divided into multiple stages with each stage designed to handle a certain category of tasks. Once a packet enters such a "PE-pipeline," it has a dedicated data path to go from one PE stage to another without rewinding or skipping. The functionality of each PE is also affected by the hardware designer. Since PEs are allocated to different tasks in advance, each one can be optimized for dedicated tasks, resulting in different kinds of PEs in a single processor. For example, each kind of PE can have its own optimized instruction set. Software should cooperate with an underlying hardware platform to make the partitioned tasks balanced among processing elements. Otherwise the over-loaded stage will become the performance bottleneck. Such a requirement makes software modification a difficult job.

*Agere PayloadPlus.*   The PayloadPlus network processor family includes the fast pattern processor (FPP), the routing switch processor (RSP), and the Agere system interface

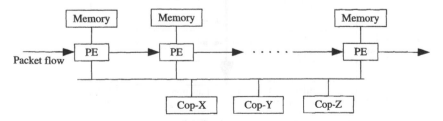

**Figure 16.7**   Pipeline mode of PE organization.

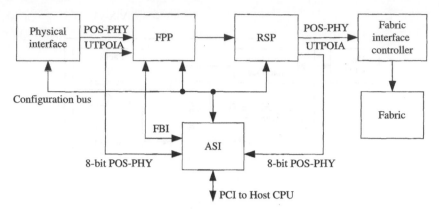

**Figure 16.8** Line card structure using Agere PayloadPlus.

(ASI). The programmable FPP performs wire-speed classification and analysis for multiple protocols at layer 2 through 7. The RSP performs various queuing, traffic management, traffic shaping, and packet modification functions on traffic flows in a fully programmable way. The ASI provides a PCI interface to a host processor for control and management functions, including routing table and virtual circuit updates, hardware configuration, and exception handling. It also assists the FPP in policing both cell and packet-based traffic, maintaining state information on data flows and capturing statistics. Figure 16.8 shows a line card system using Agere PayloadPlus. The FPP and RSP, together with Physical Interface and Switch Fabric, form a pipelined-based, communications-focused architecture.

The internal structure of FPP is shown in Figure 16.9. The *Input framer* receives packet/cell data from PHY devices or management information from the ASI. The data

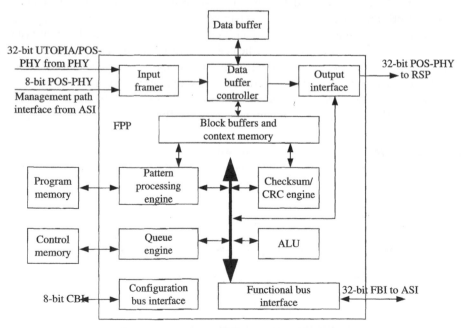

**Figure 16.9** Agere FPP internal architecture.

buffer controller manages movement of data blocks between the data buffer, input framer, block buffers, and output interface. The output interface transmits Protocol Data Units (PDUs) and their classification results to the RSP or other downstream logic. The block buffers and context memory stores the blocks currently being processed, and the configuration information for the context. The pattern-processing engine (PPE) is programmed with a simple protocol processing language, the functional programming language (FPL), to recognize and classify incoming packets based on a set of patterns. The checksum/CRC engine performs a generic checksum, IPv4 checksum, CRC-10, or CRC-32, as requested by the FPL program. The arithmetic logic unit (ALU) performs arithmetic functions such as addition, subtraction, shifting, and Boolean operations. The two bus interfaces, configuration bus interface and functional bus interface, are responsible for communication between the FPP and the ASI. The FPP divides the processing into two passes: the first pass stores data as 64-byte blocks and computes data offset for each block, creating a linked-list data structure that defines the reassembled PDU; the second pass processes the whole PDU. It simultaneously performs pattern matching and transmits the reassembled PDU and the results of the pattern-matching process for that PDU.

The RSP accepts PDUs and their classification information on up to 128 logical input ports. It queues them on up to 64 K programmable queues, then outputs the modified PDUs on up to 256 logical output ports. The RSP uses programmable VLIW compute-engines to process PDUs. The internal architecture of the RSP is shown in Figure 16.10. The input interface sends the incoming PDU blocks to the PDU assembler for reassembling into PDUs, and sends the FPP classification results for PDUs to the transmit queue logic. The stream editor compute engine performs PDU modification for each queue. These modifications include encapsulating PDUs into AAL5, segmenting into ATM cells with appropriate headers, and implementing IP operations (e.g., decrementing time-to-live counts and updating checksums). The traffic manager compute-engine enforces discard policies and keeps the queue statistics. The traffic shaper compute-engine ensures QoS and class of service (CoS) for each queue [17]. The output interface accepts blocks from the stream editor and sends them to the appropriate port manager and output port.

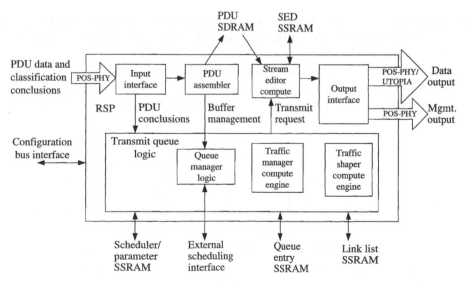

**Figure 16.10**  RSP internal architecture.

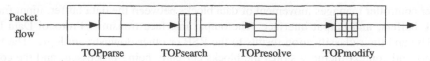

Packet flow

TOPparse        TOPsearch        TOPresolve        TOPmodify

**Figure 16.11**  Data path for each packet-processing task in EZchip NP-1.

***EZchip NP-1 and NP-2.***  NP-1 is the first duplex 10-Gbit NPU introduced to the market. As shown in Figure 16.11, NP-1 incorporates a four-stage packet processing procedure. This is as follows: (1) parse: extract different packet headers and do the corresponding analysis; (2) search: perform table look-ups through layer 2 to layer 7; (3) resolve: assign the packet to the proper port according to the destination and QoS requirements; (4) modify: modify certain fields of the packet on the basis of classification result.

As illustrated in Figure 16.12, each stage is implemented by a number of superscalar and superpipelined task optimized processing cores (TOPcores) with their own customized instruction set and data path for the specific packet processing operation. The memory bandwidth problem is resolved by a rather complicated embedded-DRAM system-on-chip technique. On-chip DRAMs, together with the dedicated search algorithms, replaces the expensive CAM. All of these efforts have dramatically improved the single-chip performance and reduced the system chip-count, power consumption, and cost [7].

NP-2 is EZchip's newer generation family of network processors that builds on EZchip's NP-1 family and further its integration. NP-2 integrates a 10-Gbit or 5-Gbit full-duplex NPU, classification engines, traffic managers, 1-Gbit and 10-Gbit MACs, and SPI4.2 interfaces in a single chip. The integration allows system vendors to deliver solutions that are cost effective as well as power and board-space efficient.

***Example of Hybrid Architecture.***  Two variations of the basic modes are shown in Figures 16.13 and 16.14, respectively. Such structures can be designed to be more adaptable to varying application requirements. But they typically make the programming task more challenging.

***Intel IXP2800.***  The Intel IXP2800 network processor [18] is a member of Intel's second-generation network processor family. It delivers 10 Gbps packet forwarding and traffic management on a single chip.

Figure 16.15 shows the internal architecture of IXP2800. The Intel XScale$^{TM}$ core is a general-purpose 32-bit RISC processor used to initialize and manage the network processor, to handle exceptions, and to perform slow path processing and other control plane tasks.

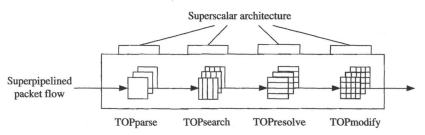

Superscalar architecture

Superpipelined packet flow

TOPparse        TOPsearch        TOPresolve        TOPmodify

**Figure 16.12**  Superpipeline and superscalar organization of processor-array for massive processing power in NP-1.

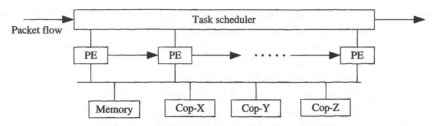

**Figure 16.13**   Parallel mode with pipeline capability.

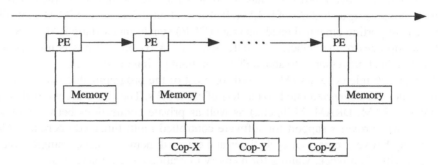

**Figure 16.14**   Pipeline mode with parallel capability.

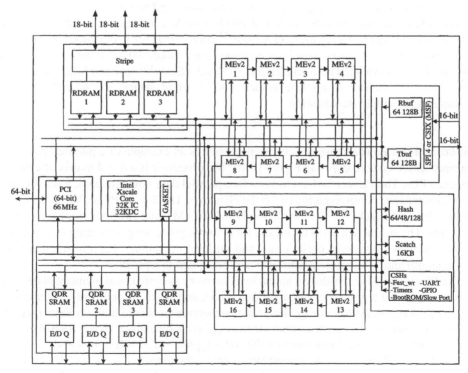

**Figure 16.15**   IXP2800 block diagram.

The media and switch fabric (MSF) interface is used to connect the IXP2800 network processor to a PHY device and/or to a switch fabric. Each of the receive and transmit interfaces can be separately configured for either SPI-4 phase 2 (System Packet Interface) for PHY devices or CSIX-L1 protocol for switch fabric interfaces. The receive and transmit ports are unidirectional and independent of each other. Each port has a clock, a control signal, a parity signal, and 16 data signals. Rbuf is a RAM that holds received data. It stores received data in sub-blocks, and is accessed by Microengines or the Intel XScale™ core reading the received information. Tbuf is a RAM that holds data and status to be transmitted. All elements within a Tbuf partition are transmitted in order.

The IXP2800 network processor has controllers for three Rambus DRAM (RDRAM) channels, supporting up to 2 GB of DRAM. It also has four independent SRAM controllers, with each supporting pipelined quad data rate (QDR) synchronous static RAM (SSRAM) and/or a coprocessor that adheres to QDR signaling. A 64-bit PCI bus is used either to connect to a host processor or to attach PCI-compliant peripheral devices.

There are 16 microengines (MEs) used for most of the programmable per-packet processing. They are connected into two clusters of eight MEs. They have access to all shared resources (SRAM, DRAM, MSF, etc.) as well as private connections between adjacent MEs. The ME provides support for software controlled multi-threaded operation. Given the disparity between processor cycle times and external memory times, a single thread of execution will often block, waiting for memory operations to complete. Having multiple threads allows for threads to interleave operation – there is often at least one thread ready to run while others are blocked. In addition to various kinds of local memories, the MEs also provide some special hardware blocks to assist certain packet processing tasks such as CRC, pseudo random number generation, multiplication, and so on.

The scratchpad unit provides 16 KB of on-chip SRAM memory that can be used for general-purpose operations by the Intel XScale™ core and the MEs. IXP2800 also provides 16 hardware rings that can be used for communication between MEs and the core. The hash unit provides a polynomial hash accelerator. The Intel XScale™ core and MEs can use it to offload hash calculations in applications such as ATM virtual channel/virtual path (VC/VP) lookup and IP 5-tuple classification.

**Cisco Toaster2.** The Toaster2 network processor is an example of a parallel, pipelined multiprocessor system, shown in Figure 16.16. The processor is a 4 × 4 matrix of custom-designed PEs. The PEs are laid out to form four parallel data flow pipelines. Each pipeline has four stages and corresponds to a row in the PE matrix. The Toaster PE is a VLIW core with independent data cache, 12 KB instruction RAM (IRAM), and two four-stage instruction pipelines. The instruction set is optimized for network processing, including fast lookups, atomic memory operations, preset tasks, and bit-level operations. Each instruction is 64 bits in length and is segmented, with each part being tied to a pipeline.

The PEs in each column share a hierarchical memory system. Local memory of each PE is in the form of a register file, a 64-byte data cache, and space for context (Toaster unit of data for packet processing) storage. Large data structures are stored in the column memory devices. The on-chip (internal) column memory (ICM) is typically a 16 KB SRAM device. The off-chip (external) column memory (XCM) is typically a 32 MB SDRAM device [19]. The packet interface consists of two subblocks called the input header buffer (IHB), which is used to receive Toaster contexts, and the output header buffer (OHB), which is used to transmit contexts. The route processor interface (RPI) provides access to all resources

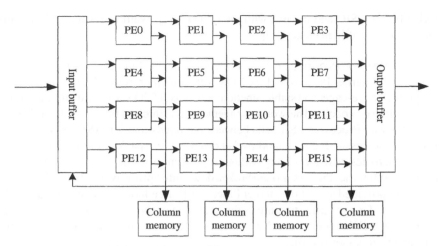

**Figure 16.16**   Architecture of Cisco's Toaster2 network processor.

internal to the Toaster2 as well as the XCM. In addition to resource access, the RPI block also maintains a set of synchronized timers that are accessed via individual processors.

Toaster2 has been designed to support either centralized or distributed configurations. An example of a system of centralized configuration is shown in Figure 16.17. Packets are received or transmitted through media-specific interfaces. Valid packets are stored in a packet buffer while the corresponding context is sent to Toaster2 for processing. A context includes the first *n* bytes of each packet, and a packet descriptor carrying the necessary information about the packet, such as the length of the received packet and a handle that will be used to associate the forwarding result with the body of the packet stored in the packet buffer. A forwarding task can be divided into eight software pipeline stages. Each packet is processed by one of the four pipelines. After being processed, the context is transferred to

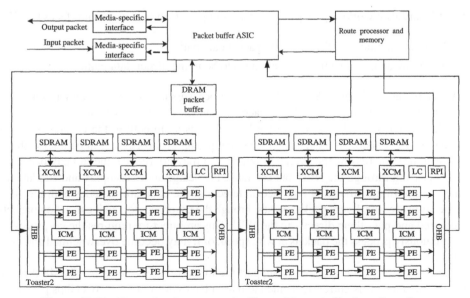

**Figure 16.17**   Example of a system using Toaster2 in centralized configuration.

the packet buffer ASIC and merged with the packet body, waiting for transmission under the control of the traffic manager [19].

***Juniper's Internet Processor II.*** The architecture of Juniper router is based on a "Switch fabric–Internet Processor II–JUNOS software" hierarchy. Switch fabric is dedicated to performance-eager and stable functions whereas JUNOS software provides full flexibility for routing protocol and network management. The Internet Processor II, derived from its former Internet Processor ASIC, sits between the fixed-function ASIC and the general-purpose microprocessor. It can support packet classification, packet filtering, policing, traffic shaping, statistics, and accounting without significant penalties on the forwarding rate.

Functions of Internet Processor II are broken down into "primitives". The following three primitives are provided as part of Internet Processor II: tree lookup, table lookup, and filter program. The order and basic structure of the execution of the three primitives are under of the control of the JUNOS software. New releases of the software will bring newer features to the Internet Processor II [20].

## 16.2   CO-PROCESSORS FOR PACKET CLASSIFICATION

The classification processing is an important functionality and generally comprises the bottleneck of the network processing unit (NPU) performance. Typically, co-processors are provided to offload this function. These devices can be divided into two categories, that is, TCAM-based and algorithm-based. This section first describes an interface standard for a co-processor recommended by the network processing forum (NPF), that is, LA-1 bus (look aside interface), followed by the introduction of several typical chips of the two types of co-processors.

### 16.2.1   LA-1 Bus

The NPF hardware working group has two task groups to standardize the interfaces for NPs:

- A streaming interface for complete packet data path.
- A look-aside interface that does not need to be in the direct data path.

As can be seen in Figure 16.18, NPU and co-processors may operate in either look-aside (LA) or streaming mode. The LA interface is intended for devices located adjacent to a NPU that offloads certain tasks from the NPU. In this architecture, the co-processor sits beside the NPU outside of the datapath, enabling packet co-processing in parallel with the NPU operation, increasing the overall throughput. It may not receive the full payload of all packets passing through the NPU, but can make the design more complex and add latency to the system. In the streaming interface architecture, the datapath includes both the NPU and the co-processor. Every packet passes through the co-processor, so it can act on packets as required and pass them directly to the NPU. This architecture requires the co-processor to continuously process the packets at wire speed, or it may become overwhelmed and drop packets.

The LA-1 interface is targeted to support the lookup requirements for OC-48 through OC-192 line rates. It is currently defined to have a bandwidth of about 6.4 Gbps per direction, which is sufficient for lookups at 10 Gbps (OC-192) packet rate. The packet count

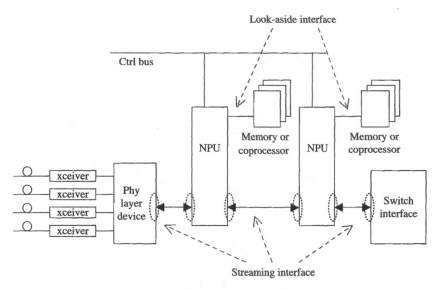

**Figure 16.18**   Linecard system block diagram.

assumptions are based on line-rate performance using 40-byte packets and 144-bit search keys [21].

LA-1 is a memory-mapped interface modeled after a synchronous separate I/O DDR SRAM interface and QDR is the basis for it. Using a DDR interface, data is clocked on the rising and falling edges of the clock signals. This effectively doubles the bandwidth of the interface without increasing the clock speed or the bus width. Overall, the LA-1 interface operates at clock speeds between 133 and 250 MHz. It supports unidirectional 18-bit read and write interfaces. These data inputs and outputs operate simultaneously, thus eliminating the need for high-speed bus turnarounds (i.e., no dead cycles are present).

The main bus signals are listed in Figure 16.19. Access to each port is accomplished using a common 24-bit address bus. Addresses for reads and writes are latched on rising edges of K and K# input clocks, respectively. Each address location is associated with two 16-bit data words that burst sequentially into or out of the device. Since data can be transferred into and

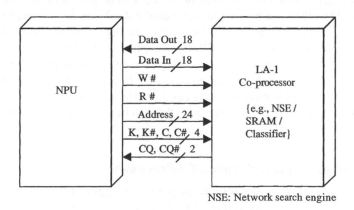

**Figure 16.19**   LA-1 bus interface signals.

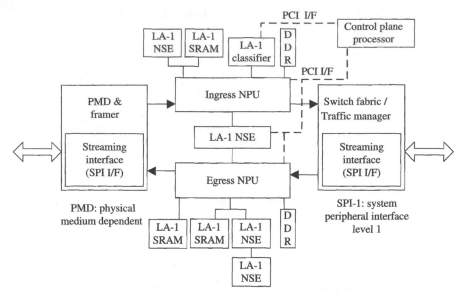

**Figure 16.20**   LA-1 co-processor configurations and connections.

out of the device on every rising edge of K, K#, and CQ, CQ# (or C, C#) clocks respectively, memory bandwidth is maximized while simplifying overall design through the elimination of bus turnarounds. As the LA-1 interface uses a memory-mapped structure, a network processor can use the LA-1 address bus to initiate co-processor actions by reading and writing to memory mapped registers. Reads and writes to these memory-mapped registers in an LA-1 network search engine (NSE) allow the packet processor to issue search instructions to the NSE, retrieve returned results, and provide in-band management for NSE databases. NSEs are discussed in Section 16.2.2.

Figure 16.20 shows different LA-1 configurations for a typical line card application. One of the biggest advantages of using the LA-1 interface is the capability to support devices in a multi-drop configuration (i.e., multiple devices connected to the same interface). Hence system designers can support an NSE, SRAM, classifier and/or other LA-1 compatible devices on the same bus at the same time.

In some scenarios, two different types of devices can be placed on the same bus (i.e., NSE and SRAM). NSEs can be used to maintain the databases for different applications that need to be searched, and SRAM can be used for storing associated data. NSE searches require more write bandwidth whereas SRAMs are generally read intensive, so having two separate data buses allows the network-processing element to write to an NSE and read from an SRAM simultaneously without wasting any LA-1 bandwidth. Multiple configurations can be supported by adding more than one LA-1 interface to a co-processor. As shown in Figure 16.20, an NSE has two LA-1 interfaces that can be used to share databases between ingress and egress NPUs [22].

### 16.2.2   TCAM-Based Classification Co-Processor

***IDT Network Search Engines and Search Accelerators.***   IDT has developed NSEs and search accelerators that utilize IDT's TCAM technology and high-performance logic technology. The NSE portfolio includes a pin-compatible family with a high performance interface available in $64K \times 36$ to $512 \times 36$ configurations as well as products that glue-lessly interface to many leading packet processing silicon solutions such as those supporting an LA-1 interface. IDT also recently introduced a family of search accelerator products that supports core search speeds up to 250 MSPS with multi-search capability of 1 billion searches per second, an innovating 80-bit interface with optimized supports for complex IPv6 policy lookups, and integrated error correction code for improved data integrity.

An NSE with a TCAM core and an LA-1 (QDRII) interface may be connected directly to the QDR LA-1 interface of an NPU. Within a single clock cycle, the NPU may initiate an NSE search via the QDR LA-1 write data bus and obtain a search result via the QDR LA-1 read data bus. To accommodate the complex multi-threaded execution environment of today's NPUs, LA-1 NSE incorporates schedulers and mailboxes so that requests, results, and exceptions associated with various NPU threads can be properly handled. Beyond the basic search operation, additional NSE performance may be gained through architectural features such as reducing the number of NPU off-chip accesses by initiating multiple database searches using a single key as well as returning multiple match results from a single-database search. Further performance gains are possible through better implementation of address caches and flow tables by using intelligent learning operations, activity monitoring, and the notification of stale or aged database entries. The remainder of this section focuses on IDT's NSEs with QDR a single LA-1 interface: the IDT75K62134 (9 Mbit, $128 K \times 72$-bit) and IDT75K52134 (4 Mbit, $64 K \times 72$-bit) devices [23–25].

The IDT75K62134 and IDT75K52134 NSEs are designed to seamlessly connect to NPUs with LA-1-compliant interfaces operating up to 250 MHz. Up to four NSE devices can be directly connected to one QDR LA-1 interface, and up to eight devices can be cascaded from each of the four NSEs connected to the QDR LA-1 bus using point-to-point cascading to form on bank, also known as a search machine. In this way, up to 32 devices can interface with one NPU, as can be seen in Figure 16.21. Each bank allows a single database size of up to one million 72-bit entries while operating at maximum frequency. Each NSE supports 16 databases, 128 contexts, and 64 72-bit global mask registers (GMRs) that are shared across all contexts. The width of each database can be selected to be 36, 72, or 144 bits wide or can be programmed to be from 32 to 576 bits wide in increments of 32 bits.

Figure 16.22 illustrates the internal architecture of the IDT NSE with a single LA-1 interface. The NSE can perform a number of operations to support database maintenance

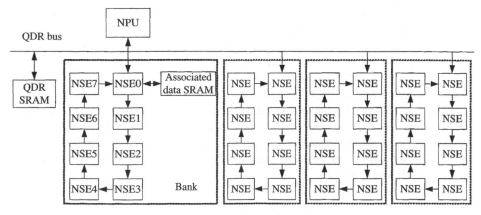

**Figure 16.21**  NSE configuration.

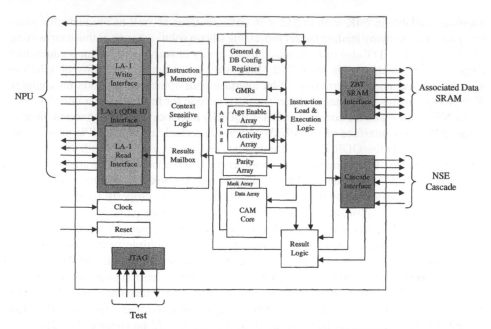

**Figure 16.22** Architecture block diagram of the IDT NSE.

and searches. These operations include lookup, multi-hit lookup, multi-database lookup, re-issue multi-database lookup, learn, and multi-hit invalidate. Each data entry in the NSE has a valid bit that can be set, cleared, or left unchanged by using the appropriate instruction. Additional database maintenance support includes aging with age enable and activity arrays that provide independent aging control per data entry. A separate aging count interval is supported per database.

The NSE search and maintenance operations are initiated by writing to the NSE using the LA-1 interface. The operation command is encoded on the address lines, and the search key is presented on the data bus. The operation is placed in the instruction memory, where it is associated with a specified context that is often connected to a specified thread of execution in the NPU. Once a thread places a request in the instruction memory, the execution logic block presents the search operation, consisting of the global mask, the search key, and a CAM instruction to the TCAM core. The index results are stored in a mailbox for fetching by the associated thread of execution in the NPU. When a search is performed, the NSE can be optionally configured to fetch a 32-bit entry from the associated data SRAM. Results are read from the mailbox using the LA-1 interface. When the execution thread receives the result word, a "done" bit indicates if the rest of the result is valid. If the result's read operation occurs before the NSE operation is completed, the done bit is not set, and the application must reissue the read command. Hit and multi-hit bits further qualify the result.

The execution block is also responsible for monitoring activities and indicating the lack of activities of entries being monitored. In addition, the execution unit maintains parity on the TCAM array, which can be interrogated through a background scrub operation using the parity check instruction.

The internal core of the NSE is divided into 4 K × 72-bit segments. There are 32 segments in the 75K62134 and 16 segments in the 75K52134. Databases are composed of a subset of these segments. To conserve power, only the segments that belong to the database being

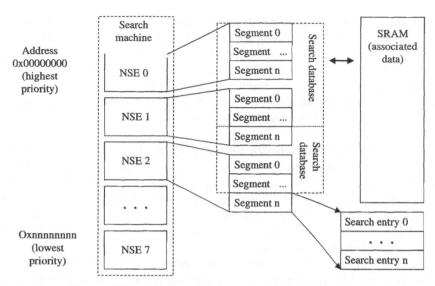

**Figure 16.23**    Search machine and logical database structure.

searched are powered up. The NSE instruction specifies a unique database on each operation. Figure 16.23 shows the logic structure for the database.

The IDT NSE also provides a set of comprehensive software packages for development support that includes system-level architectural models (SLAMs), data plane macros, complete product development diagnostics, and operational example applications, as well as a robust, production-quality control plane software library called the initialization, management, and search (IMS) library for runtime support.

IDT provides the IDT75KTA062134-200 development board to further accelerate application software development, as can be seen in Figure 16.24. The 75KTA062134-200

**Figure 16.24**    75KTA062134-200 development board photograph.

compliments the Intel IXDP2400 Development Platform to provide a complete hardware search accelerated network processing development platform. Utilizing the IDT 9M NSE with QDR LA-1 interface (IDT75K62134), the 75KTA062134-200 enables Intel IXDP2400 Development Platform to achieve 100 million searches per second (MSPS) using a 200 MHz QDR II bus frequency. Additionally, resources on the module include an on-board zero bus turnaround (ZBT) SRAM that allows for the storage of NSE associated data, and a QDR SRAM that is integrated for auxiliary NPU memory.

***Cypress Ayama™ 20000 Network Search Engine.*** Cypress Ayama™ 20000 is a high-performance, pipelined, ternary NSE that provides a seamless interface to commercial network processors via the LA-1 interface. An Ayama 20000 device can interface with up to two NPUs using two separate LA-1 interfaces. This family consists of devices of multiple densities, including 512 K (18-Mbit) and 256 K (9-Mbit) entries. It includes a full T-CAM array with per-bit masking, enabling efficient searches for the applications including flow classification, lookup and packet forwarding.

Figure 16.25 shows the Ayama 20000 connected in a system. Ayama 20000 device supports up to two NPU LA-1 interfaces, one to an ingress NPU and another to an egress NPU. Both the NPUs are able to perform searches on the same database, eliminating the need for the redundant memory storage devices or NSEs. The Fast Link™ NSE expansion interface connects Ayama 20000 to a cascade of multiple NSEs. In Figure 16.25, two different classes of NSEs are simultaneously connected to the Ayama 20000 device. A class

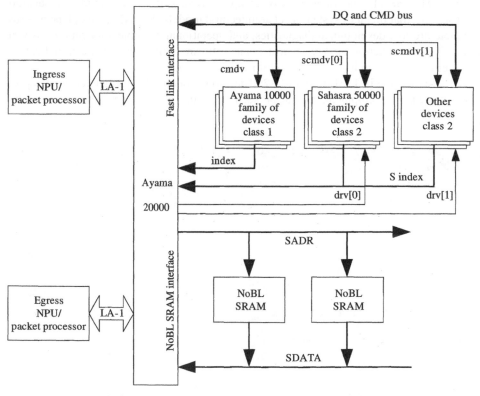

**Figure 16.25** Ayama 20000 connected to heterogeneous mix of NSEs.

is defined as a group of NSEs sharing the same latency. The cascading of NSE devices allows NPUs to perform searches on different databases via the same LA-1 interface. The NPU can use the LA-1 port to access network policy information, QoS information and the destination port information for a data packet. The cascaded NSE devices share the same data queue (DQ) and command (CMD) bus, which supplies the search data and search parameters. The search results for each class are returned via individual result bus. This prevents contention due to different latencies that the NSE devices may have. The Ayama 20000 has an internal SRAM memory controller that resolves latency issues of the cascaded NSE devices. The search results returned from the NSEs are indices of the associated data in the SRAM. A SRAM lookup can be performed using their indices. The Ayama 20000 offloads SRAM lookup overhead from the NPUs by automatically performing associated data lookups, NSE lookups and associated data management as an atomic instruction. The Ayama 20000 communicates with the external SRAM via the No Bus Latency™ (NoBL™) SRAM interface.

Figure 16.26 shows the internal block diagram of the Ayama 20000. The Ayama 20000 device has an internal NSE, an age memory block, one or two LA-1 interfaces (depending on the configuration), a NoBL SRAM interface, an external NSE interface and a control and arbitration block. The internal NSE performs database lookups, supporting up to 266 MSPS. The LA-1 interfaces connect directly to the commercial NPU. It also supports the SRAM interface standard QDR-I, running a burst of 2, at 133, 167, or 200 MHz and QDR-II, running a burst of 2 or a burst of 4, at 250 MHz. The SRAM interface connects to the external SRAM for associated data lookups. The age memory block keeps track of the frequency of usage for each database entry. If a database entry has not been used for a certain amount of time, the entry will be marked in the age memory. The information stored in the age memory can be used as the criteria for replacing or filtering out the older database entries. The control and arbitration block commands the rest of the circuitry inside the Ayama 20000 device.

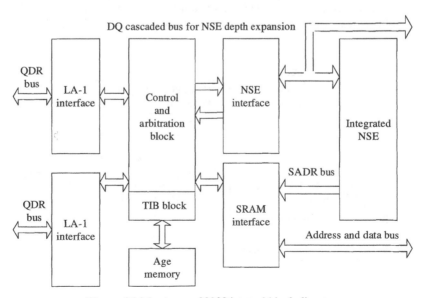

**Figure 16.26** Ayama 20000 internal block diagram.

### 16.2.3 Algorithm-Based Classification Co-Processor

*IDT PAX.port 2500^TM Content Inspection Engine.* The PAX.port 2500^TM is an application specific standard product (ASSP) content inspection engine (CIE) with streaming interfaces. It is optimized for full layer 7 content inspection and regular expression matching at OC-48 in content aware networking equipment, web switches/load balancers, multi-service switches, IP service gateways, cable modem termination systems, edge routers, network security devices, and broadband wireless networking equipment [26, 27].

The PAX.port 2500 is optimized for use in flow-through applications with in-band classification at OC-48 or multi-gigabit Ethernet line rates. The PAX.port 2500 can be connected in a system either as a flow-through pre-processor or as a look-aside co-processor.

Figure 16.27 shows a PAX.port 2500 connected as a flow-through pre-processor in a line card. The PAX.port 2500 receives each packet from the input interface and prepends the classification results on the output interface. The input and output buses are identical. Up to three dedicated SRAM pattern memories contain the classification policies. A separate PCI host interface is used for programming and configuration. An IDT SRAM and/or NSE subsystem can be used by the ingress NPU to maintain stateful information for traffic flows. The classification results can be programmed to pre-extract a key, such as an IP 5-tuple, for efficient search operations to an NSE.

Figure 16.28 shows how a PAX.port 2500 can be connected as a look-aside co-processor in a line card. Typically a switch or bridge device is required to convert the SPI-3 (system peripheral interface level 3) input packet interface and output packet interface of the PAX.port 2500. This processing model allows the NPU to maintain control over which packets are passed to the PAX.port 2500. It also allows for modifications to be made to the packet prior to passing the data to the PAX.port 2500, such as trimming (i.e., stripping data that is not of interest to the PAX.port 2500), decryption, TCP termination and other functions to be performed prior to classification.

Figure 16.29 shows a simple block diagram of a PAX.port 2500. The PAX.port 2500 supports one physical SPI-3 path (input and output) configurable as one to 16 logical channels and performs wire-speed classification at a 2.5 Gbps rate for packet sizes of 40 to 1600 bytes. There are no per-channel throughput limitations. Typically, this

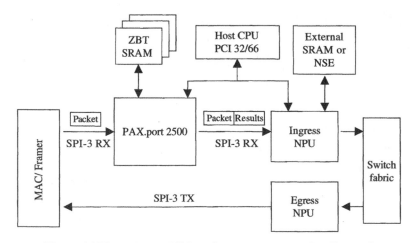

**Figure 16.27** PAX.port 2500 used as a pre-processor in a line card.

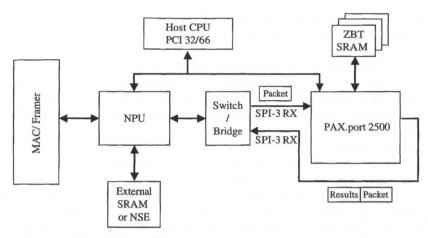

**Figure 16.28**    PAX.port 2500 used as a look-aside co-processor in a line card.

channelization maps to a single OC-48 channel, four OC-12 channels, or 16 OC-3 channels in POS applications, and various mixes of 10/100 and gigabit Ethernet channels in Ethernet applications.

The PAX.port 2500 has 15 classification cores. Each set of five classification cores has its own external memory called the pattern memory. Classification cores accept packet data and control signals from a dedicated, dynamically allocated and managed internal FIFO buffer. After classifying a packet, the classification core produces a classification result for that packet consisting of a tag (up to 64 bits) and a digest (up to 192 bits), which form a classification result together. The tag contents are programmable in a bitwise fashion and a digest is a parsed subset of the packet. Both of them can be prepended to the packet after

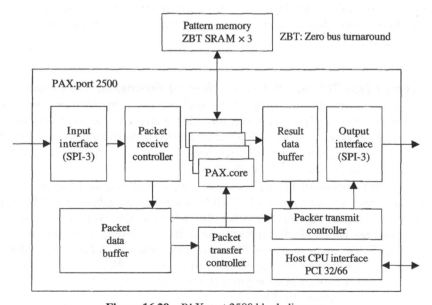

**Figure 16.29**    PAX.port 2500 block diagram.

each packet is classified and the packet is then transmitted from the PAX.port 2500 to the downstream device in the data path. The digest can also be used to store up to nine offset pointers (16 bits each).

The output interface can be overclocked by as much as 25 percent to support additional bandwidth contributed by the combined tag and digest. Classification results can also be prepended with a variable offset to overwrite up to 15 bytes at the beginning of the packet and thereby this mechanism reduces the aggregate bandwidth on the SPI-3 output interface.

The internal packet transmit controller (PTC) ensures that when classification is complete, all packets on a given virtual channel leave the device over the SPI-3 output interface in the same order in which the packets entered.

The PAX.port 2500 has three pattern memory interfaces, each providing up to 833 Mbps of classification performance for a total of 2.5 Gbps. It uses external 72-bit-wide or 36-bit-wide ZBT SRAMs to store classification policies. The number of policies depends on the complexity of policy rules for the particular application. Each of the three pattern memory interfaces is shared among five PAX.cores on a fair, round-robin basis. Each pattern memory interface can address up to 32 Mbyte of ZBT SRAM to support very large tables of complex policies.

The PAX.port 2500 has a PCI 32/66 host processor interface that provides an interface to any common central processing unit (CPU). The host processor interface provides access to option registers for configuration of the PAX.port 2500. This interface also provides the path for writing to and reading from the pattern memory.

The PAX.port 2500 classifies each packet using fully programmable classification criteria and results. Users can define any set of protocols and data patterns using IDT's high-level, non-procedural, PAX pattern description language (PDL), IDT's extensive protocol library, and application programming interfaces (APIs). Policies are loaded into external pattern memory, which the PAX.port 2500 accesses to classify the bit stream at wire speed. It is programmed using the PAX.works software development kit (SDK), which is a suite of software tools for both the development environment and the run-time execution environment. The SDK creates the pattern memory program that represents the classification rules for the PAX.port 2500.

***PMC-Sierra ClassiPI*<sup>TM</sup> *Network Classification Processor.*** The ClassiPI (classification by packet inspection) device assists network processors by offloading the complex and time-consuming task of packet classification [28]. It enables analysis and classification for all layers of a packet, including payload, at wire speed from 100 Mbps to gigabit LANs, as well as OC-48 and higher speed wide area networks (WANs). The ClassiPI PM2329 is the latest member in the ClassiPI<sup>TM</sup> family [29].

The target applications of PM2329 include: simple switching and forwarding applications that require an exact match of L2 MAC addresses (or labels as in MPLS label switching routers) and a longest prefix match of L3 addresses (for MPLS label edge routers and IP forwarding), packet filtering applications such as a firewall, virtual private network (VPN), and QoS that require match, prefix, and range checks for L2, L3, and L4 addresses, and higher-layer applications such as server-load balancing, Web caching and intrusion detection that require lookups in the payload (L7) portion of the packet.

The general architecture of a PM2329-based system is shown in Figure 16.30. The network processor or customer ASIC sits in the data path and buffers the packets upon

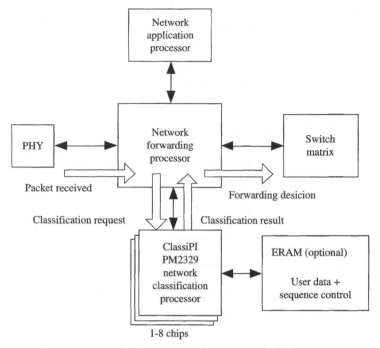

**Figure 16.30** ClassiPI-based network equipment architecture.

arrival. The ClassiPI device is attached to the generic search machine interface as a co-processor. The network processor or customer ASIC transfers the appropriate payload to the ClassiPI device depending on the type of lookup that needs to be performed. Based on the preprogrammed rule set in the ClassiPI device, the result of classification is returned to the processor that can further perform appropriate editing and forwarding of the packet. The ClassiPI supports up to two optional external SSRAMs connected using a dedicated bus, which can be used to implement more complex classification lookup sequences and to store packet parameters and user data associated with rules.

The internal architecture of PM2329 is shown in Figure 16.31. It features an efficiently pipelined architecture, enabling a continuous stream of packets to be fed into the device, while it continues to perform packet parsing, key formation, and lookup operations.

The system interface is a general-purpose synchronous SRAM interface (configurable as 32 or 64 bits wide operating in SyncBurst or ZBT mode) for connecting to a processor, packet source, or DMA (direct memory access) device. This interface is used to send packets or pre-extracted payload for classification. The results of a classification operation are placed in the result FIFO and accessed by the processor through this interface. This interface can also access the control registers that are used to configure classification operations, key selections, and the rule database. It supports up to 32 independent channels, each of which has a separate area in the packet input buffer and result FIFO, to simplify the interaction with external multi-context processors.

The field extraction engine (FEE) includes an 8 kbyte packet input buffer that can store up to 32 packets simultaneously. Whenever the external device (processor or other packet source) sends packet data to the PM2329, the packet is first deposited in the packet input buffer. The FEE can parse and extract Ethernet from layer 2 (including Ethernet II, 802.3,

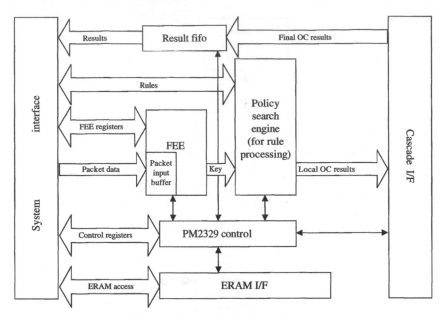

**Figure 16.31**　PM2329 block diagram.

and 802.1p/q headers), IP at layer 3, and TCP/UDP at layer 4 as well as payload data at any offset.

The policy search engine implements a set of classification functions. It performs policy-based search operation sequences, applying rules from the 16 K-deep rule memory and comparing a specified sequence of rules with the extracted key information from the FEE. It generates detailed results of those searches and returns those results (under control of the control unit) through the cascade interface to the result FIFO. The PSE performs operation cycles (OC) on packets in the order that their field extraction is complete. The processing of any one search using one key constitutes a single OC. As there could be multiple keys extracted from a packet, and as each key can be subjected to multiple searches, a packet can utilize many OCs for full processing. An OC is complete when the key is compared against a specific rule, and the results are queued in the result FIFO. The time duration of an OC depends therefore on the availability of space in the result FIFO; if the OC must wait for space, it remains active until space is available.

The control unit orchestrates the operation of the internal blocks to perform packet classification. It consists of registers required to control these operations, and state machines to perform the control functions.

The external RAM (ERAM) stores: (1) the classification program in the command RAM (C-RAM section), and (2) the user programmable data associated with every rule in the User section; (3) packet count, byte count, and timestamp statistics maintained by the device on a per-rule basis in the Stats section. The ERAM interface has a shared address bus and two data buses – one for command and the other for statistics and user data. As a consequence, two types of cycles can run on this interface. When fetching the command word, the data read from the command section of the ERAM is delivered to all devices in the cascade, whereas accesses to the statistics and user section of the ERAM are targeted between the specific PM2329 and ERAM as is determined by local on-chip ERAM configuration register in each PM2329 device.

The cascade interface is used to connect up to eight PM2329 devices to increase the number of rules in the rule database to a maximum of 128 K. Each of the devices in the cascade receives the same key but operates on different rules in parallel. The cascade interface implements a handshake mechanism to make the cascade appear as a single large device to the network processor.

## 16.3  TRAFFIC MANAGEMENT CHIPS

### 16.3.1  Overview

Traffic management is defined as the ability to control data flow across the network. A traffic management chip handles queuing and scheduling. It applies different buffering strategies so that flows can share limited buffers according to the traffic requirements. When a traffic management chip schedules cells or packets, it must make sure flows can share the limited bandwidth properly. At the same time, it will also take different protocols and QoS requirements into consideration. Nowadays, a network processor can handle flows at OC-48 or OC-192 line rate or even faster. As a workmate component of network processors, the performance of traffic management chips is becoming increasingly more critical due to the factors described above.

Traffic management chips bridge the network processor and the switch fabric. It handles numerous flows of a variety of protocols. The ingress chips process flows from the network processor before being sent to a switch fabric to resolve bandwidth congestions. It applies buffering and scheduling algorithms to these flows. This chip is also responsible for multicasting. The egress chips process data from switch fabric before data is sent to the network processor. If packets are segmented into cells in the ingress chip, reassembling the cells into an original packet is one of the important tasks of the egress chips.

There are different traffic management chips from the vendors, based on different commercial platforms and system architectures. Agere, ZettaCom, and AMCC are some of the pioneers in this field. In this section, we will discuss traffic management chips called traffic manager (TM) in more detail.

### 16.3.2  Agere's TM Chip Set

In this subsection, we will go through Agere's high-end traffic management chip set called the TM10 [30–32]. The TM10 is designed to work with the NP10, which is a network processor by Agere, to provide a complete 10 Gbps traffic management solution.

The TM10 is a high-speed, high-performance, programmable traffic management engine providing protocol data unit modification, queuing, buffer management, scheduling, and shaping.

***Architecture and Implementation.*** Figure 16.32 illustrates the data flow and major functional components of TM10. Details of the data flow and major components in TM10 are described in the following.

As shown in Figure 16.32, first, the TM10 receives PDU and its control information from a network processor or from a switch fabric. This work is done by the input interface. The PDU is the formatted data unit including protocol information, QoS parameters, and data payload. Control information is received from the NP10 through the SPI-4 interface, which

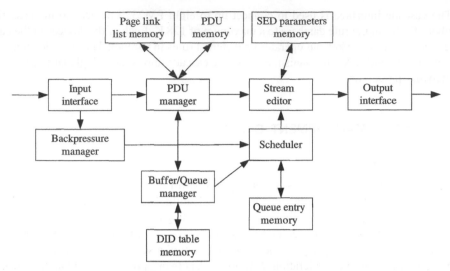

**Figure 16.32** TM10 block diagram.

is in the form of a transmit command, while control information is received from switch fabric in the form of backpressure signals for ports[1] and queues.

After that, the TM10 stores the PDUs and the related information into PDU memory. The PDU manager allocates memory pages for the incoming data. Because one packet may be segmented into multiple PDUs, these PDUs occupy more than one block and the blocks for these PDUs are linked together in the page linked list memory. The transmit commands associated with the PDUs are forwarded to the buffer and queue manager. The PDUs are segmented before being switched so that they may be interleaved while being switched. The PDU manager is in charge of reassembling egress PDUs into packets in the egress side of the switch fabric.

The buffer management process begins on the arrival of PDU and its transmit command. The buffer and queue manager checks transmit command to access the destination ID (DID) table memory. Based on the information both in the transmit command and in the DID table memory, it determines whether to queue or to discard arriving PDU. If accepted, corresponding enqueue operation will be finished by the PDU manager.

Finally, the TM10 schedules, modifies and transmits the PDUs. The scheduler determines which queue is to be serviced for the next scheduling slot. When a scheduling result is ready, the scheduled PDU will be read out from the memory and modified by the stream editor. Then the modified data block is sent to the output interface.

*Buffer and Queue Management.* The TM10 provides sophisticated and highly configurable mechanisms for buffer and queue management. It supports four types of memory management, as shown in Figure 16.33: (1) Reassembly buffer management keeps track of the number of memory pages used to reassemble PDUs as they arrive, PDUs will be enqueued after reassembly; (2) PDU buffer management keeps track of the number of memory pages that are used by enqueued PDUs; (3) Multicast staging buffer management keeps track of the control information for multicast PDUs, allows prioritizing of multicast

---

[1] These ports are not the ones when describing a router or switch. In this case, they mean queues in the structure of VOQs.

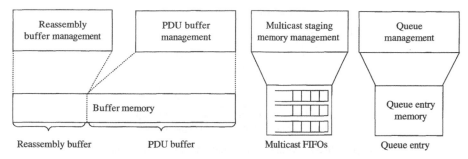

**Figure 16.33** Four types of memory management in TM10.

PDUs; (4) Queue management keeps track of the number of enqueued PDUs that belong to a particular queue or group of queues.

The first two mechanisms described above are used to protect and manage the TM10 PDU buffer. At configuration stage, the user can partition the PDU buffer into two parts: memory for reassembly and memory for enqueued PDUs.

The memory for reassembly is to allow the customization of the TM10 for specific applications or traffic conditions. The TM10 uses a set of external data buffers for PDU reassembly purposes. The reassembly space is partitioned into eight regions, corresponding to eight reassembly classes. Each reassembly class is configured with a minimum guaranteed reassembly space, as well as with a maximum usable reassembly space. This scheme allows the dynamic sharing of the reassembly space among classes. As a result of the classification process in NP10, each PDU is assigned a priority. These eight priorities are mapped into the eight priority class buffers in the reassembly buffer, respectively. These eight prioritized class buffers provide space isolation for each class. Reassembly buffer management uses a portion-sharing strategy. Each priority class buffer has a minimum and maximum threshold. The minimum threshold is the guaranteed buffer space for a certain priority class. A PDU will be accepted for reassembly if the occupation is below the minimum threshold. The maximum threshold is based on the usage of shared space and the sum of all the maximum thresholds can exceed the entire buffer space. If there is some excess shared buffer space and the occupation is below the maximum threshold, the maximum threshold can be guaranteed and a PDU will be accepted. In order to ensure that the maximum amount of reassembly memory is not exceeded, the global threshold is applied.

The TM10 uses another part of the external data buffer to store PDUs while they wait for transmission. The memory pages are tracked by the PDU buffer management process. A PDU occupies its buffer space from the time of being admitted into the PDU buffer until being transmitted out of the buffer. The TM10 provides a programmable pool-level buffer management mechanism. A buffer pool is a set of PDUs that either shares some common attributes or can be viewed as a single entity for buffer management. The TM10 supports up to 4096 such pools. For example, all flows with the same level of priority and destined for the same port can be assigned to one pool. Each of the TM10's 4096 pools is assigned a minimum (guaranteed) number of memory pages, and a maximum number of memory pages. The sum of the minimum thresholds is the guaranteed memory assigned to the pools, and the rest of the memory is shared. This means the memory space can be assigned to the pools dynamically based on their maximum thresholds, as shown in Figure 16.34. The PDU buffer management supports two forms of weighted random early detection (WRED): pool-based WRED, to protect the pool's shared memory and global shared buffer space

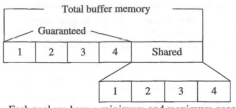

Each pool can have a minimum and maximum page
threshold. The minimum threshold is guaranteed.

**Figure 16.34** Minimum and maximum pool thresholds.

WRED, to protect all of the shared memory. These WRED mechanisms can be enabled and disabled at discretion.

Multicast staging buffer management uses a complete partition strategy. The multicast staging buffers, which are organized in the form of FIFOs, are used to temporarily hold multicast PDU information before it is added to the queue. These FIFOs are used to prioritize multicast PDUs. After a multicast PDU has been admitted into the PDU buffer space, its control information is placed in one of the eight multicast staging FIFOs. The control information remains in the FIFO while the TM10 attempts to enqueue the PDU into all the queues corresponding to the multicast group membership. The TM10 determines which of the eight FIFOs to use based on the information in the DID entry. This allows different levels of multicast priority for different multicast flows. The multicast staging FIFOs can hold the control information for up to 1 K multicast PDUs. This entire space is statically partitioned into eight FIFOs. Unlike the other managed spaces, no sharing of multicast staging FIFO space is permitted. A multicast PDU will only be admitted into the requested FIFO if its occupancy is lower than the maximum allowed value for that FIFO. When the requested FIFO is full, the multicast PDU is discarded.

Queue management is designed to protect the queue entry memory, which maintains entries for each PDU and is named QRAM by Agere. A PDU may occupy one or more buffer pages; an entry is associated with a buffer page. For unicast traffic, since the number of possible entries in the QRAM is the same as the number of PDU buffer pages, it is not possible to run out of QRAM, even when the buffer is filled with PDUs that occupy a single page. However, with the multicast case, one PDU in the PDU buffer memory can be scheduled into multiple queues, increasing the number of entries in the table. The TM10 supports up to 16 K scheduling queues. When the TM10 is ready to enqueue a PDU into a queue, it first performs the queue entry space management function, making sure that no single pool of queues uses a disproportionate amount of queue entry space. The process for queue entry space management is very similar to the process performed for PDU buffer space management. The main difference is that the queue-entry space management deals with fixed size allocations, where each allocation unit corresponds to a single queue entry. The PDU buffer space management, in contrast, deals with variable size allocation, accommodating different-sized PDUs. The queue entry space supports up to 4 K pools, with minimum and maximum thresholds per pool. Each PDU has flow-based and profile-based thresholds, as is the case with PDU buffer space management. The enqueueing decisions are made using WRED, and are based on current occupancy levels of the pools, as well as on the flow and profile of the PDU being enqueued.

These four types of memory management protect the entry buffer and payload buffer based on priority and QoS parameters. It can solve the buffer congestions in different levels.

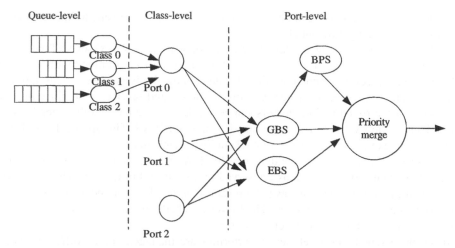

**Figure 16.35** TM10 scheduler hierarchy.

*Scheduling and Shaping.* The TM10 device uses a hierarchical scheduling structure that provides bandwidth guarantee and traffic isolation at three levels. A port-level scheduler is the first level of the hierarchical scheduling structure. The port-level scheduler arbitrates among traffic flows, which are destined for different ports. The port-level scheduler's structures for both the ingress and the egress directions are similar, and are configured separately for each case. A class-level scheduler is the second level, which can provide bandwidth and delay guarantees, fair sharing of bandwidth, and weighting among four classes. A queue-level scheduler is the bottom level of the structure. The queue-level scheduler provides fair bandwidth sharing and minimum bandwidth guarantees among the 16 K queues. The scheduling hierarchy is shown in Figure 16.35.

The port-level scheduler selects a port for service using three different kinds of schedulers as shown in Figure 16.35, including the guaranteed bandwidth scheduler (GBS), the excess bandwidth scheduler (EBS) and the backpressure scheduler (BPS). These three schedulers are serviced in a strict priority order: GBS, BPS then EBS. If the GBS has a PDU ready to transmit, it is serviced first, if there is no GBS PDU ready, the BPS scheduler is serviced next. If there are no GBS or BPS pages to transmit, the EBS scheduler will then be serviced. BPS and EBS schedule the ports in a round robin (RR) manner.

The GBS is the highest priority port scheduler. This scheduler uses a shaped virtual clock algorithm that assigns a minimum bandwidth to each port and keeps track of the next service time needed to maintain the minimum bandwidth. The virtual clock algorithm provides accurate rate-based scheduling in a form of weighted fair queuing (WFQ). It also provides a tighter delay bound than a weighted round robin scheme. An ending timestamp is calculated for each backlogged port, based on the current clock value and the length of the PDU. The scheduling mechanism works to service the PDUs with the earliest timestamps, while maintaining assigned port rates, using a set of rate groups.

At the second scheduling level, service priorities among different scheduling classes within each port are managed by a scheduler, which runs in a class-level. Within each managed port, traffic is divided into four priority classes. Schedulers of this level run a strategy called smoothed deficit weighted round robin (SDWRR) or serve the classes in strict priorities. There are four classes for each scheduler: one priority class plus three

SDWRR classes. The TM10 can be configured to use one of the scheduling schemes to serve the traffic among different classes.

Traditional implementations of deficit weighted round robin (DWRR) scheduling employ a single FIFO queue. At each scheduling event, the entire list is examined without regard to the previous scheduling event, until the allocated bandwidth is exhausted. This approach induces extremely poor performance in terms of latency and service burst, since in some cases some of the round robin members can be serviced twice before other members are serviced once. The TM10 employs a smoothed version of DWRR. This approach interleaves the transmission of packets from different scheduling events, in a two-level mechanism that ensures fairness and reduces burst and latency. In SDWRR, service is distributed on a PDU basis. PDUs from different sessions are served in a round robin fashion. The bandwidth sharing is fulfilled in a collective way that prevents one member from being accessed twice before others are accessed only once. The SDWRR scheduling algorithm is implemented in both the class- and the queue-level schedulers.

At the third scheduling level, service priorities are managed among different queues within a given class on a given port. A queue in TM10 can be viewed as a collection of virtual connections or IP flows. The virtual connections or IP flows are treated as a single entity from the traffic management perspective and addressed by queue identification (QID). The TM10 supports 16 K queues. SDWRR, as described previously, is used to serve the different queues in the class.

*Modification.* This work is finished by the stream editor (SED). The SED allows for PDU modifications to be programmed for each DID. The PDU modifications can be defined at system initialization or can be dynamically assigned during operation. PDU modifications are performed by compute engines with specifically assigned parameter values and script instruction sequences. These scripts and parameter variables are part of the programmable nature of each destination ID definition. Typical applications for PDU modifications include: encapsulating and tunneling PDUs into appropriate IP and other protocols, implementing IP operations such as decrementing time-to-live counts, IP packet fragmentation when required by the outgoing link and performing various MPLS operations such as swapping labels or pushing tags.

**Chip Set Features.** Based on the architecture we described above and strategy used in buffering and scheduling, the TM10 can achieve the following features and benefits.

TM10 can get a full 10 Gbps line rate performance with any PDU size (40 bytes or higher), supporting collaborations with both the cell-based and the frame-based switch fabrics. The TM10 has good support for multicast traffic too. By employing four types of memory management process, the TM10 can provide advanced, programmable buffer management and discarding policies. The TM10 provides up to 4096 buffer pools, each with programmable guaranteed and maximal space sizes. RED and WRED discarding policies are applied for each buffer pool. The TM10 uses per-flow buffer space thresholds for making a discard decision and per-flow and per-profile RED weights, allowing for better traffic isolation. These features enable direct support of DiffServ AF (assured forwarding), EF (expedited forwarding) and PHBs (per-hop behaviors), predictable PDU drop probability, and support for a large number of classes of service.

Hierarchical scheduling enhances advanced, programmable scheduling policies. The TM10 provides bounded delay, guaranteed bandwidth services down to byte-level granularity, as well as excellent fairness between traffic classes. Shaped virtual clock (SVC)-based shaping achieves guaranteed packet delay bounds. The TM10 supports SDWRR and strict priority policies. It can schedule up to 256 switch fabric ports, with four priority classes per port. Each traffic class within a port has a separate backpressure assertion. These scheduling capabilities can be easily programmed for different applications.

### 16.3.3   IDT TM Chip Set

A typical traffic management chip provided by IDT is called the TTM552 [33–35]. The TTM552 can be used as a standalone flow-aggregated traffic management device. Another extended chip provided by IDT is called the TTM553, which cooperates with the TTM552 and enhances the capacity of the TTM552.

The TTM552 traffic manager can perform flow-based traffic management for up to one million flows, when it is used in conjunction with the TTM552, including queuing, scheduling and buffer management. In this subsection, we will describe how the IDT TTM performs these operations.

***Architecture and Implementation.*** As shown in Figure 16.36, the TTM552 receives packets or cells channeled on the Rx traffic interface. Then it assembles the packets in the arrival reassemble queues (ARQs). Before data is stored in the buffer memory, the TTM552 performs congestion management checks based on the packet's discarding preference, forwarding label, configured thresholds, and on the measured levels of congestion. These checks may result in partial or full packet discard. If not discarded, packets or cells are stored into the buffer memory. The TTM552 places the packets in appropriate aggregated flow queues (AFQs). If the TTM552 is present, packets are placed in the appropriate flow queues (FLQ) controlled by the TTM553. At the same time, the TTM552 updates the statistics and scheduling database via the stat port.

After buffering operations, the TTM552 makes bandwidth management (scheduling) based on the configured parameters, the selected scheduling algorithms, and the received flow control and backpressure information. When a cell or a packet is scheduled, the TTM552 updates the statistics and scheduling database. Then the cell or packet is retrieved

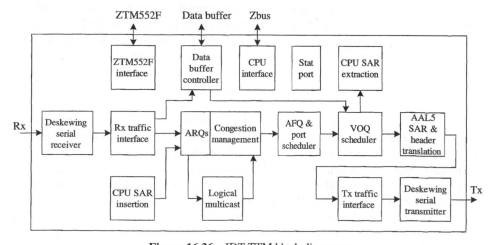

**Figure 16.36**   IDT TTM block diagram.

from the memory. After header translation is applied to the PDUs, the cell or packet is transmitted through the Tx traffic interface.

There are other functions provided by the TTM552. In the TTM552 system, multicast is supported and multicast cells are replicated by the logical multicast module. After replication, cells will be treated as unicast cells. Another function provided is that control messages from or to the CPU can be inserted or extracted over the CPU interface via the integrated segmentation and reassembly (SAR).

*Congestion Management.* Cells or packets from the network processor or switch fabric are received via the Rx traffic interface. The interface consists of an input data interface and an out-of-band flow control interface. Packets arrive at the TTM552 over the Rx traffic interface using one of the standards such as SPI-4.2, CSIX or NPSI specifications. Protocol headers of the cells or packets are examined to generate protocol independent cell (PIC) headers, and payloads of the cells or packets are extracted from the frames. If needed, they are segmented into multiple internal fixed-length cells. A loss-of-syn signal transmitted from up-stream is detected at the same time. Receipt of such a signal can either automatically trigger a training pattern transmission on the status interface that is used to communicate backpressure information to the upstream device, or simply generate an interrupt to allow software handling of the event.

The TTM552 uses ARQs to reassemble packet segments that have been interleaved by the NPU, switch fabric, CPU-SAR-generated traffic, or through logical multicast replication. The segments cannot be scheduled for departure or for next operations before they are reassembled.

Both in the ingress direction and in the egress direction, after the reassembling operations, the TTM552 should apply congestion management before cells or packets are stored into the memory, called buffering. The TTM552 performs congestion management by means of discarding threshold or congestion avoidance. When the TTM553 is present, it enables congestion management on every individual flow.

The TTM552 makes decisions to accept or discard every arriving packet based on these two types of information: current congestion conditions in the data buffer space and the thresholds configured for each queue. Each queue threshold and the memory usage are checked before the cell is accepted into the ARQ. The system can configure each of the queue levels with thresholds independently to achieve maximum flexibility in the allocation of data buffer resources. There are four levels of thresholds employed by the IDT TTM, including global data buffer maximum threshold, per port queue (PQ) maximum threshold, per AFQ maximum threshold, and per flow identification number (FIN) maximum threshold. All levels of these thresholds can be enabled or disabled. Multi-level thresholds make congestion management more flexible. The relationship of these thresholds and their operation order is shown in Figure 16.37.

There is a single, configurable global data buffer threshold. This threshold represents the entire data storage capacity that the TTM552 can sustain. If the entire data storage reaches the defined global threshold, the TTM552 discards all the arriving cells.

Similarly, there is a single, configurable discard threshold for each destination PQ. A unique maximum threshold can be set for each PQ. Same as global threshold, if the occupation of the PQ exceeds this threshold, the arriving data will be discarded.

Each AFQ can be configured with up to a group of thresholds called a set. For each AFQ, we can choose one of the 256 AFQ threshold sets. Also there is one configurable reference maximum threshold (RMT), which is always applicable to traffic arriving at the AFQ.

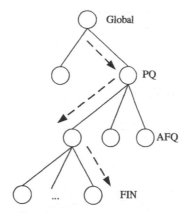

**Figure 16.37**   Congestion management of the TTM552.

Each of the 4 K AFQs has its own RMT that represents all of the memory allocated to it. When the usage exceeds the RMT value, packets or cells will be discarded. Each threshold set consists of eight configurable and selectable threshold multipliers and a configurable SOP (start of packet) flag associated with each threshold multiplier. A threshold multiplier determines the actual threshold to be applied to a packet. The actual threshold is a percentage of the AFQ's configured reference maximum threshold. The multiplier is chosen according to the priorities. If the SOP flag is active, then the result is only applied to the SOP cells.

If the TTM553 is connected, there is a single, configurable discard threshold for each destination FLQ called FIN maximum threshold. If the occupation of the FLQ exceeds this threshold, the packet belonging to this flow will be discarded.

In addition to the static threshold, the TTM552 supports congestion avoidance. It supports WRED for AFQs. The TTM552 also employs an explicit forward congestion indication (FCI) feedback mechanism for congestion avoidance. They function as indicators of local congestion that can be mapped by a downstream network processor or other protocol-aware service engines into a flow control message in the native protocol.

After performing the congestion management operations, the TTM552 stores accepted packets or cells into the memory and discards others. The TTM552 supports full packet discard (FPD) to reduce local memory congestion. When the SOP cell is discarded, the TTM552 will discard the entire packet. This method increases the efficiency of cell memory usage. When a non-SOP cell is discarded, the IDT TTM supports a version of FPD that is similar to partial packet discard (PPD). The discarding of a non-SOP cell arrival will result in all subsequent cell arrivals for the packet being discarded. A partial packet that was assembled in the ARQ or FLQ prior to the first discard is also deleted by forwarding this partial packet to the designated "trash queue."

*Queuing and Scheduling.* After congestion management, acceptable cells will be buffered into the memory in the form of queues. There are five types of queues in which data can be stored while being processed by the TTM552. They are ARQs, FLQs, AFQs, PQs, and output queues (OQs). The FLQs are only supported when the TTM553 chip is connected. In the following, we will describe the queuing structure of the TTM552.

As shown in Figure 16.38, ARQs are the first-stage of queuing for arriving packets. The TTM552 supports 2048 ARQs. The ARQs accumulate an entire packet before moving it to the next stage queuing. The next stage queuing could be FLQs if the TTM553 is connected

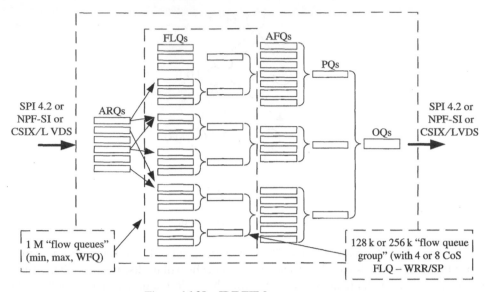

**Figure 16.38**   IDT TTM queue structure.

or AFQs if the TTM553 is absent. As mentioned in the previous part, the TTM552 starts packet accumulation when it receives an SOP cell. It moves the accumulated packet to FLQ or ARQ when it receives an EOP (end of packet) flag.

FLQs are supported when a TTM553 is connected. The TTM553 can support one million FLQs, corresponding to one million unique FINs. The FLQs are maintained by the TTM553 in its external SRAM. The TTM553 supports two modes: one-level FLQ mode and two-level FLQ mode in both the ingress and the egress directions. The one-level mode allows all one million FLQs to be scheduled directly into the AFQs. In two-level mode, four or eight FLQs are combined together and then mapped into 128 K or 256 K FLQ groups, respectively. The four or eight FLQs in each group can be scheduled before the scheduling of the FLQs. This mode adds immense flexibility.

The TTM553 standalone supports 4096 AFQs. One or more FLQs can be mapped into an AFQ. Arriving cells or packets are accumulated in ARQs before being moved into the ARQs when the TTM553 is absent. When the TTM553 is connected, any FLQs can be mapped into any AFQs based on configuration.

In the following stage, one or more AFQs can be mapped into one PQ. PQs can be used as physical ports or logical ports (virtual pipes) within an output queue. Ports can be mapped to any OQ and are "maximum rate shaped" when the TTM552 is used in the egress direction. While in the ingress direction, only one port can be mapped into one of the OQs.

The OQs correspond to the switch fabric's virtual output queues (VOQ) when the TTM552 transmits data to the switch fabric. The OQs can be viewed as physical destinations or channels when the TTM552 transmits data to a NPU or a framer. There are 1024 OQs available. However, in SPI-4.2 interface mode, only up to 16 OQs are supported for transmitting.

According to the queuing structure described above, when we use the TTM552 as a standalone chip, it manages traffic in three stages. And when the chip is connected to the TTM553, it manages traffic in 4–5 stages. The stages of traffic managing hierarchy can offer immense flexibility in configuring bandwidth on a physical channel, logical port, class, subscriber, or per-flow basis, as well as other applications. Another question is how the TTM552 cooperates with the TTM553 to finish the scheduling operations based on this queuing structure so that flows can share the limited bandwidth fairly. There are four levels of scheduling corresponding to the four stages of queuing structure except ARQs because they are dedicated to serve the reassembly and cannot be scheduled directly.

FLQs lie in the first level of hierarchy scheduling when the TTM553 is connected. These FLQs can be structured into 128 K groups of eight CoS FLQs or as 256 K groups of four CoS FLQs. FLQs can be individually configured with the following scheduling algorithms. The minimum rate algorithm is a guaranteed minimum rate of service for the FLQ. This algorithm becomes a constant bit rate (CBR)-like constant rate scheduler when other algorithms are disabled. Maximum rate algorithm controls the maximum rate for a FLQ. The available rate for a FLQ cannot exceed this value. Weight fair queuing (WFQ) is used for distributing the excess traffic when extra bandwidth is available. Strict priority and weighted round-robin (WRR) selection are only used for the FLQ within a group.

AFQs scheduling is the next level of hierarchy scheduling. There are 4096 aggregate-flow queues that can be configured with different scheduling algorithms. Same as the FLQ scheduling, the TTM552 provides two rate algorithms in this level: the minimum rate algorithm and the maximum rate algorithm. AFQ scheduling also supports dual-rate variable bit rate (VBR) shaping. This algorithm is performed using a peak rate (PCR), a maximum sustained rate (SCR) or a maximum burst size (MBS). WFQ is also used for distribution of excess traffic. If enabled, priority round-robin (PRR) or strict priority selection allows the distribution of excess bandwidth. An AFQ can be assigned to a priority level. Within the priority level, AFQs are selected on a round-robin basis.

At the third level, the TTM552 has 1024 PQs that can be individually configured with the following scheduling algorithms. PQs can be configured with a maximum rate for shaping traffic at a logical port level. This is only used in the egress direction. Ports can optionally be shaped using a calendar-based mechanism for TDM traffic with no jitter and a high-precision calendar-based shaping can be used with byte rate shaping.

At the fourth level, the TTM552 has 1024 OQs. After traffic has been serviced for departure, it goes to the OQ into which the port is mapped. In the egress direction, an OQ corresponds to a VOQ in a switch fabric, representing a destination port and CoS. In the ingress direction, an OQ is a physical port or a TDM channel of a framer. OQ selections can be round-robin or calendar-based.

Every level of scheduling can be configured to use one of the scheduling algorithms. The operational order of scheduling is opposite to the order described above. First the scheduler chooses which OQ to serve. Second the scheduler chooses a PQ within this OQ. The next is for the AFQ in the same way. Following the AFQ is the FLQ if the TTM553 is connected. Schedulers in different levels can work in parallel so that the pipelining can improve the performance of scheduling.

When scheduling is complete, the TTM552 sends data from the selected OQ to the Tx traffic interface. Before transmitting, however, there are a few modifications that the TTM552 can apply to the protocol headers of packets. If configured to do so, the TTM552 replaces the existing FIN with a new one. This is called FIN translation. The TTM552 also modifies or removes the packet header if necessary.

*Multicast.* The TTM552 supports two types of multicast. One is logical multicast and the other is spatial multicast. Logical multicast means making one or more copies of an incoming packet. The TTM552 applies this operation on the traffic received from the Rx traffic interface. Spatial multicast means sending one copy of a packet from one source port in one ingress line card to more destination ports in different egress line cards. This kind of operation is always done by a switch fabric. Logical multicast is done by the egress chips and spatial multicast by ingress chips. The bandwidth requirements of the switch fabric are minimized in this way.

Logical multicast is controlled by configuring multicast trees. A multicast tree is a data structure that describes how a packet is to be replicated. A tree has a root FIN, and one or more branches, identified by branch labels. The TTM552 performs logical multicast on a packet received on a root FIN by making one copy of the packet for each branch label in the multicast tree. Each resulting packet is identical to the original root packet with the FIN replaced by the branch FIN. The TTM552 supports up to 16,000 multicast trees. But there is an upper limit of 4096 on the total number of branch labels available to user. A branch can be reused by more than one multicast tree as shown in Figure 16.39. A multicast tree cannot have more than 4096 branches because of the upper limit.

The TTM552 classifies arriving traffic at the Rx traffic interface as either unicast or logical multicast. Unicast traffic bypasses the logical multicast engine. Logical multicast traffic is processed in the logical multicast engine. The engine first assembles PICs of a logical multicast root packet in one of the multicast ARQs. As each PIC of a root packet is received, the logical multicast engine performs congestion management checks. When a packet fails to pass the check, it is discarded. After these operations, the packet can be placed in one of the four multicast class queues (MCQs). Four MCQs provide four classes of service. The logical multicast engine selects packets from the four MCQs and replicates the root packet over their configurable multicast trees. Replicated packets behave as newly arriving unicast traffic to the later processing of TTM552.

Spatial multicasting can occur only in the ingress direction and is typically performed by a switch fabric. The ingress TTM552 assists by flagging the spatial multicast traffic going to the switch fabric and identifying the target line cards to which the traffic is to be sent. This information is passed in the form of a multicast ID or label.

***Chip Set Features.*** The TTM552 can get a full 10 Gbps line rate performance. The chip can provide per-flow queuing and scheduling. It supports up to one million configured flows when equipped with the TTM553. Scheduling can be simultaneously performed on a large number of flows, each at an individual rate of fine granularity, and with many user-configurable scheduling algorithms allowing maximum flexibility and performance.

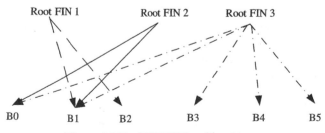

**Figure 16.39**   IDT TTM multicast trees.

Before queuing the packets or cells, the chip set executes sophisticated cell or packet admission control. Based on the information of thresholds, the chip set can support traditional discard algorithms such as maximum threshold, minimum threshold, and dynamic threshold in four different levels. If buffer memory approaches its limit because data arrival rate at the queue is greater than the departure rate, the TTM552 performs per-queue congestion management. The TTM552 can intelligently discard lower priority traffic as it arrives.

The TTM552 can also support spatial and logical multicast, satisfying the requirement of a 10 Gbps line rate.

### 16.3.4 Summary

The traffic management module plays an important role in high-performance routers. The traffic manager handles queuing and scheduling while it must consider the QoS requirements and different protocols. Because of the large number of flows managed and the very high line rate, it is difficult for the traffic manager inside a high-performance core router to complete these operations. And we cannot treat all the packets in a same way for efficiency reasons, so appropriate policing, shaping, buffering and scheduling algorithms must be developed within the TM.

From the description above, we have learned the structures, the implementations and the features of some commercial traffic management chip sets. They employ different structures and algorithms, providing different features and benefits for buffering and scheduling. They also provide configuration interfaces to users. The TM bridges the network processor and switch fabric, resolving resource congestion. They must make sure that different flows can share the memory and switch bandwidth adequately and pass through a router with lower latency.

## 16.4 SWITCHING FABRIC CHIPS

### 16.4.1 Overview

General switching principles, including various switching architectures and scheduling algorithms, have been discussed in Chapters 5 to 15. This section describes how to apply these theories to commercial applications, that is, the switching fabric chips. Generally speaking, most of today's switching fabrics beyond multi-gigabit adopt the crossbar with combined input and output queuing (CIOQ) structure.[2] In this architecture, VOQ structure is implemented in ingress ports and output queues are used in egress ports to deal with the speedup of the switching fabric. Vitesse's 872/882 and Agere's Pi40X/C are typical switching fabric chipsets using this architecture.

An alternative is to build a switching fabric using a single chip, such as Agere's Pi40SAX. The solution greatly reduces the design complexity and is often deployed in relatively lower throughput routers, for example, 40 Gbps.

In the core of the switch fabric, three different structures are used: the crossbar, the buffered crossbar, and the shared memory. The first two are space-division switching and the last one is time-division switching. Most commercial solutions support parallel and

---

[2]Share-memory is an exception as its single stage switch can only achieve 40 Gbps throughput.

multistage configurations of switching chips to achieve higher line speed and larger port numbers.

In the following section, three series of switching fabrics from Vitesse are presented. Section 16.4.3 describes the flexibly configurable cyclone switching fabric from AMCC. In Section 16.4.4, the detailed architecture of the IBM PowerPRS switching fabric is explained.[3] Finally, in Section 16.4.5, two different switching fabric solutions from Agere are described.

## 16.4.2   Switch Fabric Chip Set from Vitesse

Vitesse's [36] switch fabrics can be classified into three generations: CrossStream [37, 38], GigaStream [39], and TeraStream [40]. CrossStream, composed of a VSC870/VSC880 chip set, can perform variable-size packet switching. GigaStream is composed of VSC872/882 chip sets and cells are scheduled and switched internally. TeraStream (including two chips: VSC871 and VSC881) targets terabit core routers and uses a buffered crossbar architecture. These three chip sets represent different switching architectures and are described in detail as follows.

***CrossStream: VSC870/880 Chip Set.***  For small capacity routers, parallel bus is usually used on their backplane to support modularity and simplicity. An example would be a PCI bus-based architecture. The parallel bus architecture, however, does not scale well. A new generation of large capacity routers use high-speed serial links (HSSL) for signal transmission between the line card and the switching card on the backplane. The VSC870 and VSC880 chip set are designed based on the new generation architecture.

Figure 16.40 shows the connections between VSC870 and VSC880. Vitesse designed the CrossStream chip set that performs serial data switching between the VSC870 and the VSC880. Each serial link is a 2.125 Gbps differential signal pair. Connection request (CRQ), data, acknowledgment (ACK), and other flow control information are all multiplexed into and transferred through these serial links. The VSC870 is built into the line cards whereas the VSC880 is built into switching cards.

The VSC870 also performs bit alignment and word alignment to synchronize both itself and the VSC880. The VSC880 acts as the master, generating the bit clock. The VSC870 recovers a bit clock from the receiving HSSL and then locks to it through a phase-lock-loop (PLL). In this way, the VSC870 and VSC880 are frequency-locked to one clock source provided by the VSC880. The word alignment is achieved by shifting the word clock one bit at a time until the VSC870 detects a proper predefined word pattern.

The VSC880 is a $16 \times 16$ synchronous serial crossbar switch with each high speed I/O link running at 2.125 Gbps (2.0 Gbps for data and 0.125 Gbps for control information). The aggregate data bandwidth is 32 Gbps. The internal block diagram of VSC880 is shown in Figure 16.41, which is a typical crossbar switch fabric. CMU (clock multiplex unit) is used to generate a high-speed bit clock. DRU (data recovery unit) is designed as a delay lock loop and remains phase locked to the incoming data stream. Port logic performs the necessary logic functions, such as separating CRQs and packets, inserting acknowledgments, and so on. Switch matrix is a crossbar switch fabric and performs data transferring from input ports to output ports. The scheduling algorithm is executed in the arbitration logic block.

---

[3] Note that this series has been purchased by AMCC.

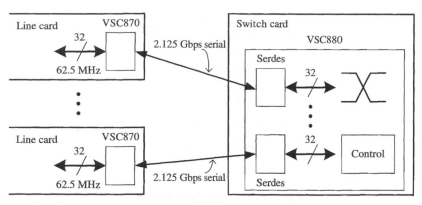

**Figure 16.40** CrossStream chip set, VSC870 and VSC880, connected by SERDES (serializer/deserializer).

In packet switching, the variable-size packet scheduling between the VSC870 and VSC880 is executed in the following three steps:

*Step* 1. The VSC870 in each line card sends multiple CRQs to the VSC880.

*Step* 2. Arbitration is performed in the VSC880. CRQs reach the switch chip on each word clock and the arbitration process takes two word clock cycles: the first cycle looks for empty output ports and the second cycle makes arbitration using the round-robin scheduling. An ACK will be sent to the corresponding VSC870 if the CRQ is granted.

*Step* 3. The VSC870 sends out packets to the granted output port after receiving an ACK from the VSC880.

Figure 16.42 shows the format of CRQs. The CRQs are inserted at the end of each packet. The beginning of a variable-size packet is indicated with a special marking word named Header. To break a match between an input and an output port, a null CRQ is sent at the end of the current packet.

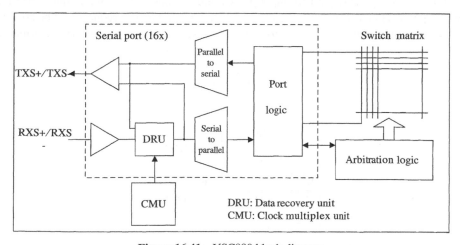

**Figure 16.41**    VSC880 block diagram.

| 10 | Header | Start of packet |
|----|--------|-----------------|
| 01 | D0 | |
| 01 | D1 | |
| | • • • | |
| 01 | DN | |
| 11 | CRQ | End of packet |
| 10 | Header | Start of packet |
| 01 | D0 | |

**Figure 16.42**    VSC870 CRQ format.

To utilize the HSSL bandwidth efficiently, a CRQ may be inserted before the end of each packet. Figure 16.43 shows the format of sending a CRQ before the end of a packet. This scheme allows the central scheduler in the VSC880 to perform arbitration while transferring data. If the CRQ word is inserted into the current data packet D words before the end of the packet, ACK results will be known at the input port when the first word of the next data packet is ready for transmission. The value D is determined based on the round trip delay from the time the port submits a CRQ until an ACK is received.

The VSC880 can support a backpressure mechanism by providing a flow control channel. The flow control channel is time shared with the signaling between the switch chip and the transceiver. The VSC880 does not take any action to prevent congestion, and only passes the state information from the output port to the input port. During the flow control, the input port stops transferring packages to that port and prevents the FIFO on the receiver side from overflowing.

CrossStream has three modes to support multicast traffic. In the first mode, it copies the multicast packets and treats them as unicast packets. In the second mode, it treats a multicast packet as a group and it can be transferred only if all of its destination requests are granted. As a result, in some conditions, it may cause a dead lock as shown in Figure 16.44. Input port 1 sends CRQs to output ports 2 and 3, and input port 4 sends CRQs to output ports 3 and 4. Obviously the request for input ports 1 and 4 cannot be granted at the same time from output 3. This dead lock can be resolved using a counter. The request will be aborted if it is not granted during a long period and therefore this mode may cause performance

| 10 | Header | Start of packet |
|----|--------|-----------------|
| 01 | D0 | |
| | • • | |
| 11 | CRQ | |
| 01 | D(N-D) | D words before |
| | • • | |
| 01 | DN | End of packet |
| 10 | Header | Start of packet |
| 01 | D0 | |

**Figure 16.43**    CRQ ahead of the end of a packet.

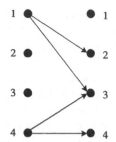

**Figure 16.44**   Example of dead lock for multicast traffic.

degradation. In the third mode, it transfers the multicast packet when parts of the requests are granted and the input port again sends a request for ungranted output ports. This mode requires the input port to buffer and reread the multicast packet until it has been transferred to all the destination ports.

The VSC870/VSC880 CrossStream can also support cell switching but the cell-mode scheduling algorithm is not integrated in the VSC880, which makes this architecture uncommon. The next generation GigaStream from Vitesse represents a typical cell switching architecture.

### GigaStream: VSC872/882 Chip Set with Bufferless Crossbar

*System Overview.* Figure 16.45 shows how to use Vitesse's GigaStream chip set to construct a CIOQ-like switching solution. The switch system is composed of two chips: the queuing engine VSC872 and the crossbar switch VSC882, respectively. The VSC872 consists of two parts, the ingress part in the left of the figure and the egress part in the right. The ingress of VSC872 provides two standard 32-bit common switch interfaces (CSIX) in the front each running up to $166\,\mathrm{Mbps} \times 32 = 5.312\,\mathrm{Gbps}$ connecting to TM or NP. The arriving frames are first sent to the frame parsing module where different kinds of frames, for example, unicast and multicast, are distinguished and sent to their corresponding queues for temporary storing.

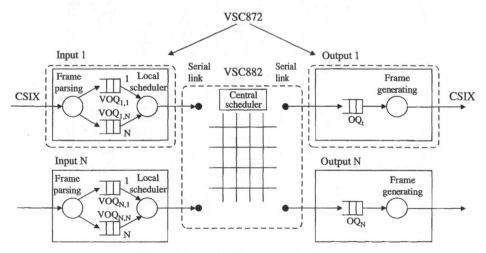

**Figure 16.45**   Architecture of GigaStream.

Because of the HOL blocking in the input queuing structure described in Chapter 5, the queuing engine VSC872 implements a VOQ instead. VSC872 provides eight serial links connecting the crossbar switch VSC882 at a speed up to 2.64384 Gbps data rate (2.5 Gbps for pure packets/cells transmission). With the execution of a sophisticated request–grant scheduling (will be illustrated later) between the local scheduler of VSC872 and the central scheduler of VSC882, the cells stored in the VOQ are scheduled and transferred to the crossbar switch VSC882 per cycle on the serial links. Since there are eight serial links in the direction to VSC882, up to eight cells can be transferred simultaneously in a same cycle to eight different VSC882s in parallel. However, each single cell is transmitted through the same crossbar switch in one cycle and there is no need to reorder at the egress of VSC872. Hence, the maximal transmission bandwidth between one VSC872 and one or more VSC882s is $8 \times 2.5\,\text{Gbps} = 20\,\text{Gbps}$, while the maximum bandwidth for the VSC872's receiving frames is $2 \times 5.312\,\text{Gbps} = 10.624\,\text{Gbps}$, providing a internal speedup of 2. Therefore, the egress of VSC872 uses an output buffer to accommodate the speedup. The cells leaving the output buffer are transformed into the correct frame pattern by the frame generating module and then sent out of the switching system.

*Queuing Architecture and Scheduling Algorithm of GigaStream.* Figure 16.46 shows the queuing system in the VSC872. The chip supports both unicast and multicast traffic. For unicast traffic, a strict high-priority (HP) and seven lower-priority (LP) queues of each VOQ are implemented. This queuing structure is replicated 16 times for its 16 output ports. For multicast traffic, the queuing architecture is similar to that of unicast traffic. When a multicast frame arrives, it is copied into all the VOQs belonging to the destination ports of the frame. The multicast VOQ is served similar to the unicast VOQ. In fact, the multicast

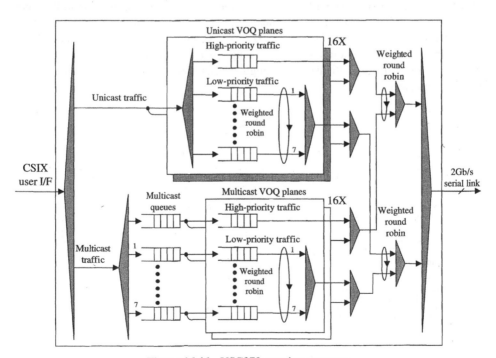

**Figure 16.46**  VSC872 queuing structure.

frame is stored in the ingress buffer as a single copy. The transfer from the multicast queue to the multicast VOQs involves only the copy of the corresponding pointers. When a multicast frame has been delivered to all of its destination ports, it is deleted from the buffer memory.

The GigaStream chip set implements three levels of scheduling. The first level generates CRQs for frames waiting in the VOQs. The second level generates a request ACK when a CRQ can be accommodated. The third level selects a queue whose frame will be sent when an ACK is received. Both the first level and the third level scheduling are executed in VSC872's local scheduler and the second level scheduling is performed in VSC882's central scheduler with an iterative matching process.

FIRST LEVEL SCHEDULING: CRQ GENERATION. For each scheduling cycle, a request can be made for one HP frame and one LP frame per VOQ. The VSC872 can generate a connection request for every non-empty HP VOQ. However, for a LP VOQ, it is allowed to send a request only when its connection cost is accumulated to be equal to or greater than the cost to gain the connection. At the end of each scheduling cycle, if current credit of any LP VOQ is below the connection cost, no request is sent and its credit is increased by a programmed weight value. If a LP VOQ credit is equal or above the connection cost, a CRQ is generated and the credit amount is debited by the connection cost at that moment.

SECOND LEVEL SCHEDULING: ACK GENERATION. The VSC882 has its own independent scheduling cycle and algorithm to generate request ACKs. This central scheduler looks at all the CRQs coming from all the local schedulers of every input port and goes through an iterative matching process similar to that of iSLIP to assign grants to requests in a fair manner. The grant process is first made only for HP CRQs. After four iterations for HP CRQs, LP CRQs are loaded and the grant process is executed for both LP CRQs and the remaining HP CRQs. In total, the VSC882 implements an algorithm that guarantees a minimum of 10 iterative matching cycles for the frame size of 40 bytes and more for a larger frame size. In theory, it requires 16 iterations to match 16 output ports to 16 input ports. This case happens only if all inputs request all the output ports and the round robin pointers are at the same location for all the output ports. By simulation and analysis, the scheduling algorithm can converge to a maximal match within four iteration steps for a $16 \times 16$ switch.

By allowing the HP CRQs first, it strictly reserves the available bandwidth for the HP traffic. This is not fair for LP traffic. After finishing the scheduling algorithm, each ACK gives the local scheduler permission to send a frame to one specific switch output.

THIRD LEVEL SCHEDULING: QUEUE GENERATION. If the local scheduler receives an ACK from the central scheduler, it must find the best frame to send to the granted switch output from its corresponding VOQs. If a HP frame is waiting, the local scheduler always selects the HP VOQ even if it is not waiting when the original CRQ is generated. If no HP frame is waiting, the "credit" is used to select a LP traffic. The credit added at the end of each scheduling cycle is the programmed weight value of the class and the connection cost is always the maximum of all class weights. "Credit" is in fact used to implement a weighted round-robin manner.

If both unicast and multicast have waiting frames to be sent, the simple weighting round-robin scheduling algorithm is used to allocate bandwidth between unicast and multicast traffic.

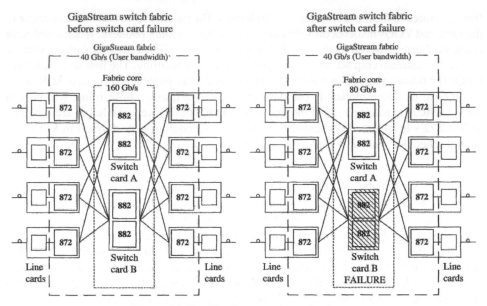

**Figure 16.47**   GigaStream active redundancy.

*Active Redundancy in GigaStream.* Figure 16.47 shows a medium scale switching system in which each VSC872 is connected to four VSC882s. Two VSC882s are in switch card A and the other two are in switch card B. The switch fabric on the left shows normal operation, where both the switch cards are working, offering a $4 \times 40\,\text{Gbps} = 160\,\text{Gbps}$ switching capacity. When one of the switch cards fails, as shown in the figure on the right, the serial links between the failed switch card and the connecting VSC872s detect link errors automatically. The VSC872s have to load-balance the traffic formerly on the failed switch to the working switch within a very short time period. Although the performance may worsen, the switching system remains working at half the throughput capacity.

*TeraStream: VSC871/881 Chip Set with Buffered Crossbar.* Vitesse's TeraStream chip set presents another type of CIOQ switch: buffered crossbar. Figure 16.48 shows a typical architecture of TeraStream, which comprises two types of chips: VSC871 and VSC881. The architecture extends the dual chip architecture of Vitesse's switching fabric.

Compared to Vitesse's former products, GigaStream and CrossStream, the new architecture gains three key advantages to achieve Terabit switching. Firstly, as shown in Figure 16.48, the 24 VSC871s are connected by 13 VSC881s in three stages. This multistage configuration of VSC881 guarantees the design of mass input ports. Secondly, through link bundling and slicing, several serial links between VSC871 and VSC881 or between neighbor VSC881s can be congregated to a single link with the aggregated bandwidth. Therefore, much higher line speed on input port can be achieved. Finally, the VSC881 implements the advanced switching structure of a buffered crossbar.

*Multistage Configuration.* The TeraStream supports both single-stage and multistage configurations. However, a multistage topology is required to achieve terabit switching capacity. A variety of multistage topologies can be constructed using the VSC881. Figure 16.49 shows some possible configurations. Historically, the Clos and Banyan architectures are very well

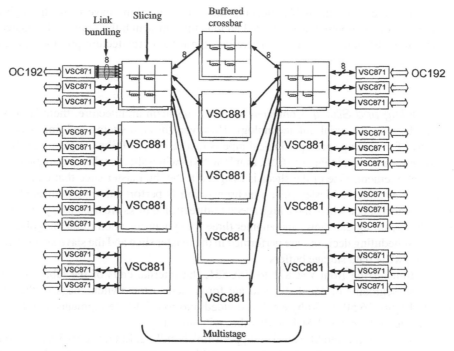

**Figure 16.48**  Typical architecture of TeraStream.

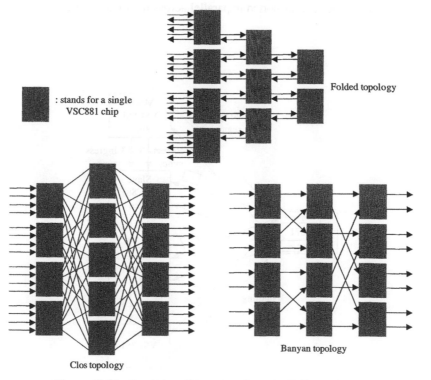

**Figure 16.49**  Possible multistage configurations of TeraStream.

known. They are "pass-through", meaning that all connections have to go through all the stages. Another topology is the folded architecture, in which the requested connectivity determines the number of stages. Therefore, the folded architecture provides a highly scalable system with fewer devices.

*Link Bundling and Slicing.* Compared to the GigaStream architecture, there is no significant advantage in serial link technology. However, through slicing and link bundling, the internal forwarding speed per logical pipe is increased to 20 Gbps, eight times that of GigaStream. As shown in Figure 16.50, four VSC881 switch slices make up a single logical core switch element. One of the slices is assigned to be the master slice that controls the remaining slave slices. Master/slave synchronization is performed via a dedicated daisy chained broadcast bus where three high speed bi-directional links are used for synchronization of the incoming data flows and another three for synchronization of the outgoing data flows. All scheduling decisions are performed in the master slice and the slave slices merely act as read/write data storage buffers.

When transferring from VSC871 to VSC881, the internal cells of the fabric are split into several segments of equal size and are forwarded to the switch slices in the same group. In Figure 16.50, an 80-byte cell is divided into four 20-byte segments and they are reconstructed at the egress VSC871 after the switching stage.

Besides slicing, the TeraStream also supports link bundling. In Figure 16.50, two groups of the four slicing links are bundled together to achieve higher forwarding speed of a single logical link. There is no further segmentation involved in link bundling. Two independent cells of the same queue are transported in parallel across the logical pipe during any given time slot.

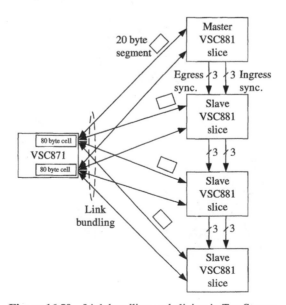

**Figure 16.50**   Link bundling and slicing in TeraStream.

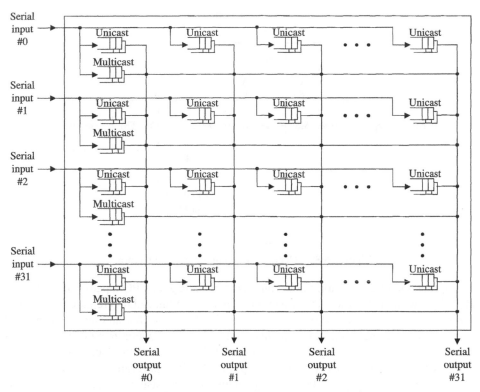

**Figure 16.51**  Crosspoint buffer structure of VSC881.

The maximal configuration of link bundling and slicing is dual link bundling plus quad slicing or quad link bundling plus dual slicing. Therefore, the maximum logical pipe bandwidth is 20 Gbps.

*Buffered Crossbar.* The internal structure of VSC881 is different from the traditional crossbar switch. It deploys a buffer in each crosspoint and is called a buffered crossbar structure. As in Figure 16.51, a unicast FIFO structure is maintained per cross point and a multicast FIFO structure is maintained per input. Each of these FIFO structures supports two priority levels: HP and LP. Each cross point unicast FIFO and input multicast FIFO support a FIFO depth up to eight cells.

The crosspoint buffered crossbar structure reduces (or avoids) the output contention. They allow the inputs to send cells to an output irrespective of simultaneous cell transfer to the same output.

### 16.4.3  Switch Fabric Chip Set from AMCC

AMCC constructs its Cyclone switching fabric [41] based on cost effectiveness. As shown in Figure 16.52, the switching fabric is not composed of a queuing engine (QE) and switch core (SW) anymore. Instead, five classes of chips are implemented together to realize packet queuing, scheduling, and switching. They are memory subsystem (MS), priority queue (PQ), arbiter (AR), crossbar (XB), and earliest deadline first queue (EDFQ). MS buffers cells, notifies PQ, and manages TM flow control credits. PQ bids AR for path to transmit cells of

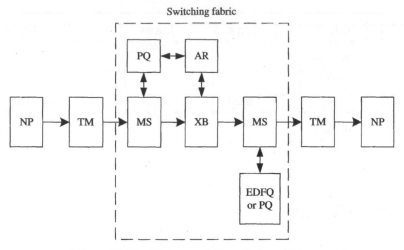

**Figure 16.52** Cyclone switching fabric architecture.

same packet and manages fabric flow control credits. AR grants PQ a path and configures XB. XB passes all cells belonging to one packet in a single link. EDFQ releases cells based on WFQ. This design method brings significant flexibility, so that an engineer can build his/her own switching fabric at minimum cost. In addition, the architecture is scalable, as extra chips can be added easily to support higher throughput or better QoS performance.

The switching fabric supports up to 40 Gbps (4 × OC192) port rate, with a maximum of 32 ports. Figure 16.53 shows a typical configuration that consists of 32 20 Gbps line cards and four 320 Gbps switch cards.

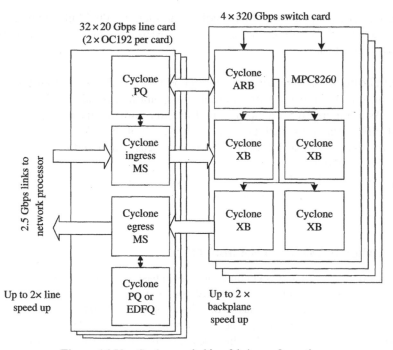

**Figure 16.53** Cyclone switching fabric configuration.

***Memory Subsystem.*** The cyclone memory subsystem block diagram is shown in Figure 16.54. Memory subsystem consists of a memory buffer (cell storage), cell/free cell list, memory management module, and serial interfaces. At the ingress port the cell sent to the memory subsystem is first de-serialized to a parallel data pattern and then stored in the memory buffer. A list of occupied cell storage and free cell storage is maintained by the memory management module and updated when any cell is stored or scheduled out. Up to 32,000 cells can be buffered in one MS. The information of new packet arrival is also passed through the queue interface to the PQ, where the packet ID is stored as output port and priority. Once a packet in PQ is granted by the AR, cells of this packet are read out from the memory buffer, serialized and transferred to the backplane continuously. In egress, cells switched by the crossbar are sent to the egress MS and stored again. Either PQ or EDFQ can be deployed at the egress to schedule cells out of the MS.

***Priority Queue.*** The PQ can be located at either the ingress ports or the egress ports. On the ingress side, the PQ buffers packet ID in a VOQ structure. Each output consists of eight CoS. Up to 32 output ports are supported per channel with a maximum of four channels per PQ. The PQ implements the deficit round robin (DRR), weighted round robin (WRR), modified deficit round robin (MDRR), and modified weighted round robin (MWRR) algorithms to generate bids to the AR via its integrated serial links. The PQ makes four bids every 32 ns to its attached ARs. On the egress side, the PQ is used to schedule packets out of the egress MS. The PQ is also responsible for flow control.

***Arbiter.*** The AR is located in the switching card configuring the XB of the same card. Up to five XBs are deployed per switching card. The AR receives bids from the PQ of every input port cards and does input–output matching using a round robin, maximal matching scheduling algorithm. The matching results are sent back through serial links to the corresponding PQ.

Besides best-effort switching, the AR also contains four TDM reservation tables to support TDM switching. Figure 16.55 shows a simple switch card architecture for optical or electrical backplanes with one AR per card.

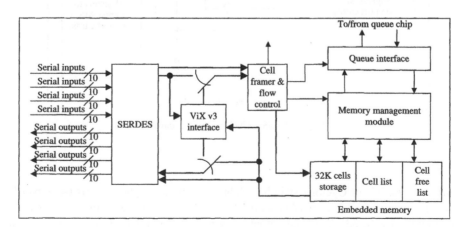

**Figure 16.54** Cyclone memory subsystem block diagram.

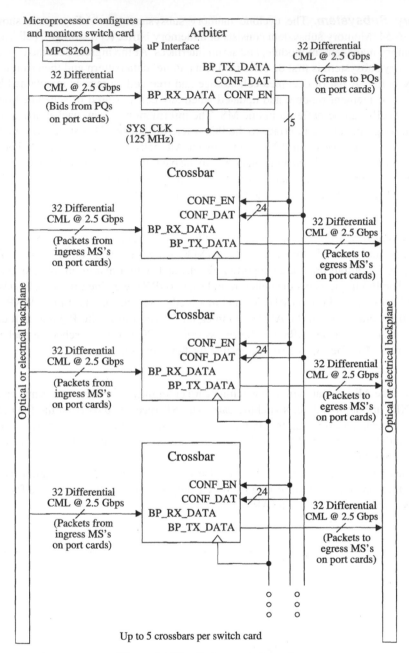

**Figure 16.55**  Cyclone switch card.

***Crossbar.*** The XB of Cyclone switching fabric is a typical synchronous 64 Gbps (data switching capacity) 32 × 32 crossbar with 2.5 Gbps line rate in each port. It is controlled and configured by the AR. When an output is not matched to any input ports, idle cells are generated for them.

***Earliest Deadline First Queue.*** The EDFQ is implemented at the egress port. It performs a WFQ algorithm to schedule packets out of egress MS. In each EDFQ, 16 schedulers are available so that up to four OC-192 channels or 16 OC-48 sub-channels can be supported by one EDFQ. The scheduling is based on flow ID, CoS, and packet length. The EDFQ also takes charge of flow control at the egress port.

### 16.4.4  Switch Fabric Chip Set from IBM (now of AMCC)

The following section explains IBM's switch chipset, which is quite different from switching architectures described in the previous sections. The overall architecture of the IBM third generation switching fabric [42] is shown in Figure 16.56. The IBM PowerPRS Q-64G is a kind of packet routing switch chip providing up to 512 Gbps aggregate throughput while the IBM PowerPRS C192 is a companion device to the Q-64G functioning as the switch core access layer between the protocol engine's OC-48 or OC-192 CSIX interfaces and the switch core. The switching fabric follows the popular topology "ingress queuing engine (IQE)–switch core (SW)–egress queuing engine (EQE)," with PowerPRS C192 as IQE and EQE and PowerPRS Q-64G as SW.

However, the switching fabric is novel in the design of 32 × 32 switch core Q-64G. It implements the shared memory mechanism and constructs the 32 × 32 switch from four 16 × 16 sub-switches mounted in port expansion by two. Figure 16.57 depicts the internal structure of the shared memory switch Q-64G. It is mainly composed of 32 input

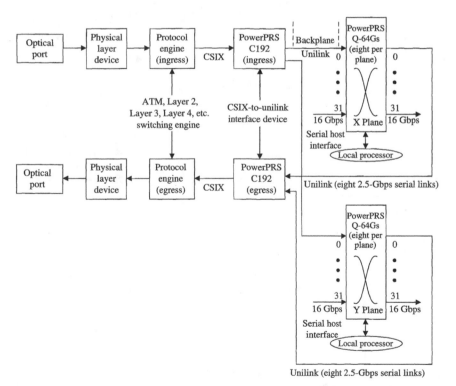

**Figure 16.56**  System view of the switching fabric with Q64-G (configured with redundant switch planes).

controllers, 32 output controllers, four sub-switch elements, and other control sections (sequencer, output queue scheduler, credit table). Each port has one input controller and one output controller. Each sub-switch is connected to half of the input controllers and half of the output controllers so that the ingress cell flows are distributed uniformly across the four sub-switches. For example, sub-switch A forwards those packets that come from input port 0–15 but head for output port 0–15.

Each component of the Q-64G switch core is described in detail using the packet forwarding path in the following.

**Sequencer.** As shown in Figure 16.57, a sequencer connects to all of the input controllers and the output controllers. It manages the access of these controllers to the shared memory of every sub-switch.

The sequencer makes scheduling in a time-division multiplexing (TDM) manner. That is, each time slot it grants the shared memory access to two input controllers and two output controllers, with one in 0–15 ports and the other in 16–31 ports. In the next time slot, it grants two other input and output ports. Finally, the sequencer visits every port in one cycle.

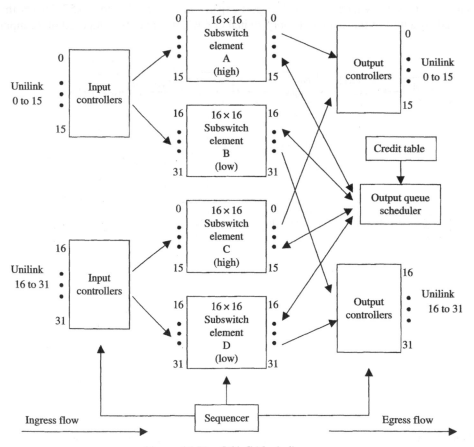

**Figure 16.57** Q64-G block diagram.

***Input Controller.*** When an input controller is granted by the sequencer, it forwards two packets at a time to the shared memory with one on the high channel (0–15 output ports) and the other on the low channel (16–31 output ports). As shown in Figure 16.57, once granted by the sequencer, the input controller of port 1 sends two packets to the shared memory of sub-switch A and sub-switch B, respectively. However, the data actually sent is the cells with equal length segmented from the packet.

The address of the destined shared memory is provided by the address manager of the corresponding sub-switch. The input controller also forwards the priority of the packet, destined memory address and the packet destination to the output queue access manager inside the sub-switch, and this address is stored in an output queue constructed one per output per priority. It is illustrated in Figure 16.58.

***16 × 16 Sub-Switch.*** The internal block of each sub-switch is shown in Figure 16.58. The key feature of this switch architecture is that it does not switch cells by connecting crosspoints anymore. Instead, it integrates 2048 10-byte rows for unicast traffic and 1024 10-byte rows for multicast traffic of shared memory per sub-switch and forwards cells by writing and reading the shared memory. The writing of the memory (cell flow in the ingress direction) is controlled by the external input controllers per input port. The reading of the memory (cell flow in the egress direction) is controlled by the output controllers per output port. Simultaneously with the cell ingress into shared memory, the address of the cell in memory is stored in the corresponding output queue, which constructs one per output per priority. Also, an external output queue scheduler is connected to every output queue of each sub-switch, gathering the occupation status of the output queue. It decides from which

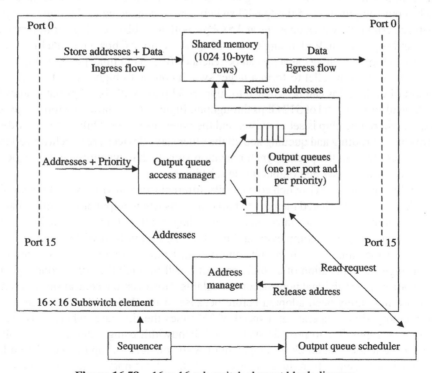

**Figure 16.58**    16 × 16 sub-switch element block diagram.

output queue the shared memory should obtain the egress cell address; that is, it controls the output packet selection when the output controller is granted by the sequencer. Moreover, an address manager is used to maintain the status of shared memory occupation and provide empty shared memory entry for external input controller.

*Output Controller.* Similar to the input controller, when an output controller is granted by the sequencer, it retrieves two packets at a time from the shared memory, one from the high channel (0–15 input ports) and the other from the low channel (16–31 input ports). As shown in the Figure 16.57, once granted by the sequencer, the output controller of port 1 receives two packets from the shared memory of sub-switch A and sub-switch C, respectively. The output packet selection is done in the output queue scheduler, and the output controller just reads data from the shared memory in the given address. After inserting some flow control information into the packet header, the output controller forwards the packet to the physical interface for serialization, and then transmits it to the egress QE. Also, the data actually received by the next egress QE is the cells with equal length segmented from the packet.

*Output Queue Scheduler.* When the output controller is granted by the sequencer, several packets can be chosen from the output queue in the corresponding port for transmitting, unlike the input controller where only the ingress packet at that cycle can be scheduled in.

An output queue scheduler has to be deployed to select packets to be scheduled out and notify the output queue to provide correct egress packet address of the shared memory. The output queue scheduler chooses egress packets by priority. However, through the implementation of a credit table, it can guarantee fixed bandwidth for every queue as well.

Each input (output) port of the Q-64G switch core is connected to the ingress (egress) QE using a serial link, which operates at 2.5 Gbps, with 8b/10b encoding for link synchronization and supervision. With a single $32 \times 32$ Q-64G chip, 2 Gbps pure data line rate and a total of 64 Gbps switching capacity can be reached. To expand link speed, multiple chips can be configured in parallel to form a larger switch core with higher port throughput. A maximum of eight chips can be reached to support 32 ports with 16 Gbps data bandwidth per port, resulting in a total of 512 Gbps throughput. Figure 16.59 shows the four chips' configuration, where one chip is set as master and the others as slaves. Only the master device performs packet routing and queuing and all the other slave devices are synchronized to the master device through the packet synchronization signals that synchronize the sequencer, shared memory addresses and output queue scheduler.

In conclusion, the Q-64G switch core is quite different from previous switching architectures. It deploys central shared memory to buffer packets when output port conflicts happen. The architecture benefits a lot in completely avoiding input–output port matching, which requires much computing complexity and much transmission bandwidth to send request and grant. At the same time, it permits an efficient handling of multicast and broadcast traffic through the replication of a single copy of a cell through the corresponding output ports as soon as the individual ports become available. However, the central shared memory architecture has rarely been adopted before because of its obvious disadvantage that the shared memory should operate at a speed of $2N$ times the line rate, where $N$ is the port number. It is impossible to provide such a high bandwidth using external central shared memory. Fortunately, the quick development of ASIC manufacturing enables the building of a buffer inside chips. To reduce the necessary shared memory bandwidth, the Q-64G switch core also introduces parallel processing inside the chip.

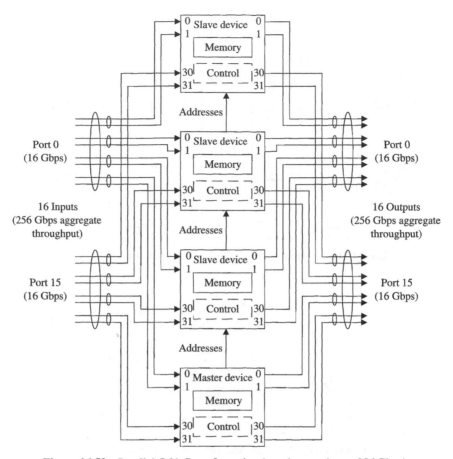

**Figure 16.59**  Parallel Q64-G configuration (speed expansion to 256 Gbps).

## 16.4.5  Switch Fabric Chip Set from Agere

The switching fabric solutions from Agere contain two main architectures. The first is built using Pi40X/C [43, 44], with similar topology to the popular three-stage structure: IQE–SW–EQE structure. The second is a single chip solution implementing Agere's new shared-memory stand-alone switch chip Pi40SAX [45]. The first topology can provide large switching capacity beyond terabits/sec, while the second provides a solution that is easy to build and control.

***Pi40X/Pi40C Chip Set for Terabit Switching.***  Figure 16.60 shows a typical switching fabric constructed using Pi40X/C. Compared to other common switching fabrics, the Pi40 series differ in two aspects. First, as shown in Figure 16.61, the IQE and EQE are located in separate Pi40X chips and an extra communication channel is built between them to communicate scheduling information. Second, more serial links are implemented in both the QE Pi40X and the XB Pi40C providing much higher bandwidth. These serial links can also be bundled freely to aggregate different line-speed links. This is shown in Figure 16.62. The Pi40X has 32 2.5 Gbps simplex serial links in line side, which can be bundled to one

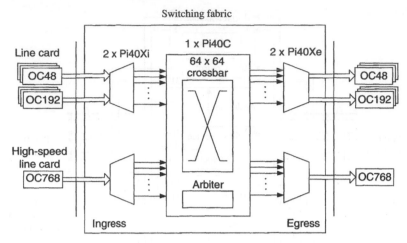

**Figure 16.60**   Agere's switching fabric with Pi40X and Pi40C chips.

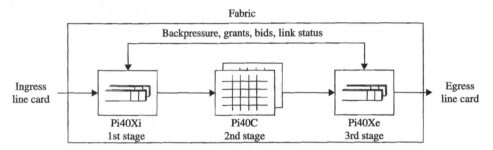

**Figure 16.61**   Pi40X ingress–egress pair communication.

OC768 channel, four OC192 channels, 16 OC48 channels, 32 OC12 channels[4], or any combination of them. The Pi40C has 64 2.5 Gbps duplex serial links providing 160 Gbps aggregate switching capacity in a single chip. Therefore, a few parallel Pi40C can support terabit switching.

*Flexible Configuration of Pi40X/C.* Since the serial links between Pi40X and Pi40C can be bundled freely, the connection patterns between them can be arbitrary. The fundamental topology is a three-stage Clos network as shown in Figure 16.63. The connections between stage 1 and 2, as well as between stage 2 and 3 are both in a fully connected pattern. Figure 16.63 shows that the switching fabric supports 1 : 1 redundancy in all the stages.

A minimal configuration of Pi40X/C is shown in Figure 16.64. Thirty-two egress serial links of Pi40X are bundled together to form a 80 Gbps virtual channel. When less serial links are bundled together more virtual channels between Pi40X and Pi40C are available. More Pi40Cs can be used to achieve higher switching capacities. A maximal configuration is shown in Figure 16.65, which provides a 2.5 Tbps throughput.

---

[4]Since there are only 32 serial links.

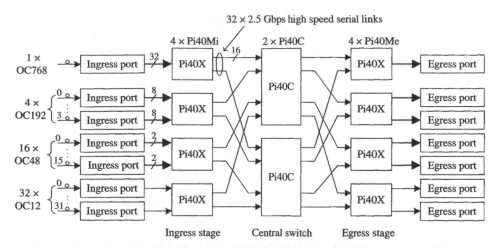

**Figure 16.62** Link bundling of Pi40X and Pi40C.

*Queuing and Scheduling in Pi40X/C.* Figure 16.66 shows the queuing and scheduling mechanism in Pi40X/C switching fabric. Note that multicast queues are not depicted there.

In the ingress QE Pi40X, cells are buffered in the internal shared memory. The memory is organized into 1024 unicast routing queues and 64 multicast routing queues. The unicast routing queues can be configured using either a simple VOQ structure or an input/output pair queuing (IOPQ) structure. Each unicast or multicast routing queue has two sub-queues, one for best-effort (BE) traffic and the other for guaranteed bandwidth (GBW) traffic. The best effort traffic will be served using a work conserving fair queuing scheduling while

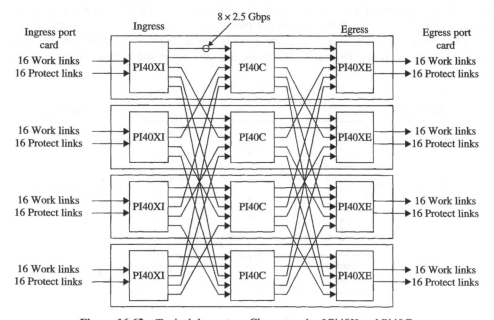

**Figure 16.63** Typical three-stage Clos network of Pi40X and Pi40C.

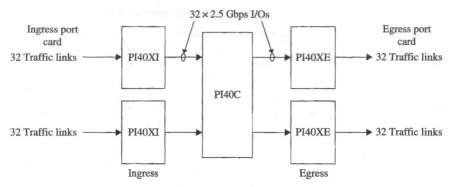

**Figure 16.64** 80 Gbps switching fabric composed of Pi40X and Pi40C.

the guaranteed traffic, most of which is real-time traffic, will be transferred through prior virtual TDM pipes.

In the egress QE Pi40X, the 1024 unicast queues are divided into different groups up to the number of line side egress links. For example, an egress Pi40X that is connected to eight OC48 links will provide $1024/8 = 128$ queues for each OC48 link. The cell destined for one of these links will be buffered in one of the corresponding 128 queues. Each group of queues is scheduled by a separate scheduler.

The scheduling of Pi40X/Pi40C chip set still follows the request–grant manner. In any given scheduling period, the GBW traffic is always prioritized over BE traffic. The GBW traffic is scheduled using a shaped virtual clock so that each GBW queue will be served once per service period. The service period of each GBW queue is a configurable value set by the user to provide proper priority. When there is no GBW traffic to schedule, a BE queue is chosen using a WRR algorithm. In every scheduling period, one queue selection is made and this request is sent to one of the connected XB Pi40C inside a previously granted cell's header. The Pi40C has an AR that decides whether to accept the request or not. Once the request is accepted, the grant signal is attached in the header of a cell destined for the requesting ports. The egress Pi40X receives the grant and further passes it to the

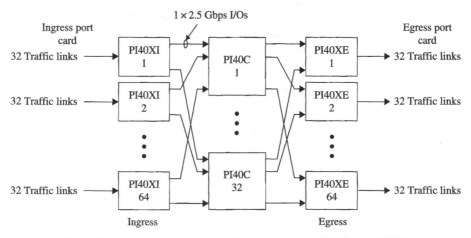

**Figure 16.65** 2.5 Tbps switching fabric composed of Pi40X and Pi40C.

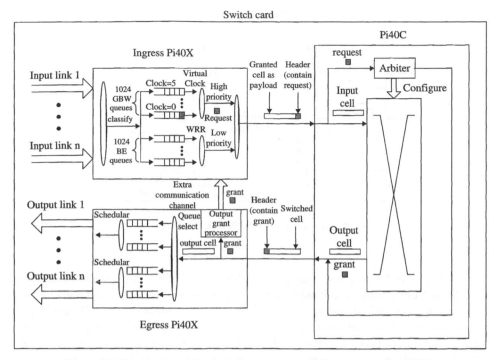

**Figure 16.66**    Queuing and scheduling structure of ingress and egress Pi40X.

ingress Pi40X in the same port card through the extra communication channel between them. Finally, the granted cell is transferred out to the XB in the next cycle.

***Pi40SAX Stand-Alone Switch Chip.*** Figure 16.67 shows another switching fabric solution from Agere, the stand-alone Pi40SAX. This switching fabric chip does not use an input-queuing structure anymore. Instead, input cells from each port are buffered in a single shared memory. Thus, there is no need to use separate ingress/egress queuing chips for each port and this greatly reduces the system's complexity. The chip performs well in building switching fabrics of edge routers. However, because of the limitation in internal shared memory's access bandwidth, the chip cannot reach a much higher switching capacity.

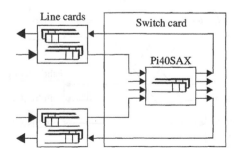

**Figure 16.67**    Switching system using Pi40SAX.

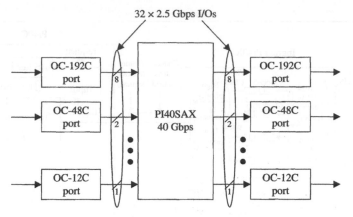

**Figure 16.68**    Pi40SAX link bundling.

From Figure 16.68, we can see that the Pi40SAX consists of 32 2.5 Gbps input and output serial links. Considering the in-band routing and framing overhead, the user bandwidth per serial link is less than 2.5 Gbps, approximately half of that, supporting an OC12 or GE port per link. To adapt to higher port rate, these links can be bundled flexibly. Eight serial links bundled together can accommodate an OC192 port and two links accommodate an OC48 port. The 32 serial links can be partitioned to any different groups, interfacing to a mixture of OC192, OC48, and other ports. Moreover, the Pi40SAX supports both the line card and the switch card redundancy. As shown in Figure 16.69, the failure of any single card does not affect the performance of the whole system.

Figure 16.70 gives an internal block diagram of Pi40SAX. Serialized data is accepted and converted into cell data (byte alignment) by the input link group (ILG), which bundles several serial links. The input port controller is responsible for directing traffic from the ILG, transferring cell payload with some control and routing information to the buffer memory controller (BMC) and the cell header to the queue manager (QM).

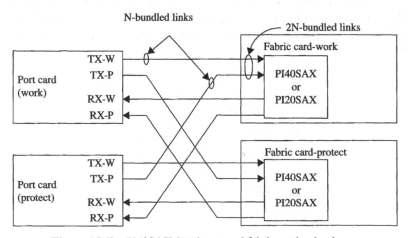

**Figure 16.69**    Pi40SAX 1 + 1 port and fabric card redundancy.

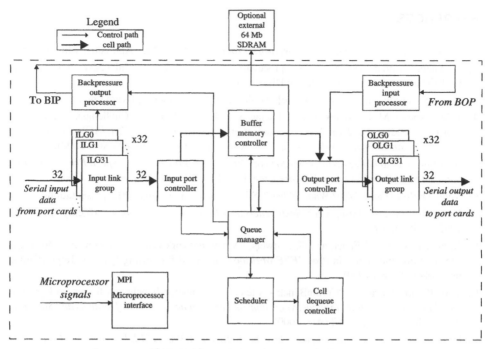

**Figure 16.70**  Pi40SAX internal block diagram.

The BMC buffers cell data in the internal shared memory, and the QM maintains cell address in 1024 unicast queues and 32 multicast branches. The 1024 unicast queues are configured either in a VOQ structure or an IOPQ implementation. Also, each unicast or multicast queue contains two sub-queues. One for GBW traffic, scheduled as the queue of shaped virtual clock, and the other for BE traffic, using the WRR scheduling. This queuing structure as well as its scheduling algorithm are the same as those of Pi40X/C.

The scheduling takes place in the scheduler and through the cell dequeue controller passed to the output port controller, where cell data is received and further sent to the output link group (OLG). The OLG serializes cell data, selects a correct output link, and finally forwards it to the port card through this link.

Extra backpressure mechanism is implemented in the Pi40SAX, differentiated into two types. One is the egress backpressure. Once a port card cannot afford to process incoming traffic from the switching fabric, it generates an egress backpressure signal and attaches it to an ingress cell header. When the cell is received by the ILG in Pi40SAX, this backpressure signal is extracted and through backpressure output/input processor sent to the output port controller, where cells destined for this busy output port are idled for a predefined number of cell cycles. The other type of backpressure is generated inside the Pi40SAX. When any of its internal queues exceeds the programmed threshold, backpressure signal is attached to a cell header and sent to the port card. Consequently, traffic heading for this queue is blocked until no backpressure signal is received.

Additionally, a microprocessor interface is available for configuring the chip and handling interrupts. Optional external SDRAM can be added to store lookup tables in multicast routing.

## REFERENCES

[1] *The Challenge for Next Generation Network Processors*, Agere Inc., Apr. 2001, white paper.

[2] N. Shah, "Understanding network processors," Master's thesis, University of California, Berkeley, Sept. 2001, Master Degree Dissertation.

[3] "Network processing forum." [Online]. Available at: http://www.npforum.org/.

[4] J. M. Rabaey, M. Potkonjak, F. Koushanfar, S.-F. Li, and T. Tuan, "Challenges and opportunities in broadband and wireless communication designs," in *Proc. IEEE/ACM International Conference on Computer Aided Design*, San Jose, California, pp. 76–82 (Nov. 2000).

[5] *Intel Internet Exchange Architecture Network Processors Flexible, Wire-Speed Processing from the Customer Premises to the Network Core*, Intel Inc., 2002, white paper.

[6] *Network Processors: Why? What? When?*, Silicon Access Inc., July 2002, presentation.

[7] *Network Processor Designs for Next-Generation Networking Equipment*, EZchip Inc., Dec. 1999, white paper.

[8] X. Nie, L. Gazsi, F. Engel, and G. Fettweis, "A new network processor architecture for high-speed communications," in *Proc. IEEE Workshop on Signal Processing Systems*, Taipei, China, pp. 548–557 (Oct. 1999).

[9] T. Wolf and M. Frankly, "CommBench – A telecommunication benchmark for network processors," in *Proc. IEEE International Symposium on Performance Analysis of Systems and Software*, Austin, Texas, pp. 154–162 (Apr. 2000).

[10] H. Liu, "A trace driven study of packet level parallelism," in *Proc. IEEE International Conference on Communications*, New York, New York, vol. 4, pp. 2191–2195 (Apr. 2002).

[11] P. Crowley, M. E. Fiuczynski, J.-L. Baer, and B. N. Bershad, "Characterizing processor architectures for programmable network interface," in *Proc. International Conference on Supercomputing*, Santa Fe, New Mexico, pp. 54–65 (May 2000).

[12] W. Bux, W. E. Denzel, T. Engbersen, A. Herkersdort, and R. P. Luijten, "Technologies and building blocks for fast packet forwarding," *IEEE Communications Magazine*, vol. 39, issue 1, pp. 70–77 (Jan. 2001).

[13] *Challenges in Designing 40-Gigabit Network Processors*, EZchip Inc., Dec. 2001, white paper.

[14] *NP-1: Reducing Router Chip-Count, Power and Cost by 80%*, EZchip Inc., June 2002, white paper.

[15] D. A. Patterson and J. L. Hennyssy, *Computer Architecture: A Quantitative Approach*, 3rd ed. Morgan Kaufmann, San Francisco, California, 2003.

[16] *PowerNP NP4GS3 Network Processor Data Sheet*, IBM Inc., Feb. 2002.

[17] B. Klein and J. Garza, "Agere systems – communications optimized payload plus network processor architecture," in *Network Processor Design: Issues and Practices*. Morgan Kaufmann, San Francisco, California, 2002, vol. 1, pp. 219–233.

[18] *Intel IXP2800 Network Processor – For OC-192/10 Gbps network edge and core applications*, Intel Inc., product brief.

[19] J. Marshall, "Cisco systems – Toaster2," in *Network Processor Design: Issues and Practices*. Morgan Kaufmann, San Francisco, California, 2002, vol. 1, pp. 235–248.

[20] *Implementing a Flexible Hardware-based Router for the New IP Infrastructure*, Juniper Inc., white paper.

[21] *LA-1 interface*. [Online]. Available at: http://www.npforum.org/ApprovedSpecs.htm

[22] H. Bhugra, *LA-1: Examining the Look-Aside Processor Interface*. [Online]. Available at: http://www.commsdesign.com/

[23] M. J. Miller, "IDT network search engine with QDR LA-1 interface," in *Network Processor Design, Issues and Practices*. Morgan Kaufmann, San Francisco, California, 2003, vol. 2, pp. 365–384.

[24] *4.5M and 9M Network Search Engine (NSE) with QDR Interface, Data Sheet*, IDT, 2002.

[25] *Network Search Engine (NSE) TCAM with QDR Interface, User's Manual*, IDT, 2002.

[26] *PAX.port 2500, Data Sheet*, IDT, 2003.

[27] *PAX.port 2500, Technical Summary*, IDT, 2003.

[28] R. T. Vineet Dujari and A. Shelat, "PMC-Sierra, Inc. – ClassiPI," in *Network Processor Design, Issues and Practices*. Morgan Kaufmann, San Francisco, California, 2002, vol. 1, pp. 291–305.

[29] *PM2329 ClassiPI Network Classification Processor Datasheet*, PMC-Sierra, Inc., 2001.

[30] *Technical Guide to the TM10-Preliminary Data Book*, Agere System Inc., Dec. 2002.

[31] *Technical Guide to the APP550 and APP530 Network Processors, Version 7*, Agere System Inc., May 2003.

[32] *Technical Guide to the APP540/520 Network Processors, Version 1*, Agere System Inc., May 2003.

[33] *ZTM Advanced Traffic Manager Product Brief*, ZettaCom Inc., May 2004.

[34] *ZTM552 Traffic Manager Preliminary Data Sheet, version 3.0*, ZettaCom Inc., Dec. 2003.

[35] *ZTM552 Traffic Management Training*, ZettaCom Inc., May 2004.

[36] Vitesse. [Online]. Available at: http://www.vitesse.com

[37] *VSC870 datasheet Rev 4.0: high performance serial backplane transceiver*, Vitesse. [Online]. Available at: http://www.vitesse.com

[38] *VSC880 datasheet Rev 4.0: high performance 16 × 16 serial crosspoint switch*, Vitesse. [Online]. Available at: http://www.vitesse.com

[39] *GigaStream intelligent switch fabric VSC872/VSC882 design manual Rev 2.2*, Vitesse. [Online]. Available at: http://www.vitesse.com

[40] *TeraStream intelligent switch fabric VSC871/VSC881 design manual Rev 1.0*, Vitesse. [Online]. Available at: http://www.vitesse.com

[41] *Cyclone Switch Fabric S8505-S8905 Product Concept, Rev0.07*, AMCC.

[42] *PowerPRS Q-64G Packet Routing Switch datasheet, initial release*, IBM.

[43] *Technical Guide to the Pi40X, Rev 18*, Agere System Inc., Mar. 2003.

[44] *Technical Guide to the Pi40C, Rev 13*, Agere System Inc., Mar. 2003.

[45] *Technical Guide to the Pi40SAX and Pi20SAX, Rev 12*, Agere System Inc., Sept. 2003.

# INDEX

16-bit cyclic redundancy check (CRC-16), 425

Abacus switch, 336
Accounting management (AM), 16
Acknowledgment (ACK), 429, 580
Active queue management, 164
Address
   aggregation, 26
   broadcaster (AB), 330, 338, 356
   copy, 222–224
   interval, 305
   lookup, 25
   prefix, 25
Admission control, 118
Agere system interface (ASI), 548
Aggregated flow queue (AFQ), 573
Application programming interface (API), 564
Application specific
   instruction processor (ASIP), 539
   integrated circuit (ASIC), 29, 351, 538
   standard product (ASSP), 562
Approximated Longest Queue Drop
   (ALQD), 172
APSARA, 251, 252
Arbiter (AR), 589
Area-based quadtree (AQT), 95
Arithmetic logic unit (ALU), 549
Arrayed-waveguide grating (AWG), 477
Arrival reassemble queue (ARQ), 573
Assured forwarding (AF), 127, 572
Asynchronous transfer mode (ATM), 2, 337, 539

ATM
   routing and concentration
     (ARC), 337, 351
   switch chip, 207
ATLANTA Switch, 398
Augmented banyan switches, 186
Availability, 116
Average rate, 116

Backbone routers, 3
Backlogged period for session, 144
Backpressure (BP), 349
   scheduler (BPS), 571
Bandwidth, 115
Banyan, 284
   switch, 176
Banyan-based switch, 185, 192, 193
Base index, 39
Batcher-
   banyan, 288
   sorting, 287
BC-16-16, 53
Beginning of packet (BOP), 422
Bernoulli arrival process, 196
Best-effort (BE), 599
Binary
   network, 333
   search, 47
   trie (1-bit trie), 29
Birkhoff-von Neumann switch, 438
Bit selection, 60

*High Performance Switches and Routers*, by H. Jonathan Chao and Bin Liu
Copyright © 2007 John Wiley & Sons, Inc.

Printed and bound by CPI Group (UK) Ltd, Croydon, CR0 4YY